Instructc

Drafting & Design

Engineering Drawing Using Manual and CAD Techniques

by

Clois E. Kicklighter, CSIT

Dean Emeritus, School of Technology
Professor Emeritus of Construction Technology
Indiana State University
Terre Haute, IN

and

Walter C. Brown

Publisher
The Goodheart-Willcox Company, Inc.
Tinley Park, Illinois
www.g-w.com

Previously published and copyrighted as *Drafting for Industry*
by the Goodheart-Willcox Company, Inc.

Manufactured in the United States of America.

Instructor's Manual
ISBN 978-1-59070-905-4

Instructor's Resource Binder
ISBN 978-1-59070-906-1

Instructor's Resource CD
ISBN 978-1-59070-907-8

2 3 4 5 6 7 8 9 – 08 – 12 11 10 09

Contents

Chapter Resources

Introduction

Drafting & Design: Engineering Drawing Using Manual and CAD Techniques provides a comprehensive approach to classroom instruction in the field of drafting. The teaching package includes the textbook, the Worksheets, the Instructor's Manual, the Instructor's Resource Binder, the Instructor's Resource CD, the *ExamView*® Assessment Suite CD, and the Instructor's PowerPoint® Presentations CD. These components contain a variety of resources to assist the drafting instructor.

The textbook and supplements provide in-depth coverage of the principles of manual (traditional) drafting and computer-aided drafting (CAD). The two approaches to drafting are taught in combination throughout the text. Numerous drafting procedures and problems are presented to illustrate the application of both methods.

The development of the textbook began with a study to identify the instruction needed by drafters in industry. Approximately 250 industrial firms were contacted to ascertain their requirements for drafting personnel ranging from technicians to designers. Most companies supplied examples of typical drawings produced by their personnel. Many companies sent copies of their drafting room manuals and other standards. These drawings and publications were carefully reviewed to include material in the text that addresses the educational needs of both beginning and advanced drafting students. Drafting problems of an "exercise" nature were kept to a minimum. Actual problems encountered in the drafting rooms of industry were included to enrich the study of drafting. The creative approach to problem solving—so essential in all technical careers today—is emphasized throughout the text.

Using the Text

Drafting & Design: Engineering Drawing Using Manual and CAD Techniques is divided into 28 chapters. The chapters are organized into five sections. The five sections are arranged by level of skill, and by the amount and type of technical information included. This provides flexibility in various teaching situations and allows the instructor to use the text in an efficient manner.

Each chapter begins with a list of objectives that will be covered in the chapter. Throughout the chapter, key technical terms are identified in ***boldface italic*** type to assist the student in comprehension of the material. By encountering key terms in this manner, the student can also quickly identify important topics when reviewing the material. In addition, certain CAD terms, such as command names and drawing functions, are identified in **boldface sans serif** type.

Each chapter concludes with a chapter summary and review questions to test student comprehension of the material. Many chapters include an Additional Resources section listing suggested materials and learning sources for further study. Most chapters feature drafting problems for students to apply skills. Design problems involving creative problem-solving techniques are included where appropriate.

Section One of the text, Introduction to Drafting Fundamentals, provides an overview of the basic skills required to produce drawings. The material in this section provides the basis for instruction needed by all students to understand the "language of industry." It covers different types of technical drawings, careers and opportunities associated with the field of drafting, and traditional drafting tools and equipment. This section also introduces the student to CAD and the advantages it presents to the drafter and industry. Common CAD tools, commands, and software packages are discussed to give the student an overview of CAD functions.

Topics covered in Section One include: Drafting and the Drafter; Traditional Drafting Equipment and Drawing Techniques; Introduction to CAD; CAD Commands and Functions; and Sketching, Lettering, and Text.

Section Two, Drafting Techniques and Skills, covers geometric constructions and basic drafting skills. It teaches the fundamentals required to complete drawings that are consistent with the accepted rules and practices of modern industry. Step-by-step procedures for developing solutions to drafting problems are featured in this section.

Topics covered in Section Two include: Basic Geometric Constructions; Advanced Geometric Constructions; Multiview Drawings; Dimensioning Fundamentals; Section Views; and Pictorial Drawings.

Section Three, Descriptive Geometry, provides students with a basic understanding of drafting skills and techniques required to understand spatial relationships and analyze problems. This section should be used with students who desire to graphically describe relationships between points, lines, intersections, and surfaces.

Topics covered in Section Three include: Auxiliary Views; Revolutions; Intersections; and Developments.

Section Four, Advanced Applications, introduces more complex topics, including geometric dimensioning and tolerancing and specialized manufacturing processes. This section is designed for students who have developed a command of drafting fundamentals and are prepared to learn dimensioning and tolerancing practices, as well as design information for products such as fasteners, cams, and gears. This section teaches the drawing techniques and terminology necessary to provide full details and specifications for the manufacture of products.

Topics covered in Section Four include: Geometric Dimensioning and Tolerancing; Working Drawings; Threads and Fastening Devices; Cams, Gears, and Splines; Drawing Management; and Manufacturing Processes.

Section Five, Drafting and Design Specializations, covers the different fields of drafting. It introduces the skills and methods involved in each drafting discipline. This section provides a basic foundation for teaching the fundamentals of each drafting specialty.

Topics covered in Section Five include: Architectural Drafting; Structural Drafting; Electrical and Electronics Drafting; Map and Survey Drafting; Welding Drafting; Technical Illustration; and Graphs and Charts.

Using the Worksheets

The Worksheets supplement contains many of the drafting problems from the textbook. It is designed for use with the text in a traditional drafting environment. However, many of the problems can also be completed using a CAD system. The problems are designed to help the student:

1. Develop basic as well as advanced drafting skills.
2. Acquire more drafting experience with less repetitive work.
3. Become knowledgeable with common drafting procedures.

The problems are closely correlated with the text and have been carefully selected to provide realistic experiences. The number of problems in the Worksheets supplement has been increased in this edition to provide a broader range of difficulty and variety.

Using the Instructor's Manual

The Instructor's Manual provides the instructor with useful ideas and instructional materials. The instructional materials help the instructor create a meaningful experience for students who are learning beginning and advanced drafting techniques.

The Instructor's Manual is organized in a manner that permits the instructor to be flexible in presentations. The instructor can move systematically from Section One through the entire text to provide instruction for classes ranging from beginning to advanced students. The instructor can also select certain chapters for presenting material of special interest to the class.

Each of the chapter resources includes chapter objectives, instructional tasks, instructional aids and assignments, and solutions to the in-text problems and activities. Solutions to the Worksheets are also given. In addition, each chapter has a chapter quiz with corresponding solutions. Many chapters also have reproducible masters for use as student handouts.

Pedagogical charts are also provided to assist in the instruction and evaluation processes. These charts contain page references correlating key topics and activities to the textbook and supplements. They include the Scope and Sequence Chart and the Basic Skills Chart.

Using the Instructor's Resource Binder

The Instructor's Resource Binder incorporates all of the elements of the Instructor's Manual and also contains the color transparencies to assist the instructor during lectures and demonstrations. The color transparencies are designed to add variety to the classroom presentation of the material. The reproducible masters provided in the chapter resources may be used as either handouts or to create additional transparencies.

Using the Instructor's Resource CD

The Instructor's Resource CD includes the contents of the Instructor's Manual and Instructor's Resource Binder in electronic form. Materials belonging to each of the chapter resources are provided as PDF files for use in Adobe® Reader®. The color transparencies are supplied as files for viewing in either Reader or PowerPoint®. In addition, many of the drafting problems from the textbook and the Worksheets are provided as DWG files on the Instructor's Resource CD. These files can be opened in AutoCAD®. Solutions to the problems are also provided as DWG files. The Instructor's Resource CD also includes a lesson plan for each chapter as well as Internet links to various industrial firms and resource providers.

Using the *ExamView*® Assessment Suite CD

The *ExamView*® Assessment Suite CD contains convenient tools for creating your own tests or quizzes in a professional format. Tests and quizzes may be generated from a question bank of more than 1500 questions. The questions range from very basic to difficult. Several styles of questions—true or false, multiple choice, matching, identification, and completion—are included. If you desire, you can add your own questions to the question bank.

Using the Instructor's PowerPoint Presentations CD

The Instructor's PowerPoint Presentations CD contains electronic slide presentations corresponding to key concepts in the text. The presentations are designed for display in the classroom. They can be used with the PowerPoint Viewer utility, which is included with the CD. Presentations are provided for each chapter in the text. They are intended as special lecture supplements to generate student interest and classroom discussion.

Organization of a Drafting Course

Drafting courses may vary in method and content. Two factors that affect the method and content are the goals for the course and the type of equipment available.

Goals for industrial education or technology education courses are primarily exploring or understanding the use of drafting in industry. Content for this type of course should be selected from Sections One, Two, and Three of the textbook.

Instructional goals for advanced industrial technology education courses and more technically oriented courses are skill building and understanding technical information. The application of drafting principles to solve graphic problems is also an important goal. In courses involving more advanced instruction, the textbook can be followed from Section One to Section Five, depending on the time available and student progress.

Teaching CAD

CAD has become an essential part of most drafting departments in industry and has been widely integrated into school drafting programs. The addition of CAD to the school drafting program does not change the fundamental *principles* of drafting, only the methods and procedures of the *process.* The computer does not do the drawing for the drafter. The drafter is still required to have drafting skills and knowledge of drafting principles. CAD brings an increase in mathematical capability and material information, and changes the process of arriving at the finished product—the drawing. Two primary advantages have been derived from the utilization of CAD. First, the actual production time has decreased. Second, the design resources are greatly enhanced by the ability to store data during the design process.

Student graduates going into industry have an advantage if they have had CAD training. Once a certain level of skill has been developed on one CAD system, a student is more apt to adapt to other CAD systems. A student should learn that the computer increases the drafter's capability, but it is the student who must understand the design and drafting process and must be able to use the computer efficiently.

Drafting instructors should become thoroughly familiar with the CAD system purchased for the program to effectively instruct the students on its use. The ease of use of the software package and CAD system will help increase productivity and the quality of drawings.

Developing a Teaching Plan

The chapter resources in this instructor's resource provide a teaching plan for each chapter of the textbook. The chapter objectives that students are expected to achieve in their study of each chapter are given. The instructor should utilize these when introducing a chapter. A list of Instructional Tasks is also presented for each chapter. The Instructional Tasks assist the instructor in planning the instructional presentation. The Instructional Aids and Assignments outline additional reference materials that may be utilized in the presentation. Suggestions for assigning the problems from the text are also given in this section.

A chapter quiz is provided for each chapter in the chapter resources. The quiz should be given to students after they complete the chapter material. Most quizzes include a performance section to further assist the instructor with student evaluation. The solutions to each quiz can be found in the chapter resources.

Teaching Techniques and Methods

Teaching methods should be varied to include instruction from the text, the Worksheets, lectures, demonstrations, interactive group discussions, multimedia presentations, films, and overhead transparencies. When appropriate, demonstrations of proper usage of manual and CAD drafting equipment should also be given. Most students learn more readily when the instructional methods are varied and more than one method is used in presenting a given lesson. As previously discussed, the chapter resource material includes instructional tasks and many other strategies for teaching each chapter.

Presenting the Assignment

Outline each assignment during the class period before the start of the new material. The following steps may be useful.

1. Give an introduction and overview of the chapter.
2. State the objectives to be achieved.
3. Assign reading material from the textbook.
4. Answer any student questions to help clarify the assignment.

Presenting the Lesson Material

When presenting the lesson material, cover each topic as completely as possible. Strive to make each subject interesting. The following steps may be useful.

1. Restate the objectives to be achieved from studying the chapter.
2. Break the lesson into its key points or parts and discuss each briefly. Short discussion periods with visual aids are very effective in presenting drafting procedures and concepts.
3. Use demonstration techniques and devices such as sketching on the chalkboard, displaying items with an overhead projector, or displaying drawings on a computer monitor.
4. Use models, "glass box" projections, and industry drawings as motivational devices to encourage learning.
5. Assign drafting problems to provide experience and practice.
6. Move among students to observe their work and to ascertain learning difficulties and additional instructional needs.
7. Relate the activity to its use and application in industry to enable students to fully understand and value the activity. Frequently refer to the purposes (objectives) for studying the chapter.

Additional Techniques in Presenting Material

Use people from industry and former students who are employed in drafting and design fields as class speakers. Multimedia presentations, films, actual machine parts, and models should be utilized to assist students in learning the material presented.

The goal of all instructional methods is to enhance the learning process and to assist students in acquiring the technical knowledge and skills taught in each chapter. Careful planning and observation is necessary to ascertain that learning is being achieved with each lesson presentation.

Additional Teaching Techniques

A variety of teaching resources and student activities can be used to encourage learning in addition to the strategies previously discussed. These include supplemental reading materials, field trips, and involvement with advisory councils, student organizations, and cooperative education. The following sections discuss additional learning opportunities that are available to the student.

Supplemental Reading

There are many resources available to drafting teachers and their students. These include supplemental reading items such as drafting room manuals, product manuals from manufacturers, prints and specification sheets from industry, catalogs, and employment brochures. Contact your advisory council members or drafting supervisors in the field for this information. School counseling personnel and employment service offices can provide brochures detailing job requirements, duties, and opportunities, as well as information on career fields related to drafting.

Field Trips

Conducting a field trip is an excellent way to promote learning. A field trip to a drafting firm can help students greatly increase their understanding of the drafting process. Check your school's field trip policy. Arrange a time for a field trip when the majority of students are available with the least amount of interference with their school schedule.

Most companies are willing to cooperate with instructors because of the mutual benefits derived from a field trip experience. Industrial companies depend on schools to a large degree to supply competent employees. Industry cooperation is greatly enhanced by the use of an active advisory council.

Field trips should be planned carefully to derive the most educational benefit. Be certain that the industry representative understands the purpose of the field trip and that you want specific goals to be obtained. Students should also be prepared by understanding the purposes of the trip. You should provide them with an overview of what they might expect to see. Brainstorming can be used to plan questions for the industry representative. These questions might include the nature of the work, career opportunities, training required, and pay scales. Student behavior is generally not a problem on field trips, but it is a good idea to remind them that they are guests of the company and are representatives of the school. Their behavior reflects on them as students and future employees.

Observations and other experiences gained on the field trip should be discussed at the next class session in order to make efficient use of this educational activity. A letter of thanks or a telephone call should follow the visit.

Advisory Councils

Advisory councils are an essential part of successful industrial and technical education programs. Advisory councils provide valuable information regarding course content, training required for employment, equipment needs, and employment opportunities. They also can provide resources such as speakers, surplus supplies, and equipment. Advisory councils are most helpful when they are informed and understand the program. They can provide the needed support to school administrators, community officials, and other groups when developing a program.

Members of an advisory council are selected from employees and management representatives of the particular occupational field served by the program. A council usually consists of five to seven members depending on the size of the program. Your state education agency can provide additional information on the selection and use of advisory councils.

Student Organizations

There are several student organizations on a local, state, and national level that offer many benefits to drafting students. These organizations help students acquire leadership skills, develop desirable character traits, and build school pride. Some of these organizations are SkillsUSA, the American Design Drafting Association (ADDA), and the International Technology Education Association (ITEA). Check with your state education agency for additional information.

Cooperative Education Opportunities

Most educational institutions have programs sponsored by a joint effort between industry and the school. The programs provide cooperative work experience for students. These programs provide part-time, in-school related training and work experience in an occupational field on a part-time basis. A student is usually allowed to work 15–20 hours per week. A training plan and schedule is developed by the instructor-coordinator who teaches the related class. This person also visits the student periodically on the job to coordinate the two facets of the training program. Students receive school credit for what they "learn" and pay for what they "earn."

Measuring Student Achievement

Drafting is the language of industry—the ability to communicate with others regarding industrial processes and products. This requires that a degree of understanding of drafting and a degree of skill in its use must be developed. These are the goals of a drafting program. Visualization of objects or products is an important facet of understanding and using drafting in an industrial setting. Instructors should strive to assist students in developing their ability to visualize objects early in the drafting program. This allows a student to successfully represent objects using multiview projection or pictorial drawing. Once students are able to visualize objects, other drafting components such as line conventions, dimensioning, and constructing special views can be developed more readily.

Students are expected to develop verbal communication skills, build social behavioral skills, and manage their time well, regardless of their future employment. Drafting instructors must also help to develop these skills in their students.

Evaluation Techniques

Effective instruction is dependent, in part, on evaluation of student progress toward the accomplishment of objectives of the course. When students are held responsible and provided with an appraisal of their progress, strong motivation is likely to result. Evaluation of student progress also provides instructors with information necessary to adjust their teaching emphasis.

Quizzes have been provided for each chapter in this instructor's resource. Instructors may choose to give the chapter quiz after each chapter, select questions from several chapter quizzes and give a test over the chapters of a section, or combine the quizzes into a term examination.

Appropriate drawing problems provide an excellent source of material for the performance evaluation of student progress. Evaluation of student progress in the ability to use the design method should also be included, as this is an important area of learning for all students. The instructor may provide basic criteria as outlined in Chapter 1 and use problems in the text, or take advantage of student-suggested problems.

Promoting Your Program

In addition to providing an effective instructional program in drafting, the instructor must also allow time for the public relations aspect of promoting the program. This means working with groups and individuals inside and outside of the school. The ultimate goal of the instructor is to assist others in understanding the value of the drafting program and its contribution to a student's educational preparation, the school as a whole, and the community.

An instructor can build good public relations and support for the drafting program. This will allow instructors to serve present and future students more effectively because of greater pride and appreciation for the program. In promoting your drafting program, it is best to present the positive values of your program rather than to dwell on the negative aspects of other offerings. Sound public relations should result in people becoming aware of the benefits of the program. Suggestions for promoting your program include:

1. Create opportunities for other teachers, administrators, board members, and industry personnel to visit the program.
2. Display student work in showcases and on bulletin boards both inside and outside the laboratory.
3. Plan public relations activities in connection with school open house events, parent visitation days, and visits by "feeder" schools.
4. Prepare articles for local community and school newspapers and professional journals. Be sure to post such articles in prominent places around school. These articles may feature special work of students, class projects, and projects performed for the school or other organizations. Articles on former students and their success in drafting employment as well as articles on advisory council meetings are also appropriate.
5. Invite outside representatives to speak in class—industry personnel, advisory council members, and former students. Follow up the presentation with a news article.
6. Arrange for your students to make presentations before industry association groups, service clubs, and other community organizations on topics concerning class projects and activities.
7. Work with other faculty members on interdisciplinary projects where drafting students can make a contribution.

Resource Materials

The chapter resources in this instructor's resource offer suggestions for using instructional resource materials for each of the 28 chapters in the textbook. Many of the chapters in the text include an Additional Resources section listing resource providers. The following are some general resources and resource providers related to design, drafting, and CAD that the instructor may find useful.

Manuals, Books, and Catalogs

ASME Codes and Standards
American Society of Mechanical Engineers (ASME)
Information Central Orders/Inquiries
PO Box 2300
Fairfield, NJ 07007-2300
www.asme.org

Engineering Standards
IHS, Inc.
321 Inverness Drive South
Englewood, CO 80112
www.global.ihs.com

Machinery's Handbook
Industrial Press, Inc.
989 Avenue of the Americas
New York, NY 10018
www.industrialpress.com

Occupational Outlook Handbook
US Bureau of Labor Statistics
Government Printing Office
200 Constitution Ave., NW
Washington, DC 20210
www.bls.gov

In addition to these resources, catalogs of precision tools, gears, and instruments are available from various manufacturers. Also available are journals published by industrial and trade associations.

Periodicals

American Machinist
Penton Media, Inc.
1300 E. 9th Street
Cleveland, OH 44114
www.americanmachinist.com

Automation Weekly
Automation Resources, Inc.
11000 Prairie Lakes Dr.
Suite 450
PO Box 44759
Eden Prairie, MN 55344
www.automation.com

Cadalyst
Questex Media Group, Inc.
275 Grove Street, Suite 2-130
Newton, MA 02466
www.cadalyst.com

CADCAMNet
7100 N Broadway, Suite 2-P
Denver, CO 80221
www.cadcamnet.com

Computer Graphics World
COP Communications, Inc.
620 W. Elk Ave.
Glendale, CA 91204
www.cgw.com

Design News
225 Wyman Street
Waltham, MA 02451
www.designnews.com

Machine Design
Penton Media, Inc.
1300 E. 9th Street
Cleveland, OH 44114
www.machinedesign.com

Managing Automation
Thomas Publishing Company
5 Penn Plaza, 9th Floor
New York, NY 10001
www.managingautomation.com

PC Magazine
Ziff Davis Media
28 East 28th Street
New York, NY 10016
www.pcmag.com

Tech Directions
832 Phoenix Drive
Ann Arbor, MI 48108
www.techdirections.com

Agencies and Associations

American Design Drafting Association (ADDA)
105 East Main Street
Newbern, TN 30859
www.adda.org

American Institute of Architects (AIA)
1735 New York Ave., NW
Washington, DC 20006
www.aia.org

American National Standards Institute (ANSI)
1819 L Street, NW, 6th Floor
Washington, DC 20036
www.ansi.org

American Society of Mechanical Engineers (ASME)
PO Box 2300
Fairfield, NJ 07007-2300
www.asme.org

American Welding Society (AWS)
550 N.W. LeJeune Road
Miami, FL 33126
www.aws.org

Association for Career and
Technical Education (ACTE)
1410 King St.
Alexandria, VA 22314
www.acteonline.org

International Technology
Education Association (ITEA)
1914 Association Drive, Suite 201
Reston, VA 20191-1539
www.iteaconnect.org

National Association of
Industrial Technology (NAIT)
3300 Washtenaw Ave., Suite 220
Ann Arbor, MI 48104
www.nait.org

SkillsUSA
PO Box 3000
Leesburg, VA 20177-0300
www.skillsusa.org

Audiovisual Materials

A variety of audiovisual materials are available to enhance the drafting curriculum. Contact the following companies for assistance in selecting the appropriate educational materials.

H.W. Wilson
950 University Ave.
Bronx, NY 10452
www.hwwilson.com

Brodhead Garrett Co.
100 Paragon Parkway
Mansfield, OH 44903
www.brodheadgarrett.com

L.S. Starrett Co.
121 Crescent Street
Athol, MA 01331
www.starrett.com

Minnesota Mining and Manufacturing Co. (3M)
Meeting and Presentation Solutions
3M Center
St. Paul, MN 55144
www.3m.com

RMI Media Productions
1365 N. Winchester Street
Olathe, KS 66061
www.rmimedia.com

Goodheart-Willcox Welcomes Your Input

If you have comments, corrections, or suggestions regarding the textbook or its supplements, please send them to:

Managing Editor—Technology
Goodheart-Willcox Co., Inc.
18604 West Creek Drive
Tinley Park, IL 60477
www.g-w.com

Basic Skills Chart

The Basic Skills Chart identifies skill-building activities in the ***Drafting & Design: Engineering Drawing Using Manual and CAD Techniques*** teaching package. These activities specifically encourage the development of basic academic skills. Included are activities in the textbook, Worksheets, and Instructor's Resources. The academic areas addressed in the chart include reading, writing, verbal (other than reading and writing), math, science, and analytical.

Activities are broken down by chapter, and a page number is given to locate the activity. Hands-on activities are identified with the symbol ✍ preceding the activity listing.

	Chapter 1	Chapter 2
Reading	**Text:** Drafting as a problem-solving tool (24); careers in drafting (31); careers related to drafting (33); Activity 11 (39); Activity 12 (40); Activity 15 (40); Activity 20 (40). **IR:** Transparency 1-1, *Problem Solving;* Reproducible Master 1-1, *Types of Technical Drawings;* Reproducible Master 1-2, *The Design Method;* Reproducible Master 1-3, *Types of Models;* Instructional Task 1.	**Text:** ✍Drafting media (44); sheet format (58). **IR:** Transparency 2-1, *Applications of Line Conventions;* Reproducible Master 2-1, *Drafting Equipment;* Reproducible Master 2-2, *Line Conventions.*
Writing	**Text:** Drafting as a communication tool (22); Activity 2 (38); Activity 3 (38); Activity 5 (39); ✍Activity 7 (39); Activity 11 (39); Activity 12 (40); Activity 20 (40). **IR:** Instructional Task 2.	**Text:** ✍Drawing pencils (46); Alphabet of Lines (47); ✍erasing and erasing tools (51); ✍neatness in drafting (52); ✍drafting instrument procedures (59); ✍using a protractor (62); ✍using a compass (63); ✍drafting templates (65); ✍irregular curves (68); ✍pencil techniques with instruments (69); ✍inking (69); ✍Problems 1–24. **Worksheets:** ✍2-1: *Alphabet of Lines;* ✍2-5: *Instrument Drafting;* ✍2-6: *Instrument Drafting;* ✍2-7: *Circles, Arcs, and Irregular Curves;* ✍2-8: *Instrument Drawings;* ✍2-9: *Instrument Drawings;* ✍2-10: *Instrument Drawings;* ✍2-11: *Instrument Drawings;* ✍2-12: *Throttle Guide Gate;* ✍2-13: *Guide Plate;* ✍2-14: *Clevis;* ✍2-15: *Bracket;* ✍2-16: *Gasket.*
Verbal	**Text:** Drafting as a problem-solving tool (24); ✍Activity 1 (38); ✍Activity 6 (39); Activity 10 (39); Activity 15 (40); Activities 17–20 (40). **IR:** Instructional Task 6.	
Math	**Text:** Drafting as a problem-solving tool (24); Activity 4 (38).	**Text:** ✍Drafting equipment (42); ✍scales (53); sheet format (58); ✍drafting instrument procedures (59); ✍using a protractor (62); ✍using a compass (63); ✍dividers (66); ✍Problems 1–24. **Worksheets:** ✍2-2: *Architect's Scale;* ✍2-3: *Decimal Inch Scales;* ✍2-4: *Metric Scale.* **IR:** Transparency 2-2, *Mechanical Engineer's Scales;* Instructional Task 3.
Science	**Text:** Models (29).	
Analytical	**Text:** Drafting as a problem-solving tool (24); drafting as a design tool (27); models (29); Activities 3–4 (38); Activities 5–6 (39); ✍Activity 7 (39); Activities 8–9 (39); Activity 11 (39); Activity 12 (40); ✍Activity 14 (40). **IR:** Transparency 1-1, *Problem Solving;* Instructional Tasks 3, 4, 7, 10.	

	Chapter 3	Chapter 4
Reading	**Text:** What is CAD? (77); mechanical CAD applications (80); general purpose CAD packages (85); advanced mechanical drafting and modeling CAD packages (89); AEC CAD packages (93); Activity 1 (100). **IR:** Reproducible Master 3-1, *CAD System Components;* Reproducible Master 3-2, *Benefits of CAD.*	**Text:** File management commands (102); display control commands (114); dimensioning commands (115); drawing aids (115); layers (117); colors and linetypes (118); blocks and attributes (118); 3D drawing and viewing commands (119); 3D animation and rendering commands (121). **IR:** Reproducible Master 4-1, *Drawing Commands;* Reproducible Master 4-2, *Editing and Inquiry Commands;* Reproducible Master 4-3, *Display Control Commands;* Reproducible Master 4-4, *Dimensioning Commands;* Reproducible Master 4-5, *Drawing Aids;* Reproducible Master 4-6, *File Management Commands and Utility Functions;* Reproducible Master 4-7, *Types of CAD Models.*
Writing	**IR:** Instructional Tasks 6, 7, 8.	**Text:** ✍Drawing Problems 1–12 (125–129). **IR:** Instructional Task 10.
Verbal	**Text:** Activity 3 (100). **IR:** Instructional Tasks: 1, 6, 7, ✍8, 9.	**IR:** Instructional Task 17.
Math		**Text:** Coordinate systems (102); drawing commands (104); editing and inquiry commands (108).
Science	**Text:** CAD workstation (82).	
Analytical	**Text:** Why use CAD? (78); selecting a CAD package (84); Activities 1–4 (100).	**Text:** Layers (117); colors and linetypes (118); blocks and attributes (118); Activities 1–2, 4 (125); ✍Drawing Problems 1–12 (125–129).

	Chapter 5	Chapter 6
Reading	**Text:** Sketching equipment (131); transfer type and overlays (149); ✍Creating text on CAD drawings (150). **IR:** Instructional Task 1.	
Writing	**Text:** ✍Sketching techniques (132); technical lettering overview (139); ✍pencil techniques (140); styles of lettering (140); guidelines (141); ✍single-stroke Gothic lettering (142); lettering with ink (148); ✍Sketching Problems 1–5 (155–157); ✍Lettering Problems 1–17 (157–158); ✍Drawing Problems 1–12 (159–161). **Worksheets:** ✍5-1: *Sketching Lines;* ✍5-2: *Sketching Angles;* ✍5-3: *Sketching Circles and Arcs;* ✍5-4: *Sketching Ellipses and Irregular Curves;* ✍5-5: *Sketching Objects;* ✍5-6: *Sketching Objects;* ✍5-7: *Sketching Objects;* ✍5-8: *Sketching Objects;* ✍5-9: *Sketching Objects;* ✍5-10: *Vertical Gothic Lettering;* ✍5-11: *Inclined Gothic Lettering,* ✍5-12: *Lettering Notes.* **IR:** Reproducible Master 5-3, *Single-Stroke Gothic Lettering.* **IR:** Instructional Tasks 2, 3, 4, 5, 7, 8, 9.	**Text:** Problems and Activities 1–22 (212). **Worksheets:** ✍6-8: *Outside Caliper.*
Math	**IR:** Instructional Task 5.	**Text:** ✍Constructing lines (164); ✍constructing angles (169); ✍constructing polygons (173); ✍constructing circles and arcs (191); ✍Problems and Activities 1–28 (212). **Worksheets:** ✍6-1: *Geometric Constructions;* ✍6-2: *Geometric Constructions;* ✍6-3: *Geometric Constructions;* ✍6-4: *Geometric Constructions;* ✍6-5: *Geometric Constructions;* ✍6-6: *Geometric Constructions;* ✍6-7: *Geometric Constructions.* **IR:** Transparency 6-1, *Bisecting a Line;* Transparency 6-2, *Dividing a Line;* Transparency 6-3, *Regular Polygons;* Reproducible Master 6-1, *Bisecting an Angle;* Reproducible Master 6-2, *Constructing Tangents;* Instructional Tasks 1, 2, 3, 4, 5, 6, 7.
Analytical	**Text:** ✍Drawing Problems 1–12 (159–161).	

	Chapter 7	Chapter 8
Reading		**Text:** Visualizing an object from a multiview drawing (259), ✍Problems and Activities (267–268).
Writing		**Text:** ✍Conventional drafting practices (253); ✍Problems and Activities (263–268); ✍Drawing Problems 1–31 (269–280). **Worksheets:** ✍8-1: *Missing Line Problems;* ✍8-2: *Missing View Problems;* ✍8-3: *End Clamp;* ✍8-4: *Stop Block;* ✍8-5: *Link Coupler;* ✍8-6: *Stop Bracket;* ✍8-7: *Pillow Block;* ✍8-8: *Sheet Stop Pivot Bracket;* ✍8-9: *Sliding Pulley Hub;* ✍8-10: *Hub Clamp;* ✍8-11: *Single Bearing Hanger;* ✍8-12: *V-Block;* ✍8-13: *Lower Straight Anvil;* ✍8-14: *Flange;* ✍8-15: *Variable Gear Cover.* **IR:** Instructional Task 4.
Math	**Text:** ✍Conic sections (213); ✍constructing other curves (228); ✍Problems and Activities 1–12 (239). **Worksheets:** ✍7-1: *Geometric Constructions;* ✍7-2: *Geometric Constructions.* **IR:** Transparency 7-1, *Conic Sections;* Reproducible Master 7-1, *Constructing Conic Sections;* Instructional Tasks 1, 2, 3, 4.	**Text:** Orthographic projection (243); first-angle and third-angle projections (257); ✍laying out a drawing (260). **IR:** Reproducible Master 8-2, *Projecting Points between Views;* Reproducible Master 8-3, *Projecting Normal and Inclined Surfaces.*
Analytical	**Text:** ✍Problems and Activities 1, 3, 6 (239).	**Text:** Orthographic projection (243); ✍conventional drafting practices (253); first-angle and third-angle projections (257); visualizing an object from a multiview drawing (259); ✍Problems and Activities (263–268); ✍Drawing Problems 1–31 (269–280). **Worksheets:** 8-1: *Missing Line Problems;* 8-2: *Missing View Problems.* **IR:** Transparency 8-1, *The Glass Box;* Transparency 8-2, *The Glass Box Unfolded;* Transparency 8-3, *Projecting Oblique Surfaces;* Instructional Tasks 1, 2, 3, 5.

	Chapter 9	Chapter 10
Reading	**Text:** Dimensioning CAD drawings (301). **IR:** Reproducible Master 9-1, *Rules for Good Dimensioning.*	**Text:** Cutting-plane lines (315); projection and placement of section views (316); types of section views (318); ✍conventional sectioning practices (323); material symbols in section views (327); hatching section views on CAD drawings (327). **IR:** Reproducible Master 10-1, *Types of Section Views.*
Writing	**Text:** Elements in dimensioning (282); dimensioning features for size (288); dimensioning features for location (295); unnecessary dimensions (298); notes (298); ✍rules for good dimensioning (299); ✍Drawing Problems 1–20 (309–314). **Worksheets:** ✍9-1: *Dimensioning Elements;* ✍9-2: *Spacer Block;* ✍9-3: *Clamp Plate;* ✍9-4: *Flange;* ✍9-5: *Bracket;* ✍9-6: *Outlet Check Valve;* ✍9-7: *Cylinder Rod Guide Bracket;* ✍9-8: *Bracket.* **IR:** Reproducible Master 9-1, *Rules for Good Dimensioning;* Reproducible Master 9-3, *Rectangular Coordinate Dimensioning;* Reproducible Master 9-4, *Unidirectional and Aligned Dimensions;* Reproducible Master 9-5, *Rectangular Coordinate Dimensioning;* Instructional Tasks 2, 7, 8.	**Text:** Section lines (316); ✍conventional sectioning practices (323); material symbols in section views (327); ✍Drawing Problems 1–28 (331–346). **Worksheets:** ✍10-1: *Box End Cap;* ✍10-2: *Sleeve;* ✍10-3: *Orifice;* ✍10-4: *Sleeve Pressure Regulator;* ✍10-5: *Piston;* ✍10-6: *Handwheel;* ✍10-7: *Lower Eccentric;* ✍10-8: *Right-Hand Cap;* ✍10-9: *Pitot Override Cover;* ✍10-10: *Pivot Pin;* ✍10-11: *Hub;* ✍10-12: *Sheave;* ✍10-13: *Barrel;* ✍10-14: *Tool Holder Bushing;* ✍10-15: *Fan Bracket.* **IR:** Instructional Task 2.
Math	**Text:** Dimensioning systems (285); ✍Drawing Problems 1–20 (309–314). **Worksheets:** ✍9-2: *Spacer Block;* ✍9-3: *Clamp Plate;* ✍9-4: *Flange;* ✍9-5: *Bracket.* **IR:** Transparency 9-1, *Decimal Inch Dimensioning;* Transparency 9-2, *Dimensioning Arcs and Curves;* Transparency 9-3, *Dimensioning Round Holes;* Reproducible Master 9-2, *Inch-Metric Equivalents;* Instructional Tasks 1, 3, 4, 5, 6.	**Text:** ✍Conventional sectioning practices (323); ✍Drawing Problems 1–28 (331–346).
Analytical	**Text:** ✍Drawing Problems 1–20 (309–314).	**Text:** ✍Drawing Problems 1–28 (331–346). **IR:** Instructional Tasks 1, 2, 3.

	Chapter 11	Chapter 12
Reading	**Text:** Types of pictorial projections (347).	**IR:** Transparency 12-1, *Secondary Auxiliary View.*
Writing	**Text:** ✍Axonometric projection (349); ✍oblique projections and drawings (376); ✍perspective drawings (381); ✍Problems and Activities 1–2 (397); ✍Drawing Problems 1–32 (397–405). **Worksheets:** ✍11-1: *Incline Block;* ✍11-2: *Brace Block;* ✍11-3: *Mounting Flange;* ✍11-4: *V-Block;* ✍11-5: *Box Angle;* ✍11-6: *Angle Bracket;* ✍11-7: *Drawing Curved Surfaces in Isometric;* ✍11-8: *U-Strap;* ✍11-9: *Pulley;* ✍11-10: *Wear Plate;* ✍11-11: *Shaft Support;* ✍11-12: *Box Parallel;* ✍11-13: *Mounting Bracket;* ✍11-14: *Two-Point Perspective Drawing.* **IR:** Reproducible Master 11-1, *Perspective Grid*; Instructional Tasks 2, 3, 4, 5, 6, 7.	**Text:** ✍Primary auxiliary views (408); ✍secondary auxiliary views (419); ✍Problems and Activities 1–16 (428–436); ✍Drawing Problems 1–6 (437–439). **Worksheets:** ✍12-8: *Bracket;* ✍12-9: *Stripper Bracket;* ✍12-10: *Cutter Block.* **IR:** Instructional Tasks 2, 11, 12, 13.
Math	**Text:** ✍Axonometric projection (349); ✍oblique projections and drawings (376); ✍perspective drawings (381); ✍Drawing Problems 1–32 (397–405). **IR:** Instructional Tasks 4, 5, 6, 7.	**Text:** ✍Primary auxiliary views (408); ✍secondary auxiliary views (419); ✍Problems and Activities 1–16 (428–436); ✍Drawing Problems 1–6 (437–439). **Worksheets:** ✍12-1: *Auxiliary Projections;* ✍12-2: *Auxiliary Projections;* ✍12-3: *Auxiliary View Construction;* ✍12-4: *Auxiliary View Construction;* ✍12-5: *Secondary Auxiliary View Construction;* ✍12-6: *Secondary Auxiliary View Construction;* ✍12-7: *Secondary Auxiliary Projections.* **IR:** Instructional Tasks 3, 4, 5, 6, 7, 8, 9, 10, 13, 14, 15.
Analytical	**Text:** Activity 2 (397); ✍Drawing Problems 1–32 (397–405). **IR:** Instructional Task 1.	**Text:** ✍Problems and Activities 1–16 (428–436); ✍Drawing Problems 1–6 (437–439). **Worksheets:** ✍12-1: *Auxiliary Projections;* ✍12-2: *Auxiliary Projections;* ✍12-3: *Auxiliary View Construction;* ✍12-4: *Auxiliary View Construction;* ✍12-5: *Secondary Auxiliary View Construction;* ✍12-6: *Secondary Auxiliary View Construction;* ✍12-7: *Secondary Auxiliary Projections.* **IR:** ✍Transparency 12-1, *Secondary Auxiliary View;* Instructional Tasks 1, 11, 12.

	Chapter 13	Chapter 14
Reading	**IR:** Transparency 13-1, *Revolving a Plane to Locate the Edge View.*	**Text:** Types of intersections (464); ✍spatial relationships (464); summary of projection methods applied in locating intersections (497). **Worksheets:** ✍14-2: *Intersections of Lines.* **IR:** Transparency 14-1, *Types of Surfaces;* Transparency 14-2, *Visibility of Crossing Lines in Space.*
Writing	**Text:** ✍Revolution procedures (442); ✍Drawing Problems 1–3 (460–461). **Worksheets:** ✍13-5: *Primary Revolutions;* ✍13-6: *Successive Revolutions.*	**Text:** ✍Spatial relationships (464); ✍intersection procedures (472); ✍Problems and Activities 1–11 (498–507). **Worksheets:** ✍14-2: *Intersections of Lines.*
Math	**Text:** ✍Revolution procedures (442); ✍Problems and Activities 1–8 (456–459); ✍Drawing Problems 1–3 (460–461). **Worksheets:** ✍13-1: *Revolutions;* ✍13-2: *Revolutions;* ✍13-3: *Revolutions;* ✍13-4: *Revolutions;* ✍13-5: *Primary Revolutions;* ✍13-7: *True Length Lines.* **IR:** Reproducible Master 13-1, *Revolution Method;* Instructional Tasks 2, 3, 4, 5, 6, 7, 8, 9, 10, 11.	**Text:** ✍Spatial relationships (464); ✍intersection procedures (472). **Worksheets:** ✍14-1: *Intersections of Lines;* ✍14-3: *Line Visibility;* ✍14-4: *Piercing Points;* ✍14-5: *Piercing Points;* ✍14-6: *Perpendicular Lines;* ✍14-7: *Intersection of Planes;* ✍14-8: *Intersection of a Plane and Prism;* ✍14-9: *Intersection of Prisms.* **IR:** Transparency 14-3, *Intersection of Planes;* Reproducible Master 14-1, *Visibility of a Line and a Plane in Space;* Reproducible Master 14-2, *Piercing Point of a Line and a Plane;* Instructional Task 2.
Analytical	**Text:** ✍Revolution procedures (442); ✍Problems and Activities 1–8 (456–459); ✍Drawing Problems 1–3 (460–461). **Worksheets:** ✍13-1: *Revolutions;* ✍13-2: *Revolutions;* ✍13-3: *Revolutions;* ✍13-4: *Revolutions;* ✍13-5: *Primary Revolutions.* **IR:** Transparency 13-1, *Revolving a Plane to Locate the Edge View;* Instructional Task 1.	**Text:** ✍Problems and Activities 1–4 (498–501). **Worksheets:** ✍14-1: *Intersections of Lines;* ✍14-3: *Line Visibility;* ✍14-4: *Piercing Points;* ✍14-7: *Intersection of Planes;* ✍14-8: *Intersection of a Plane and Prism;* ✍14-9: *Intersection of Prisms.* **IR:** Transparency 14-2, *Visibility of Crossing Lines in Space;* Instructional Tasks 3, 4, 5, 6, 7, 8, 9, 10, 11, 12, 13, 14, 15, 16, 17, 18, 19, 20, 21, 22, 23, 24.

	Chapter 15	Chapter 16
Reading	**Text:** Types of developments (510).	**Text:** Tolerancing fundamentals (550); tolerancing terms (550); selection of fits (558); geometric dimensioning and tolerancing (559); surface texture (572); geometric dimensioning and tolerancing on CAD drawings (574). **IR:** Transparency 16-2, *Feature Control Frame;* Transparency 16-3, *Surface Texture Symbol;* Reproducible Master 16-1, *Geometric Characteristic Symbols and Modifying Symbols;* Reproducible Master 16-2, *Positional Tolerancing for Feature Pattern Location;* Reproducible Master 16-3, *Dimensioning Symbols;* Reproducible Master 16-4, *Geometric Dimensioning and Tolerancing Symbols;* Reproducible Master 16-5, *Positional Tolerancing;* Instructional Task 4.
Writing	**Text:** ✍Development procedures (510); Problems and Activities 1–8 (537–545); ✍Design Problem 3 (545); ✍Drawing Problems 1–2 (545–547). **Worksheets:** ✍15-1: *Rectangular Prism Development;* ✍15-2: *Rectangular Prism Development;* ✍15-3: *Oblique Prism Development;* ✍15-4: *Truncated Cylinder Development;* ✍15-5: *Two-Piece Pipe Elbow Development;* ✍15-6: *Three-Piece Pipe Elbow Development;* ✍15-7: *Oblique Cylinder Development;* ✍15-8: *Truncated Pyramid Development;* ✍15-9: *Truncated Oblique Pyramid Development;* ✍15-10: *Cone Development;* ✍15-11: *Truncated Cone Development;* ✍15-12: *Transition Piece Development.* **IR:** Reproducible Master 15-1, *Development of a Rectangular Prism;* Reproducible Master 15-2, *Development of a Cylinder with an Inclined Bevel;* Instructional Tasks 2, 3, 4.	**Text:** ✍Application of tolerances (555); tolerances of form, profile, orientation, and runout (565); surface texture (572); ✍Drawing Problems 1–9 (578–586). **Worksheets:** ✍16-1: *Differential Spider;* ✍16-2: *Slide Nut;* ✍16-3: *Alignment Block;* ✍16-4: *Ring Plate;* ✍16-5: *Left Z-Axis Support;* ✍16-6: *Y-Axis Drive Cover Bracket.* **IR:** Instructional Tasks 2, 5.
Verbal		**IR:** Instructional Task 1.
Math	**Text:** ✍Development procedures (510); ✍Design Problems 1–5 (545). **IR:** Transparency 15-1, *Development of a Truncated Pyramid;* Transparency 15-2, *Development of a Truncated Right Cone;* Instructional Tasks 5, 6, 7, 8, 9, 10, 11, 12, 13, 14.	**Text:** ✍Application of tolerances (555); tolerances of location (562); surface texture (572). **IR:** Transparency 16-1, *Applications of Tolerances.*
Analytical	**Text:** ✍Design Problems 1–5 (545).	**Text:** Selection of fits (558).

	Chapter 17	Chapter 18
Reading	**Text:** Types of working drawings (587); block formats on working drawings (594); standards for drafting (596); the design and drafting process (596). **IR:** Reproducible Master 17-1, *Types of Working Drawings;* Instructional Tasks 1, 2, 3.	**Text:** Thread terminology (616); thread forms (617); thread series (618); thread classes (618); single and multiple threads (618); thread specifications (619); bolts and screws (629); washers and retaining rings (636); nuts (636); rivets (639); pin fasteners, keys, and springs (640). **IR:** Transparency 18-1, *Thread Representations;* Reproducible Master 18-1, *Thread Terminology;* Reproducible Master 18-2, *Thread Forms;* Reproducible Master 18-3, *Thread Note;* Instructional Task 2.
Writing	**Text:** ✍Functional drafting techniques (602); ✍Drawing Problems 1–9 (603–613); ✍Design Problems (614). **Worksheets:** ✍17-1: *Components Bracket;* ✍17-2: *Mating Components Bracket;* ✍17-3: *Cover Bracket;* ✍17-4: *Hanger Bolt;* ✍17-5: *Battery Bracket;* ✍17-6: *Valve;* ✍17-7: *Bracket;* ✍17-8: *Center Base Frame;* ✍17-9: *PC Card Bracket;* ✍17-10: *Gear Cover Plate;* ✍17-11: *Hydraulic Dechuck Piston;* ✍17-12: *Roller for Brick Elevator;* ✍17-13: *Metering Sleeve;* ✍17-14: *Tube Transfer;* ✍17-15: *Idler Gear Shaft;* ✍17-16: *Duct Casting;* ✍17-17: *Focusing Base.* **IR:** Instructional Task 4.	**Text:** Thread specifications (619); ✍thread representations (620); ✍bolts and screws (629); ✍Problems and Activities 1–20 (532–533); ✍Drawing Problems 1–8 (645–650). **Worksheets:** ✍18-1: *Bolts and Nuts;* ✍18-2: *Threaded Block;* ✍18-3: *Special Adjusting Screw;* ✍18-4: *Spindle Ram Screw;* ✍18-5: *Shank.* **IR:** Instructional Tasks 3, 4, 5, 6, 7, 8, 9.
Math	**Worksheets:** ✍17-10: *Gear Cover Plate;* ✍17-11: *Hydraulic Dechuck Piston;* ✍17-12: *Roller for Brick Elevator.*	**Text:** Single and multiple threads (618). **Worksheets:** ✍18-1: *Bolts and Nuts;* ✍18-2: *Threaded Block;* ✍18-3: *Special Adjusting Screw;* ✍18-4: *Spindle Ram Screw;* ✍18-5: *Shank.*
Analytical	**Text:** ✍Design Problems (614). **Worksheets:** ✍17-10: *Gear Cover Plate;* ✍17-11: *Hydraulic Dechuck Piston;* ✍17-12: *Roller for Brick Elevator.*	**Worksheets:** ✍18-3: *Special Adjusting Screw;* ✍18-4: *Spindle Ram Screw.*

	Chapter 19	Chapter 20
Reading	**Text:** ✍Cams (653); gears (663); splines (675). **IR:** Reproducible Master 19-1, *Spur Gear Terminology;* Reproducible Master 19-2, *Bevel Gear Terminology;* Reproducible Master 19-3, *Worm Gear Terminology;* Instructional Task 6.	**Text:** Traditional methods of reproducing drawings (681); traditional methods of reproducing prints (685); storing drawings (687); reproducing, distributing, and storing CAD drawings (687). **IR:** Transparency 20-1, *Reproduction Prints.*
Writing	**Text:** ✍Cams (653); gears (663); ✍Problems and Activities 1–16 (679–680). **Worksheets:** ✍19-1: *Cam Layout;* ✍19-2: *Cam Design Problem;* ✍19-3: *Spur Gear;* ✍19-4: *Bevel Gear;* ✍19-5: *Gear Assembly.* **IR:** Instructional Tasks 2, 5, 7, 8, 9, 10.	**Text:** ✍Problems and Activities 1–3, 6–7 (690). **IR:** ✍Instructional Task 5.
Verbal		**Text:** ✍Problems and Activities 6–7 (690). **IR:** Instructional Task 5.
Math	**Text:** ✍Cams (653); gears (663); ✍Problems and Activities 1–16 (679–680). **Worksheets:** ✍19-1: *Cam Layout;* ✍19-2: *Cam Design Problem;* ✍19-3: *Spur Gear;* ✍19-4: *Bevel Gear;* 19-5: *Gear Assembly.* **IR:** Transparency 19-1, *Cam Displacement Diagram and Cam Layout;* Instructional Task 4.	
Science	**Text:** ✍Cams (653); gears (663).	**Text:** Traditional methods of reproducing prints (685).
Analytical	**Text:** ✍Problems and Activities 9–10, 16 (679–680). **Worksheets:** ✍19-1: *Cam Layout;* ✍19-2: *Cam Design Problem;* ✍19-3: *Spur Gear;* ✍19-4: *Bevel Gear;* ✍19-5: *Gear Assembly.* **IR:** Instructional Task 10.	**Text:** ✍Problems and Activities 4–5 (690).

	Chapter 21	Chapter 22
Reading	**Text:** Machine processes (692); surface texture (700); linking design and manufacturing (701); computer-aided drafting (CAD) (701); computer-aided manufacturing (CAM) (704); computer-integrated manufacturing (CIM) (711). **IR:** Reproducible Master 21-1, *Machine Processes;* Reproducible Master 21-2, *Automated Manufacturing System;* Instructional Task 6.	**Text:** Types of architectural drawings (716). **IR:** Reproducible Master 22-1, *Architectural Material Symbols;* Reproducible Master 22-2, *Floor Plan;* Instructional Tasks 2, 3, 4, 5, 6, 7.
Writing	**IR:** Instructional Task 10.	**Text:** ✍Problems and Activities 1–4 (733–734). **Worksheets:** ✍22-1. **IR:** Instructional Tasks 1, 2, 3, 5, 7.
Verbal	**IR:** Instructional Tasks 2, 10, 11.	
Math	**Text:** Computer numerical control machining (697).	**Worksheets:** ✍22-1: *Architectural Drawings.*
Analytical		**Worksheets:** ✍22-1: *Architectural Drawings.*

	Chapter 23	Chapter 24
Reading	**Text:** Structural wood construction (736); structural steel construction (738); structural steel drafting (739); concrete construction (740); concrete construction drafting (745). **IR:** Reproducible Master 23-1, *Welded Wire Reinforcement;* Reproducible Master 23-2, *Beam Data;* Instructional Tasks 1, 4.	**Text:** Electrical and electronics drawings (750). **IR:** Reproducible Master 24-1, *Industrial Control Schematic Diagram;* Instructional Task 3.
Writing	**Text:** ✍Problems and Activities 1–3 (747).	**Text:** Electrical and electronics drawings (750); ✍Problems and Activities 1–6 (757–760). **Worksheets:** ✍24-1: *Electrical Symbols;* ✍24-2: *Electrical Power System;* ✍24-3: *Schematic Diagram.* **IR:** Instructional Tasks 2, 3, 4.
Math	**Text:** ✍Problems and Activities 1–3 (747).	
Science		**Text:** Integrated circuits (755).
Analytical	**Text:** ✍Problems and Activities 1–3 (747).	

	Chapter 25	Chapter 26
Reading	**Text:** Mapping and surveying terms (761); types of maps (763); gathering map data (768). **IR:** Transparency 25-1, *Contour Map.*	**Text:** Welding processes (780); types of welded joints (782); types of welds (782); weld symbols (782); standard welding symbol (783). **IR:** Reproducible Master 26-1, *Welding Processes;* Reproducible Master 26-2, *Types of Welds;* Reproducible Master 26-3, *Weld Symbols;* Reproducible Master 26-4, *Elements in a Welding Symbol.*
Writing	**Text:** Map format elements (768); map drafting techniques (771). **Worksheets:** ✍25-1: *Topographic Map;* ✍25-2: *Map Traverse.* **IR:** Instructional Task 3.	**Text:** ✍Activities 1–2 (789); ✍Drawing Problems 1–5 (789–794). **Worksheets:** ✍26-1: *Joint Designs;* ✍26-2: *Lubricator Tank Base.* **IR:** Instructional Task 3.
Verbal	**IR:** Instructional Task 4.	
Math	**Text:** Map format elements (768); map drafting techniques (771); ✍Problems and Activities 1–4 (777–778). **Worksheets:** ✍25-1: *Topographic Map;* ✍25-2: *Map Traverse.*	**Worksheets:** ✍26-2: *Lubricator Tank Base.*
Science	**Text:** Gathering map data (768). **IR:** Instructional Task 1.	**Text:** Welding processes (780).
Analytical	**Worksheets:** ✍25-1: *Topographic Map;* ✍25-2: *Map Traverse.*	**Text:** ✍Activities 1–2 (789). **Worksheets:** ✍26-2: *Lubricator Tank Base.*

	Chapter 27	Chapter 28
Reading	**Text:** Types of technical illustrations (795).	**Text:** Types of graphs and charts (805).
Writing	**Text:** Basic illustration techniques (797); ✍Problems and Activities 1–4 (804). **Worksheets:** ✍27-1: *Bearing Mount;* ✍27-2: *Slotted Angle Plate.* **IR:** Instructional Tasks 2, 3, 4, 5.	**Text:** ✍Problems and Activities 1–6 (813). **Worksheets:** ✍28-1: *Line Graph.*
Verbal	**IR:** ✍Instructional Task 1.	
Math		**Text:** Types of graphs and charts (805). **Worksheets:** ✍28-1: *Line Graph.* **IR:** Transparency 28-1, *Index Bar Graph.*
Analytical		**Text:** ✍Problems and Activities 1–6 (813). **Worksheets:** ✍28-1: *Line Graph.* **IR:** Instructional Tasks 1, 2, 3, 4, 5, 6, 7, 8, 9.

Scope and Sequence Chart

The Scope and Sequence Chart identifies the major concepts presented in each chapter of the *Drafting & Design: Engineering Drawing Using Manual and CAD Techniques* text. The chart is divided into five sections, which include Chapters 1–5, 6–11, 12–15, 16–21, and 22–28. Within these sections, entries are identified by a bold chapter number. Topics follow the chapter number for easy reference.

Section 1—Introduction to Drafting (Chapters 1–5)

Care and Use of Drafting Tools and Equipment

2: Drafting equipment (42); drafting media (44); drawing pencils (46); erasing and erasing tools (51); scales (53); using a protractor (62); using a compass (63); drafting templates (65); dividers (66); irregular curves (68).

5: Sketching equipment (131); transfer type and overlays (149).

Safe and Efficient Work Practices and Techniques

2: Drafting equipment (42); drawing pencils (46); Alphabet of Lines (47); neatness in drafting (52); scales (53); sheet format (58); drafting instrument procedures (59); using a protractor (62); using a compass (63); drafting templates (65); dividers (66); irregular curves (68); pencil techniques with instruments (69); inking (70).

5: Sketching techniques (132); technical lettering overview (139); pencil techniques (140); styles of lettering (140); guidelines (141); single-stroke Gothic lettering (142); lettering with ink (148); transfer type and overlays (149).

Basic Skills in Communication, Math, and Science

1: Drafting as a communication tool (22).

5: Sketching techniques (132); single-stroke Gothic lettering (142).

Design and Problem-Solving Processes

1: Drafting as a problem-solving tool (24); drafting as a design tool (27); models (29).

Computer Applications and Literacy

3: What is CAD? (77); why use CAD? (78); mechanical CAD applications (80); CAD workstation (82); selecting a CAD package (84); general purpose CAD packages (85); advanced mechanical drafting and modeling CAD packages (89); AEC CAD packages (93).

4: File management commands (102); coordinate systems (102); drawing commands (104); editing and inquiry commands (108); display control commands (114); dimensioning commands (115); drawing aids (115); layers (117); colors and linetypes (118); blocks and attributes (118); 3D drawing and viewing commands (119); 3D animation and rendering commands (121).

5: Creating text on CAD drawings (150).

Career Information and Employment Skills

1: Drafting as a design tool (27); careers in drafting (31); careers related to drafting (33).

Section 2—Drafting Techniques and Skills (Chapters 6–11)

Care and Use of Drafting Tools and Equipment

6: Constructing lines (164); constructing angles (169); constructing polygons (173); constructing circles and arcs (191).

Safe and Efficient Work Practices and Techniques

6: Constructing lines (164); constructing angles (169); constructing polygons (173); constructing circles and arcs (191).
7: Conic sections (213); constructing other curves (228).
8: Orthographic projection (243); conventional drafting practices (253); first-angle and third-angle projections (257); visualizing an object from a multiview drawing (259); laying out a drawing (260).
9: Elements in dimensioning (282); dimensioning features for size (288); dimensioning features for location (295); unnecessary dimensions (298); notes (298); rules for good dimensioning (299).
10: Projection and placement of section views (316); types of section views (318); conventional sectioning practices (323); material symbols in section views (327).
11: Axonometric projection (349); oblique projections and drawings (376); perspective drawings (381).

Basic Skills in Communication, Math, and Science

6: Constructing lines (164); constructing angles (169); constructing polygons (173); constructing circles and arcs (191).
7: Conic sections (213); constructing other curves (228).
8: Orthographic projection (243); first-angle and third-angle projections (257); visualizing an object from a multiview drawing (259); laying out a drawing (260).
9: Elements in dimensioning (282); dimensioning systems (285); dimensioning features for size (288); dimensioning features for location (295); notes (298).
10: Cutting-plane lines (315); section lines (316); types of section views (318).
11: Types of pictorial projections (347); axonometric projection (349); oblique projections and drawings (376); perspective drawings (381).

Design and Problem-Solving Processes

6: Constructing lines (164); constructing angles (169); constructing polygons (173); constructing circles and arcs (191).
7: Conic sections (213); constructing other curves (228).
8: Orthographic projection (243); visualizing an object from a multiview drawing (259); laying out a drawing (260).
9: Elements in dimensioning (282).
10: Types of section views (318).
11: Axonometric projection (349); oblique projections and drawings (376); perspective drawings (381).

Computer Applications and Literacy

6: Constructing lines (164); constructing angles (169); constructing polygons (173); constructing circles and arcs (191).
7: Conic sections (213); constructing other curves (228).
8: Laying out a drawing (260).
9: Dimensioning CAD drawings (301).
10: Hatching section views on CAD drawings (327).
11: Axonometric projection (349); oblique projections and drawings (376).

Section 3—Descriptive Geometry (Chapters 12–15)

Safe and Efficient Work Practices and Techniques

13: Revolution procedures (442).
14: Intersection procedures (472); summary of projection methods applied in locating intersections (497).
15: Development procedures (510).

Basic Skills in Communication, Math, and Science

12: Primary auxiliary views (408); secondary auxiliary views (419).
14: Spatial relationships (464).
15: Development procedures (510).

Design and Problem-Solving Processes

12: Primary auxiliary views (408); secondary auxiliary views (419).
13: Revolution procedures (442).
14: Types of intersections (464); spatial relationships (464); intersection procedures (472).
15: Types of developments (510); development procedures (510).

Computer Applications and Literacy

12: Primary auxiliary views (408); secondary auxiliary views (419).
13: Revolution procedures (442).
14: Intersection procedures (472).
15: Development procedures (510).

Section 4—Advanced Applications (Chapters 16–21)

Safe and Efficient Work Practices and Techniques

16: Application of tolerances (555).
17: Standards for drafting (596); functional drafting techniques (602).
18: Thread terminology (616); thread forms (617); thread series (618); thread classes (618); single and multiple threads (618); thread specifications (619); thread representations (620); bolts and screws (629); washers and retaining rings (636); nuts (636); rivets (639); pin fasteners, keys, and springs (640).
19: Cams (653); gears (663); splines (675).
20: Storing drawings (687).
21: Computer numerical control machining (697).

Basic Skills in Communication, Math, and Science

16: Tolerancing fundamentals (550); tolerancing terms (550); geometric dimensioning and tolerancing (559).
18: Thread terminology (616).
19: Gears (663).
20: Traditional methods of reproducing drawings (681); traditional methods of reproducing prints (685).
21: Surface texture (700).

Design and Problem-Solving Processes

16: Application of tolerances (555); selection of fits (558); geometric dimensioning and tolerancing (559); tolerances of location (562); tolerances of form, profile, orientation, and runout (565); surface texture (572).
17: Types of working drawings (587); block formats on working drawings (594); the design and drafting process (596); applications of working drawings (596).
21: Machine processes (692); computer numerical control machining (697); computer-aided drafting (CAD) (701); computer-aided manufacturing (CAM) (704); computer-integrated manufacturing (CIM) (711).

Computer Applications and Literacy

16: Geometric dimensioning and tolerancing on CAD drawings (574).
19: Cams (653).
20: Reproducing, distributing, and storing CAD drawings (687).
21: Computer numerical control machining (697); computer-aided drafting (CAD) (701); computer-aided manufacturing (CAM) (704); computer-integrated manufacturing (CIM) (711).

Social and Cultural Impacts of Technology

17: Standards for drafting (596).
20: Traditional methods of reproducing drawings (681).
21: Linking design and manufacturing (701); computer-aided manufacturing (CAM) (704); computer-integrated manufacturing (CIM) (711).

Section 5—Drafting and Design Specializations (Chapters 22–28)

Safe and Efficient Work Practices and Techniques

24: Electrical and electronics drawings (750).
25: Gathering map data (768); map drafting techniques (771).
26: Weld symbols (782); standard welding symbol (783).
27: Basic illustration techniques (797).

Basic Skills in Communication, Math, and Science

25: Mapping and surveying terms (761); types of maps (763); map format elements (768).
28: Types of graphs and charts (805).

Design and Problem-Solving Processes

22: Types of architectural drawings (716).
23: Structural wood construction (736); structural steel construction (738); structural steel drafting (739); concrete construction (740); concrete construction drafting (745).
24: Electrical and electronics drawings (750).
26: Welding processes (780); types of welded joints (782); types of welds (782).
27: Types of technical illustrations (795).

Computer Applications and Literacy

24: Integrated circuits (755).
25: Gathering map data (768).

Career Information and Employment Skills

27: Types of technical illustrations (795); basic illustration techniques (797).

Section 1 Introduction to Drafting

Drafting and the Drafter

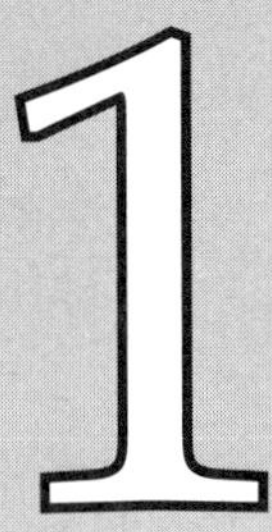

Learning Objectives

After studying this chapter, the student will be able to:

- Define the role of drafting in industry.
- Explain the purpose of technical drawings.
- Describe how sketches are used to communicate ideas.
- List and describe the four steps in the design method.
- Explain the importance of models in industry.
- Identify the types of careers available in drafting and related fields.
- Describe the educational background and skills required for careers in drafting and related fields.
- Describe the duties associated with different types of careers in drafting.

Instructional Resources

Text: pages 21–40

Review Questions, pages 37–38

Problems and Activities, pages 38–39

Instructor's Resource

Instructional Tasks

Instructional Aids and Assignments

Chapter 1 Quiz

Reproducible Masters

- Reproducible Master 1-1: *Types of Technical Drawings.* Common types of technical drawings are illustrated. Shown are a freehand sketch, a mechanical drawing, a set of drawings, and a presentation drawing.
- Reproducible Master 1-2: *The Design Method.* The steps in the design method are listed and explained. The four steps are problem definition, preliminary solutions, preliminary solution refinement, and decision and implementation.
- Reproducible Master 1-3: *Types of Models.* The three common types of models—scale models, mockups, and prototypes—are identified and defined for discussion purposes. This handout can be used as a transparency.

Color Transparencies (Binder/IRCD only)

- Transparency 1-1: *Problem Solving.* The three basic classifications of problems are shown.
- Transparency 1-2: *Conceptual Model.* A conceptual model such as this computer-generated rendering of a race car can be very useful as a communication, problem-solving, or design tool.
- Transparency 1-3: *Careers in Drafting.* Six traditional drafting careers are identified.

Instructional Tasks

1. Explain how drafting serves as a graphic language.
   - Display some working drawings and discuss the view arrangements. Explain how drafting symbols are used to communicate information.
2. Discuss the use of sketching to serve as a communication tool.
   - Show students several types of sketches.
3. Describe how a sketch is typically different from a mechanical drawing.
   - Display a mechanical drawing and a sketch. Have students list the differences between the two.
4. Explain how a presentation drawing may be used to communicate information.
   - Ask students to select one or two presentation drawings from a large collection. Have them explain why the selected drawings communicate the information in the best manner.
5. Discuss the various types of problems that may be encountered by a problem solver.
   - Discuss the three categories of problems—well-structured problems, semi-structured problems, and nonstructured problems.

6. Define *problem solving*.
   - Have students explain the elements of the following terms: problem, design, and design method.
7. Identify and describe the four steps in the design method.
   - Discuss each step. Have students use the steps to solve a problem.
8. Discuss the use and types of models in the design process.
   - Display actual models used in industry.
9. Identify careers in drafting and related fields. Also identify the duties and educational requirements associated with these careers.
   - Discuss the nature of the work, entry requirements, job potential, and rewards of the various careers.
   - Post news articles regarding careers and opportunities in drafting on the classroom bulletin board.
   - Post on the bulletin board examples of industrial drawings and ask students to comment.
10. Organize design groups and have them solve problems.
   - Have students study several problems needing solutions, such as a means of elevating a car for an oil change, a way to store tools in a home workshop, or a plan for creating a study area at home with book storage and a writing area.
   - Invite a representative of industry to speak to the class on problem solving.

Instructional Aids and Assignments

1. Show the class a multimedia presentation or film on creative problem solving.
2. Show photographs or slides of solutions to problems worked out by previous groups.
3. Show the class a multimedia presentation or film on drafting careers and careers in related fields.
4. Display industrial drawings and prints in class.
5. Invite an architect, drafter, engineer, or industrial designer to speak to the class.
6. Display the basic types of equipment and supplies the students will be using.
7. Assign the problems and activities in the text.

Answers to Review Questions, Text

Pages 37–38

1. technical
2. Graphic
3. The primary purpose of drafting is to communicate an idea, plan, or object to some other person.
4. American National Standards Institute (ANSI)
5. Sketches, mechanical drawings, sets of drawings, and presentation drawings.
6. Sketches
7. Mechanical
8. The purpose of a presentation drawing is to secure acceptance of the proposed product.
9. Problem solving is the process of seeking practical solutions to a problem.
10. A well-structured problem.
11. Divergent
12. The design method is a systematic procedure for approaching a design problem and arriving at a solution.
13. Problem definition, development of preliminary solutions, preliminary solution refinement, and decision and implementation.
14. defined
15. Brainstorming
16. model
17. mockup
18. A full-size operating model of an actual object.
19. senior drafting
20. layout
21. design
22. Architect, industrial designer, and engineer.

Solutions to Problems and Activities, Text

Pages 38–39

1. Students will have collected examples of drawings that represent as many of the following types or purposes as possible:
   A. Idea sketch.
   B. Technical drawing.
   C. Manufacturing or construction drawing.
   D. Presentation drawing.
   E. Reference drawing.
   F. Patent drawing.

G. Advertising drawing.
H. Service or maintenance drawing.
Discuss why each drawing represents the category it is in.

2. Students will have made a list of several problems for each of the following categories:
A. Well-structured problems.
B. Semi-structured problems.
C. Nonstructured problems.
Discuss why each problem is placed in a specific category.
3. Organize the class into several groups, and have a brainstorming session to list as many useful items as possible that can be made from each item suggested. Include all items, regardless of practicality. For example:
A. Bale of straw.
Archery target, high jump landing pad, safety bumper on the curve of a mini-car racetrack, bedding for garden plants, punching bag, etc.
4. Organize the class into several groups. List possible solutions to the problems. For example:
C. Make a 1″ square hole in the side of a tin can.
Drill a series of small holes in the shape of a square; drill a hole to insert tin snips and cut the square hole; make a square punch and die and punch the hole; drill a hole and file corners into a square.
5. Have the students make a list of six or more items not currently available that have sales potential. This can be done in groups or individually. Examples of items include special tool holders, safety devices for machinery, etc.
6. Organize groups and monitor their progress in following the steps in the design method.
7. Assign this problem to small groups or to individuals. Monitor their progress in the use of the design method in arriving at the final solution. Sketches and instrument drawings should reflect their knowledge and skill in design drafting.
8. Assign this problem to small groups or to individuals. Suggest that they start by thinking of jobs that need to be done and determine whether a small gasoline engine could be used. Other equipment, such as fan blades or pulleys, can also be used.
9. Use the same approach and procedure as in Problem 8.
10. Suggest students do some reading on the career field of the person to be interviewed and prepare an outline of information to be sought in the interview. Have the students present their reports to the class.
11. Suggest sources of information the students can use, such as the library, trade journals, or references on famous persons. Have students present their reports to the class.
12. Discuss with the class the procedure to follow when problems occur in industry. A person using the design method studies and resolves the problem. Students should view the school or community problem in this way, research the needs, and develop a satisfactory solution. You may want to invite a school or community leader to class to discuss the problem at the start, and invite him or her back to comment on the solution when it is presented.
13. Observe the number of words required to describe the object. Have another student read it to see if there is adequate information to construct the object described.
14. Compare the clarity of information provided by the written narrative and the sketch.
15. The report should describe the individual's background, entry into drafting, and his or her related career.
16. Student collections should reveal many uses and applications of drafting that are typical of the types of jobs found in industry.
17. Students should be encouraged to read about the career of the person to be interviewed. A topical outline to aid in the interview should include such items as educational and experience requirements, entry jobs, progressive job levels after entry, nature of the work, and financial and fringe benefits of the work.
18. The report should reveal a number of consumer activities where drafting is useful.
19. Many students will be able to obtain prints through their family, relatives, or friends. As the instructor, you may want to have a few industrial prints on hand to discuss drafting applications.
20. Most communities have a well-known architect, engineer, or industrial designer in private practice who would be willing to participate in an interview or provide information. City, county, and state architects or engineers are other potential candidates.

Answers to Chapter 1 Quiz

1. A. communicate an idea, plan, or object to some other person
2. C. American National Standards Institute
3. D. All of the above.
4. B. a set of drawings
5. A. convergent thinking
6. B. prototype
7. C. Prove out the product design.
8. C. design
9. D. industrial designer
10. B. graphic
11. A. Checker
12. A. Problem definition
    B. Preliminary solutions
    C. Preliminary solution refinement
    D. Decision and implementation

Chapter Quiz 1

Drafting and the Drafter

Name ______________________________

Period____________ Date____________ Score ____________

Multiple Choice

Choose the answer that correctly completes the statement. Write the corresponding letter in the space provided.

_____ 1. The primary purpose of preparing a technical drawing is to _____.
A. communicate an idea, plan, or object to some other person
B. sketch a possible solution to a problem
C. communicate an idea to the public
D. confirm an idea

_____ 2. *ANSI* is the acronym for _____.
A. Associated National Standards Industry
B. Association of National Standards Institute
C. American National Standards Institute
D. American National Scale Illustration

_____ 3. Sketches may be made in _____ form.
A. freehand
B. detailed
C. schematic
D. All of the above.

_____ 4. The information needed for production of an object is contained in _____.
A. the specifications
B. a set of drawings
C. the prospectus
D. None of the above.

_____ 5. The process of arriving at a solution for a well-structured problem is usually accomplished through _____.
A. convergent thinking
B. divergent thinking
C. intellectual discourse
D. manufacturing analysis

_____ 6. An original full-size operating model of an actual object is called a _____.
A. mockup
B. prototype
C. fixture
D. pilot model

Name ____

______ 7. Which of the following is *not* a duty of a detail drafter?
A. Prepare detail drawings.
B. Revise drawings.
C. Prove out the product design.
D. Prepare bills of material.

______ 8. A _____ drafter is a senior level drafter and represents the highest level of drafting skill.
A. detail
B. layout
C. design
D. trainee

______ 9. The _____ is concerned with the development of solutions to three-dimensional problems involving esthetics, materials, manufacturing processes, human factors, and creativity.
A. technical illustrator
B. checker
C. design drafter
D. industrial designer

______ 10. Drafting is sometimes referred to as the "language of industry" and may be described as a _____ language.
A. written
B. graphic
C. scientific
D. spoken

______ 11. Of the following positions, which is likely to have the greatest drafting knowledge and skill?
A. Checker
B. Trainee drafter
C. Detail drafter
D. Layout drafter

Completion

Write the correct answer in the space provided.

12. List in order the four steps of the design method.

A. ____

B. ____

C. ____

D. ____

Types of Technical Drawings

Freehand Sketch

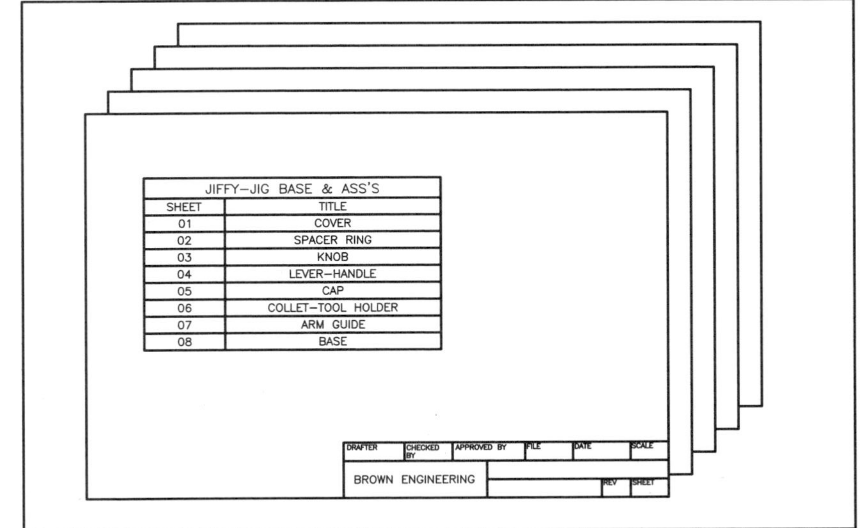

Set of Drawings

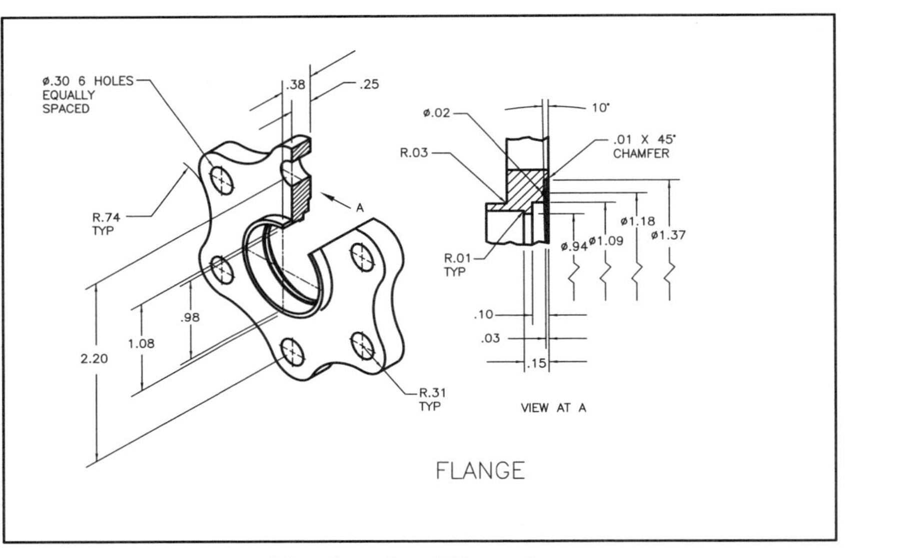

Mechanical Drawing

Presentation Drawing

RM 1-1

The Design Method

Step 1 Problem Definition

- Make a problem statement
- List the requirements
- Specify limitations or restrictions
- Conduct research

Step 2 Preliminary Solutions

- Brainstorm
- List possible solutions

Step 3 Preliminary Solution Refinement

- Combine all ideas
- Make rough sketches

Step 4 Decision and Implementation

- Prepare a decision chart
- Rate possible solutions
- Select the best solution
- Prepare a working drawing

RM 1-2

Types of Models

Models are used to improve communication between technical personnel. Models are also used to provide greater visualization of problems and solutions by nontechnical and management employees.

Scale Models

A scale model is a replica of the actual or proposed object. The model can be smaller or larger than the object. However, proportions and overall appearance should be accurate. Some scale models are working models.

Mockups

A mockup is a full-size model that simulates an actual machine or part. It represents a more realistic appearance than a typical scale model. A mockup is not operational.

Prototypes

A prototype is a full-size operating model of the actual object. A prototype is usually the first full-size working model constructed by workers. Each part is made individually. The purpose of a prototype is to correct design and operation flaws before starting production.

RM 1-3

Traditional Drafting Equipment and Drawing Techniques

Learning Objectives

After studying this chapter, the student will be able to:

- Identify and describe how to use basic drafting tools.
- List and explain the types of lines in the Alphabet of Lines.
- Describe how to make drawings to scale.
- Use drafting tools and basic drawing techniques to make drawings.

Instructional Resources

Text: pages 41–76

Review Questions, page 71

Drawing Problems, pages 72–76

Worksheets: pages 7–22

- Worksheet 2-1: *Alphabet of Lines*
- Worksheet 2-2: *Architect's Scale*
- Worksheet 2-3: *Decimal Inch Scales*
- Worksheet 2-4: *Metric Scale*
- Worksheet 2-5: *Instrument Drafting*
- Worksheet 2-6: *Instrument Drafting*
- Worksheet 2-7: *Circles, Arcs, and Irregular Curves*
- Worksheet 2-8: *Instrument Drawings*
- Worksheet 2-9: *Instrument Drawings*
- Worksheet 2-10: *Instrument Drawings*
- Worksheet 2-11: *Instrument Drawings*
- Worksheet 2-12: *Throttle Guide Gate*
- Worksheet 2-13: *Guide Plate*
- Worksheet 2-14: *Clevis*
- Worksheet 2-15: *Bracket*
- Worksheet 2-16: *Gasket*

Instructor's Resource

Instructional Tasks

Instructional Aids and Assignments

Chapter 2 Quiz

Reproducible Masters

- Reproducible Master 2-1: *Drafting Equipment.* A list of instruments and equipment recommended for most drafting work is shown. This handout can be used as a transparency.
- Reproducible Master 2-2: *Line Conventions.* Accepted line conventions are shown for lines in the Alphabet of Lines.

Procedure Checklist

Color Transparencies (Binder/IRCD only)

- Transparency 2-1: *Applications of Line Conventions.* Shown are standard line weights and conventions used in drafting.
- Transparency 2-2: *Mechanical Engineer's Scales.* Partial mechanical engineer's scales for full size, half size, and quarter size scales are shown to assist students in learning how to read the scale.

Instructional Tasks

1. Identify by name and demonstrate the use of basic drafting instruments.
   - Arrange a display of the drafting instruments students will be expected to use in class. Discuss the care and maintenance of these instruments.
   - Demonstrate the use of each instrument in connection with the instructional content.
2. Explain how to select and use drafting media, pencils, and erasers.
   - Discuss qualities desired in drafting media, pencils, and erasers.
   - Display samples of drafting media, pencils, and erasers. Discuss their applications, advantages, and limitations, such as erasability without "ghosting," reproduction of quality prints, stability, and cost.
3. Explain how to measure and lay out drawings to scale.
   - Demonstrate measuring to scale and laying off measurements.

- Prepare a sheet of premeasured lines (see the sample shown here) as a handout for students to measure in class. A key prepared on clear plastic will be helpful in checking student work.
- Discuss the selection of the proper scale in making a drawing.

4. Identify the lines in the Alphabet of Lines and demonstrate their use in drafting.
   - Discuss the width of lines and their distinguishing characteristics and use.
   - Display some industrial prints. Point out the use of the various lines.

Instructional Aids and Assignments

1. Show multimedia presentations or films on the use and care of drafting instruments.
2. Display an overhead transparency to demonstrate how to read a scale.
3. Display an overhead transparency showing the Alphabet of Lines.
4. Show the class a set of industrial drawings to show applications of the Alphabet of Lines.
5. Assign the one-view drawing problems from the textbook or Worksheets. The number of problems is sufficient to assign a minimum number to all students and to identify problems that may be done for extra credit. Some problems may be used for the performance section of the chapter quiz.

Answers to Review Questions, Text

Page 71

1. instrument
2. Triangles
3. drafting machine
4. media
5. Vellum
6. Answer may include any three of the following: Standard wooden pencils, rectangular leads, mechanical lead holders, and thin leads.
7. 7B to 9H
8. Conical and wedge.
9. Alphabet of Lines
10. visible
11. dash
12. crosshatching
13. Centerlines represent axes of symmetrical parts, circles, and paths of motion.
14. dimension
15. Break
16. A smudged area on a copy of a drawing caused by damage from erasing or mishandling.
17. Flat and triangular.
18. full-divided
19. An architect's scale.
20. mechanical
21. meter
22. quarter
23. title block
24. inclined
25. protractor
26. A compass.
27. templates
28. Dividers
29. An irregular curve or French curve.

Solutions to Drawing Problems, Text

Pages 72–76

Student work should look like the following drawings. The problem number and title are indicated on each problem sheet.

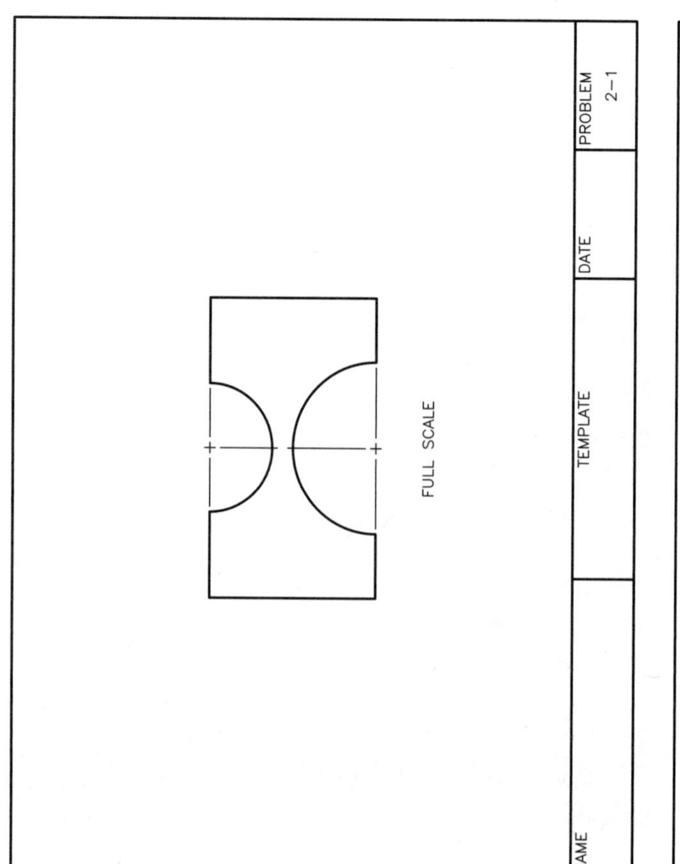

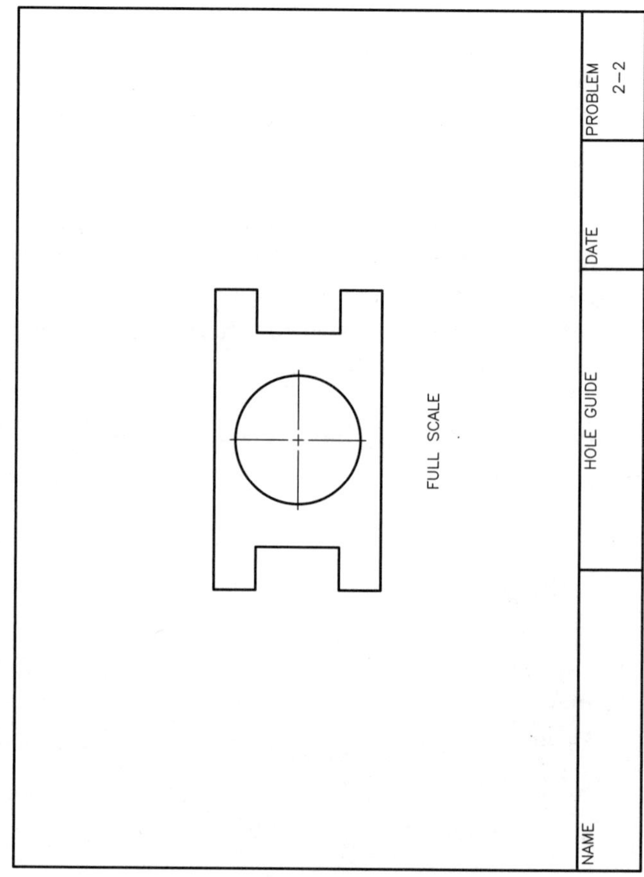

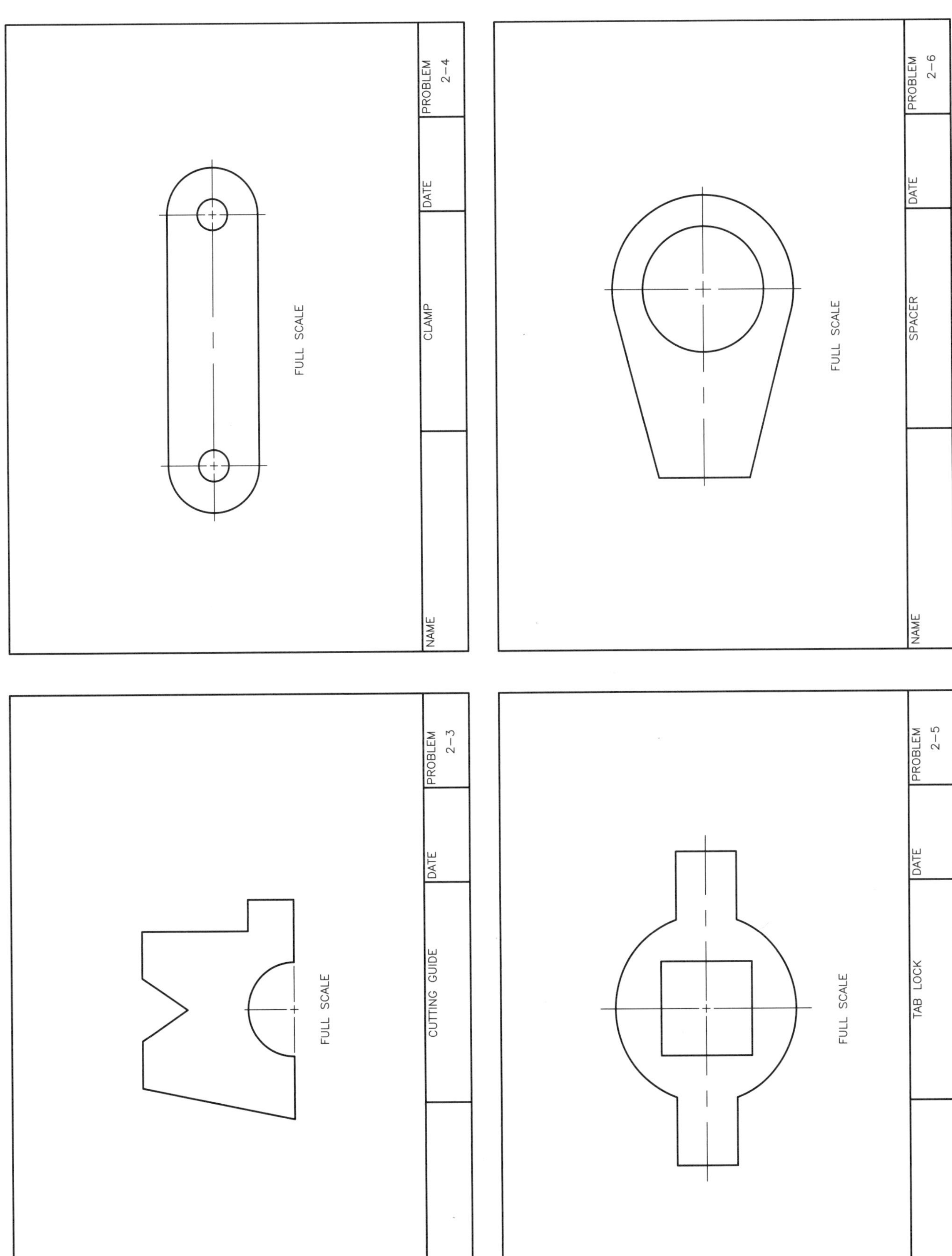
FULL SCALE
PROBLEM 2–4
DATE
CLAMP
NAME
FULL SCALE
PROBLEM 2–6
DATE
SPACER
NAME
FULL SCALE
PROBLEM 2–3
DATE
CUTTING GUIDE
NAME
FULL SCALE
PROBLEM 2–5
DATE
TAB LOCK
NAME

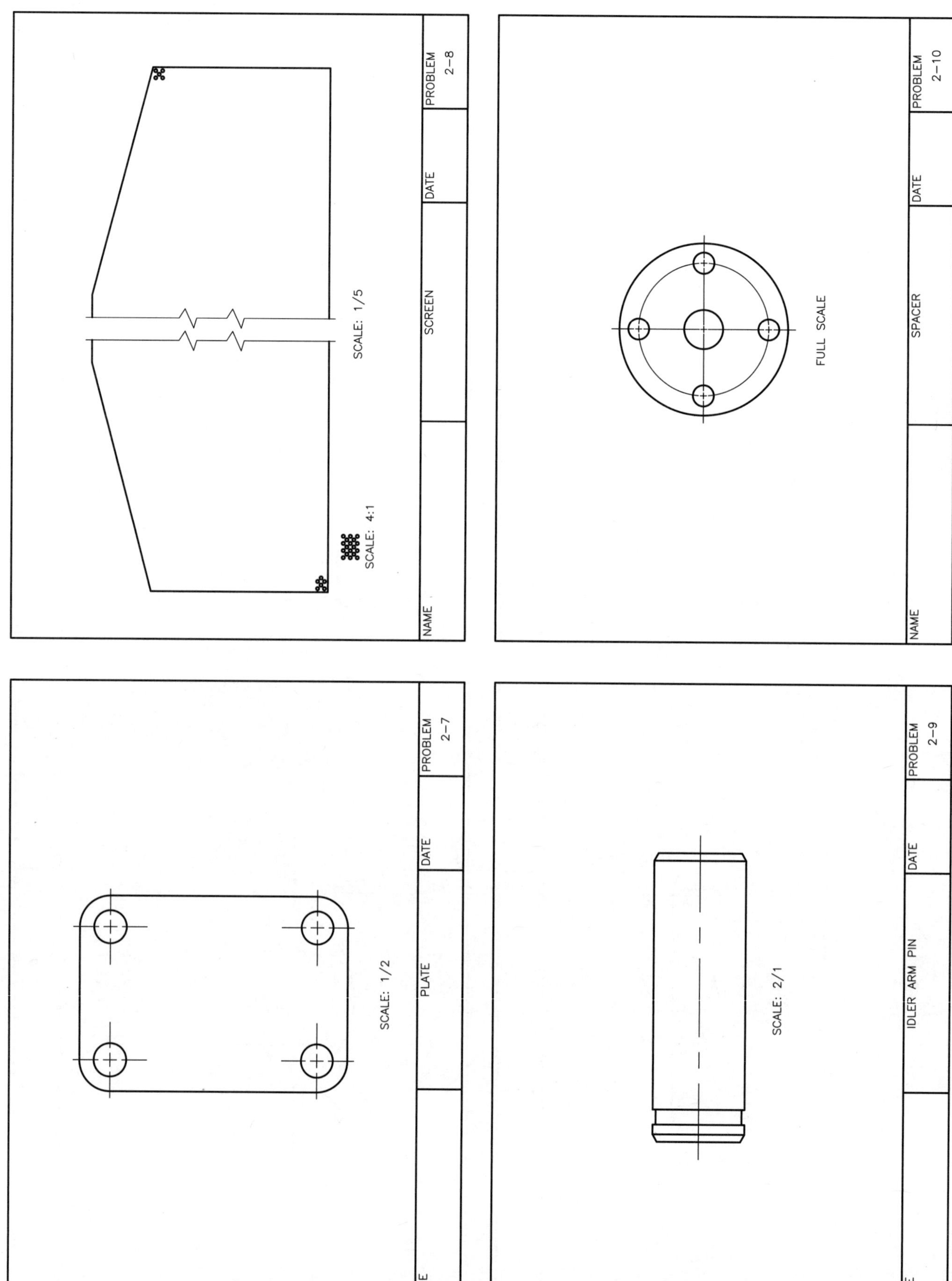

PROBLEM
2–8
DATE
SCREEN
NAME
SCALE: 1/5
SCALE: 4:1
PROBLEM
2–10
DATE
SPACER
NAME
FULL SCALE
PROBLEM
2–7
DATE
PLATE
NAME
SCALE: 1/2
PROBLEM
2–9
DATE
IDLER ARM PIN
NAME
SCALE: 2/1

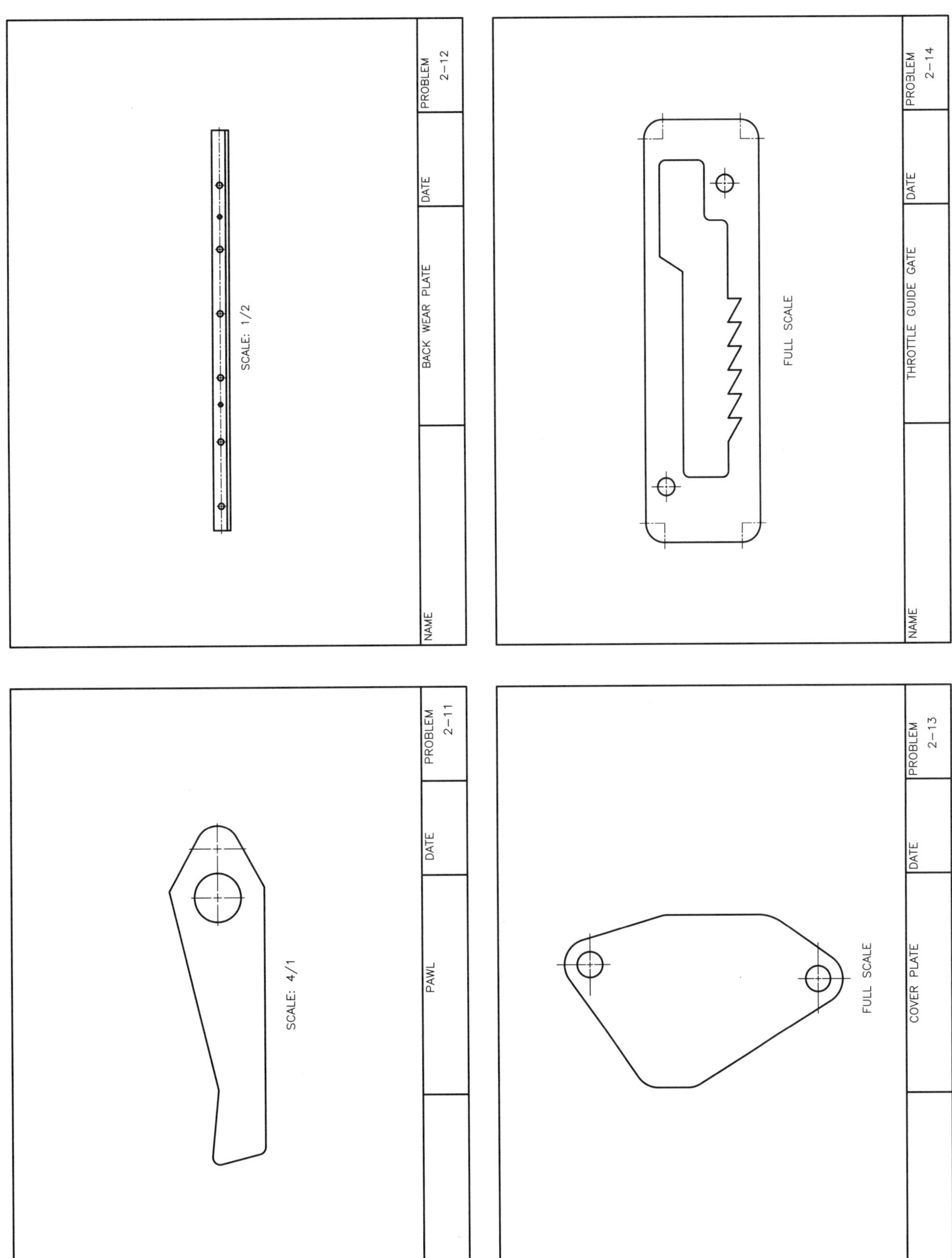
PROBLEM 2–12
DATE
BACK WEAR PLATE
NAME
SCALE: 1/2
PROBLEM 2–14
DATE
THROTTLE GUIDE GATE
NAME
FULL SCALE
PROBLEM 2–11
DATE
PAWL
NAME
SCALE: 4/1
PROBLEM 2–13
DATE
COVER PLATE
NAME
FULL SCALE

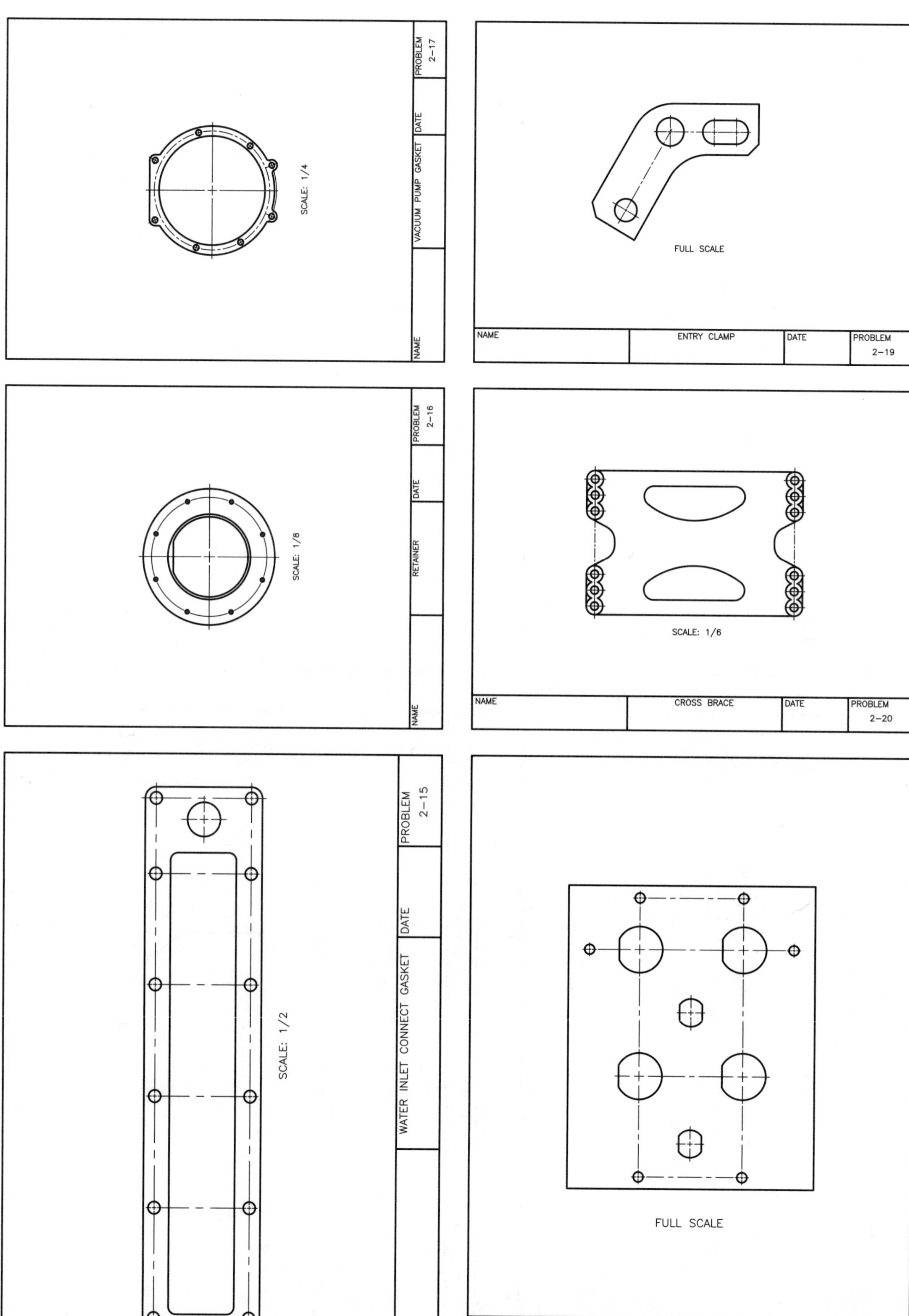
PROBLEM 2-17
DATE
VACUUM PUMP GASKET
NAME
SCALE: 1/4
FULL SCALE
NAME
ENTRY CLAMP
DATE
PROBLEM 2-19
PROBLEM 2-16
DATE
RETAINER
NAME
SCALE: 1/8
SCALE: 1/6
NAME
CROSS BRACE
DATE
PROBLEM 2-20
PROBLEM 2-15
DATE
WATER INLET CONNECT GASKET
NAME
SCALE: 1/2
FULL SCALE
NAME
FRONTAL PLATE
DATE
PROBLEM 2-18

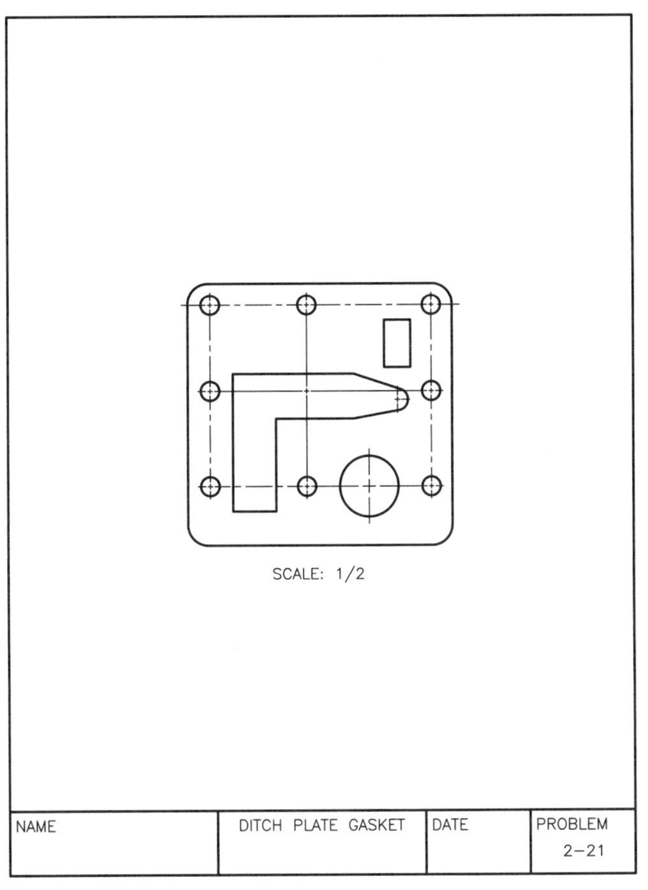
SCALE: 1/2
NAME
DITCH PLATE GASKET
DATE
PROBLEM
2–21

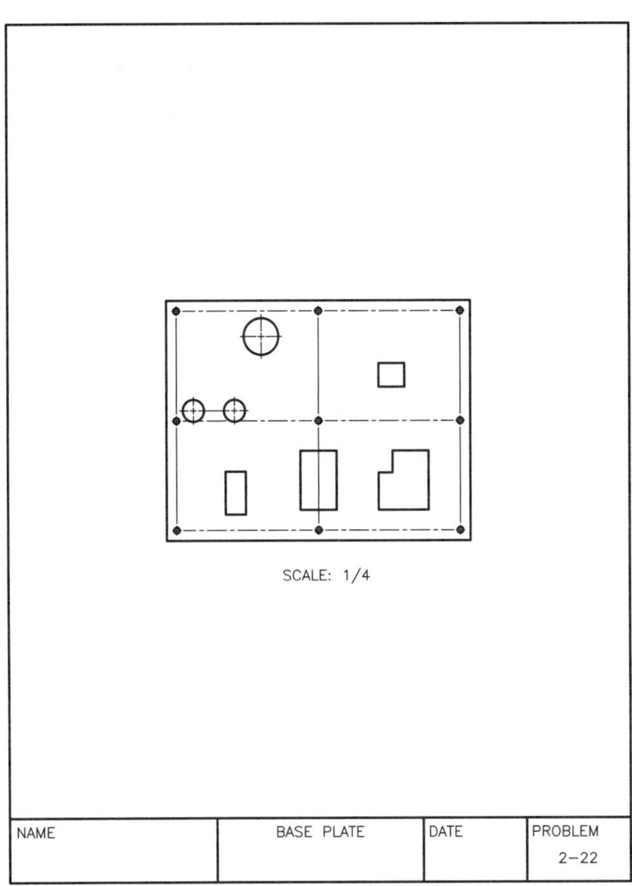
SCALE: 1/4
NAME
BASE PLATE
DATE
PROBLEM
2–22

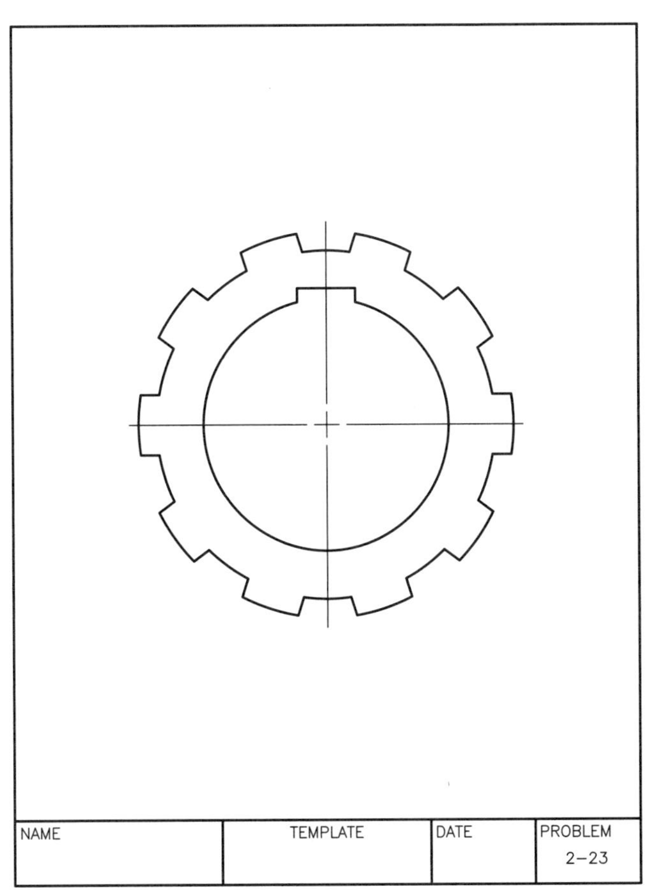
NAME
TEMPLATE
DATE
PROBLEM
2–23

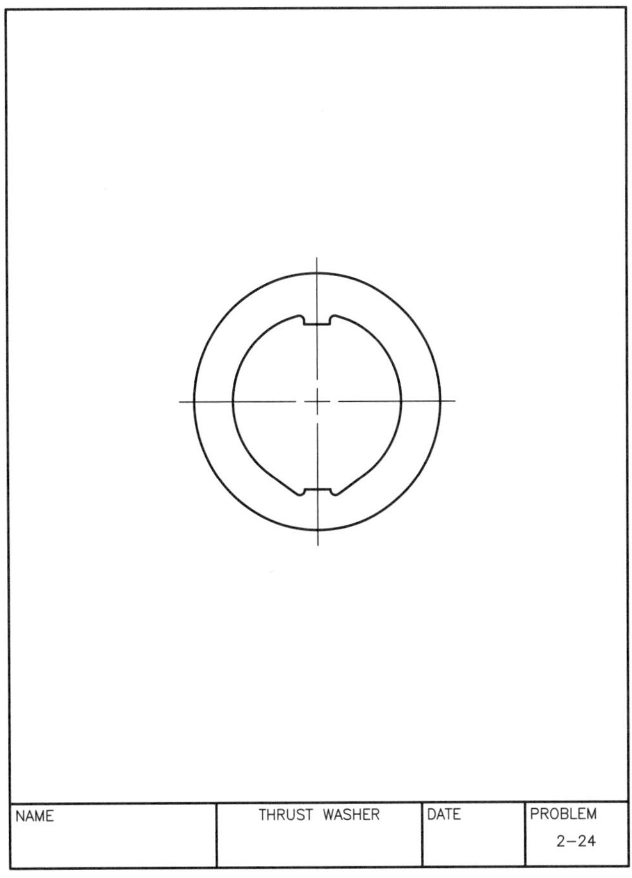
NAME
THRUST WASHER
DATE
PROBLEM
2–24

Solutions to Worksheets

Pages 7–22

1. Worksheets 2-1 through 2-5 only:
   Observe for line uniformity, spacing, and endings. You may wish to prepare a transparency for checking measured lines.
2. Worksheets 2-6 through 2-16:
   Student work should look like the following drawings. The problem number and title are indicated on each problem sheet.

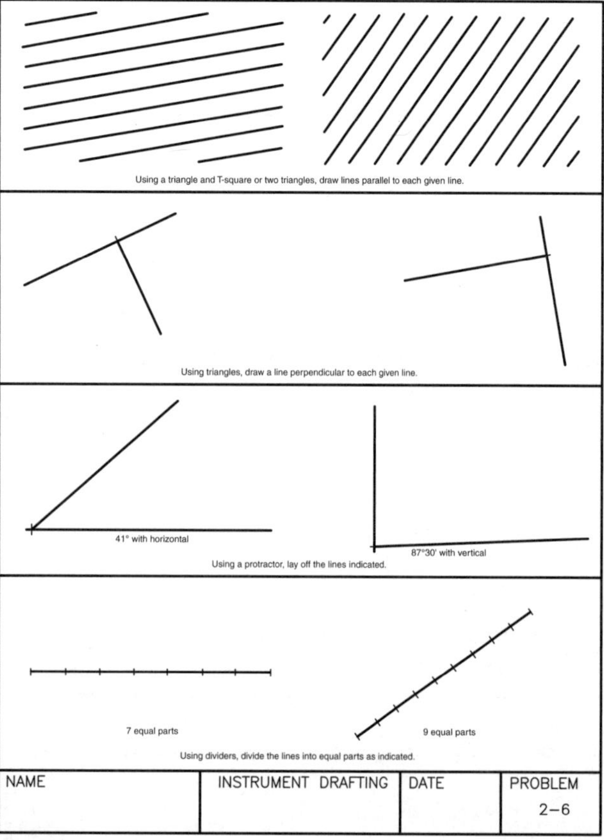

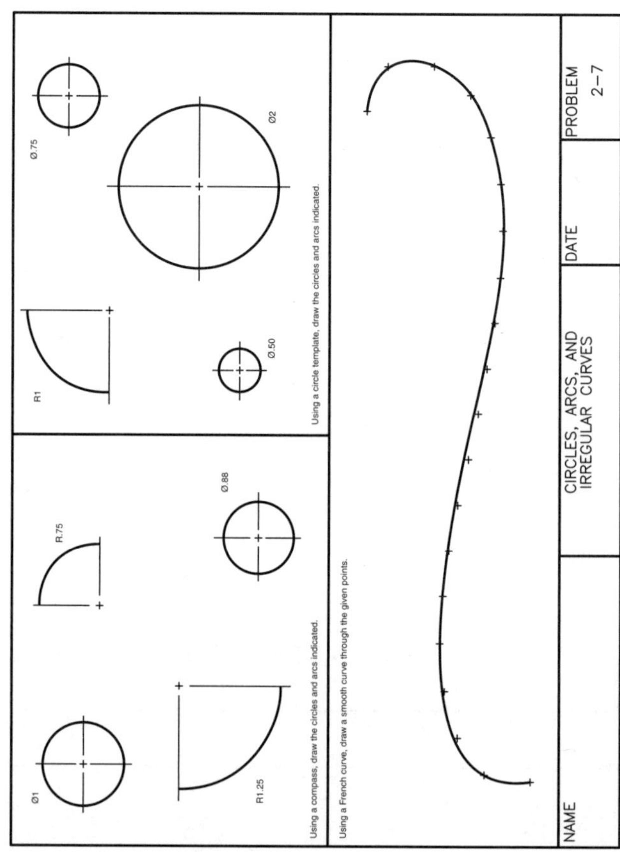

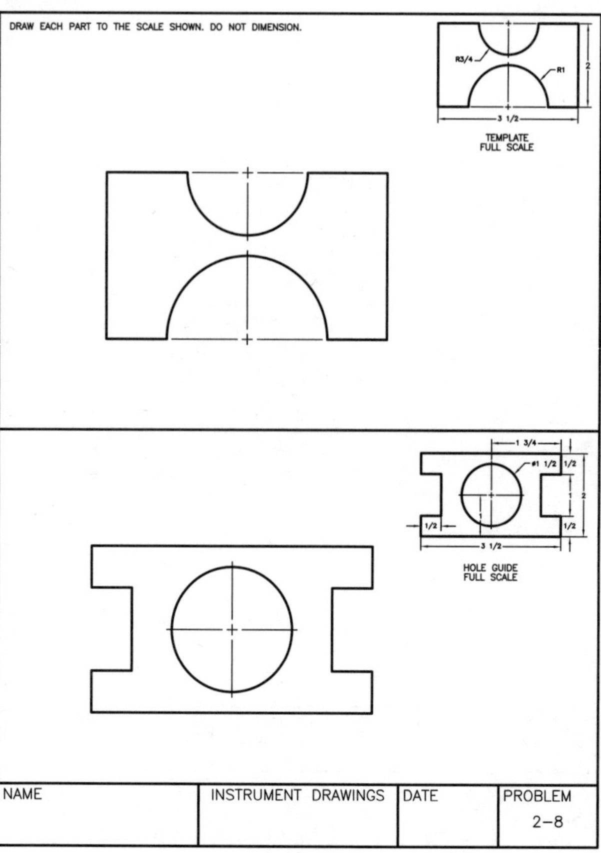

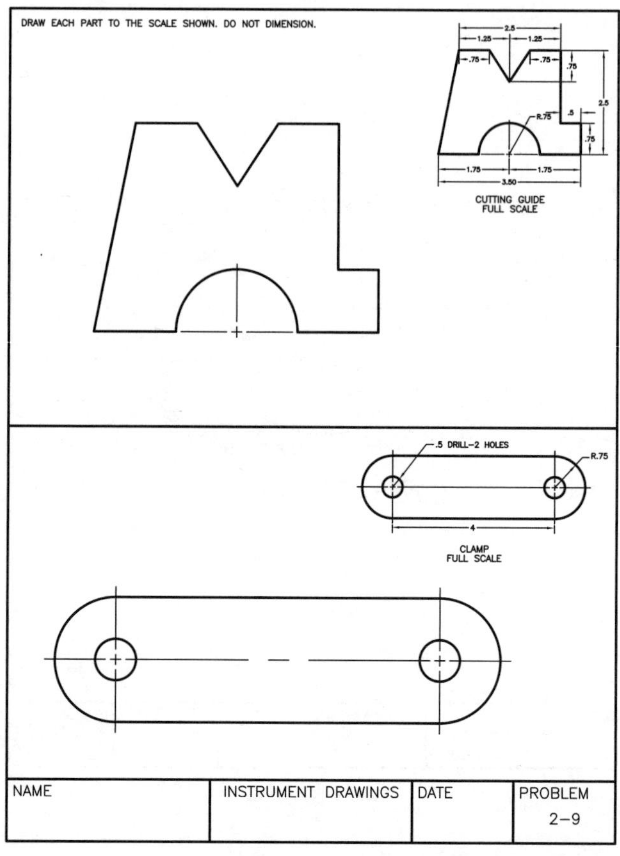

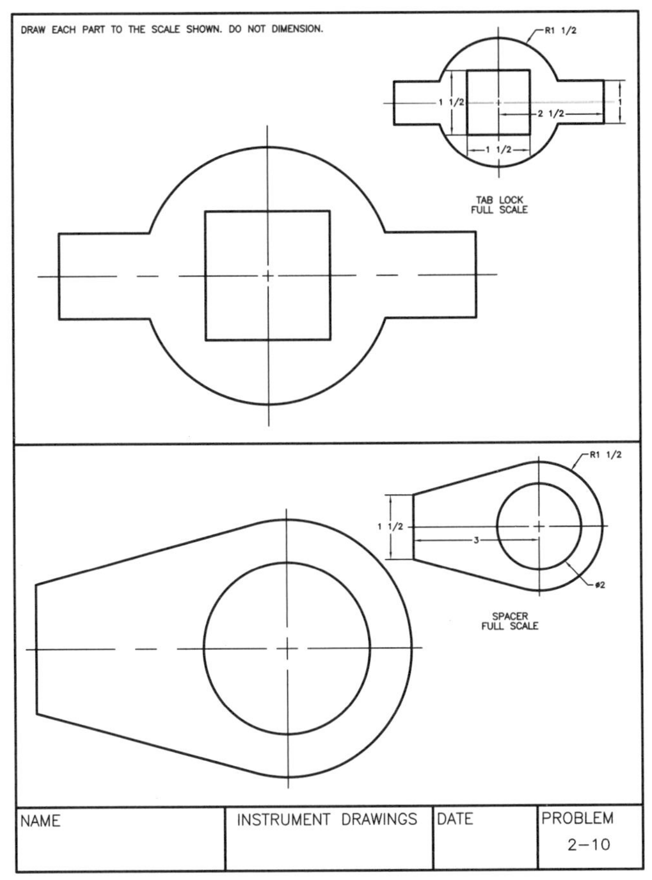
DRAW EACH PART TO THE SCALE SHOWN. DO NOT DIMENSION.
R1 1/2
1 1/2
2 1/2
1 1/2
TAB LOCK
FULL SCALE
R1 1/2
1 1/2
3
ø2
SPACER
FULL SCALE
NAME
INSTRUMENT DRAWINGS
DATE
PROBLEM
2–10

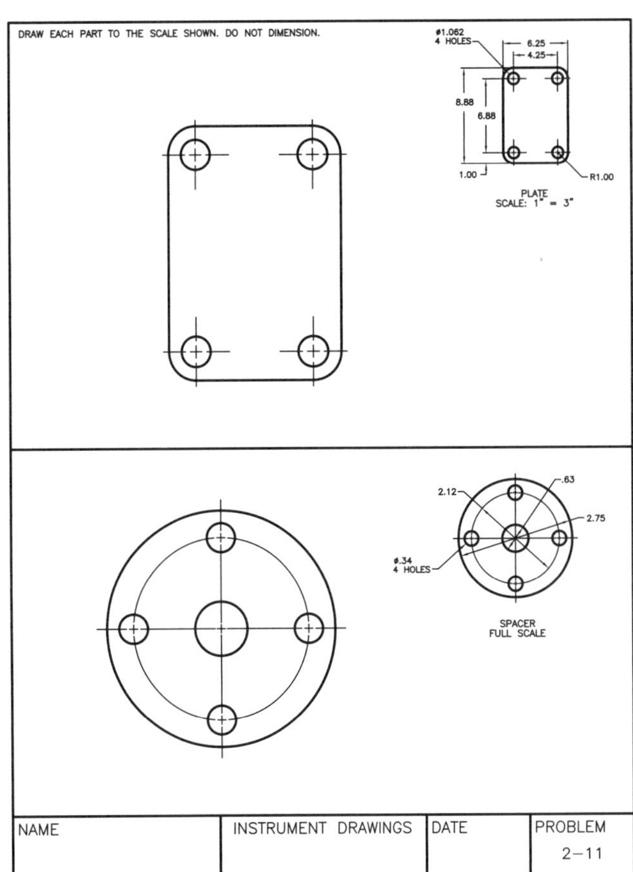
DRAW EACH PART TO THE SCALE SHOWN. DO NOT DIMENSION.
ø1.062
4 HOLES
6.25
4.25
8.88
6.88
1.00
R1.00
PLATE
SCALE: 1" = 3"
2.12
.63
2.75
ø.34
4 HOLES
SPACER
FULL SCALE
NAME
INSTRUMENT DRAWINGS
DATE
PROBLEM
2–11

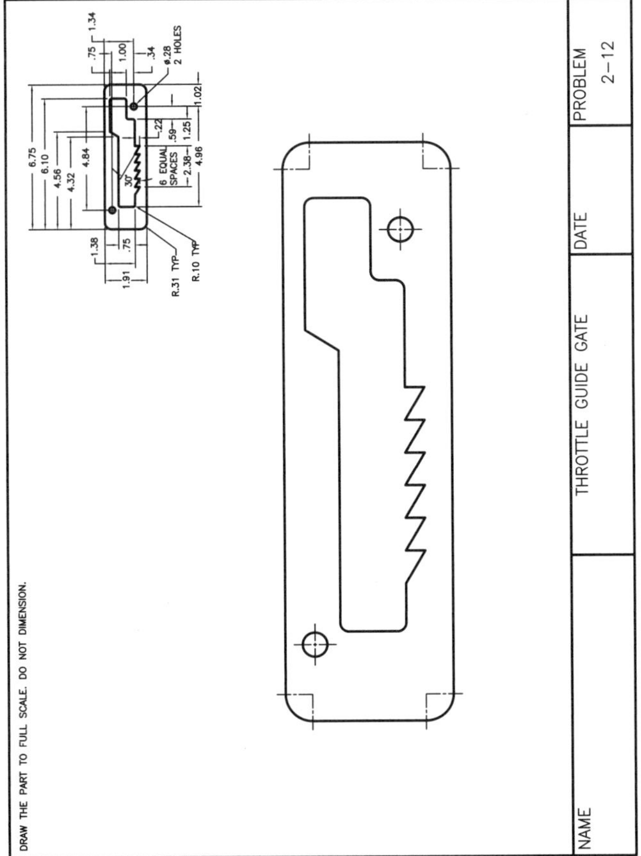
DRAW THE PART TO FULL SCALE. DO NOT DIMENSION.
1.34
.75
1.00
.34
ø.28
2 HOLES
1.02
6.75
6.10
4.56
4.32
4.84
.22
.59
1.25
6 EQUAL SPACES
2.38
4.96
30°
1.38
.75
1.91
R.31 TYP
R.10 TYP
PROBLEM
2–12
DATE
THROTTLE GUIDE GATE
NAME

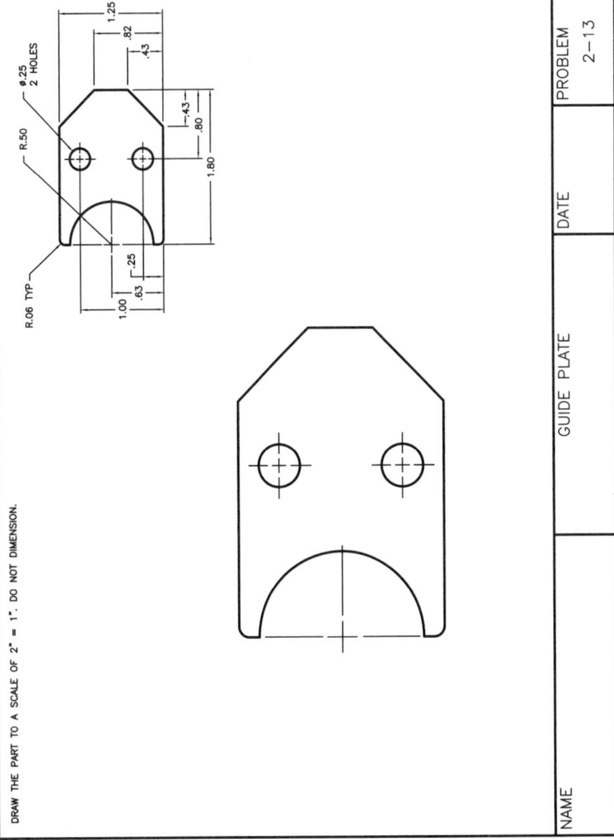
DRAW THE PART TO A SCALE OF 2" = 1". DO NOT DIMENSION.
1.25
.82
.43
ø.25
2 HOLES
R.50
.43
.80
1.80
R.06 TYP
.25
.63
1.00
PROBLEM
2–13
DATE
GUIDE PLATE
NAME

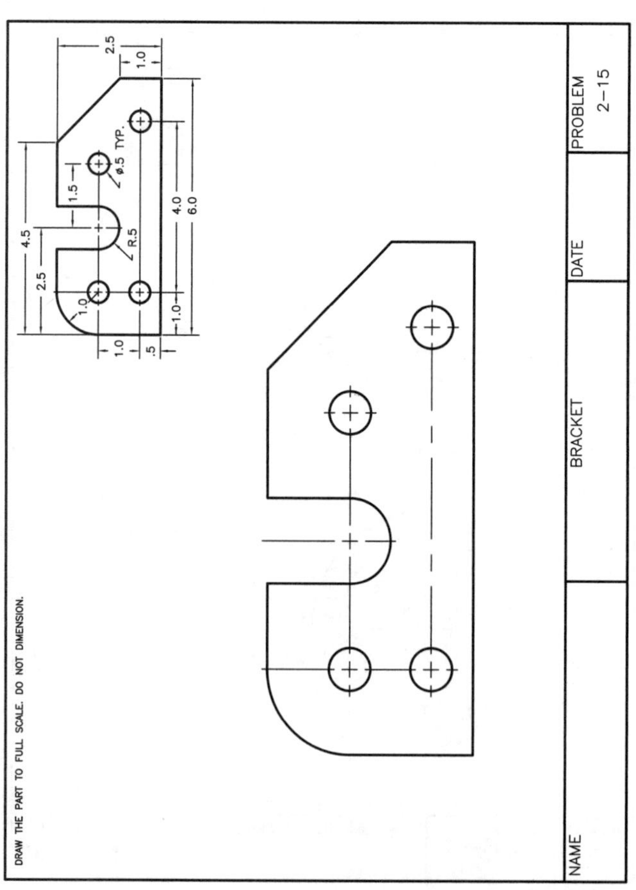
DRAW THE PART TO FULL SCALE. DO NOT DIMENSION.
NAME
BRACKET
DATE
PROBLEM
2–15

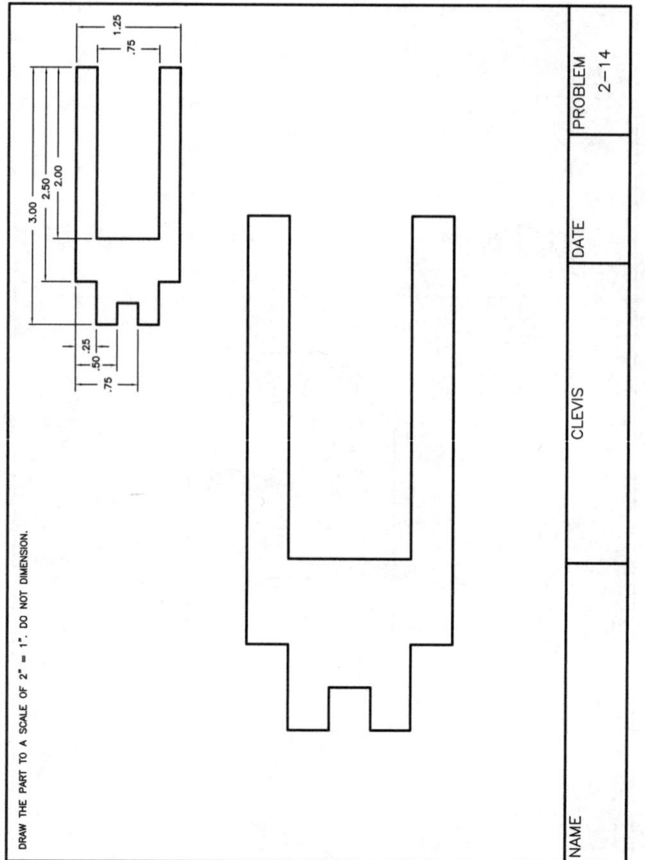
DRAW THE PART TO A SCALE OF 2" = 1". DO NOT DIMENSION.
NAME
CLEVIS
DATE
PROBLEM
2–14

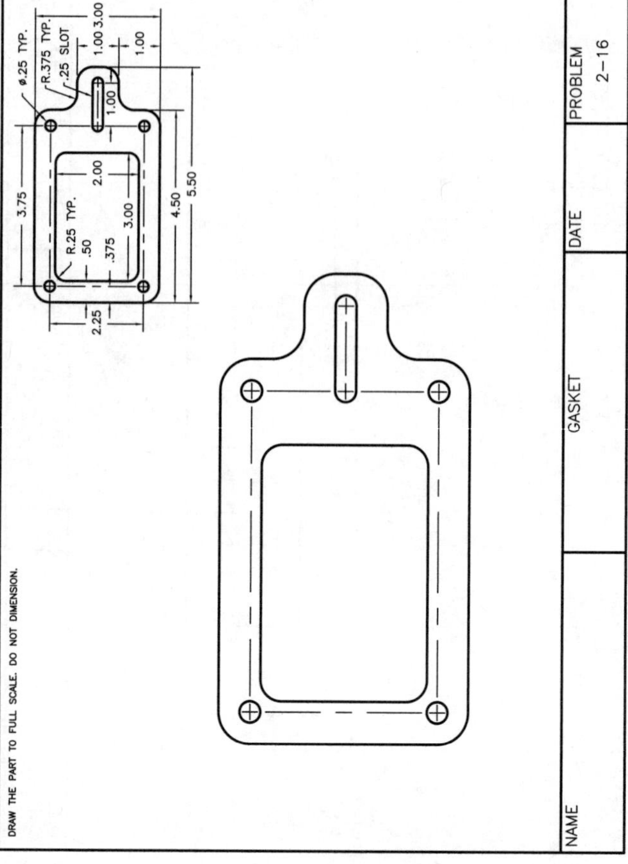
DRAW THE PART TO FULL SCALE. DO NOT DIMENSION.
NAME
GASKET
DATE
PROBLEM
2–16

Answers to Chapter 2 Quiz

1. C. Drafting machine
2. D. 4H
3. B. civil engineer's
4. C. polyester film
5. A. To show an internal feature.
6. A. Centerlines
7. D. Section
8. D. hidden
9. C. phantom
10. D. using light construction lines for initial layout
11. C. protractor
12. A. Beam compass
13. A. Object line
    B. Centerline
    C. Phantom line
    D. Hidden line
    E. Cutting-plane line
14. A. 3-3/4″
    B. 8-1/4″
    C. 19′-9″
    D. 20′-0″
    E. 38′-6″
    F. 5.1″
    G. 9.9″
    H. 14.3″
    I. 4.84″
    J. 4100′
    K. 127 mm
    L. 98 mm
    M. 232 mm
    N. 11.5 m
    O. 42 cm
15. The following illustration shows how to place a 30°-60° triangle and a 45° triangle to draw a line 15° to vertical.

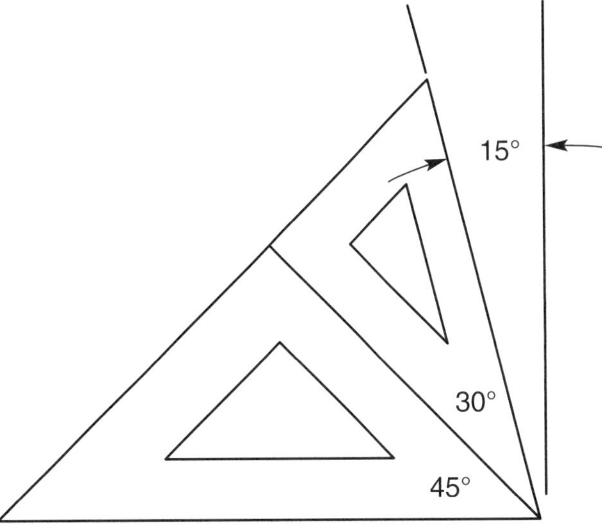

16. Refer to the drawings given in the *Solutions to Drawing Problems, Text* section for the problem selected from the textbook.

Chapter Quiz

Traditional Drafting Equipment and Drawing Techniques

Name ____________________

Period ____________ Date ____________ Score ____________

Multiple Choice

Choose the answer that correctly completes the statement. Write the corresponding letter in the space provided.

_____ 1. What drafting device combines the functions of several basic instruments?
A. Parallel straightedge
B. Protractor
C. Drafting machine
D. T-square

_____ 2. Which of the following drafting leads is the least likely to smudge the drawing?
A. 7B
B. 2H
C. 3H
D. 4H

_____ 3. The 50 scale is commonly found on a(n) _____ scale.
A. architect's
B. civil engineer's
C. mechanical engineer's
D. metric

_____ 4. The drafting media with the greatest dimensional stability is _____.
A. paper
B. tracing paper
C. polyester film
D. vellum

_____ 5. Why is a short break line on the drawing of a machine part used?
A. To show an internal feature.
B. To reduce the length of the drawing.
C. To show the cross-sectional shape of a part.
D. None of the above.

_____ 6. _____ are thin lines composed of long and short dashes alternately spaced with a long dash at each end.
A. Centerlines
B. Hidden lines
C. Object lines
D. Section lines

Name ______________________________

_____ 7. _____ lines are used to represent surfaces exposed by a cutting plane.
A. Border
B. Hidden
C. Object
D. Section

_____ 8. A(n) _____ line represents a surface behind another surface.
A. object
B. section
C. phantom
D. hidden

_____ 9. A(n) _____ line is used to represent an alternate position of a part.
A. object
B. section
C. phantom
D. break

_____ 10. "Ghosting" on a drawing can best be avoided by _____.
A. using a steel erasing knife
B. using heavy pressure with an electric erasing machine
C. backing the drawing with a thin metal sheet
D. using light construction lines for initial layout

_____ 11. Angles for inclined lines are measured with a(n) _____.
A. compass
B. drafting template
C. protractor
D. irregular curve

_____ 12. Which drafting tool is used for drawing very large circles and arcs?
A. Beam compass
B. Dividers
C. Triangle
D. Parallel straightedge

Identification

13. Identify the following lines. Write your answers in the spaces provided.

_____ A.

_____ B.

_____ C.

_____ D.

_____ E.

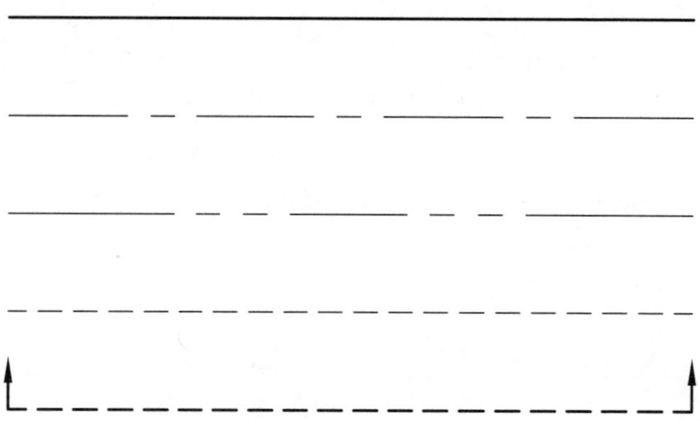

Name ____________________

14. Measure the following line lengths using the scale indicated. Record each measurement in the space provided.

Architect's Scale

Civil Engineer's Scale (Inches)

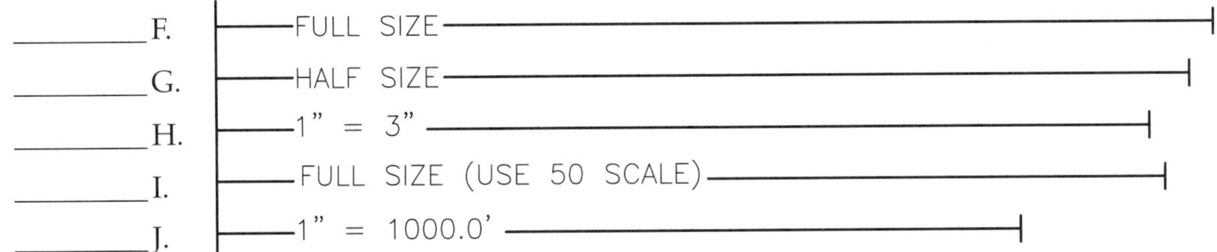

Metric Scale

Drafting Performance

15. Indicate by a freehand sketch how to draw a line at 15° to vertical using the 30°-60° and 45° triangles.

Name ____

16. Make a one-view drawing of a problem selected by your instructor from the Drawing Problems section of Chapter 2 in your textbook.

Drafting Equipment

The equipment and supplies listed below are adequate for most drafting work. Check with your instructor before purchasing any equipment.

Instruments

- Small compass with pen attachment
- Large compass with pen attachment
- Lengthening bar
- Friction joint dividers
- Technical pen
- Lead holder
- Box of leads
- Screwdriver

Other Equipment

- Drawing board or drawing table
- T-square with 24" plastic edge
- 10" 30°-60° triangle
- 8" 45° triangle
- Architect's and engineer's scales
- Lettering device
- Protractor
- Irregular (French) curve
- Circle and ellipse templates
- Erasing shield
- Soft rubber eraser
- Vinyl eraser
- Dusting brush
- Sketch pad
- Drawing paper and tracing paper (or vellum)
- Drafting tape
- Drafting pencils or mechanical lead holder
- Sandpaper pad, file, or lead pointer

RM 2-1

Line Conventions

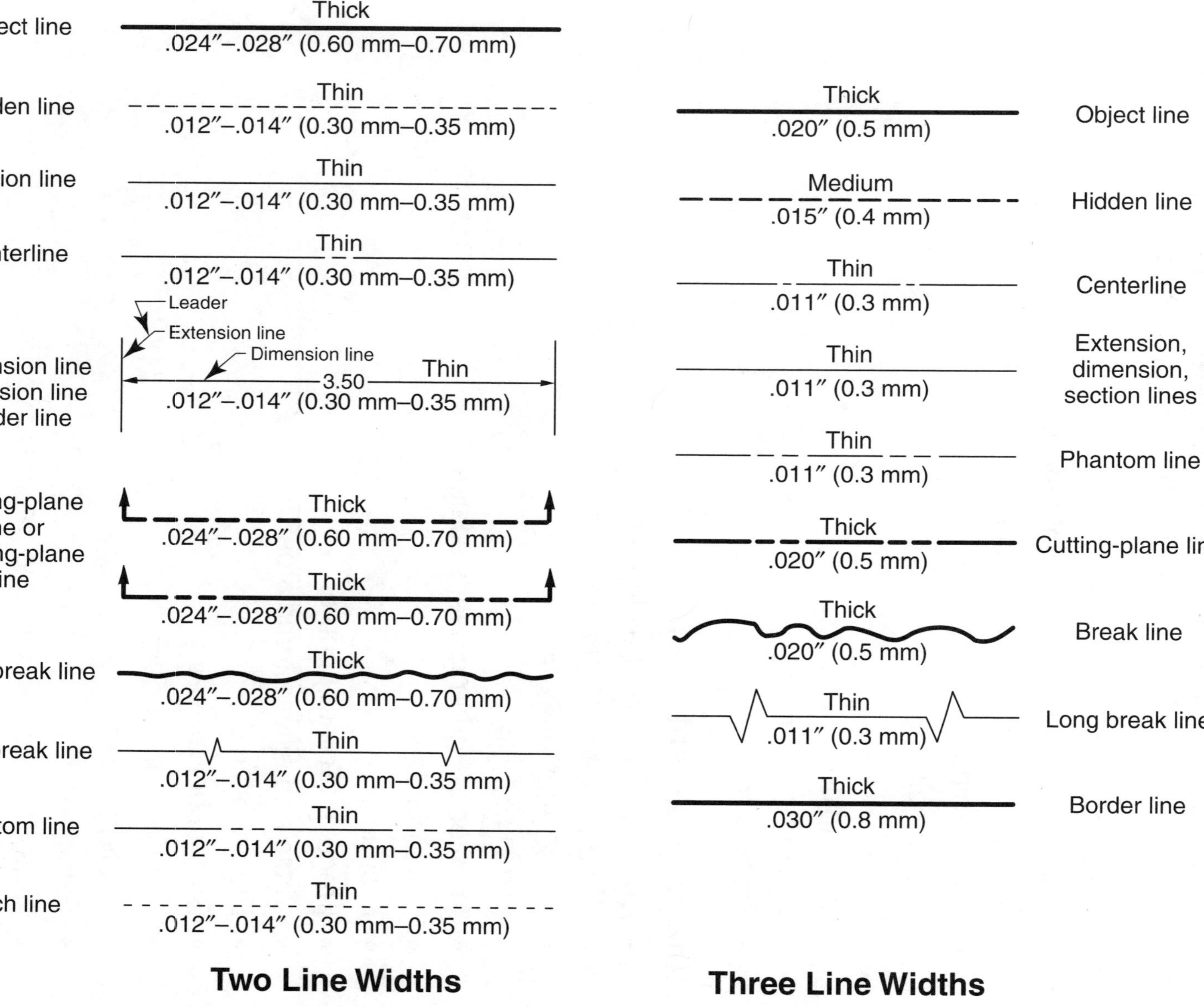

RM 2-2

Procedure Checklist

Traditional Drafting Equipment and Drawing Techniques

Name ____

Observable Items	Completed		Comments	Instructor Initials
	Yes	No		
1. Draws the lines in the Alphabet of Lines.				
2. Erases lines properly.				
3. Reads a scale.				
4. Lays out measurements with a scale.				
5. Lays out a border and title block.				
6. Draws horizontal lines.				
7. Draws vertical lines.				
8. Draws inclined lines.				
9. Draws parallel lines.				
10. Draws a line perpendicular to an inclined line.				
11. Measures angles.				
12. Draws arcs and circles.				
13. Draws symbols using a template.				
14. Divides a line using dividers.				
15. Draws irregular curves.				
16. Inks a drawing.				

Instructor Signature ____

Introduction to CAD

Learning Objectives

After studying this chapter, the student will be able to:

- Explain computer-aided drafting and design.
- Identify common applications for CAD in different areas of drafting.
- List the components of a typical CAD workstation.
- Identify features of CAD software and how they should be evaluated when selecting a program.
- Explain the advantages of specific CAD applications.

Instructional Resources

Text: pages 77–100

Review Questions, pages 99–100

Problems and Activities, page 100

Instructor's Resource

Instructional Tasks

Instructional Aids and Assignments

Chapter 3 Quiz

Reproducible Masters

- Reproducible Master 3-1: *CAD System Components.* The common parts of a CAD workstation are listed and explained.
- Reproducible Master 3-2: *Benefits of CAD.* The most significant time- and money-saving benefits of CAD are listed and explained.

Procedure Checklist

Color Transparencies (Binder/IRCD only)

- Transparency 3-1: *CAD Rendering.* Shown is a CAD-generated rendering of an engine block and exhaust manifold.
- Transparency 3-2: *Solid Modeling Methods.* Common methods for creating three-dimensional solid models from two-dimensional drawing geometry are illustrated.
- Transparency 3-3: *Parametric Modeling.* Shown is a parametric model created with an advanced mechanical drafting and modeling CAD package.

Instructional Tasks

1. Discuss how CAD is used in the drafting and design process.
   - Invite a representative from industry to discuss the advantages of CAD in the design and drafting process.
2. Describe the components of a CAD workstation.
   - Show a multimedia presentation or film on CAD workstations.
   - Display photographs of various CAD system components. Use a variety of products from different manufacturers.
3. Explain data storage devices and their advantages.
   - Use photos or an actual computer setup to explain storage devices and functions.
4. Discuss and compare different types of display devices.
   - Use photos or an actual computer setup to explain the functions of display devices.
5. Discuss and compare different types of input and output devices.
   - Use photos or an actual computer setup to explain the functions of input devices.
   - Demonstrate the use of a plotter or printer.
6. Discuss the development of CAD from the 1950s to the present.
   - Have one or more students report on the growth of CAD.
7. Discuss the changes and benefits brought about by CAD.
   - Assign one or more students to prepare a report on the changes brought about by CAD.

8. Discuss the job qualifications for a CAD designer/drafter.
   - Have one or more students prepare a report on CAD employment opportunities. If possible, have them interview industry or employment service personnel. Have them make use of the *Occupational Outlook Handbook* and other career references.
9. Discuss the application of CAD within various industries.
   - Organize a small discussion panel to discuss CAD applications in various industries. The panel can be made up of students or industry personnel.

Instructional Aids and Assignments

1. Show multimedia presentations or films on CAD applications in industry.
2. Invite members of advisory councils or industry personnel to speak to the class.
3. Display and/or discuss articles from CAD publications relative to products, operations, methods, and career opportunities.
4. Arrange a tour of a drafting firm using CAD.
5. Assign the Problems and Activities in the textbook.

Answers to Review Questions, Text

Pages 99–100

1. computer-aided drafting
2. software
3. CAD saves time and money.
4. symbol library
5. C. true size
6. isometric, oblique
7. workstation
8. B. keyboard
9. monitor
10. video card
11. output
12. C. It produces very high-quality line reproductions in color.
13. General purpose, advanced mechanical drafting and modeling, and AEC CAD packages.
14. Objects
15. hatch
16. D. Drawing.
17. Layers
18. Surface models and solid models.
19. sweep
20. attributes
21. plan

Answers to Chapter 3 Quiz

1. A. output
2. B. Revising drawings.
3. C. video
4. D. monitor
5. C. 17″
6. B. keyboard
7. A. trackball
8. B. digitizer puck
9. B. vectors
10. D. pen plotter
11. B. Layers
12. C. loft

Chapter Quiz 3

Introduction to CAD

Name ____

Period__________________ Date__________________ Score ________________

Multiple Choice

Choose the answer that correctly completes the statement. Write the corresponding letter in the space provided.

_______ 1. Devices such as plotters, printers, and monitors are called _____ devices.
- A. output
- B. dedicated
- C. serial
- D. optional

_______ 2. In which area does CAD drawing provide true time savings?
- A. Making original drawings.
- B. Revising drawings.
- C. Working with a client.
- D. None of the above.

_______ 3. The _____ card is the device that transmits data from the CPU to the monitor.
- A. network
- B. mouse
- C. video
- D. output

_______ 4. The _____ provides visual feedback on what the computer is doing and what you are doing with the computer.
- A. mouse
- B. sound card
- C. digitizing tablet
- D. monitor

_______ 5. In general, a CAD monitor should be at least _____ in size.
- A. 12″
- B. 15″
- C. 17″
- D. 21″

_______ 6. The most common input device is a _____.
- A. mouse
- B. keyboard
- C. puck
- D. digitizing tablet

Name ____

________ 7. A(n) _____ is like an upside-down mouse.
A. trackball
B. digitizing tablet
C. light pen
D. All of the above.

________ 8. Tablet menus are generally used with a _____.
A. graphics adapter
B. digitizer puck
C. mouse
D. None of the above.

________ 9. Pen plotters draw lines as _____.
A. raster images
B. vectors
C. clusters
D. small dots

________ 10. The _____ is the most popular traditional device for producing high-quality CAD line drawings.
A. laser printer
B. inkjet printer
C. thermal plotter
D. pen plotter

________ 11. _____ are similar to transparent drawing sheets on which objects are drawn.
A. Hatch patterns
B. Layers
C. Primitives
D. Parameters

________ 12. A _____ is a type of solid model created by extruding one or more profiles along a rail.
A. primitive
B. sweep
C. loft
D. constraint

CAD System Components

Central Processing Unit (CPU)

- Processor
- Memory (RAM)
- Input/output interfaces

Monitor

- CRT (Cathode ray tube)
- LCD (Liquid crystal display)

Graphics Adapter

- VGA (Video graphics array)
- SVGA (Super video graphics array)
- XGA (Extended graphics array)
- UVGA (Ultra VGA)

Input and Pointing Devices

- Keyboard
- Mouse
- Trackball
- Digitizing tablet with a puck or stylus

CAD Software

- General purpose CAD packages
- Advanced mechanical drafting and modeling CAD packages
- AEC CAD packages

Output Devices

- Pen plotter
- Inkjet plotter
- Inkjet printer
- Laser printer

RM 3-1

Benefits of CAD

The productivity gained by using a modern CAD system when compared to traditional drafting is well documented. Some of the primary areas responsible for the increased productivity are drawing speed, drawing quality, drawing modification, flexibility, scale, and analysis.

Drawing Speed

Most drafting tasks are accomplished much faster when made with the tools of a CAD system in comparison to the tools of traditional drafting. The ability to copy objects and the use of symbols from symbol libraries make this rule a reality.

Drawing Quality

Quality gained through the use of a CAD system is most notable in the areas of accuracy and line quality. The width of each line is exactly as specified and all lines are uniform in color. There are no eraser marks on a CAD drawing, and each object is located accurately in the desired position.

Drawing Modification

Modifying a drawing is one of the most time-consuming tasks of the drafter. Editing functions that are a part of every CAD software package make drawing modifications quick and easy. Changes can be made in seconds and new copies produced in minutes.

Flexibility

Completed drawings made with a CAD system can be printed, plotted, or displayed with different types of presentation media. CAD drawings also offer greater communication between the many individuals and departments involved in the design and manufacturing process. Anyone needing information about a drawing can access it on a workstation via a computer network. This helps in the development of standards and helps prevent mistakes in documentation.

Scale

In almost all cases, CAD drawings are made at full size. Plotting scales are then calculated for drawings that require different scale sizes. This provides more control over drawing scales and reduces the chance for error.

Analysis

Many types of analyses may be performed when using a CAD system designed for manufacturing applications. Examples include analyses for durability, strength, and potential points of failure. The result is a better product at a lower cost to the consumer.

RM 3-2

CAD Commands and Functions

Learning Objectives

After studying this chapter, the student will be able to:

- List several general categories of commands used in popular CAD programs.
- Explain how points and objects are located using a coordinate system.
- Explain the use of linear, angular, and leader dimensioning.
- Identify and describe drawing aids.
- Discuss the purposes of colors, linetypes, and layers.
- Explain layer naming conventions as related to CAD drawings.
- Describe 3D drawing.
- Explain rendering.
- Explain animation.

Instructional Resources

Text: pages 101–130

Review Questions, pages 124–125

Problems and Activities, page 125

Drawing Problems, pages 126–130

Instructor's Resource

Instructional Tasks

Instructional Aids and Assignments

Chapter 4 Quiz

Reproducible Masters

- Reproducible Master 4-1: *Drawing Commands*. Shown are the most common drawing commands used in a general purpose CAD program.
- Reproducible Master 4-2: *Editing and Inquiry Commands*. Shown are the most common editing and inquiry commands used in a general purpose CAD program.
- Reproducible Master 4-3: *Display Control Commands*. Shown are the most common display control commands used in a general purpose CAD program.
- Reproducible Master 4-4: *Dimensioning Commands*. Shown are the most common dimensioning commands used in a general purpose CAD program.
- Reproducible Master 4-5: *Drawing Aids*. Shown are the most common drawing aids used in a general purpose CAD program.
- Reproducible Master 4-6: *File Management Commands and Utility Functions*. Shown are the most common file management commands and utility functions used in a general purpose CAD program.
- Reproducible Master 4-7: *Types of CAD Models*. The three basic types of CAD models are described.

Procedure Checklist

Color Transparencies (Binder/IRCD only)

- Transparency 4-1: *CAD Coordinate Entry*. The three basic types of coordinate entry used in making CAD drawings are illustrated.
- Transparency 4-2: *Layer Management*. A drawing created with layers to distinguish different objects and linetypes is shown. The layers are identified by name and color in a table to illustrate how they are assigned to objects in the drawing.
- Transparency 4-3: *CAD Models*. The three basic types of CAD-generated models are shown.

Instructional Tasks

1. Explain the basic interface of a CAD program and discuss how to start and save a drawing file.
   - Discuss basic CAD functions and features. Demonstrate the commands used to start and save drawing files.
2. Demonstrate how to set up a drawing.
   - Discuss drawing templates.

3. Describe how to select or enter a given command.
   - Demonstrate different selection and entry methods for entering commands. Have a student follow for clarification.
4. Demonstrate the use of the Cartesian coordinate system.
   - Show a multimedia presentation or film on the Cartesian coordinate system.
5. Introduce drawing commands and their use.
   - Demonstrate the use of drawing commands. Explain common drawing command options.
6. Discuss how to construct drawing objects.
   - Demonstrate the construction of lines, circles, and arcs. Have a student follow for clarification.
7. Demonstrate how to add text to a drawing.
   - Demonstrate the use of text commands.
8. Demonstrate the addition of section lines in a view.
   - Explain hatching and discuss hatch symbols used to represent different materials.
9. Introduce editing commands and their use.
   - Demonstrate the use of editing commands. Explain common editing command options.
10. Introduce inquiry commands and their use.
    - Have a student list some of the most common inquiry commands. Compare the use of these commands to manual drafting practice.
11. Introduce display control commands and their use.
    - Demonstrate the use of display control commands.
12. Demonstrate how to dimension a drawing.
    - Show examples of different dimensioning commands and methods.
13. Discuss drawing aids used in constructing drawings.
    - Describe the different types of drawing aids and demonstrate their use.
14. Introduce layers and describe how they are used.
    - Explain the purpose of layers. Show examples of drawings that have items assigned to many different layers, such as an architectural floor plan or an electronics drawing.
15. Demonstrate the use, selection, creation, and storage of symbols.
    - Explain how to create and save symbols for repeated use.
16. Discuss common procedures for plotting a drawing.
    - Define plotting terms and controls. Display a check plot and a final plot.
17. Discuss file management.
    - Lead a discussion on the proper ways to manage files.
18. Introduce three-dimensional (3D) drawing and viewing methods.
    - Discuss the different types of CAD models. Demonstrate the use of 3D viewing commands.
19. Introduce 3D animation and rendering commands.
    - Discuss the common terms associated with rendering. Present a simple animation of a CAD model.

Instructional Aids and Assignments

1. Show the class a set of industrial drawings where changes have been made or need to be made.
2. Assign the Problems and Activities in the textbook.
3. Assign the Drawing Problems in the textbook.
4. For additional student experience, select problems from other parts of the text.

Answers to Review Questions, Text

Pages 124–125

1. commands
2. Pull-down
3. File management commands.
4. template
5. X, Y
6. Drawing
7. Answer may include any four of the following: By center and radius; by center and diameter; by three points on the circle; by two points on the circle; and by radius and two lines or two circles to which the circle should be tangent.

8. arc
9. ellipse
10. polygon
11. **Text**
12. **Hatching**
13. C. **Dimension**
14. **Erase**
15. **Undo**
16. **Scale**
17. round
18. boundary
19. copy
20. **Area**
21. Answer may include any three of the following: **Zoom**, **Pan**, **View**, and **Redraw**/**Regenerate**.
22. magnification
23. **Linear**, **Angular**, **Diameter**, **Radius**, and **Leader**.
24. leader
25. drawing aids
26. Grid snap and object snap.
27. layer
28. Blocks
29. schedules
30. pictorial
31. wireframe
32. user coordinate system
33. An animation is a series of still images played sequentially at a very fast rate.

Solutions to Drawing Problems, Text

Pages 126–130

Student work should look like the following drawings. The problem number and title are indicated on each problem sheet. Evaluate the competence of the student in completing the drawing. Review the printed drawing for accuracy.

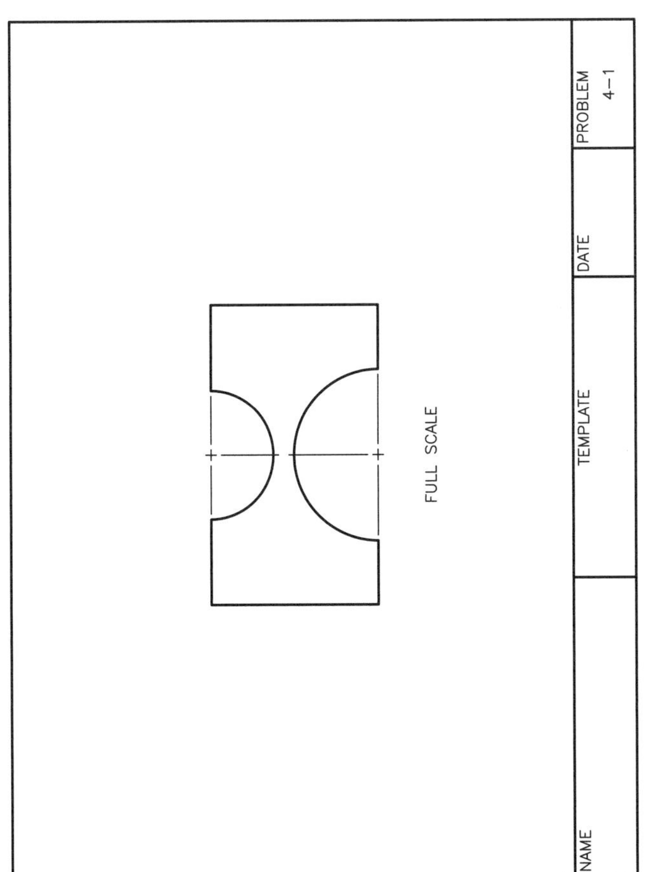

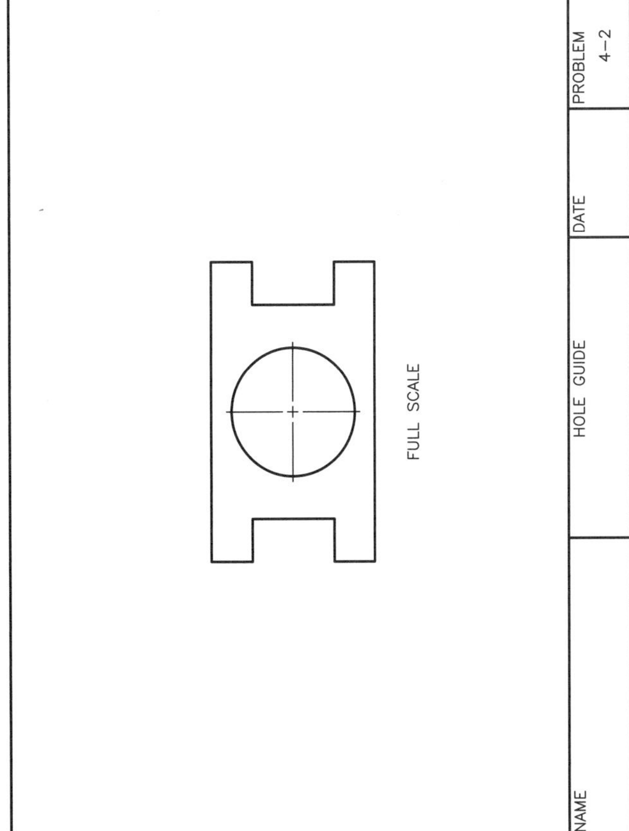

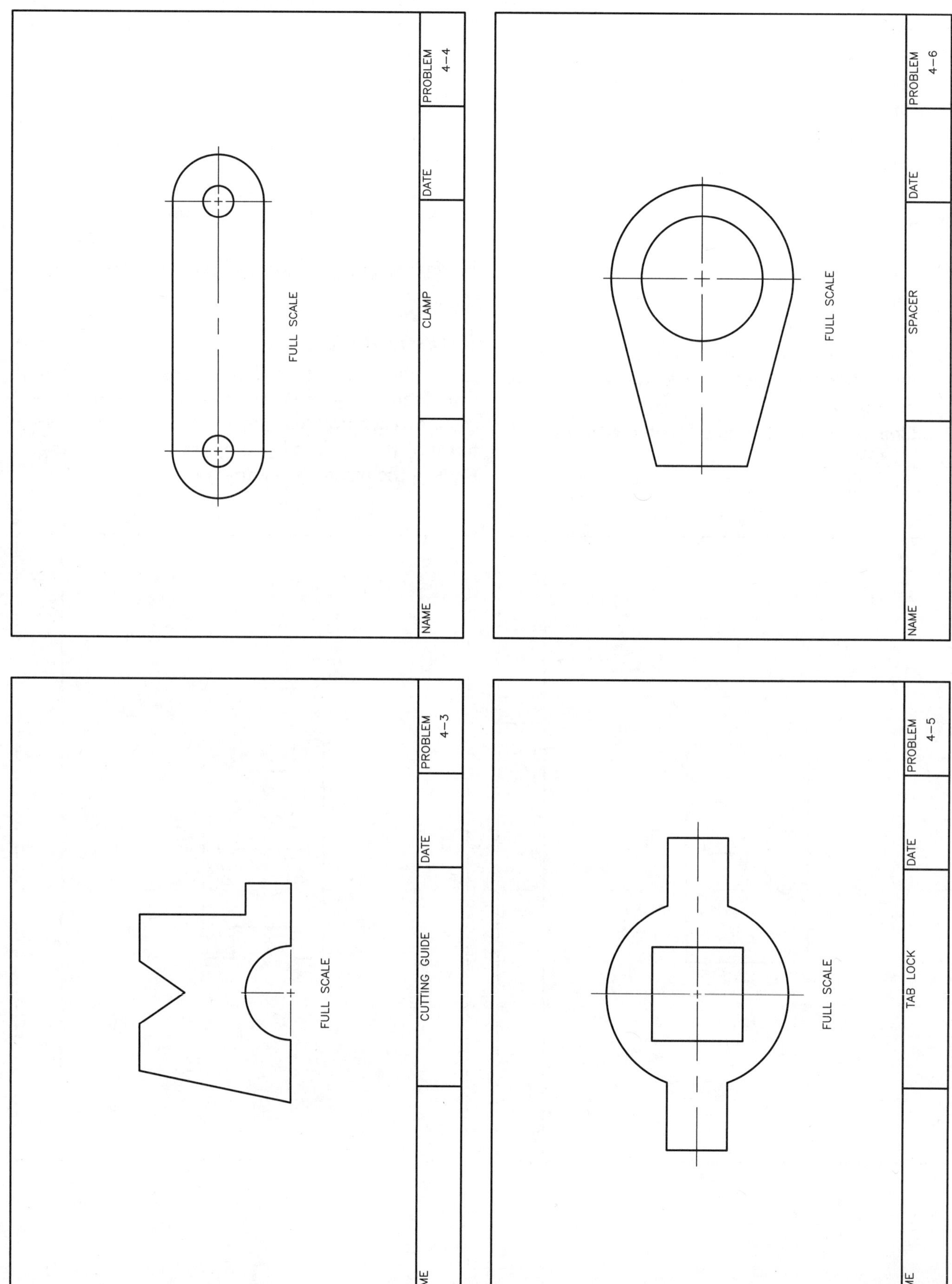

FULL SCALE
PROBLEM 4–4
DATE
CLAMP
NAME
FULL SCALE
PROBLEM 4–6
DATE
SPACER
NAME
FULL SCALE
PROBLEM 4–3
DATE
CUTTING GUIDE
NAME
FULL SCALE
PROBLEM 4–5
DATE
TAB LOCK
NAME

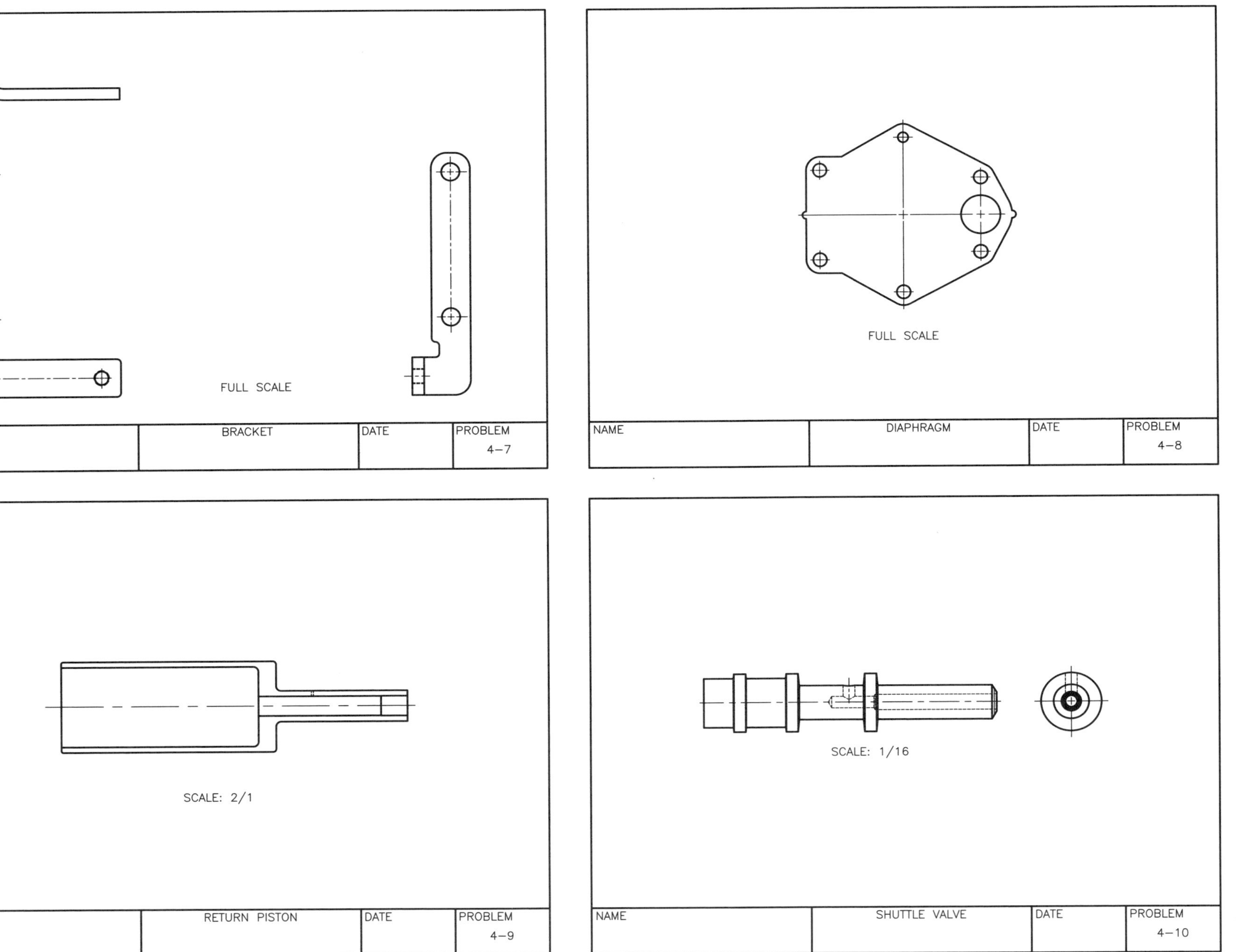
FULL SCALE
NAME
BRACKET
DATE
PROBLEM 4-7
FULL SCALE
NAME
DIAPHRAGM
DATE
PROBLEM 4-8
SCALE: 2/1
NAME
RETURN PISTON
DATE
PROBLEM 4-9
SCALE: 1/16
NAME
SHUTTLE VALVE
DATE
PROBLEM 4-10

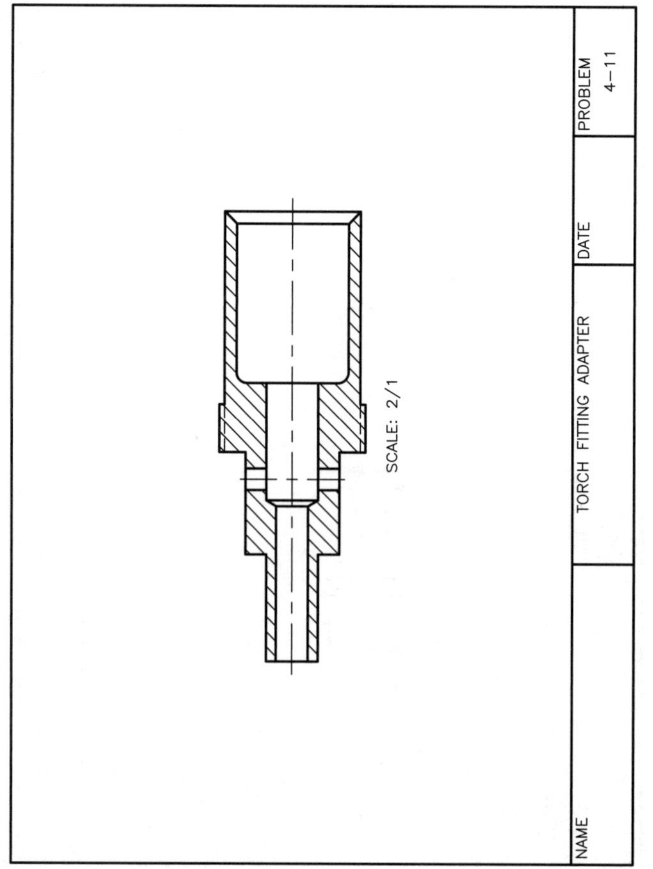

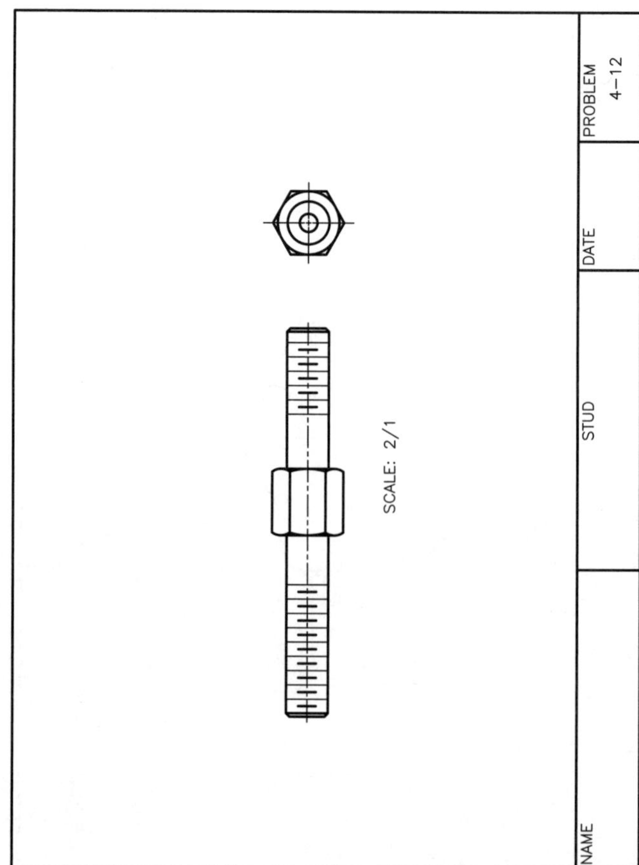

Answers to Chapter 4 Quiz

1. C. template
2. D. shows data stored for an object
3. A. **Move**
4. D. drawing
5. A. **Erase**, **Move**, and **Copy**
6. B. Starting point, center, and endpoint
7. C. spline
8. B. **Hatch**
9. C. **Array**
10. D. To increase or decrease the magnification factor.
11. D. **Pan**
12. C. text
13. B. inquiry
14. D. diameter dimensioning
15. A. layers
16. D. Z
17. B. attribute

Chapter Quiz 4

CAD Commands and Functions

Name ____________________

Period ____________ Date ____________ Score ____________

Multiple Choice

Choose the answer that correctly completes the statement. Write the corresponding letter in the space provided.

_____ 1. A _____ is a drawing file with preconfigured user settings.
A. grid
B. block
C. template
D. wireframe

_____ 2. The **List** command _____.
A. displays the files on the hard drive
B. compiles a list of objects used in the drawing
C. creates a list of layers in the drawing
D. shows data stored for an object

_____ 3. The **Copy** command functions in a similar manner to the _____ command except that it places a copy of the selected objects at the specified location.
A. **Move**
B. **Array**
C. **Rotate**
D. **Scale**

_____ 4. The **Line**, **Arc**, and **Circle** commands are _____ commands.
A. editing
B. dimensioning
C. inquiry
D. drawing

_____ 5. Commands that provide for the modification of a drawing include _____.
A. **Erase**, **Move**, and **Copy**
B. **Text**, **Erase**, and **Move**
C. **Move**, **Circle**, and **Copy**
D. **Copy**, **Erase**, and **Text**

_____ 6. Which of the following is *not* a method of drawing a circle?
A. Center and radius
B. Starting point, center, and endpoint
C. Center and diameter
D. Two points on the circle

Name ______________________________

_______ 7. A _____ is a smooth curve that passes through a series of control points specified by the user.

A. fillet

B. round

C. spline

D. ellipse

_______ 8. Which command is used to add section lines or fill patterns to a drawing?

A. **Layer**

B. **Hatch**

C. **Mirror**

D. **Block**

_______ 9. Which command is used to make multiple copies of selected objects in a rectangular or circular pattern?

A. **Fillet**

B. **Mirror**

C. **Array**

D. **Extend**

_______ 10. What is the function of the **Zoom** command?

A. To speed up regeneration.

B. To move the drawing in the display window from one location to another.

C. To move to the next drawing.

D. To increase or decrease the magnification factor.

_______ 11. Which of the following is *not* an editing command?

A. **Erase**

B. **Trim**

C. **Scale**

D. **Pan**

_______ 12. Commands that place notes and lettering on a drawing are called _____ commands.

A. editing

B. display control

C. text

D. plotting

_______ 13. To obtain a measurement of distance or area, a CAD drafter uses _____ commands.

A. display control

B. inquiry

C. text

D. editing

_______ 14. The **Linear** dimensioning command is used for all of the following except _____.

A. dimensioning a horizontal distance

B. dimensioning a vertical distance

C. dimensioning an inclined line

D. diameter dimensioning

Name ____

________ 15. The use of _____ is similar to placing different objects in a drawing on separate sheets as in overlay drafting.

A. layers
B. linetypes
C. snap
D. ortho

________ 16. The _____ axis represents the "vertical" axis in three-dimensional drawing.

A. V
B. X
C. Y
D. Z

________ 17. A(n) _____ is text information saved with a block.

A. layer
B. attribute
C. linetype
D. grid

Drawing Commands

The drawing commands of a CAD program make up the heart of the program's drawing capability. These commands are used to create objects on screen.

Line

The **Line** command is the most frequently used command. It is used to draw lines.

Double Line

The **Double Line** command is used to create walls on floor plans and similar objects in other applications.

Point

The **Point** command is used to create point objects for construction and location purposes.

Arc

The **Arc** command is used to draw partial circles.

Circle

The **Circle** command allows circles to be drawn in several different ways.

Spline

The **Spline** command allows the creation of a smooth curve through a series of points.

Ellipse

The **Ellipse** command is used to draw ellipses and elliptical arcs.

Polygon

The **Polygon** command enables the construction of regular polygons.

Rectangle

The **Rectangle** command usually provides at least two methods of construction—specifying the dimensions and dragging.

Sketch

The **Sketch** command allows freehand lines to be drawn with a pointing device.

Text

The **Text** command allows text to be placed on a drawing.

Hatch

The **Hatch** command is used to hatch an area of a drawing.

RM 4-1

Editing and Inquiry Commands

Editing commands allow the user to modify drawings in several ways. Inquiry commands are designed to list data for selected objects and calculate distances and areas.

Erase

The **Erase** command provides for the removal of objects from the drawing permanently.

Undo

The **Undo** command reverses the last command.

Move

The **Move** command allows one or more objects to be moved from one location to another without changing orientation.

Copy

The **Copy** command places a copy of an object at a specified location, leaving the original in place.

Mirror

The **Mirror** command draws a mirror image of an existing object.

Rotate

The **Rotate** command is used to alter the orientation of an object on the drawing.

Scale

The size of existing objects may be changed using the **Scale** command.

Fillet

The **Fillet** command generates a smoothly fitted arc between two lines, arcs, or circles.

Chamfer

The **Chamfer** command trims two intersecting lines a specific distance from the intersection and adds a connecting line.

Trim

The **Trim** command is used to shorten an object to its intersection with another object.

Extend

Using the **Extend** command, an existing object can be lengthened to end at a boundary edge.

Stretch

The **Stretch** command is used to move a selected portion of a drawing while maintaining connections to parts of the drawing left in place.

Array

The **Array** command makes multiple copies of selected objects in a circular or rectangular pattern.

Properties

The **Properties** command permits the examination of data stored for an object.

Distance

The **Distance** command determines the distance and angle between two points.

Area

The **Area** command calculates the area of an enclosed space.

RM 4-2

Display Control Commands

Display commands govern how a drawing is displayed on the monitor.

Zoom

The **Zoom** command increases or decreases the apparent size of objects on screen even though their actual size remains constant.

Pan

The **Pan** command moves the drawing in the display window from one location to another. Using this command is similar to "shifting" the paper.

View

The **View** command can be used to speed the process of displaying different views when constant switching back and forth between views on a large drawing is necessary.

Redraw

The **Redraw** command "cleans up" the display by removing marker blips from the screen.

Regenerate

The **Regenerate** command forces the program to regenerate the drawing and redraw the screen.

RM 4-3

Dimensioning Commands

The dimensioning commands of a CAD program speed the process of dimensioning lengths, distances, and angles on a drawing. Most CAD programs provide for automated dimensioning.

Linear

The **Linear** dimensioning command represents a group of commands related to dimensioning. This group of commands includes the following:

- **Horizontal**. Draws a horizontal dimension line.
- **Vertical**. Draws a vertical dimension line.
- **Aligned**. Draws a dimension line parallel to a specified line.
- **Rotated**. Draws a dimension line at a specific angle.
- **Baseline**. Continues a dimension from another dimension.
- **Continue**. Continues a dimension from the previous dimension.

Angular

The **Angular** dimensioning command is used to dimension the angle between two lines. This command generates an arc to indicate the angle.

Diameter

The **Diameter** dimensioning command is used to dimension the diameter of a circle.

Radius

The **Radius** dimensioning command is used to perform radius dimensioning.

Leader

The **Leader** dimensioning command is used to draw a specific or local note.

RM 4-4

Drawing Aids

Drawing aids are designed to speed up the drawing process and maintain accuracy at the same time. The most common drawing aids are listed here.

Grid

The grid function creates a reference grid of dots to be displayed on screen.

Snap

The snap function allows the cursor to "snap" to snap grid points. This function is similar to the grid function, except the snap grid is not visible.

Object snap

The object snap function allows the cursor to "connect" to points already in the drawing.

Ortho

The ortho mode ensures that all lines drawn using a pointing device will be orthogonal with respect to the grid.

Isometric snap

The isometric snap grid provides three axes for making isometric drawings. The axes are oriented at 30°, 90°, and 150°.

RM 4-5

File Management Commands and Utility Functions

File management commands allow the user of a CAD program to start, save, and open drawing files. Utility functions include commands and features used to access help, rename objects, and specify user settings.

New

The **New** command starts a new drawing file.

Save

The **Save** command writes the current state of the drawing to disk.

Open

The **Open** command accesses a drawing that has been previously saved.

Quit

The **Quit** command exits the program and does not update the file unless specified.

Help

The **Help** command provides user assistance.

Rename

The **Rename** command changes the name of an object, such as a block, layer, linetype, or text style.

System Variables

System variables are used to specify various modes and settings until changed.

RM 4-6

Types of CAD Models

Three-dimensional models serve a number of important functions. They help drafters and others visualize objects and test designs. A model can be shaded to produce a more realistic appearance and rotated to show the object from different angles. Solid models can be analyzed for mass properties. The three basic types of CAD-generated models are listed here.

Wireframe models

Wireframe models are created by connecting points on an object. The points represent intersections of lines. Connecting the points makes the object appear three-dimensional. A wireframe model is the simplest type of CAD model.

Surface models

Surface models are constructed by connecting edges. In basic terms, a surface model begins with a wireframe model. Each plane of the object is then converted to a surface as if a sheet of material were to cover the frame. Surface models can typically be enhanced with color, texture, and lighting.

Solid models

A solid model is the most realistic type of CAD model. Instead of recognizing only surfaces, the computer treats the object as a solid object made up of solid material. Solid models can be created in several different ways. They can be constructed from basic building shapes called primitives. They can also be constructed from two-dimensional geometry. Solid models are typically rendered with materials and lighting to create a more realistic appearance. Solid models can be analyzed for mass, volume, material properties, and other types of data.

RM 4-7

Procedure Checklist

CAD Commands and Functions

Name ____

Observable Items	Completed		Comments	Instructor Initials
	Yes	No		
1. Creates a new drawing file and saves it to disk.				
2. Selects and inputs commands.				
3. Enters coordinates and locates points on screen.				
4. Uses drawing aids.				
5. Constructs objects using drawing commands.				
6. Uses layer functions.				
7. Uses object snaps.				
8. Modifies objects using editing commands.				
9. Uses text commands.				
10. Uses dimensioning commands.				
11. Uses inquiry commands.				
12. Uses display control commands.				
13. Creates and inserts symbols.				
14. Hatches section views.				
15. Plots drawings.				
16. Manages drawing files.				

Instructor Signature ____

Sketching, Lettering, and Text

Learning Objectives

After studying this chapter, the student will be able to:

- Explain the role of sketching in technical communication.
- Describe accepted techniques for sketching.
- Identify different styles of lettering.
- List and describe industry standards used for lettering on drawings.
- Explain how guidelines are used to determine the height and slope of lettering.
- Draw single-stroke Gothic lettering.
- Describe the CAD functions used for creating text.

Instructional Resources

Text: pages 131–161

Review Questions, pages 154–155

Problems and Activities, pages 155–158

Drawing Problems, pages 159–161

Worksheets: pages 23–34

- Worksheet 5-1: *Sketching Lines*
- Worksheet 5-2: *Sketching Angles*
- Worksheet 5-3: *Sketching Circles and Arcs*
- Worksheet 5-4: *Sketching Ellipses and Irregular Curves*
- Worksheet 5-5: *Sketching Objects*
- Worksheet 5-6: *Sketching Objects*
- Worksheet 5-7: *Sketching Objects*
- Worksheet 5-8: *Sketching Objects*
- Worksheet 5-9: *Sketching Objects*
- Worksheet 5-10: *Vertical Gothic Lettering*
- Worksheet 5-11: *Inclined Gothic Lettering*
- Worksheet 5-12: *Lettering Notes*

Instructor's Resource

Instructional Tasks

Instructional Aids and Assignments

Chapter 5 Quiz

Reproducible Masters

- Reproducible Master 5-1: *Orthographic Sketching Grid*. Shown is a sketching grid for students to use when drawing problems involving orthographic projection.
- Reproducible Master 5-2: *Isometric Sketching Grid*. Shown is a sketching grid for students to use when drawing problems involving isometric views.
- Reproducible Master 5-3: *Single-Stroke Gothic Lettering*. The letters of the alphabet are shown on a grid to illustrate proper proportion in lettering.

Procedure Checklist

Instructional Tasks

1. Describe the purpose of sketching and its importance in drafting.
   - Discuss the uses and applications of sketches.
   - Explain the process of "thinking through" solutions to drafting problems.
2. Explain the sketching technique.
   - Discuss the pencil grip and the hand and arm position that create a relaxed, comfortable position.
3. Discuss how to sketch straight lines.
   - To encourage students to draw lightweight lines during the layout and construction phases of sketching, have them draw a heavy line and then erase it. Next, have them draw a light line and erase it. The results should convince students that light construction lines should be used until they are ready to "heavy-in" a sketch.
   - Demonstrate the technique of sketching straight lines.
4. Explain how to sketch circles, arcs, and ellipses.
   - Discuss the different methods of sketching circles, arcs, and ellipses.

- Select one method for each shape and demonstrate it.
5. Sketch objects to proportion.
   - Discuss the pencil-sight and unit methods of estimating proportion.
6. Identify common styles of lettering and the industry standard.
   - Display some industrial drawings and discuss the styles used.
   - Discuss the reasons why Gothic lettering is the industry standard.
   - Comment on architectural styles of lettering.
7. Explain how to draw guidelines for height and slope.
   - Discuss the importance of guidelines.
   - Discuss mechanical drawing devices for constructing guidelines.
   - Demonstrate how to lay out Gothic letters.
8. Discuss how to form single-stroke Gothic letters.
   - Demonstrate proper hand and arm position and movement.
   - Emphasize the importance of proportion, stability, and quality in lettering.
9. Demonstrate how to letter words, lines, and notes.
   - Discuss the composition of words, sentences, and notes involving two or more lines.
   - Discuss the size of letters on various types and sizes of drawings.
10. Introduce text commands used in CAD drafting.
    - Discuss the general procedure for creating text on a drawing.
11. Explain the purpose of text styles.
    - Discuss the common settings used to determine the appearance of text.
    - Explain different justification settings used for text.

Instructional Aids and Assignments

1. Show multimedia presentations or films on the techniques of sketching.
2. Prepare a transparency of a sketch showing lightweight lines and finished lines.
3. Display large-size lettering charts showing specific strokes in forming letters.
4. Display industrial drawings showing the extent of use and clarity of lettering on technical drawings.
5. Assign the number of problems necessary to achieve the proper skill level in the various phases of sketching. Use the problems in the text or use Worksheets 5-1 through 5-9. The number of problems is sufficient to assign a minimum number to all students and to identify problems that may be done for extra credit. Some problems may be used for the performance section of the chapter quiz.
6. Assign the lettering problems in the text or use Worksheets 5-10 through 5-12.
7. It is not intended that students do all of the lettering problems and exercises given in this chapter. Rather, the number of different problems and activities given should enable you to select those that are most appropriate for the particular group of students in your class.
8. It may be more effective to assign enough lettering exercises to familiarize students with the proper techniques, and then expect continued improvement in clarity and uniformity of lettering on successive drawing problems.

Answers to Review Questions, Text

Pages 154–155

1. freehand
2. grid
3. 1 1/2″
4. end
5. perpendicular
6. Vertical
7. inclined
8. The centerline method, the enclosing square method, the hand-pivot method, and the free-circle method.
9. The free-ellipse method.
10. irregular
11. Proportion
12. lettering
13. text
14. B. HB, F, or H
15. Roman, Italic, Text, and Gothic.
16. Gothic
17. Guidelines
18. above

19. O
20. 1/8″
21. Notes
22. A technical pen.
23. It is used to ink letters and symbols.
24. text
25. font
26. Left, right, center, middle, and aligned.

Solutions to Problems and Activities, Text

Sketching Problems, Pages 155–157

For Problem 1, observe the uniformity, straightness, slope, and endings of lines. Also observe the size of angles. For Problems 2 and 3, observe the uniformity of circles, arcs, and ellipses. For Problems 4 and 5, evaluate student work for line uniformity, accuracy, and sketching technique.

Lettering Problems, Pages 157–158

For Problems 6–17, students should use the techniques suggested for obtaining lettering that is uniform and clear. Observe students as they work for the proper use of guidelines, clarity, and spacing of letters, words, and sentences. An effective way of calling attention to lettering quality is to bring several industrial prints to class. Have students review the clarity and uniformity of the lettering used. Students should understand that the neatness and clarity of a drawing are greatly affected by the dimensions and notes that the drafter places on the drawing.

For Problems 18–20, evaluate student work for accuracy and appearance. The text should be uniform in height and should have the proper justification. Check that the correct text style settings are used.

Solutions to Drawing Problems, Text

Pages 159–161

Student work should look like the following drawings. The problem number and title are indicated on each problem sheet.

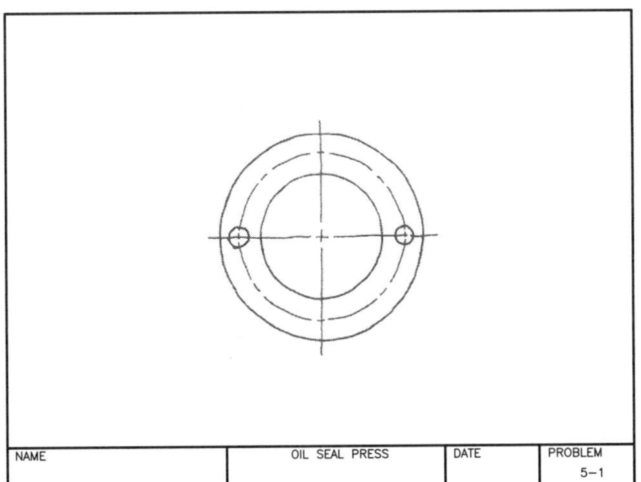

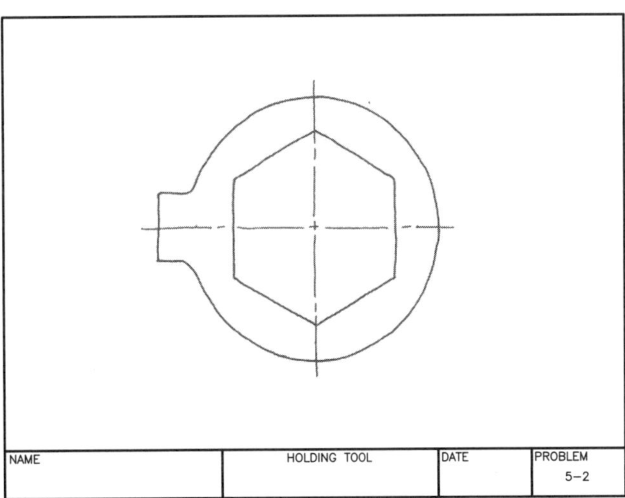

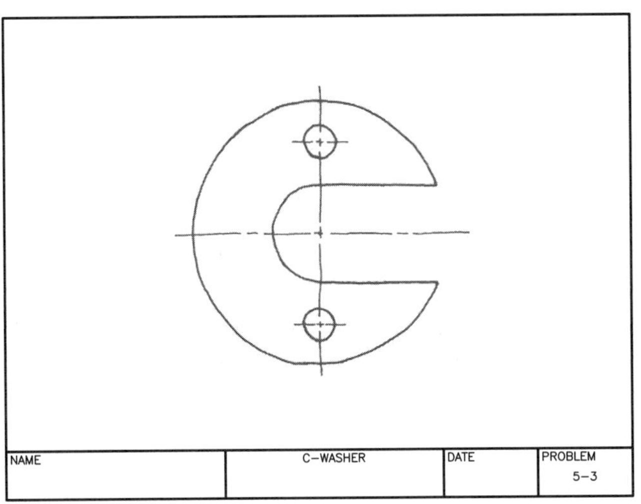

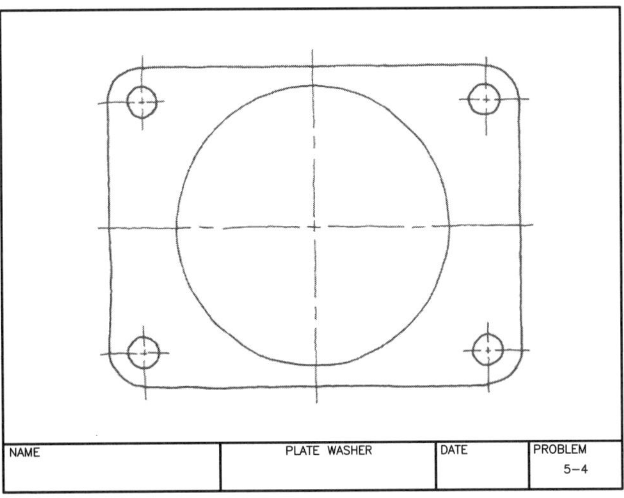

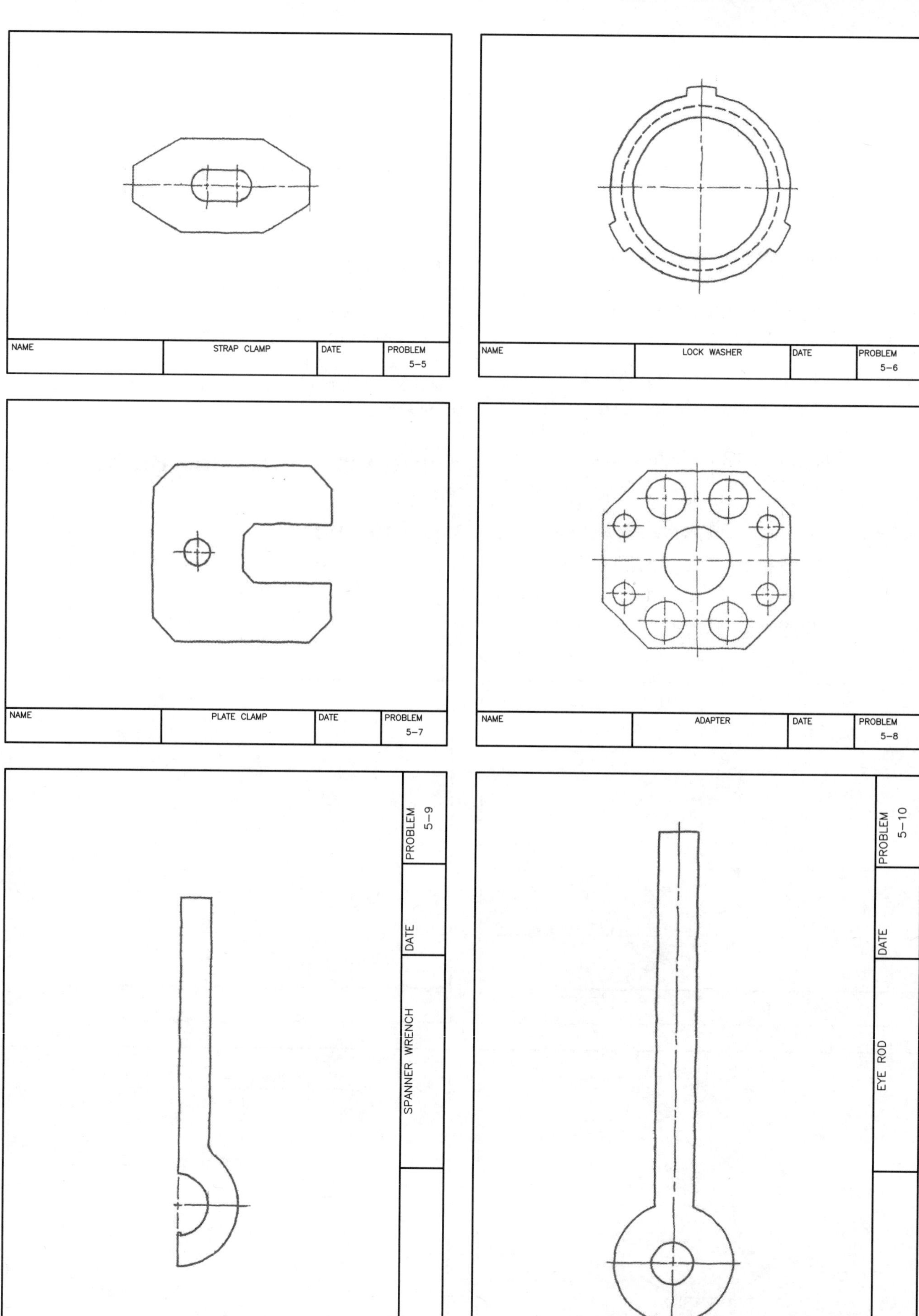
NAME
STRAP CLAMP
DATE
PROBLEM
5-5
NAME
LOCK WASHER
DATE
PROBLEM
5-6
NAME
PLATE CLAMP
DATE
PROBLEM
5-7
NAME
ADAPTER
DATE
PROBLEM
5-8
PROBLEM
5-9
DATE
SPANNER WRENCH
NAME
PROBLEM
5-10
DATE
EYE ROD
NAME

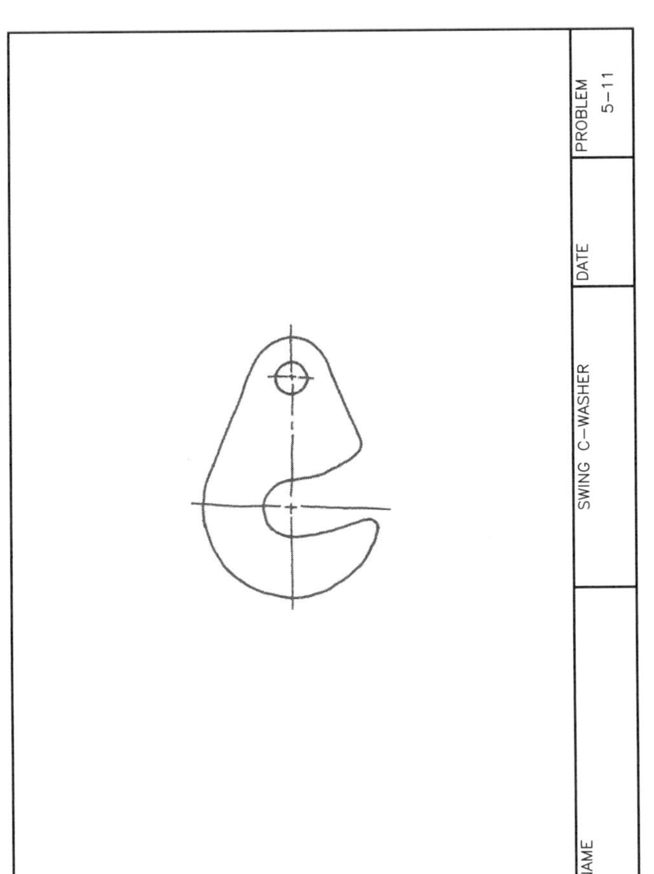
PROBLEM
5–11
DATE
SWING C–WASHER
NAME

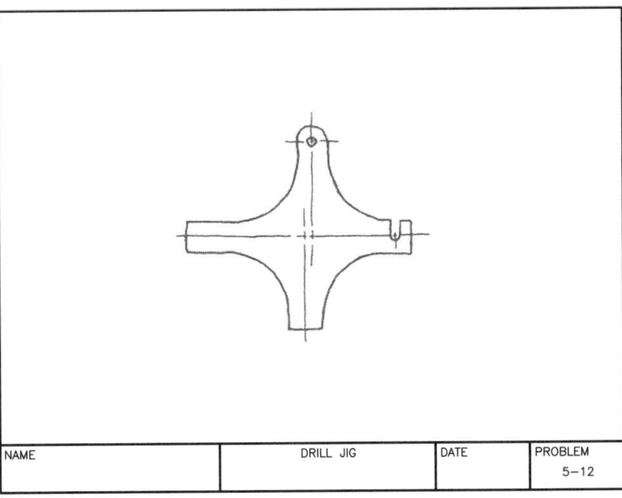
NAME
DRILL JIG
DATE
PROBLEM
5–12

Solutions to Worksheets

Pages 23–34

1. Worksheets 5-1 through 5-4:
   Observe the uniformity, straightness, slope, and endings of lines. Observe the size of angles. Observe the uniformity of circles, arcs, and ellipses.
2. Worksheets 5-5 through 5-9:
   Student work should look similar to the drawings shown below. The problem number and title are indicated on each problem sheet.
3. Worksheets 5-10 through 5-12:
   Students should complete each section by lettering the alphabet and notes in the size shown. Students should repeat the alphabet as many times as space permits. Observe for characteristics of good lettering—staying within vertical and horizontal guidelines, maintaining proportion and proper spacing, and drawing well-formed letters.

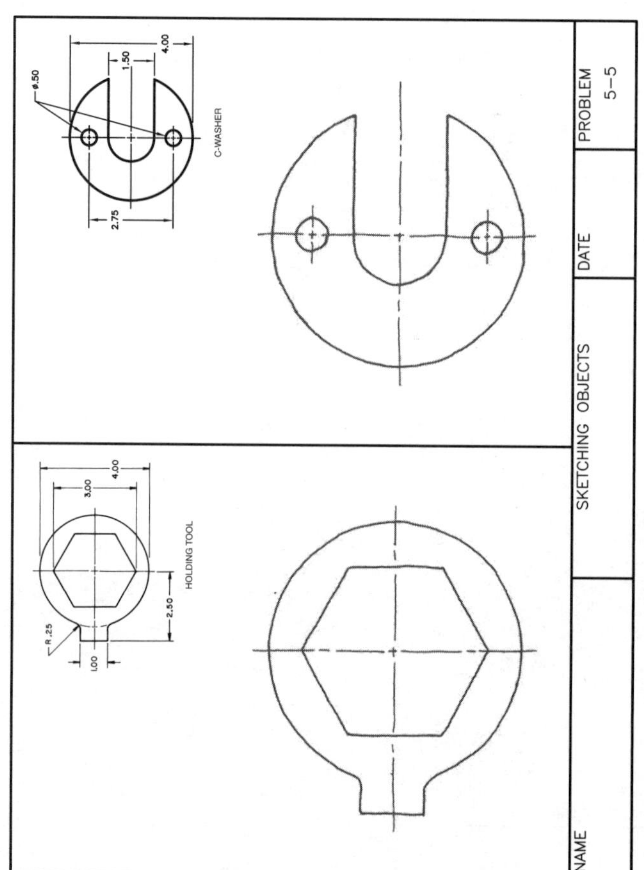

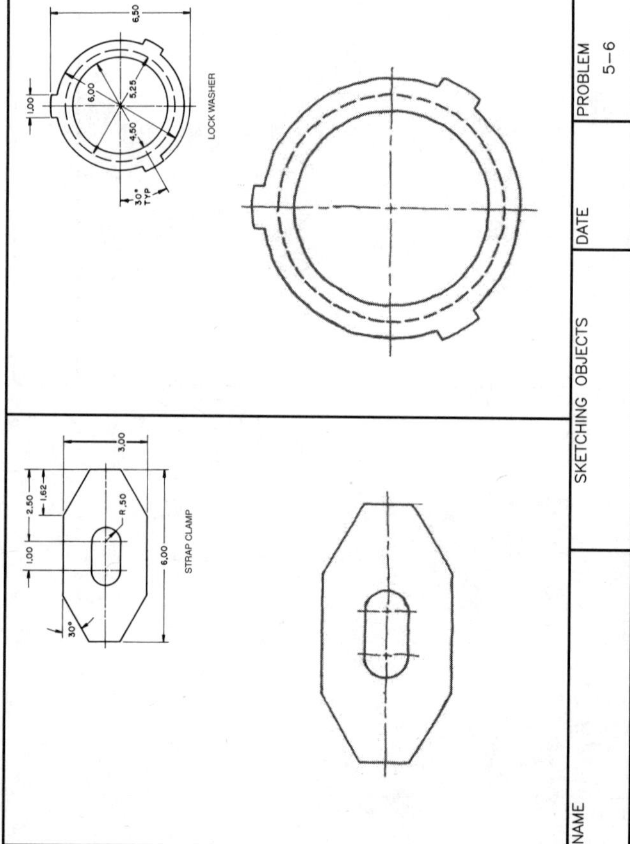

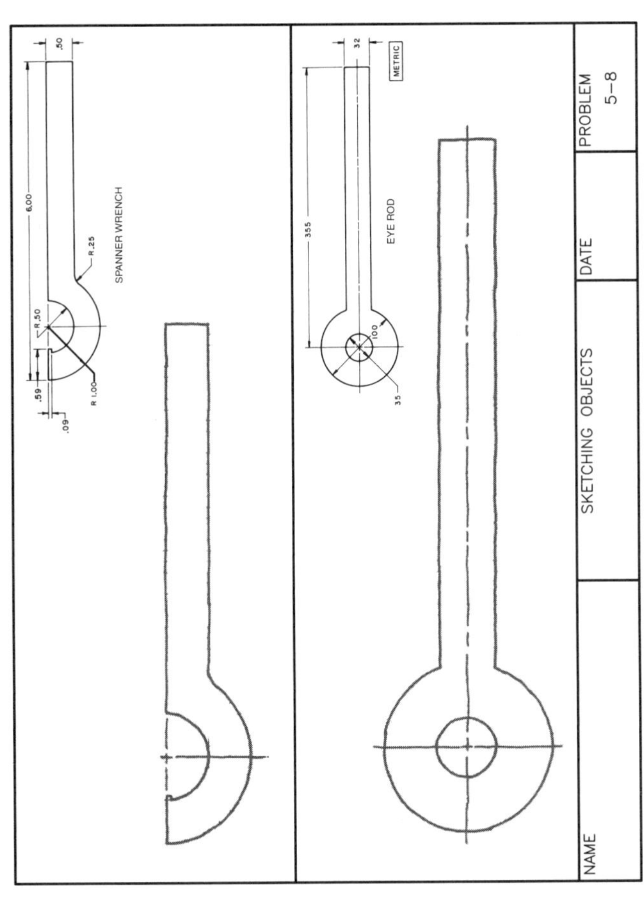
SPANNER WRENCH
EYE ROD
METRIC
NAME
SKETCHING OBJECTS
DATE
PROBLEM
5–8

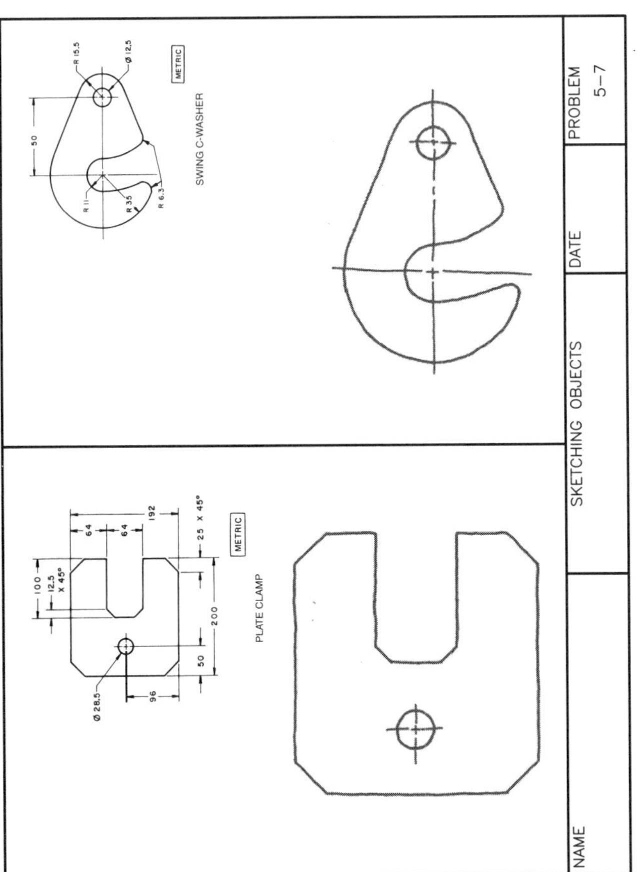
PLATE CLAMP
METRIC
SWING C-WASHER
METRIC
NAME
SKETCHING OBJECTS
DATE
PROBLEM
5–7

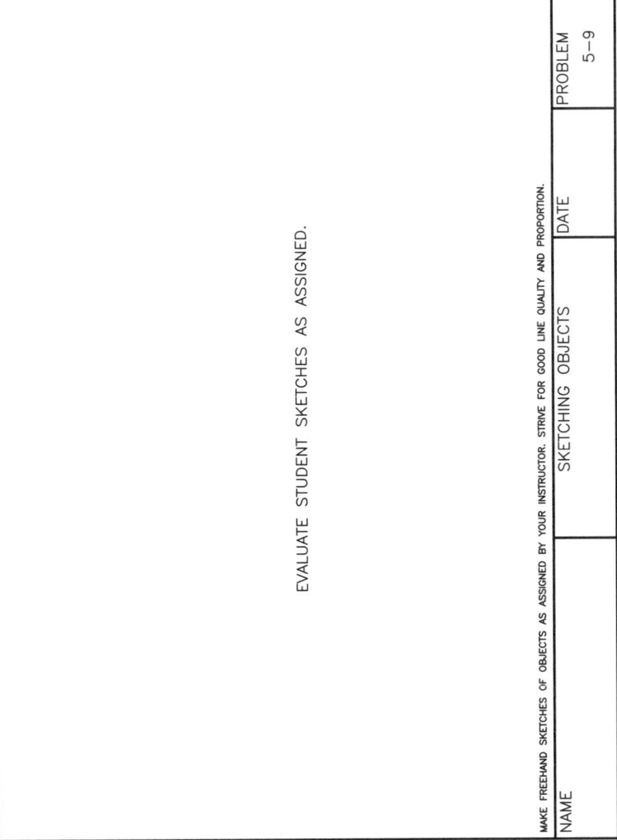
EVALUATE STUDENT SKETCHES AS ASSIGNED.
MAKE FREEHAND SKETCHES OF OBJECTS AS ASSIGNED BY YOUR INSTRUCTOR. STRIVE FOR GOOD LINE QUALITY AND PROPORTION.
NAME
SKETCHING OBJECTS
DATE
PROBLEM
5–9

Answers to Chapter 5 Quiz

1. D. All of the above.
2. C. termination point of the line
3. B. Rotate the paper slightly to develop a comfortable orientation.
4. C. To develop the ability to construct technical sketches without the use of aids.
5. D. with a firm grip and approximately 1 1/2″ from the lead point
6. C. Compass method.
7. C. free-ellipse
8. B. proportion
9. B. HB, F, or H
10. C. To maintain a conical point on the lead.
11. A. A lettering guide.
12. D. Twice the height of the whole number.
13. A. horizontally
14. C. Gothic
15. B. 1/8″
16. D. two-thirds
17. A. one letter space
18. B. two letter spaces
19. Refer to the drawings given in the *Solutions to Drawing Problems, Text* section for the problem selected from the textbook.
20. Refer to the drawings given in the *Solutions to Drawing Problems, Text* section for the problem selected from the textbook.

Chapter Quiz 5

Sketching, Lettering, and Text

Name ____

Period____________________ Date____________________ Score ________________

Multiple Choice

Choose the answer that correctly completes the statement. Write the corresponding letter in the space provided.

_______ 1. How are sketches useful to the drafter?
A. Sketches provide a means of thinking through a problem.
B. Sketches may be an initial step in planning an instrument drawing.
C. Sketches provide a quick and simple way of sharing an idea.
D. All of the above.

_______ 2. When sketching straight lines, your eye should be on the _____.
A. pencil
B. line that is being drawn
C. termination point of the line
D. top of the sheet

_______ 3. Which of the following is a useful technique when sketching straight or curved lines?
A. Change hands when drawing lines on the opposite side of the sheet.
B. Rotate the paper slightly to develop a comfortable orientation.
C. Use two pencils when drawing parallel lines.
D. Always keep your eye on the beginning point of the line.

_______ 4. What is the aim of freehand technical sketching?
A. To improve poor lettering ability.
B. To replace traditional instrument drawings.
C. To develop the ability to construct technical sketches without the use of aids.
D. None of the above.

_______ 5. When sketching, the pencil should be held _____.
A. tightly to assure firm, straight lines
B. close to the lead point for better control
C. quite loose and relaxed for easy movement
D. with a firm grip and approximately 1 1/2″ from the lead point

_______ 6. Which of the following is *not* considered to be a freehand method of sketching circles and arcs?
A. Centerline method.
B. Enclosing square method.
C. Compass method.
D. Free-circle method.

Name ____

________ 7. The fastest method of sketching ellipses is the _____ method.
A. rectangular
B. trammel
C. free-ellipse
D. compass

________ 8. The most important element in a technical sketch, in order for it to convey an accurate description, is _____.
A. correct line weight
B. proportion
C. straightness of lines
D. curvature of lines

________ 9. What is the most appropriate hardness of lead to be used for lettering?
A. 4B, B, or HB
B. HB, F, or H
C. H, 2H, or 4H
D. 4H

________ 10. Why should the pencil be rotated frequently during the lettering of a drawing?
A. To keep the pencil from becoming "sweaty."
B. To reduce finger cramps.
C. To maintain a conical point on the lead.
D. To release tension in the hand.

________ 11. What is one useful device that may be used in constructing freehand lettering?
A. A lettering guide.
B. A protractor.
C. A scale to draw straight lines.
D. No aids may be used in freehand lettering.

________ 12. What is the recommended overall height of fractions in freehand lettering?
A. The same height as the whole number.
B. One-half the height of the whole number.
C. Two-thirds the height of the whole number.
D. Twice the height of the whole number.

________ 13. General notes on drawings should be oriented so that they can be read _____.
A. horizontally
B. vertically
C. either horizontally or vertically
D. Any angle is acceptable.

________ 14. The standard style of lettering on drawings is _____.
A. Roman
B. German Text
C. Gothic
D. Italic

Name ____

________ 15. The minimum height of lettering on drawings usually is _____.
A. 1/16″
B. 1/8″
C. 1/4″
D. 1/2″

________ 16. The spacing between lines of lettering in notes should be _____ the height of letters on the drawing.
A. one-quarter
B. one-half
C. one-third
D. two-thirds

________ 17. Spacing between words within a note is _____.
A. one letter space
B. two letter spaces
C. three letter spaces
D. four letter spaces

________ 18. Spacing between sentences within a note is _____.
A. one letter space
B. two letter spaces
C. three letter spaces
D. one letter space plus the period

Drafting Performance

19. Make a one-view technical sketch of a problem selected by your instructor from the Drawing Problems section of Chapter 5 in your textbook.

Name ______________________________

20. Letter a note from a problem selected by your instructor from the Lettering Problems section of Chapter 5 in your textbook.

Orthographic Sketching Grid

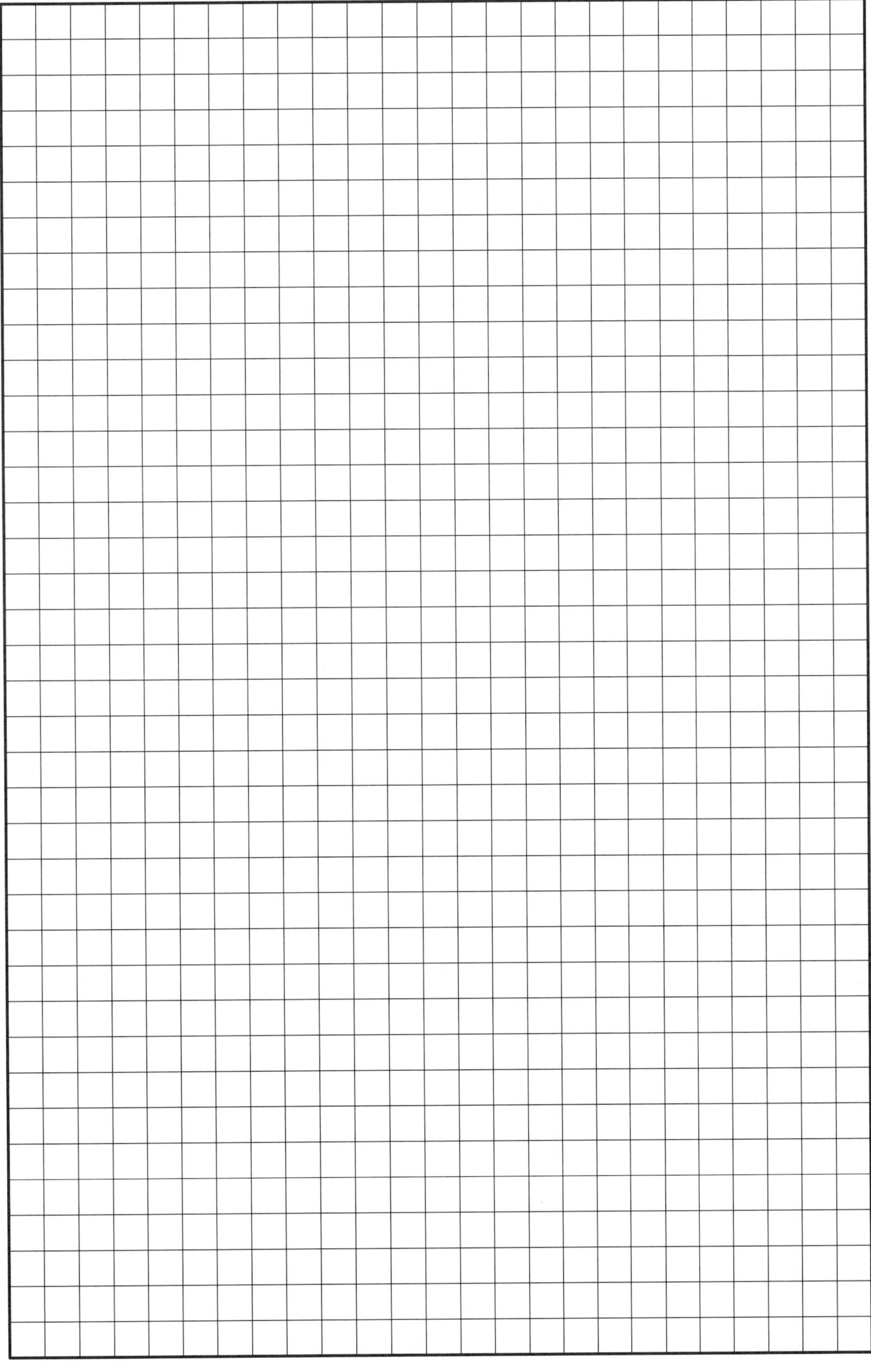

RM 5-1

Isometric Sketching Grid

RM 5-2

Single-Stroke Gothic Lettering

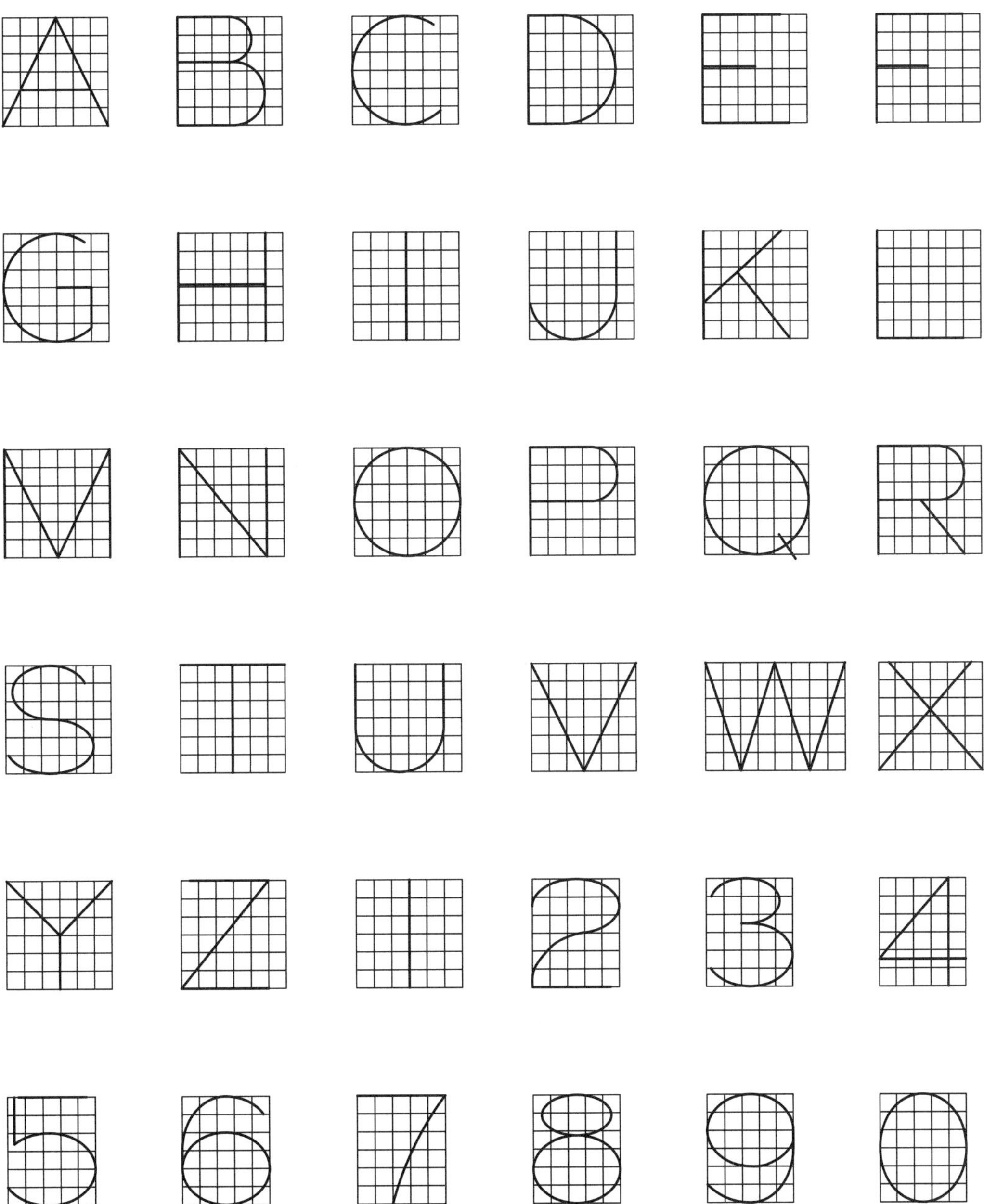

Source: ANSI

RM 5-3

Procedure Checklist

Sketching, Lettering, and Text

Name ______________________________

Observable Items	Completed		Comments	Instructor Initials
	Yes	No		
1. Sketches horizontal lines.				
2. Sketches vertical lines.				
3. Sketches inclined lines.				
4. Sketches angles.				
5. Sketches circles and arcs.				
6. Sketches ellipses.				
7. Sketches irregular curves.				
8. Sketches objects.				
9. Forms letters.				
10. Uses guidelines in lettering.				
11. Composes words and sentences.				
12. Places notes on drawings.				
13. Letters with ink.				
14. Letters with a mechanical device.				
15. Letters with transfer type.				

Instructor Signature ______________________________

Section 2 Drafting Techniques and Skills

Basic Geometric Constructions

Learning Objectives

After studying this chapter, the student will be able to:

- Use manual drafting tools and methods to make geometric constructions.
- Use CAD commands and methods to make geometric constructions.
- Draw, bisect, and divide lines.
- Construct, bisect, and transfer angles.
- Draw triangles, squares, hexagons, and octagons.
- Use special techniques to construct regular polygons.
- Construct circles and arcs.

Instructional Resources

Text: pages 163–212

Review Questions, pages 210–211

Problems and Activities, pages 211–212

Worksheets: pages 35–42

- Worksheet 6-1: *Geometric Constructions*
- Worksheet 6-2: *Geometric Constructions*
- Worksheet 6-3: *Geometric Constructions*
- Worksheet 6-4: *Geometric Constructions*
- Worksheet 6-5: *Geometric Constructions*
- Worksheet 6-6: *Geometric Constructions*
- Worksheet 6-7: *Geometric Constructions*
- Worksheet 6-8: *Outside Caliper*

Instructor's Resource

Instructional Tasks

Instructional Aids and Assignments

Chapter 6 Quiz

Reproducible Masters

- Reproducible Master 6-1: *Bisecting an Angle.* Shown are the steps required to bisect an angle.
- Reproducible Master 6-2: *Constructing Tangents.* Shown are procedures for constructing an arc through a given point and tangent to a line, constructing an arc tangent to two circles, and constructing an arc tangent to a line and a circle.

Procedure Checklist

Color Transparencies (Binder/IRCD only)

- Transparency 6-1: *Bisecting a Line.* Shown are manual construction methods for bisecting a line.
- Transparency 6-2: *Dividing a Line.* Shown is the step-by-step procedure for dividing a line into proportional parts.
- Transparency 6-3: *Regular Polygons.* Common regular polygons are shown. The included angle is identified for each.

Instructional Tasks

1. Discuss the various procedures for making geometric constructions with straight lines.
   - Demonstrate the geometric functions of bisecting, laying out through a point, and dividing into a number of equal parts.
   - Have class members study objects in the classroom and identify the geometric shapes they see.
2. Discuss how to construct, bisect, and transfer angles.
   - Demonstrate the geometric functions applicable to angles.
   - Display examples of machine parts and architectural pieces. Have students identify the geometric shapes contained in each.
3. Discuss how to construct triangles.
   - Demonstrate the geometric functions applicable to triangles.
4. Discuss how to construct squares.
   - Demonstrate the geometric functions applicable to squares.
5. Discuss how to construct various types of polygons.
   - Demonstrate the geometric functions applicable to polygons.

- Present several industrial drawings and identify the geometric forms used in the drawings.

6. Discuss how to transfer plane figures.
   - Demonstrate the geometric functions applicable to transferring plane figures.
7. Discuss how to construct circles and arcs.
   - Demonstrate the geometric functions applicable to circles and arcs.

Instructional Aids and Assignments

1. Display models of geometric forms.
2. Display machine parts and architectural pieces representative of geometric shapes.
3. Show multimedia presentations or films on the application of geometry to drafting and design.
4. In an open area, lay out various geometric forms such as angles, triangles, and other polygons. Make use of the 3-4-5 method of forming a right angle. Lay out a rectangle (approximating the size of a house foundation) and check for squareness by measuring the diagonals.
5. Assign the number of problems necessary to achieve the proper skill level in making geometric constructions. Use the problems in the text or use Worksheets 6-1 through 6-8. The number of problems is sufficient to assign a minimum number to all students and to identify problems that may be done for extra credit. Some problems may be used for the performance section of the chapter quiz.

Answers to Review Questions, Text

Pages 210–211

1. geometry
2. bisect
3. **Line**
4. T-square
5. The **Offset** command.
6. compass
7. The vertical line method and the inclined line method.
8. The **Divide** command.
9. The **Rotate** and **Align** commands.
10. perpendicular
11. Polar
12. D. Trapezoid
13. An equilateral triangle.
14. The **Polygon** command is used for drawing regular polygons with three or more sides.
15. An isosceles triangle.
16. 90
17. square
18. **Inscribed**
19. A. 108°
20. hexagon
21. **Copy**
22. Draw a rectangle to enclose the plane figure.
23. The **Scale** command.
24. arc
25. The **Circle** command.
26. tangent
27. The **Trim** command.
28. rectified
29. pi (π)
30. The circumference, radius, area, and center point location.
31. chord

Solutions to Problems and Activities, Text

Pages 211–212

Student work should look like the following drawings. The problem number and title are indicated on each problem sheet.

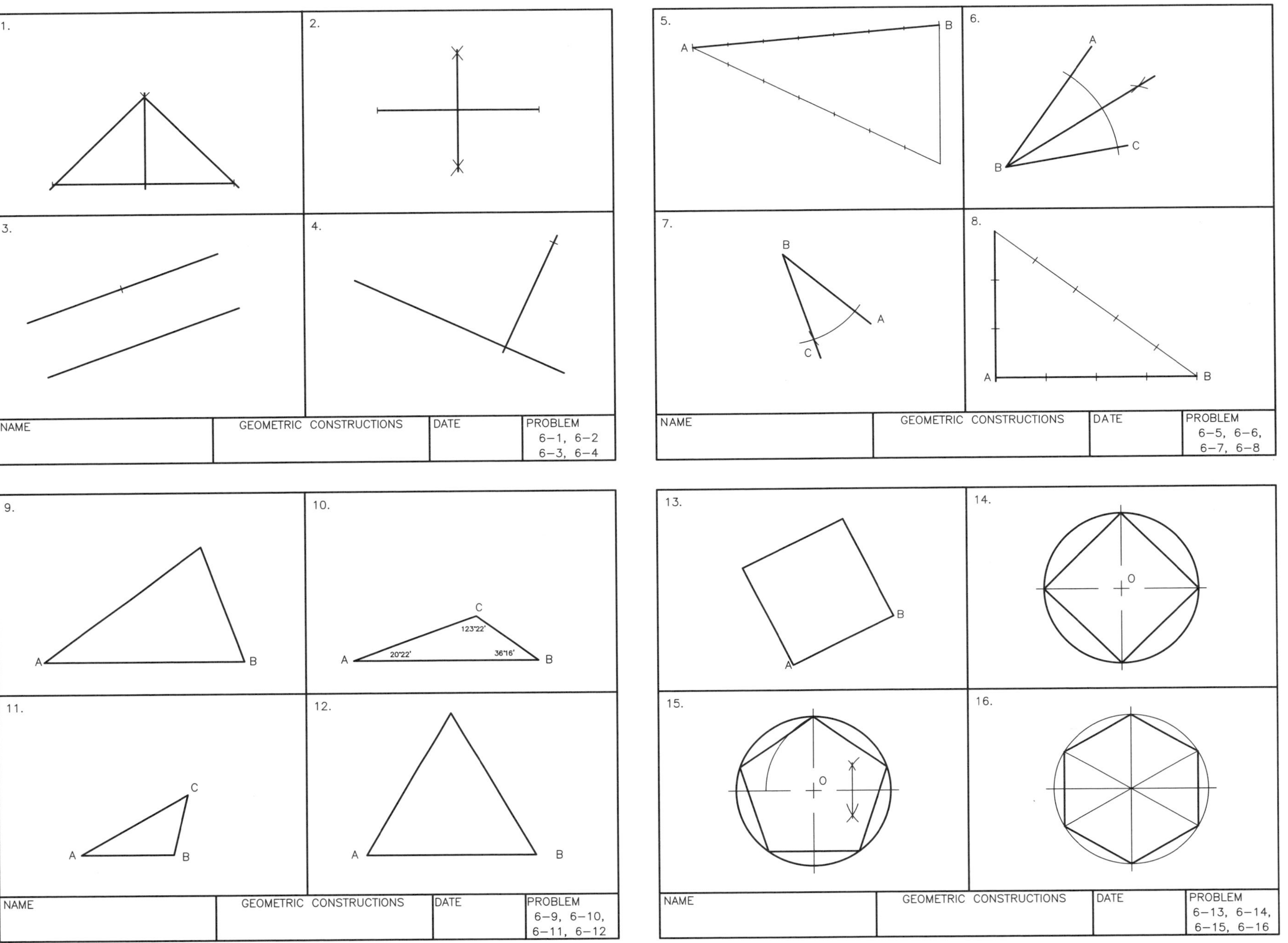
1.
2.
3.
4.
NAME
GEOMETRIC CONSTRUCTIONS
DATE
PROBLEM 6–1, 6–2 6–3, 6–4
5.
6.
7.
8.
NAME
GEOMETRIC CONSTRUCTIONS
DATE
PROBLEM 6–5, 6–6, 6–7, 6–8
9.
10.
123°22'
20°22'
36°16'
11.
12.
NAME
GEOMETRIC CONSTRUCTIONS
DATE
PROBLEM 6–9, 6–10, 6–11, 6–12
13.
14.
15.
16.
NAME
GEOMETRIC CONSTRUCTIONS
DATE
PROBLEM 6–13, 6–14, 6–15, 6–16

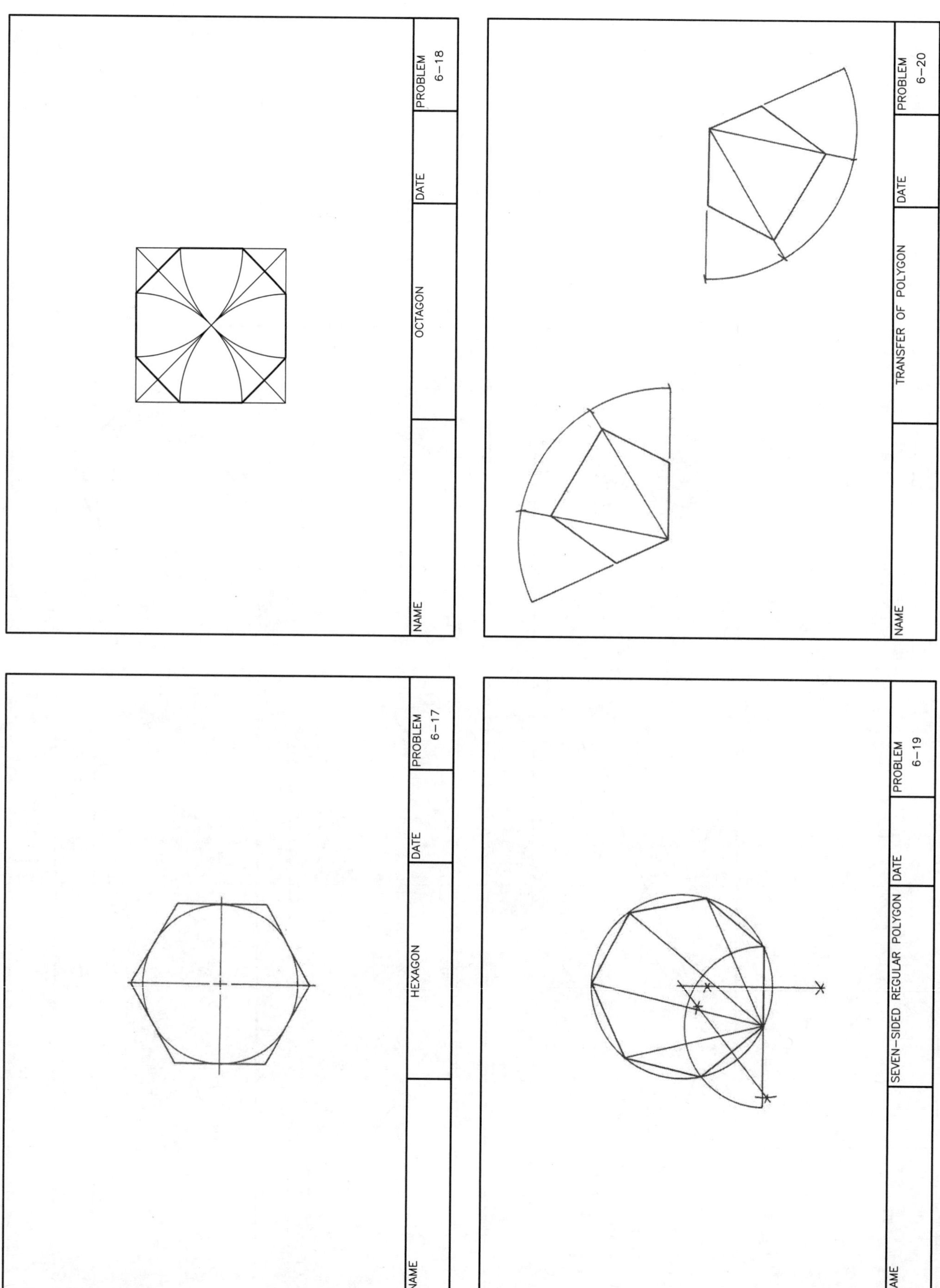

PROBLEM
6–18
DATE
OCTAGON
NAME
PROBLEM
6–20
DATE
TRANSFER OF POLYGON
NAME
PROBLEM
6–17
DATE
HEXAGON
NAME
PROBLEM
6–19
DATE
SEVEN–SIDED REGULAR POLYGON
NAME

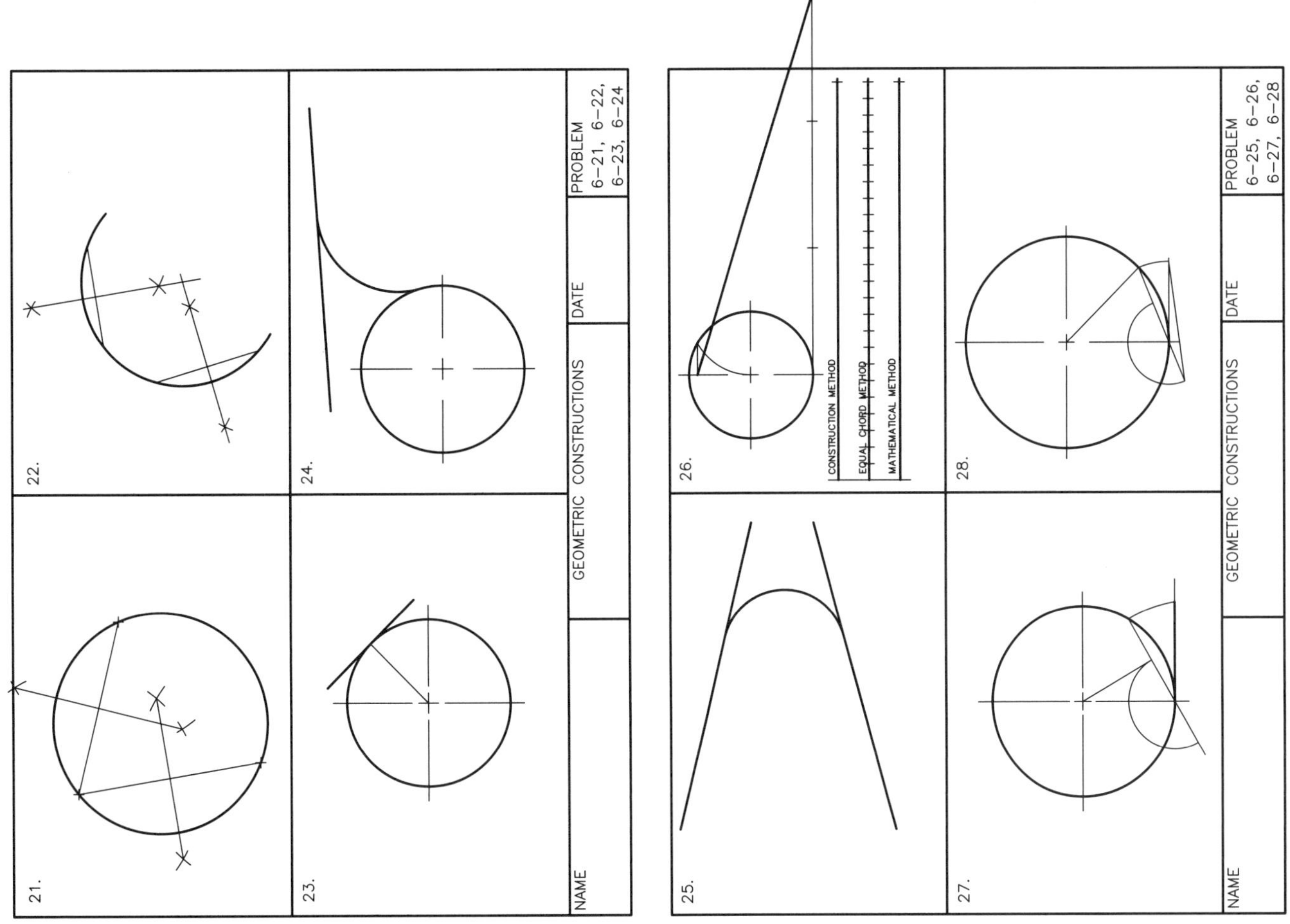
21.
22.
23.
24.
PROBLEM
6–21, 6–22,
6–23, 6–24
DATE
GEOMETRIC CONSTRUCTIONS
NAME
25.
26.
CONSTRUCTION METHOD
EQUAL CHORD METHOD
MATHEMATICAL METHOD
27.
28.
PROBLEM
6–25, 6–26,
6–27, 6–28
DATE
GEOMETRIC CONSTRUCTIONS
NAME

Solutions to Worksheets
Pages 35–42

Student work should look like the following drawings. The problem number and title are indicated on each problem sheet.

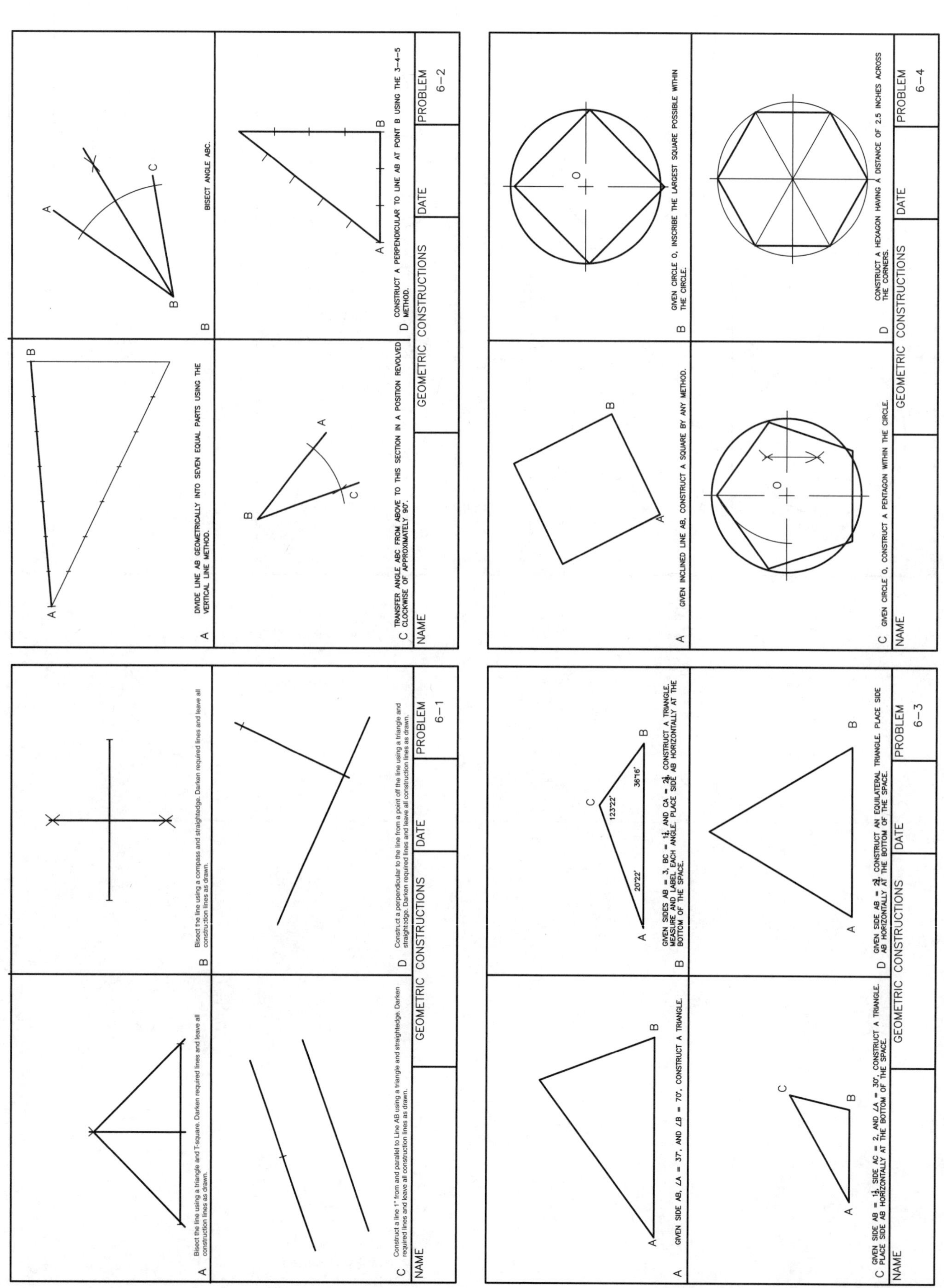

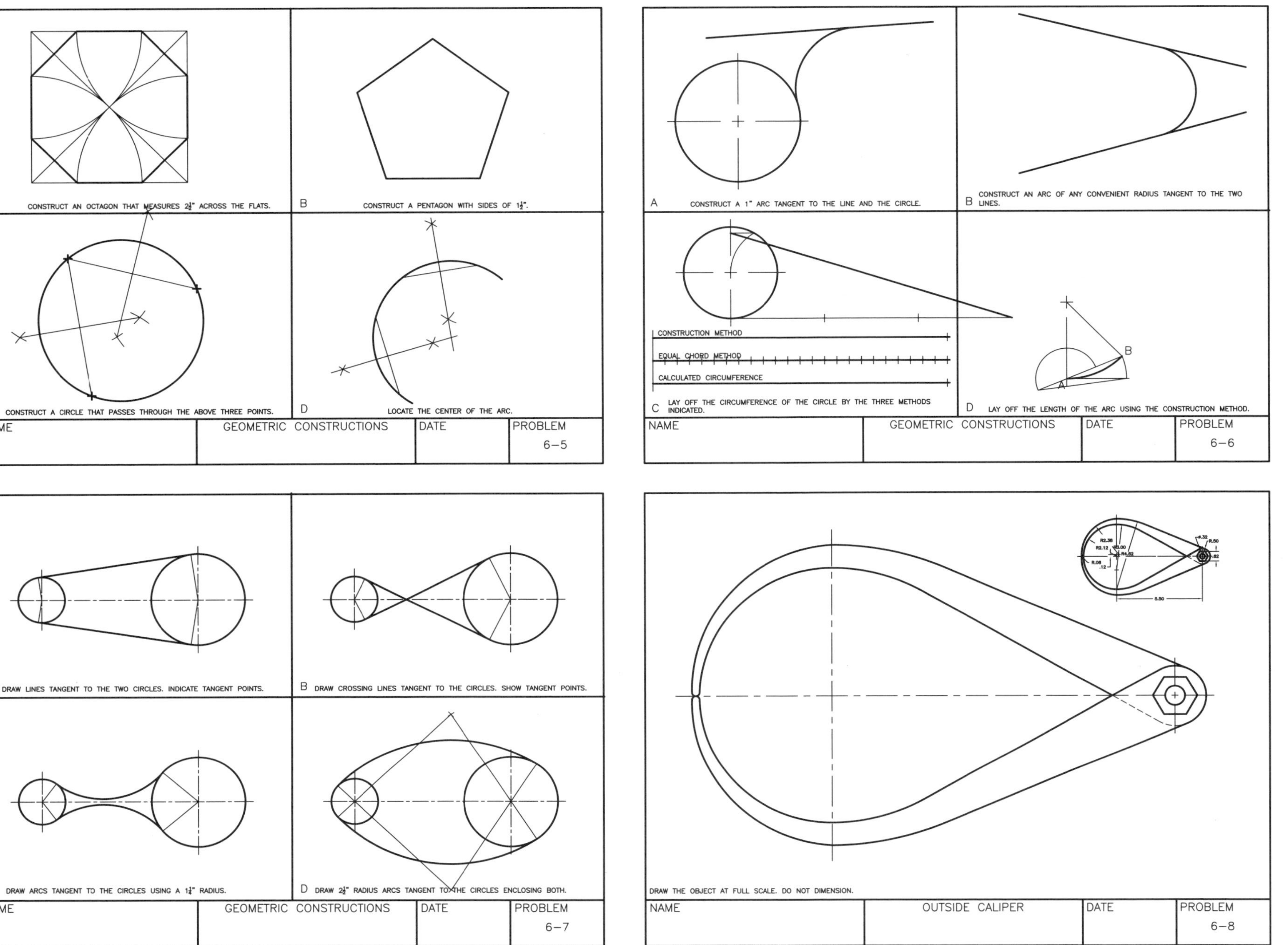

A CONSTRUCT AN OCTAGON THAT MEASURES 2½" ACROSS THE FLATS.
B CONSTRUCT A PENTAGON WITH SIDES OF 1½".
C CONSTRUCT A CIRCLE THAT PASSES THROUGH THE ABOVE THREE POINTS.
D LOCATE THE CENTER OF THE ARC.
NAME
GEOMETRIC CONSTRUCTIONS
DATE
PROBLEM 6–5
A CONSTRUCT A 1" ARC TANGENT TO THE LINE AND THE CIRCLE.
B CONSTRUCT AN ARC OF ANY CONVENIENT RADIUS TANGENT TO THE TWO LINES.
CONSTRUCTION METHOD
EQUAL CHORD METHOD
CALCULATED CIRCUMFERENCE
C LAY OFF THE CIRCUMFERENCE OF THE CIRCLE BY THE THREE METHODS INDICATED.
B
A
D LAY OFF THE LENGTH OF THE ARC USING THE CONSTRUCTION METHOD.
NAME
GEOMETRIC CONSTRUCTIONS
DATE
PROBLEM 6–6
A DRAW LINES TANGENT TO THE TWO CIRCLES. INDICATE TANGENT POINTS.
B DRAW CROSSING LINES TANGENT TO THE CIRCLES. SHOW TANGENT POINTS.
C DRAW ARCS TANGENT TO THE CIRCLES USING A 1¼" RADIUS.
D DRAW 2½" RADIUS ARCS TANGENT TO THE CIRCLES ENCLOSING BOTH.
NAME
GEOMETRIC CONSTRUCTIONS
DATE
PROBLEM 6–7
DRAW THE OBJECT AT FULL SCALE. DO NOT DIMENSION.
NAME
OUTSIDE CALIPER
DATE
PROBLEM 6–8

Answers to Chapter 6 Quiz

1. D. All of the above.
2. C. Compass
3. A. Rectangle
4. B. **Offset**
5. A. equilateral
6. D. Scale, straightedge, and triangle.
7. B. Compass and triangle.
8. B. **Rotate**
9. C. six
10. C. **Polygon**
11. A. Specifying the center point and radius.
12. D. All of the above.
13. C. circle or square
14. The student answer should be similar to the construction shown in **Figure 6-19** in the text.
15. The student answer should be similar to the construction shown in **Figure 6-31** in the text.

Chapter Quiz

Basic Geometric Constructions

Name ____

Period ______________ Date ______________ Score ______________

Multiple Choice

Choose the answer that correctly completes the statement. Write the corresponding letter in the space provided.

_______ 1. Acceptable solutions to geometric constructions depend on _____.
- A. using the proper procedure
- B. accuracy
- C. careful work
- D. All of the above.

_______ 2. Which of the following instruments can be used to bisect a line?
- A. Protractor
- B. French curve
- C. Compass
- D. Triangle

_______ 3. What common polygon has opposite sides equal with all interior angles 90°?
- A. Rectangle
- B. Rhomboid
- C. Trapezoid
- D. Triangle

_______ 4. The _____ command is typically used to draw parallel lines.
- A. **Trim**
- B. **Offset**
- C. **Divide**
- D. **Extend**

_______ 5. A(n) _____ triangle always has three sides equal and three angles equal.
- A. equilateral
- B. isosceles
- C. right
- D. scalene

_______ 6. The following instruments should be used in dividing a line into a number of equal parts:
- A. Straightedge and triangle.
- B. Straightedge and two triangles.
- C. Straightedge and scale.
- D. Scale, straightedge, and triangle.

Name ____

_______ 7. To transfer an angle, the following instruments should be used:
A. Scale and triangle.
B. Compass and triangle.
C. Scale and compass.
D. Scale and straightedge.

_______ 8. The _____ command is used to transfer an angle.
A. **Move**
B. **Rotate**
C. **Stretch**
D. **Mirror**

_______ 9. A hexagon has _____ sides.
A. four
B. five
C. six
D. seven

_______ 10. The _____ command provides the quickest way to create an equilateral triangle.
A. **Line**
B. **Rectangle**
C. **Polygon**
D. **Array**

_______ 11. What is the default method for drawing a circle with the **Circle** command?
A. Specifying the center point and radius.
B. Specifying the radius and selecting two points of tangency.
C. Specifying two points along the diameter.
D. Specifying three points through which the circle passes.

_______ 12. Which of the following is an acceptable method of obtaining the length of the circumference of a circle?
A. Construction method.
B. Equal chord method.
C. **List** command.
D. All of the above.

_______ 13. To construct an octagon when the distance across the flats is known, you start by constructing a(n) _____.
A. circle
B. square
C. circle or square
D. equilateral triangle

Name ______________________________

Drafting Performance

14. Construct a triangle with the following side lengths given: Base = 2.25″, Side 1 (clockwise from base) = 1.75″, and Side 2 = 1.00″. Show your construction lines if you are drawing manually.

15. Construct a hexagon having a distance across the flats of 1.75″. Show your construction lines if you are drawing manually.

Bisecting an Angle

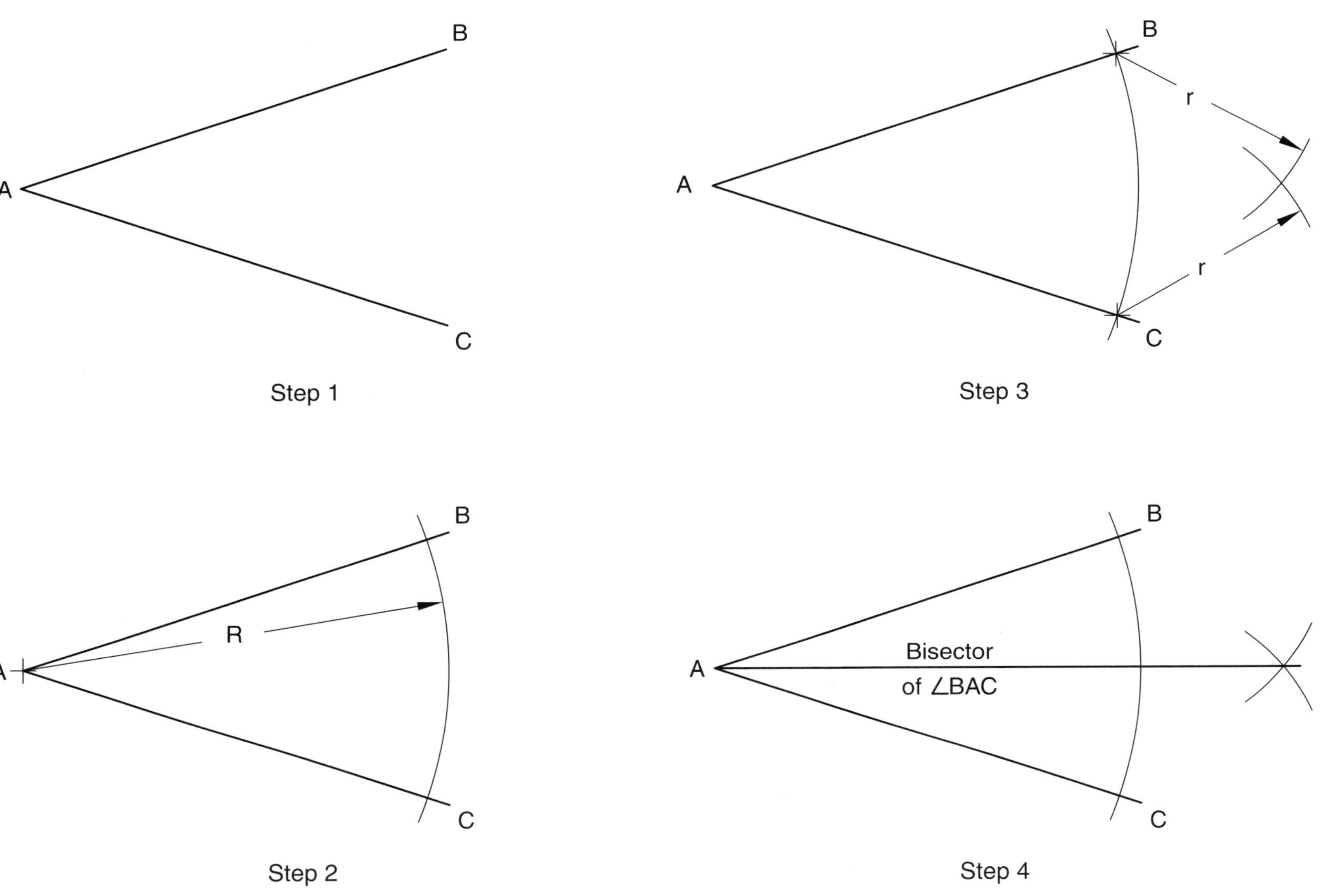

RM 6-1

Constructing Tangents

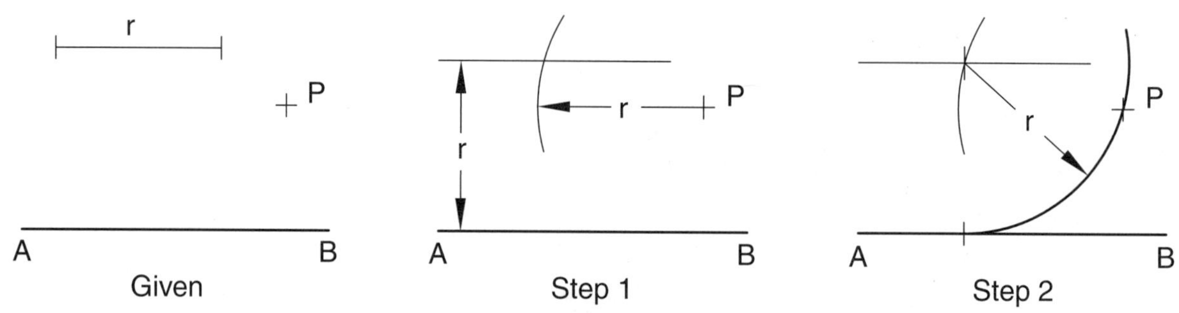

Constructing an arc through a given point and tangent to a line

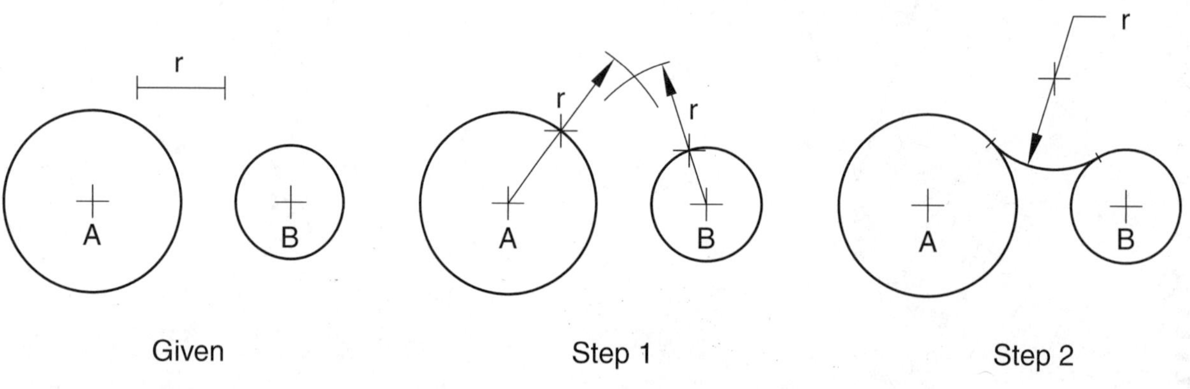

Constructing an arc tangent to two circles

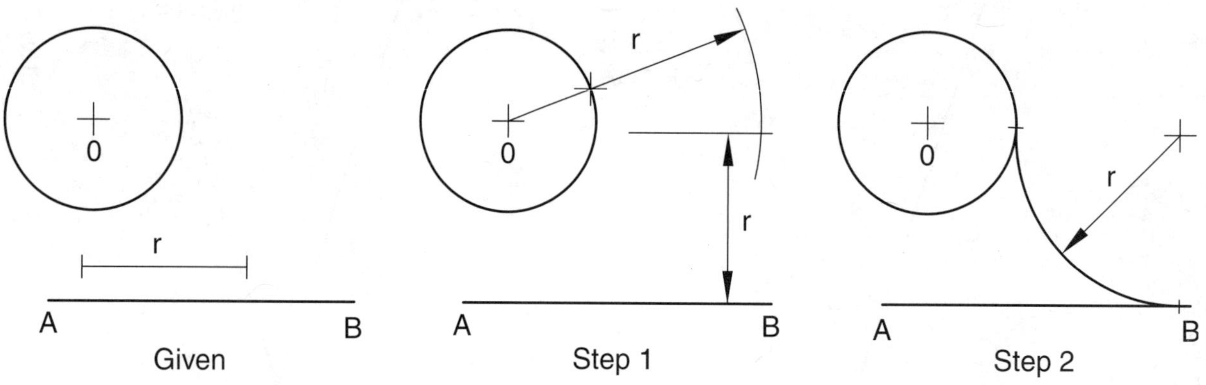

Constructing an arc tangent to a line and a circle

RM 6-2

Procedure Checklist

Basic Geometric Constructions

Name ____________________

Observable Items	Completed		Comments	Instructor Initials
	Yes	No		
1. Constructs lines.				
2. Divides lines.				
3. Constructs angles.				
4. Bisects angles.				
5. Constructs triangles.				
6. Constructs squares.				
7. Constructs other types of polygons.				
8. Transfers plane figures.				
9. Constructs circles and arcs.				
10. Draws tangents to circles and arcs.				
11. Lays out lengths of circles and arcs.				

Instructor Signature ____________________

Advanced Geometric Constructions

Learning Objectives

After studying this chapter, the student will be able to:

- Use manual drafting and CAD procedures to make geometric constructions.
- Construct ellipses.
- Construct parabolas.
- Construct hyperbolas.
- Draw special geometric curves used in drafting, including the spiral of Archimedes, helical curves, cycloids, and involutes.

Instructional Resources

Text: pages 213–239

Review Questions, page 238

Problems and Activities, page 239

Worksheets: pages 43–44

- Worksheet 7-1: *Geometric Constructions*
- Worksheet 7-2: *Geometric Constructions*

Instructor's Resource

Instructional Tasks

Instructional Aids and Assignments

Chapter 7 Quiz

Reproducible Masters

- Reproducible Master 7-1: *Constructing Conic Sections.* Shown are procedures for constructing an ellipse, a parabola, and a hyperbola.

Procedure Checklist

Color Transparencies (Binder/IRCD only)

- Transparency 7-1: *Conic Sections.* Shown are the sections formed when a plane passes through a right circular cone.

Instructional Tasks

1. Discuss the various procedures for constructing ellipses.
   - Demonstrate each geometric construction method for ellipses.
   - Demonstrate how to use an ellipse template.
2. Discuss the procedures for constructing parabolas.
   - Demonstrate each geometric construction method for parabolas.
   - Display photos showing uses of parabolas in construction.
3. Discuss the procedures for constructing hyperbolas.
   - Demonstrate each geometric construction method for hyperbolas.
4. Discuss the procedures for constructing other types of curves.
   - List and describe applications of other types of geometric curves.

Instructional Aids and Assignments

1. Display models and/or photos of structures involving advanced geometric shapes.
2. Assign the number of problems necessary to achieve the proper skill level in making geometric constructions. Use the problems in the text or use Worksheets 7-1 and 7-2. The number of problems is sufficient to assign a minimum number to all students and to identify problems that may be done for extra credit. Some problems may be used for the performance section of the chapter quiz.

Answers to Review Questions, Text

Page 238

1. cone
2. ellipse
3. major, minor
4. An instrument used for constructing curves.
5. The **Ellipse** command.

6. The **Arc** option.
7. ellipse
8. A parabola.
9. The **Spline** command.
10. asymptotes
11. **Spline**
12. equilateral
13. rotary, reciprocal
14. A helix.
15. cycloid
16. An epicycloid.
17. A hypocycloid.
18. The curve formed when a tightly drawn chord unwinds from around a circle or a polygon.

Solutions to Problems and Activities, Text

Page 239

Student work should look like the following drawings. The problem number and title are indicated on each problem sheet.

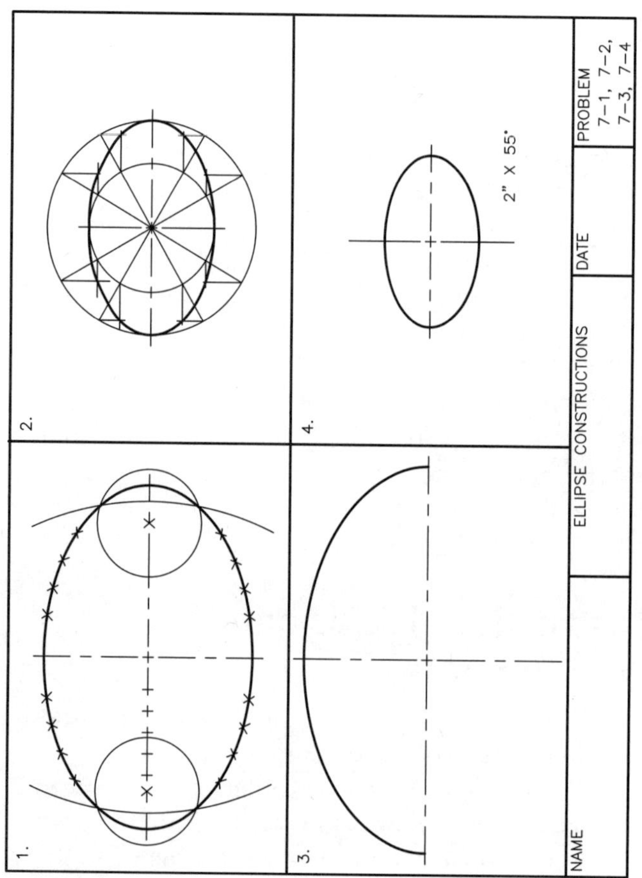

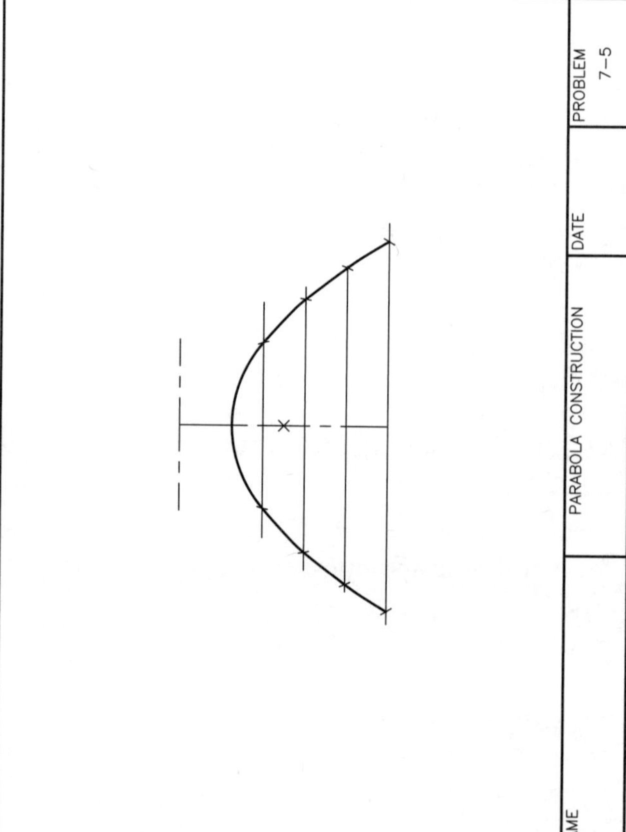

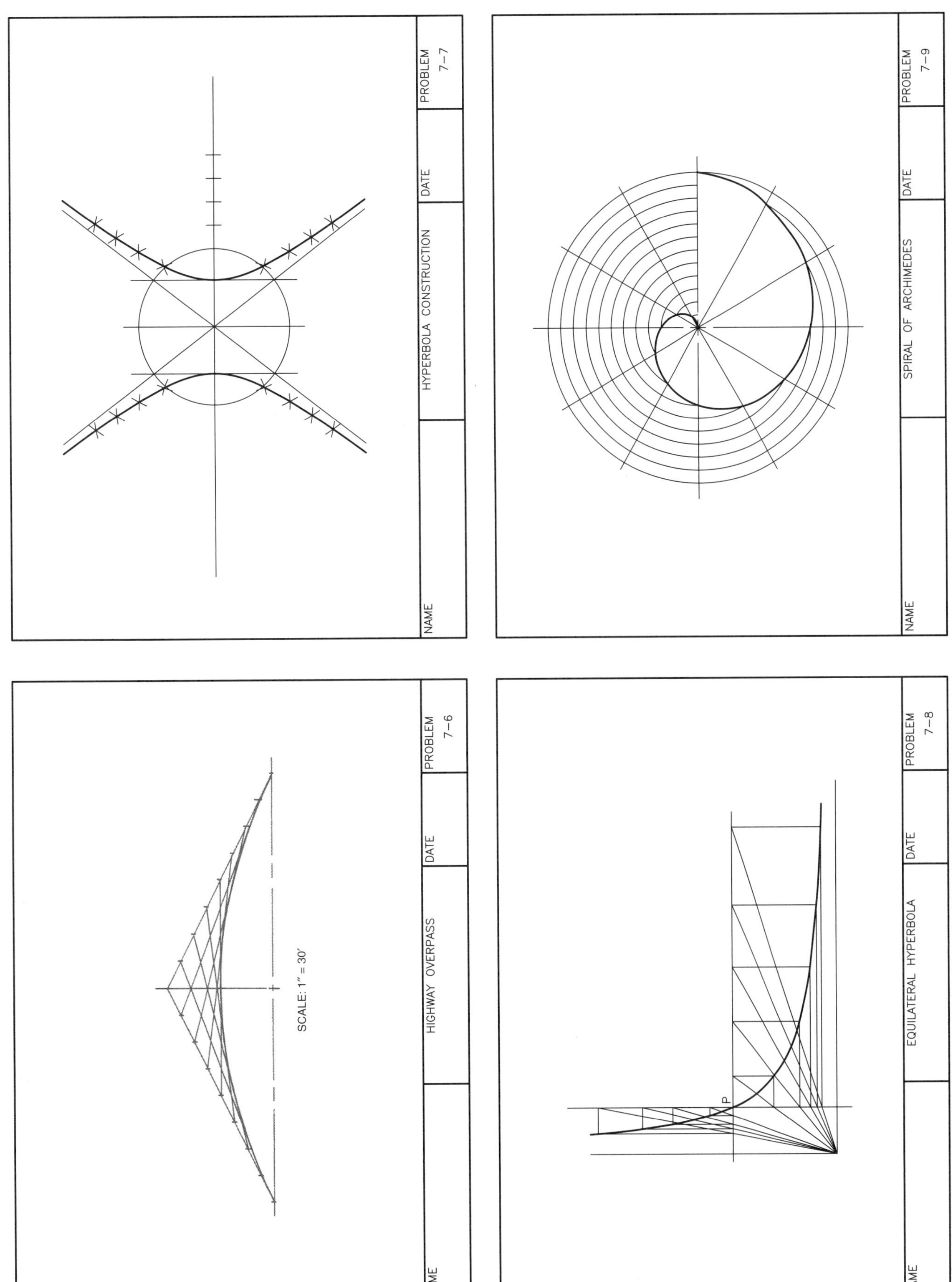
PROBLEM
7–7
DATE
HYPERBOLA CONSTRUCTION
NAME
PROBLEM
7–9
DATE
SPIRAL OF ARCHIMEDES
NAME
PROBLEM
7–6
DATE
HIGHWAY OVERPASS
NAME
SCALE: 1″ = 30′
PROBLEM
7–8
DATE
EQUILATERAL HYPERBOLA
NAME
P

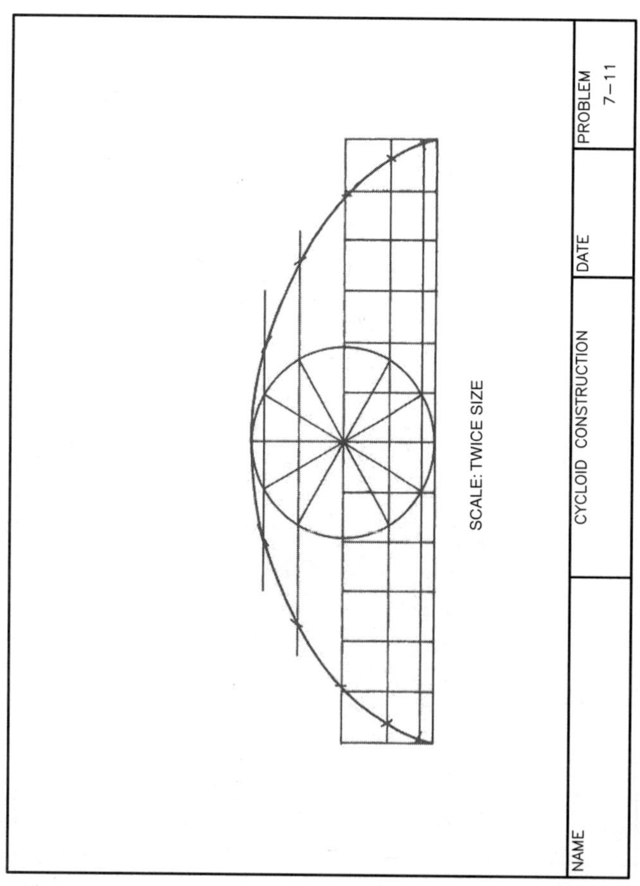
SCALE: TWICE SIZE
NAME
CYCLOID CONSTRUCTION
DATE
PROBLEM
7–11

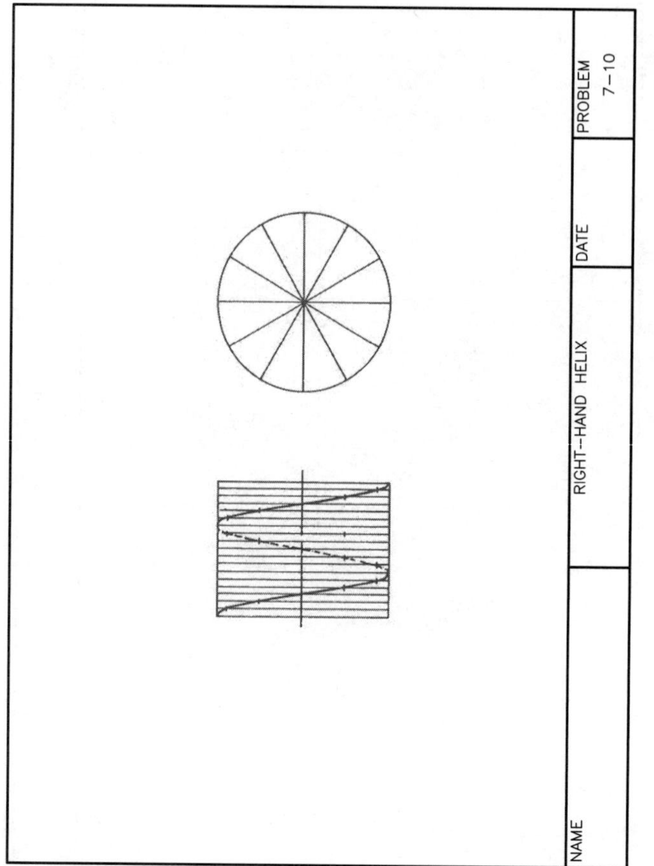
NAME
RIGHT–HAND HELIX
DATE
PROBLEM
7–10

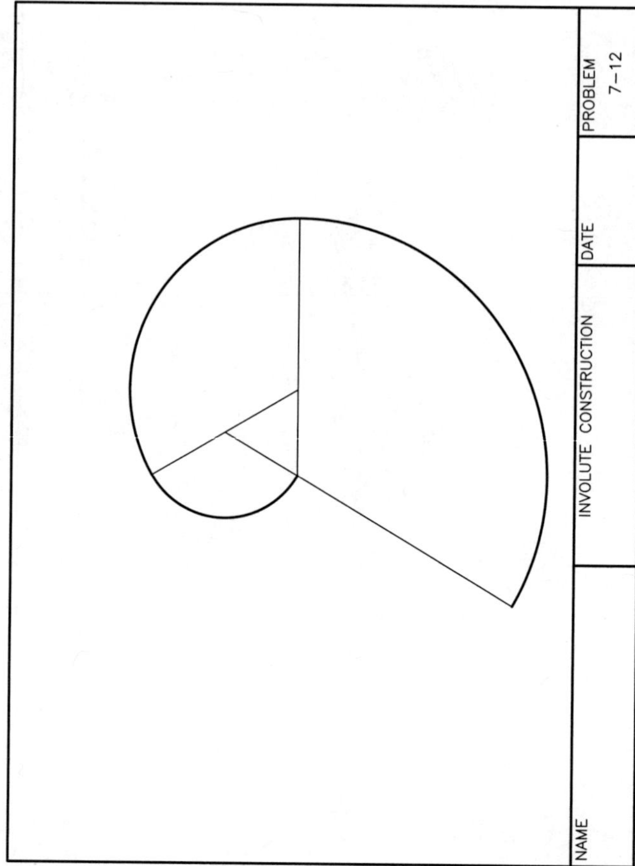
NAME
INVOLUTE CONSTRUCTION
DATE
PROBLEM
7–12

Solutions to Worksheets

Pages 43–44

Student work should look like the following drawings. The problem number and title are indicated on each problem sheet.

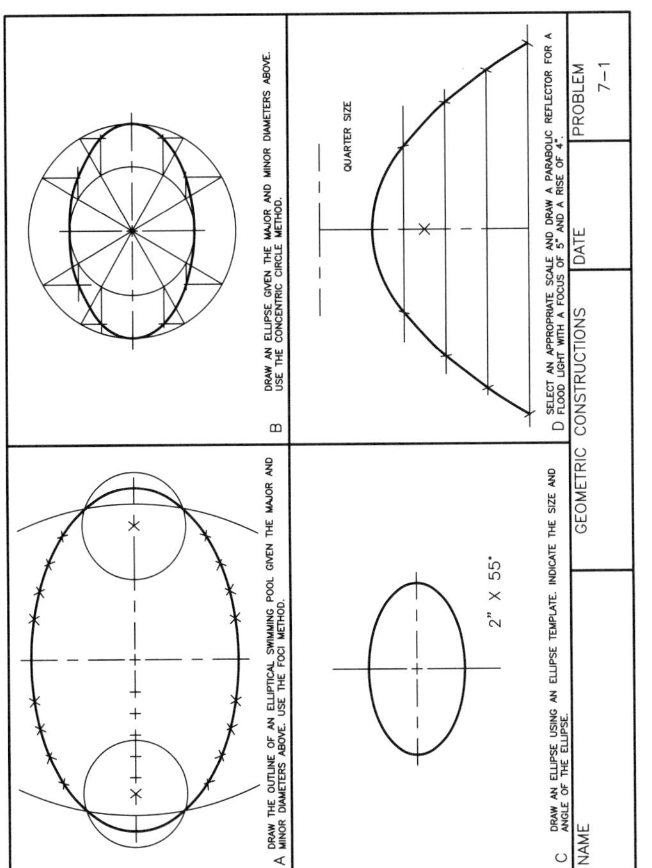

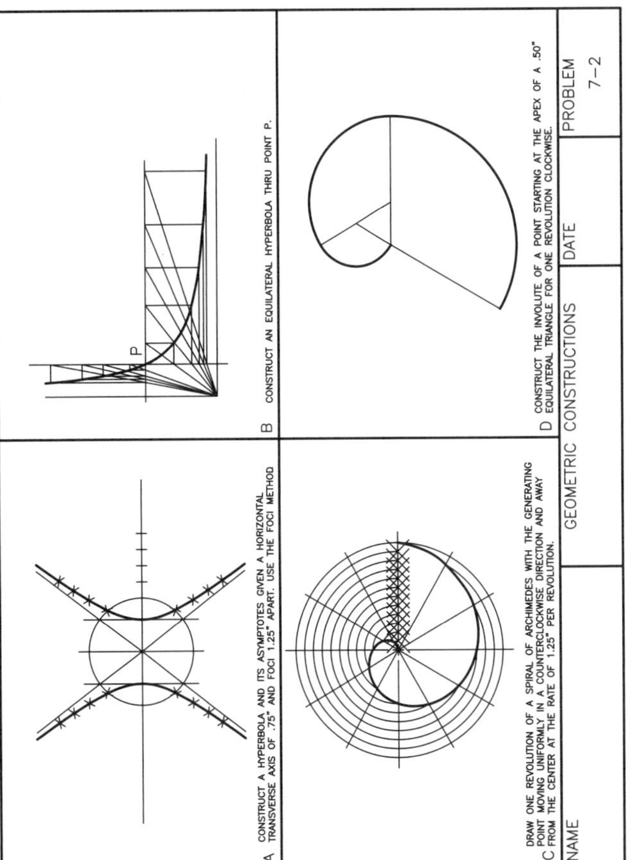

Answers to Chapter 7 Quiz

1. C. conic sections
2. B. ellipse
3. D. hyperbola
4. A. spiral of Archimedes
5. B. endpoint of one axis
6. B. **Spline**
7. D. **Arc**
8. B. helix
9. C. cycloid
10. D. involute
11. The student answer should be similar to one of the ellipse constructions shown in the text.
12. The student answer should be similar to the construction shown in Figure 7-28 in the text.

Chapter Quiz

Advanced Geometric Constructions

Name ____________________

Period__________ Date__________ Score __________

Multiple Choice

Choose the answer that correctly completes the statement. Write the corresponding letter in the space provided.

_______ 1. Curved shapes produced by passing planes through a right circular cone are known as _____.
A. foci
B. involutes
C. conic sections
D. asymptotes

_______ 2. A(n) ____ is formed when a plane is passed through a right circular cone, making an angle with the axis greater than that made by the elements.
A. circle
B. ellipse
C. parabola
D. hyperbola

_______ 3. A(n) ____ is formed when a plane is passed through a right circular cone, making an angle with the axis smaller than that made by the elements.
A. circle
B. ellipse
C. parabola
D. hyperbola

_______ 4. A(n) _____ is formed by a point moving uniformly around and away from a fixed point.
A. spiral of Archimedes
B. helix
C. cycloid
D. involute

_______ 5. By default, the _____ is specified first when using the **Ellipse** command to draw an ellipse.
A. center point
B. endpoint of one axis
C. midpoint of one axis
D. ellipse angle

Name ____

________ 6. The _____ command can be used to draw a complex curve such as a parabola.
A. **Ellipse**
B. **Spline**
C. **Circle**
D. **Offset**

________ 7. The **Start, Center, Angle** option of the _____ command can be used to draw an involute of a square.
A. **Polygon**
B. **Spline**
C. **Ellipse**
D. **Arc**

________ 8. A(n) _____ is best described as the path of a point moving around a cylinder at a uniform rate and parallel to the axis of the cylinder.
A. spiral of Archimedes
B. helix
C. cycloid
D. involute

________ 9. When a circle rolls along a straight line, the path of a fixed point on the circumference of the circle forms a(n) _____.
A. spiral of Archimedes
B. helix
C. cycloid
D. involute

________ 10. The _____ is the curve formed when a tightly drawn chord unwinds from around a circle or a polygon such as a triangle or square.
A. spiral of Archimedes
B. helix
C. cycloid
D. involute

Drafting Performance

11. Construct an ellipse having a major axis of 1 1/2″ and a minor axis of 1″. Use the method specified by your instructor. Use a separate sheet of paper if necessary.

Name ____

12. Draw an involute of an equilateral triangle having 1/2″ sides. Use the method specified by your instructor. Use a separate sheet of paper if necessary.

Constructing Conic Sections

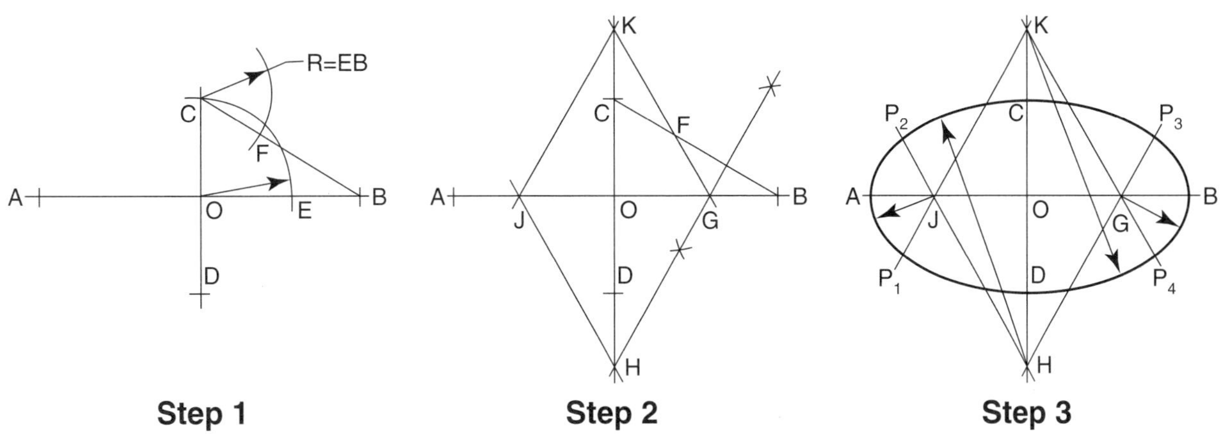

Ellipse
Four-center approximate method

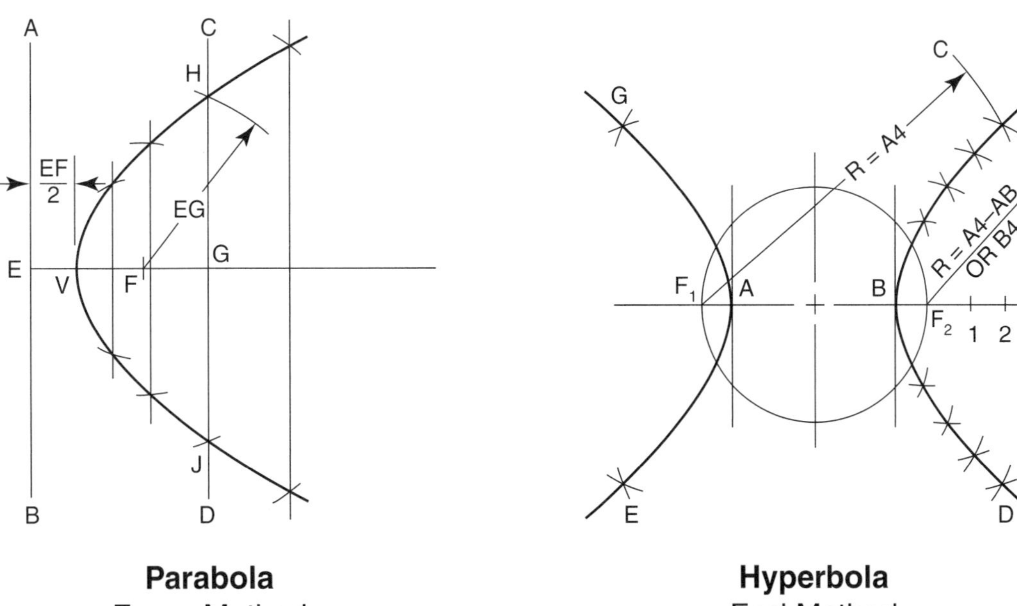

Parabola
Focus Method

Hyperbola
Foci Method

RM 7-1

Procedure Checklist

Advanced Geometric Constructions

Name ____

Observable Items	Completed		Comments	Instructor Initials
	Yes	No		
1. Constructs an ellipse using: A. The foci method.				
B. The concentric circle method.				
C. The parallelogram method.				
D. The four-center approximate method.				
E. The trammel method.				
F. The **Ellipse** command.				
G. An ellipse template.				
2. Constructs a parabola using: A. The focus method.				
B. The tangent method.				
C. The **Spline** command.				
D. Two given points.				
3. Constructs a hyperbola using the foci method.				
4. Constructs a spiral of Archimedes.				
5. Constructs a helix.				
6. Constructs a cycloid.				
7. Constructs an epicycloid.				
8. Constructs a hypocycloid.				
9. Constructs an involute.				

Instructor Signature ______________________________________

Multiview Drawings

Learning Objectives

After studying this chapter, the student will be able to:

- Explain the principles of orthographic projection.
- Identify the number and types of views needed to make a multiview drawing.
- Use orthographic projection to create multiview drawings.
- Explain the differences between third-angle projection and first-angle projection.

Instructional Resources

Text: pages 241–280

Review Questions, page 262–263

Problems and Activities, pages 263–268

Drawing Problems, pages 269–280

Worksheets: pages 45–59

- Worksheet 8-1: *Missing Line Problems*
- Worksheet 8-2: *Missing View Problems*
- Worksheet 8-3: *End Clamp*
- Worksheet 8-4: *Stop Block*
- Worksheet 8-5: *Link Coupler*
- Worksheet 8-6: *Stop Bracket*
- Worksheet 8-7: *Pillow Block*
- Worksheet 8-8: *Sheet Stop Pivot Bracket*
- Worksheet 8-9: *Sliding Pulley Hub*
- Worksheet 8-10: *Hub Clamp*
- Worksheet 8-11: *Single Bearing Hanger*
- Worksheet 8-12: *V-Block*
- Worksheet 8-13: *Lower Straight Anvil*
- Worksheet 8-14: *Flange*
- Worksheet 8-15: *Variable Gear Cover*

Instructor's Resource

Instructional Tasks

Instructional Aids and Assignments

Chapter 8 Quiz

Reproducible Masters

- Reproducible Master 8-1: *Location of Principal Views.* The proper locations of the three principal views (the top, front, and right side views) are shown.
- Reproducible Master 8-2: *Projecting Points Between Views.* The horizontal, frontal, and profile views of a point and a line are given to show the proper method of projecting points between views.
- Reproducible Master 8-3: *Projecting Normal and Inclined Surfaces.* An object with normal surfaces and an object with an inclined surface are shown to illustrate proper projection techniques.

Procedure Checklist

Color Transparencies (Binder/IRCD only)

- Transparency 8-1: *The Glass Box.* The "glass box" is illustrated to help students visualize the three primary views of an object.
- Transparency 8-2: *The Glass Box Unfolded.* The "glass box" is shown unfolded to reveal the six possible object views.
- Transparency 8-3: *Projecting Oblique Surfaces.* An oblique surface is projected to each of the three primary views to show how it appears in each view.

Instructional Tasks

1. Define the terms *multiview drawing* and *orthographic projection.*
   - Show a multimedia presentation or film on the orthographic projection system.
   - Discuss the orthographic projection system and the importance of proper selection and relationships of views.
2. Discuss how to select the views of an object for a multiview drawing.
   - Demonstrate the projection of views with the aid of the "glass box." (Avoid objects with hidden lines.)

- Demonstrate the projection of points, lines, and surfaces.
- Use a transparency with overlays (preferably in color) to demonstrate the projection of views.

3. Discuss how to project views with hidden lines and surfaces.
   - Demonstrate the projection of hidden lines and surfaces.
   - Discuss how the precedence of lines is determined.
   - Discuss removed and partial views.
4. Discuss how to apply conventional drafting practices.
   - Explain the purpose of conventional drafting practices.
   - Demonstrate the use of conventional drafting practices.
5. Discuss first-angle and third-angle projection.
   - Identify the four quadrants and their projection planes.
   - Discuss the similarities and differences between drawings made using first-angle and third-angle projection.
   - Discuss the importance of using the correct procedure to lay out a drawing.

Instructional Aids and Assignments

1. Show a multimedia presentation or film on multiview drawing.
2. Display a "glass box" and suitable machine parts or objects to demonstrate orthographic projection.
3. Assign the *Multiview Problems with Missing Lines* and *Multiview Drawings with Missing Views* problems from the text or assign Worksheets 8-1 and 8-2.
4. Prepare a chart for the class and assign the *Identifying Points, Lines, and Surfaces* problems in the text.
5. Assign and discuss the answers to the *Reading a Drawing* problem in the text.
6. Assign the drawing problems in the textbook. The number of problems is sufficient to assign a minimum number to all students and to identify problems that may be done for extra credit. Some problems may be used for the performance section of the chapter quiz.

Answers to Review Questions, Text

Pages 262–263

1. A multiview drawing is the major type of drawing used in drafting. It is a projection drawing that incorporates several views on one drawing and describes a three-dimensional object in two dimensions.
2. The front view.
3. orthographic projection
4. The frontal plane, horizontal plane, and profile plane.
5. frontal
6. point
7. straight line
8. Horizontal, vertical, inclined, and oblique.
9. Vertical
10. Inclined
11. Oblique
12. top
13. perpendicular
14. rectangle
15. The front view.
16. The stock thickness.
17. Give primary consideration to selection of the front view; consider space requirements of the entire drawing; choose between two equally important views unless space or other factors prohibit; and consider the number of views to be drawn.
18. hidden lines
19. Visible
20. fillet, round
21. runout
22. third-angle
23. Third-angle

Solutions to Problems and Activities, Text

Multiview Drawings with Missing Lines, Page 263

Student work should look like the drawings shown in Problem Sheet 8-1.

Multiview Drawings with Missing Views, Page 263

Student work should look like the drawings shown in Problem Sheet 8-2.

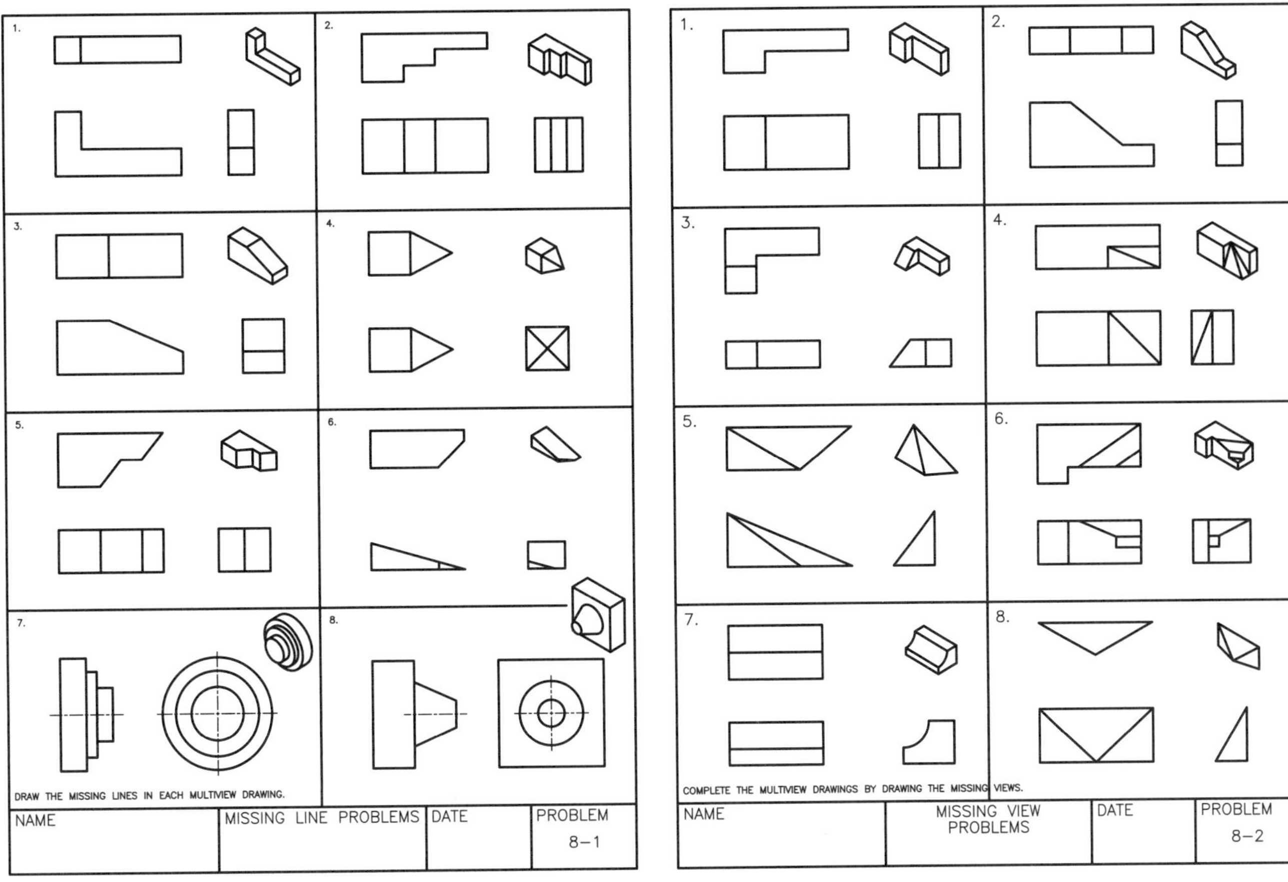
1.
2.
3.
4.
5.
6.
7.
8.
DRAW THE MISSING LINES IN EACH MULTIVIEW DRAWING.
NAME
MISSING LINE PROBLEMS
DATE
PROBLEM
8–1
1.
2.
3.
4.
5.
6.
7.
8.
COMPLETE THE MULTIVIEW DRAWINGS BY DRAWING THE MISSING VIEWS.
NAME
MISSING VIEW PROBLEMS
DATE
PROBLEM
8–2

Identifying Points, Lines, and Surfaces, Page 266

	Pictorial View			Front View			Side View			Top View		
	Problem A											
	Point	Line	Surface	Point	Line	Surface	Point	Line	Surface	Point	Line	Surface
1		9-8	D	30				35-36			23-26	V
2			C		28-29				Y		22-25	
3			B			X		33-37			24-26	
4			E	30				35-36	Z		23-26	
5			A		27-28		33					W
	Problem B											
1			A		3-6		17					W
2			D			Z		13-15				F
3			D		6-10			12-16	E	18		
4			B			Y		11-14			1-2	
5			B		4-5	Y	11				1-2	
	Problem C											
1			A		28-30			34-36				U
2			B		29-31				Y			V
3		4-7			29-30		35				23-24	
4			C			W		34-39			25-27	
5			E		30-33				Z		22-27	
	Problem D											
1			A		26-27			31-32 31-33			23-24	U
2			D		27-30				Z		22-25	
3		2-6	C			X	35	31-35			23-25	
4			B			W			Y			V

Reading a Drawing, Page 267

1. Left profile and frontal (or frontal and right profile).
2. FORK BRACKET
3. 63346
4. 2″ stock
5. P-1
   R-12
   S-11
   T-2
   U-4
   V-6
   W-7
   X-10
   Y-8
   Z-9
6. The two views presented are the most descriptive. A top view would not improve clarity.
7. A recessed cylinder, confirmed in the other view.
8. 17/64
9. No. 7 (.201)
10. .625

Solutions to Drawing Problems, Text

Pages 269–280

Student work should look like the following drawings. The problem number and title are indicated on each problem sheet.

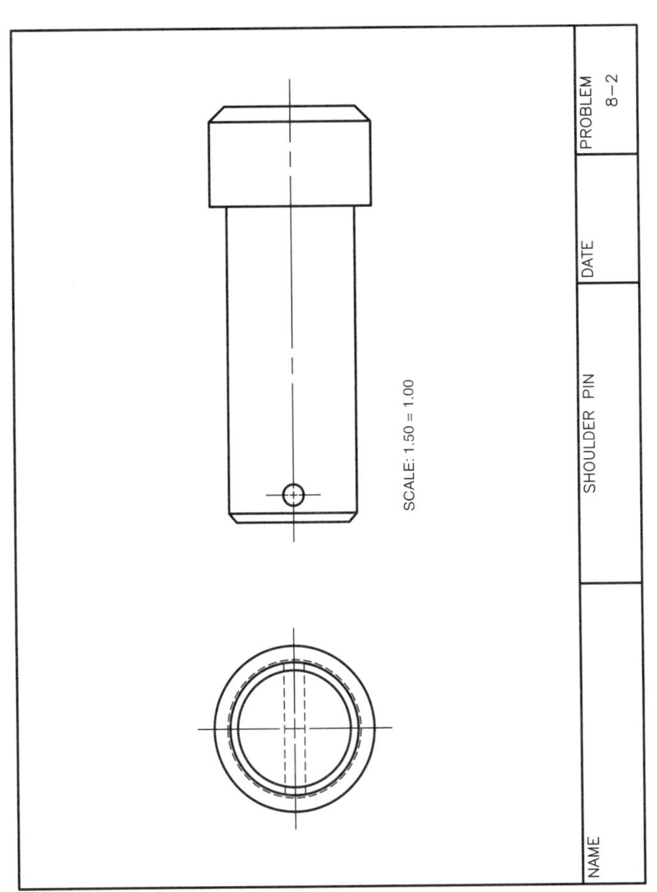
PROBLEM
8–2
DATE
SHOULDER PIN
NAME
SCALE: 1.50 = 1.00

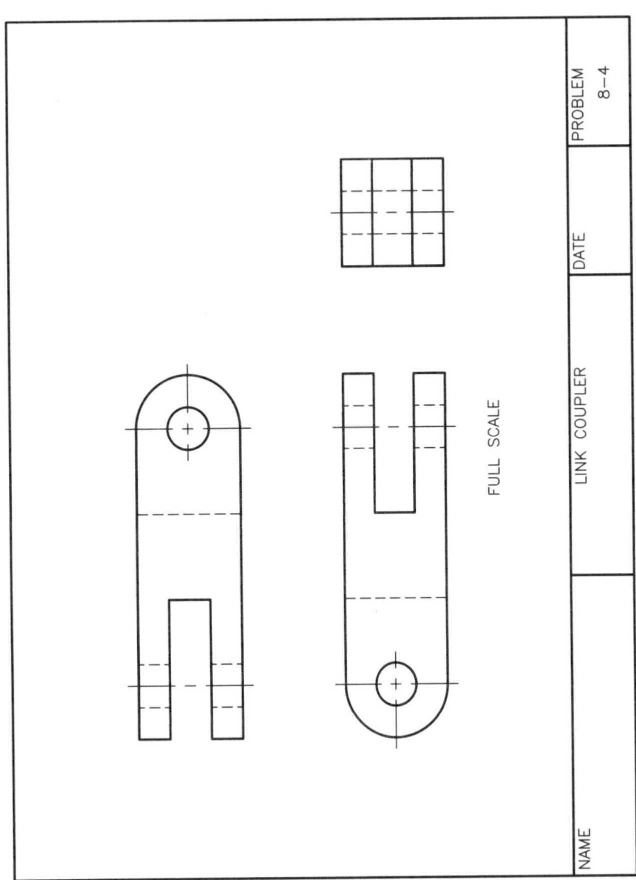
PROBLEM
8–4
DATE
LINK COUPLER
NAME
FULL SCALE

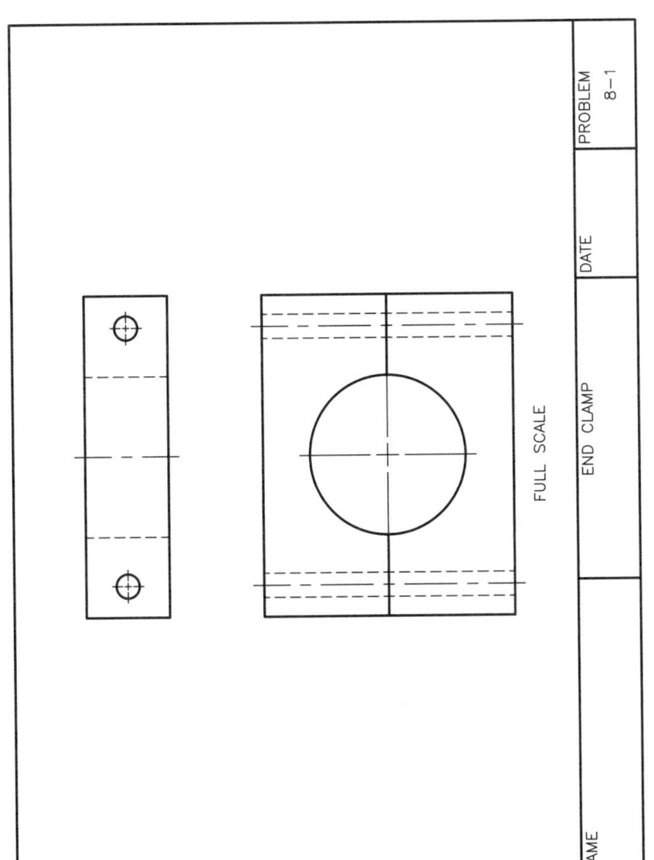
PROBLEM
8–1
DATE
END CLAMP
NAME
FULL SCALE

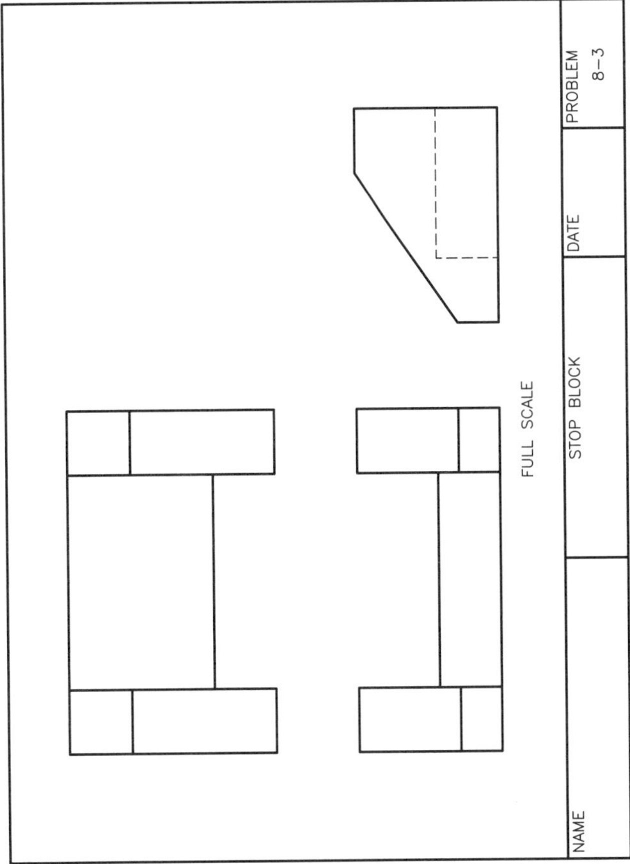
PROBLEM
8–3
DATE
STOP BLOCK
NAME
FULL SCALE

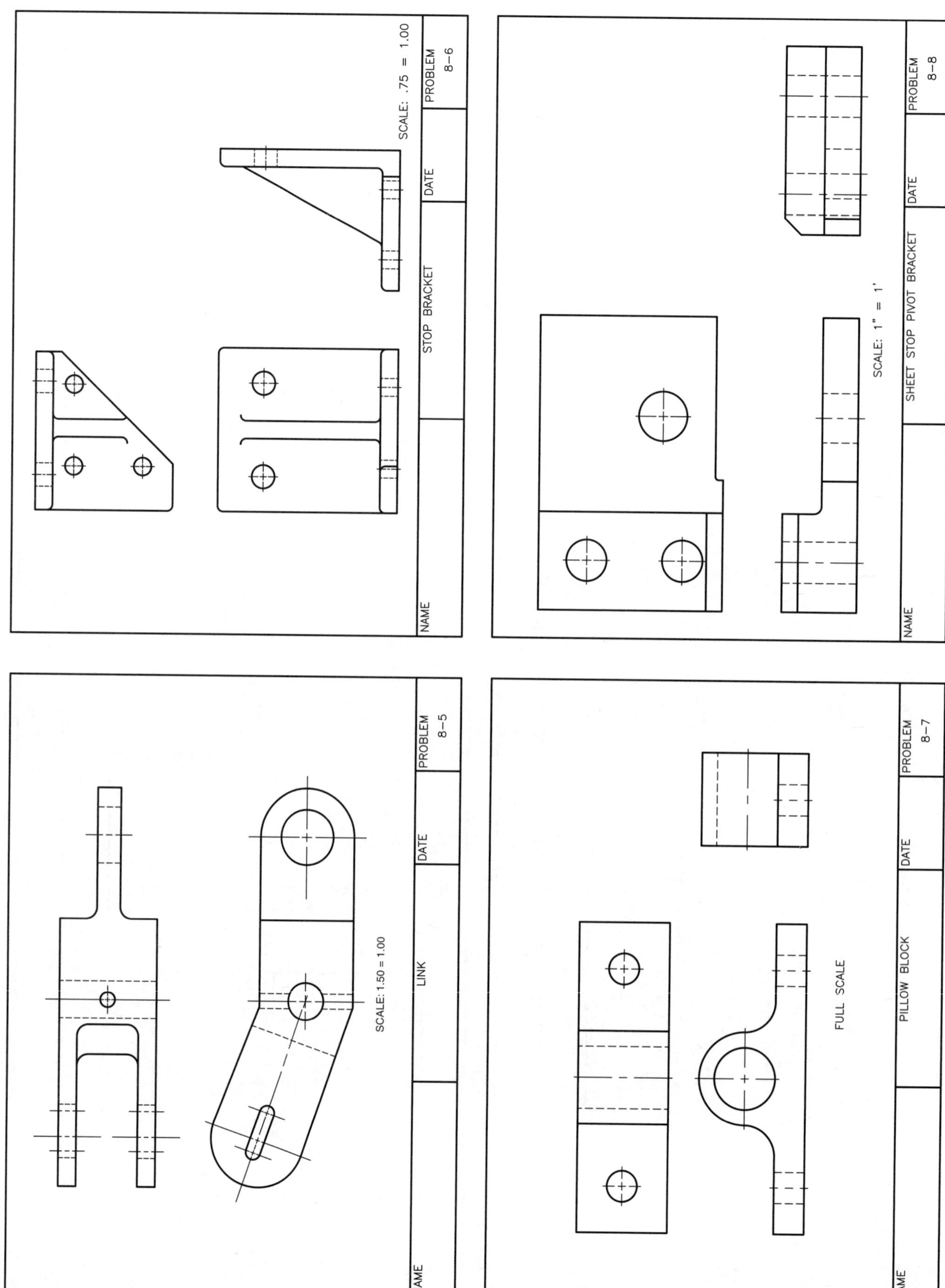
SCALE: .75 = 1.00
PROBLEM
8–6
DATE
STOP BRACKET
NAME
PROBLEM
8–8
DATE
SHEET STOP PIVOT BRACKET
SCALE: 1" = 1'
NAME
PROBLEM
8–5
DATE
LINK
SCALE: 1.50 = 1.00
NAME
PROBLEM
8–7
DATE
PILLOW BLOCK
FULL SCALE
NAME

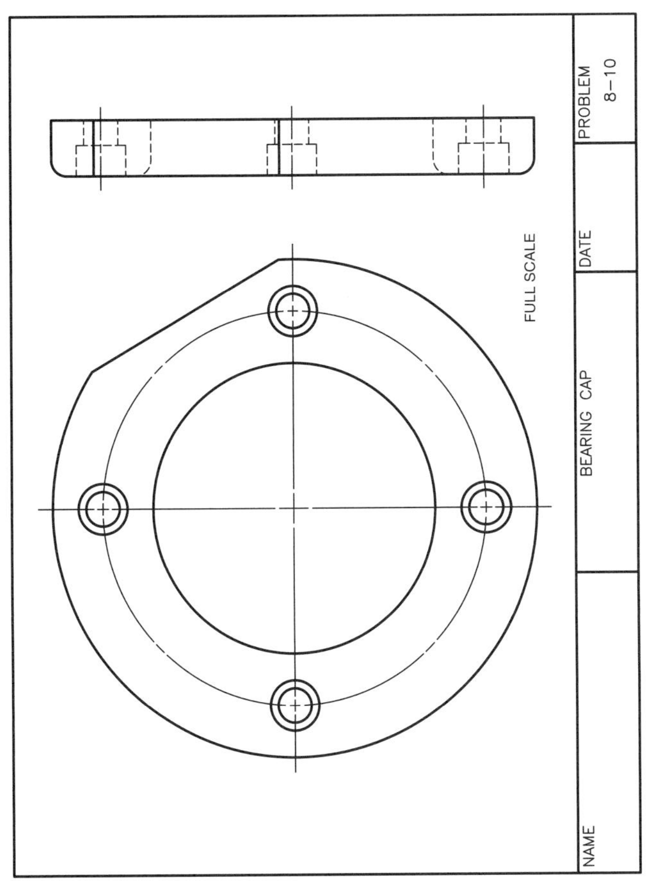
PROBLEM
8–10
DATE
BEARING CAP
NAME
FULL SCALE

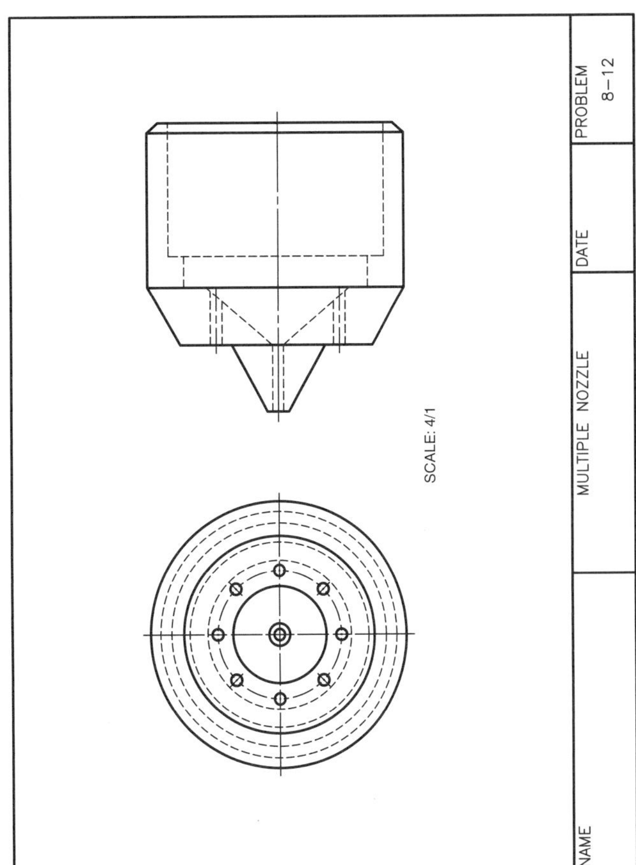
PROBLEM
8–12
DATE
MULTIPLE NOZZLE
NAME
SCALE: 4/1

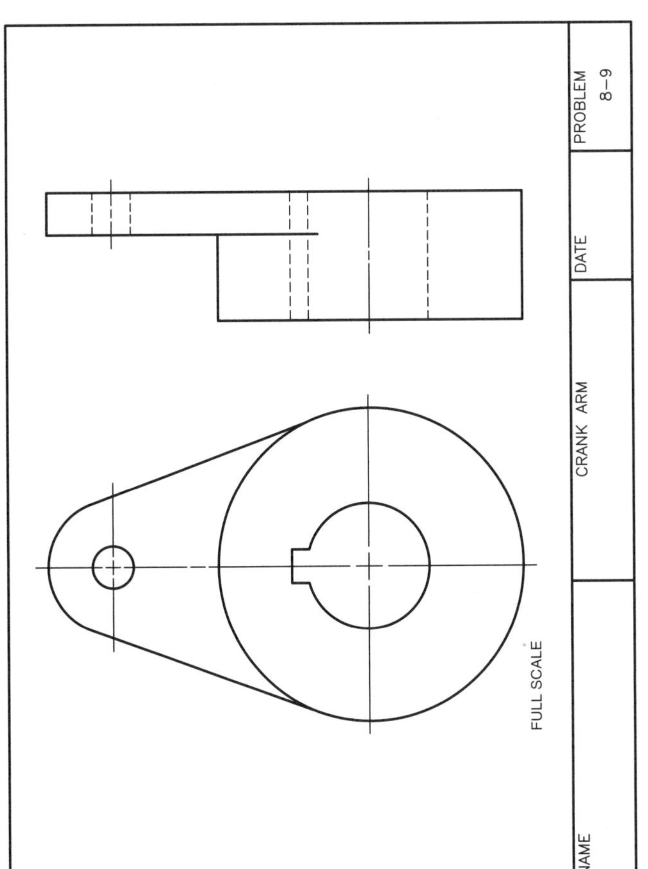
PROBLEM
8–9
DATE
CRANK ARM
NAME
FULL SCALE

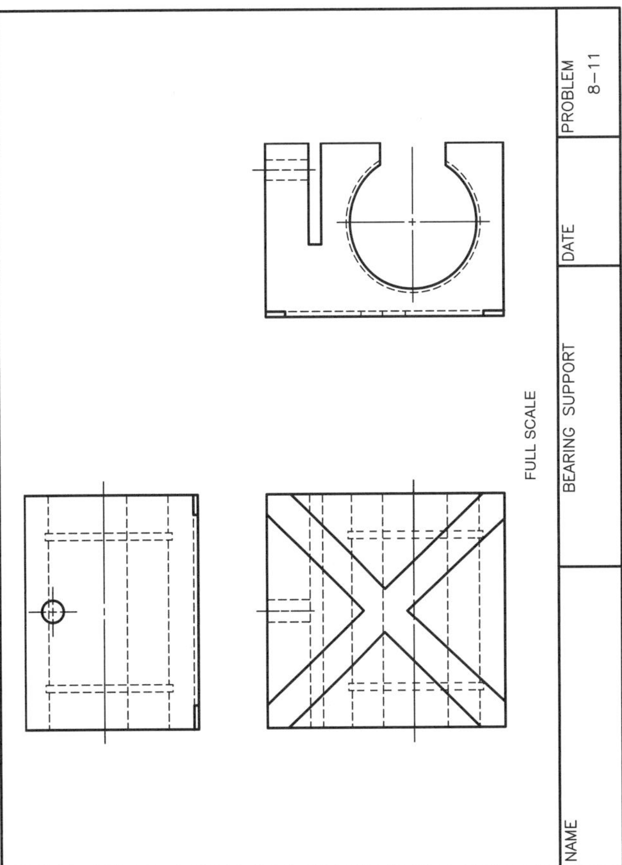
PROBLEM
8–11
DATE
BEARING SUPPORT
NAME
FULL SCALE

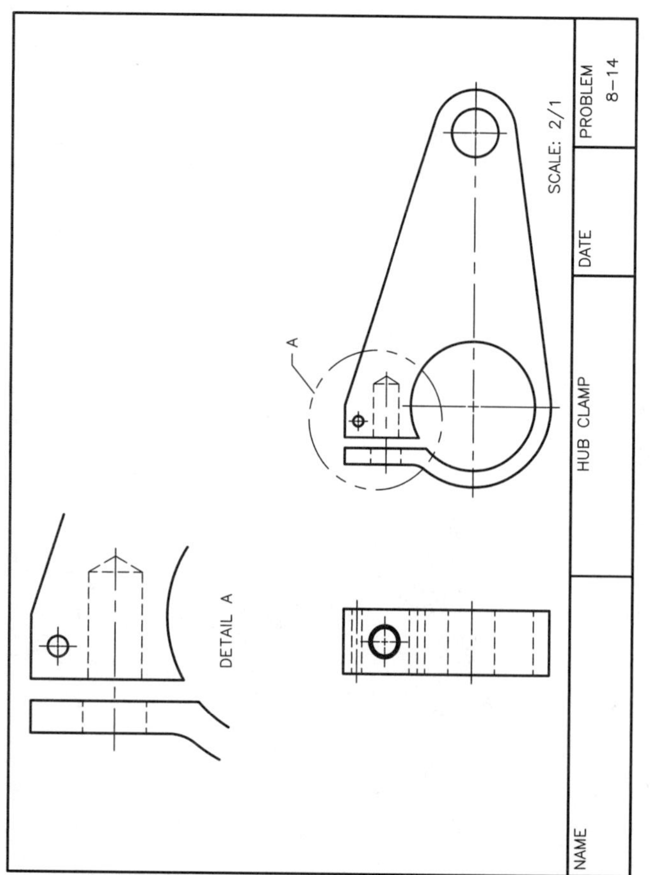
SCALE: 2/1
A
DETAIL A
NAME
HUB CLAMP
DATE
PROBLEM
8–14

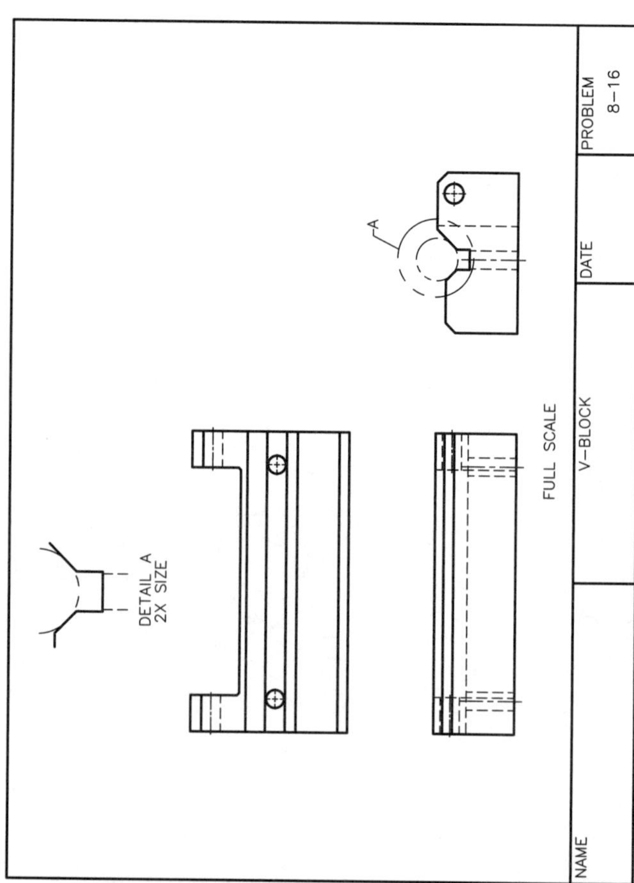
A
DETAIL A
2X SIZE
FULL SCALE
NAME
V–BLOCK
DATE
PROBLEM
8–16

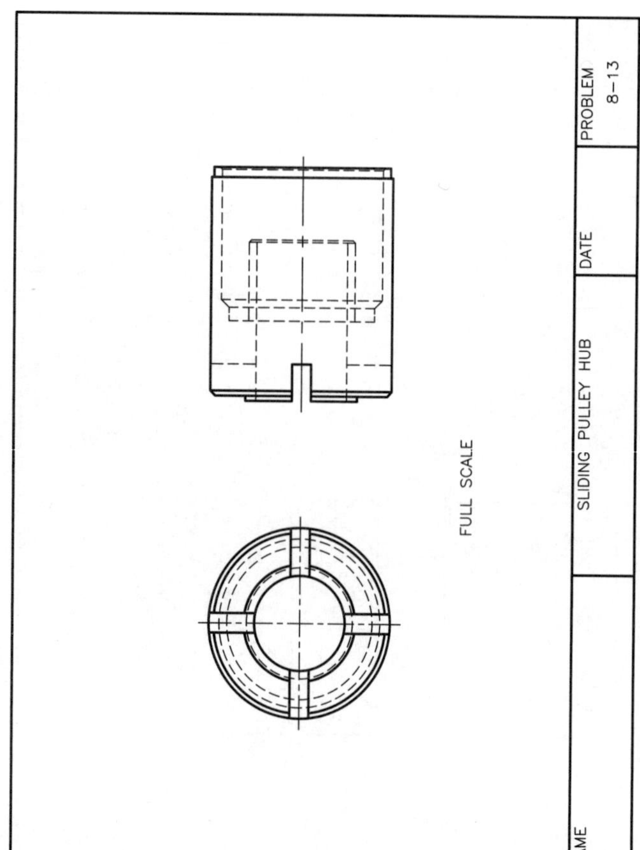
FULL SCALE
NAME
SLIDING PULLEY HUB
DATE
PROBLEM
8–13

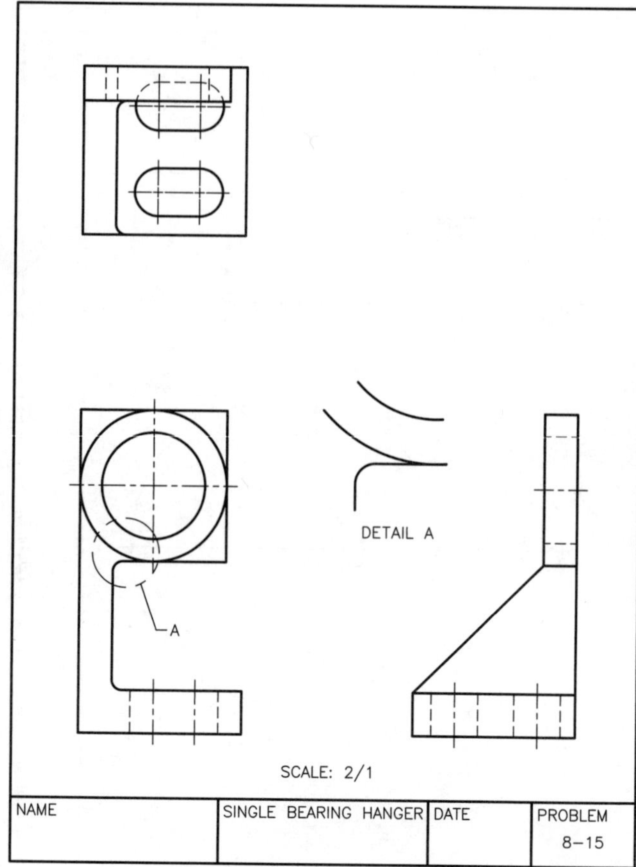
DETAIL A
A
SCALE: 2/1
NAME
SINGLE BEARING HANGER
DATE
PROBLEM
8–15

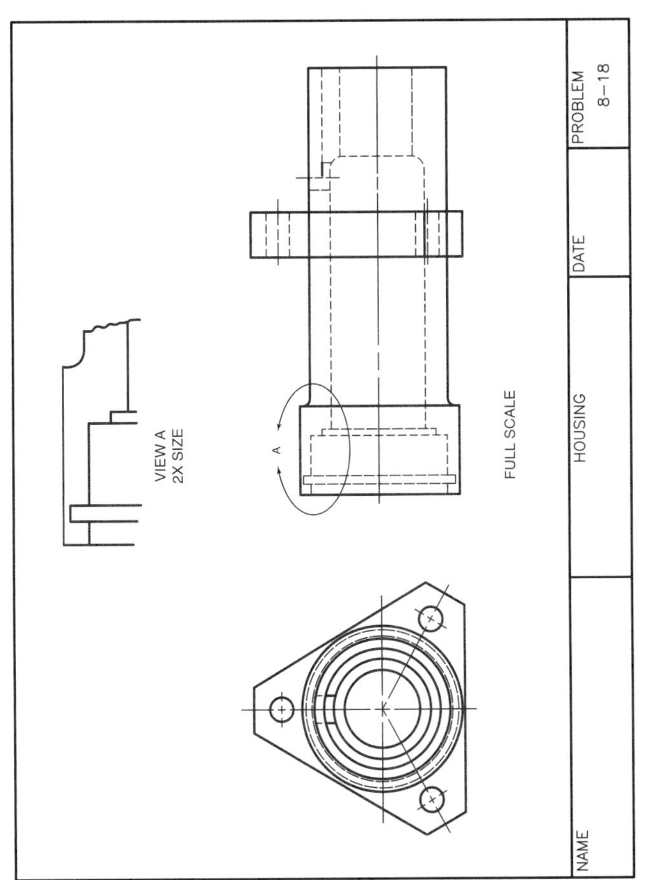
VIEW A
2X SIZE
A
FULL SCALE
HOUSING
NAME
DATE
PROBLEM
8–18

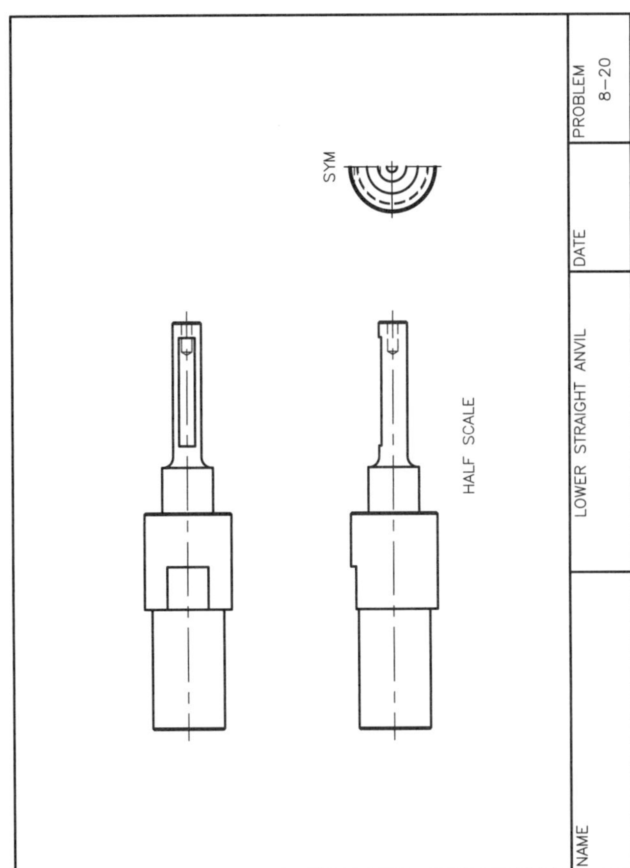
SYM
HALF SCALE
LOWER STRAIGHT ANVIL
NAME
DATE
PROBLEM
8–20

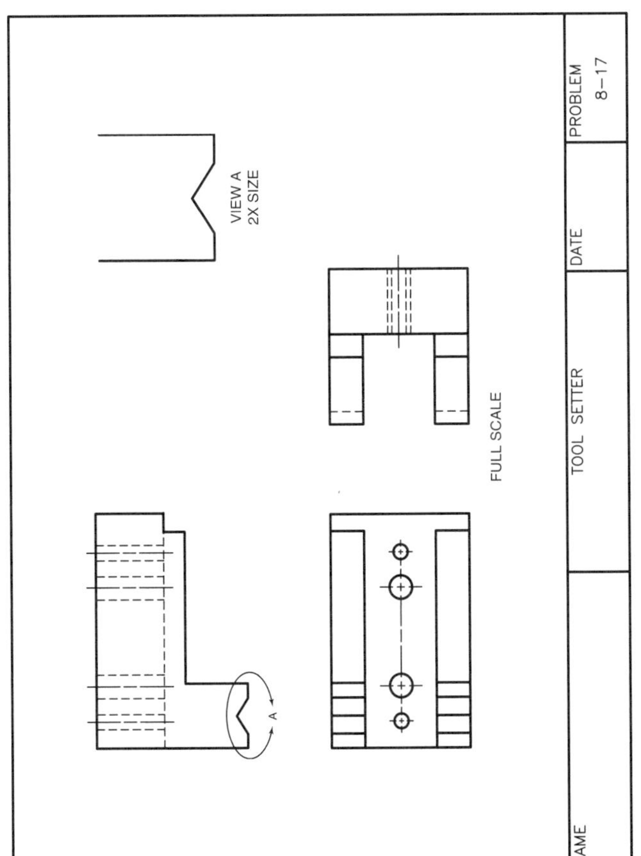
VIEW A
2X SIZE
A
FULL SCALE
TOOL SETTER
NAME
DATE
PROBLEM
8–17

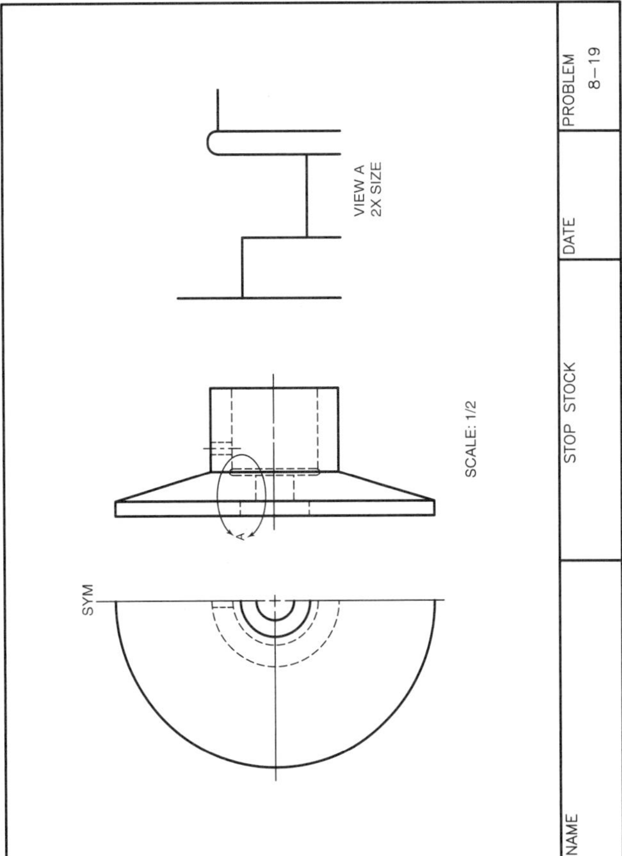
VIEW A
2X SIZE
A
SYM
SCALE: 1/2
STOP STOCK
NAME
DATE
PROBLEM
8–19

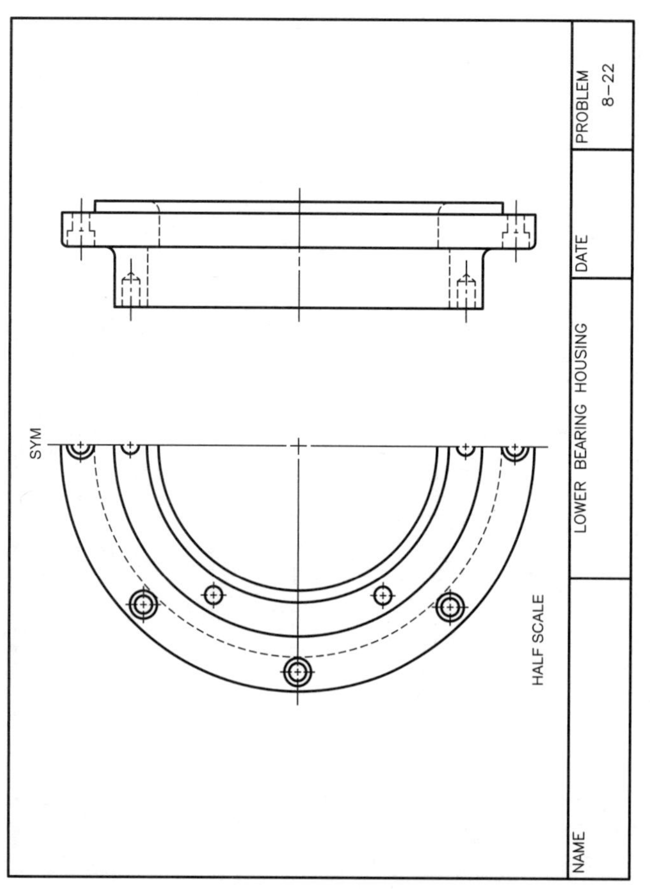
PROBLEM
8–22
DATE
LOWER BEARING HOUSING
NAME
HALF SCALE
SYM

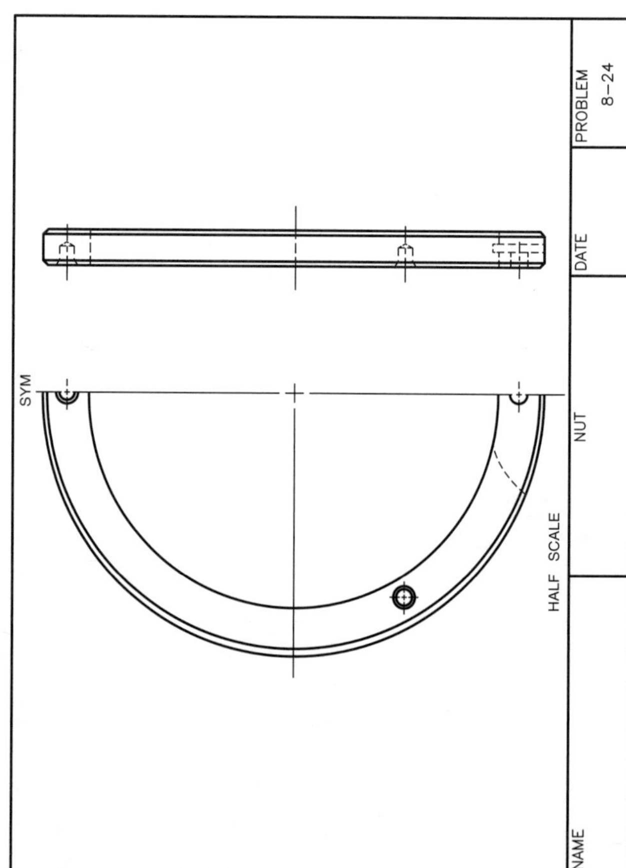
PROBLEM
8–24
DATE
NUT
NAME
HALF SCALE
SYM

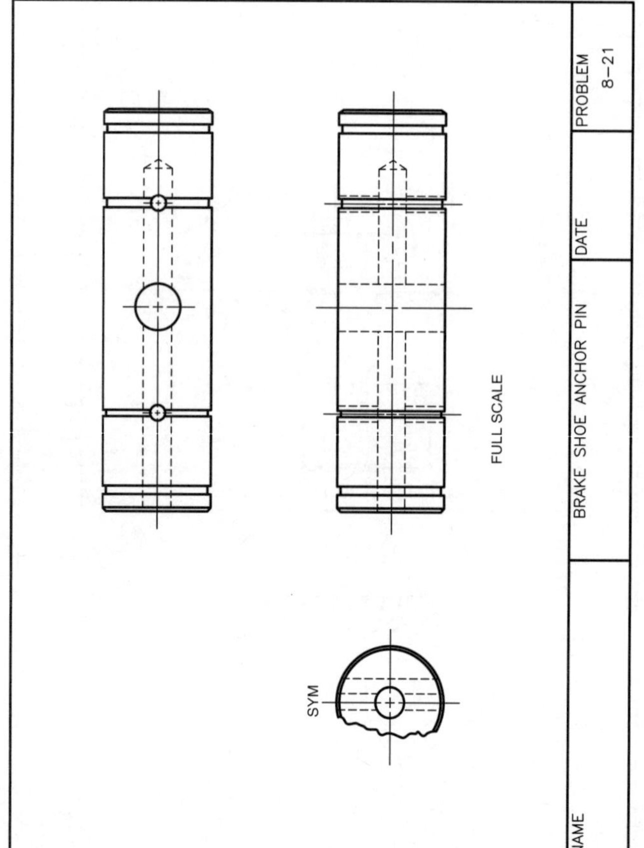
PROBLEM
8–21
DATE
BRAKE SHOE ANCHOR PIN
NAME
FULL SCALE
SYM

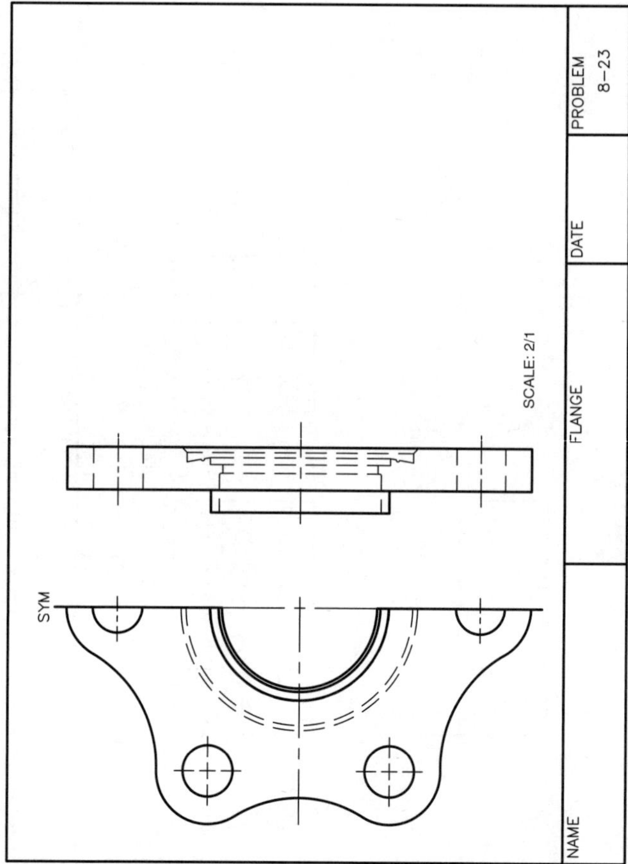
PROBLEM
8–23
DATE
FLANGE
NAME
SCALE: 2/1
SYM

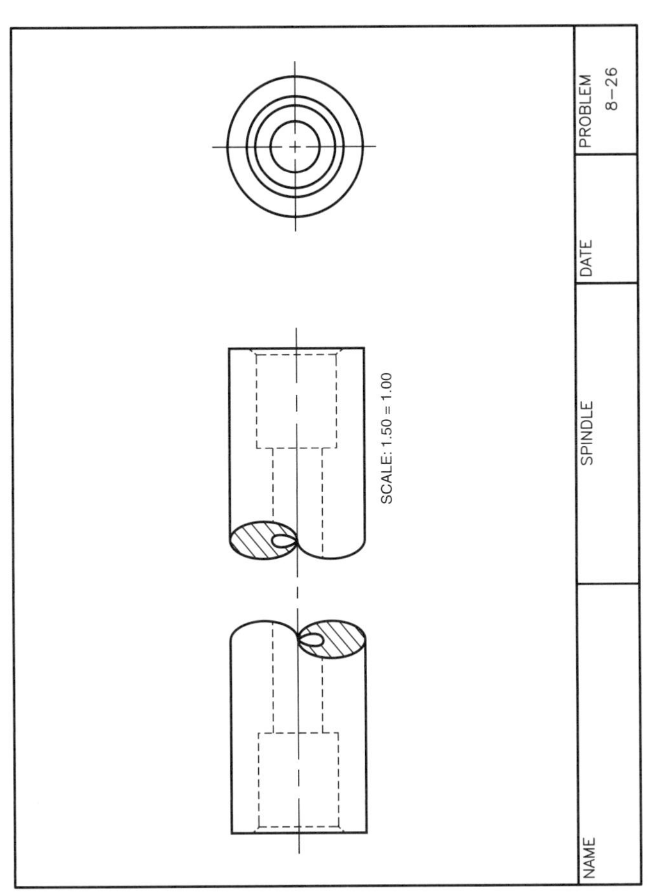
PROBLEM
8–26
DATE
SPINDLE
NAME
SCALE: 1.50 = 1.00

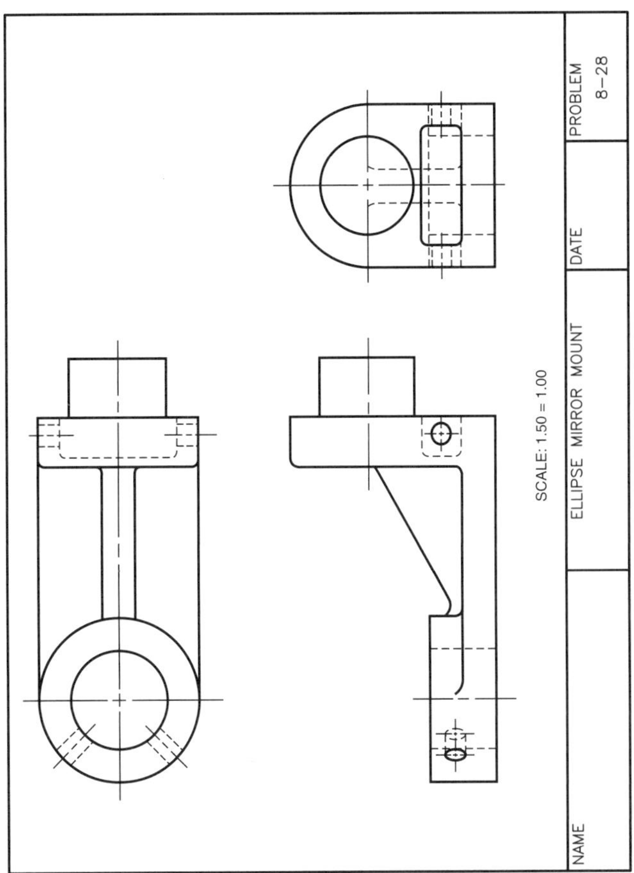
PROBLEM
8–28
DATE
ELLIPSE MIRROR MOUNT
NAME
SCALE: 1.50 = 1.00

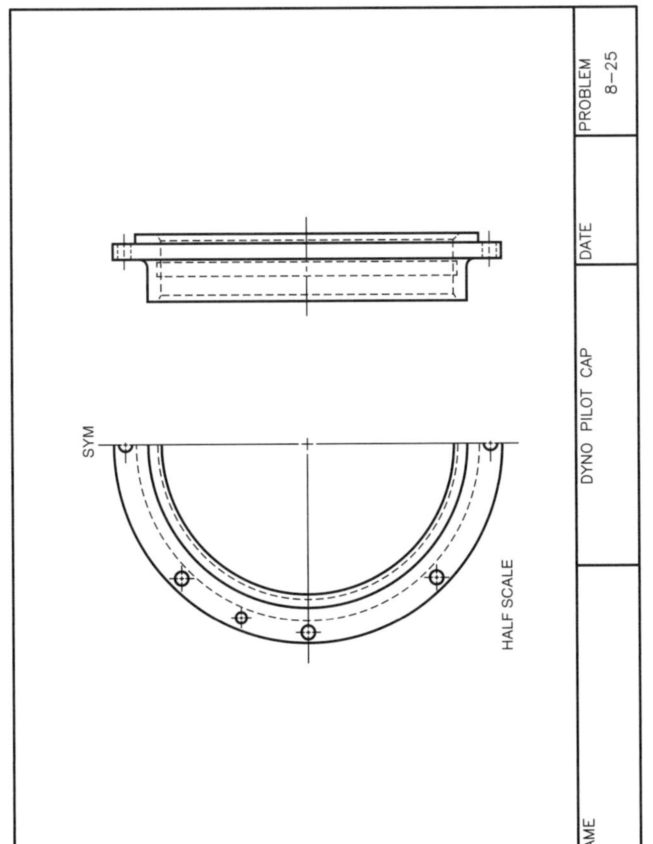
PROBLEM
8–25
DATE
DYNO PILOT CAP
NAME
SYM
HALF SCALE

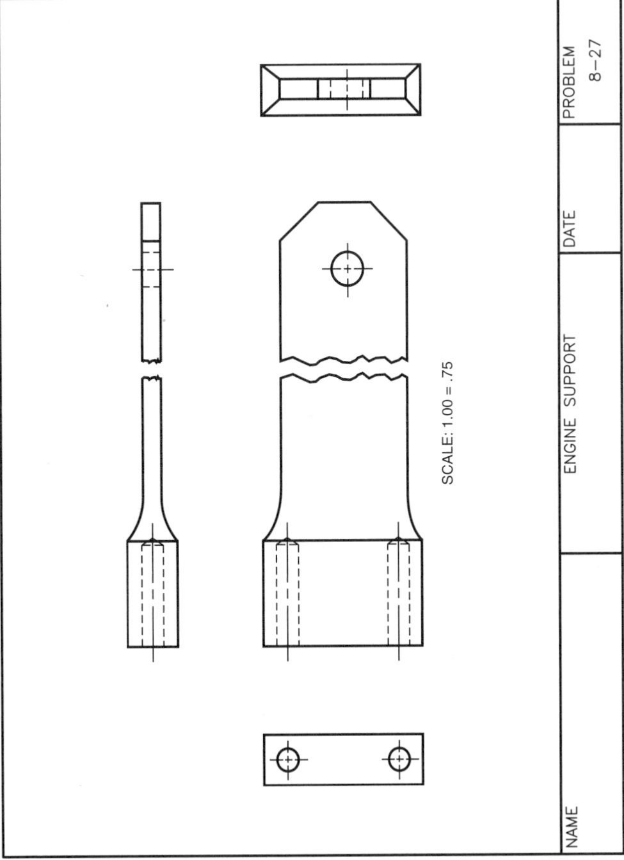
PROBLEM
8–27
DATE
ENGINE SUPPORT
NAME
SCALE: 1.00 = .75

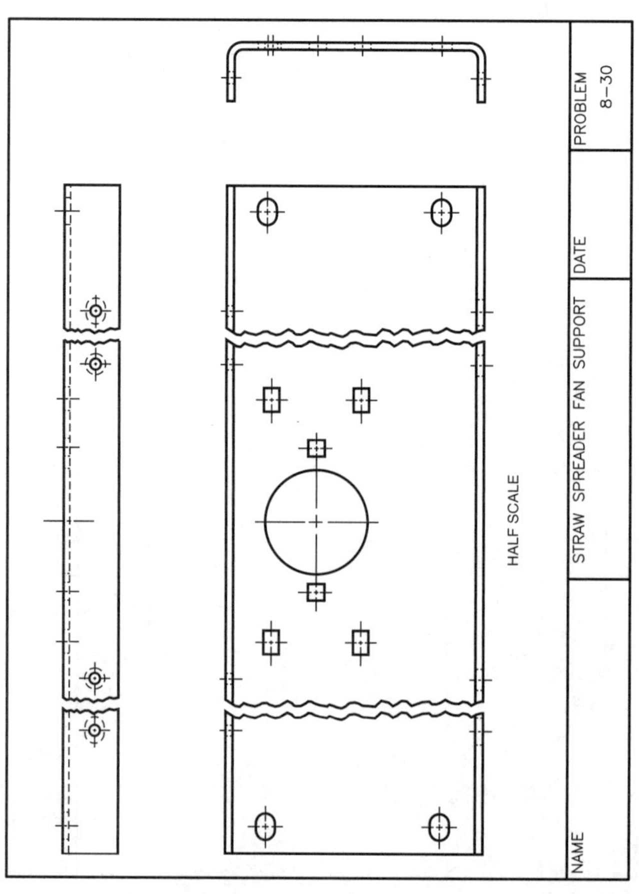
PROBLEM
8–30
DATE
STRAW SPREADER FAN SUPPORT
HALF SCALE
NAME

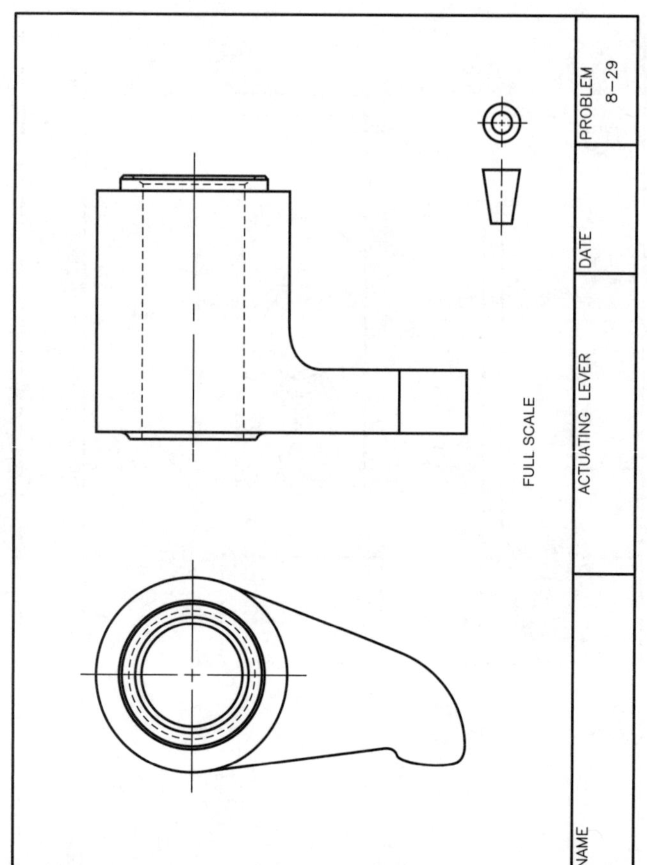
PROBLEM
8–29
DATE
ACTUATING LEVER
FULL SCALE
NAME

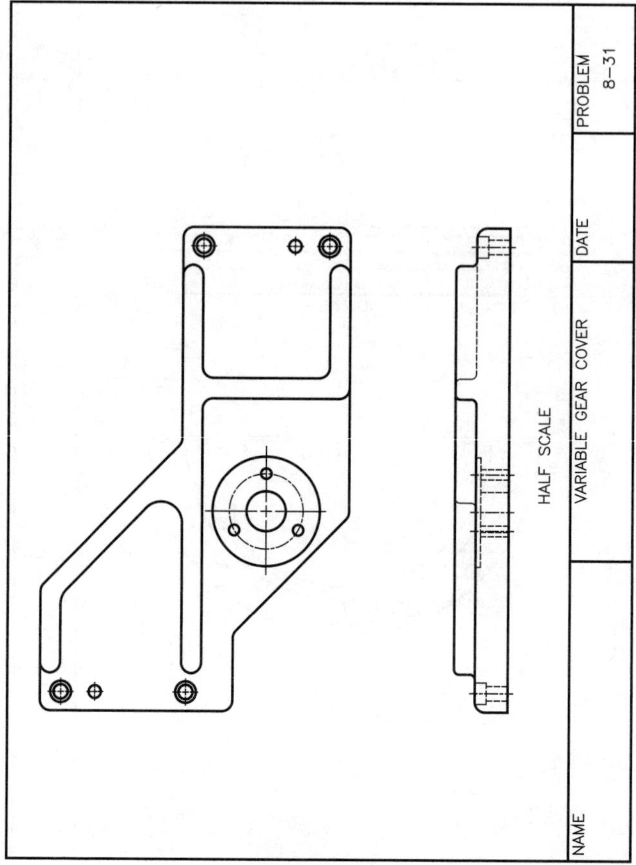
PROBLEM
8–31
DATE
VARIABLE GEAR COVER
HALF SCALE
NAME

Solutions to Worksheets

Pages 45–59

Student work should look like the following drawings. The problem number and title are indicated on each problem sheet.

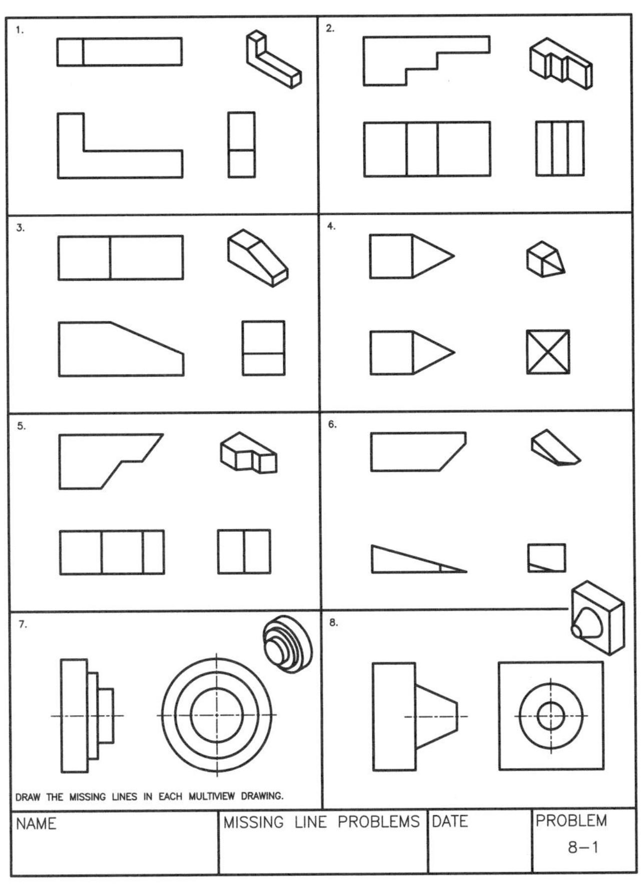

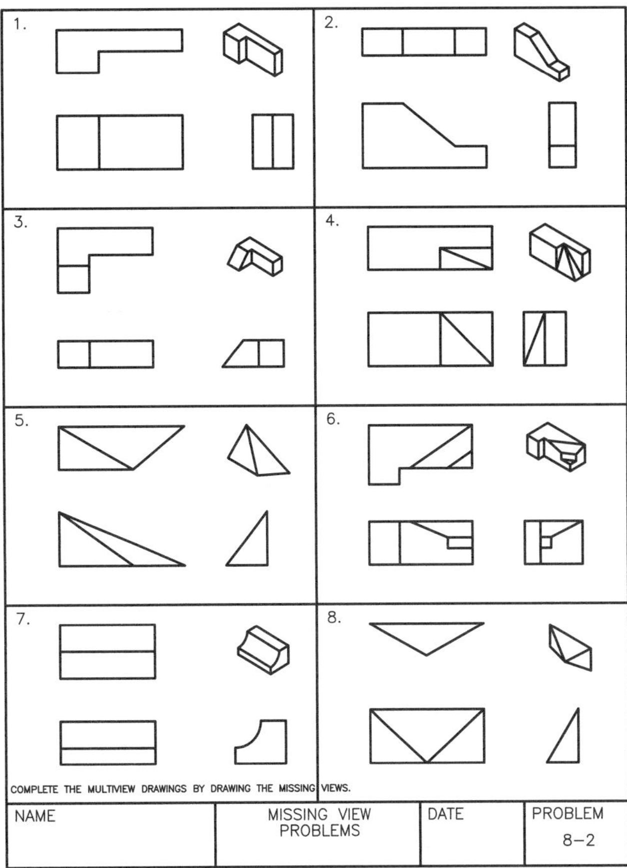

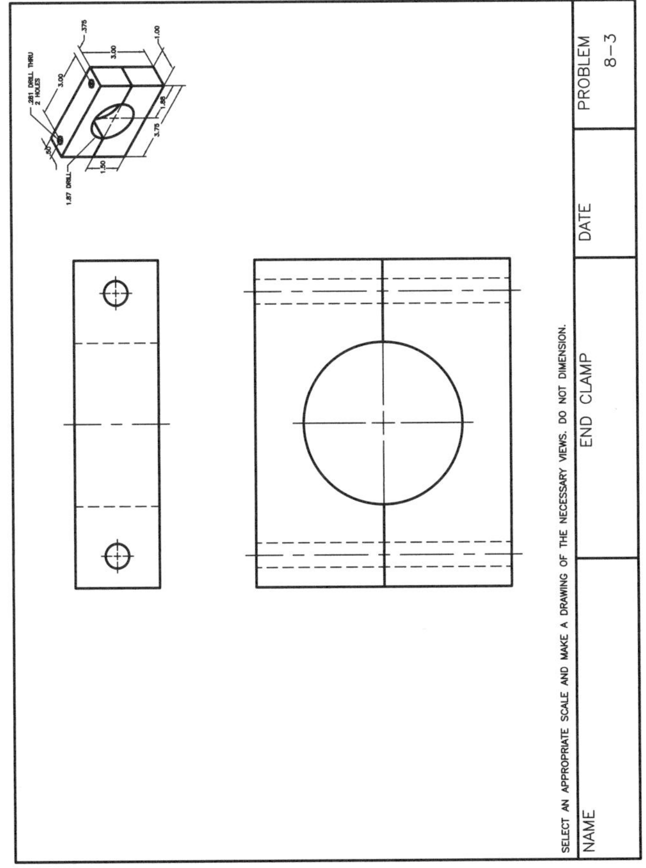

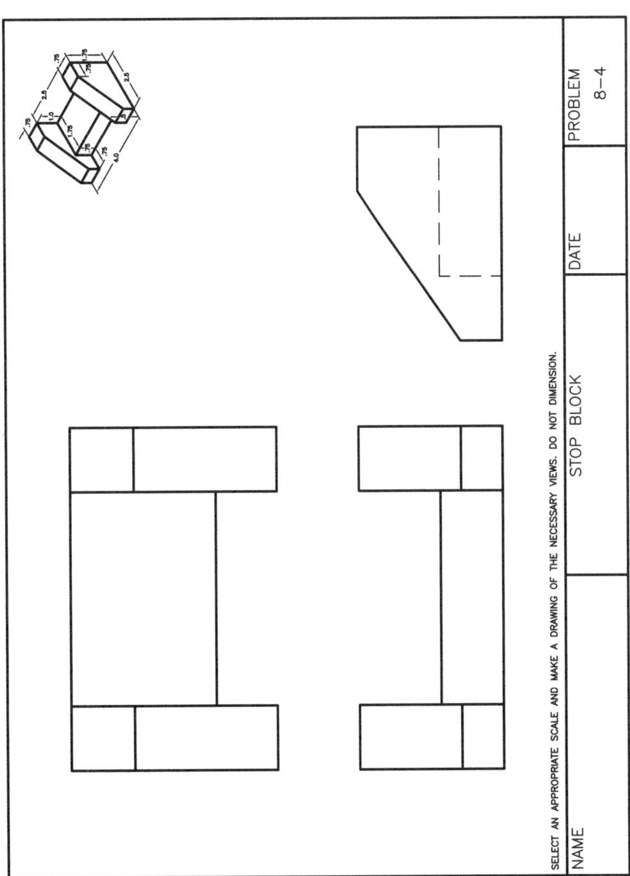

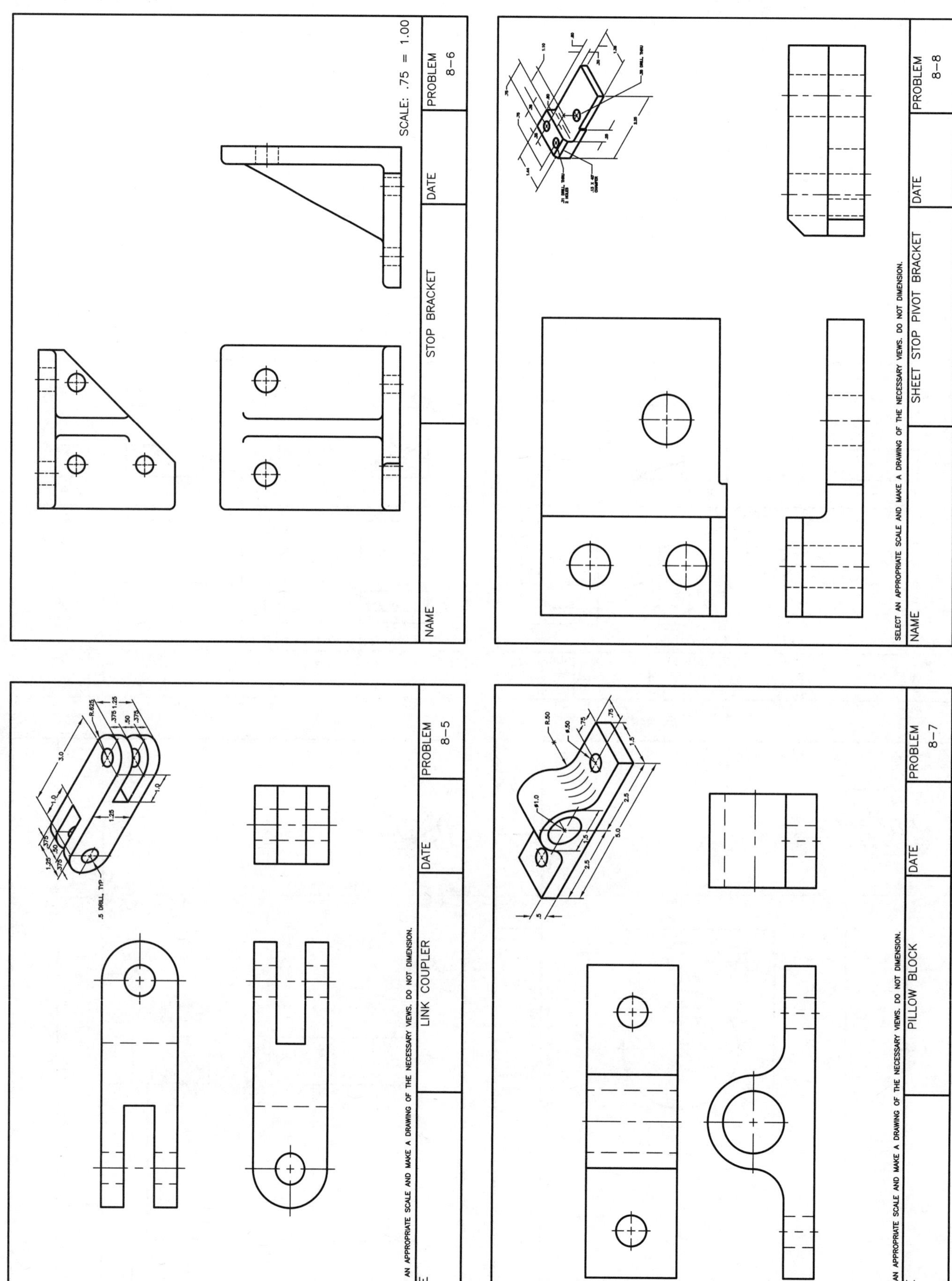
SCALE: .75 = 1.00
NAME
STOP BRACKET
DATE
PROBLEM
8–6
SELECT AN APPROPRIATE SCALE AND MAKE A DRAWING OF THE NECESSARY VIEWS. DO NOT DIMENSION.
NAME
SHEET STOP PIVOT BRACKET
DATE
PROBLEM
8–8
SELECT AN APPROPRIATE SCALE AND MAKE A DRAWING OF THE NECESSARY VIEWS. DO NOT DIMENSION.
NAME
LINK COUPLER
DATE
PROBLEM
8–5
.5 DRILL, TYP
SELECT AN APPROPRIATE SCALE AND MAKE A DRAWING OF THE NECESSARY VIEWS. DO NOT DIMENSION.
NAME
PILLOW BLOCK
DATE
PROBLEM
8–7

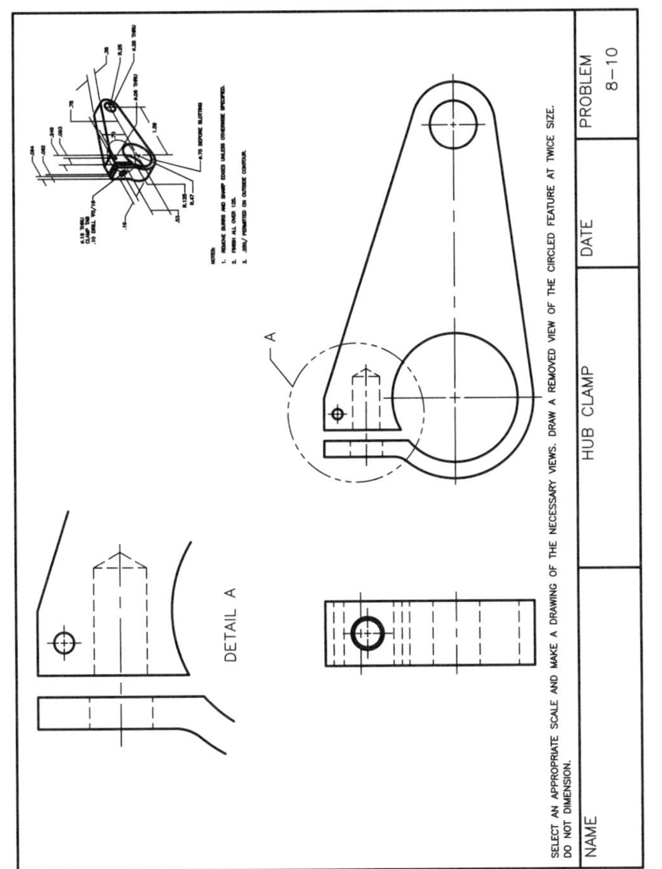
A
DETAIL A
SELECT AN APPROPRIATE SCALE AND MAKE A DRAWING OF THE NECESSARY VIEWS. DRAW A REMOVED VIEW OF THE CIRCLED FEATURE AT TWICE SIZE.
DO NOT DIMENSION.
NAME
HUB CLAMP
DATE
PROBLEM
8–10

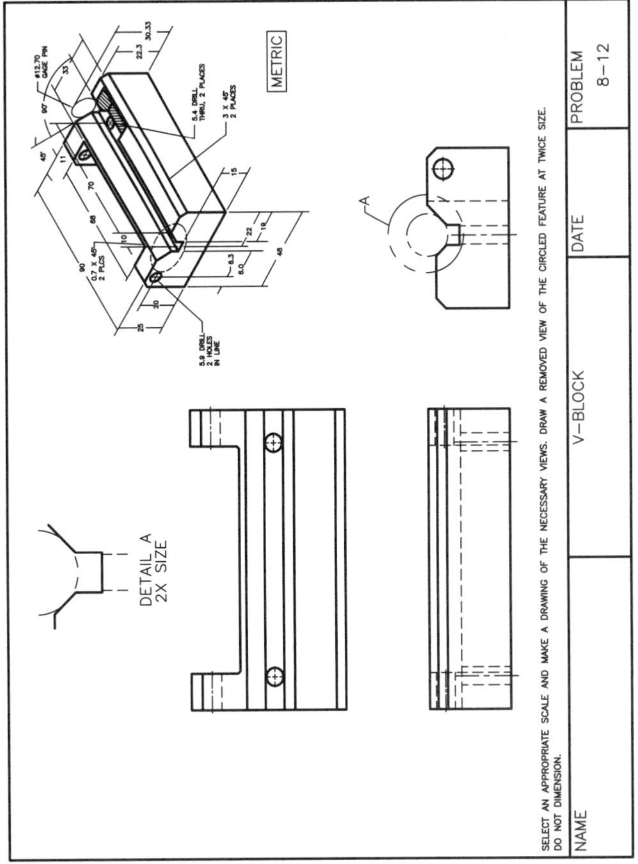
METRIC
A
DETAIL A
2X SIZE
SELECT AN APPROPRIATE SCALE AND MAKE A DRAWING OF THE NECESSARY VIEWS. DRAW A REMOVED VIEW OF THE CIRCLED FEATURE AT TWICE SIZE.
DO NOT DIMENSION.
NAME
V–BLOCK
DATE
PROBLEM
8–12

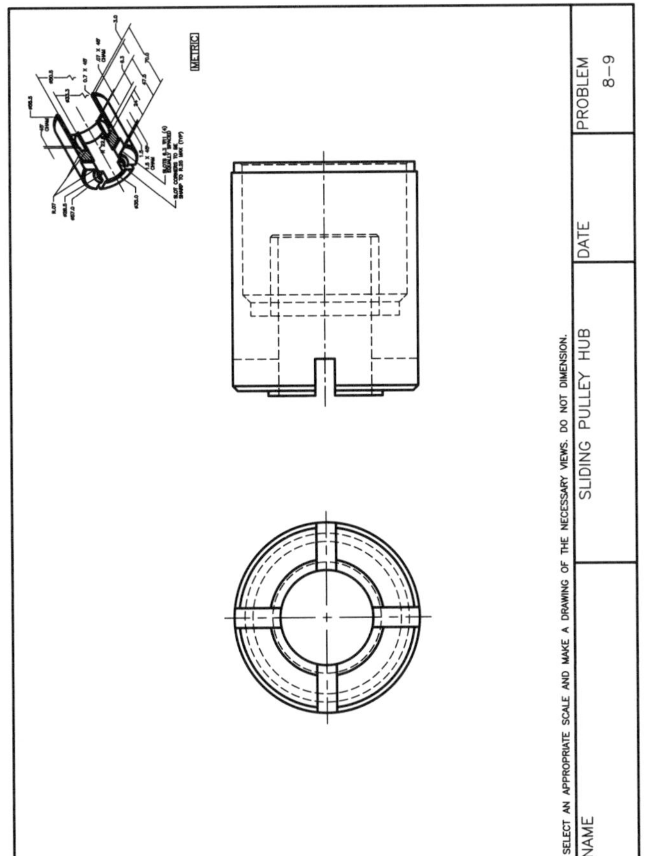
METRIC
SELECT AN APPROPRIATE SCALE AND MAKE A DRAWING OF THE NECESSARY VIEWS. DO NOT DIMENSION.
NAME
SLIDING PULLEY HUB
DATE
PROBLEM
8–9

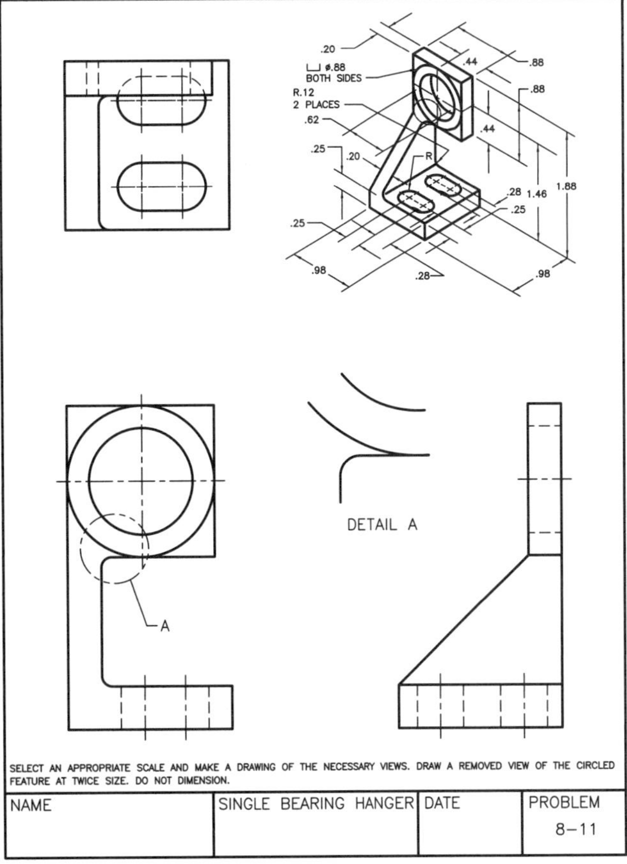
.20
⌴ ⌀.88
BOTH SIDES
R.12
2 PLACES
.62
.25
.20
R
.44
.88
.88
.44
.28
1.46
1.88
.25
.25
.98
.28
.98
A
DETAIL A
SELECT AN APPROPRIATE SCALE AND MAKE A DRAWING OF THE NECESSARY VIEWS. DRAW A REMOVED VIEW OF THE CIRCLED FEATURE AT TWICE SIZE. DO NOT DIMENSION.
NAME
SINGLE BEARING HANGER
DATE
PROBLEM
8–11

Answers to Chapter 8 Quiz

1. D. "orthographic projection"
2. B. To the right of the front view and in line with the front view.
3. C. Oblique
4. D. The orientation that orients all surfaces parallel to the frontal plane of projection.
5. B. Flat parts made from relatively thin sheet stock.
6. D. fillet
7. C. Object lines, hidden lines, cutting-plane lines, centerlines.
8. B. Third-angle, first-angle
9. B. represented by an object line
10. D. First-angle and third-angle projection drawings differ mainly in how the object is projected and the positions of the views.
11. A. Front
    B. Top or plan
    C. Side or end
12. A. First-angle projection
    B. Third-angle projection
13. Refer to the drawings given in the *Solutions to Drawing Problems, Text* section for the problem selected from the textbook.

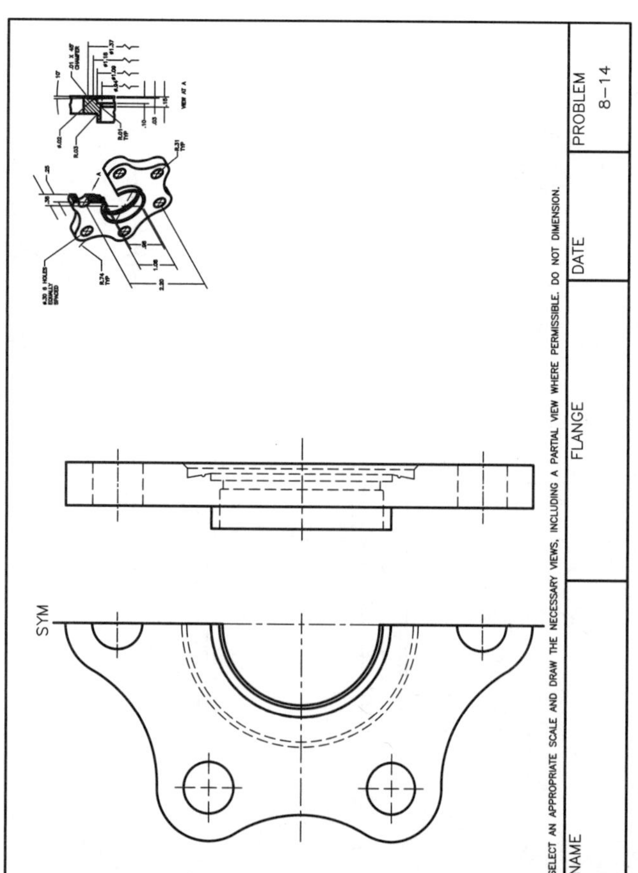

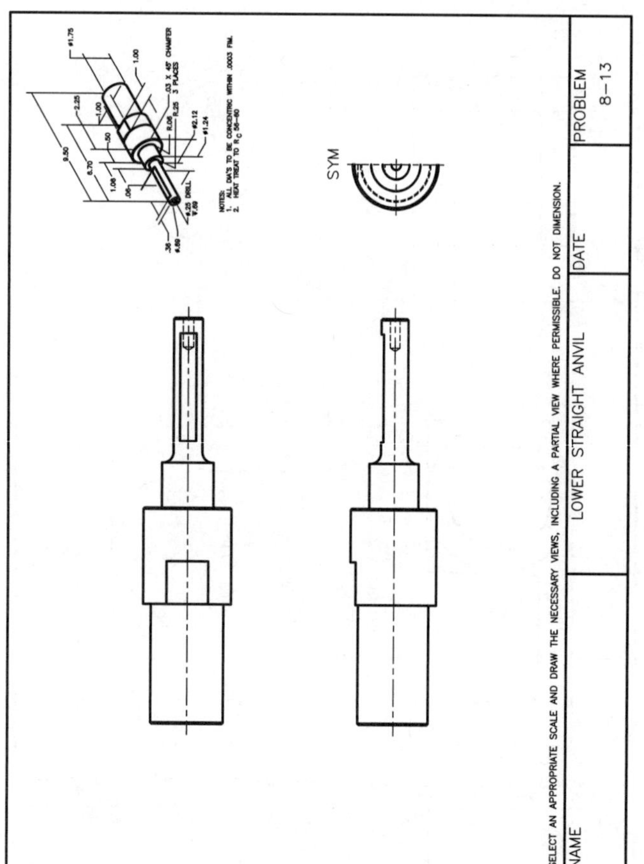

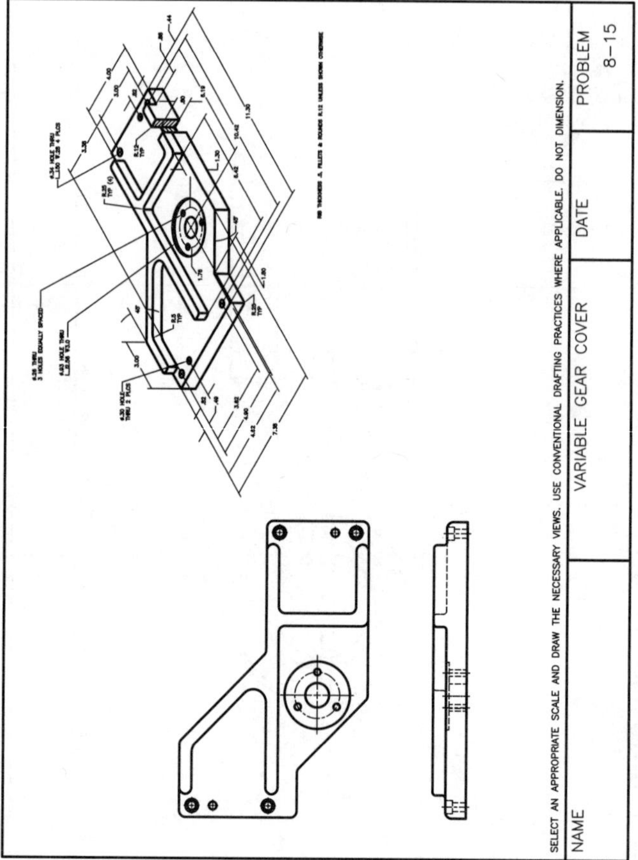

Chapter Quiz 8

Multiview Drawings

Name ____

Period ____________ Date ____________ Score ____________

Multiple Choice

Choose the answer that correctly completes the statement. Write the corresponding letter in the space provided.

_____ 1. In drafting, the terms "multiview" and _____ are used interchangeably.
A. "dimetric projection"
B. "trimetric projection"
C. "isometric projection"
D. "orthographic projection"

_____ 2. In third-angle projection, where is the right side view located?
A. To the left of the front view and in line with the top view.
B. To the right of the front view and in line with the front view.
C. To the right of the front view and in line with the top view.
D. A right side view is not typically drawn.

_____ 3. What type of line never appears as true length in any of the principal planes of projection?
A. Normal
B. Hidden
C. Oblique
D. All lines appear true length in one or more of the principal planes of projection.

_____ 4. Which of the following is *not* a factor to be considered when selecting the front view of an object?
A. The most representative contour or shape of the object.
B. The natural or functioning position of the object.
C. The orientation that produces the fewest hidden lines in all views.
D. The orientation that orients all surfaces parallel to the frontal plane of projection.

_____ 5. Which of the following types of parts may be adequately shown in one view by adding a note for thickness?
A. Cylindrical parts.
B. Flat parts made from relatively thin sheet stock.
C. Very small parts.
D. All parts require at least two views.

_____ 6. A small rounded interior corner is known as a _____.
A. radius
B. chamfer
C. round
D. fillet

Name ______________________________

_______ 7. What is the priority of importance that governs precedence of lines when certain lines coincide in the projection of views?
A. Cutting-plane lines, object lines, hidden lines, centerlines.
B. Centerlines, object lines, hidden lines, cutting-plane lines.
C. Object lines, hidden lines, cutting-plane lines, centerlines.
D. Hidden lines, object lines, cutting-plane lines, centerlines.

_______ 8. _____ projection is used in the United States and Canada while most European countries use _____ projection.
A. First-angle, third-angle
B. Third-angle, first-angle
C. Second-angle, third-angle
D. Third-angle, fourth-angle

_______ 9. Fillets and rounds on drawings are _____.
A. not represented since there is no sharp line of intersection
B. represented by an object line
C. represented by a centerline
D. represented by a phantom line

_______ 10. Which of the following is true in relation to first-angle and third-angle projection?
A. Third-angle projection is used primarily in European countries.
B. The frontal projection plane is between the viewer and the object in first-angle projection.
C. First-angle projection drawings have more lines and surfaces shown.
D. First-angle and third-angle projection drawings differ mainly in how the object is projected and the positions of the views.

Completion

Write the correct answer in the space provided.

11. Give the name of the principal view shown in each projection plane.

A. Frontal plane ______________________________

B. Horizontal plane ______________________________

C. Profile plane ______________________________

Identification

12. Identify the following projection symbols. Write your answers in the spaces provided.

A. ______________________ B. ______________________

Drafting Performance

13. Select the necessary views and prepare a drawing of a problem selected by your instructor from the Drawing Problems section of Chapter 8 in your textbook.

Location of Principal Views

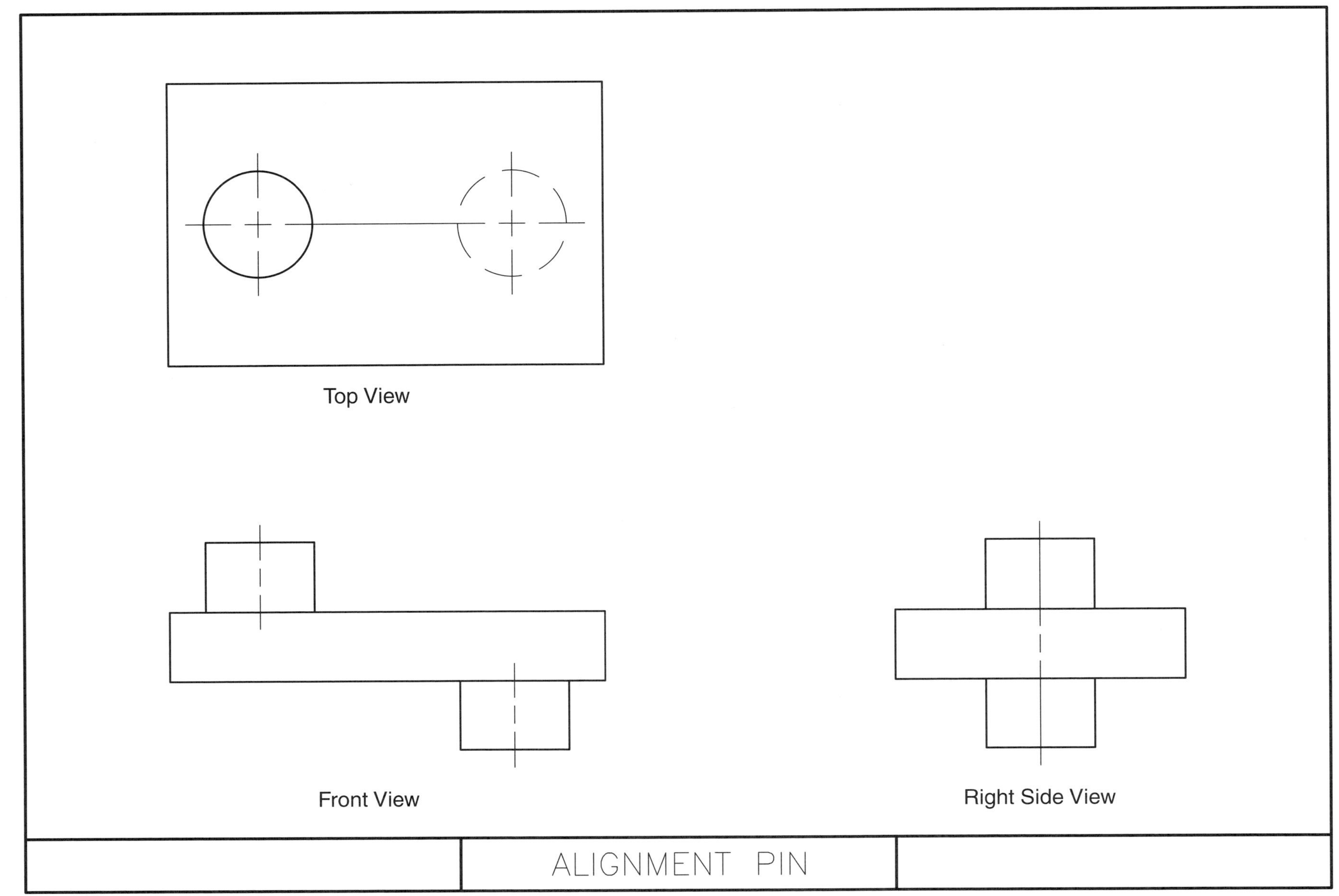

RM 8-1

Projecting Points Between Views

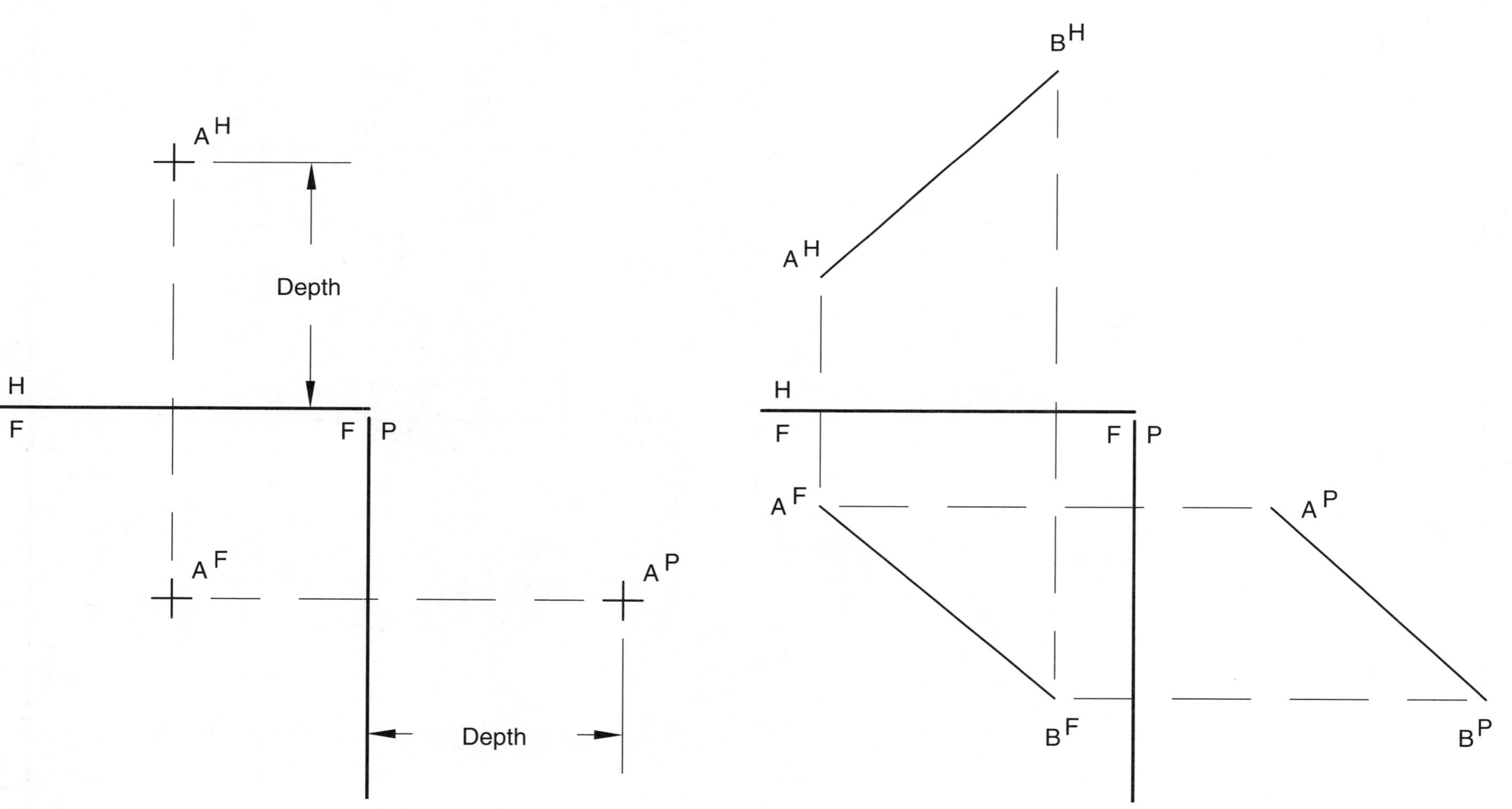

RM 8-2

Projecting Normal and Inclined Surfaces

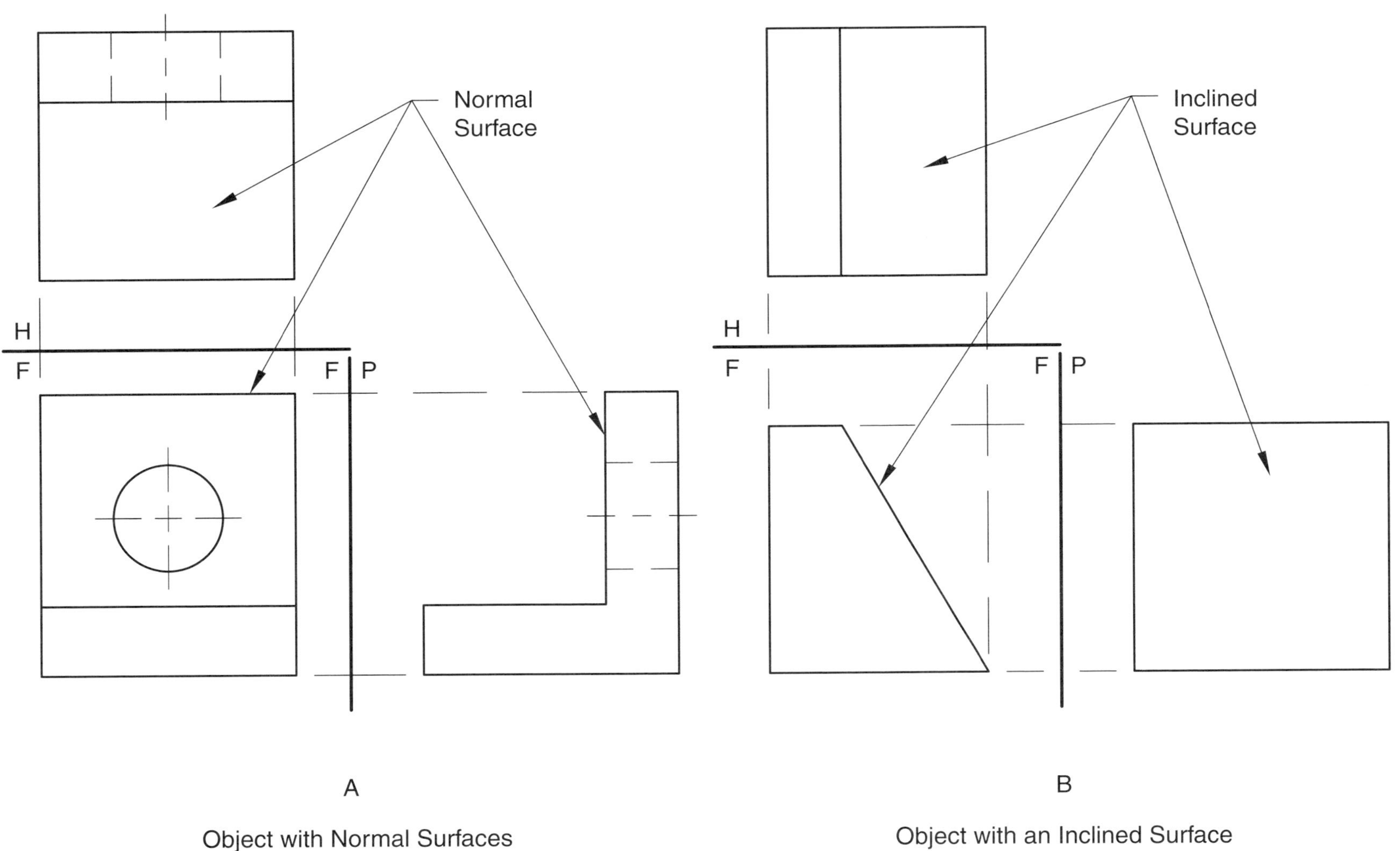

A

Object with Normal Surfaces

B

Object with an Inclined Surface

RM 8-3

Procedure Checklist

Multiview Drawings

Name ____

Observable Items	Completed		Comments	Instructor Initials
	Yes	No		
1. Projects points in multiviews.				
2. Projects lines in multiviews.				
3. Constructs a multiview drawing.				
4. Selects views.				
5. Constructs removed views.				
6. Constructs partial views.				
7. Visualizes objects for multiview drawings.				

Instructor Signature ____

Dimensioning Fundamentals

Learning Objectives

After studying this chapter, the student will be able to:

- Define size and location dimensions.
- Explain the drawing conventions used for dimension, extension, and leader lines.
- Describe standard conventions used in inch dimensioning and metric dimensioning.
- Identify and explain common dimensioning systems used in drafting.
- Explain the purpose of general and local notes.
- List the general rules for good dimensioning practice.
- Describe the common commands and methods used in dimensioning CAD drawings.
- Dimension drawings using accepted conventions.

Instructional Resources

Text: pages 281–314

Review Questions, pages 308–309

Drawing Problems, pages 309–314

Worksheets: pages 60–67

- Worksheet 9-1: *Dimensioning Elements*
- Worksheet 9-2: *Spacer Block*
- Worksheet 9-3: *Clamp Plate*
- Worksheet 9-4: *Flange*
- Worksheet 9-5: *Bracket*
- Worksheet 9-6: *Outlet Check Valve*
- Worksheet 9-7: *Cylinder Rod Guide Bracket*
- Worksheet 9-8: *Bracket*

Instructor's Resource

Instructional Tasks

Instructional Aids and Assignments

Chapter 9 Quiz

Reproducible Masters

- Reproducible Master 9-1: *Rules for Good Dimensioning*. The rules for good dimensioning presented in the text are shown in this handout to provide easy access when students are making drawings.
- Reproducible Master 9-2: *Inch-Metric Equivalents*. The Inch-Metric Equivalents chart presented in the Reference Section of the textbook is shown in this handout to provide easy access for students.
- Reproducible Master 9-3: *Size and Location Dimensions*. The proper practices for placing size and location dimensions are shown.
- Reproducible Master 9-4: *Unidirectional and Aligned Dimensions*. The unidirectional and aligned systems of dimensioning are shown for identical objects.
- Reproducible Master 9-5: *Rectangular Coordinate Dimensioning*. The object shown is dimensioned using rectangular coordinate dimensioning.

Procedure Checklist

Color Transparencies (Binder/IRCD only)

- Transparency 9-1: *Decimal Inch Dimensioning*. Proper practices for placing decimal inch dimensions are shown.
- Transparency 9-2: *Dimensioning Arcs and Curves*. Accepted conventions for dimensioning arcs and curves are shown.
- Transparency 9-3: *Dimensioning Round Holes*. Accepted conventions for dimensioning round holes are shown.

Instructional Tasks

1. Define the terms *size dimensions* and *location dimensions*.
    - Show a multimedia presentation or film on dimensioning.
    - Clarify the differences between size dimensions and location dimensions.
2. Explain how to correctly draw dimension, extension, and leader lines.
    - Discuss the elements of good dimensioning practices.

3. Discuss the unidirectional and aligned systems of dimensioning.
    - Clarify the differences between unidirectional and aligned dimensioning.
4. Discuss how to apply dimensions using fractional inch, decimal inch, and metric dimensioning.
    - List and explain accepted rules for applying dimensions.
5. Discuss the application of dimensions for size.
    - List and explain dimensioning conventions for different geometric shapes.
6. Discuss the application of dimensions for location.
    - Explain the differences between point-to-point, coordinate, tabular, and ordinate dimensioning.
7. Explain how to place notes on a drawing.
    - Discuss proper form and placement for drawing notes.
    - Demonstrate the construction of arrowheads.
    - Discuss the characteristics of drawing notes.
    - Demonstrate proper size, spacing, and alignment of notes on drawings.
    - Differentiate between general and local notes.
8. List and explain the rules for good dimensioning.
    - Discuss the importance of good dimensioning practices.

Instructional Aids and Assignments

1. Show a multimedia presentation or film on dimensioning practices.
2. Display examples of industrial drawings illustrating good dimensioning practices.
3. Show a multimedia presentation or film on the metric system.
4. Invite a professional from industry to speak on dimensioning practices.
5. Assign the drawing problems in the textbook. The number of problems is sufficient to assign a minimum number to all students and to identify problems that may be done for extra credit. Some problems may be used for the performance section of the chapter quiz.

Answers to Review Questions, Text

Pages 308–309

1. Size dimensions and location dimensions.
2. size
3. location
4. thin
5. termination
6. C. .375″ to 1″
7. The termination of a dimension.
8. Leaders
9. Dimensional
10. one-third
11. A. .125″
12. Unidirectional dimensioning and aligned dimensioning.
13. millimeters
14. Decimal inch dimensioning, fractional dimensioning, metric dimensioning, and dual dimensioning.
15. Decimal inch
16. Fractional dimensioning
17. comma
18. inch, metric
19. Size
20. radius
21. circles
22. Straight-line or diagonal-line serrations on a part used to provide a better grip or interference fit.
23. B. countersink
24. keyseat
25. undercut
26. point-to-point
27. Rectangular coordinate dimensioning and polar coordinate dimensioning.
28. When a large number of similar features is to be located.
29. tolerances
30. Notes
31. .125
32. parallel
33. Notes that convey information applying to the entire drawing.
34. style
35. Dimensioning
36. Linear dimensioning, angular dimensioning, radial dimensioning, leader dimensioning, and ordinate dimensioning.
37. **Leader**

Solutions to Drawing Problems, Text

Pages 309–314

Student work should look like the following drawings. The problem number and title are indicated on each problem sheet. For Problems 9-1 through 9-6, dimension figures should not be included with the dimensions if students are drawing the problems manually.

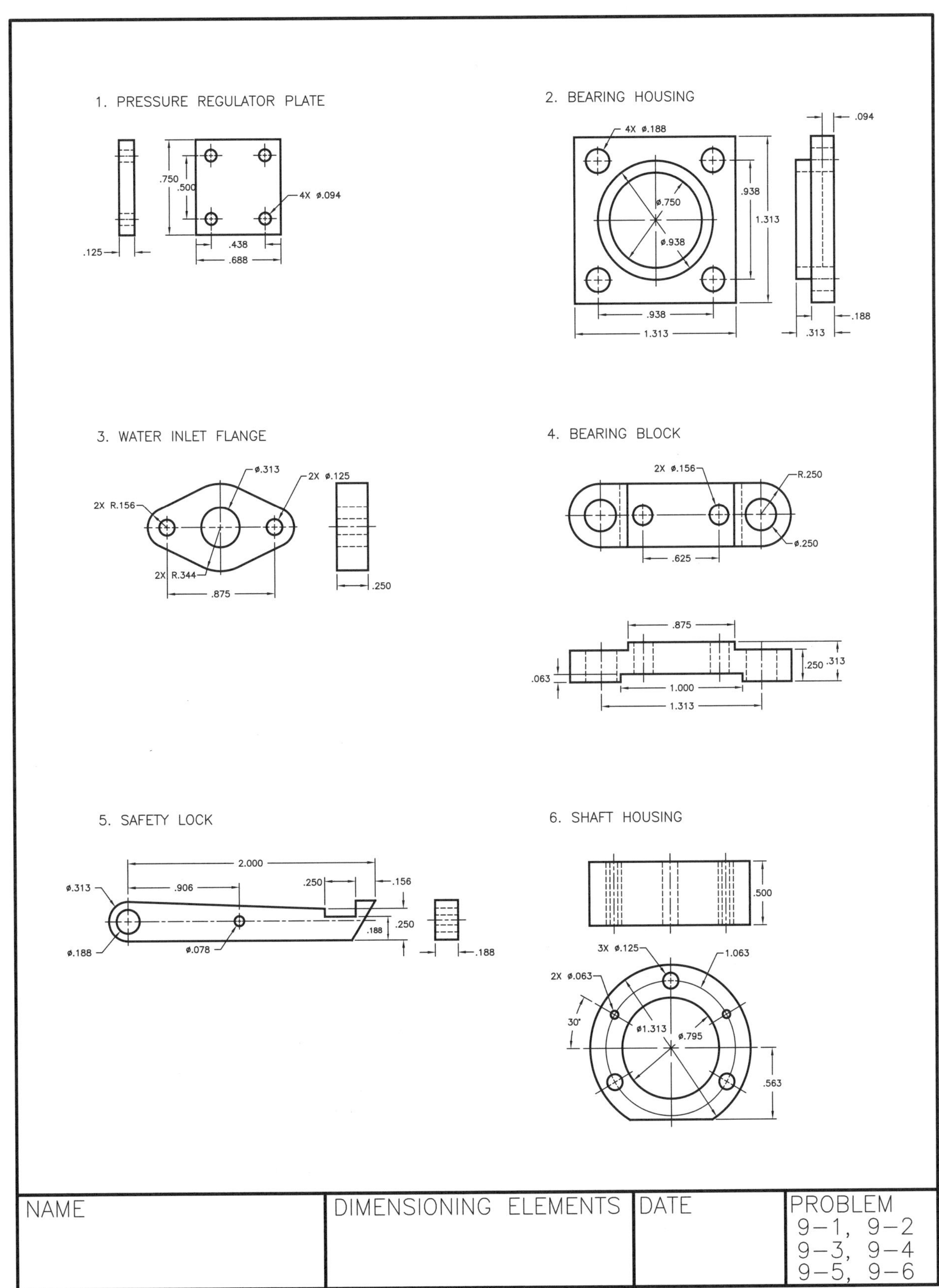

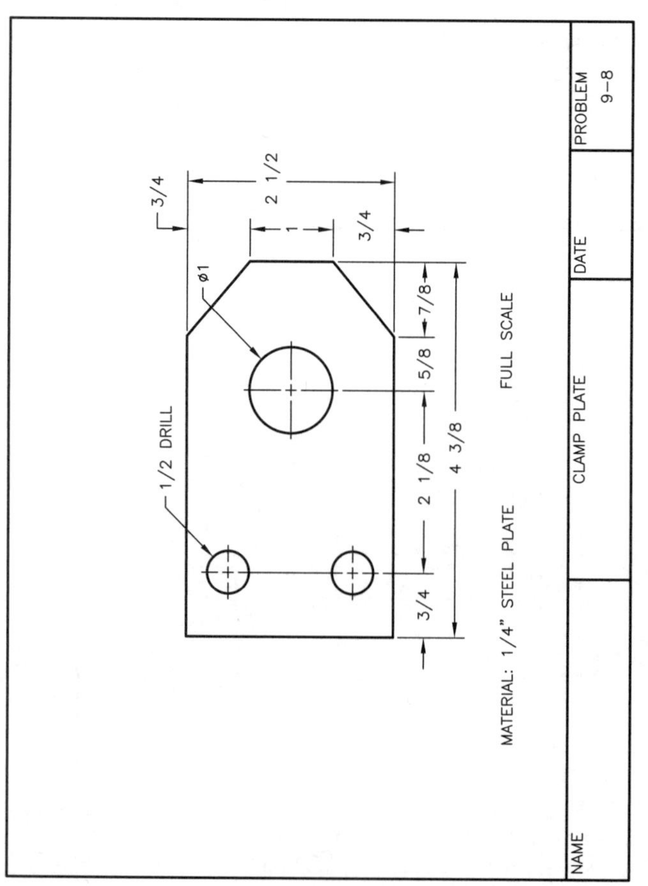

MATERIAL: 1/4" STEEL PLATE
FULL SCALE
1/2 DRILL
Ø1
CLAMP PLATE
PROBLEM 9-8
DATE
NAME

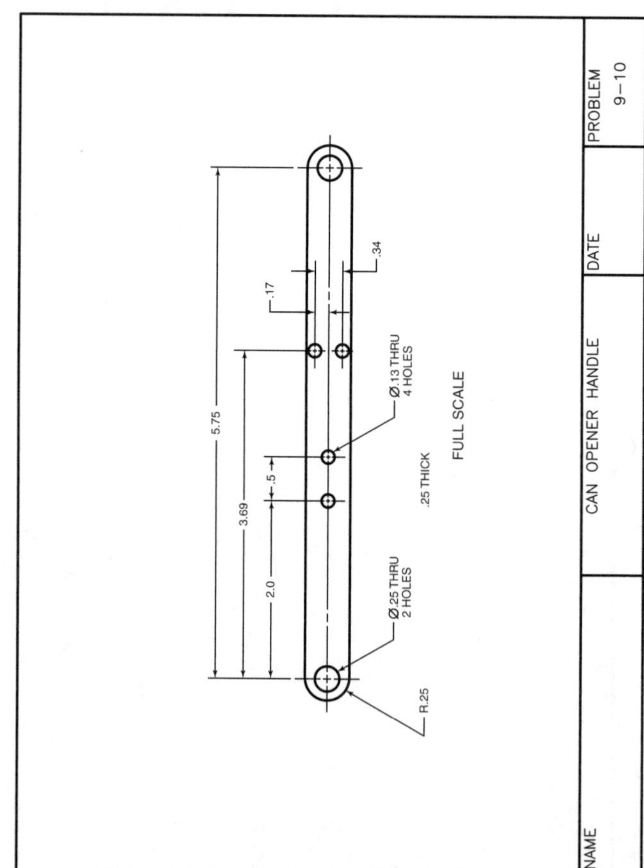

Ø.13 THRU 4 HOLES
Ø.25 THRU 2 HOLES
R.25
.25 THICK
FULL SCALE
CAN OPENER HANDLE
PROBLEM 9-10
DATE
NAME

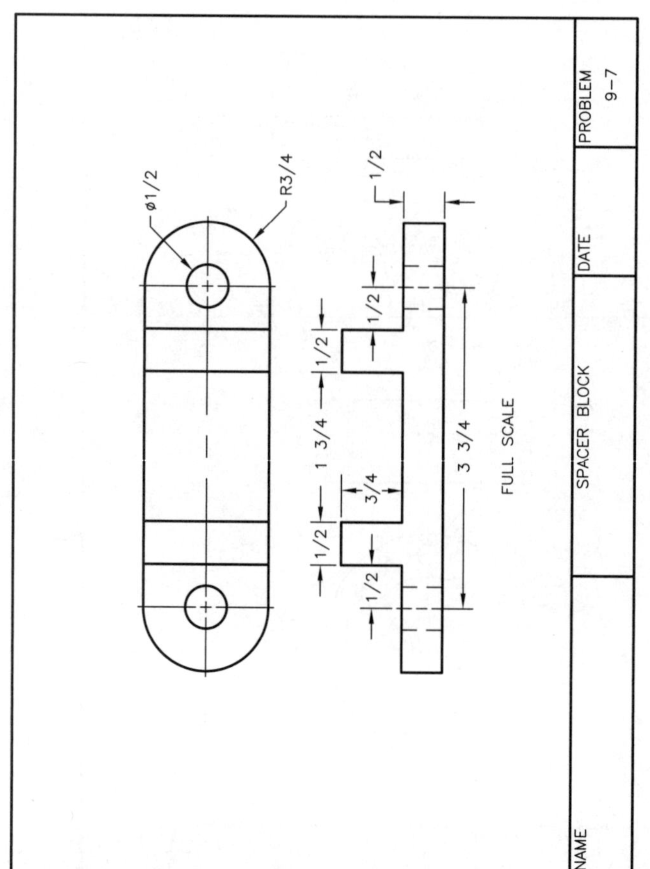

Ø1/2
R3/4
FULL SCALE
SPACER BLOCK
PROBLEM 9-7
DATE
NAME

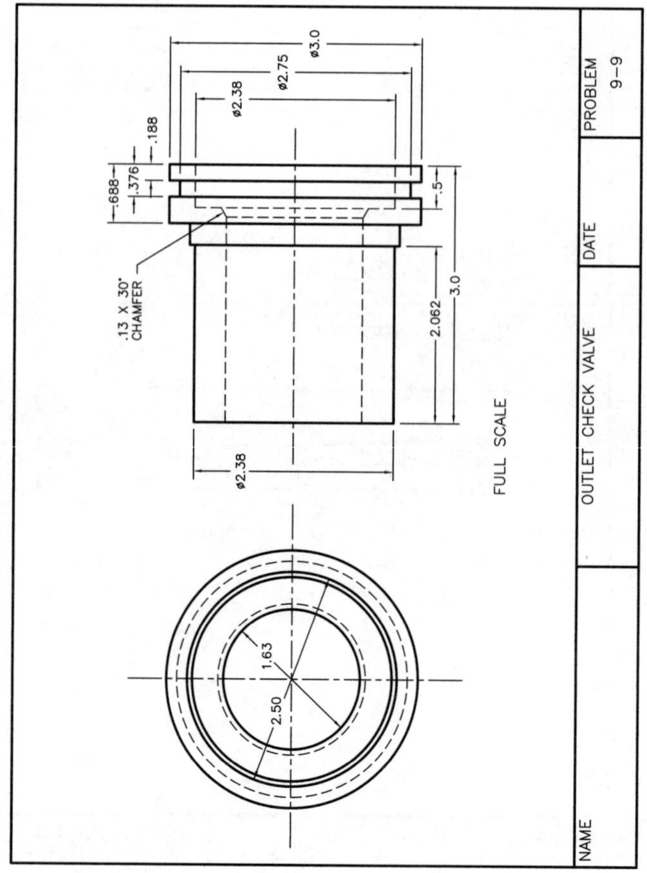

.13 X 30° CHAMFER
FULL SCALE
OUTLET CHECK VALVE
PROBLEM 9-9
DATE
NAME

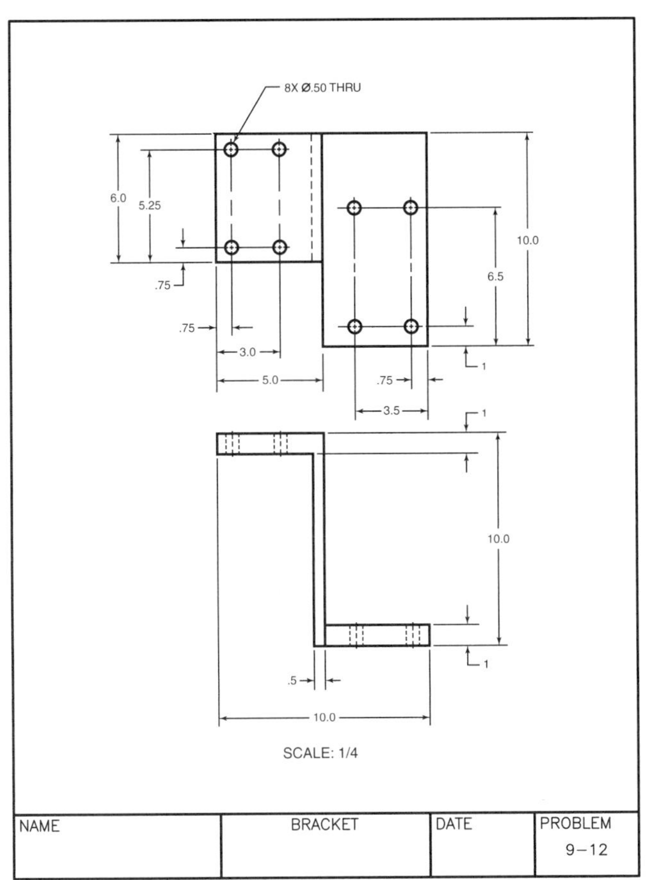
8X Ø.50 THRU
6.0
5.25
.75
.75
3.0
5.0
.75
3.5
10.0
6.5
1
1
10.0
1
.5
10.0
SCALE: 1/4
NAME
BRACKET
DATE
PROBLEM
9–12

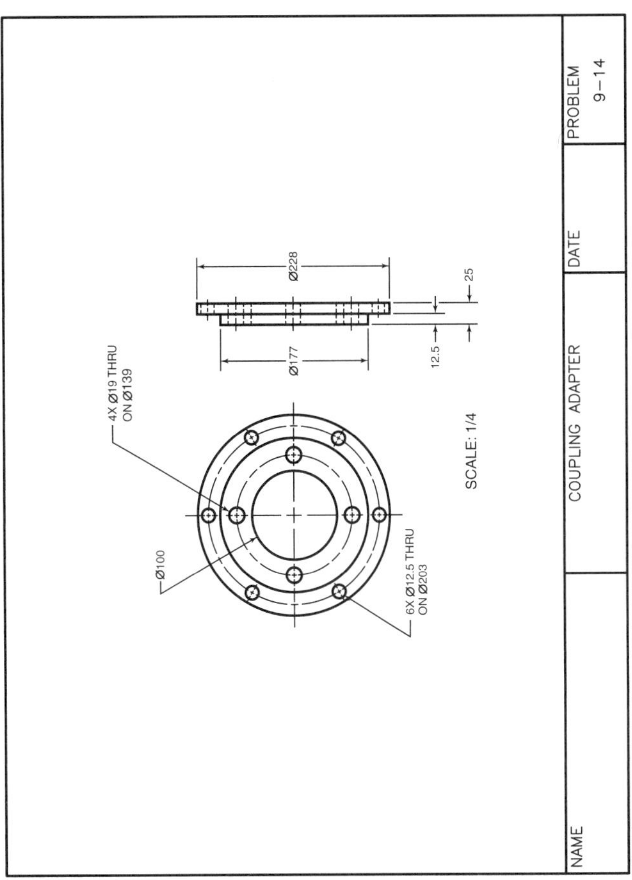
Ø228
25
Ø177
12.5
4X Ø19 THRU
ON Ø139
Ø100
6X Ø12.5 THRU
ON Ø203
SCALE: 1/4
PROBLEM
9–14
DATE
COUPLING ADAPTER
NAME

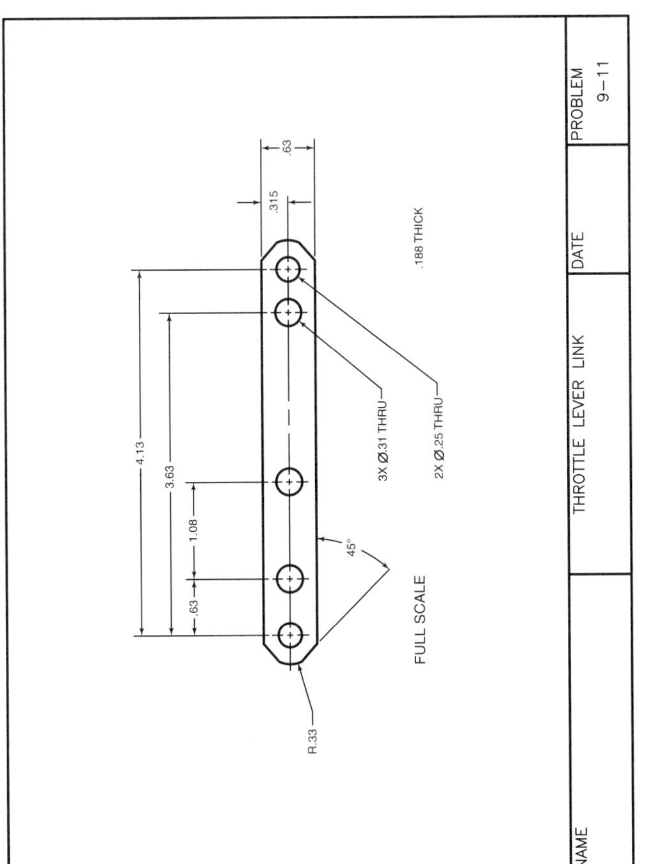
.63
.315
.188 THICK
4.13
3.63
1.08
.63
3X Ø.31 THRU
2X Ø.25 THRU
45°
R.33
FULL SCALE
PROBLEM
9–11
DATE
THROTTLE LEVER LINK
NAME

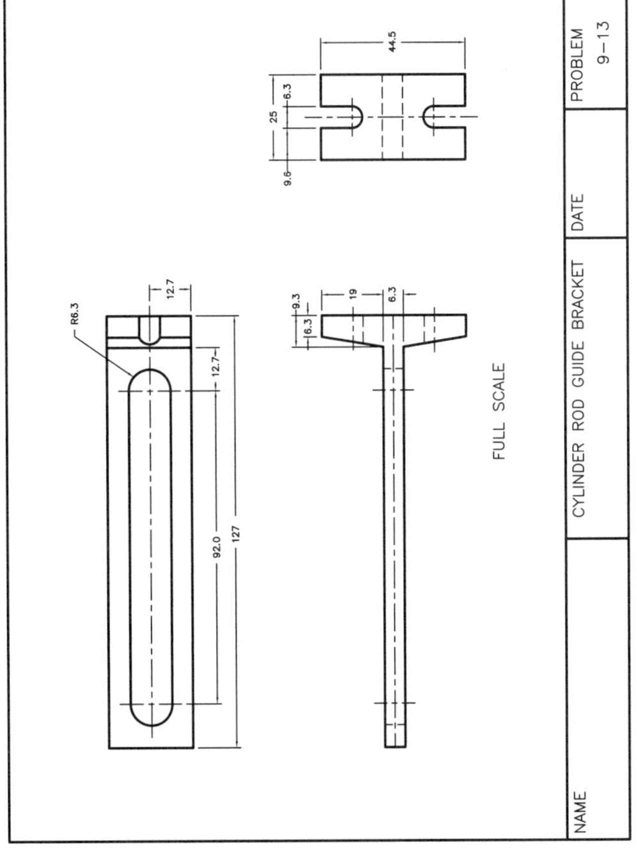
44.5
25
6.3
9.6
R6.3
12.7
12.7
92.0
127
9.3
6.3
19
6.3
FULL SCALE
PROBLEM
9–13
DATE
CYLINDER ROD GUIDE BRACKET
NAME

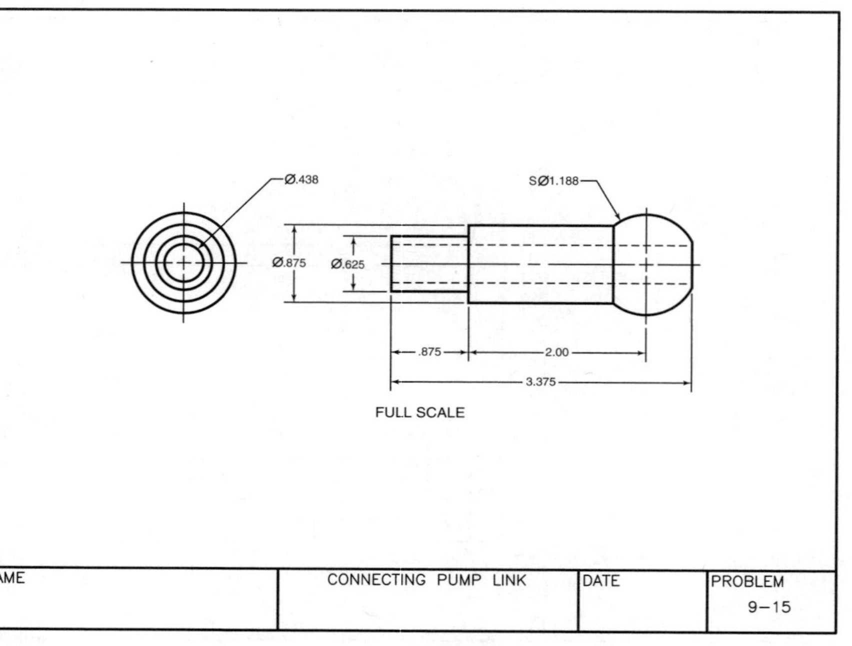
Ø.438
SØ1.188
Ø.875
Ø.625
.875
2.00
3.375
FULL SCALE
NAME
CONNECTING PUMP LINK
DATE
PROBLEM 9–15

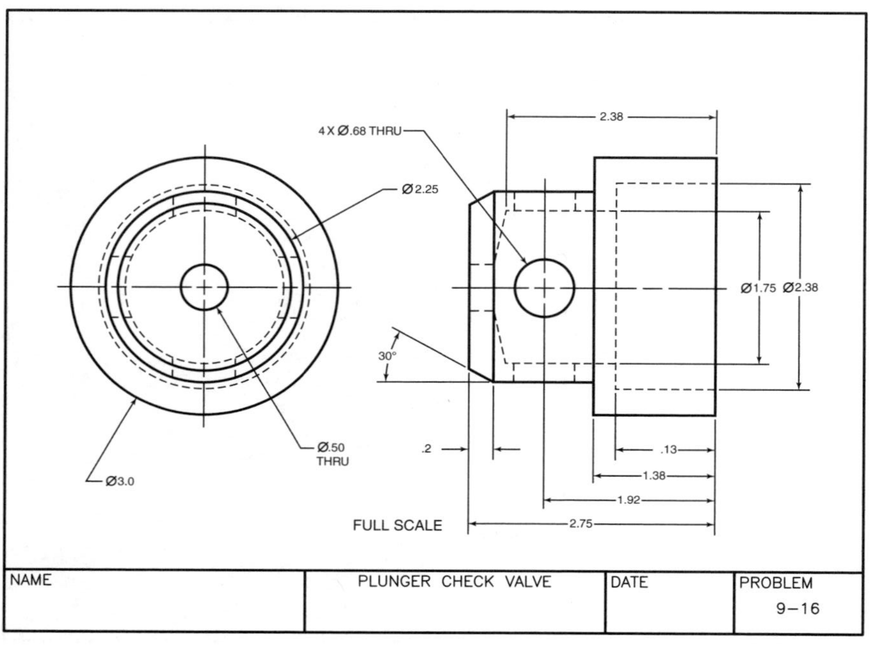
4 X Ø.68 THRU
Ø2.25
2.38
Ø1.75 Ø2.38
30°
Ø.50 THRU
Ø3.0
.2
.13
1.38
1.92
2.75
FULL SCALE
NAME
PLUNGER CHECK VALVE
DATE
PROBLEM 9–16

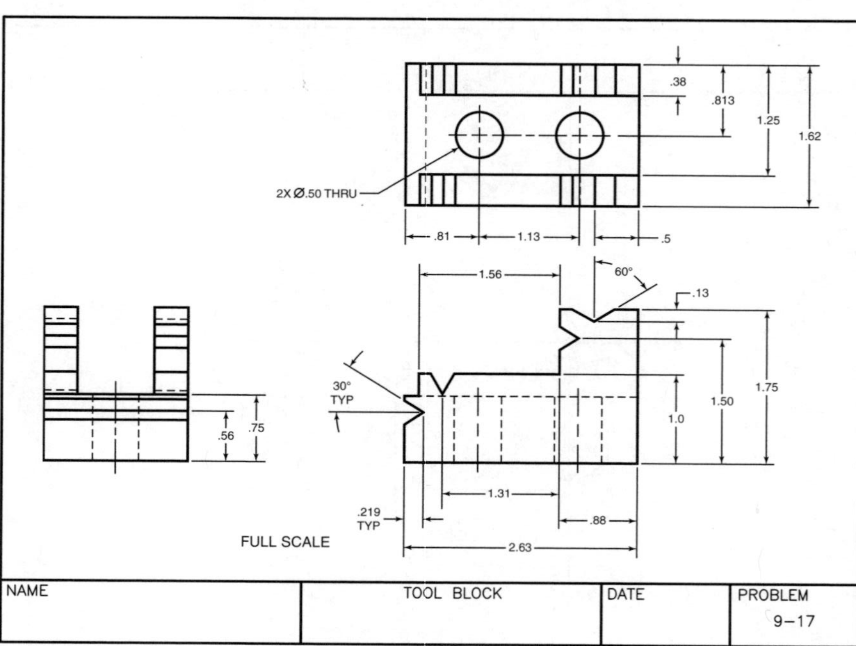
.38
.813
1.25
1.62
2X Ø.50 THRU
.81
1.13
.5
1.56
60°
.13
30° TYP
1.0
1.50
1.75
.56
.75
1.31
.219 TYP
.88
2.63
FULL SCALE
NAME
TOOL BLOCK
DATE
PROBLEM 9–17

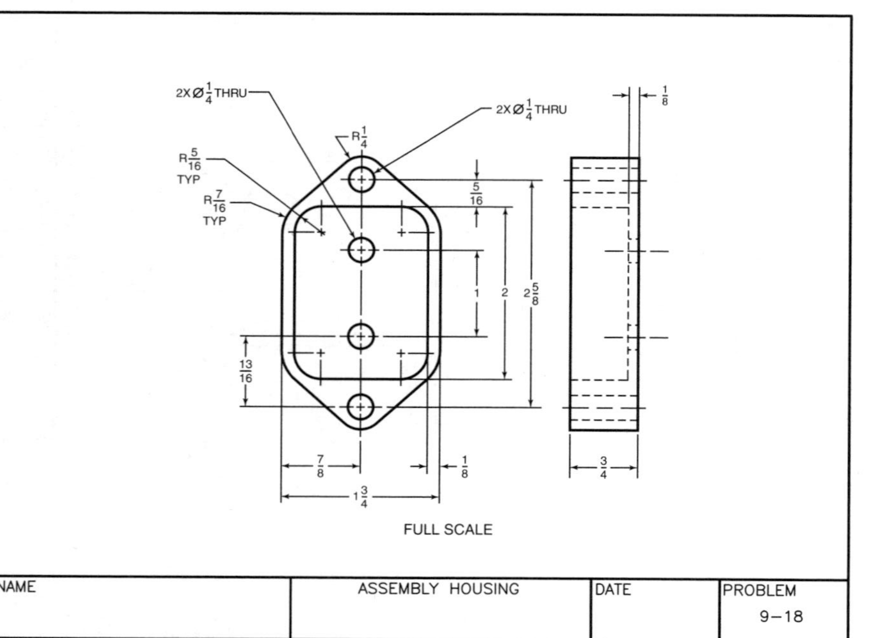
2X Ø $\frac{1}{4}$ THRU
2X Ø $\frac{1}{4}$ THRU
R $\frac{1}{4}$
R $\frac{5}{16}$ TYP
R $\frac{7}{16}$ TYP
$\frac{5}{16}$
1
2
$2\frac{5}{8}$
$\frac{13}{16}$
$\frac{7}{8}$
$\frac{1}{8}$
$1\frac{3}{4}$
$\frac{1}{8}$
$\frac{3}{4}$
FULL SCALE
NAME
ASSEMBLY HOUSING
DATE
PROBLEM 9–18

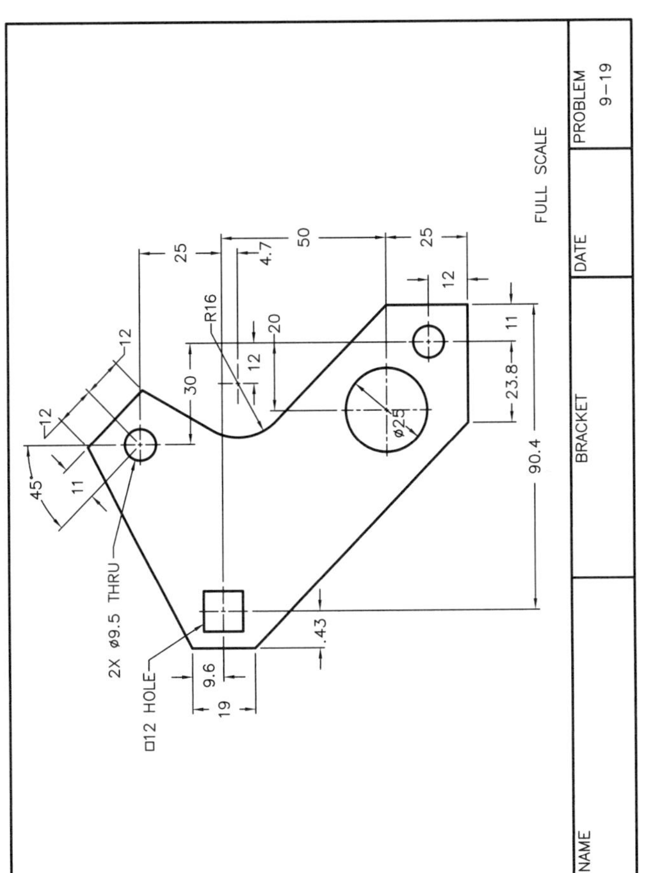
PROBLEM 9–19
FULL SCALE
DATE
BRACKET
NAME
25
50
25
4.7
12
R16
20
12
30
12
12
45°
11
11
23.8
90.4
⌀25
2X ⌀9.5 THRU
□12 HOLE
9.6
19
.43

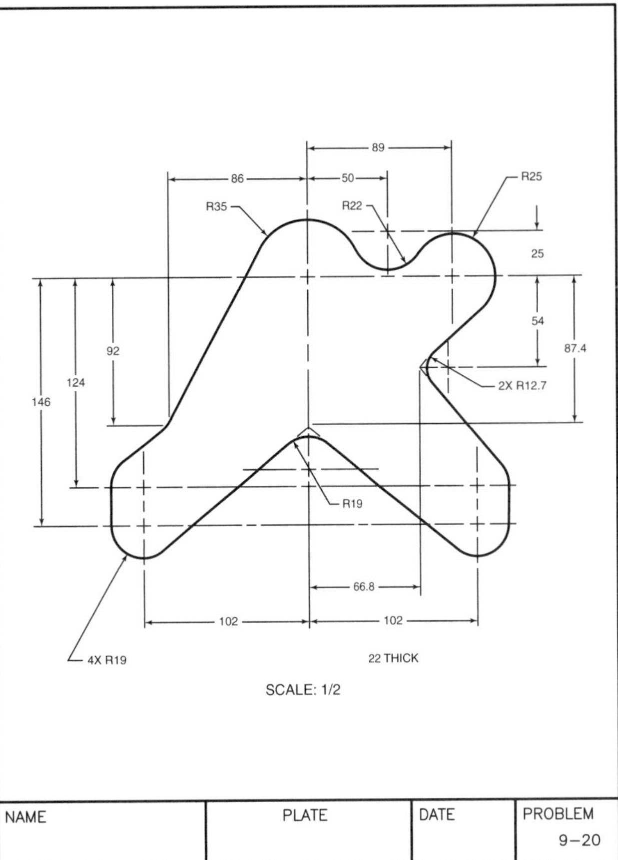
89
86
50
R35
R22
R25
25
54
87.4
92
124
146
2X R12.7
R19
66.8
102
102
4X R19
22 THICK
SCALE: 1/2
NAME
PLATE
DATE
PROBLEM 9–20

Solutions to Worksheets

Pages 60–67

Student work should look like the following drawings. The problem number and title are indicated on each problem sheet.

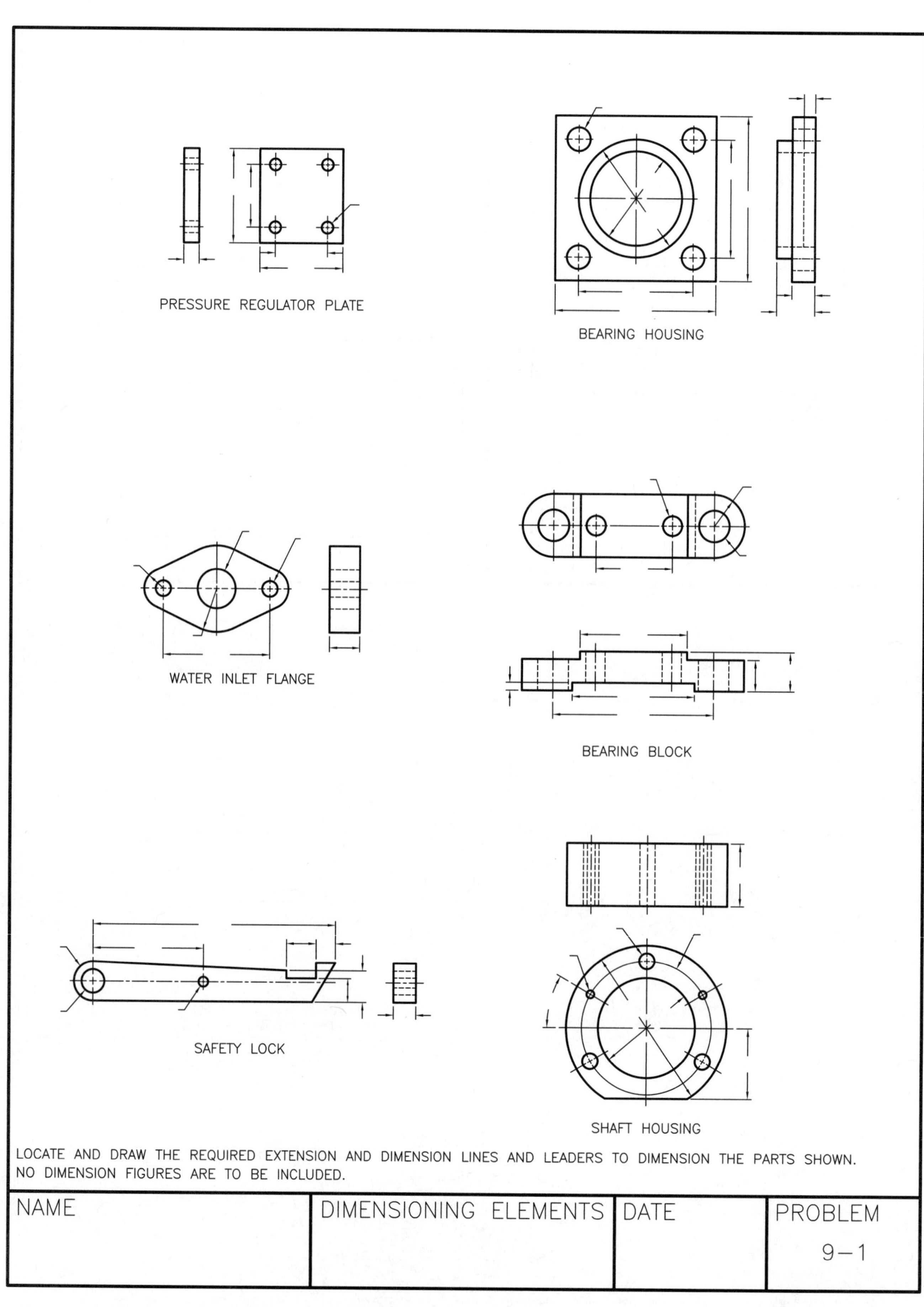

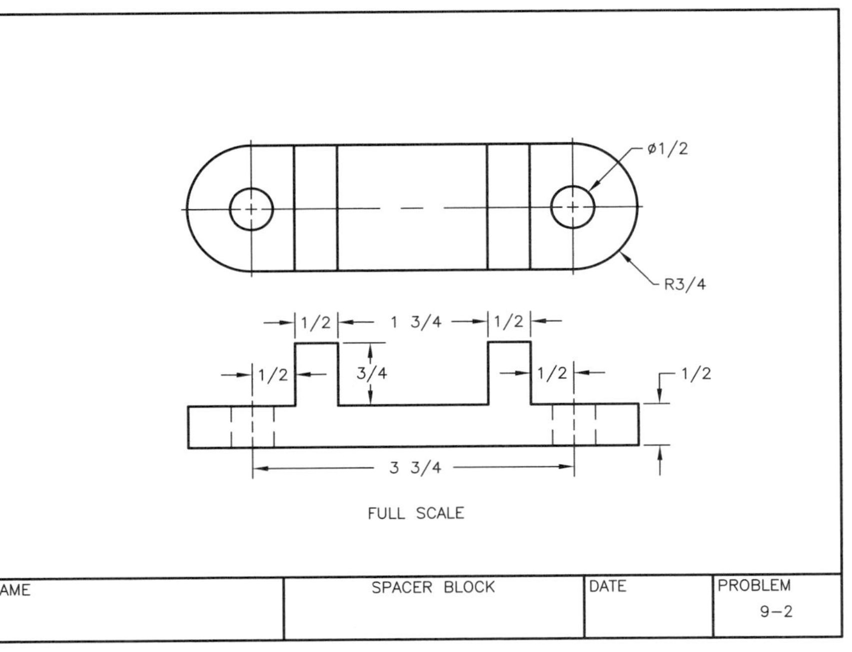
ø1/2
R3/4
1/2
1 3/4
1/2
1/2
3/4
1/2
1/2
3 3/4
FULL SCALE
NAME
SPACER BLOCK
DATE
PROBLEM
9-2

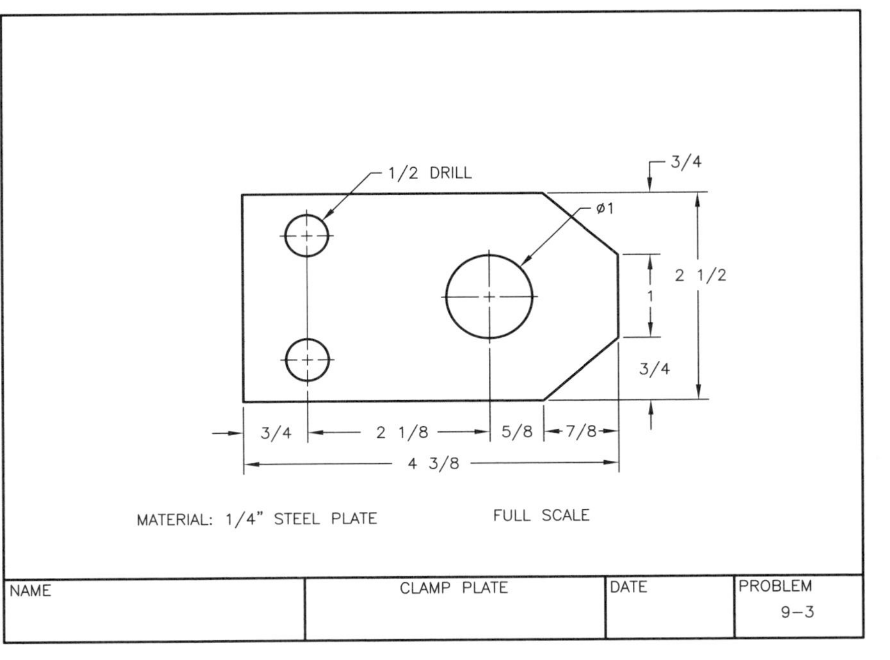
1/2 DRILL
3/4
ø1
2 1/2
1
3/4
3/4
2 1/8
5/8
7/8
4 3/8
MATERIAL: 1/4" STEEL PLATE
FULL SCALE
NAME
CLAMP PLATE
DATE
PROBLEM
9-3

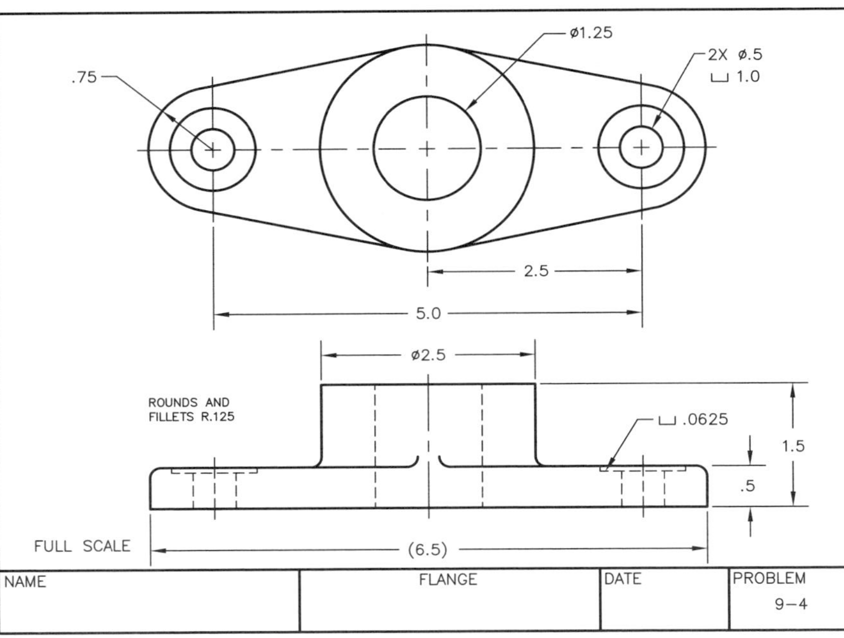
ø1.25
.75
2X ø.5
⌴ 1.0
2.5
5.0
ø2.5
ROUNDS AND
FILLETS R.125
⌴ .0625
1.5
.5
FULL SCALE
(6.5)
NAME
FLANGE
DATE
PROBLEM
9-4

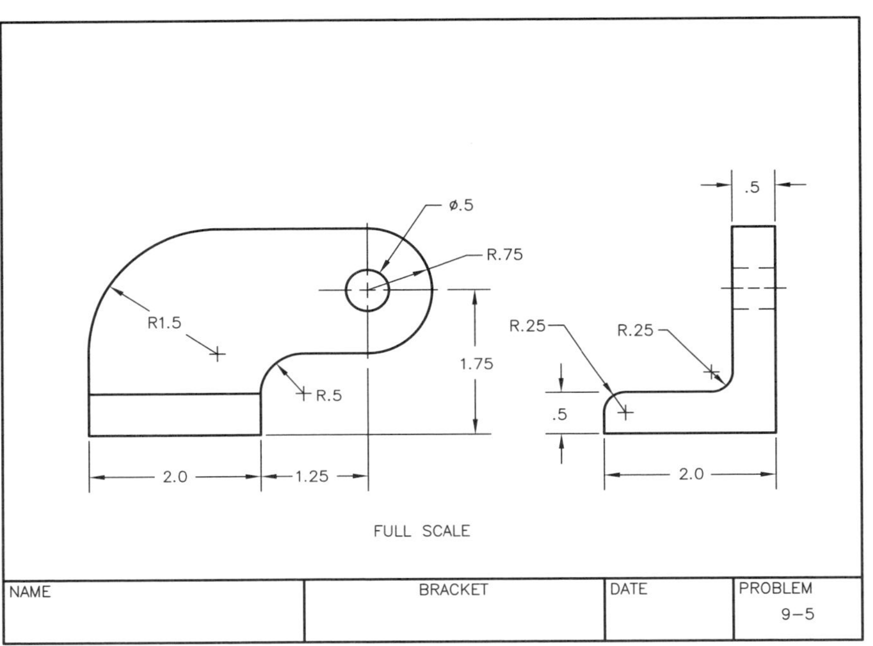
.5
ø.5
R.75
R1.5
R.25
R.25
1.75
R.5
.5
2.0
1.25
2.0
FULL SCALE
NAME
BRACKET
DATE
PROBLEM
9-5

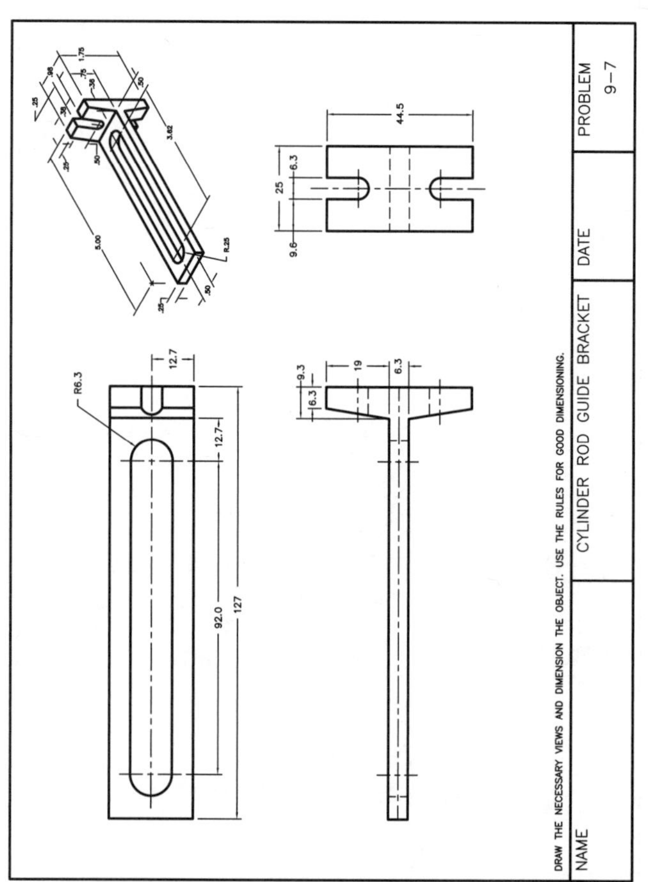

Answers to Chapter 9 Quiz

1. C. centerline
2. A. dot
3. A. Dimensions should be placed between the views to which they relate and outside the outline of the part.
4. C. unidirectional
5. B. coordinate
6. C. Avoid crossing dimension lines with extension lines or leaders whenever possible.
7. size, location
8. local
9. Refer to the drawings given in the *Solutions to Drawing Problems, Text* section for the problem selected from the textbook.

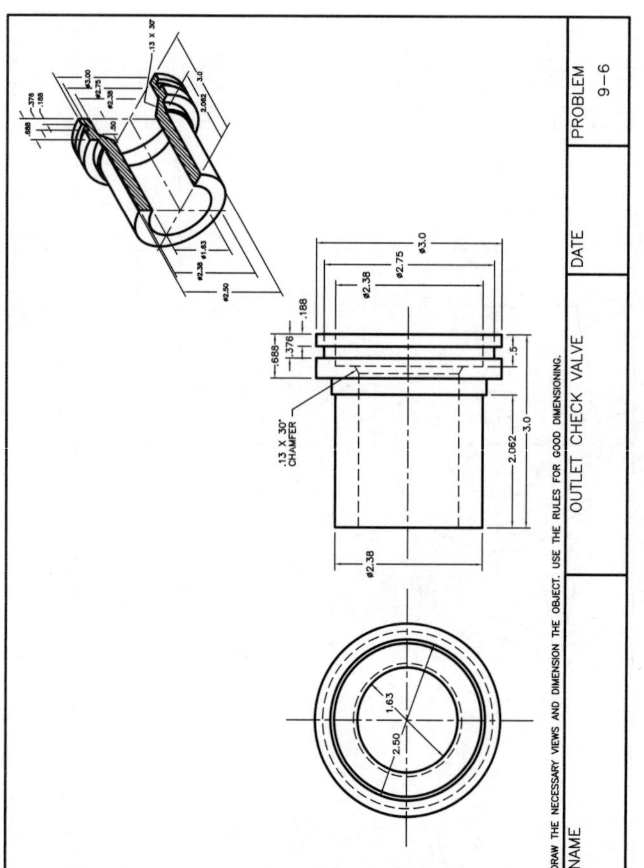

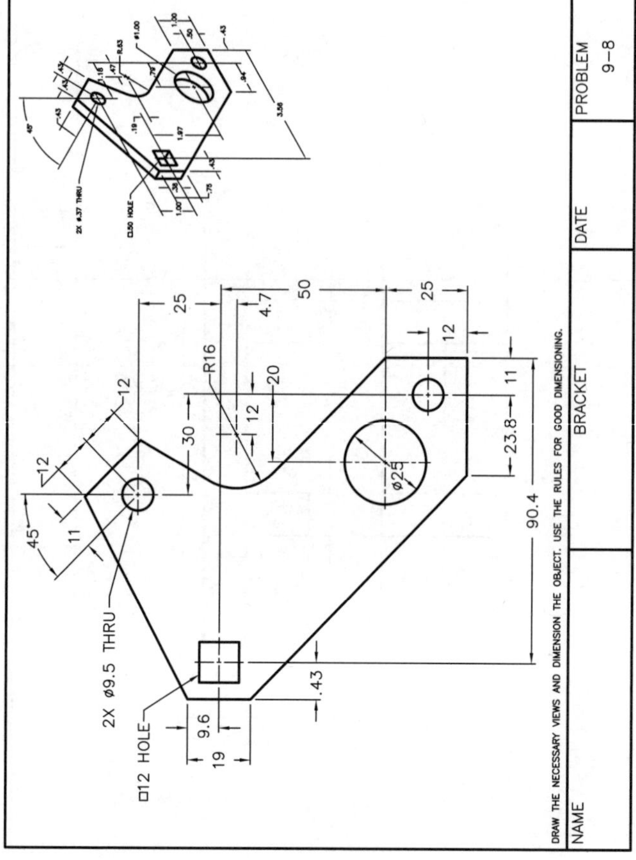

Chapter Quiz 9

Dimensioning Fundamentals

Name ____________________

Period__________ Date__________ Score __________

Multiple Choice

Choose the answer that correctly completes the statement. Write the corresponding letter in the space provided.

_____ 1. The width of a dimension line is the same as that of a(n) _____.
A. object line
B. border line
C. centerline
D. short break line

_____ 2. A leader line terminates with a(n)_____ when a surface finish is being called out.
A. dot
B. slash
C. arrow
D. No terminating symbol is used.

_____ 3. Which of the following statements is true concerning the placement of dimensions?
A. Dimensions should be placed between the views to which they relate and outside the outline of the part.
B. Dimensions should be placed on hidden lines rather than visible outlines.
C. Dimensions should be repeated on each view.
D. Three-fourths of the dimensions should be placed on the front view.

_____ 4. In the _____ dimensioning system, all dimension figures are placed to be read from the bottom of the drawing.
A. aligned
B. decimal inch
C. unidirectional
D. dual

_____ 5. The following drawing is an example of _____ dimensioning.
A. point-to-point
B. coordinate
C. tabular
D. ordinate

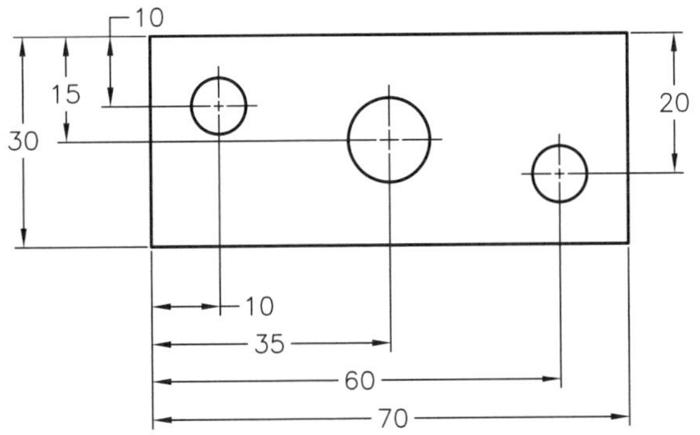

Name ____________________

_______ 6. Of the following, which is considered good dimensioning practice?
A. Dimension lines should be drawn thicker than object lines.
B. Aligned dimensioning is the preferred practice in comparison to unidirectional dimensioning.
C. Avoid crossing dimension lines with extension lines or leaders whenever possible.
D. Duplicate dimensions take extra time but add to the clarity of a drawing.

Completion

Write the correct answer in the space provided.

7. The two general types of dimensions used on drawings are _____ and _____ dimensions.
8. Notes that provide specific information, such as the size of a hole, are referred to as _____ notes.

Drafting Performance

9. Select the necessary views and prepare a drawing of a problem selected by your instructor from the Drawing Problems section of Chapter 9 in your textbook. Dimension the drawing using proper dimensioning practices.

Rules for Good Dimensioning

The following rules will serve as guides to good dimensioning practices.

- Take time to plan the location of dimension lines. Avoid crowding by providing adequate room for spacing (at least .40″ (10 mm) for the first line and .25″ (6 mm) for successive lines).
- Dimension lines should be thin and should contrast noticeably with object lines on the drawing.
- Dimension each feature in the view that most completely shows the characteristic contour of that feature.
- Dimensions should be placed between the views to which they relate and outside the outline of the part.
- Extension lines are gapped away from the object approximately .06" (1.5 mm) and extend beyond the dimension line approximately .125" (3 mm). Extension lines may cross other extension lines or object lines when necessary. Avoid crossing dimension lines with extension lines or leaders whenever possible.
- Show dimensions between points, lines, or surfaces that have a necessary and specific relation to each other.
- Dimensions should be placed on visible outlines rather than hidden lines.
- State each dimension clearly so that it can be interpreted in only one way.
- Dimensions must be sufficiently complete for size, form, and location of features so that no calculating or assuming of distances or locations is necessary.
- Avoid duplication of dimensions. Only dimensions that provide essential information should be shown.
- In chain dimensioning, one dimension in a dimension chain should be omitted (architectural and structural drawing excepted) to avoid location of a feature from more than one point.

RM 9-1

Inch-Metric Equivalents

INCHES		MILLI-METERS
FRACTIONS	DECIMALS	
	.00394	.1
	.00787	.2
	.01181	.3
1/64	.015625	.3969
	.01575	.4
	.01969	.5
	.02362	.6
	.02756	.7
1/32	.03125	.7938
	.0315	.8
	.03543	.9
	.03937	1.00
3/64	.046875	1.1906
1/16	.0625	1.5875
5/64	.078125	1.9844
	.07874	2.00
3/32	.09375	2.3813
7/64	.109375	2.7781
	.11811	3.00
1/8	.125	3.175
9/64	.140625	3.5719
5/32	.15625	3.9688
	.15748	4.00
11/64	.171875	4.3656
3/16	.1875	4.7625
	.19685	5.00
13/64	.203125	5.1594
7/32	.21875	5.5563
15/64	.234375	5.9531
	.23622	6.00
1/4	.2500	6.35
17/64	.265625	6.7469
	.27559	7.00
9/32	.28125	7.1438
19/64	.296875	7.5406
5/16	.3125	7.9375
	.31496	8.00
21/64	.328125	8.3344
11/32	.34375	8.7313
	.35433	9.00
23/64	.359375	9.1281
3/8	.375	9.525
25/64	.390625	9.9219
	.3937	10.00
13/32	.40625	10.3188
27/64	.421875	10.7156
	.43307	11.00
7/16	.4375	11.1125
29/64	.453125	11.5094

INCHES		MILLI-METERS
FRACTIONS	DECIMALS	
15/32	.46875	11.9063
	.47244	12.00
31/64	.484375	12.3031
1/2	.5000	12.70
	.51181	13.00
33/64	.515625	13.0969
17/32	.53125	13.4938
35/64	.546875	13.8907
	.55118	14.00
9/16	.5625	14.2875
37/64	.578125	14.6844
	.59055	15.00
19/32	.59375	15.0813
39/64	.609375	15.4782
5/8	.625	15.875
	.62992	16.00
41/64	.640625	16.2719
21/32	.65625	16.6688
	.66929	17.00
43/64	.671875	17.0657
11/16	.6875	17.4625
45/64	.703125	17.8594
	.70866	18.00
23/32	.71875	18.2563
47/64	.734375	18.6532
	.74803	19.00
3/4	.7500	19.05
49/64	.765625	19.4469
25/32	.78125	19.8438
	.7874	20.00
51/64	.796875	20.2407
13/16	.8125	20.6375
	.82677	21.00
53/64	.828125	21.0344
27/32	.84375	21.4313
55/64	.859375	21.8282
	.86614	22.00
7/8	.875	22.225
57/64	.890625	22.6219
	.90551	23.00
29/32	.90625	23.0188
59/64	.921875	23.4157
15/16	.9375	23.8125
	.94488	24.00
61/64	.953125	24.2094
31/32	.96875	24.6063
	.98425	25.00
63/64	.984375	25.0032
1	1.0000	25.4000

RM 9-2

Size and Location Dimensions

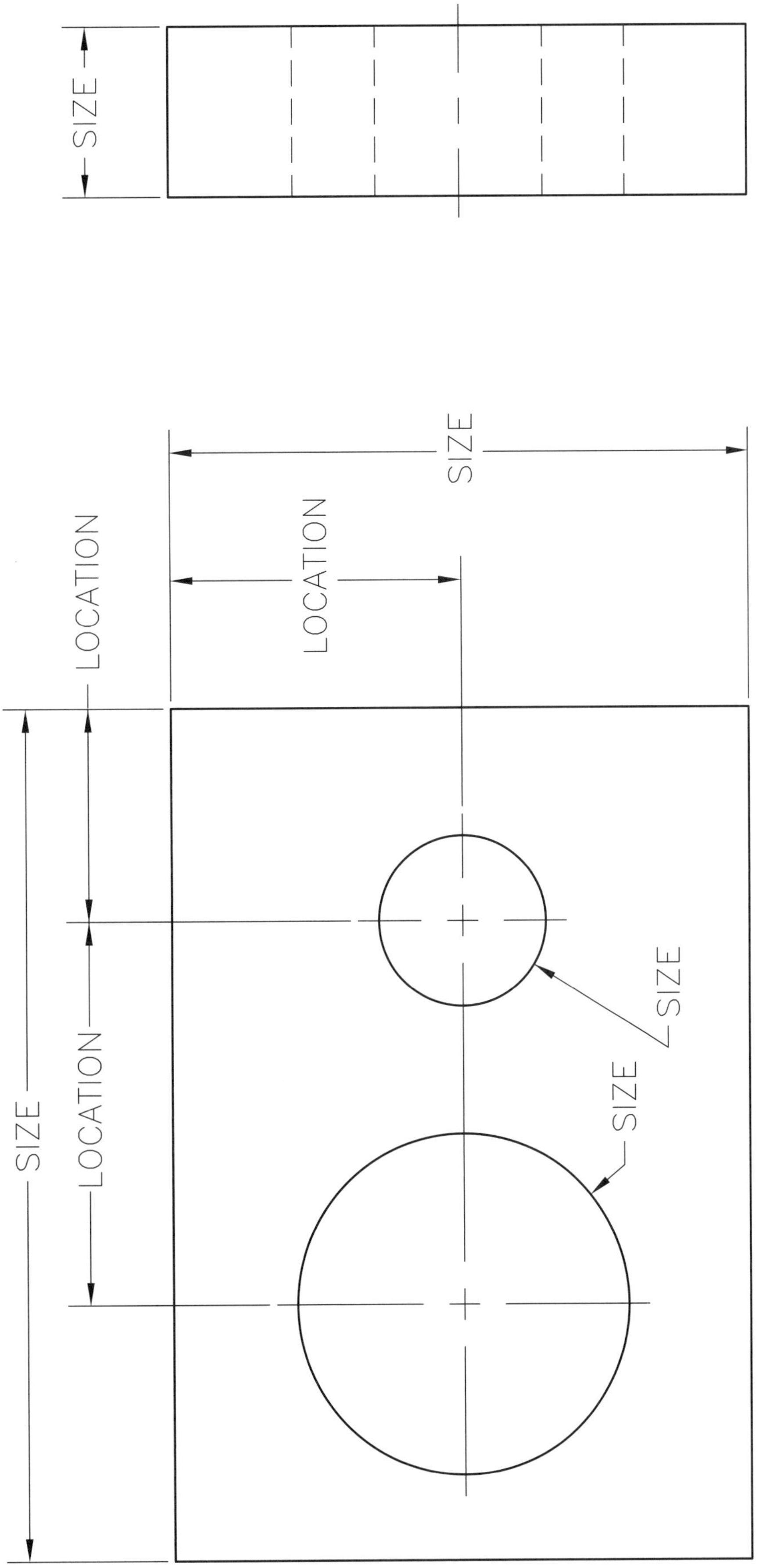

SIZE
SIZE
LOCATION
LOCATION
SIZE
LOCATION
SIZE
SIZE

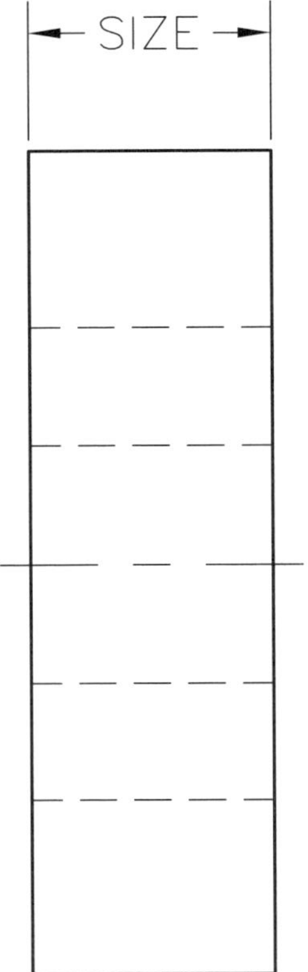

RM 9-3

Unidirectional and Aligned Dimensions

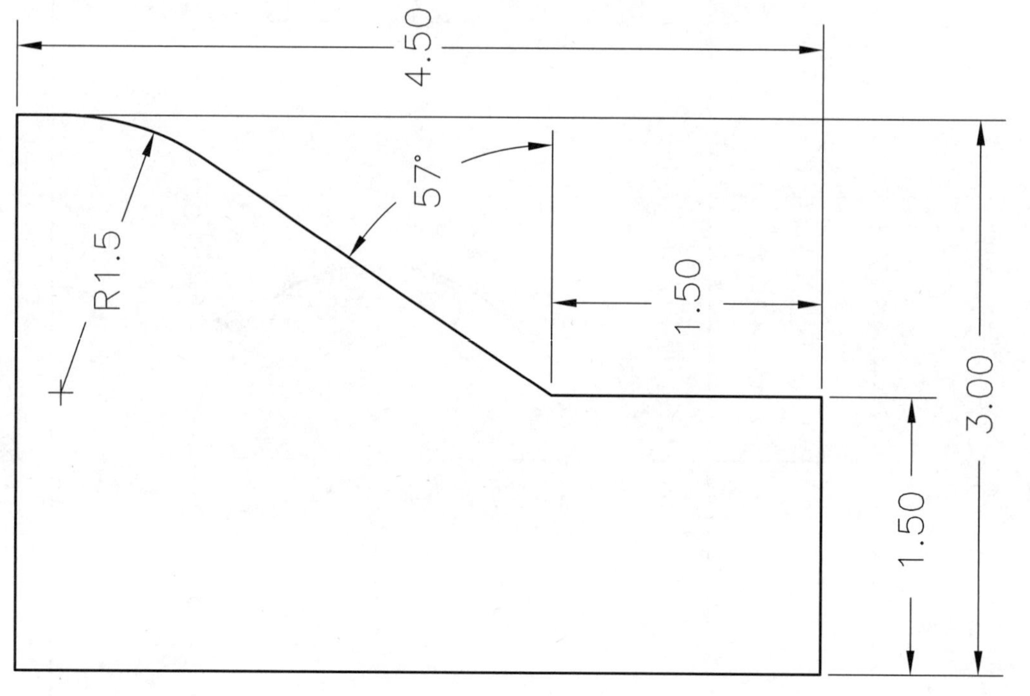

Unidirectional Dimensions

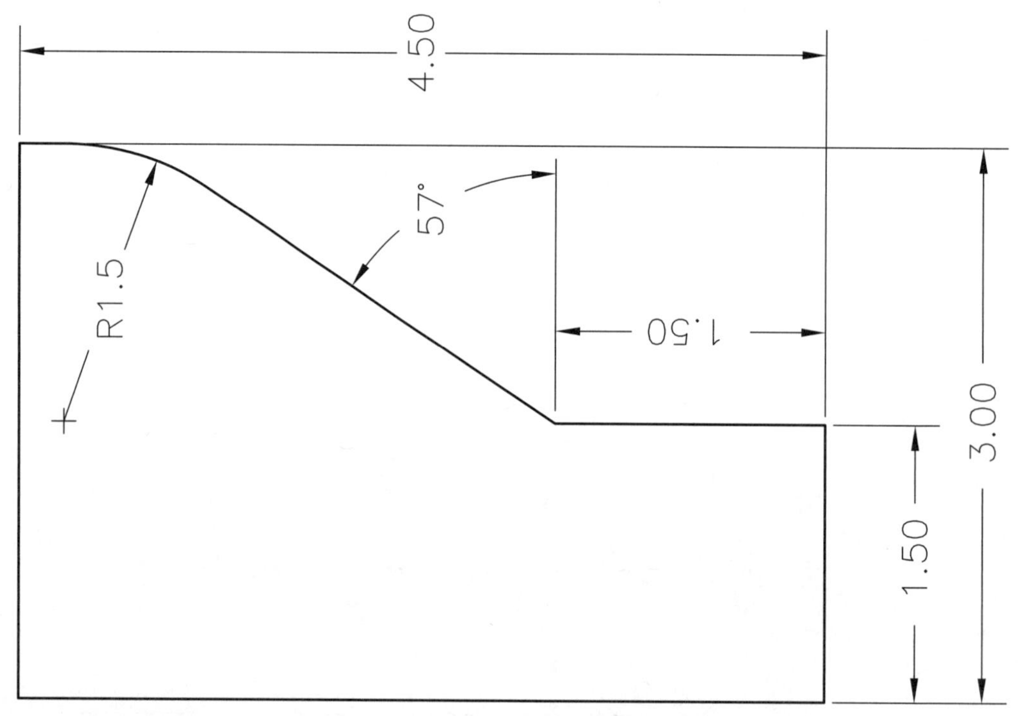

Aligned Dimensions

RM 9-4

Rectangular Coordinate Dimensioning

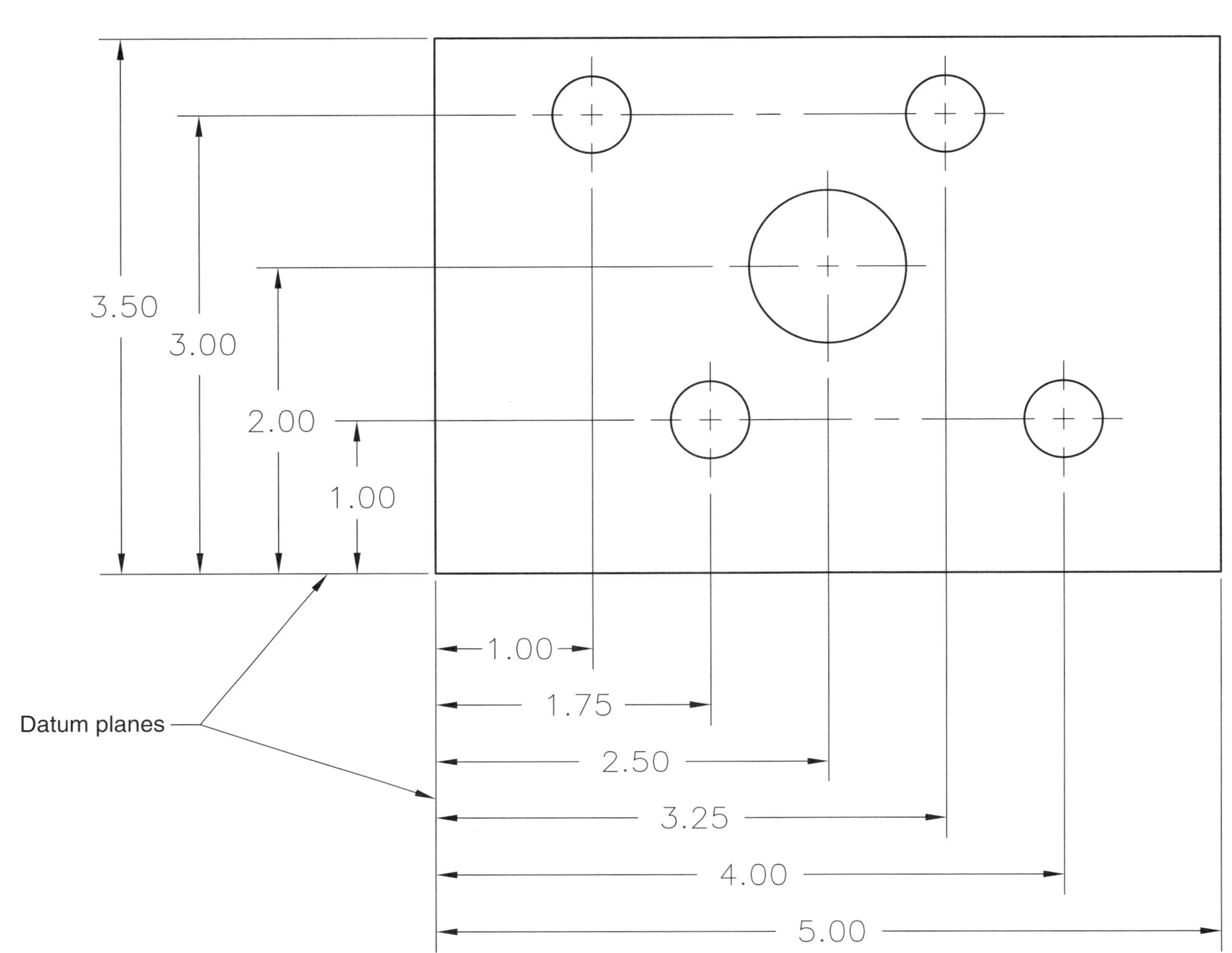

RM 9-5

Procedure Checklist

Dimensioning Fundamentals

Name ______________________________

Observable Items	Completed		Comments	Instructor Initials
	Yes	No		
1. Draws dimension lines.				
2. Draws extension lines.				
3. Draws leaders.				
4. Constructs arrowheads.				
5. Adds fractional dimensions.				
6. Adds decimal dimensions.				
7. Dimensions fillets and corners.				
8. Dimensions angles.				
9. Dimensions chamfers.				
10. Dimensions features using symbols.				
11. Dimensions irregular curves.				
12. Dimensions a drawing using tabular dimensioning.				
13. Adds notes to a drawing.				

Instructor Signature ______________________________

Section Views

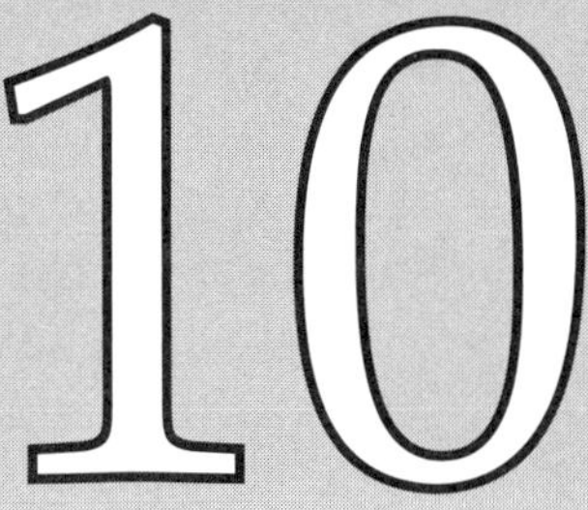

Learning Objectives

After studying this chapter, the student will be able to:

- Visualize a section view along a cutting plane.
- Construct section views.
- Draw various types of sections.
- Apply conventional drafting practices in sectioning.
- Describe how section views are created in CAD drafting.

Instructional Resources

Text: pages 315–346

Review Questions, pages 330–331

Drawing Problems, pages 331–346

Worksheets: pages 68–82

- Worksheet 10-1: *Box End Cap*
- Worksheet 10-2: *Sleeve*
- Worksheet 10-3: *Orifice*
- Worksheet 10-4: *Sleeve Pressure Regulator*
- Worksheet 10-5: *Piston*
- Worksheet 10-6: *Handwheel*
- Worksheet 10-7: *Lower Eccentric*
- Worksheet 10-8: *Right-Hand Cap*
- Worksheet 10-9: *Pitot Override Cover*
- Worksheet 10-10: *Pivot Pin*
- Worksheet 10-11: *Hub*
- Worksheet 10-12: *Sheave*
- Worksheet 10-13: *Barrel*
- Worksheet 10-14: *Tool Holder Bushing*
- Worksheet 10-15: *Fan Bracket*

Instructor's Resource

Instructional Tasks

Instructional Aids and Assignments

Chapter 10 Quiz

Reproducible Masters

- Reproducible Master 10-1: *Types of Section Views*. The common types of section views are identified and defined.
- Reproducible Master 10-2: *Thin Sections*. Two examples of objects drawn as thin sections are shown.

Procedure Checklist

Color Transparencies (Binder/IRCD only)

- Transparency 10-1: *Full Section*. A drawing of an object with a full section view is shown.
- Transparency 10-2: *Half Section*. A drawing of an object with a half section view is shown.
- Transparency 10-3: *Revolved Sections*. Drawings of several objects with revolved section views are shown.
- Transparency 10-4: *Removed Sections*. Several removed section views from a single object are shown.
- Transparency 10-5: *Offset Section*. A drawing of an object with an offset section view is shown.
- Transparency 10-6: *Broken-Out Section*. A drawing of an object with a broken-out section view is shown.
- Transparency 10-7: *Aligned Section*. A drawing of an object with an aligned section view is shown.

Instructional Tasks

1. Visualize a section view along a cutting plane.
   - Discuss the purpose of section views.
   - Discuss how the viewing direction is determined for a given section view.
   - Display a cutaway of a machine part to show a section view of the interior.
   - Show a multimedia presentation, film, or color transparency of a section view.
2. Explain how to construct section views.
   - Discuss the projection and placement of views.
   - Demonstrate the construction of section lines.

- Discuss the representation of lines behind the cutting plane.

3. Explain how to apply conventional sectioning practices.
   - Discuss the purpose of conventional sectioning practices.
   - Discuss the types of conventional sectioning practices and their uses.

Instructional Aids and Assignments

1. Show a multimedia presentation or film on section views.
2. Display machine parts and architectural examples that have portions cut away to expose interior detail.
3. Show examples of industrial drawings with section views.
4. Assign the drawing problems in the textbook. The number of problems is sufficient to assign a minimum number to all students and to identify problems that may be done for extra credit. Some problems may be used for the performance section of the chapter quiz.

Answers to Review Questions, Text

Pages 330–331

1. cutting plane
2. They indicate the direction in which the section is viewed.
3. section
4. The **Hatch** command.
5. 45
6. 1/8, 3/16
7. Yes.
8. Answer may include any five of the following: Full sections, half sections, revolved sections, removed sections, offset sections, broken-out sections, aligned sections, thin sections, auxiliary sections, partial sections, phantom sections, and unlined sections.
9. full
10. half
11. revolved
12. removed
13. offset
14. aligned
15. auxiliary
16. A hidden section.
17. "S"
18. D. None of the above features are typically sectioned.
19. under
20. hatching
21. The ANSI31 pattern.
22. hatch boundary

Solutions to Drawing Problems, Text

Pages 331–346

Student work should look like the following drawings. The problem number and title are indicated on each problem sheet.

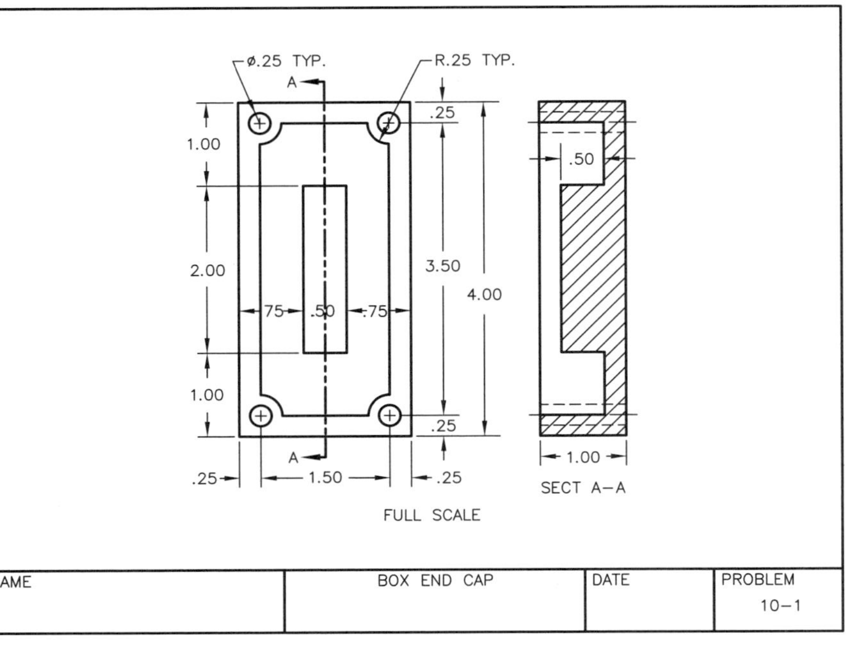
ø.25 TYP.
R.25 TYP.
A
A
.25
.25
1.00
2.00
1.00
3.50
4.00
.75
.50
.75
.50
.25
1.50
.25
1.00
SECT A–A
FULL SCALE
NAME
BOX END CAP
DATE
PROBLEM
10–1

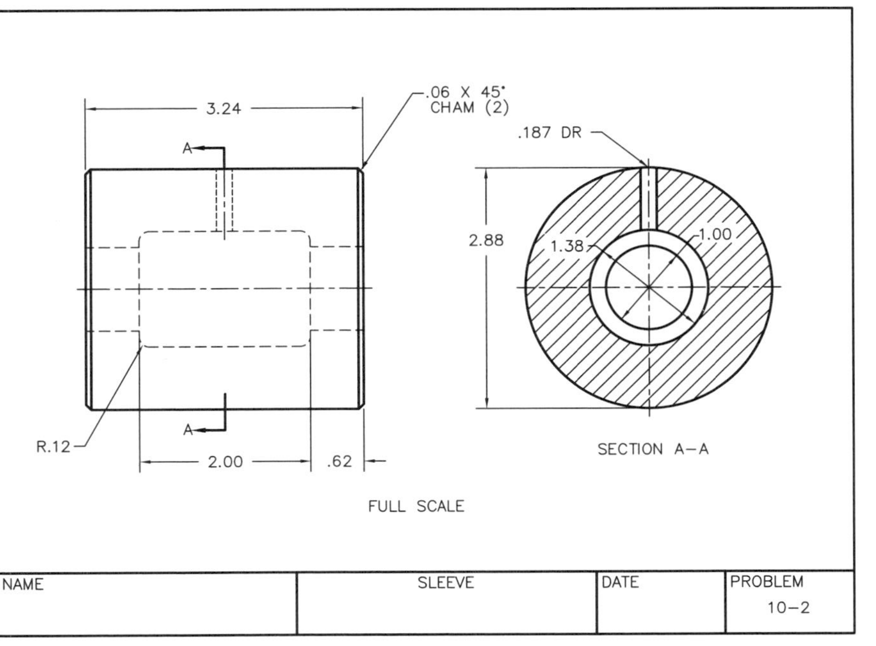
3.24
.06 X 45°
CHAM (2)
.187 DR
A
A
2.88
1.38
1.00
R.12
2.00
.62
SECTION A–A
FULL SCALE
NAME
SLEEVE
DATE
PROBLEM
10–2

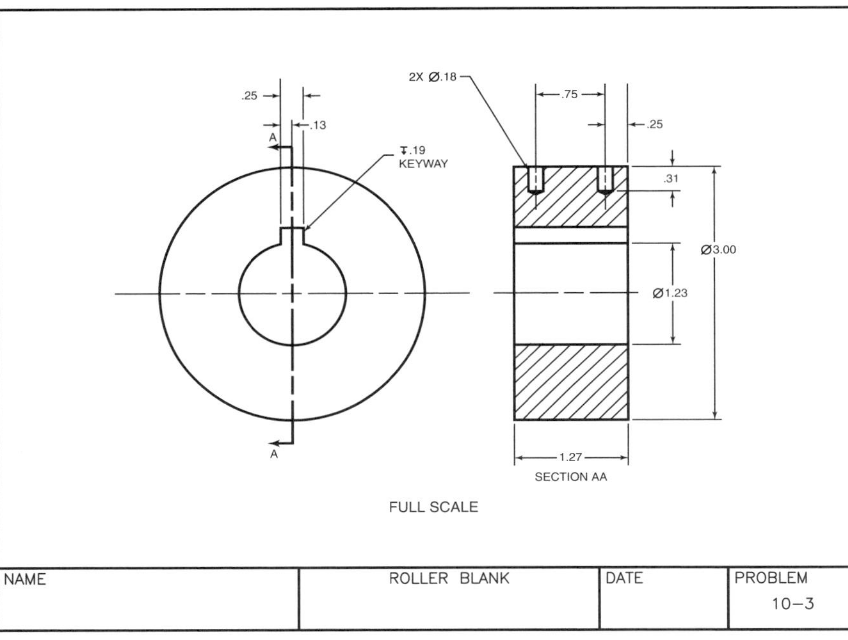
2X Ø.18
.25
.13
A
A
⊽.19
KEYWAY
.75
.25
.31
Ø3.00
Ø1.23
1.27
SECTION AA
FULL SCALE
NAME
ROLLER BLANK
DATE
PROBLEM
10–3

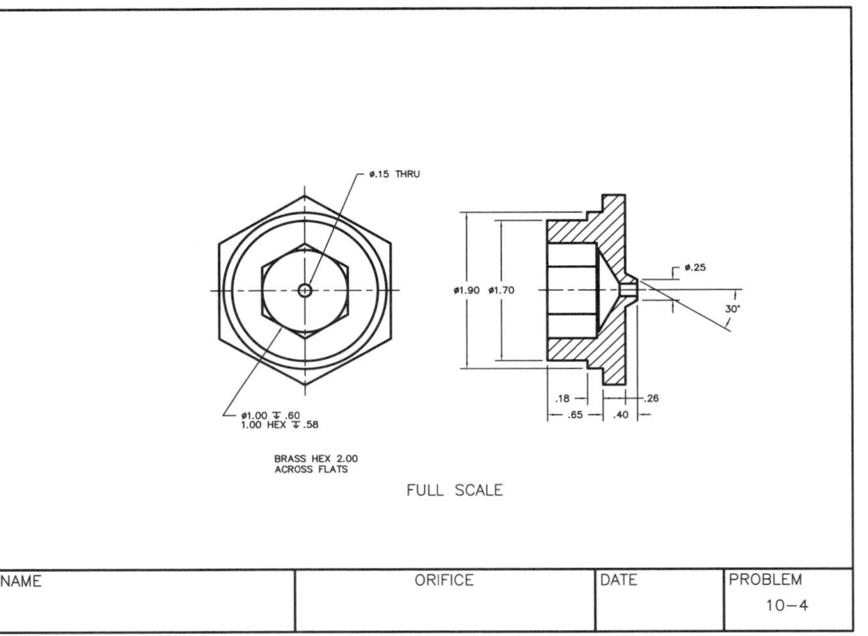
ø.15 THRU
ø.25
ø1.90 ø1.70
30°
.18
.26
.65
.40
ø1.00 ⊽.60
1.00 HEX ⊽.58
BRASS HEX 2.00
ACROSS FLATS
FULL SCALE
NAME
ORIFICE
DATE
PROBLEM
10–4

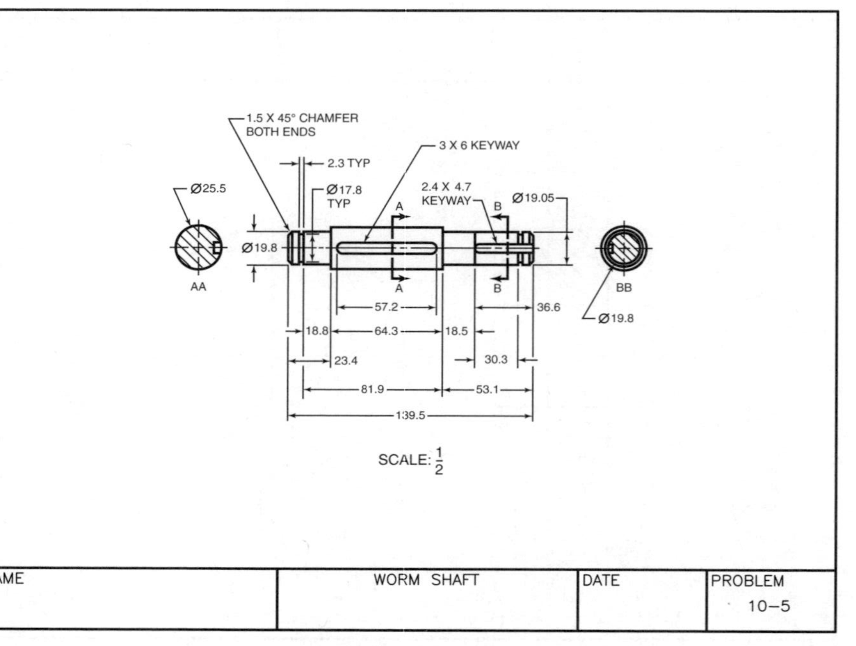
1.5 X 45° CHAMFER
BOTH ENDS
3 X 6 KEYWAY
2.3 TYP
Ø25.5
Ø17.8
TYP
2.4 X 4.7
KEYWAY
Ø19.05
Ø19.8
AA
BB
57.2
36.6
18.8
64.3
18.5
23.4
30.3
81.9
53.1
139.5
SCALE: 1/2
NAME
WORM SHAFT
DATE
PROBLEM
10–5

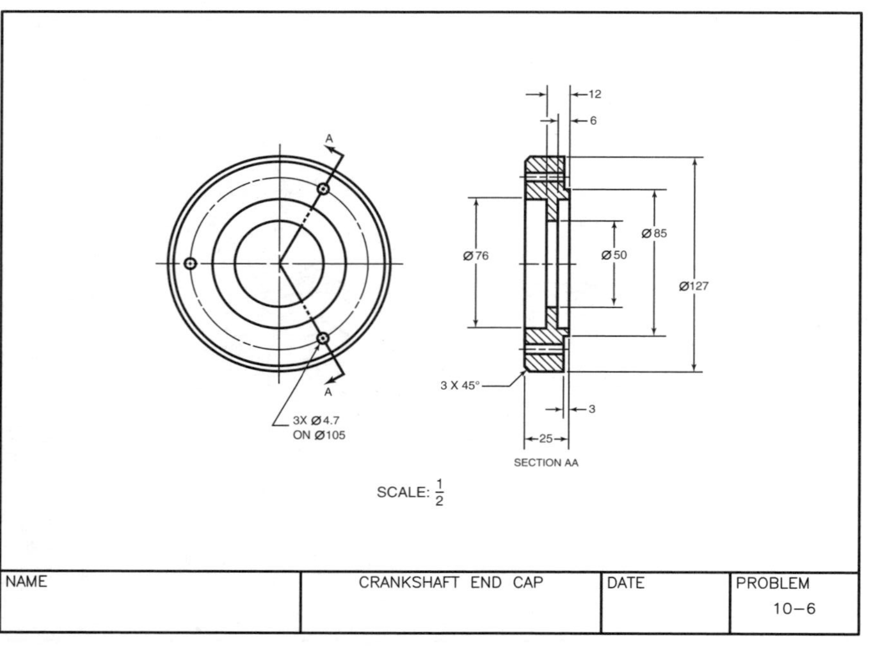
12
6
Ø85
Ø76
Ø50
Ø127
3 X 45°
3
3X Ø4.7
ON Ø105
25
SECTION AA
SCALE: 1/2
NAME
CRANKSHAFT END CAP
DATE
PROBLEM
10–6

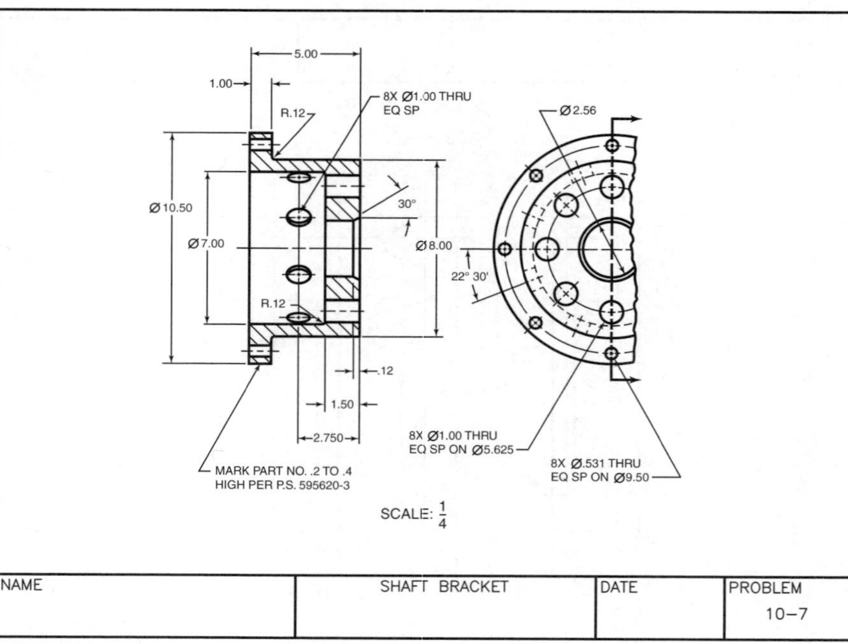
5.00
1.00
8X Ø1.00 THRU
EQ SP
R.12
Ø2.56
Ø10.50
30°
Ø7.00
Ø8.00
22° 30'
.12
1.50
2.750
8X Ø1.00 THRU
EQ SP ON Ø5.625
8X Ø.531 THRU
EQ SP ON Ø9.50
MARK PART NO. .2 TO .4
HIGH PER P.S. 595620-3
SCALE: 1/4
NAME
SHAFT BRACKET
DATE
PROBLEM
10–7

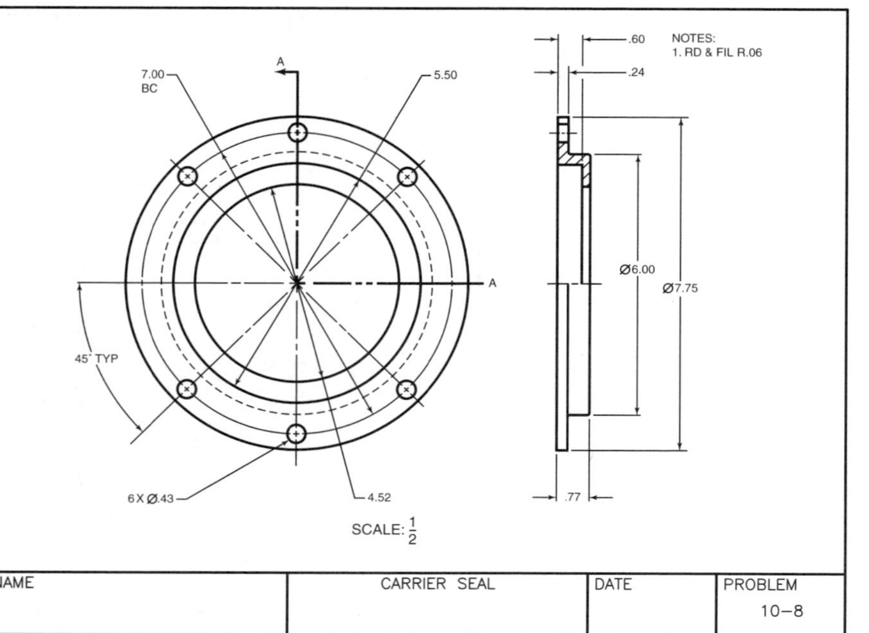
.60
NOTES:
1. RD & FIL R.06
7.00
BC
5.50
.24
Ø6.00
Ø7.75
45° TYP
6 X Ø.43
4.52
.77
SCALE: 1/2
NAME
CARRIER SEAL
DATE
PROBLEM
10–8

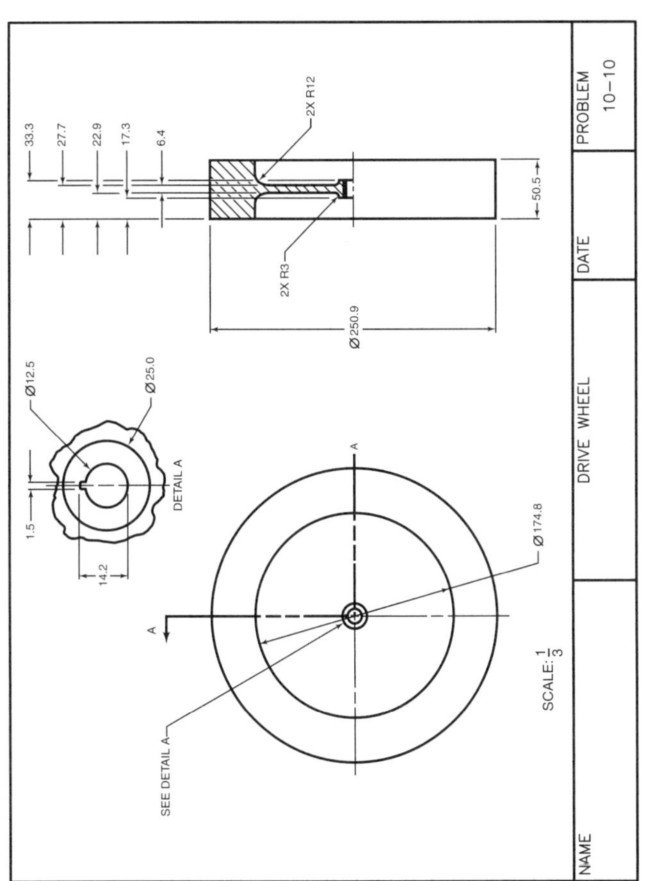
PROBLEM
10–10
DATE
DRIVE WHEEL
NAME
SCALE: 1/3
SEE DETAIL A
DETAIL A
Ø12.5
Ø25.0
1.5
14.2
Ø174.8
Ø250.9
2X R12
2X R3
50.5
33.3
27.7
22.9
17.3
6.4

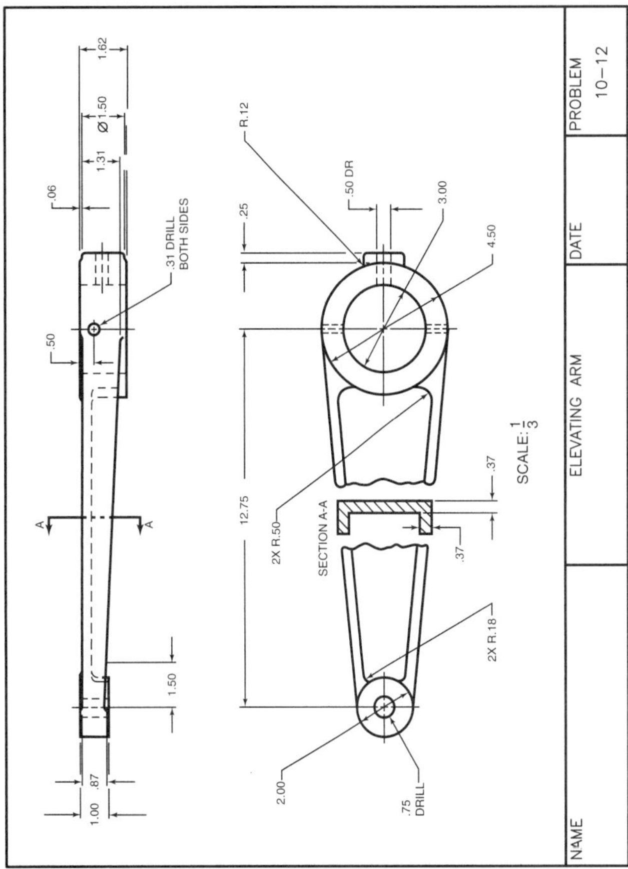
PROBLEM
10–12
DATE
ELEVATING ARM
NAME
SCALE: 1/3
SECTION A-A
.31 DRILL
BOTH SIDES
.75
DRILL
2X R.50
2X R.18
R.12
.50 DR
3.00
4.50
12.75
2.00
1.62
Ø1.50
1.31
.06
.50
.25
.37
.37
1.50
1.00
.87

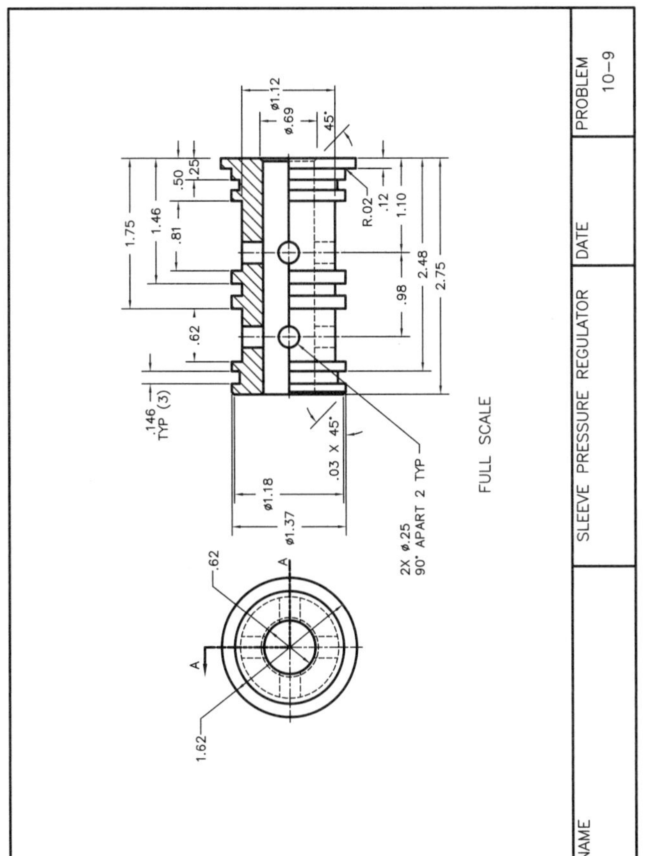
PROBLEM
10–9
DATE
SLEEVE PRESSURE REGULATOR
NAME
FULL SCALE
2X ø.25
90° APART 2 TYP
.03 X 45°
45°
R.02
.146
TYP (3)
ø1.18
ø1.37
ø1.12
ø.69
1.75
1.46
.81
.50
.25
.62
.12
1.10
.98
2.48
2.75
.62
1.62

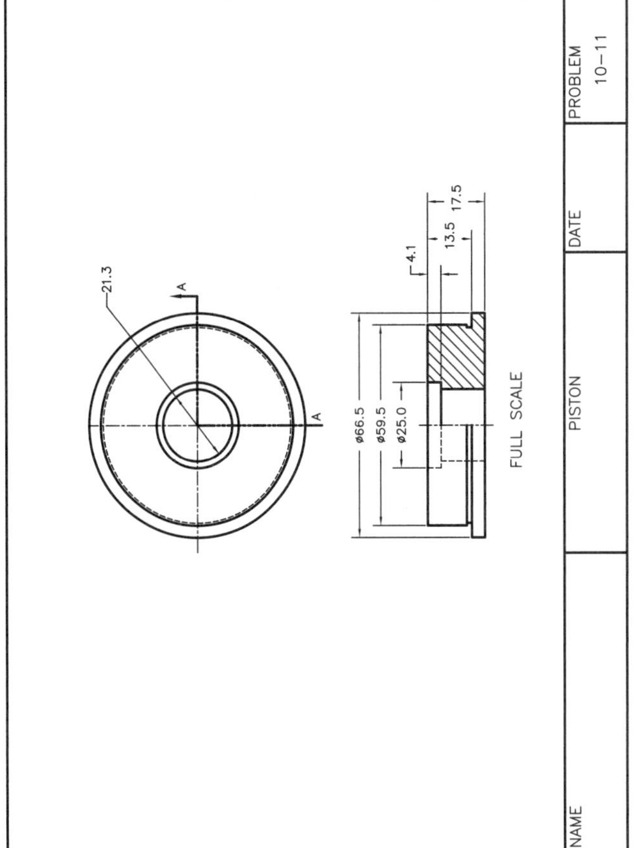
PROBLEM
10–11
DATE
PISTON
NAME
FULL SCALE
21.3
ø66.5
ø59.5
ø25.0
4.1
13.5
17.5

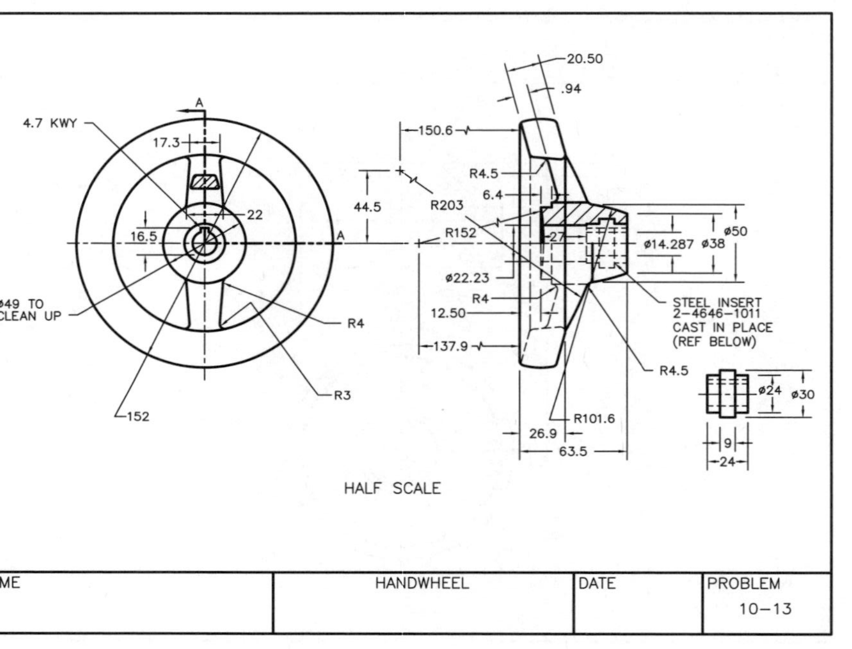

4.7 KWY
⌀49 TO CLEAN UP
STEEL INSERT 2–4646–1011 CAST IN PLACE (REF BELOW)
HALF SCALE
NAME
HANDWHEEL
DATE
PROBLEM
10–13

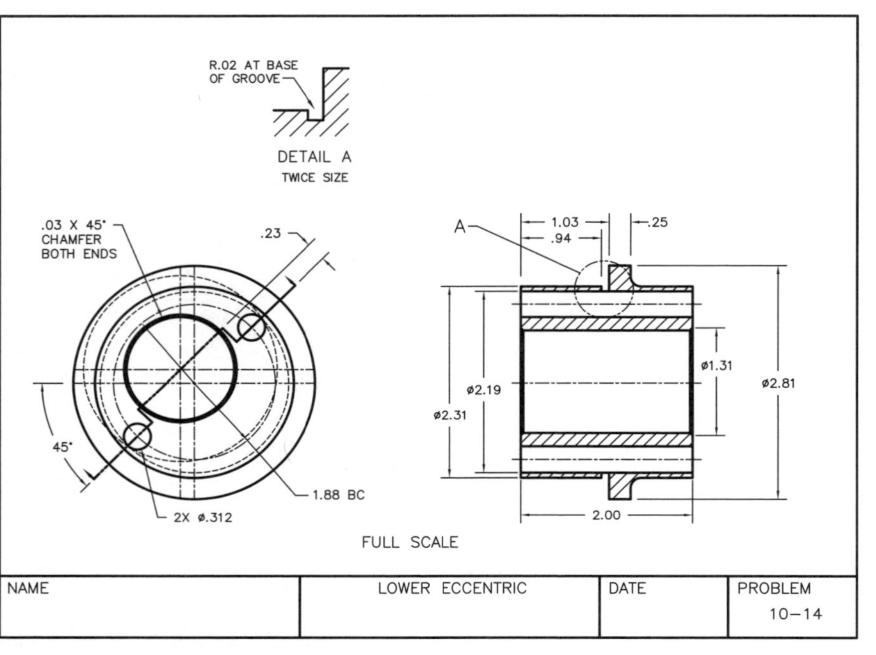

R.02 AT BASE OF GROOVE
DETAIL A
TWICE SIZE
.03 X 45° CHAMFER BOTH ENDS
2X ⌀.312
1.88 BC
FULL SCALE
NAME
LOWER ECCENTRIC
DATE
PROBLEM
10–14

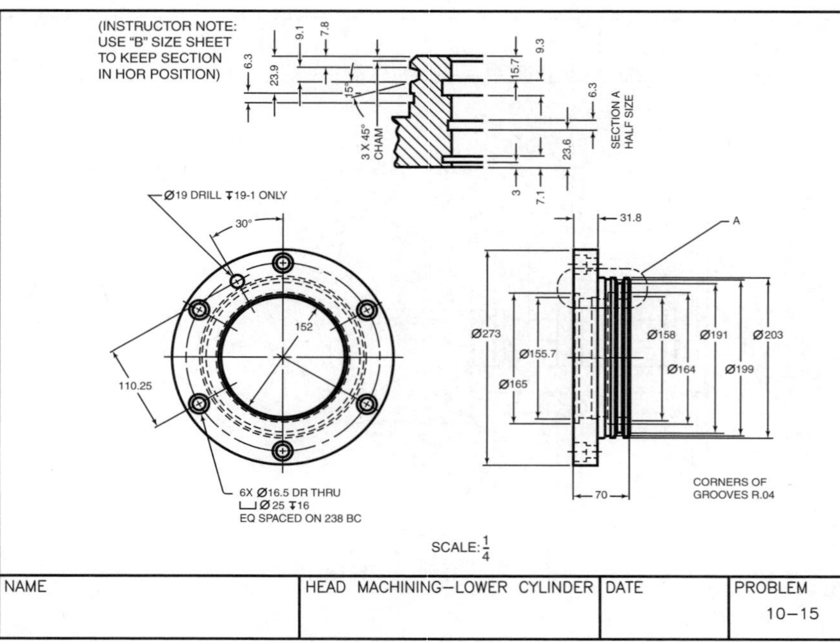

(INSTRUCTOR NOTE: USE "B" SIZE SHEET TO KEEP SECTION IN HOR POSITION)
3 X 45° CHAM
SECTION A
HALF SIZE
Ø19 DRILL ↧19-1 ONLY
6X Ø16.5 DR THRU
⌴Ø25 ↧16
EQ SPACED ON 238 BC
CORNERS OF GROOVES R.04
SCALE: 1/4
NAME
HEAD MACHINING–LOWER CYLINDER
DATE
PROBLEM
10–15

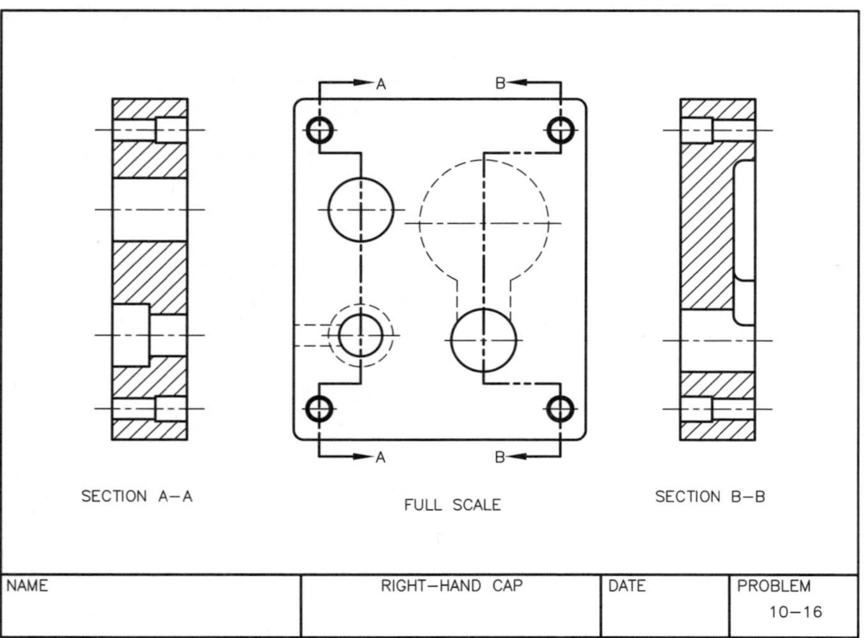

SECTION A–A
FULL SCALE
SECTION B–B
NAME
RIGHT–HAND CAP
DATE
PROBLEM
10–16

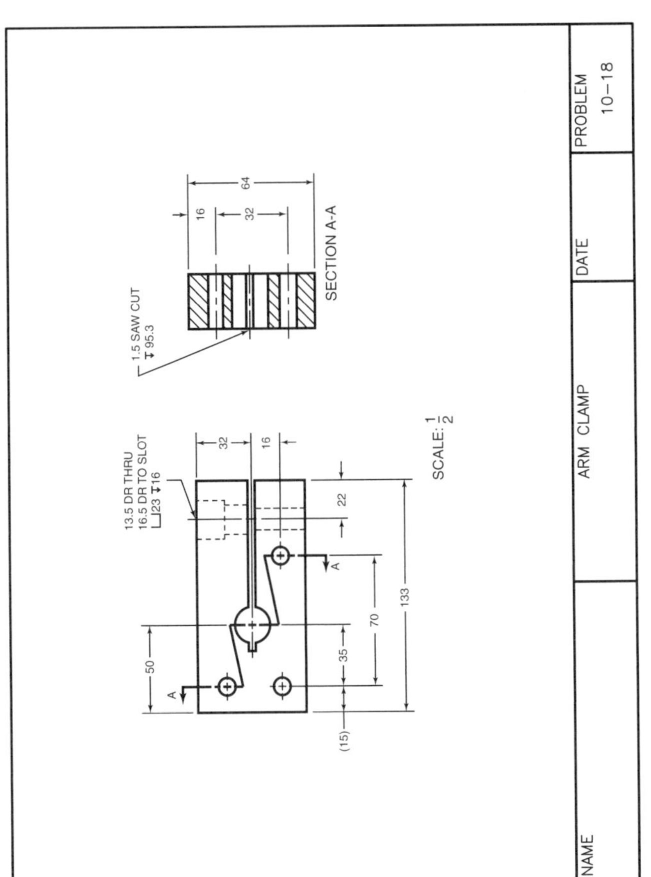
PROBLEM 10–18
DATE
ARM CLAMP
NAME
SCALE: 1/2
SECTION A-A
1.5 SAW CUT ↧95.3
13.5 DR THRU
16.5 DR TO SLOT
⌴23 ↧16
64
16
32
50
22
70
133
35
(15)
A

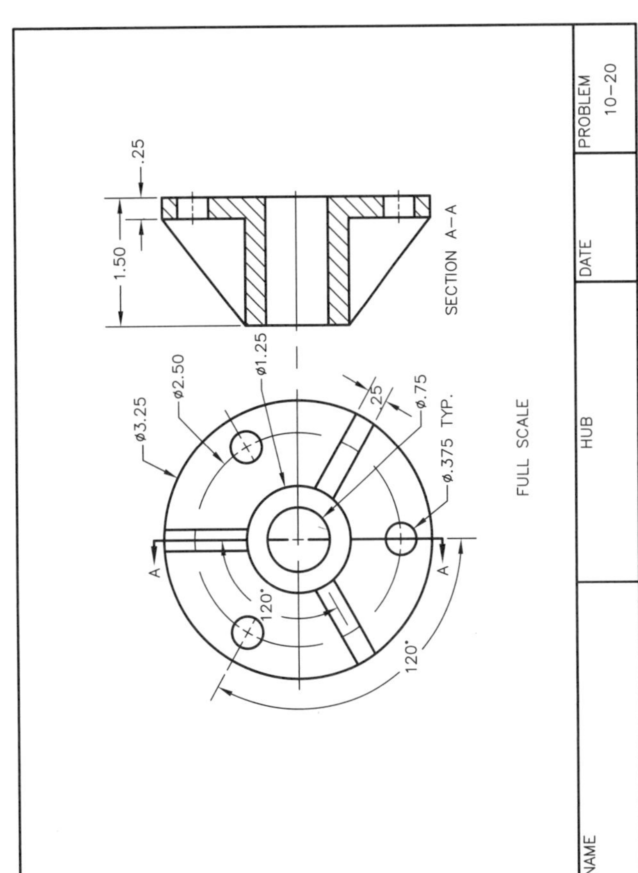
PROBLEM 10–20
DATE
HUB
NAME
FULL SCALE
SECTION A–A
.25
1.50
ø3.25
ø2.50
ø1.25
ø.75
ø.375 TYP.
120°
A

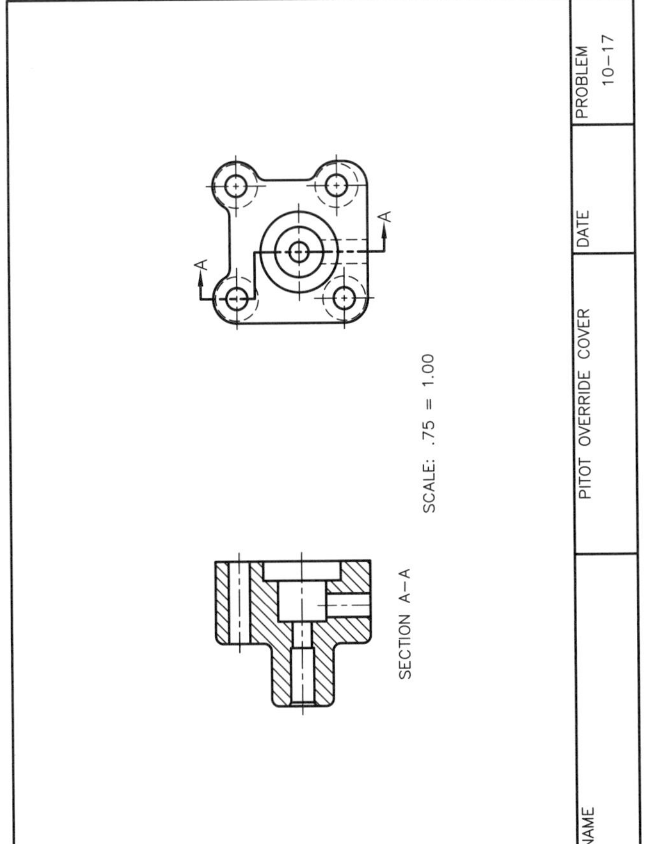
PROBLEM 10–17
DATE
PITOT OVERRIDE COVER
NAME
SCALE: .75 = 1.00
SECTION A–A
A

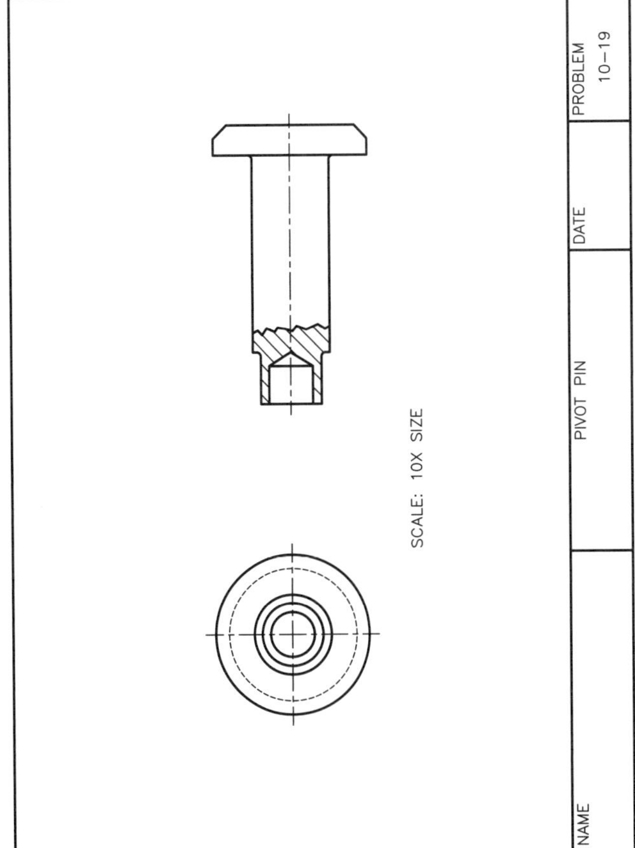
PROBLEM 10–19
DATE
PIVOT PIN
NAME
SCALE: 10X SIZE

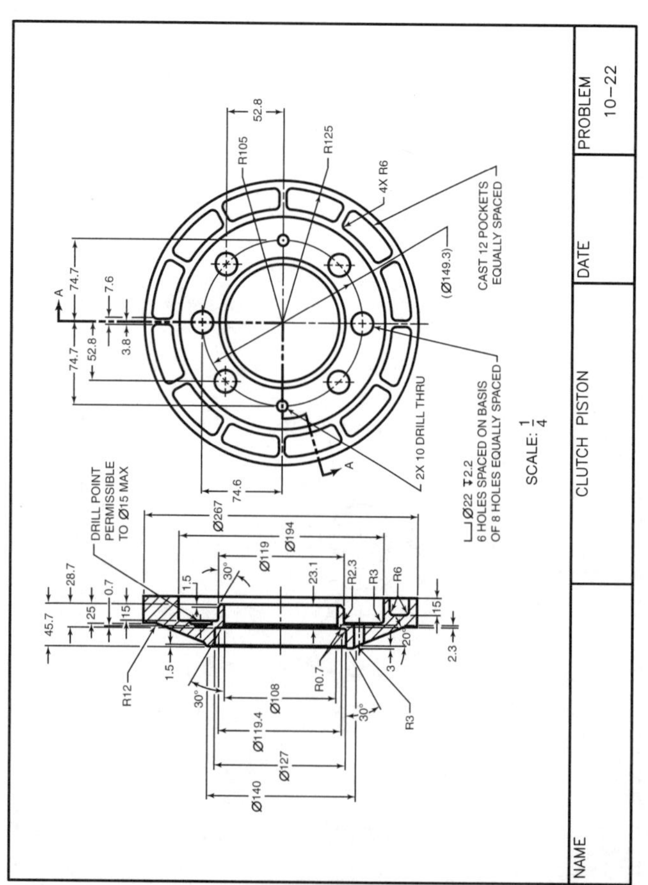
PROBLEM
10–22
DATE
CLUTCH PISTON
NAME
SCALE: 1/4
2X 10 DRILL THRU
CAST 12 POCKETS
EQUALLY SPACED
4X R6
DRILL POINT
PERMISSIBLE
TO Ø15 MAX

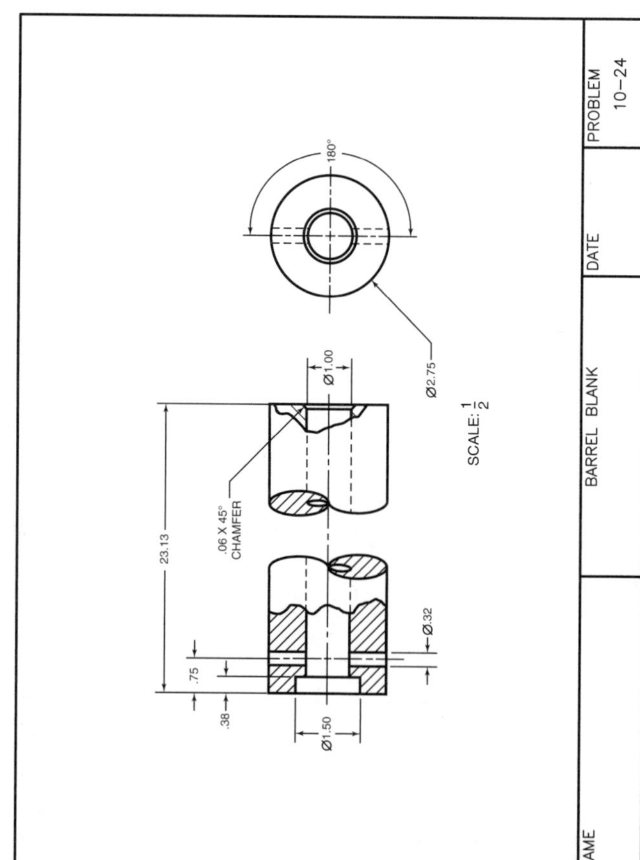
PROBLEM
10–24
DATE
BARREL BLANK
NAME
SCALE: 1/2
.06 X 45°
CHAMFER

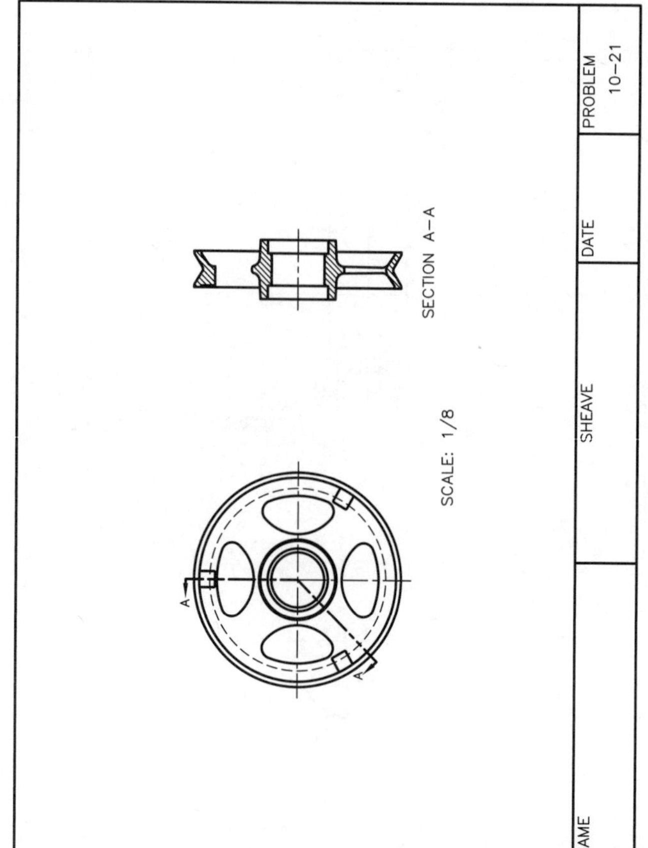
PROBLEM
10–21
DATE
SHEAVE
NAME
SCALE: 1/8
SECTION A–A

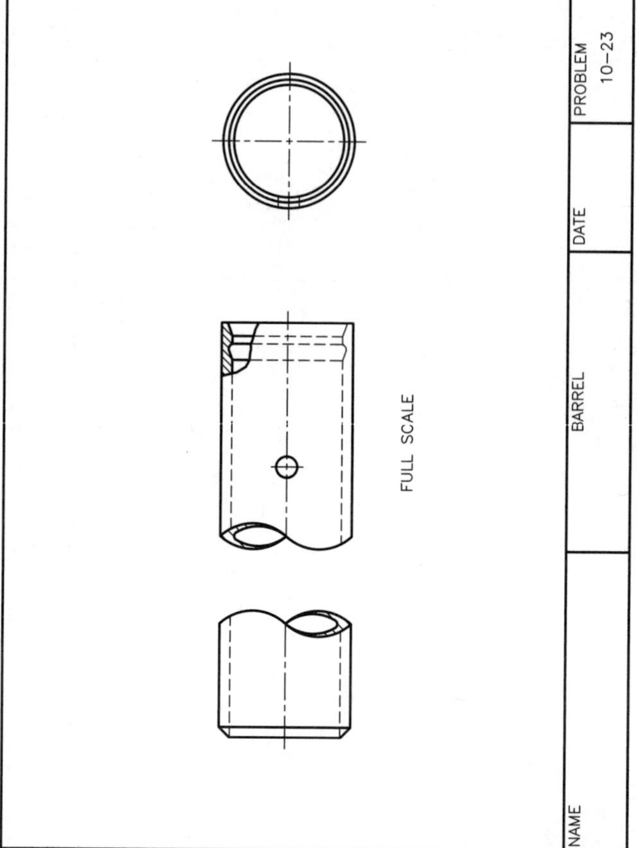
PROBLEM
10–23
DATE
BARREL
NAME
FULL SCALE

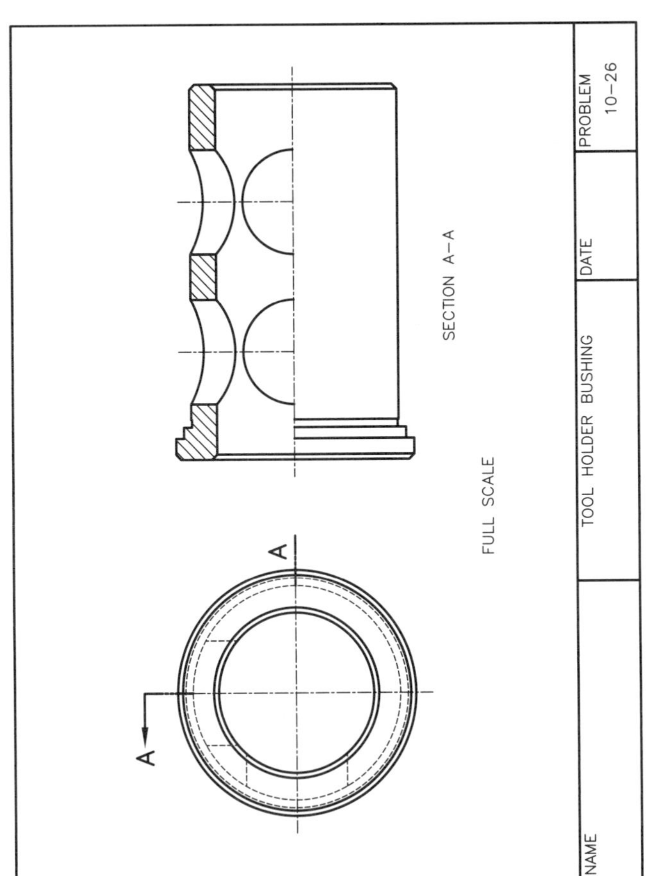
SECTION A–A
FULL SCALE
A
A
PROBLEM 10–26
DATE
TOOL HOLDER BUSHING
NAME

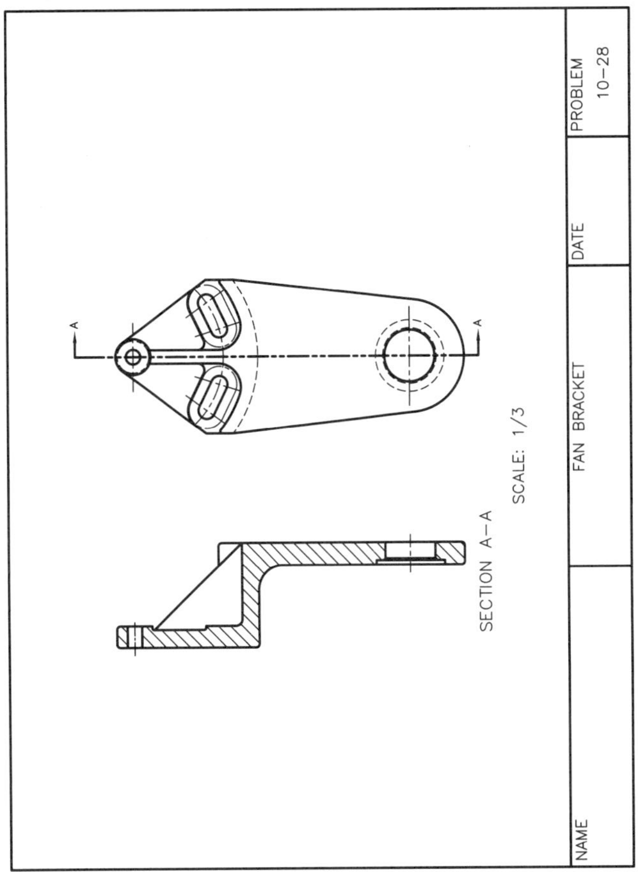
A
A
SECTION A–A
SCALE: 1/3
PROBLEM 10–28
DATE
FAN BRACKET
NAME

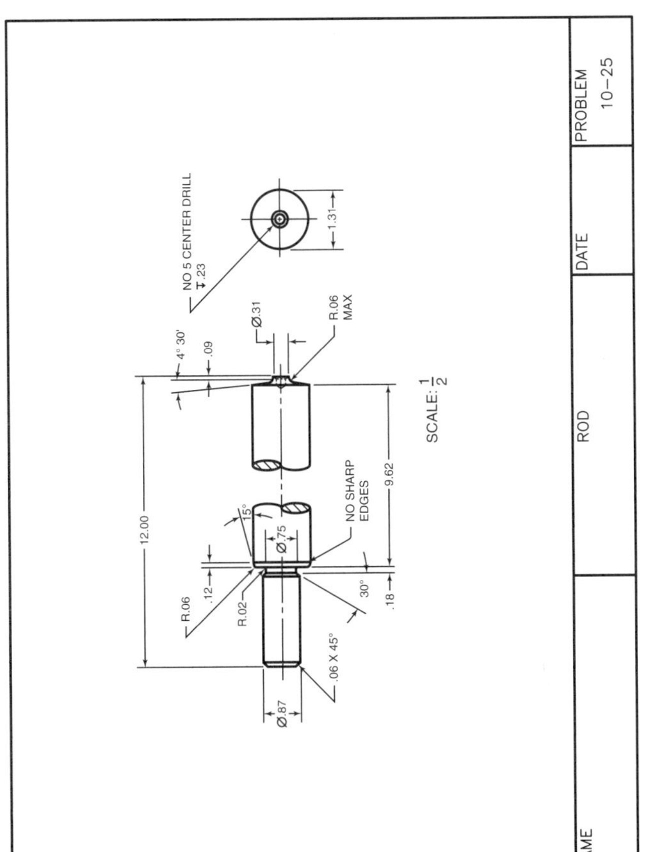
NO 5 CENTER DRILL
↧.23
4° 30'
.09
Ø.31
R.06
MAX
1.31
12.00
9.62
15°
Ø.75
NO SHARP
EDGES
.12
R.06
R.02
30°
.18
.06 X 45°
Ø.87
SCALE: 1/2
PROBLEM 10–25
DATE
ROD
NAME

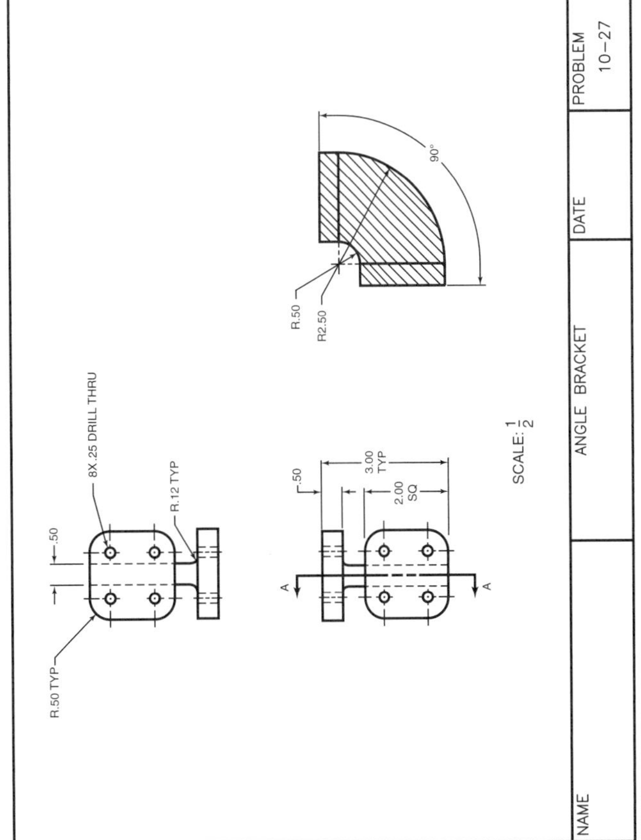
90°
R.50
R2.50
8X .25 DRILL THRU
R.12 TYP
.50
R.50 TYP
.50
3.00
TYP
2.00
SQ
A
A
SCALE: 1/2
PROBLEM 10–27
DATE
ANGLE BRACKET
NAME

Solutions to Worksheets

Pages 68–82

Student work should look like the following drawings. The problem number and title are indicated on each problem sheet.

DRAW AND DIMENSION THE NECESSARY VIEWS OF THE OBJECT, INCLUDING A FULL SECTION.
NAME
SLEEVE
DATE
PROBLEM 10–2
SECTION A–A

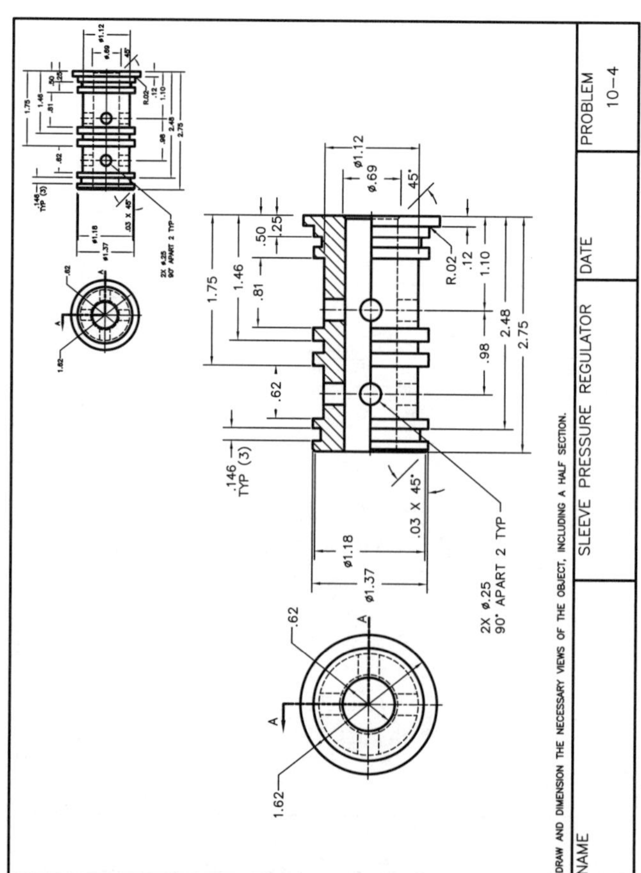

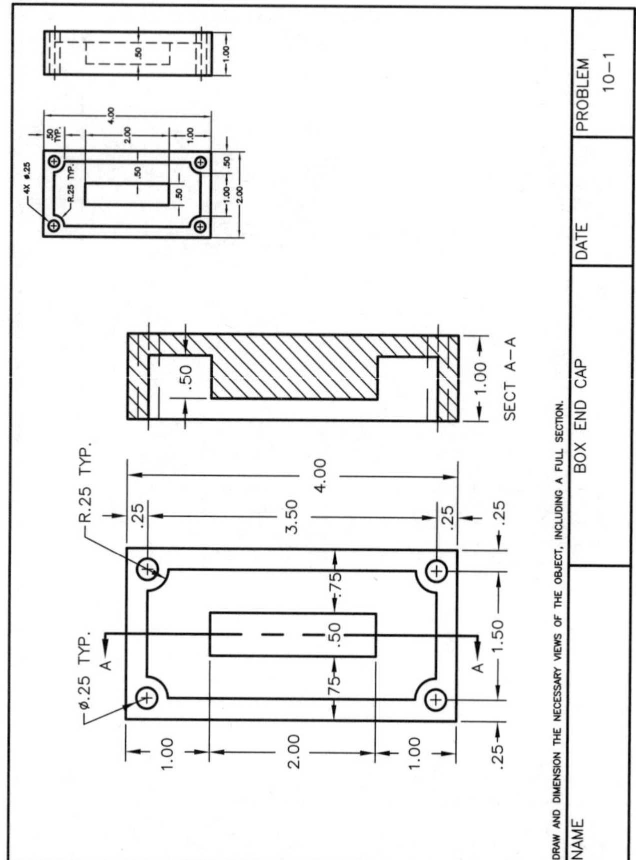

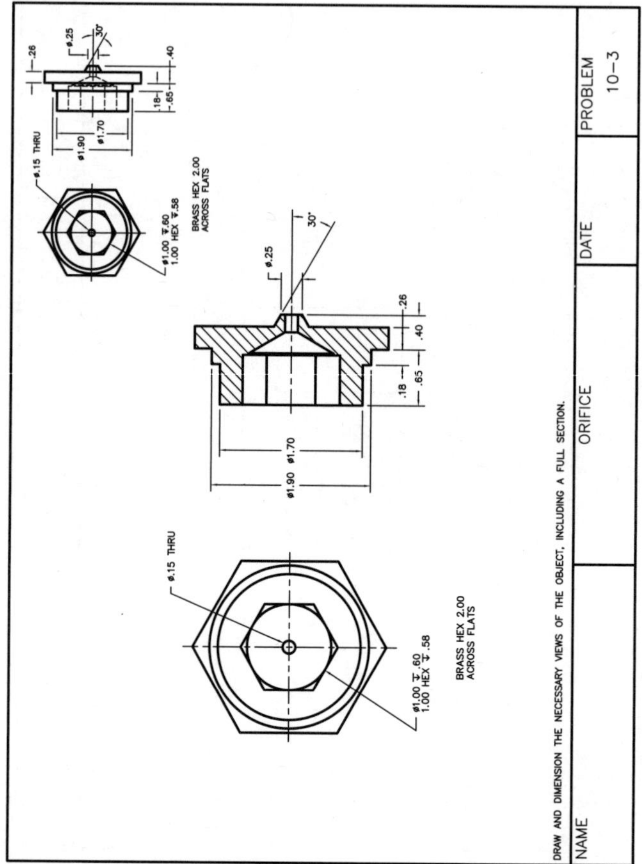

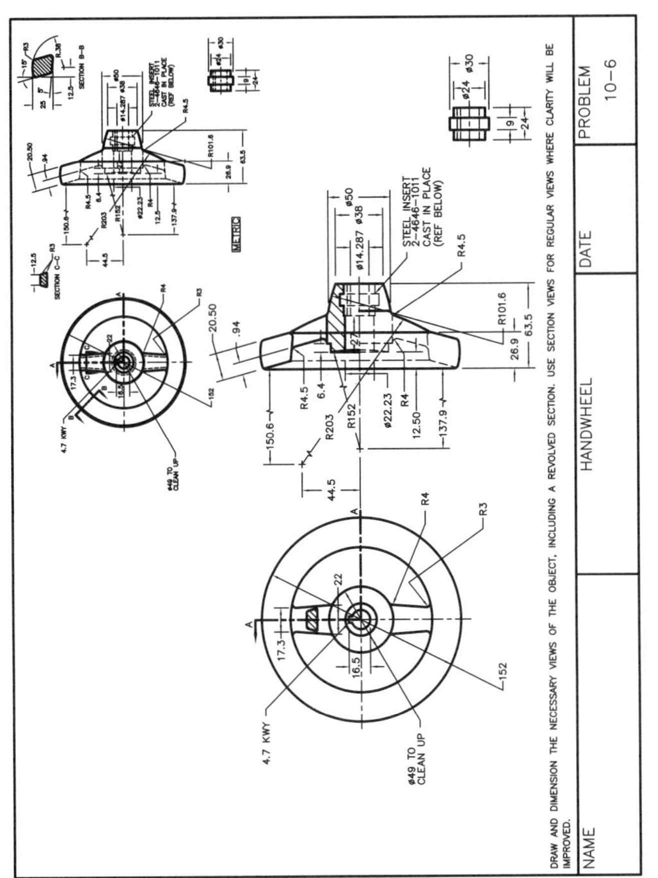
DRAW AND DIMENSION THE NECESSARY VIEWS OF THE OBJECT, INCLUDING A REVOLVED SECTION. USE SECTION VIEWS FOR REGULAR VIEWS WHERE CLARITY WILL BE IMPROVED.
NAME
HANDWHEEL
DATE
PROBLEM
10–6
4.7 KWY
ø49 TO
CLEAN UP
STEEL INSERT
2–466–1011
CAST IN PLACE
(REF BELOW)
METRIC
152
R3
R4
R4.5
R101.6
R152
R203
ø50
ø38
ø14.287
ø22.23
ø24
ø30
17.3
16.5
22
20.50
.94
150.6
137.9
44.5
6.4
12.50
26.9
63.5
9
24

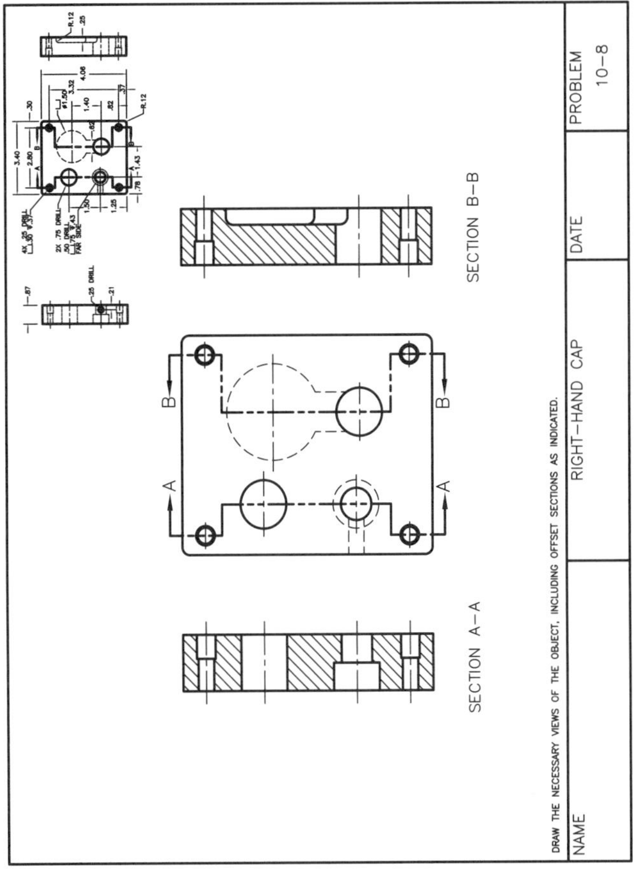
DRAW THE NECESSARY VIEWS OF THE OBJECT, INCLUDING OFFSET SECTIONS AS INDICATED.
NAME
RIGHT–HAND CAP
DATE
PROBLEM
10–8
SECTION A–A
SECTION B–B
A
B

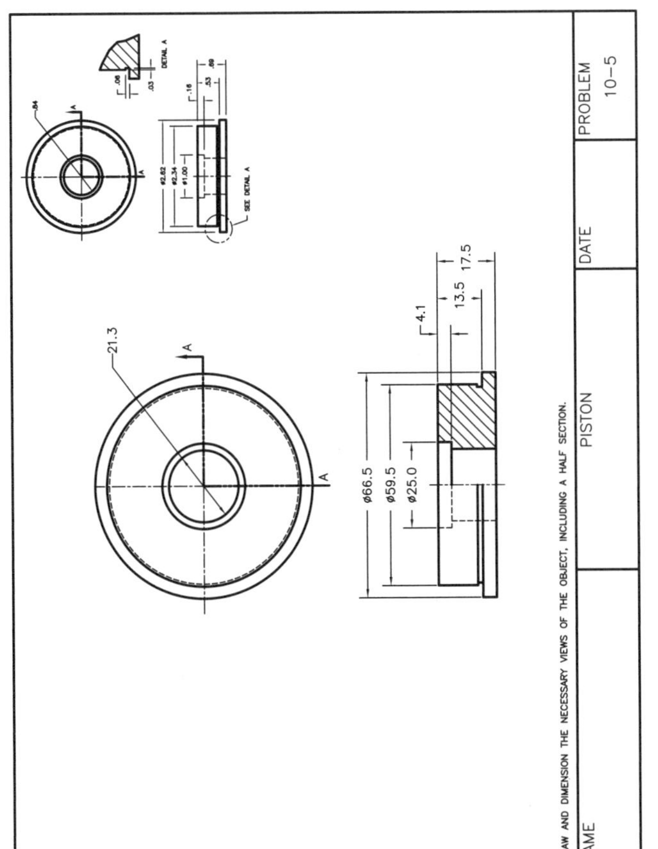
DRAW AND DIMENSION THE NECESSARY VIEWS OF THE OBJECT, INCLUDING A HALF SECTION.
NAME
PISTON
DATE
PROBLEM
10–5
21.3
A
ø66.5
ø59.5
ø25.0
4.1
13.5
17.5

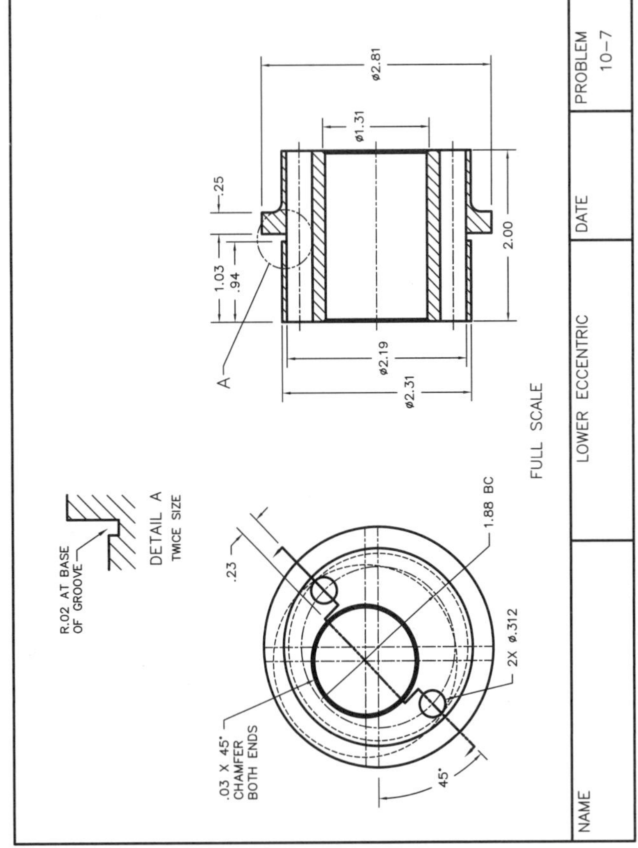
NAME
LOWER ECCENTRIC
DATE
PROBLEM
10–7
FULL SCALE
R.02 AT BASE
OF GROOVE
DETAIL A
TWICE SIZE
.03 X 45°
CHAMFER
BOTH ENDS
.23
1.88 BC
2X ø.312
45°
A
1.03
.94
.25
ø2.81
ø1.31
ø2.19
ø2.31
2.00

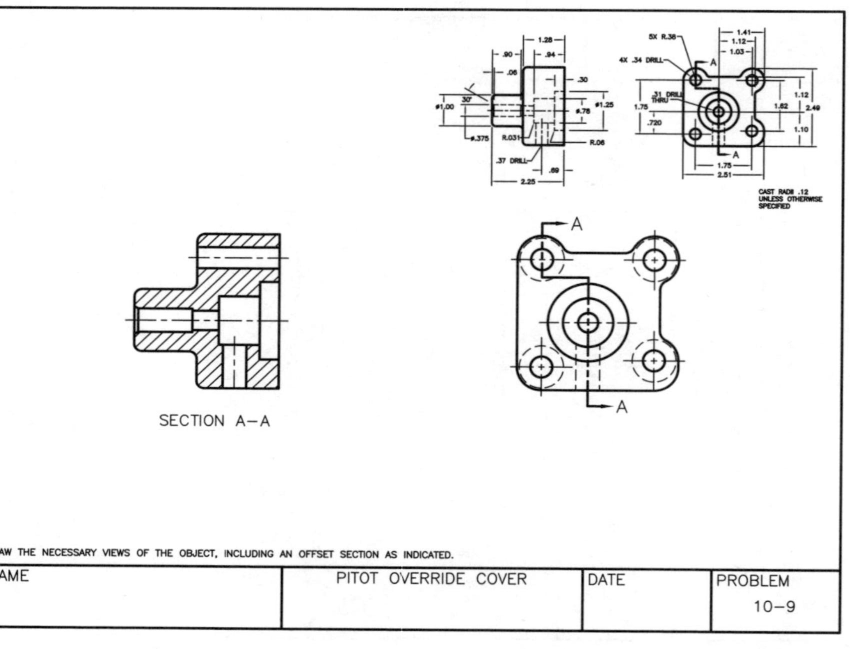
SECTION A–A
DRAW THE NECESSARY VIEWS OF THE OBJECT, INCLUDING AN OFFSET SECTION AS INDICATED.
NAME
PITOT OVERRIDE COVER
DATE
PROBLEM
10–9

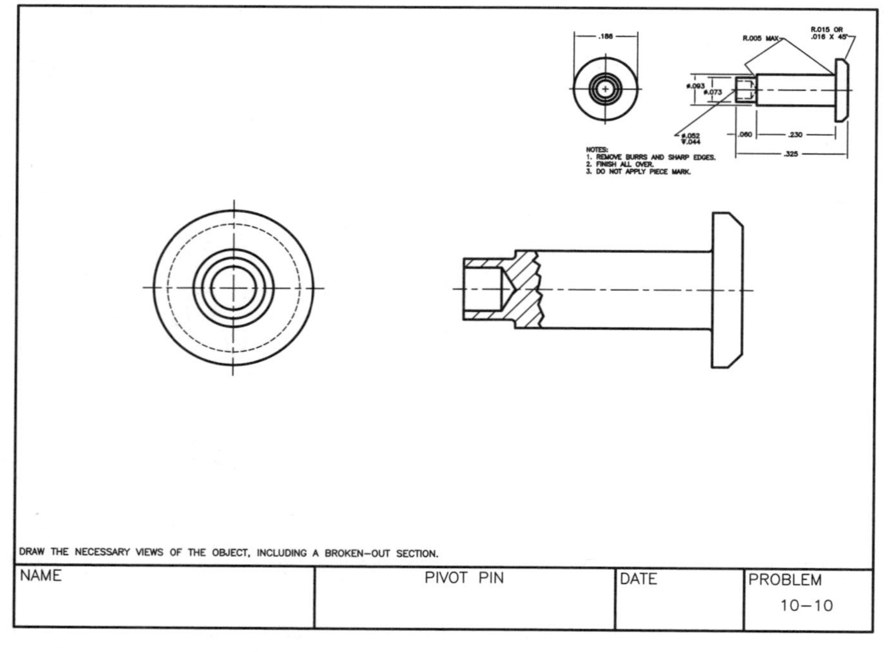
NOTES:
1. REMOVE BURRS AND SHARP EDGES.
2. FINISH ALL OVER.
3. DO NOT APPLY PIECE MARK.
DRAW THE NECESSARY VIEWS OF THE OBJECT, INCLUDING A BROKEN-OUT SECTION.
NAME
PIVOT PIN
DATE
PROBLEM
10–10

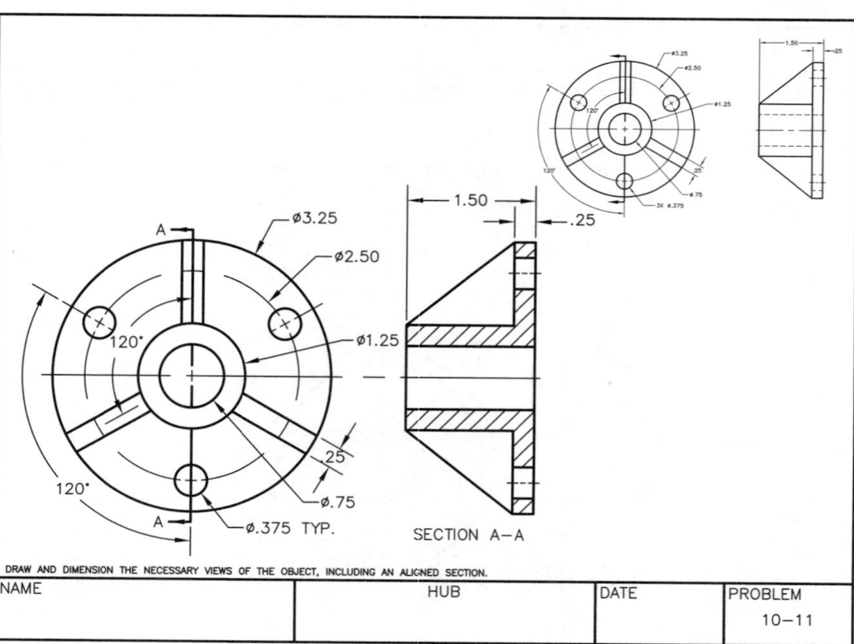
⌀3.25
⌀2.50
⌀1.25
.25
⌀.75
⌀.375 TYP.
120°
120°
1.50
.25
SECTION A–A
DRAW AND DIMENSION THE NECESSARY VIEWS OF THE OBJECT, INCLUDING AN ALIGNED SECTION.
NAME
HUB
DATE
PROBLEM
10–11

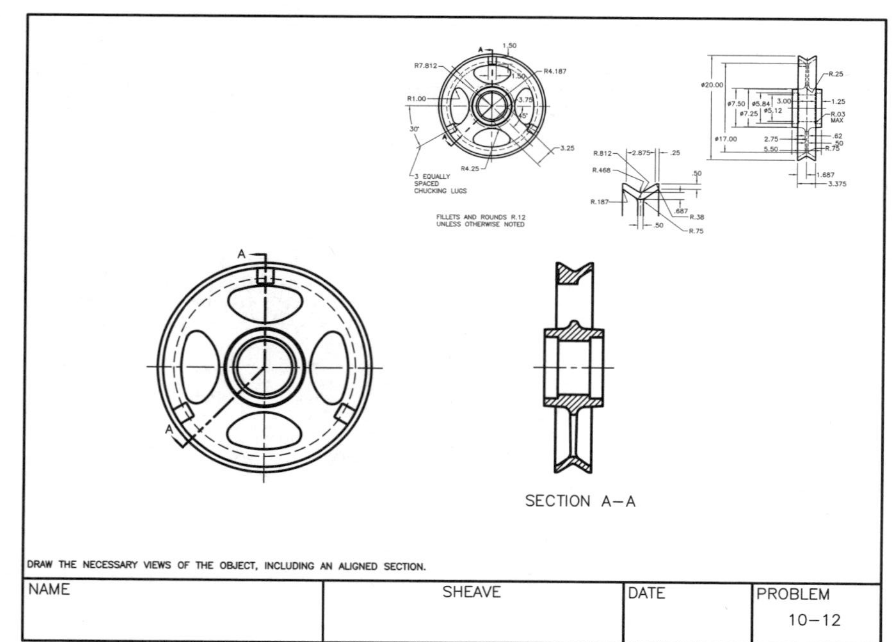
FILLETS AND ROUNDS R.12 UNLESS OTHERWISE NOTED
SECTION A–A
DRAW THE NECESSARY VIEWS OF THE OBJECT, INCLUDING AN ALIGNED SECTION.
NAME
SHEAVE
DATE
PROBLEM
10–12

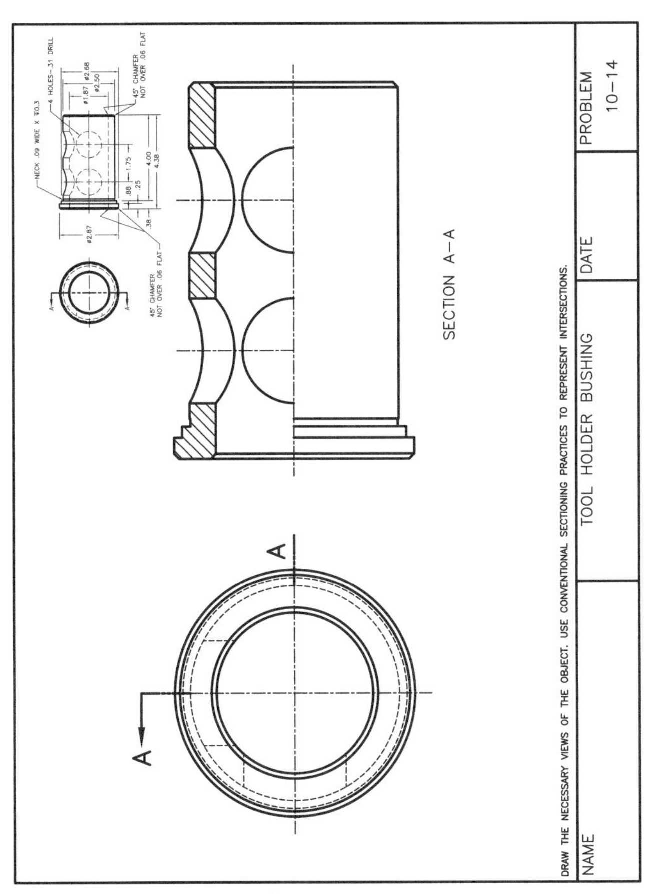

SECTION A–A
A
A
DRAW THE NECESSARY VIEWS OF THE OBJECT. USE CONVENTIONAL SECTIONING PRACTICES TO REPRESENT INTERSECTIONS.
NAME
TOOL HOLDER BUSHING
DATE
PROBLEM
10–14

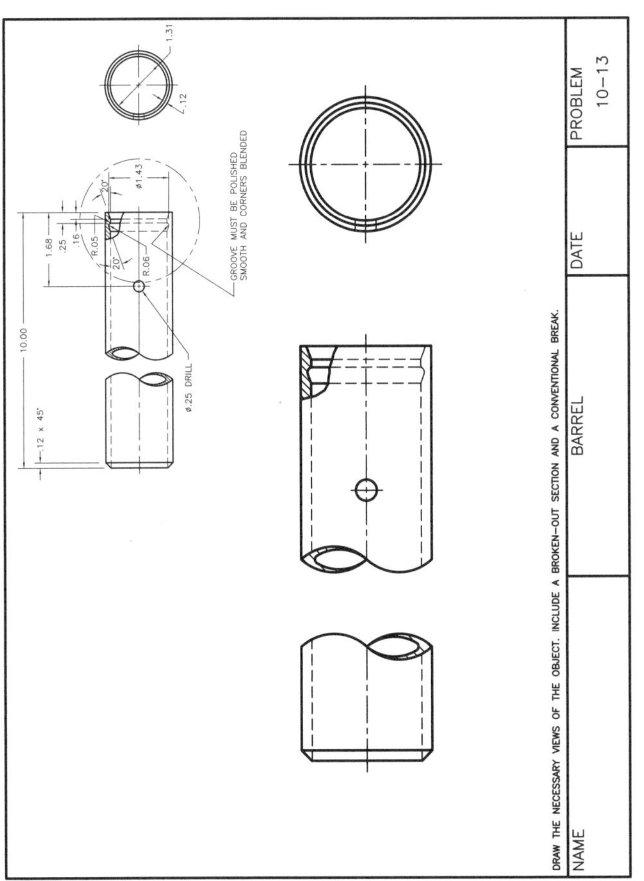

GROOVE MUST BE POLISHED SMOOTH AND CORNERS BLENDED
⌀.25 DRILL
10.00
.12 × 45°
DRAW THE NECESSARY VIEWS OF THE OBJECT. INCLUDE A BROKEN-OUT SECTION AND A CONVENTIONAL BREAK.
NAME
BARREL
DATE
PROBLEM
10–13

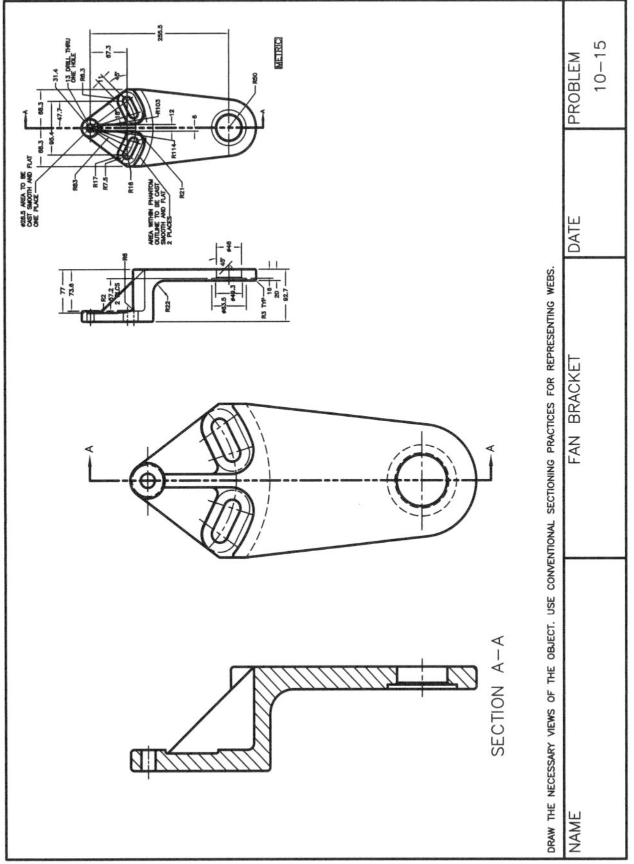

METRIC
SECTION A–A
DRAW THE NECESSARY VIEWS OF THE OBJECT. USE CONVENTIONAL SECTIONING PRACTICES FOR REPRESENTING WEBS.
NAME
FAN BRACKET
DATE
PROBLEM
10–15

Answers to Chapter 10 Quiz

1. D. All of the above.
2. B. When the object has one major centerline and it is obvious the section is taken along the centerline.
3. A. When they are needed for clarity.
4. B. half
5. D. Offset section.
6. D. removed
7. Refer to the drawings given in the *Solutions to Drawing Problems, Text* section for the problem selected from the textbook.

Chapter Quiz 10

Section Views

Name ____________________

Period__________ Date__________ Score __________

Multiple Choice

Choose the answer that correctly completes the statement. Write the corresponding letter in the space provided.

_____ 1. What is the purpose of a section view?
A. To show interior construction.
B. To show hidden features that cannot be shown clearly by hidden lines.
C. To show the shape of exterior features.
D. All of the above.

_____ 2. When can a cutting-plane line be omitted?
A. When there are too many features to show the cutting plane clearly.
B. When the object has one major centerline and it is obvious the section is taken along the centerline.
C. When the cutting-plane line cannot be drawn as a straight line.
D. The cutting-plane line must always be shown.

_____ 3. When should hidden lines behind the cutting plane be shown?
A. When they are needed for clarity.
B. When they don't coincide with other lines.
C. Hidden lines are never shown behind the cutting plane.
D. Hidden lines are always shown behind the cutting plane.

_____ 4. A _____ section of a symmetrical object shows the internal and external features in the same view.
A. full
B. half
C. removed
D. revolved

_____ 5. What type of section has a cutting plane that is not one continuous plane?
A. Full section.
B. Revolved section.
C. Removed section.
D. Offset section.

_____ 6. A section view that appears apart from the regular view is known as a(n) _____ section.
A. half
B. broken-out
C. offset
D. removed

Name ____________________

Drafting Performance

7. Locate the cutting-plane line and prepare a multiview drawing of a problem selected by your instructor from the Drawing Problems section of Chapter 10 in your textbook. Include a section view and dimension the drawing.

Types of Section Views

A ***section view*** is the view "seen" beyond an imaginary cutting plane. A ***cutting plane*** passes through an object at a right angle to the direction of sight.

Full Section

A ***full section*** is a view where the cutting plane passes entirely through an object. The cross section behind the cutting plane is exposed to view.

Half Section

A ***half section*** shows the internal and external features of an object in the same view. This type of view is useful for showing details of symmetrical objects. Only one-half of the object is sectioned along the axis of symmetry.

Revolved Section

A ***revolved section*** is obtained by passing a cutting plane through the centerline or axis of the part to be sectioned. The cross section is then rotated 90° in place to expose the section.

Removed Section

A ***removed section*** is one that has been moved out of its normal projected position in the standard arrangement of views.

Offset Section

The cutting plane for an ***offset section*** is not a single plane. The cutting plane is stepped, or offset, to pass through features that lie in more than one plane.

Broken-Out Section

A ***broken-out section*** shows interior details where less than a half section is required to convey the necessary information. The partial section appears in place on the regular view. Break lines are used to limit the sectioned area.

Aligned Section

In an ***aligned section***, features such as spokes, holes, and ribs are drawn as if rotated into, or out of, the cutting plane. It is used when true projection would be confusing.

Thin Section

A ***thin section*** is used for a part that is too thin for section lining. The material for the section may be shown solid.

RM 10-1

Thin Sections

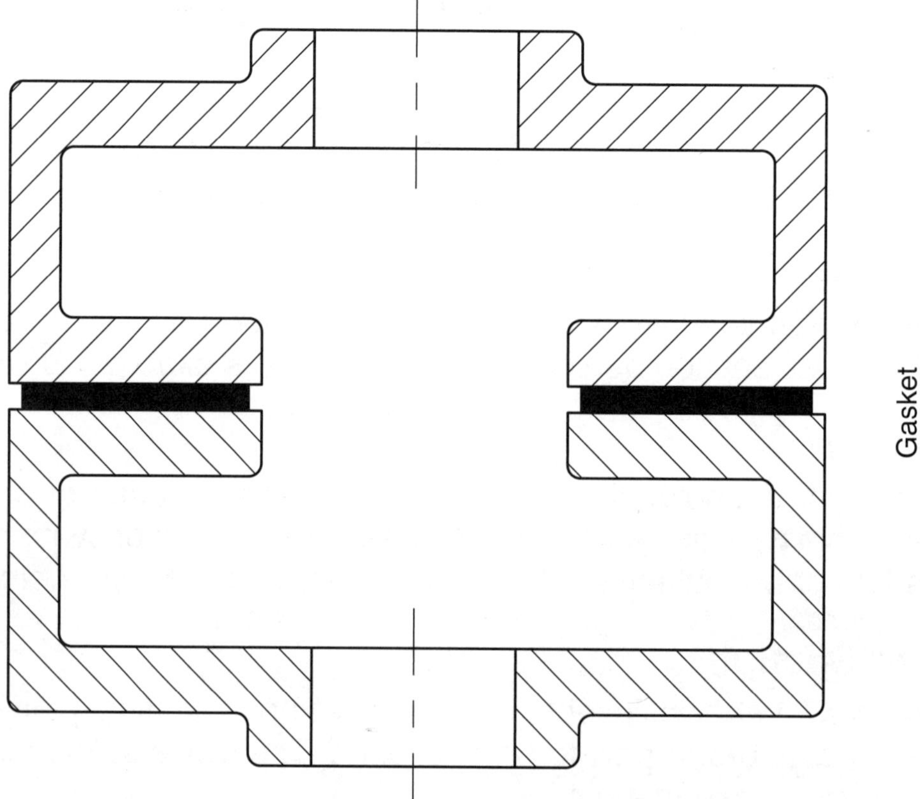

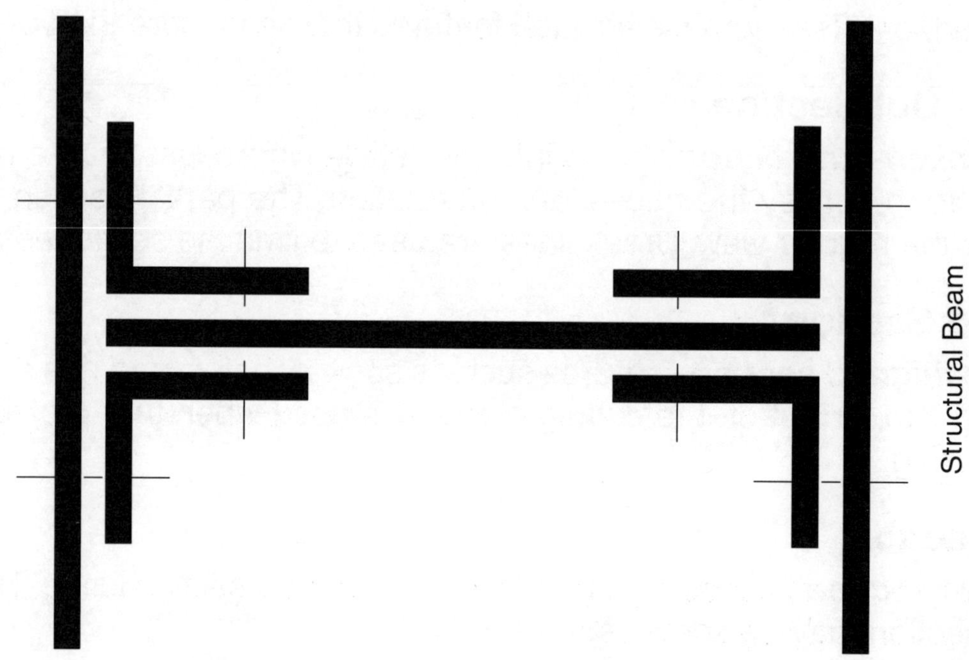

RM 10-2

Procedure Checklist

Section Views

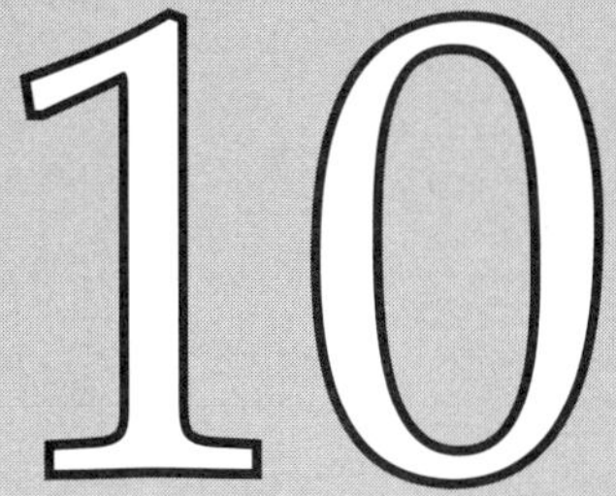

Name ____

Observable Items	Completed		Comments	Instructor Initials
	Yes	No		
1. Determines a location for a cutting plane and projects a section view.				
2. Draws a cutting-plane line.				
3. Draws section lines.				
4. Draws a full section.				
5. Draws a half section.				
6. Draws a revolved section.				
7. Draws an offset section.				
8. Draws a thin section.				
9. Draws material symbols.				

Instructor Signature ____

Pictorial Drawings

Learning Objectives

After studying this chapter, the student will be able to:

- List the three basic types of pictorial drawings and explain the purpose of each.
- Explain the principles of axonometric projection.
- Draw isometric, dimetric, and trimetric views.
- Draw oblique views.
- Draw one-point and two-point perspective views.
- Describe how pictorial views are created in CAD drafting.

Instructional Resources

Text: pages 347–405

Review Questions, pages 396–397

Drawing Problems, pages 397–405

Worksheets: pages 83–96

- Worksheet 11-1: *Incline Block*
- Worksheet 11-2: *Brace Block*
- Worksheet 11-3: *Mounting Flange*
- Worksheet 11-4: *V-Block*
- Worksheet 11-5: *Box Angle*
- Worksheet 11-6: *Angle Bracket*
- Worksheet 11-7: *Drawing Curved Surfaces in Isometric*
- Worksheet 11-8: *U-Strap*
- Worksheet 11-9: *Pulley*
- Worksheet 11-10: *Wear Plate*
- Worksheet 11-11: *Shaft Support*
- Worksheet 11-12: *Box Parallel*
- Worksheet 11-13: *Mounting Bracket*
- Worksheet 11-14: *Two-Point Perspective Drawing*

Instructor's Resource

Instructional Tasks

Instructional Aids and Assignments

Chapter 11 Quiz

Reproducible Masters

- Reproducible Master 11-1: *Four-Center Approximate Method.* Shown is the procedure for constructing isometric ellipses using the four-center approximate method.
- Reproducible Master 11-2 *Perspective Grid.* Shown is a perspective grid to be used by students in constructing two-point perspective drawings.
- Reproducible Master 11-3: *Oblique Drawings.* The three types of oblique drawings are shown for the same object. Each drawing is labeled with the receding axis angle.

Procedure Checklist

Color Transparencies (Binder/IRCD only)

- Transparency 11-1: *Types of Pictorials.* Five basic types of pictorial drawings are shown for comparison.
- Transparency 11-2: *Axonometric Drawings.* The three types of axonometric drawings are shown with axis angles identified.
- Transparency 11-3: *Oblique Drawings.* The three types of oblique drawings are shown. Each drawing is labeled with the receding axis angle.
- Transparency 11-4: *One-Point Perspective Method.* Shown is the procedure for drawing a one-point perspective.
- Transparency 11-5: *Two-Point Perspective Method.* Shown is the procedure for drawing a two-point perspective.
- Transparency 11-6: *CAD-Generated Model.* Shown is a photorealistic computer-generated rendering of a custom-built motorcycle.

Instructional Tasks

1. Identify and discuss the three basic types of pictorial drawings and their subtypes.
    - Show a multimedia presentation or film on pictorial drawings and their construction.
    - Discuss the advantages and limitations of each type of pictorial drawing.

2. Explain how to construct isometric views.
   - Discuss how to select a viewing position.
   - Demonstrate the construction of isometric lines and nonisometric lines.
   - Demonstrate the construction of isometric ellipses.
   - Demonstrate the construction of irregular curves in isometric drawings.
3. Explain how to dimension axonometric drawings.
   - Discuss correct and incorrect practices used in isometric dimensioning.
4. Explain how to construct dimetric views.
   - Discuss how to select the surfaces to be emphasized in the view.
   - Demonstrate the construction of a dimetric scale.
5. Explain how to construct trimetric views.
   - Discuss how to select the surfaces to be emphasized in the view.
6. Explain how to construct oblique views.
   - Discuss the selection of the viewing position.
   - Demonstrate oblique dimensioning practices.
7. Explain how to construct perspective views.
   - Demonstrate the construction of one-point perspective drawings.
   - Demonstrate the construction of two-point perspective drawings.
   - Demonstrate the construction of circles and irregular curves in perspective drawings.
   - Discuss the use of perspective grids and drawing boards.

Instructional Aids and Assignments

1. Show a multimedia presentation or film featuring pictorial drawings.
2. Display simple machine or architectural parts that are suitable for students to sketch and draw pictorially.
3. Assign the drawing problems in the textbook. The number of problems is sufficient to assign a minimum number to all students and to identify problems that may be done for extra credit. Some problems may be used for the performance section of the chapter quiz.

Answers to Review Questions, Text

Pages 396–397

1. A three-dimensional representation showing the width, height, and depth of an object.
2. Pictorial drawings are widely used for assembly drawings, piping diagrams, service and repair manuals, sales catalogs, and technical training manuals.
3. perspective
4. perpendicular
5. inclined
6. Isometric, dimetric, and trimetric.
7. D. 120°
8. isometric
9. Isometric drawings tend to be larger.
10. isometric
11. Isometric snap.
12. By locating the endpoints on isometric lines and then drawing the lines.
13. By locating the endpoints of the sides and connecting the endpoints.
14. Circles and arcs appear as ellipses or partial ellipses in isometric drawings.
15. Ellipses can be drawn using the four-center approximate method, the coordinate method, or an isometric ellipse template.
16. The **Ellipse** command.
17. coordinate
18. section
19. Unidirectional dimensioning.
20. 120
21. The tendency for long objects to appear distorted.
22. two
23. The angle at which the object is viewed.
24. trimetric
25. two
26. Cavalier, cabinet, and general.
27. It presents a distorted appearance for objects when the depth approaches or exceeds the width.
28. cabinet
29. 45° and 30°
30. arcs, circles
31. One-point (parallel), two-point (angular), and three-point.
32. station point
33. Points in space where all parallel lines meet.

34. vertical
35. vanishing
36. two-point
37. picture
38. coordinate
39. vanishing point

Solutions to Drawing Problems, Text

Pages 397–405

Student work should look like the following drawings. The problem number and title are indicated on each problem sheet.

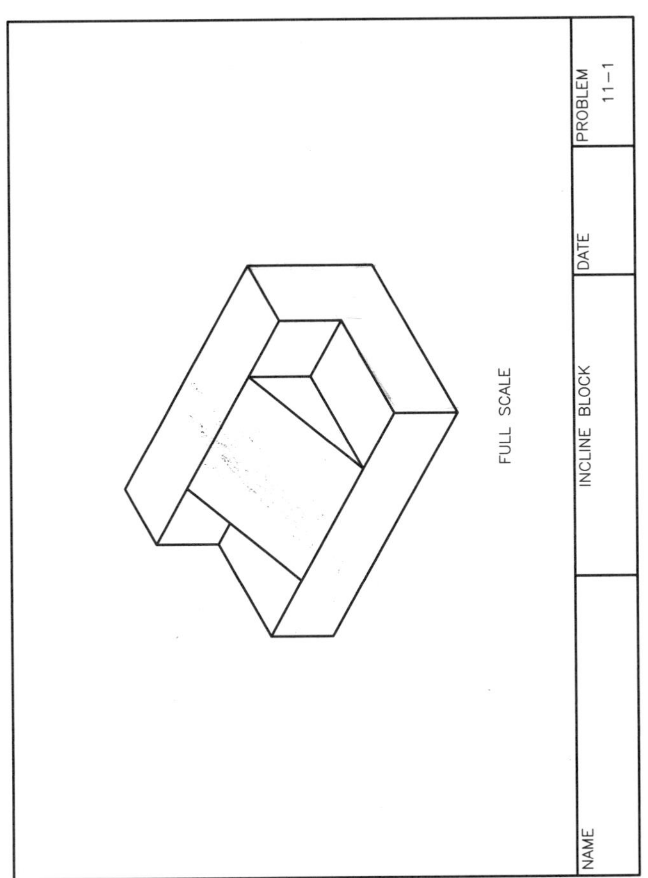

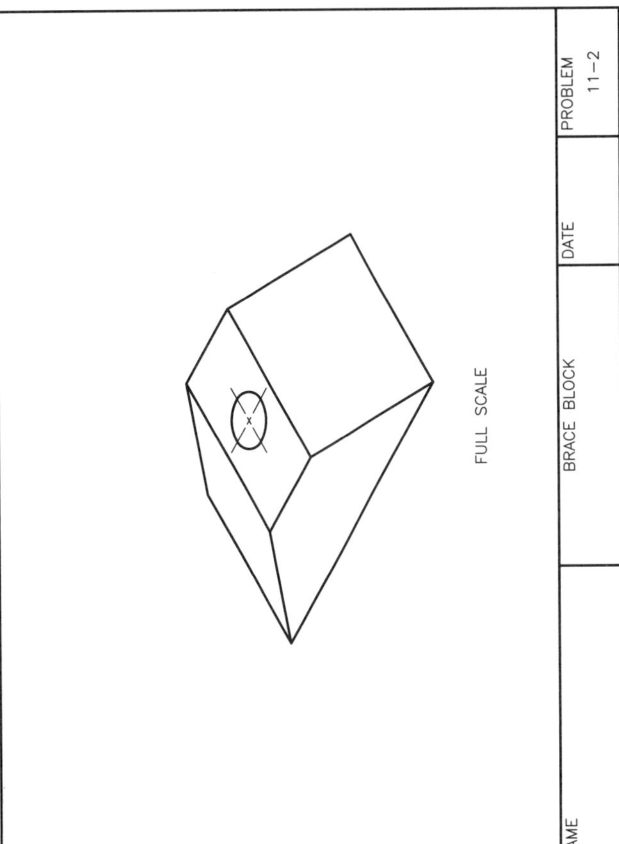

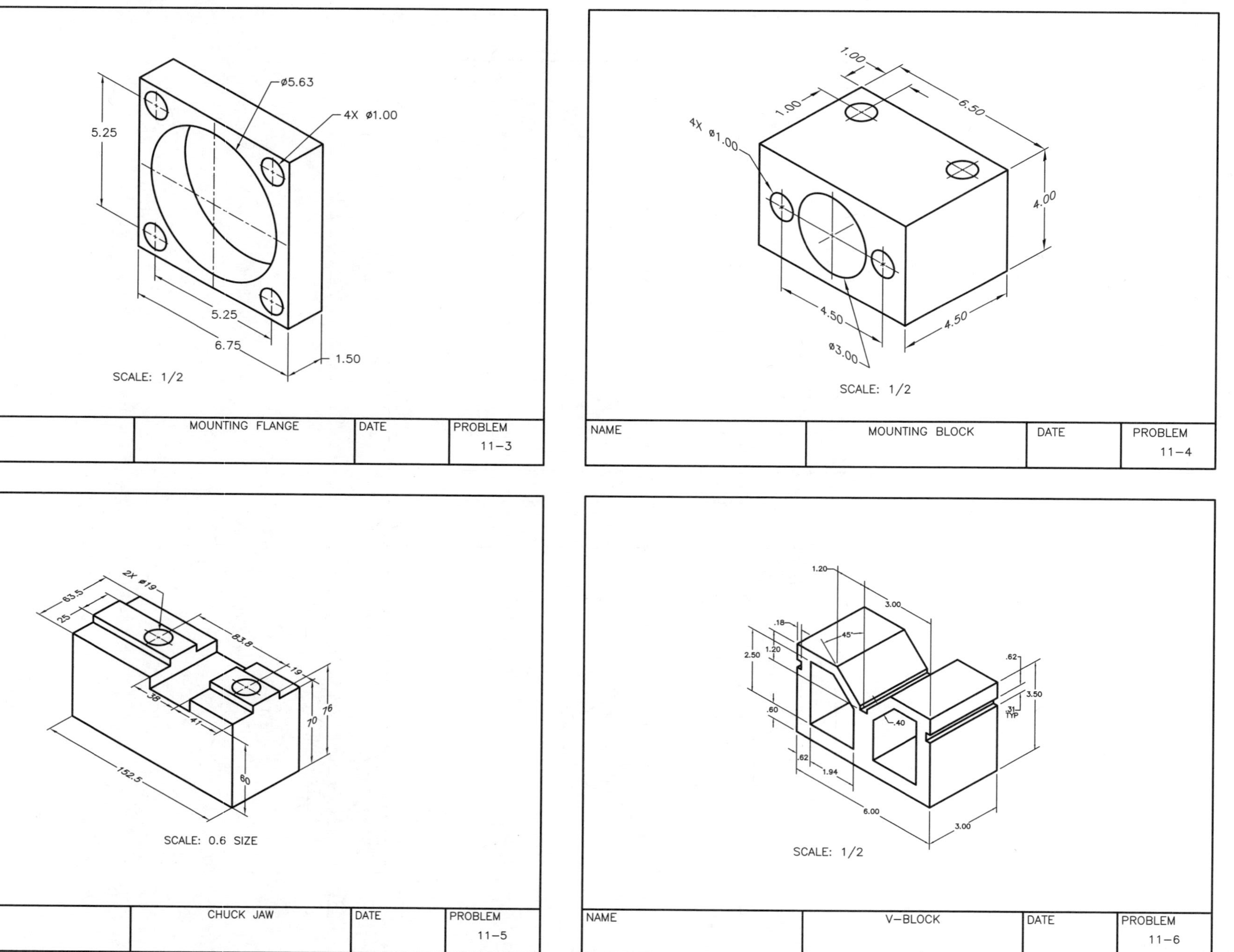

⌀5.63
4X ⌀1.00
5.25
5.25
6.75
1.50
SCALE: 1/2
NAME
MOUNTING FLANGE
DATE
PROBLEM
11–3
1.00
1.00
6.50
4X ⌀1.00
4.00
4.50
4.50
⌀3.00
SCALE: 1/2
NAME
MOUNTING BLOCK
DATE
PROBLEM
11–4
2X ⌀19
63.5
25
83.8
19
38
41
70
76
152.5
60
SCALE: 0.6 SIZE
NAME
CHUCK JAW
DATE
PROBLEM
11–5
1.20
3.00
.18
45°
2.50
1.20
.62
3.50
.31 TYP
.60
.40
.62
1.94
6.00
3.00
SCALE: 1/2
NAME
V–BLOCK
DATE
PROBLEM
11–6

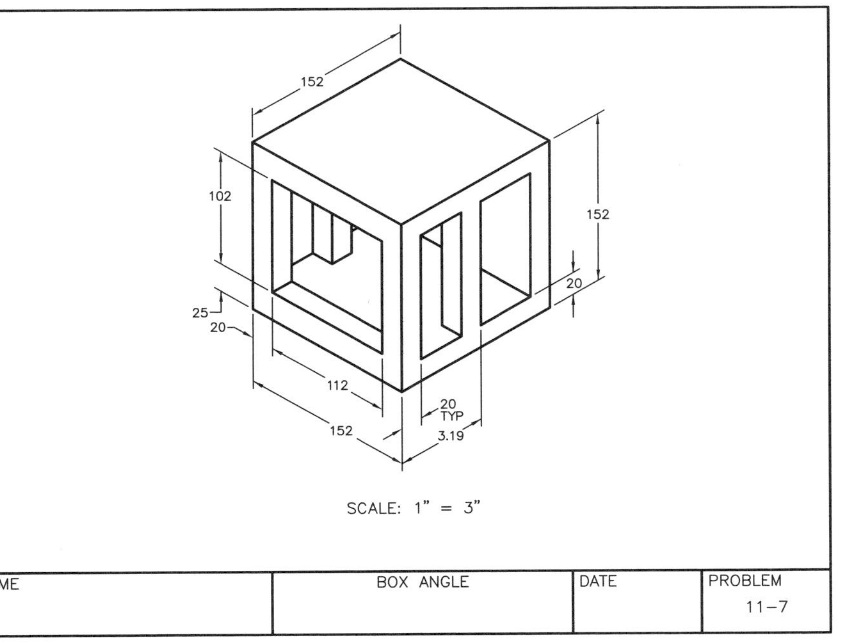

152
102
152
20
25
20
112
152
20 TYP
3.19
SCALE: 1" = 3"
NAME
BOX ANGLE
DATE
PROBLEM
11–7

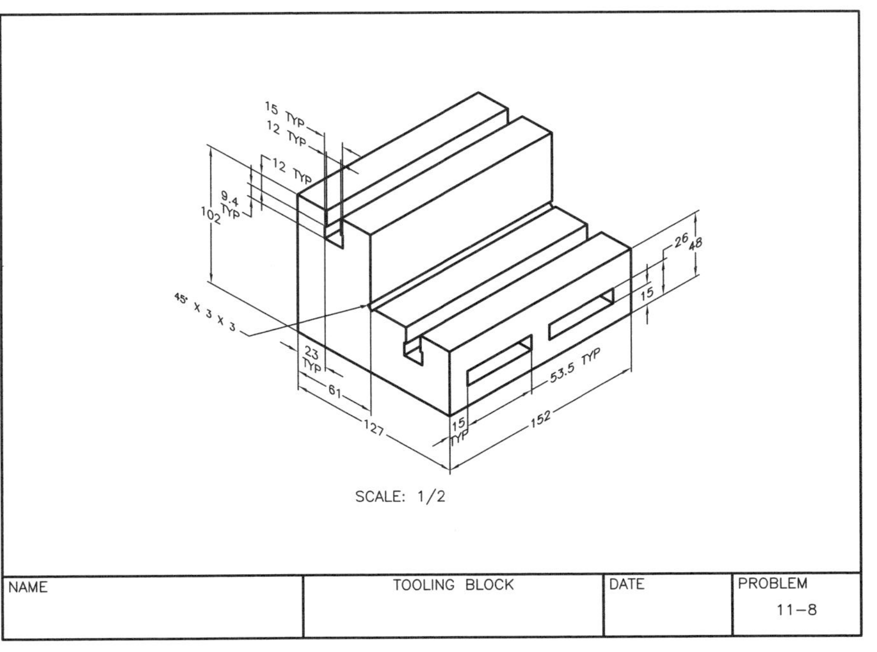

15 TYP
12 TYP
12 TYP
9.4 TYP
102
45° X 3 X 3
23 TYP
61
127
15 TYP
152
53.5 TYP
15
26
48
SCALE: 1/2
NAME
TOOLING BLOCK
DATE
PROBLEM
11–8

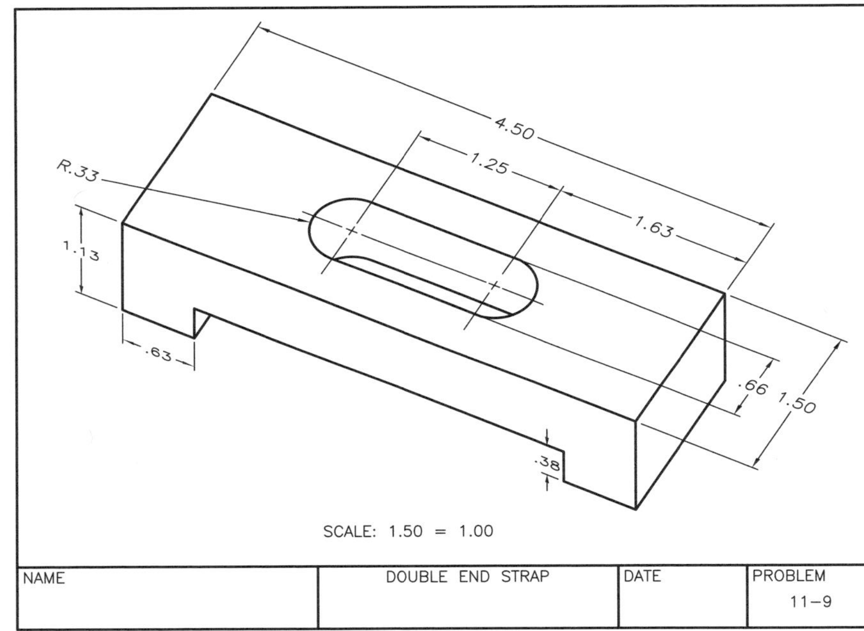

4.50
1.25
1.63
R.33
1.13
.63
.66
1.50
.38
SCALE: 1.50 = 1.00
NAME
DOUBLE END STRAP
DATE
PROBLEM
11–9

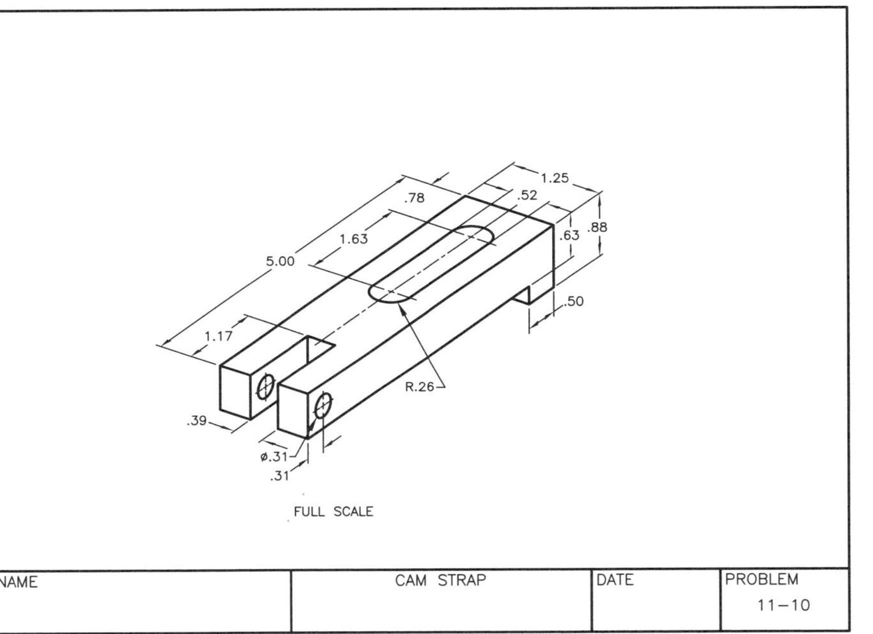

1.25
.78
.52
1.63
.63
.88
5.00
.50
1.17
R.26
.39
⌀.31
.31
FULL SCALE
NAME
CAM STRAP
DATE
PROBLEM
11–10

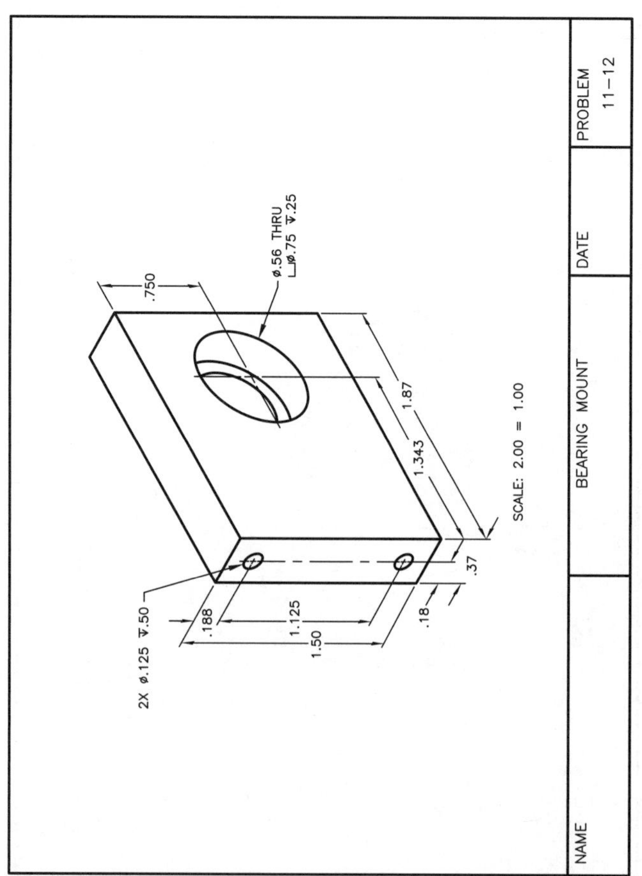

.750
⌀.56 THRU
⌴⌀.75 ↧.25
1.87
1.343
2X ⌀.125 ↧.50
.188
1.125
1.50
.18
.37
SCALE: 2.00 = 1.00
NAME
BEARING MOUNT
DATE
PROBLEM
11–12

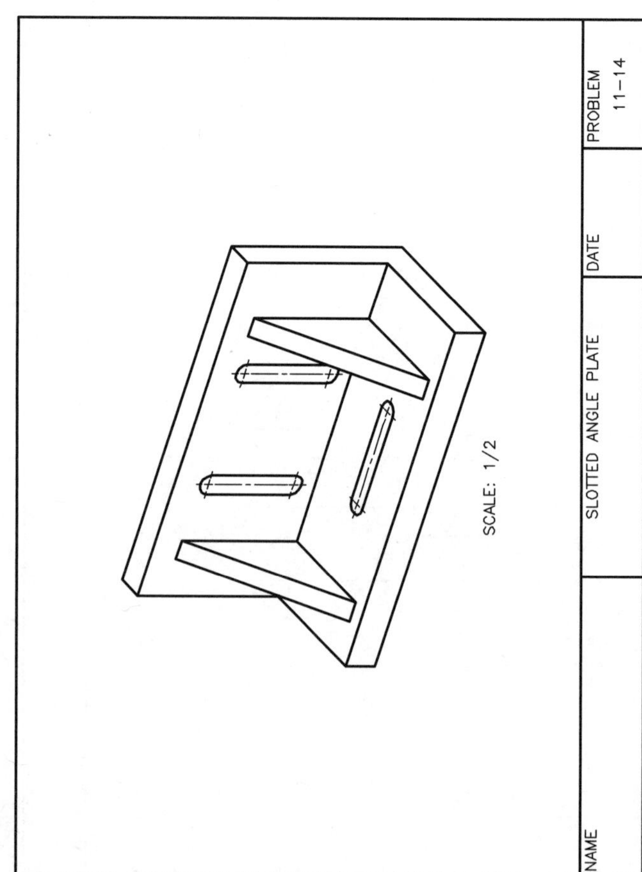

SCALE: 1/2
NAME
SLOTTED ANGLE PLATE
DATE
PROBLEM
11–14

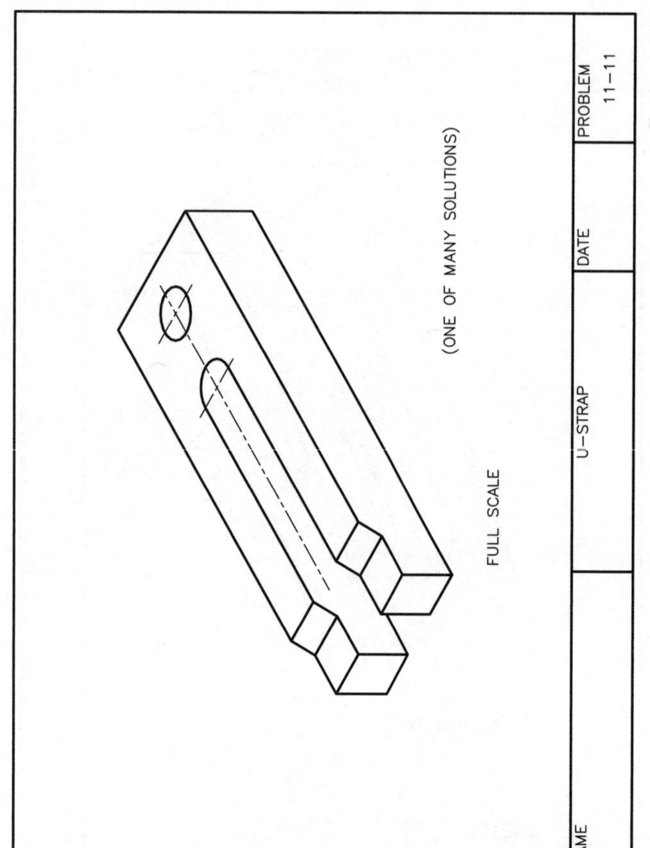

(ONE OF MANY SOLUTIONS)
FULL SCALE
NAME
U-STRAP
DATE
PROBLEM
11–11

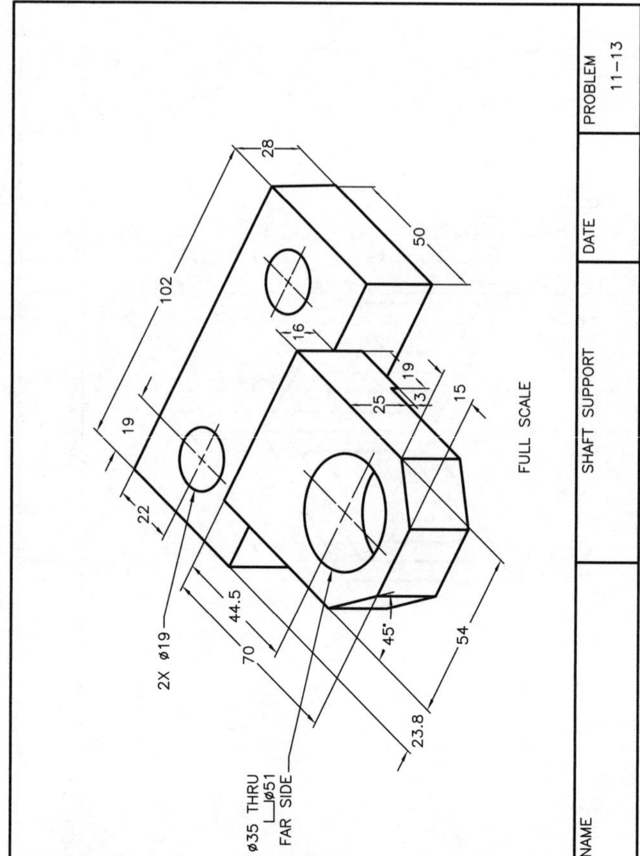

28
102
50
16
19
3
25
15
19
22
2X ⌀19
44.5
70
45°
54
23.8
⌀35 THRU
⌴⌀51
FAR SIDE
FULL SCALE
NAME
SHAFT SUPPORT
DATE
PROBLEM
11–13

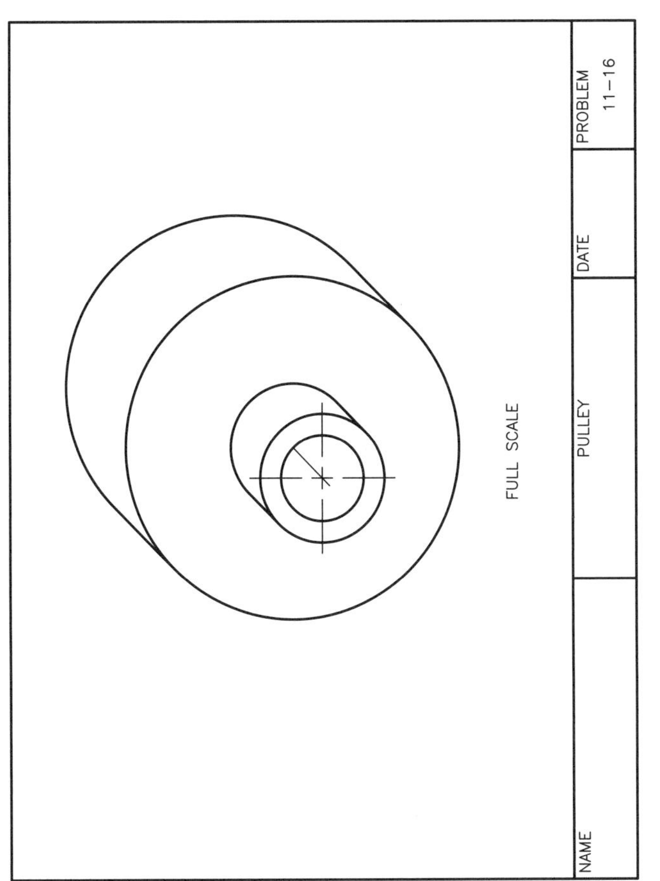
FULL SCALE
PULLEY
PROBLEM
11–16
DATE
NAME

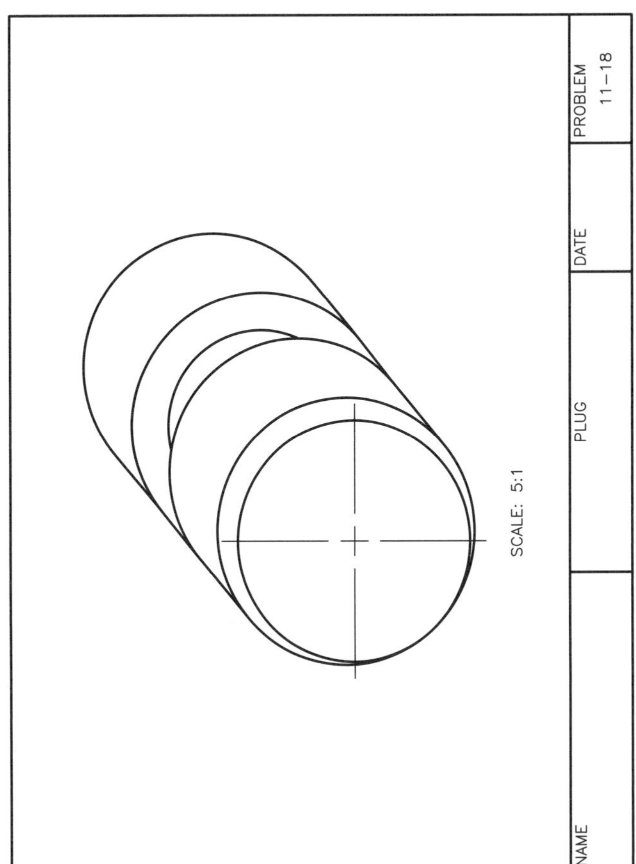
SCALE: 5:1
PLUG
PROBLEM
11–18
DATE
NAME

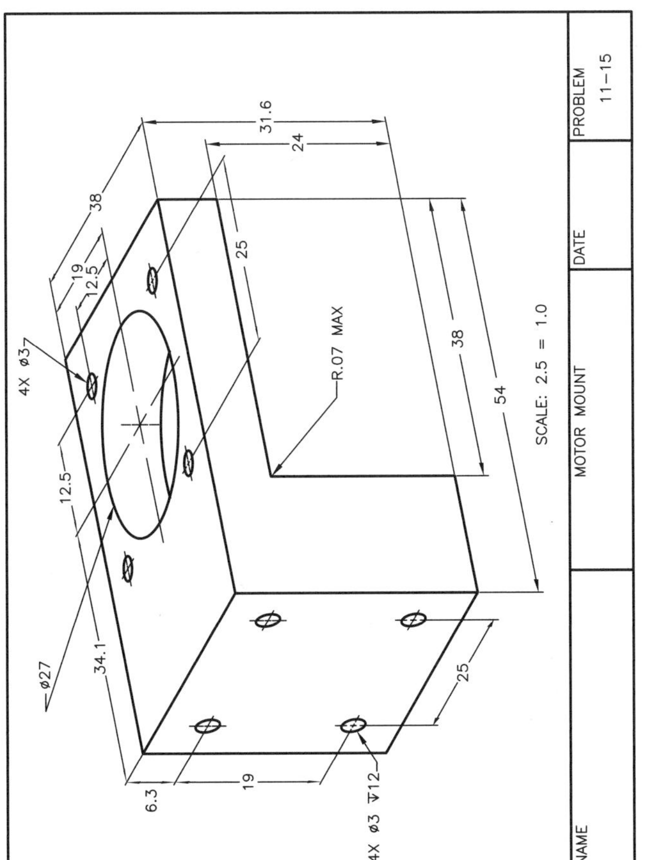
31.6
24
38
19
12.5
25
4X ⌀3
R.07 MAX
38
54
12.5
⌀27
34.1
25
6.3
19
4X ⌀3 ↧12
SCALE: 2.5 = 1.0
MOTOR MOUNT
PROBLEM
11–15
DATE
NAME

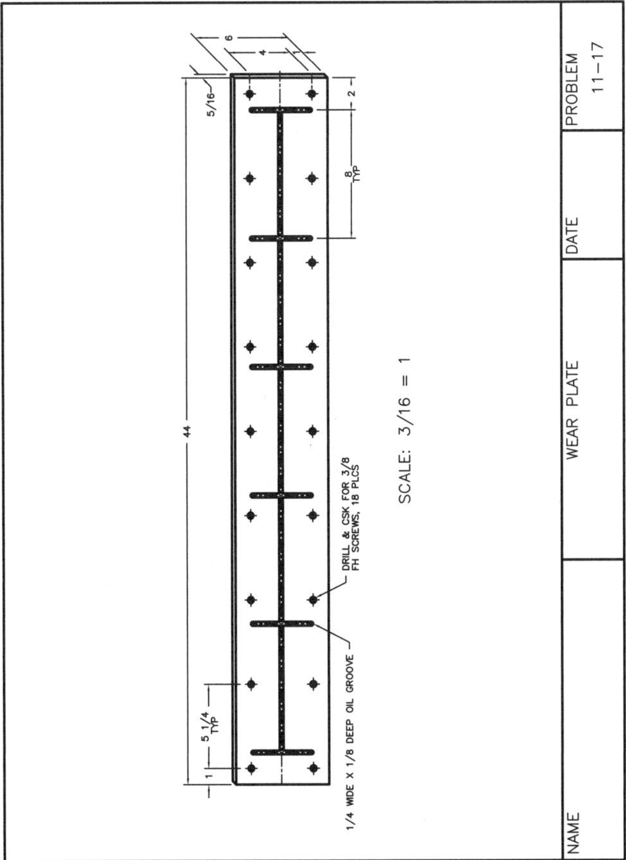
6
4
5/16
2
8
TYP
44
DRILL & CSK FOR 3/8
FH SCREWS, 18 PLCS
1/4 WIDE X 1/8 DEEP OIL GROOVE
5 1/4
TYP
1
SCALE: 3/16 = 1
WEAR PLATE
PROBLEM
11–17
DATE
NAME

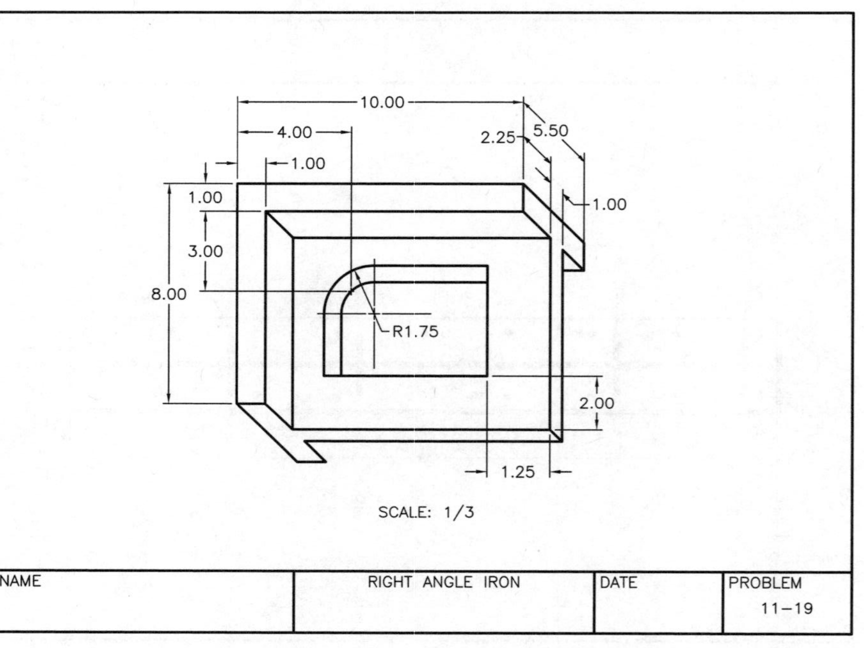
10.00
4.00
1.00
2.25
5.50
1.00
1.00
3.00
8.00
R1.75
2.00
1.25
SCALE: 1/3
NAME
RIGHT ANGLE IRON
DATE
PROBLEM
11-19

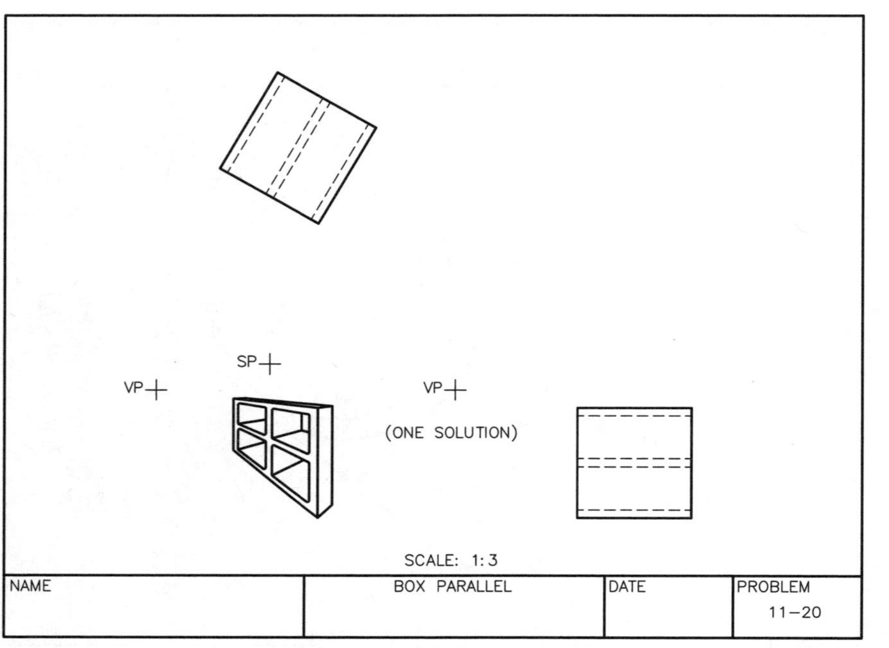
SP
VP
VP
(ONE SOLUTION)
SCALE: 1:3
NAME
BOX PARALLEL
DATE
PROBLEM
11-20

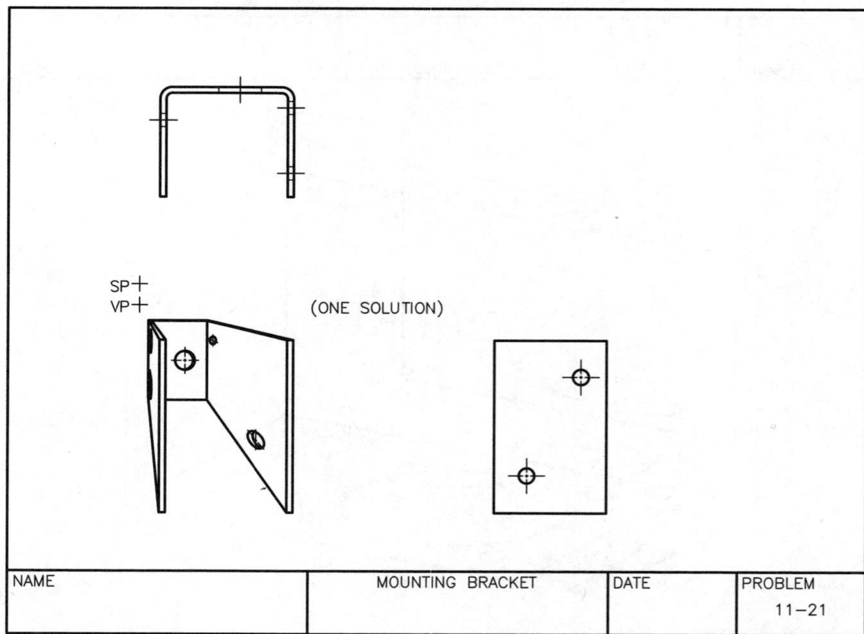
SP
VP
(ONE SOLUTION)
NAME
MOUNTING BRACKET
DATE
PROBLEM
11-21

Solutions to Worksheets

Pages 83–96

Student work should look like the following drawings. The problem number and title are indicated on each problem sheet.

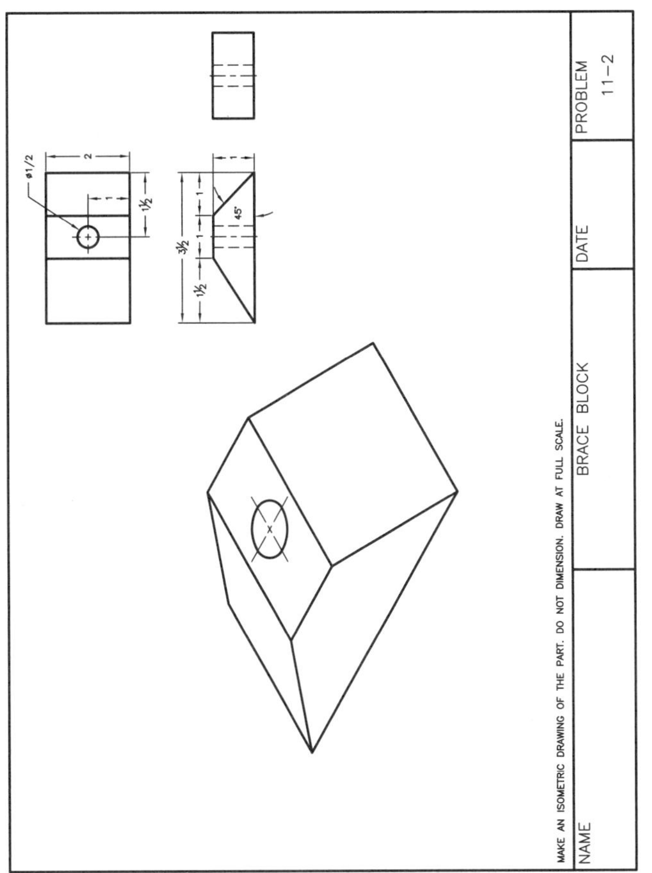

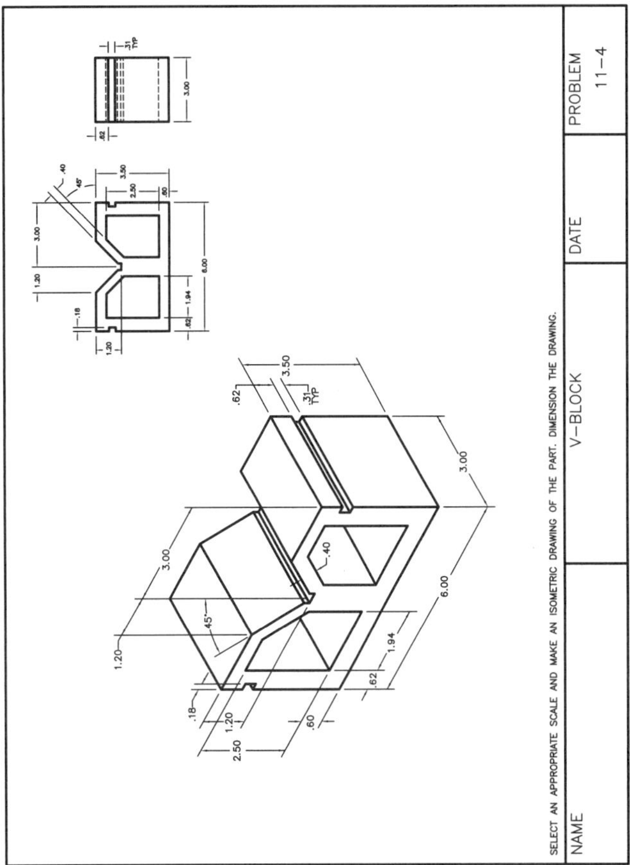

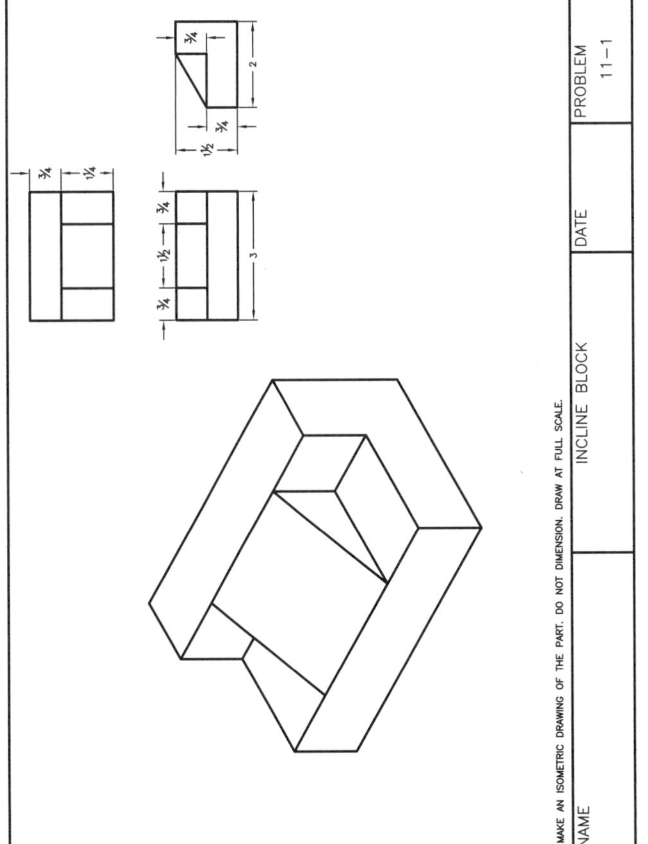

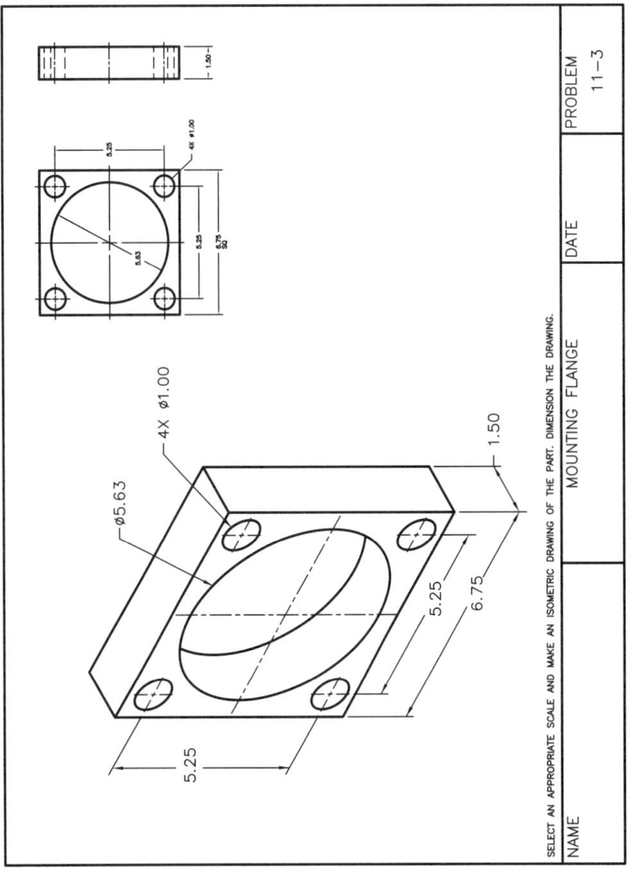

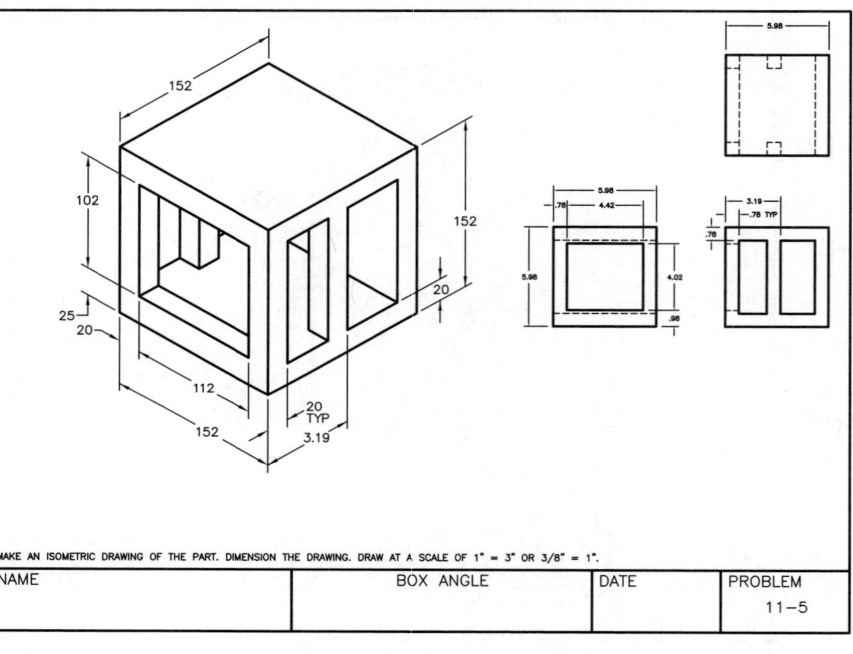
152
102
152
25
20
20
112
152
20
TYP
3.19
5.98
5.98
.78
4.42
5.98
4.02
.98
3.19
.78 TYP
.78
MAKE AN ISOMETRIC DRAWING OF THE PART. DIMENSION THE DRAWING. DRAW AT A SCALE OF 1" = 3" OR 3/8" = 1".
NAME
BOX ANGLE
DATE
PROBLEM
11–5

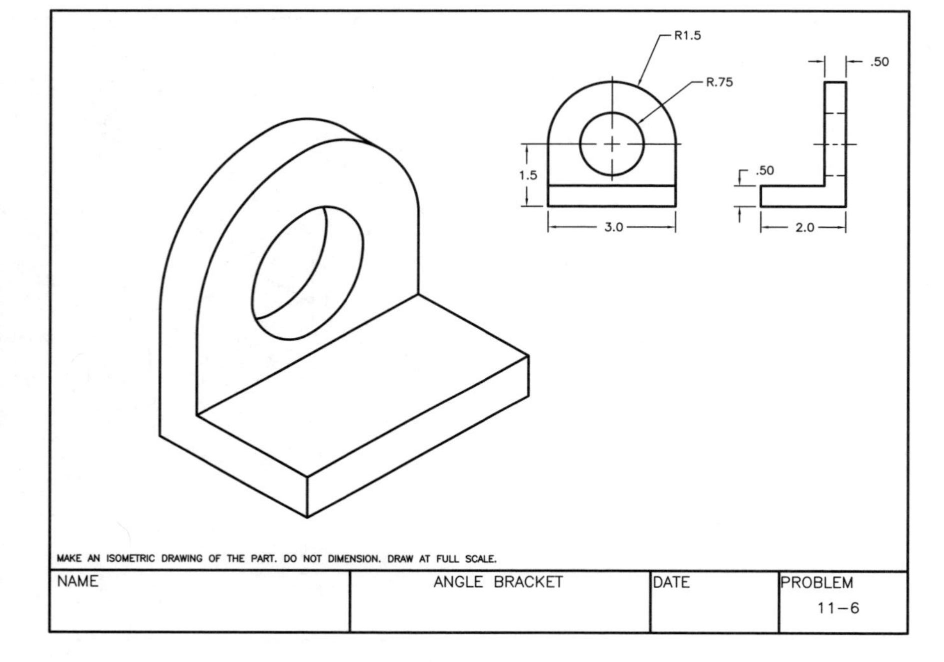
R1.5
R.75
.50
1.5
.50
3.0
2.0
MAKE AN ISOMETRIC DRAWING OF THE PART. DO NOT DIMENSION. DRAW AT FULL SCALE.
NAME
ANGLE BRACKET
DATE
PROBLEM
11–6

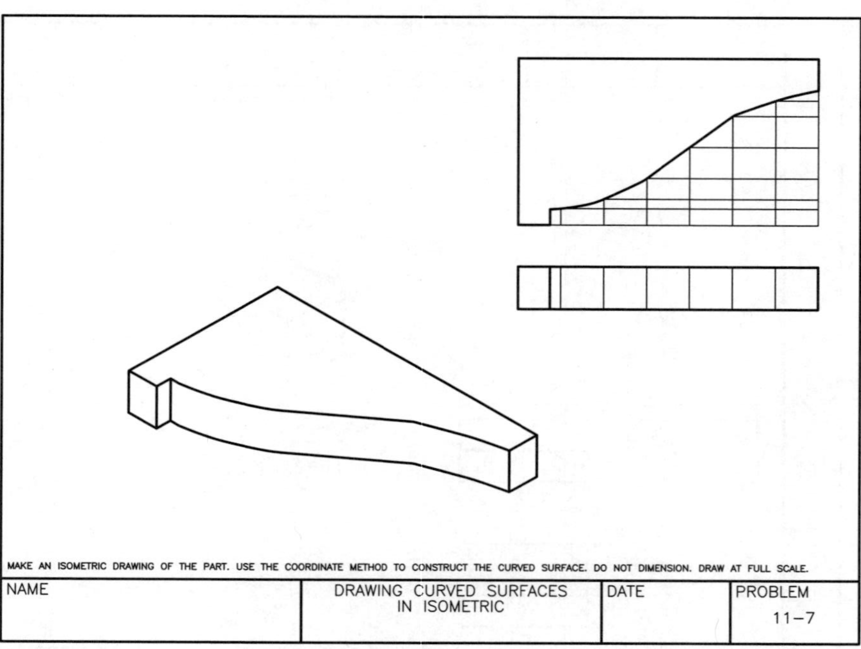
MAKE AN ISOMETRIC DRAWING OF THE PART. USE THE COORDINATE METHOD TO CONSTRUCT THE CURVED SURFACE. DO NOT DIMENSION. DRAW AT FULL SCALE.
NAME
DRAWING CURVED SURFACES IN ISOMETRIC
DATE
PROBLEM
11–7

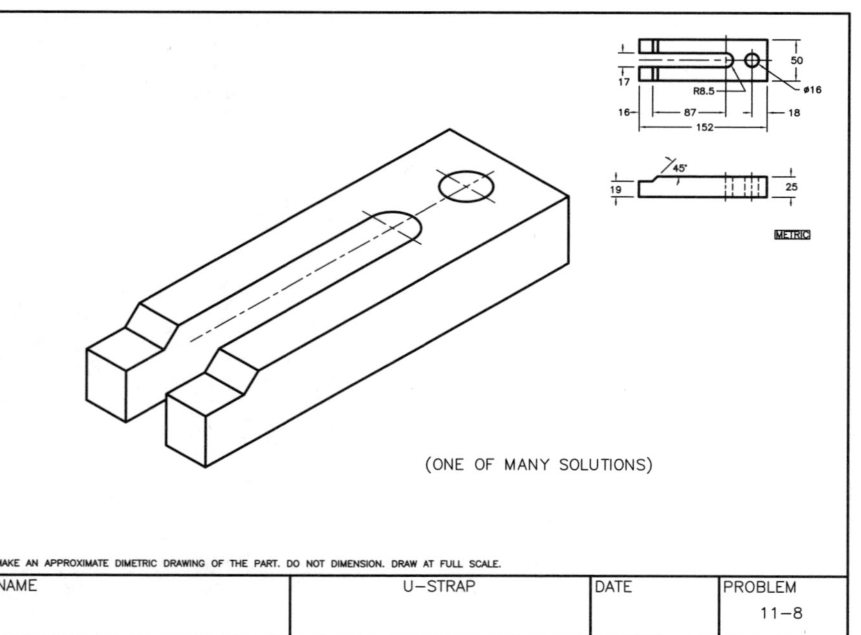
50
17
R8.5
ø16
16
87
18
152
45°
19
25
METRIC
(ONE OF MANY SOLUTIONS)
MAKE AN APPROXIMATE DIMETRIC DRAWING OF THE PART. DO NOT DIMENSION. DRAW AT FULL SCALE.
NAME
U–STRAP
DATE
PROBLEM
11–8

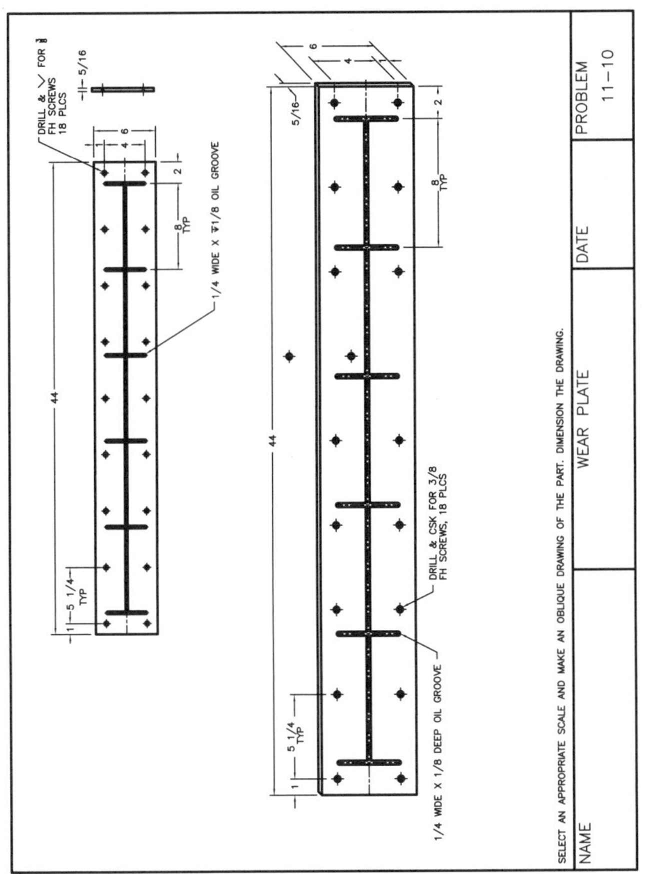
SELECT AN APPROPRIATE SCALE AND MAKE AN OBLIQUE DRAWING OF THE PART. DIMENSION THE DRAWING.
NAME
DATE
PROBLEM
11-10
WEAR PLATE
DRILL & CSK FOR 3/8 FH SCREWS, 18 PLCS
1/4 WIDE X 1/8 DEEP OIL GROOVE
1/4 WIDE X ⊽1/8 OIL GROOVE
44
5 1/4 TYP
8 TYP
5/16

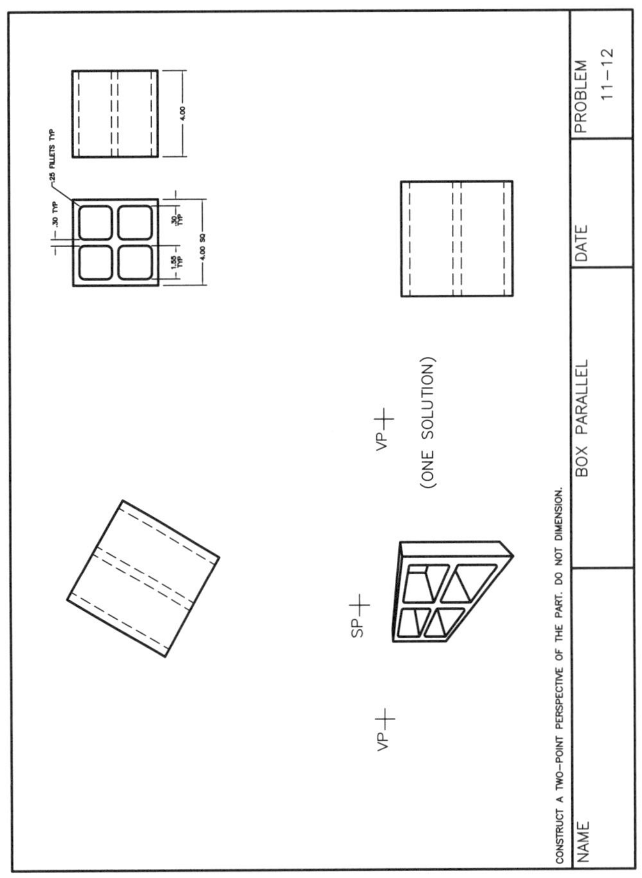
CONSTRUCT A TWO-POINT PERSPECTIVE OF THE PART. DO NOT DIMENSION.
NAME
DATE
PROBLEM
11-12
BOX PARALLEL
VP
SP
VP
(ONE SOLUTION)
.25 FILLETS TYP
4.00 SQ
4.00

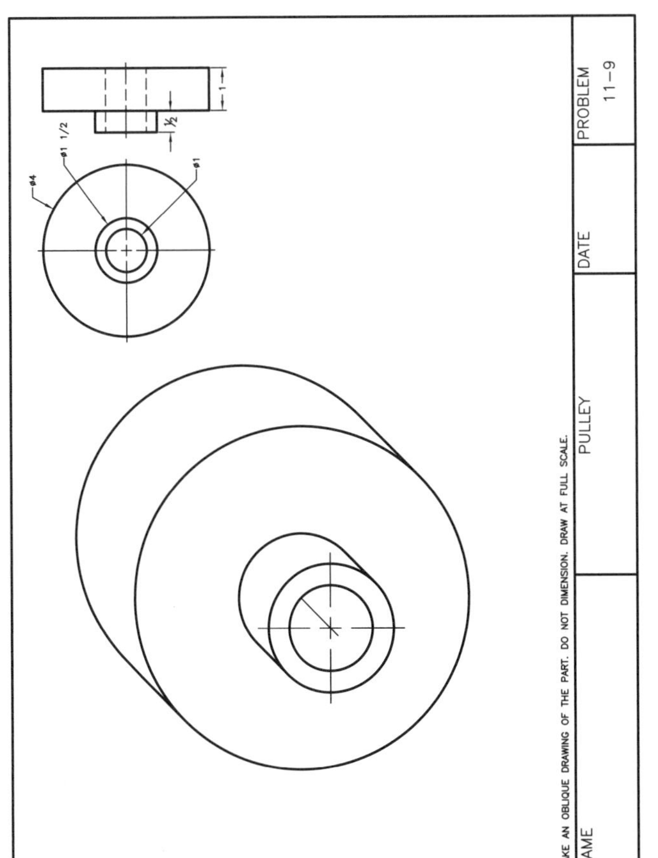
MAKE AN OBLIQUE DRAWING OF THE PART. DO NOT DIMENSION. DRAW AT FULL SCALE.
NAME
DATE
PROBLEM
11-9
PULLEY
ø4
ø1 1/2
ø1
1
½

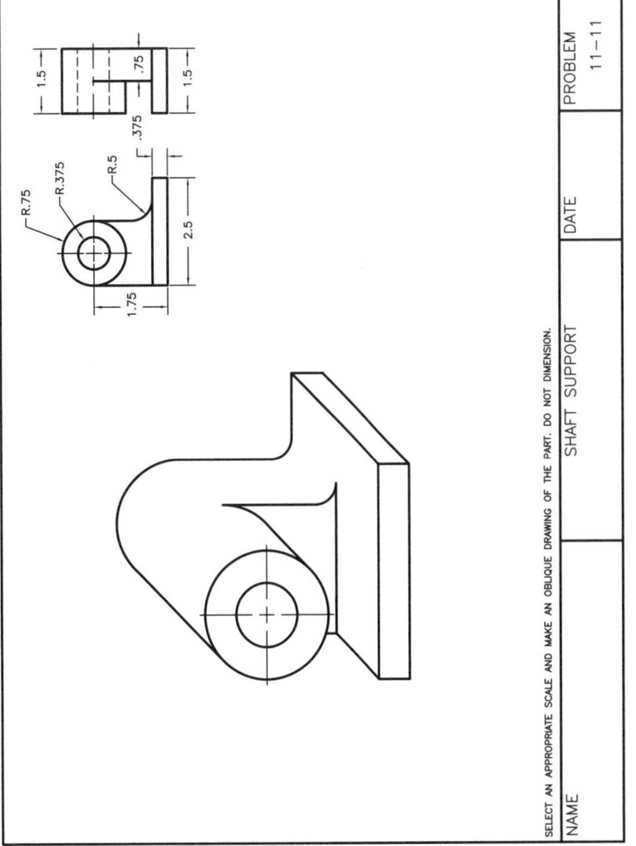
SELECT AN APPROPRIATE SCALE AND MAKE AN OBLIQUE DRAWING OF THE PART. DO NOT DIMENSION.
NAME
DATE
PROBLEM
11-11
SHAFT SUPPORT
R.75
R.375
R.5
.375
2.5
1.75
1.5
.75
1.5

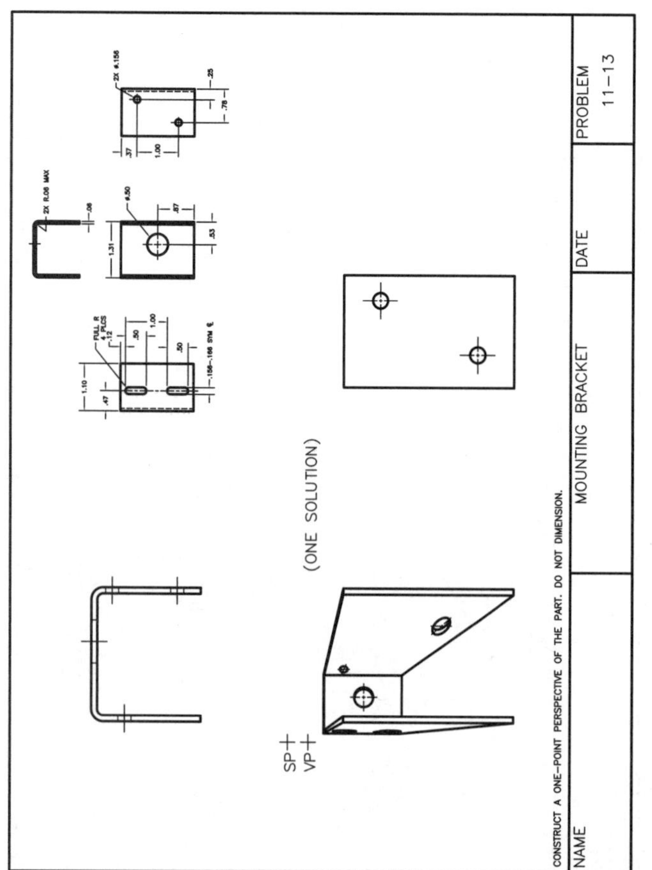

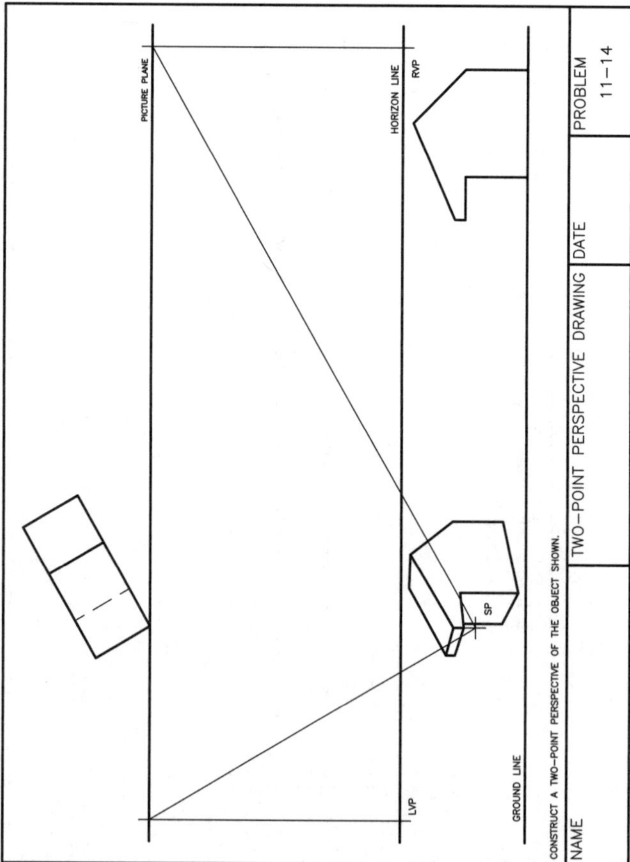

Answers to Chapter 11 Quiz

1. A. axonometric
2. A. isometric
3. B. Objects that are projected are oriented at different viewing angles.
4. B. All three object faces make different angles with the plane of projection.
5. C. cavalier
6. D. Perspective
7. B. perspective
8. D. nonisometric
9. D. The **Circle** command.
10. A. the coordinate method
11. Refer to the drawings given in the *Solutions to Drawing Problems, Text* section for the problem selected from the textbook.

Chapter Quiz

Pictorial Drawings

Name ______________________________

Period__________ Date__________ Score __________

Multiple Choice

Choose the answer that correctly completes the statement. Write the corresponding letter in the space provided.

________ 1. In _____ projection, the lines of sight are perpendicular to the plane of projection.
A. axonometric
B. oblique
C. parallel perspective
D. angular perspective

________ 2. In _____ projection, the three principal faces of a rectangular object are equally inclined to the plane of projection and the three axes make equal angles with each other.
A. isometric
B. dimetric
C. trimetric
D. perspective

________ 3. What is the primary difference between dimetric and isometric projection?
A. A dimetric projection is easier to construct than an isometric projection.
B. Objects that are projected are oriented at different viewing angles.
C. The object axes in a dimetric projection are drawn at three different scales.
D. None of the object faces in a dimetric projection are equally inclined to the plane of projection.

________ 4. Which of the following is true in relation to trimetric projection?
A. Two of the object axes make equal angles with each other.
B. All three object faces make different angles with the plane of projection.
C. A trimetric projection appears smaller than a dimetric projection.
D. A trimetric projection is easier to construct than an isometric projection.

________ 5. A _____ oblique drawing uses true length measurements along the depth axis.
A. general
B. cabinet
C. cavalier
D. parallel

________ 6. Which of the following types of pictorial drawings gives the most realistic view of an object?
A. Isometric
B. Dimetric
C. Oblique
D. Perspective

Name ____

_______ 7. Parallel lines on an object remain parallel in all pictorial drawings except _____ drawings.
A. axonometric
B. perspective
C. oblique
D. trimetric

_______ 8. Inclined lines in multiview drawings become _____ lines in isometric drawings.
A. horizontal
B. vertical
C. isometric
D. nonisometric

_______ 9. Which of the following is *not* used for drawing ellipses in axonometric drawings?
A. The four-center approximate method.
B. The coordinate method.
C. Isometric ellipse templates.
D. The **Circle** command.

_______ 10. Irregular curves in pictorial drawings can be constructed by use of _____.
A. the coordinate method
B. isometric ellipse templates
C. the four-center approximate method
D. the **Polygon** command

Drafting Performance

11. Select the best viewing orientation and construct a drawing of a problem selected by your instructor from the Drawing Problems section of Chapter 11 in your textbook.

Four-Center Approximate Method

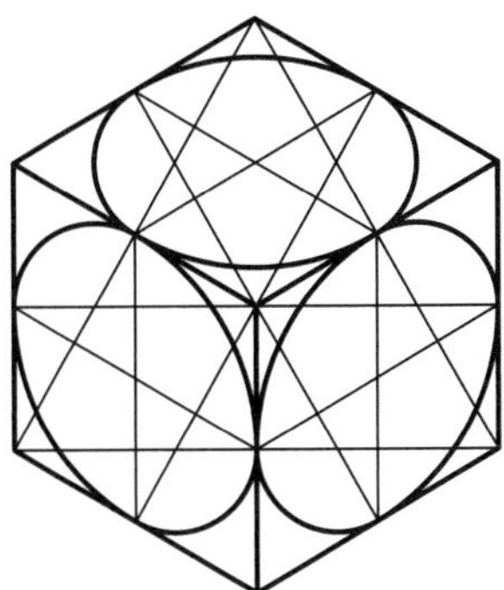

Ellipse positions

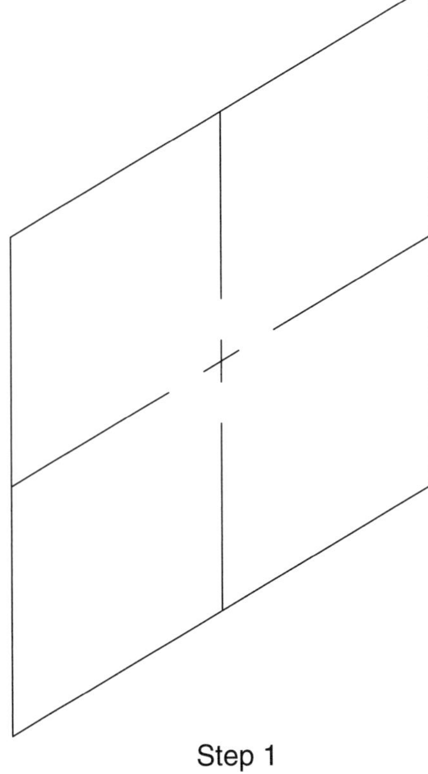

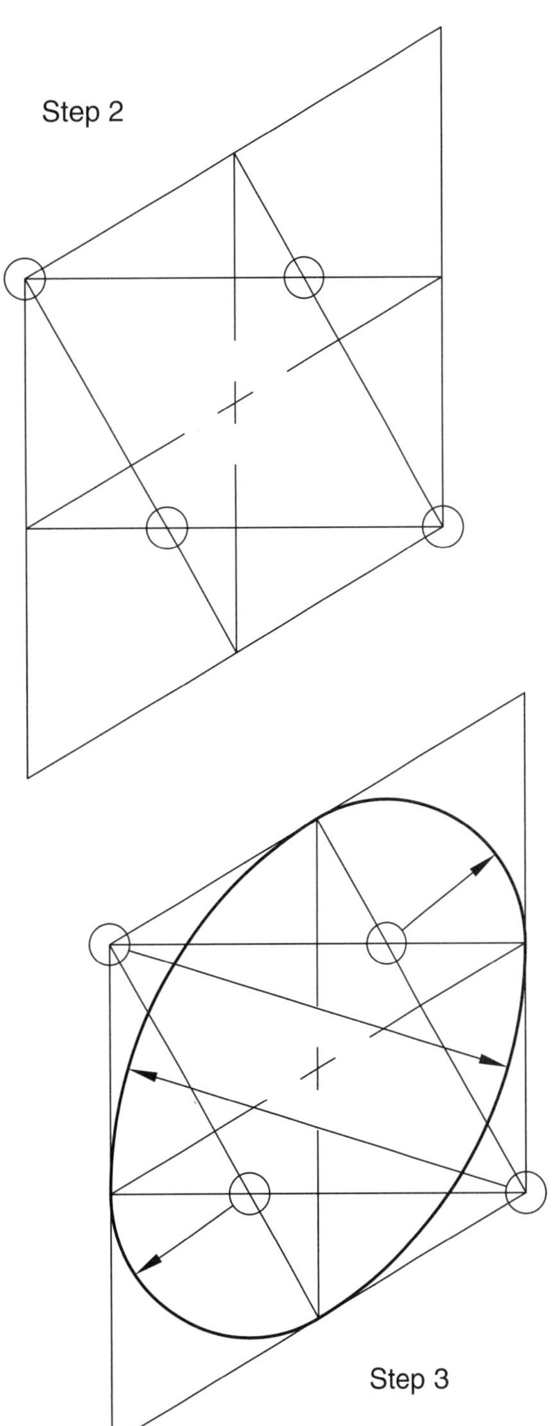

RM 11-1

Perspective Grid

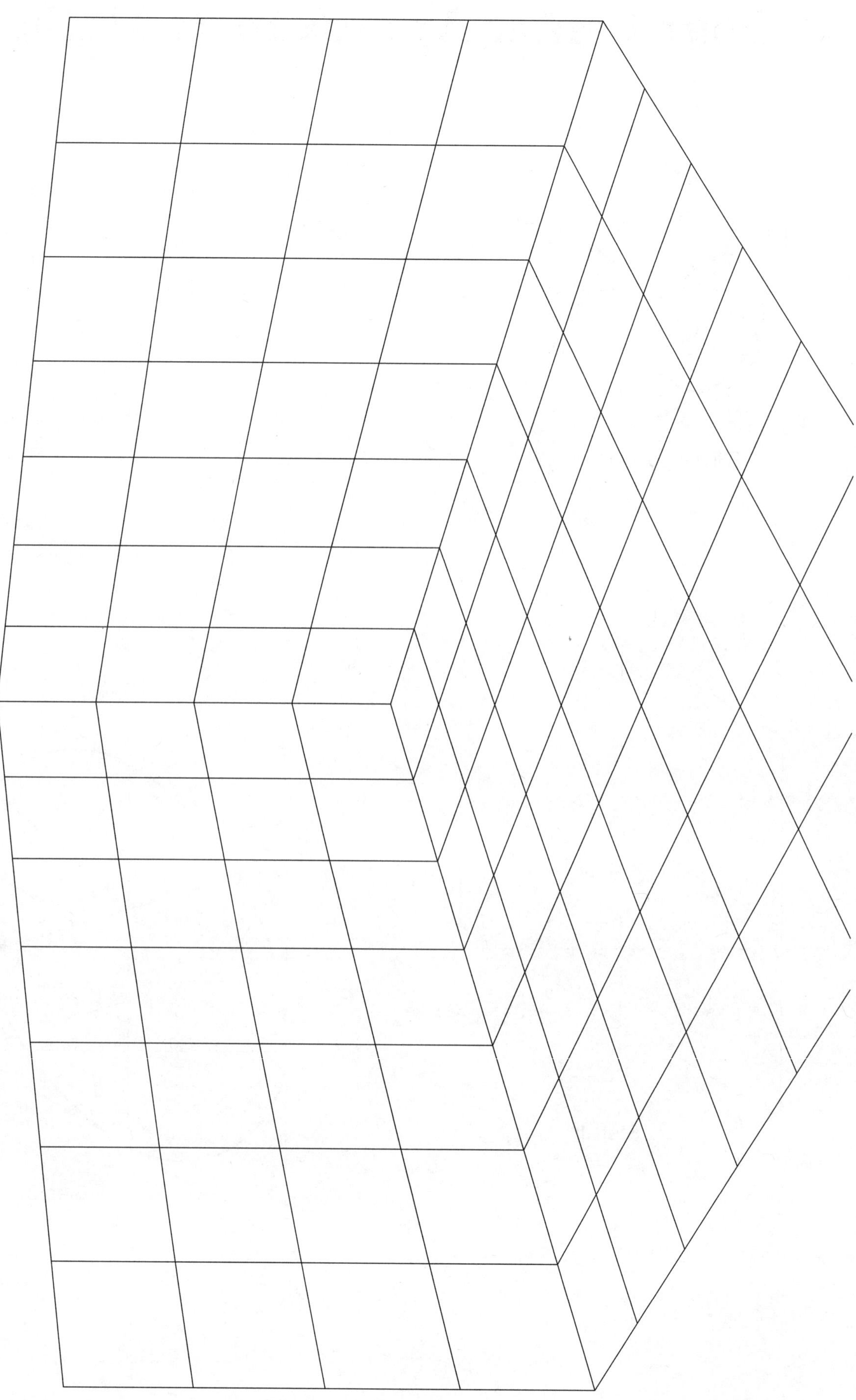

RM 11-2

Oblique Drawings

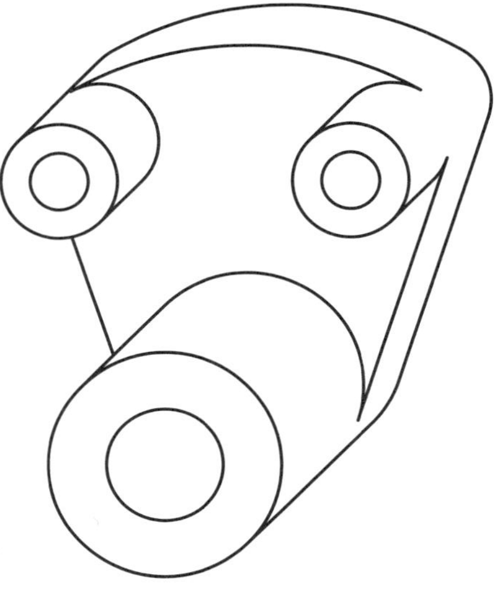

Cavalier Oblique
Full depth at 45°

Cabinet Oblique
Half depth at 45°

General Oblique
Three-quarter depth at 30°

RM 11-3

Procedure Checklist

Pictorial Drawings

Name ____

Observable Items	Completed		Comments	Instructor Initials
	Yes	No		
1. Constructs isometric drawings.				
2. Constructs isometric circles and arcs using: A. The four-center approximate method.				
B. The coordinate method.				
C. An isometric ellipse template.				
D. The **Ellipse** command.				
3. Constructs irregular curves in isometric drawings.				
4. Draws isometric section views.				
5. Dimensions isometric drawings.				
6. Constructs trimetric drawings.				
7. Dimensions trimetric drawings.				
8. Constructs oblique drawings.				
9. Dimensions oblique drawings.				
10. Constructs perspective drawings.				
11. Constructs circles in perspective views.				
12. Draws irregular curves in perspective views.				

Instructor Signature ____

Section 3 Descriptive Geometry

Auxiliary Views

Learning Objectives

After studying this chapter, the student will be able to:

- List the basic types of auxiliary views and explain the purpose of each type.
- Describe the common applications of auxiliary views.
- Explain the projection procedures for creating auxiliary views.
- Draw primary and secondary auxiliary views using manual and CAD methods.

Instructional Resources

Text: pages 407–439

Review Questions, page 428

Problems and Activities, pages 428–436

Drawing Problems, pages 437–439

Worksheets: pages 97–106

- Worksheet 12-1: *Auxiliary Projections*
- Worksheet 12-2: *Auxiliary Projections*
- Worksheet 12-3: *Auxiliary View Construction*
- Worksheet 12-4: *Auxiliary View Construction*
- Worksheet 12-5: *Secondary Auxiliary View Construction*
- Worksheet 12-6: *Secondary Auxiliary View Construction*
- Worksheet 12-7: *Secondary Auxiliary Projections*
- Worksheet 12-8: *Bracket*
- Worksheet 12-9: *Stripper Bracket*
- Worksheet 12-10: *Cutter Block*

Instructor's Resource

Instructional Tasks

Instructional Aids and Assignments

Chapter 12 Quiz

Reproducible Masters

- Reproducible Master 12-1: *Primary Auxiliary View*. Shown is a frontal auxiliary view.
- Reproducible Master 12-2: *Auxiliary View Used to Construct a Principal View*. The process of using an auxiliary view for the completion of a principal view is shown.

Procedure Checklist

Color Transparencies (Binder/IRCD only)

- Transparency 12-1: *Secondary Auxiliary View*. The solution to a secondary auxiliary view problem is shown.

Instructional Tasks

1. Define the term *auxiliary view*.
   - Discuss the relationship of auxiliary views to normal views.
2. Clarify the purpose of primary auxiliary views.
   - Ask students to draw primary auxiliary views of several classroom objects.
   - Use a transparency to demonstrate the projection of a primary auxiliary view.
3. Discuss the procedure for determining the true size and shape of an inclined surface.
   - Use step-by-step instruction and give examples of determining the true size and shape of an inclined surface.
4. Discuss the procedure for locating a point in an auxiliary view.
   - Clarify the importance of the location of a point in an auxiliary view as a basis for understanding all subsequent views.
   - Demonstrate the procedure for locating a point in an auxiliary view.
5. Discuss the procedure for locating a true length line in an auxiliary view.
   - Discuss the usefulness of an auxiliary view in finding the true length of a line.
   - Use transparencies with overlays to demonstrate the location of a true length line.
6. Define the term *slope*.
   - Using ordinary classroom objects, discuss and demonstrate the procedure for determining the slope of a line.

7. Discuss how to determine the true angle between a line and a principal plane.
   - Demonstrate the procedure for determining the true angle between a line and a principal plane.
8. Discuss how to determine the true angle between two planes.
   - Use transparencies to demonstrate how to locate the true angle between two planes.
9. Explain how circles and irregular curves are projected in auxiliary views.
   - Discuss manual and CAD methods for projecting circles and irregular curves in auxiliary views.
10. Discuss the purpose for and construction of a principal view with the aid of an auxiliary view.
    - Using an ordinary object, demonstrate the construction of a principal view with the aid of an auxiliary view.
11. Explain the need for secondary auxiliary views of objects.
    - Instruct students to compile a list of applications needing secondary auxiliary views.
12. Explain the need for secondary auxiliary views of objects.
    - Instruct students to compile a list of applications needing secondary auxiliary views.
13. Explain how to construct the point view of a line in a secondary view.
    - Draw several views (top and front views) of lines. Demonstrate the correct procedure in order to project the proper view.
14. Discuss how to determine the true angle between two planes in a secondary auxiliary view.
    - Use transparencies to demonstrate how to determine the true angle between two planes in a secondary auxiliary view.
15. Discuss applications for determining the true size of an oblique plane.
    - Demonstrate how to determine the true size of an oblique plane using an architectural example.

Instructional Aids and Assignments

1. Display transparencies with overlays showing auxiliary view projection methods.
2. Display machine or architectural parts with inclined surfaces or features. With a contrasting color, paint the inclined or oblique surface to be projected.
3. Assign the drawing problems in the textbook. The number of problems is sufficient to assign a minimum number to all students and to identify problems that may be done for extra credit. Some problems may be used for the performance section of the chapter quiz.

Answers to Review Questions, Text

Page 428

1. An auxiliary view is a supplementary view used to provide a true size and shape description of an object surface (typically an inclined surface).
2. size, shape
3. D. All of the above.
4. Primary and secondary.
5. successive
6. An auxiliary view projected from an orthographic view.
7. inclined
8. true length
9. slope
10. dihedral
11. The **Ellipse** and **Spline** commands.
12. ellipse templates
13. Oblique
14. primary, principal
15. line of sight
16. point, edges
17. oblique

Solutions to Problems and Activities, Text

Pages 428–436

Student work should look like the following drawings. The problem number and title are indicated on each problem sheet.

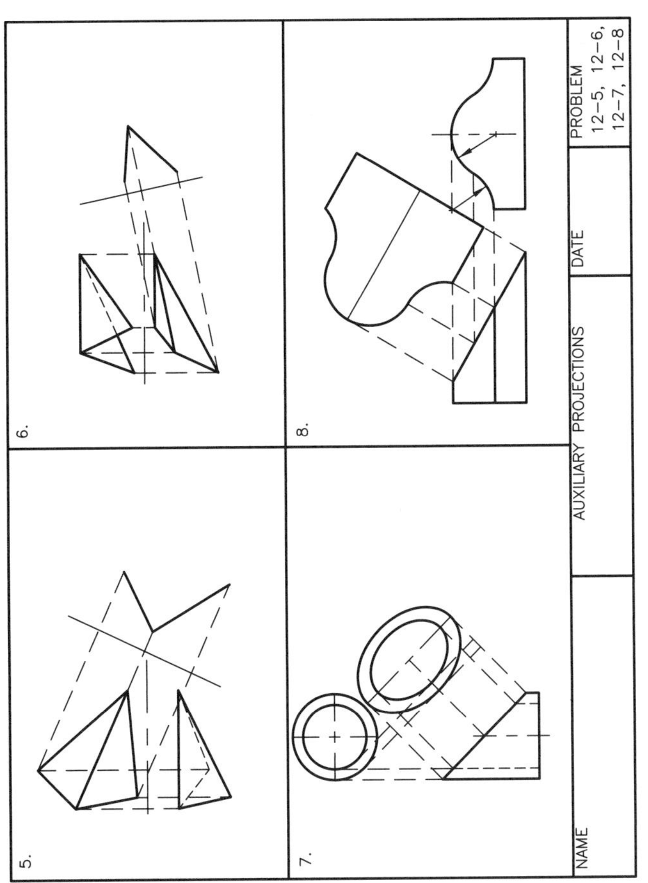
PROBLEM
12–5, 12–6,
12–7, 12–8
DATE
AUXILIARY PROJECTIONS
NAME
5.
6.
7.
8.

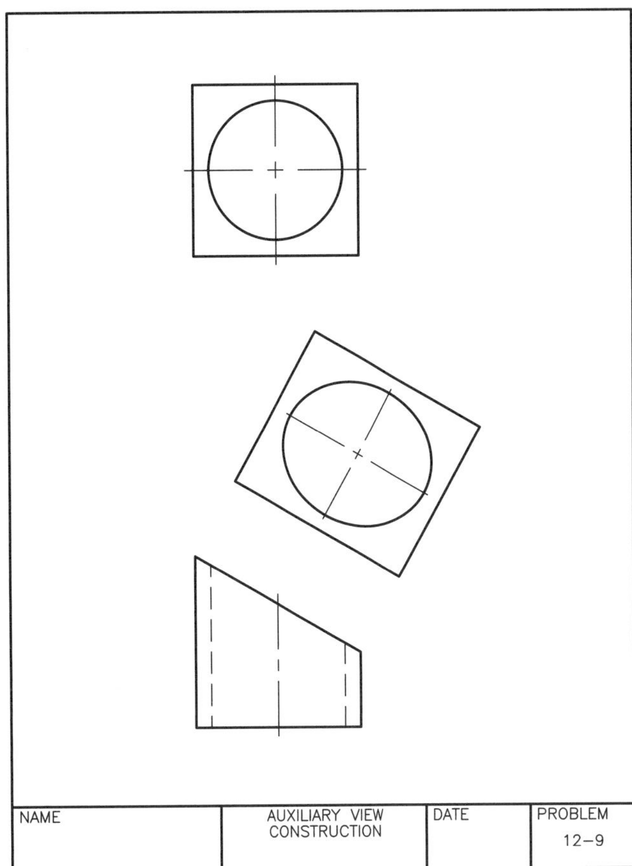
NAME
AUXILIARY VIEW
CONSTRUCTION
DATE
PROBLEM
12–9

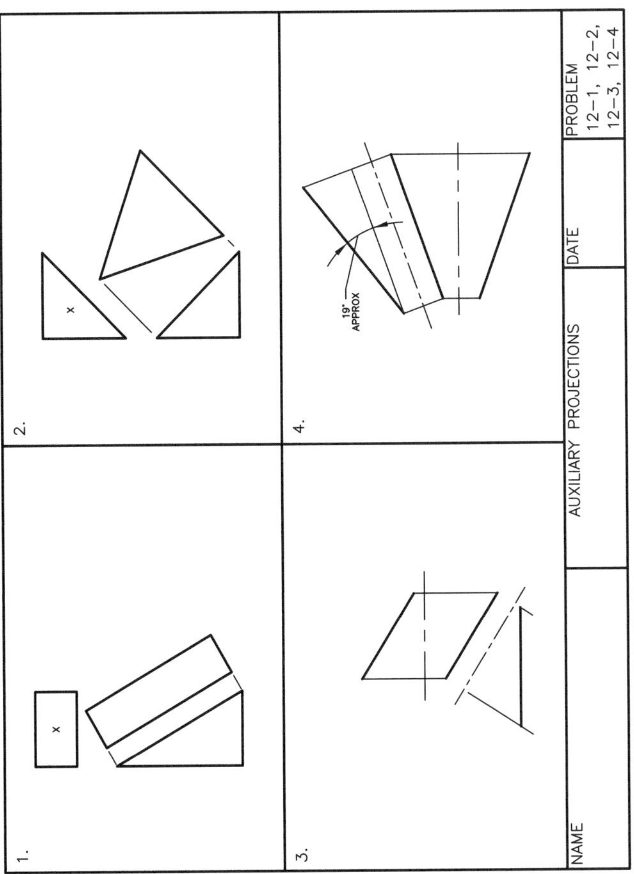
PROBLEM
12–1, 12–2,
12–3, 12–4
DATE
AUXILIARY PROJECTIONS
NAME
1.
2.
3.
4.
19° APPROX

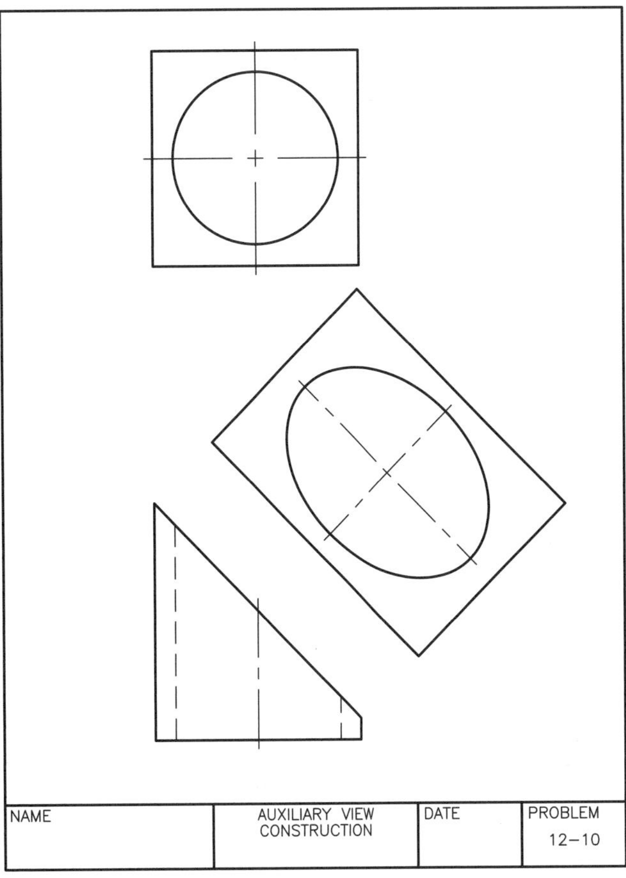
NAME
AUXILIARY VIEW
CONSTRUCTION
DATE
PROBLEM
12–10

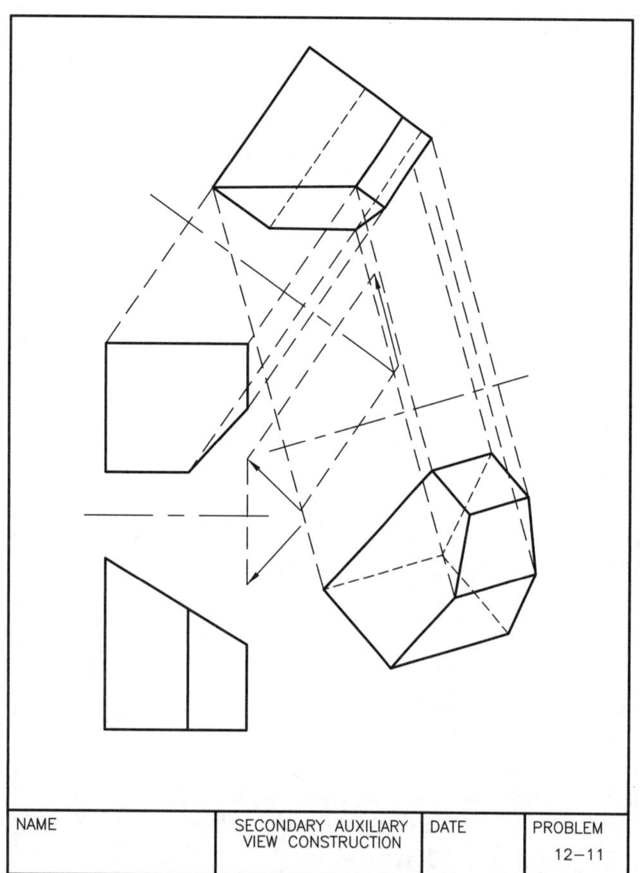
NAME
SECONDARY AUXILIARY VIEW CONSTRUCTION
DATE
PROBLEM
12–11

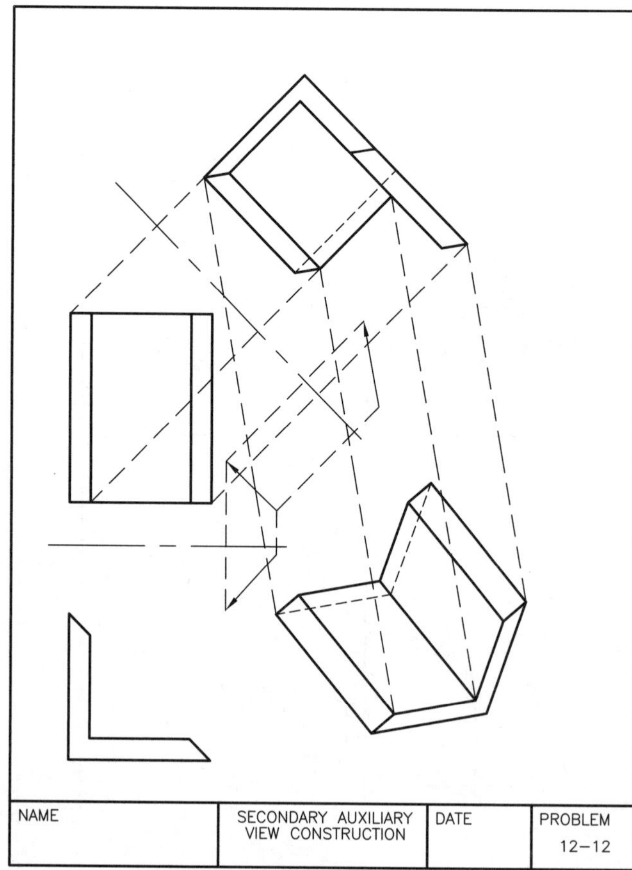
NAME
SECONDARY AUXILIARY VIEW CONSTRUCTION
DATE
PROBLEM
12–12

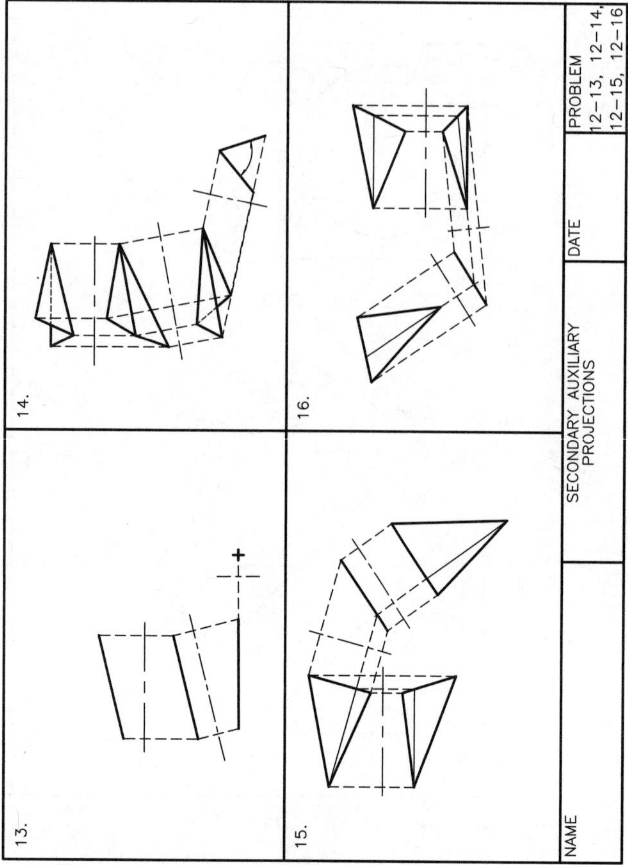
14.
16.
13.
15.
PROBLEM
12–13, 12–14,
12–15, 12–16
DATE
SECONDARY AUXILIARY PROJECTIONS
NAME

Solutions to Drawing Problems, Text
Pages 437–439

Student work should look like the following drawings. The problem number and title are indicated on each problem sheet.

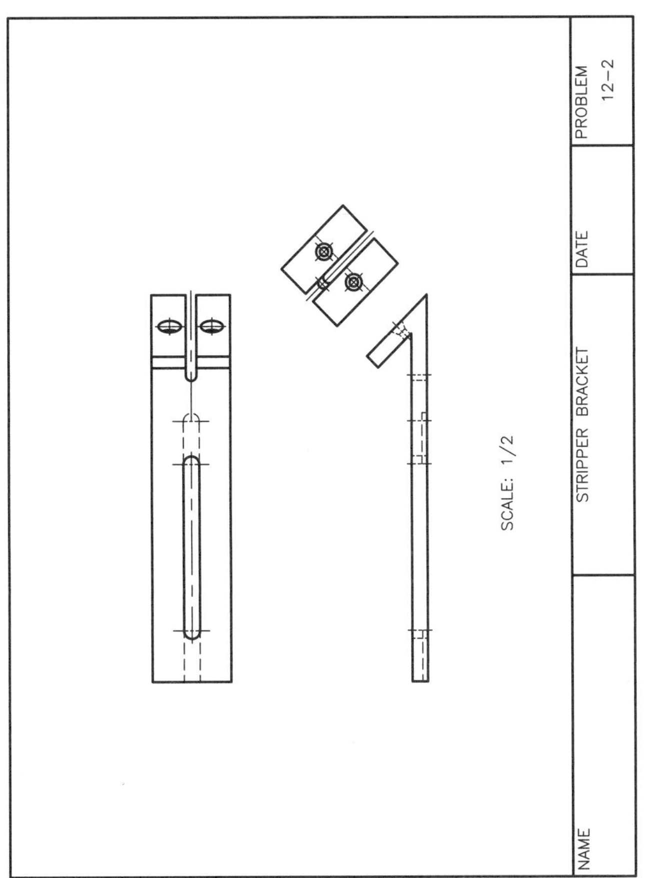

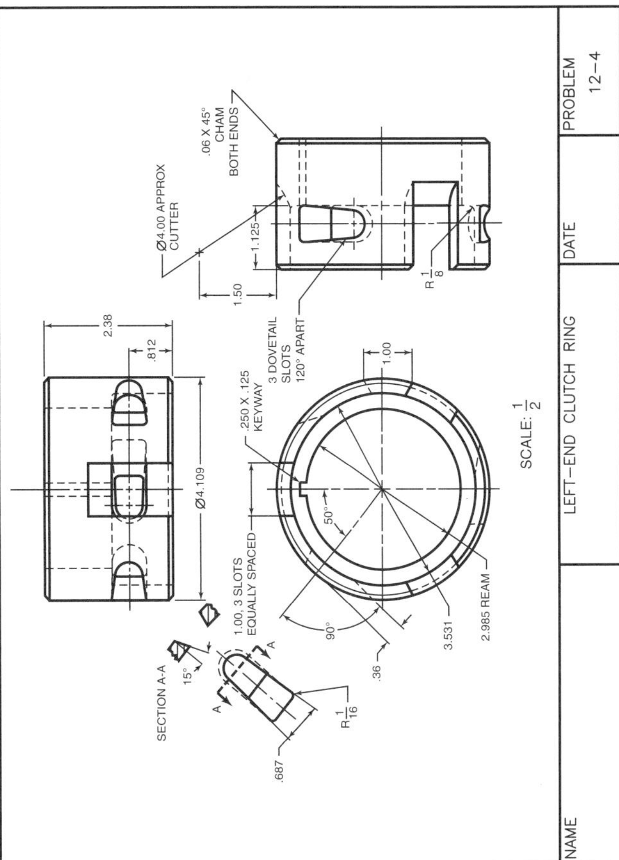

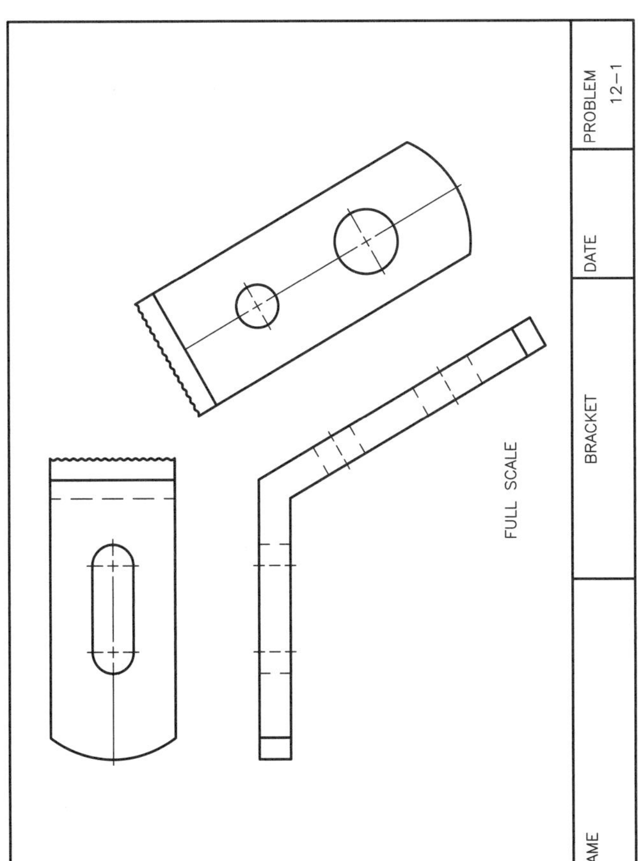

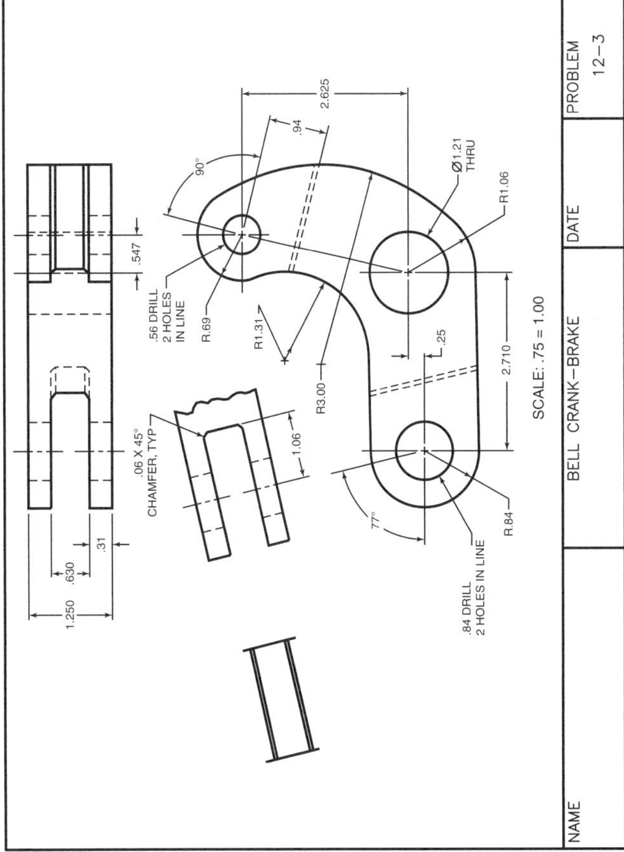

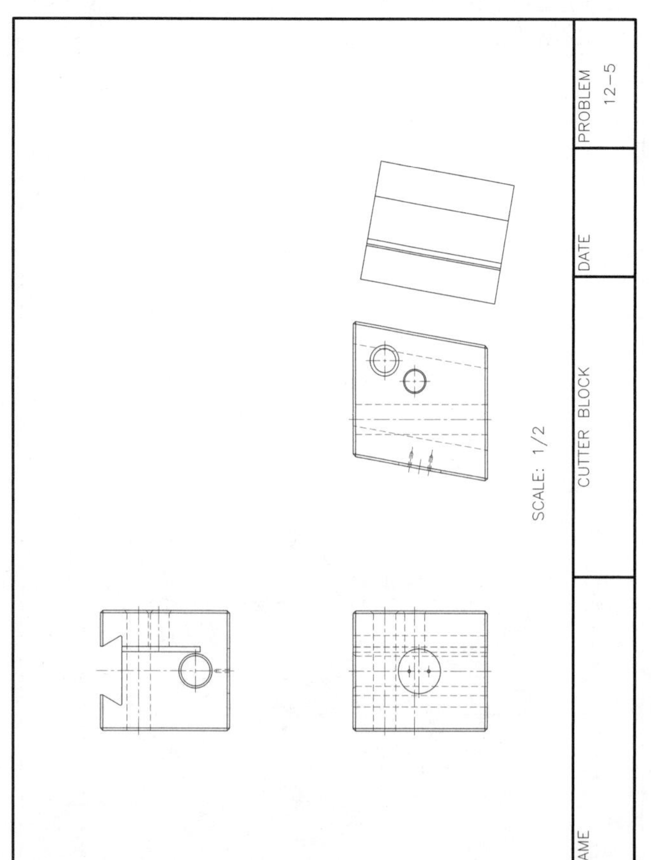

PROBLEM
12–5
DATE
CUTTER BLOCK
NAME
SCALE: 1/2

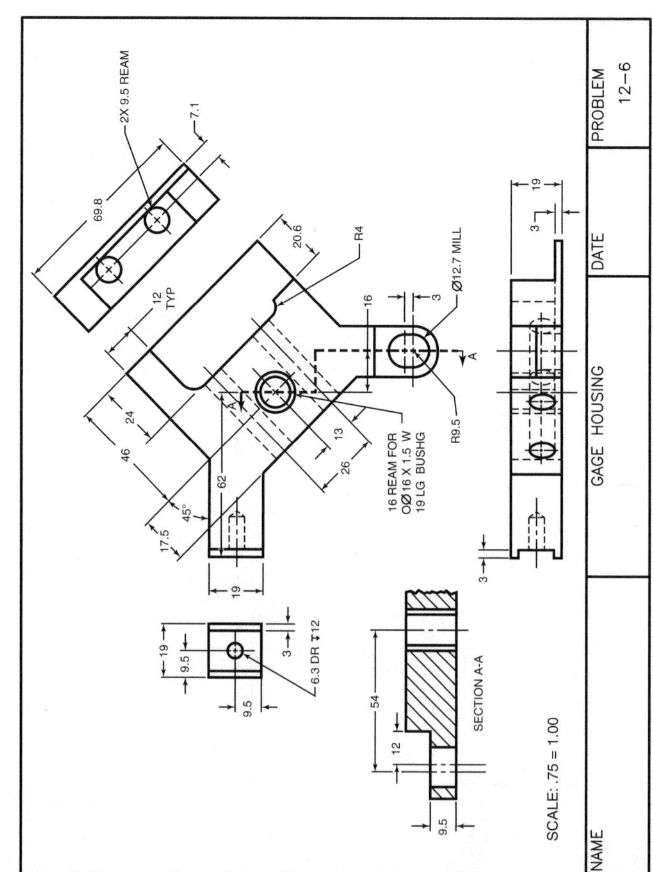

PROBLEM
12–6
DATE
GAGE HOUSING
NAME
SCALE: .75 = 1.00
2X 9.5 REAM
16 REAM FOR
OØ16 X 1.5 W
19 LG BUSHG
Ø12.7 MILL
R9.5
R4
12
TYP
6.3 DR ↧12
SECTION A-A

Solutions to Worksheets

Pages 97–106

Student work should look like the following drawings. The problem number and title are indicated on each problem sheet.

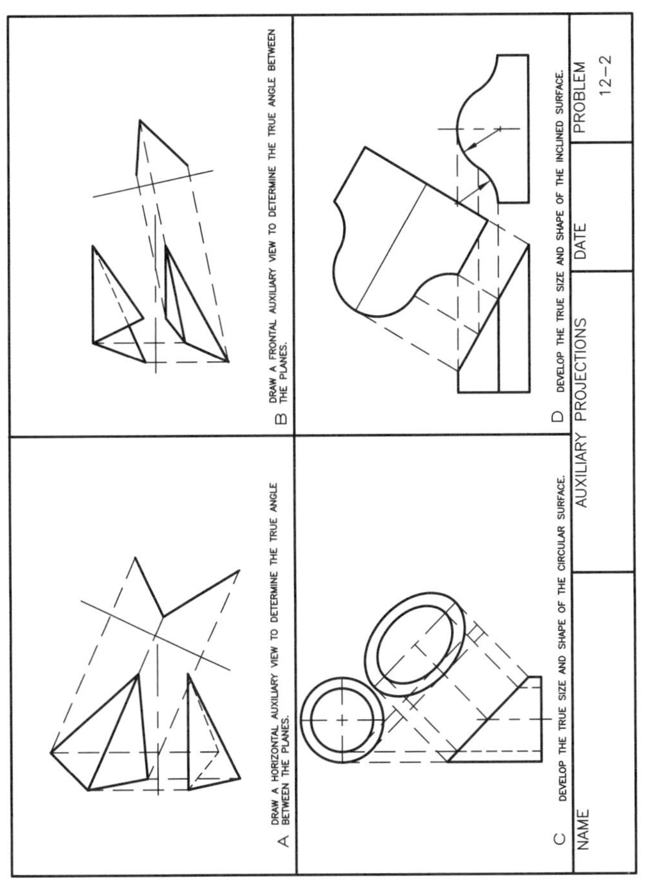

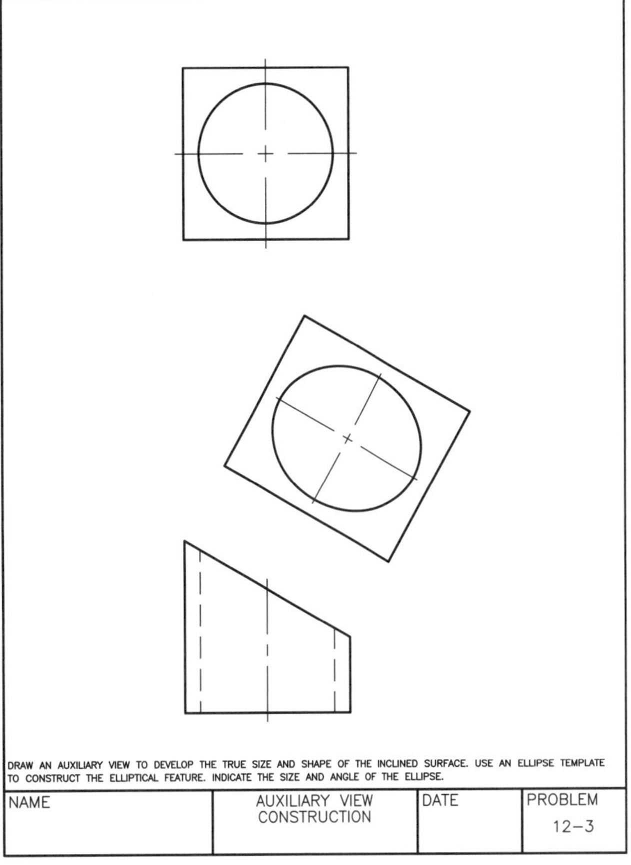

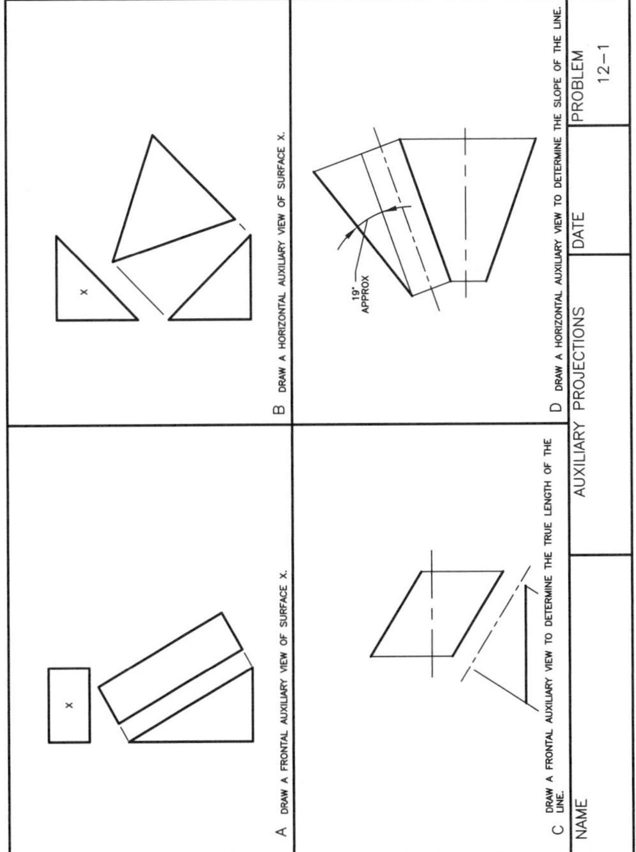

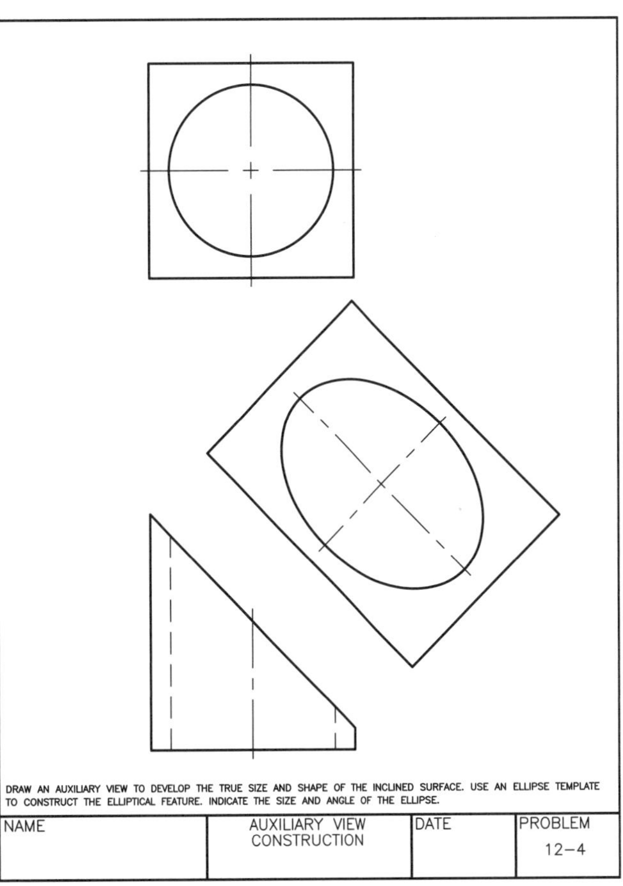

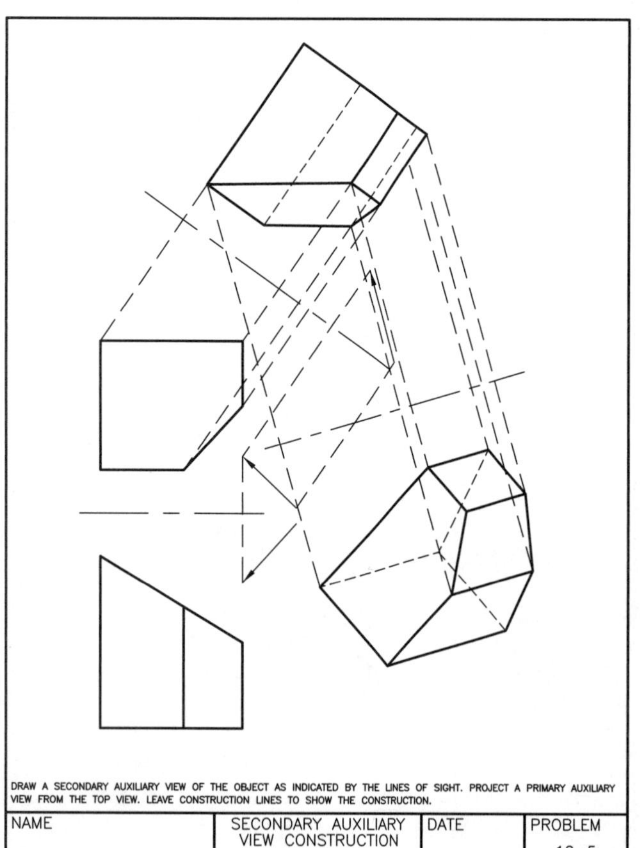
DRAW A SECONDARY AUXILIARY VIEW OF THE OBJECT AS INDICATED BY THE LINES OF SIGHT. PROJECT A PRIMARY AUXILIARY VIEW FROM THE TOP VIEW. LEAVE CONSTRUCTION LINES TO SHOW THE CONSTRUCTION.
NAME
SECONDARY AUXILIARY VIEW CONSTRUCTION
DATE
PROBLEM
12–5

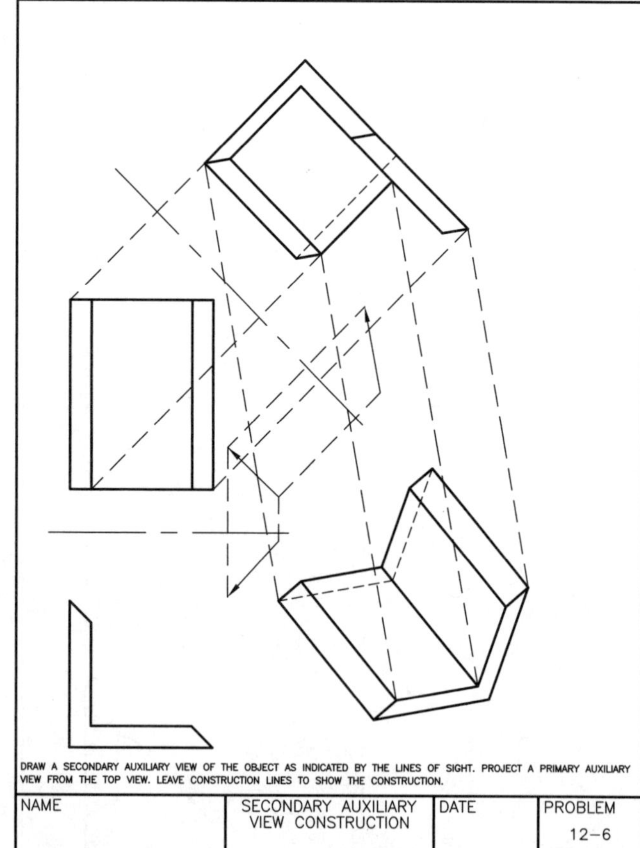
DRAW A SECONDARY AUXILIARY VIEW OF THE OBJECT AS INDICATED BY THE LINES OF SIGHT. PROJECT A PRIMARY AUXILIARY VIEW FROM THE TOP VIEW. LEAVE CONSTRUCTION LINES TO SHOW THE CONSTRUCTION.
NAME
SECONDARY AUXILIARY VIEW CONSTRUCTION
DATE
PROBLEM
12–6

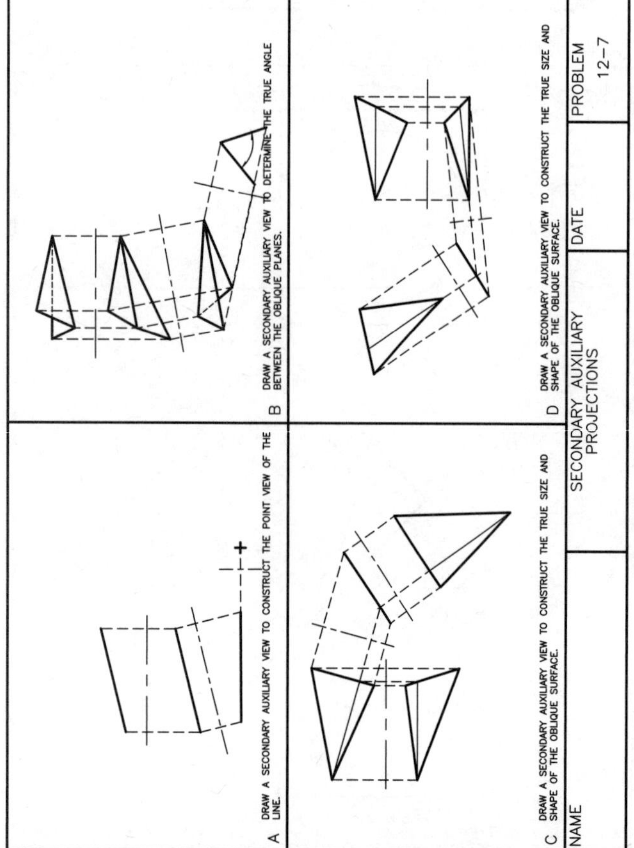
A DRAW A SECONDARY AUXILIARY VIEW TO CONSTRUCT THE POINT VIEW OF THE LINE.
B DRAW A SECONDARY AUXILIARY VIEW TO DETERMINE THE TRUE ANGLE BETWEEN THE OBLIQUE PLANES.
C DRAW A SECONDARY AUXILIARY VIEW TO CONSTRUCT THE TRUE SIZE AND SHAPE OF THE OBLIQUE SURFACE.
D DRAW A SECONDARY AUXILIARY VIEW TO CONSTRUCT THE TRUE SIZE AND SHAPE OF THE OBLIQUE SURFACE.
NAME
SECONDARY AUXILIARY PROJECTIONS
DATE
PROBLEM
12–7

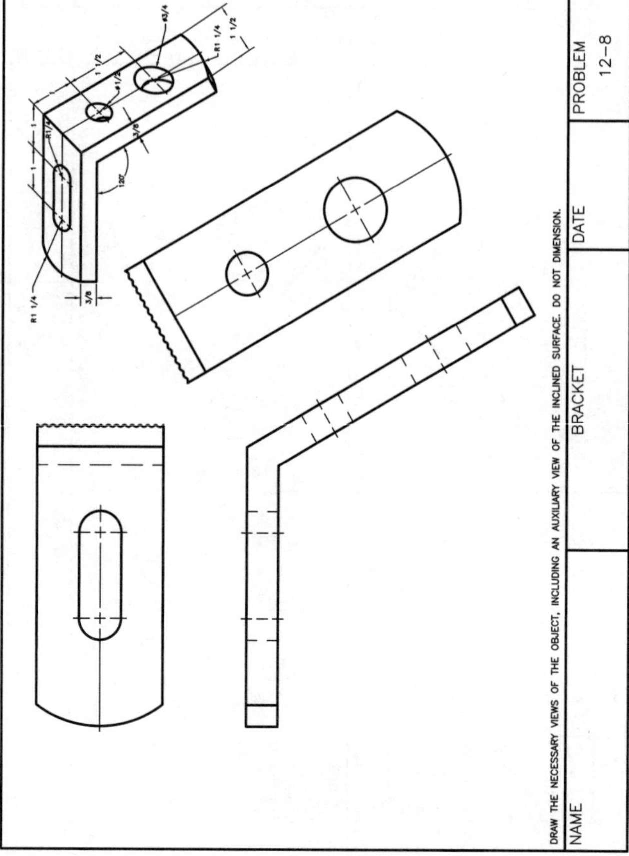
DRAW THE NECESSARY VIEWS OF THE OBJECT, INCLUDING AN AUXILIARY VIEW OF THE INCLINED SURFACE. DO NOT DIMENSION.
NAME
BRACKET
DATE
PROBLEM
12–8

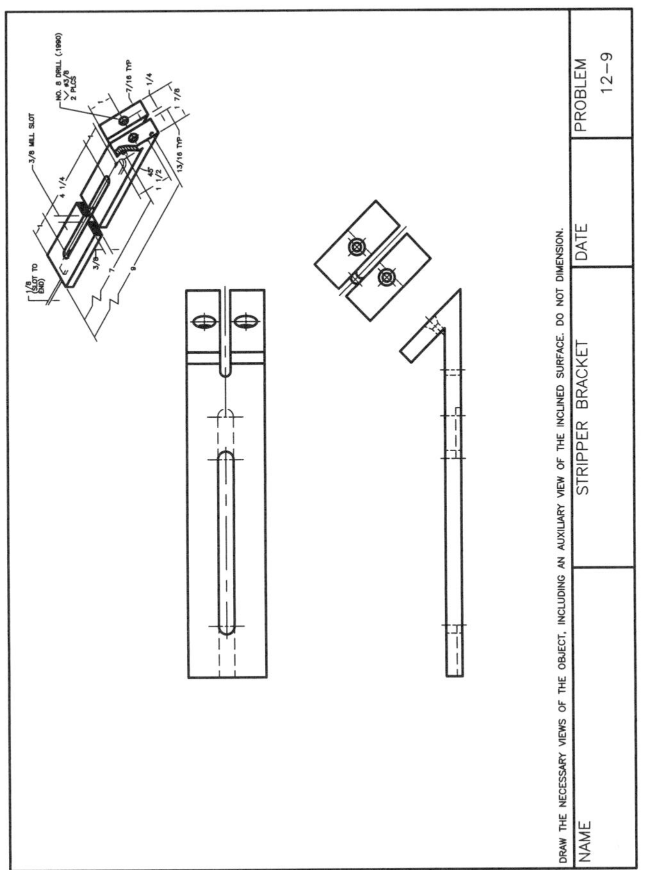

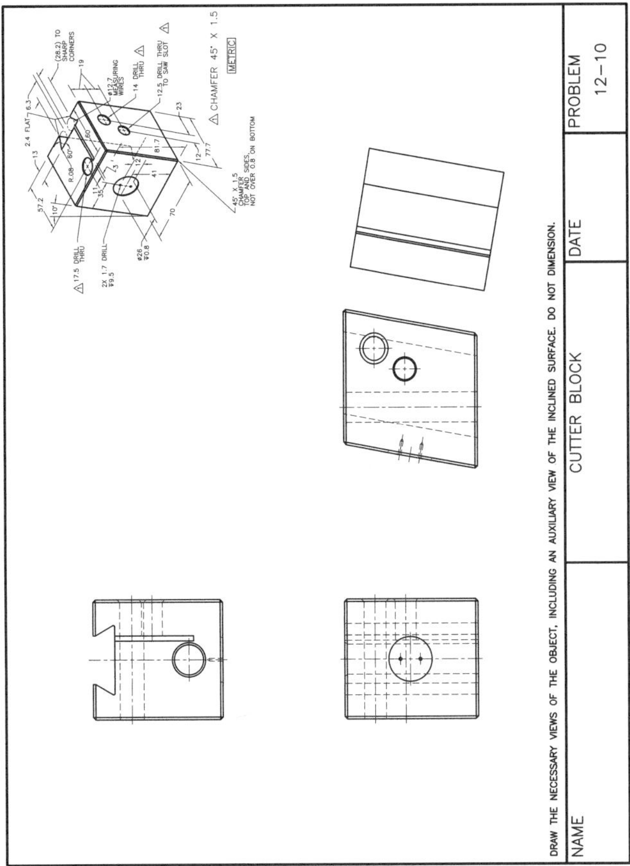

Answers to Chapter 12 Quiz

1. D. All of the above.
2. B. Primary and secondary.
3. A. one
4. C. An oblique line.
5. B. secondary auxiliary
6. B. The slope of a line.
7. B. The true shape of an oblique surface.
8. Refer to the drawings given in the *Solutions to Problems and Activities, Text* section or the *Solutions to Drawing Problems, Text* section for the problem selected from the textbook.

Chapter Quiz

Auxiliary Views

Name ______________________________

Period______________ Date______________ Score ______________

Multiple Choice

Choose the answer that correctly completes the statement. Write the corresponding letter in the space provided.

_______ 1. What type of information is provided by auxiliary views?
- A. The true length of a line.
- B. The edge view of a plane.
- C. The true angle between planes.
- D. All of the above.

_______ 2. What are the two primary types of auxiliary views?
- A. Primary and successive.
- B. Primary and secondary.
- C. Secondary and successive.
- D. Partial and successive.

_______ 3. A primary auxiliary view is perpendicular to _____ of the principal views.
- A. one
- B. two
- C. three
- D. A primary auxiliary view is not perpendicular to any of the principal views.

_______ 4. Which of the following lines requires an auxiliary view to find the true length?
- A. A normal line.
- B. A horizontal line.
- C. An oblique line.
- D. None of the above.

_______ 5. The true size and shape of an oblique surface will be shown in the _____ view.
- A. primary auxiliary
- B. secondary auxiliary
- C. successive auxiliary
- D. normal

_______ 6. Which of the following can be found by the use of a primary auxiliary view?
- A. The true size of an oblique plane.
- B. The slope of a line.
- C. The true angle between two planes when the line of intersection is an oblique line.
- D. None of the above.

Name ____________________

________ 7. Which of the following requires the use of a secondary auxiliary view?
A. The true length of an inclined line.
B. The true shape of an oblique surface.
C. The point view of a horizontal line.
D. All of the above.

Drafting Performance

8. Draw a solution of a problem selected by your instructor from Chapter 12 in your textbook. Leave construction lines on the drawing.

Primary Auxiliary View

A primary auxiliary view may be projected from any one of the normal views. As shown here, a frontal auxiliary view is projected from the front view.

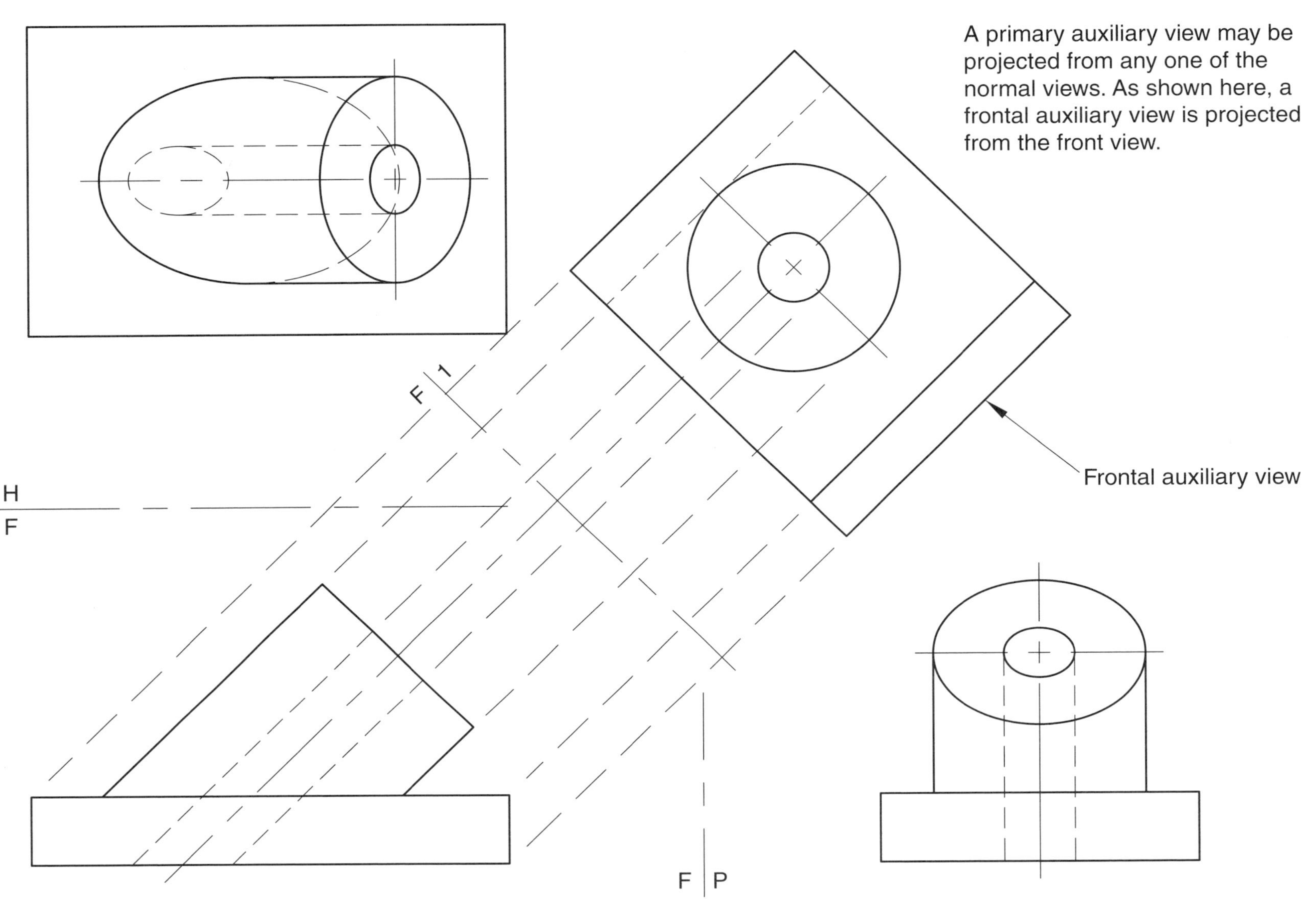

RM 12-1

Auxiliary View Used to Construct a Principal View

Given: Profile view and partial front view

Required: Complete the front and profile views with information developed through an auxiliary view

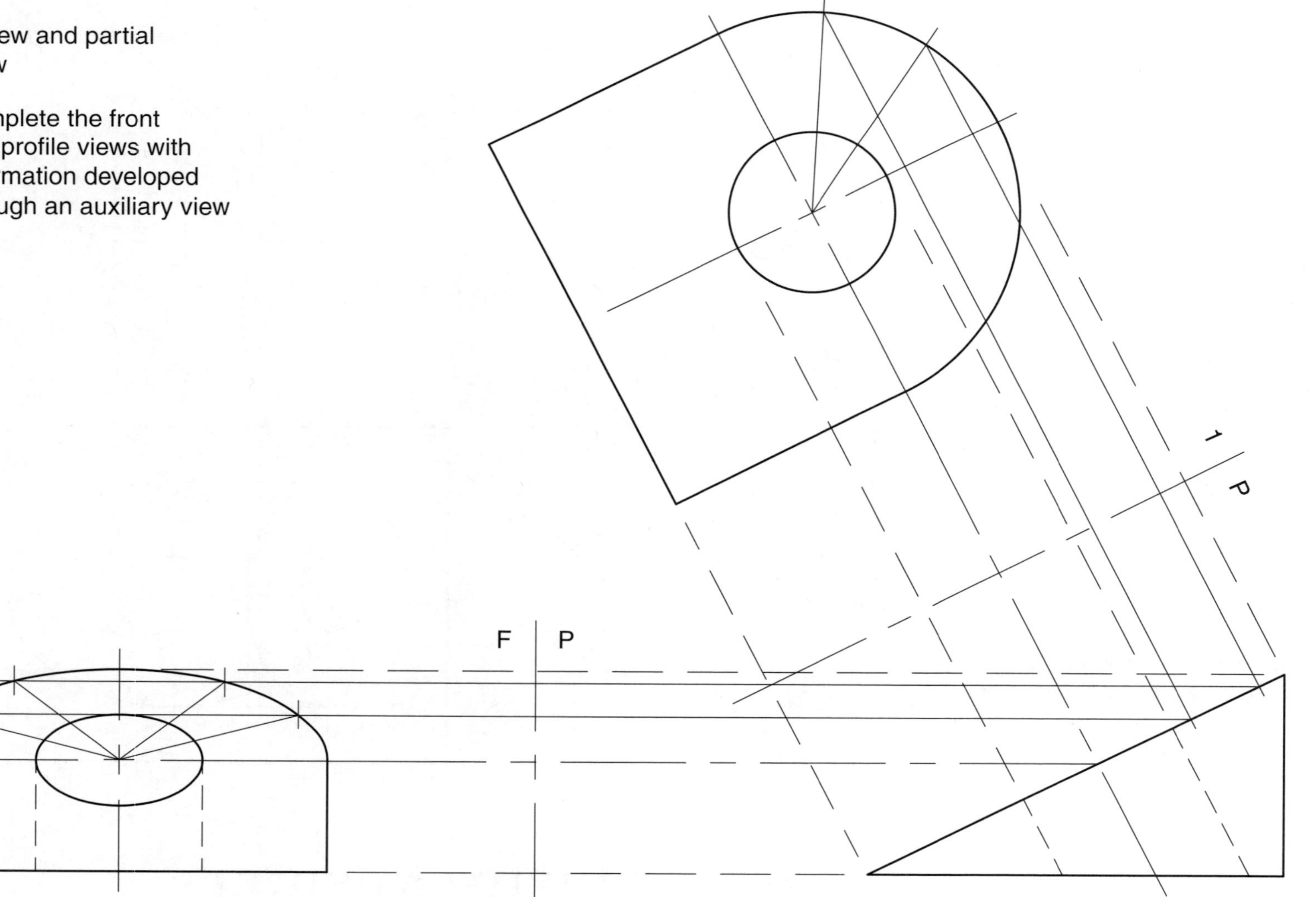

RM 12-2

Procedure Checklist

Auxiliary Views

Name ______________________________

Observable Items	Completed		Comments	Instructor Initials
	Yes	No		
1. Develops primary auxiliary views to construct: A. The location of a point.				
B. A true length line.				
C. The true size and shape of an inclined surface.				
2. Develops secondary auxiliary views to construct: A. The point view of a line.				
B. The true angle between two planes.				
C. The true size and shape of an oblique plane.				

Instructor Signature ______________________________

Revolutions

Learning Objectives

After studying this chapter, the student will be able to:

- Explain and apply the principles of revolution.
- Create revolved views using manual and CAD procedures.
- Revolve a line to determine its true length.
- Revolve a line to determine the true angle between the line and a principal plane.
- Revolve a plane to determine its true size.
- Determine the true angle between planes using the revolution method.

Instructional Resources

Text: pages 441–461

Review Questions, page 456

Problems and Activities, pages 456–459

Drawing Problems, pages 460–461

Worksheets: pages 107–113

- Worksheet 13-1: *Revolutions*
- Worksheet 13-2: *Revolutions*
- Worksheet 13-3: *Revolutions*
- Worksheet 13-4: *Revolutions*
- Worksheet 13-5: *Primary Revolutions*
- Worksheet 13-6: *Successive Revolutions*
- Worksheet 13-7: *True Length Lines*

Instructor's Resource

Instructional Tasks

Instructional Aids and Assignments

Chapter 13 Quiz

Reproducible Masters

- Reproducible Master 13-1: *Revolution Method.* A drawing of a cone is illustrated to show the method of developing the true length of a line by revolution.

Procedure Checklist

Color Transparencies (Binder/IRCD only)

- Transparency 13-1: *Revolving a Plane to Locate the Edge View.* The process of revolving a plane to locate the edge view is shown.

Instructional Tasks

1. Explain the meaning of the term *revolution.*
   - Discuss the relationship of revolved views to auxiliary views.
   - Show examples of machine or architectural parts for which the revolution method would be useful in defining features.
2. Discuss the common spatial relationships that can be obtained through the use of revolution.
   - Use the element of a cone to demonstrate the principles of revolution.
3. Explain how to use the revolution method to find the true length of a line.
   - Demonstrate the revolution method. Use appropriate transparencies.
4. Explain how to use the revolution method to determine the true angle between a line and a principal plane.
   - Using ordinary objects, demonstrate the procedure for determining the true angle between a line and a principal plane.
5. Explain how to use the revolution method to revolve a plane to determine its true size.
   - Use transparencies and step-by-step instruction to demonstrate how to revolve a plane to determine its true size.
6. Explain how to use the revolution method to locate the edge view of a plane.
   - Use transparencies and step-by-step instruction to demonstrate how to revolve a plane to locate the edge view.
7. Explain how to use the revolution method to determine the true angle between two planes.

- Discuss applications for determining the true angle between two planes.

8. Explain how to use the revolution method to determine the true angle between two intersecting oblique planes.
   - Demonstrate how to use the auxiliary and revolution methods to determine the true angle between two intersecting oblique planes.
9. Explain how to trace the path of revolution of a point about an oblique axis.
   - Ask students to name machine designs where tracing the path of revolution of a point about an oblique axis would apply.
   - Using transparencies, demonstrate how to revolve a point about an oblique axis.
10. Explain how to construct a primary revolution.
    - Using an ordinary classroom object, demonstrate how to revolve an object about an axis perpendicular to a principal plane.
11. Explain how to construct a successive revolution.
    - Use step-by-step instruction, along with any appropriate object, to demonstrate successive revolution of an object to determine the true size of an oblique surface.

Instructional Aids and Assignments

1. Display transparencies with overlays showing the method of revolution.
2. Display machine or architectural parts with inclined or oblique surfaces.
3. Show a multimedia presentation or film on the revolution method.
4. Assign the drawing problems in the textbook. The number of problems is sufficient to assign a minimum number to all students and to identify problems that may be done for extra credit. Some problems may be used for the performance section of the chapter quiz.

Answers to Review Questions, Text

Page 456

1. Revolution is a method in which spatial relationships are defined by rotating or revolving parts.
2. auxiliary
3. revolved
4. points, lines, planes
5. By creating three-dimensional views of models.
6. The **Orbit** and **Rotate 3D** commands.
7. **Rotate**
8. length
9. true
10. An edge view of the plane.
11. line of intersection
12. A clear view of an object, the true length of a line, or the true size of a surface.
13. successive

Solutions to Problems and Activities, Text

Pages 456–459

Student work should look like the following drawings. The problem number and title are indicated on each problem sheet.

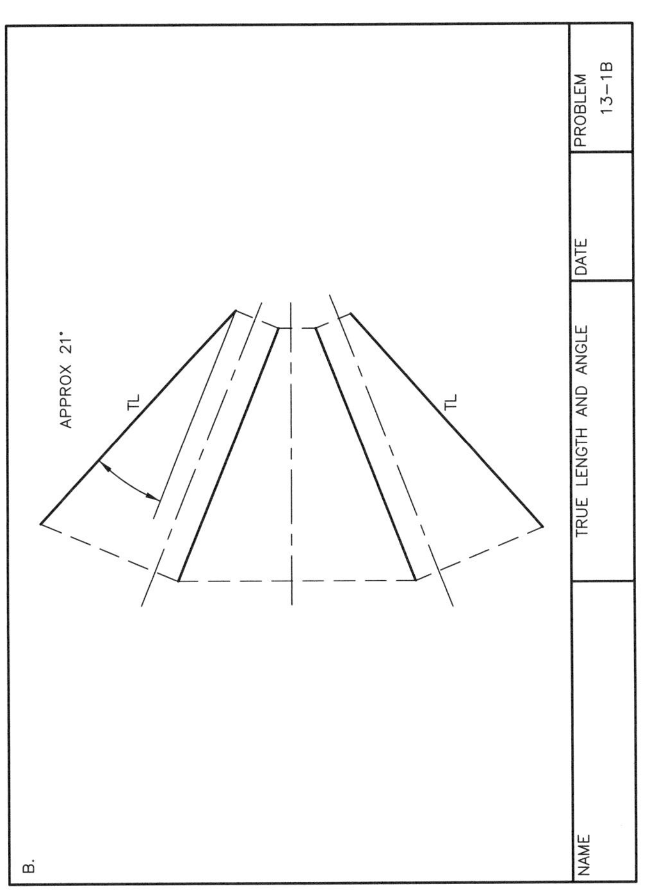
B.
APPROX 21°
TL
TL
NAME
TRUE LENGTH AND ANGLE
DATE
PROBLEM
13–1B

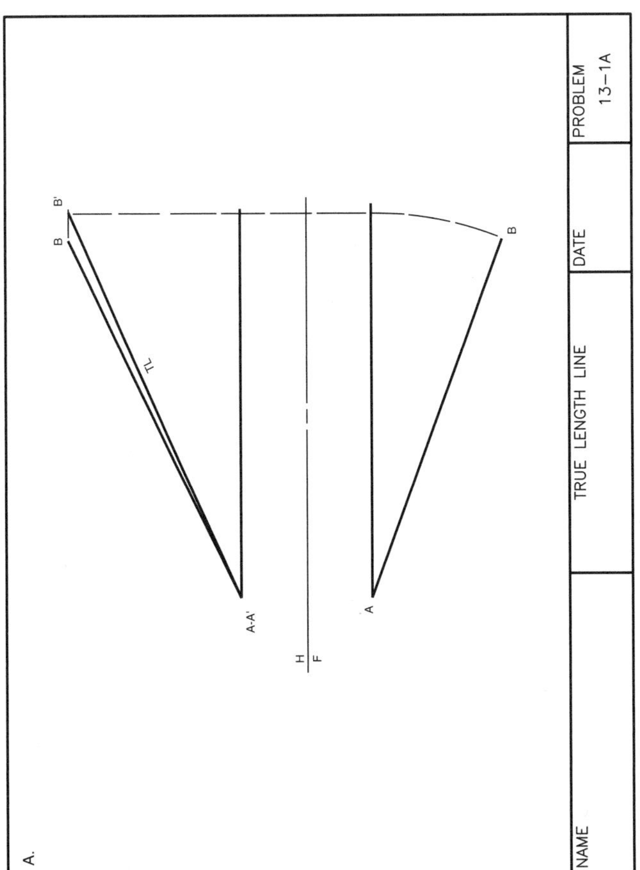
A.
B
B'
TL
A-A'
H
F
A
B
NAME
TRUE LENGTH LINE
DATE
PROBLEM
13–1A

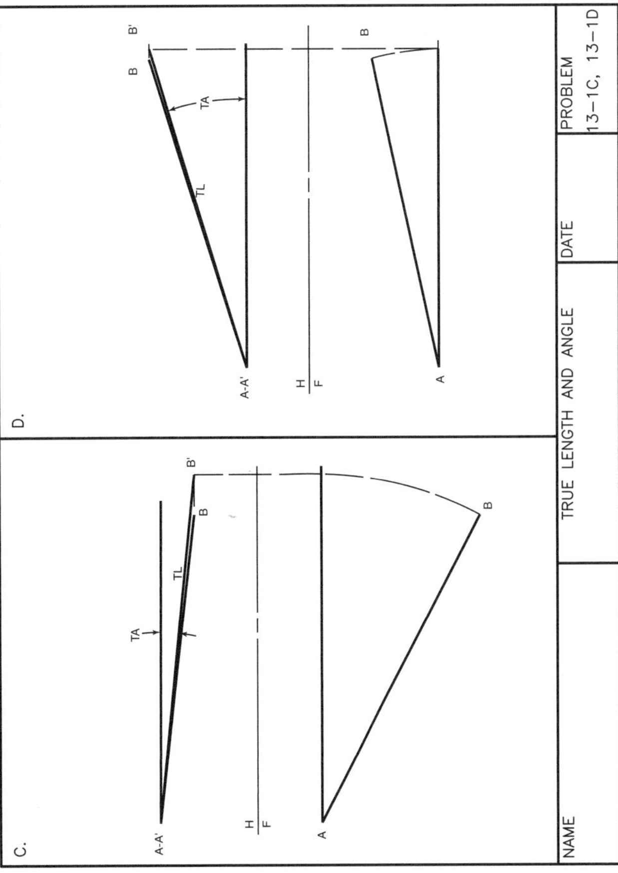
C.
A-A'
TA
TL
B
B'
H
F
A
B
D.
B
B'
TA
TL
A-A'
H
F
B
A
NAME
TRUE LENGTH AND ANGLE
DATE
PROBLEM
13–1C, 13–1D

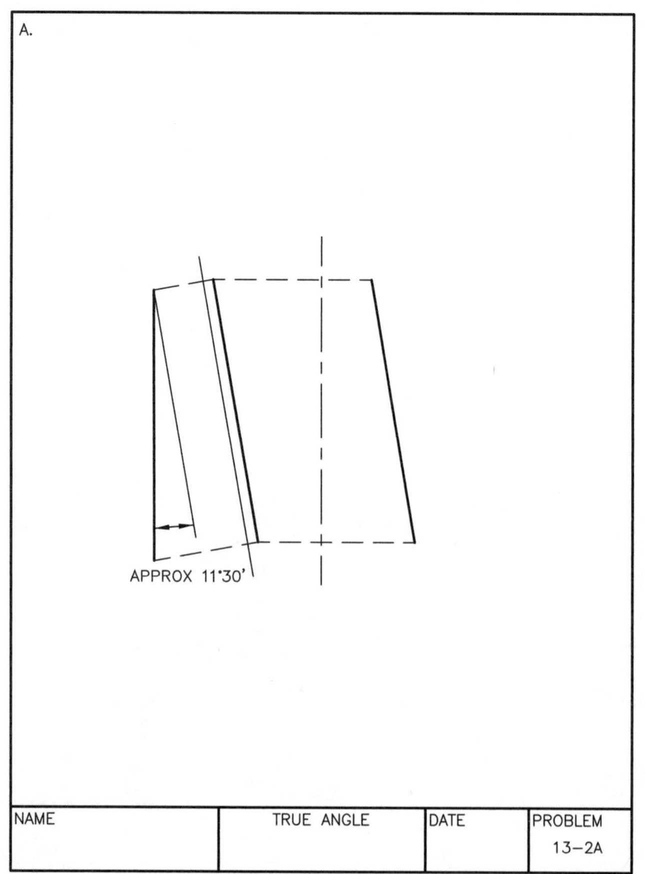
A.
APPROX 11°30'
NAME
TRUE ANGLE
DATE
PROBLEM
13–2A

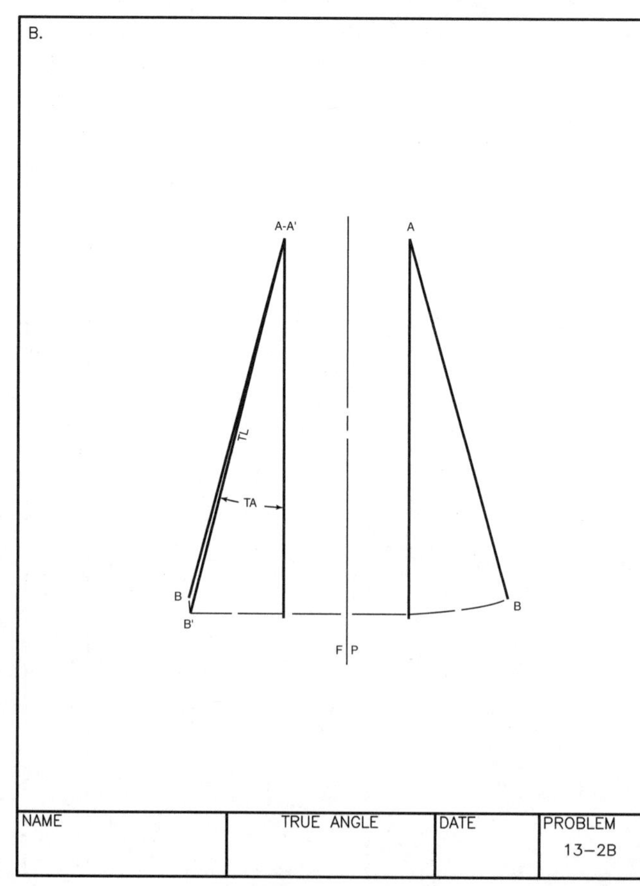
B.
A-A'
A
TL
TA
B
B'
B
F P
NAME
TRUE ANGLE
DATE
PROBLEM
13–2B

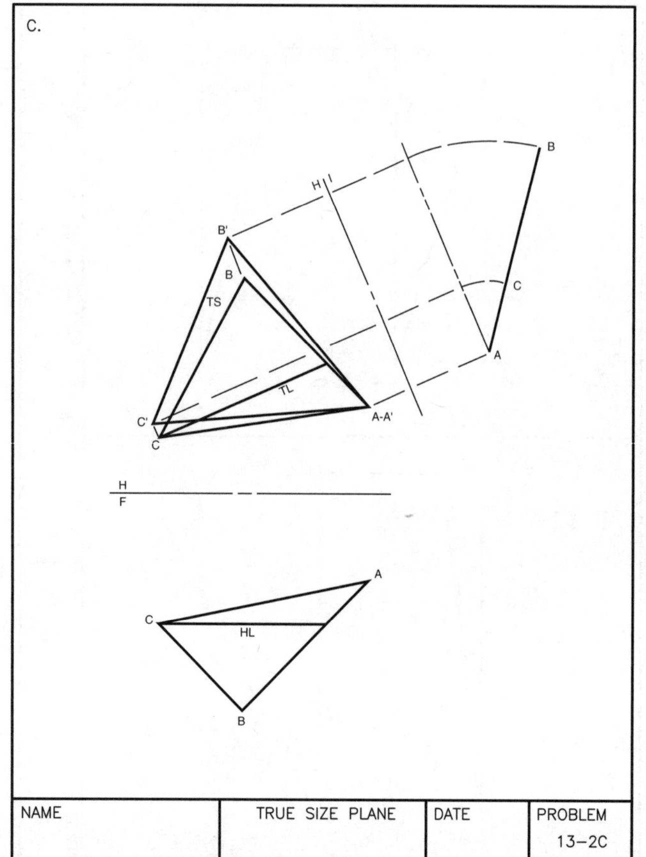
C.
B
H I
B'
B
TS
C
A
TL
C'
C
A-A'
H
F
A
C
HL
B
NAME
TRUE SIZE PLANE
DATE
PROBLEM
13–2C

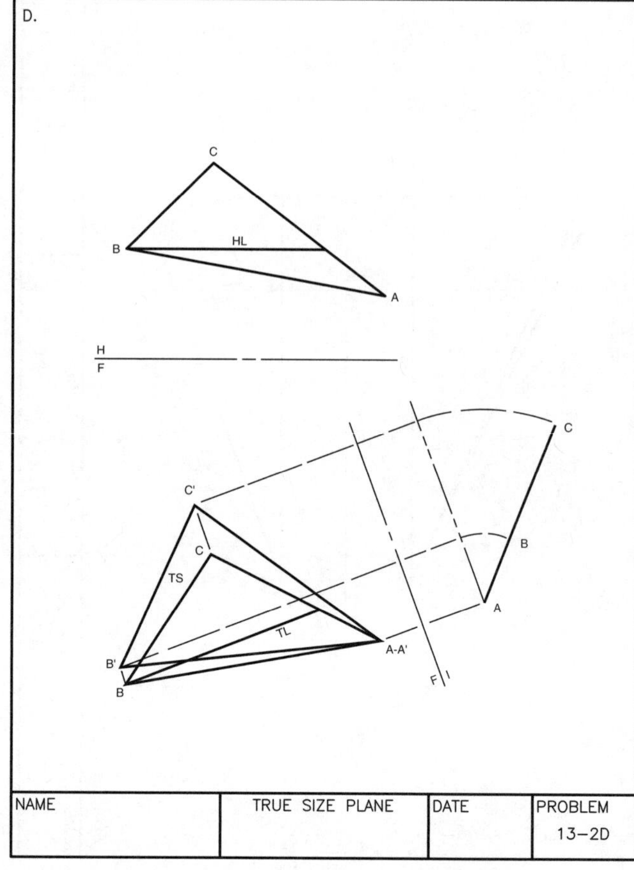
D.
C
B
HL
A
H
F
C
C'
C
B
TS
A
TL
A-A'
B'
B
F I
NAME
TRUE SIZE PLANE
DATE
PROBLEM
13–2D

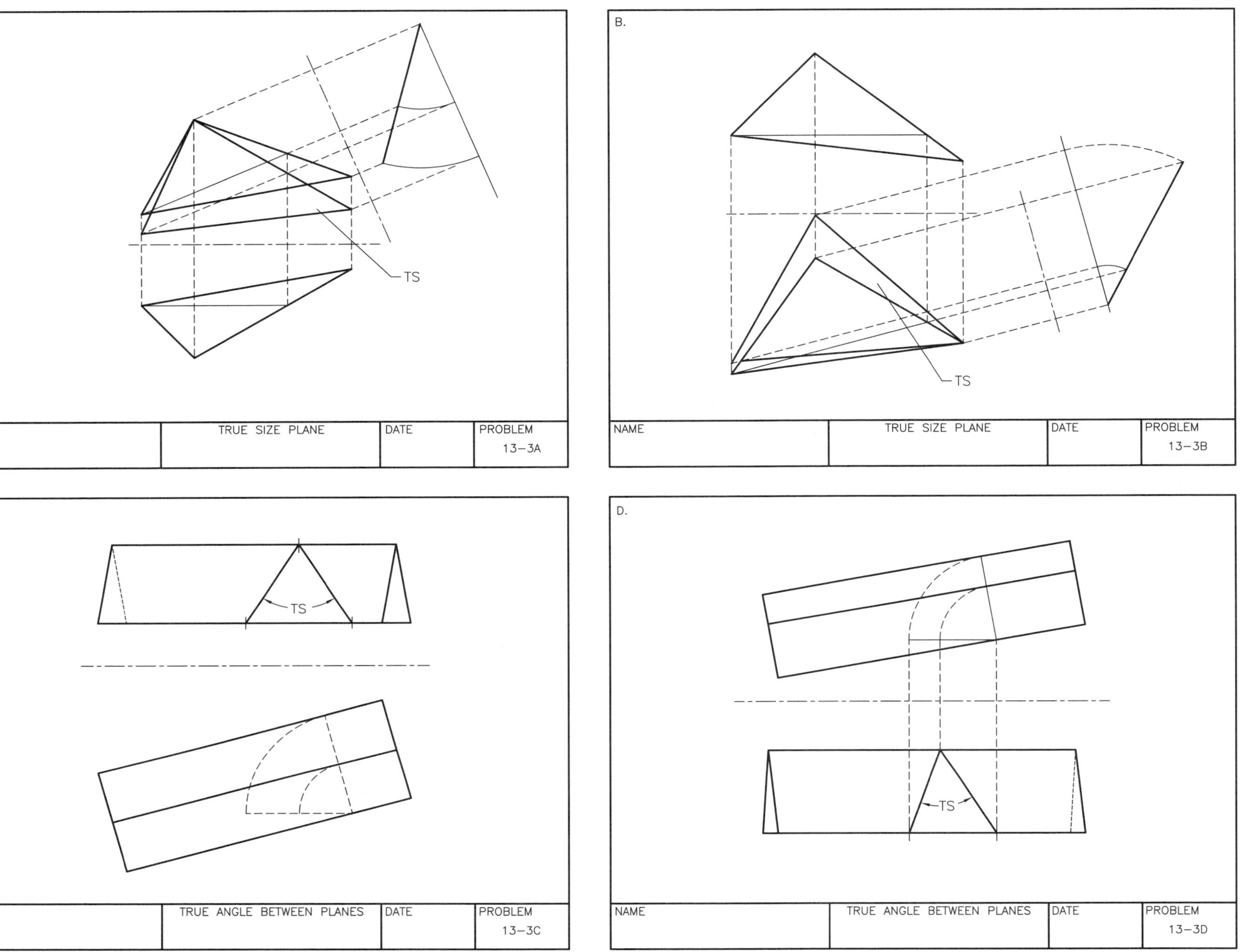

A.
TS
NAME
TRUE SIZE PLANE
DATE
PROBLEM
13–3A
B.
TS
NAME
TRUE SIZE PLANE
DATE
PROBLEM
13–3B
C.
TS
NAME
TRUE ANGLE BETWEEN PLANES
DATE
PROBLEM
13–3C
D.
TS
NAME
TRUE ANGLE BETWEEN PLANES
DATE
PROBLEM
13–3D

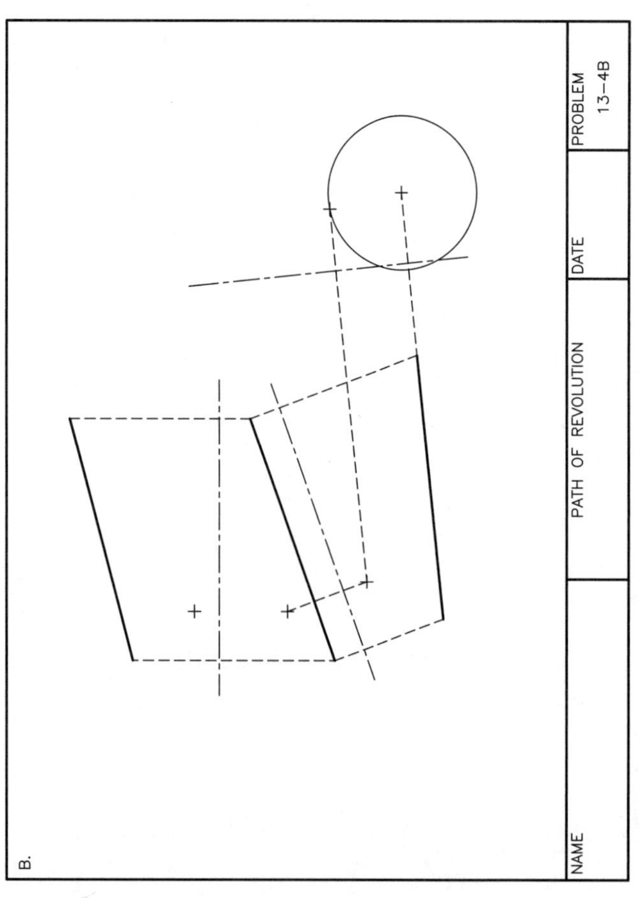
PROBLEM
13–4B
DATE
PATH OF REVOLUTION
NAME
B.

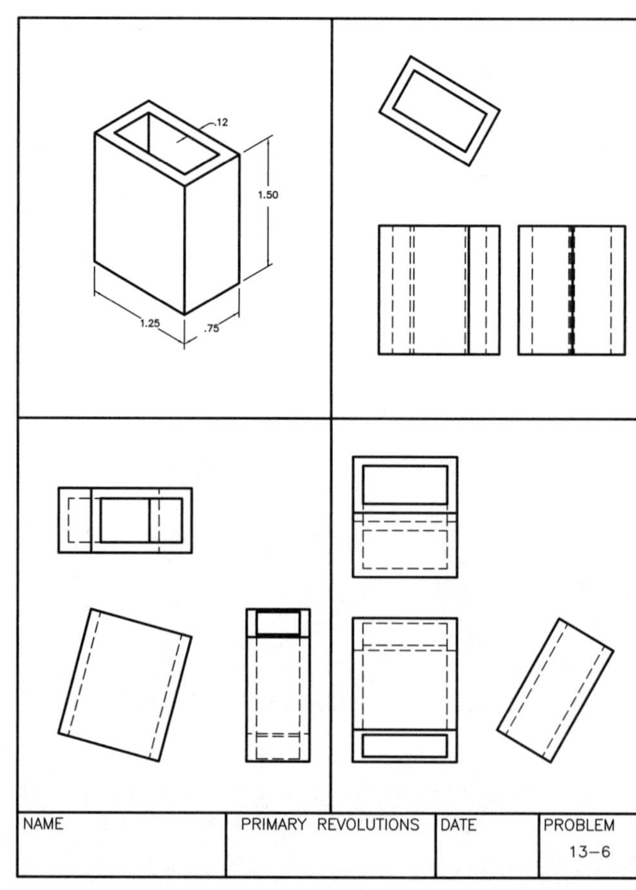
.12
1.50
1.25
.75
NAME
PRIMARY REVOLUTIONS
DATE
PROBLEM
13–6

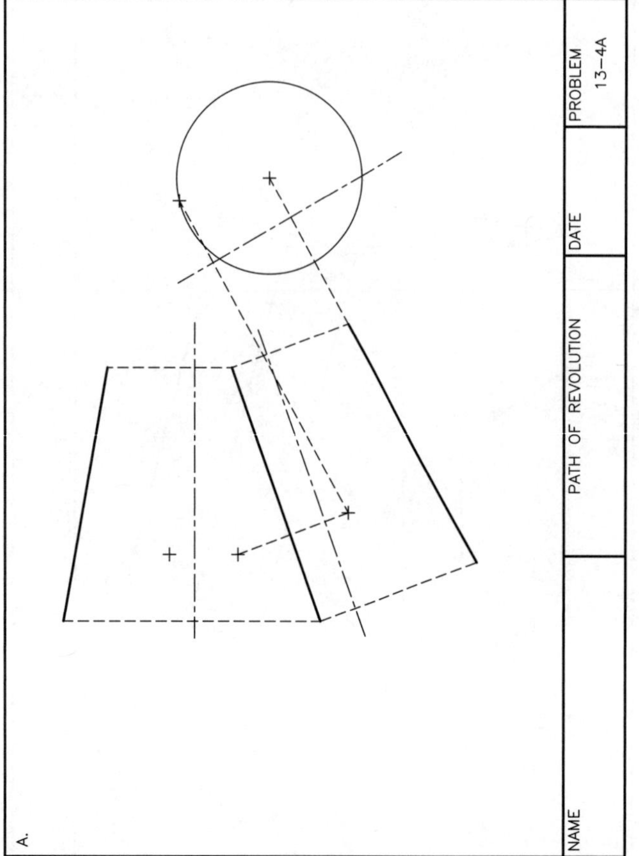
PROBLEM
13–4A
DATE
PATH OF REVOLUTION
NAME
A.

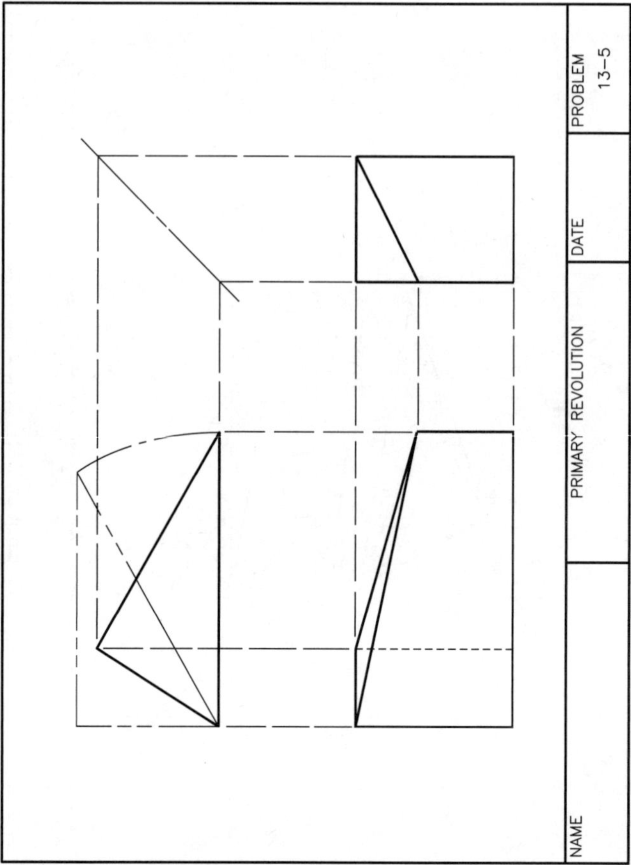
PROBLEM
13–5
DATE
PRIMARY REVOLUTION
NAME

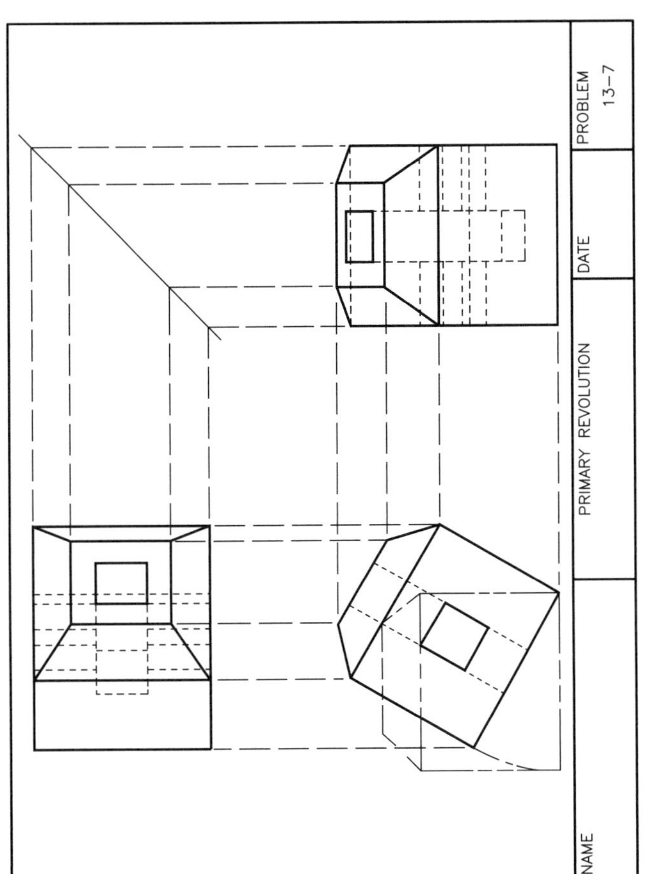
PROBLEM
13–7
DATE
PRIMARY REVOLUTION
NAME

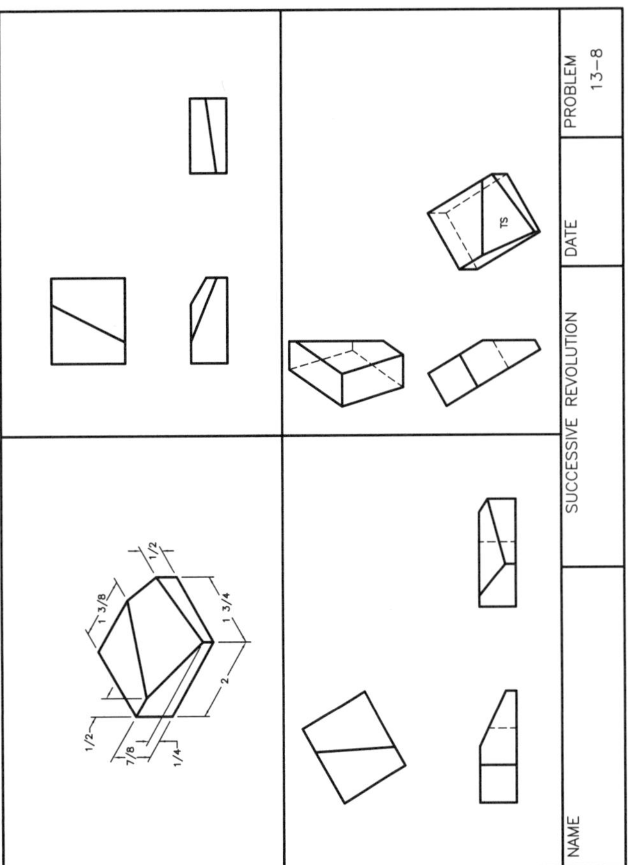
PROBLEM
13–8
DATE
SUCCESSIVE REVOLUTION
NAME
1/2
1 3/8
1 3/4
2
1/2
7/8
1/4
TS

Solutions to Drawing Problems, Text

Pages 460–461

Student work should look like the following drawings. The problem number and title are indicated on each problem sheet.

HL A
LEG A
LEG B
HL B
LEG C
HL C
TL C
TL A
LEGS A AND C
LEG B
TL B
METRIC
SCALE: 1:25
NAME
SUPPORT BRACKET
DATE
PROBLEM
13–1

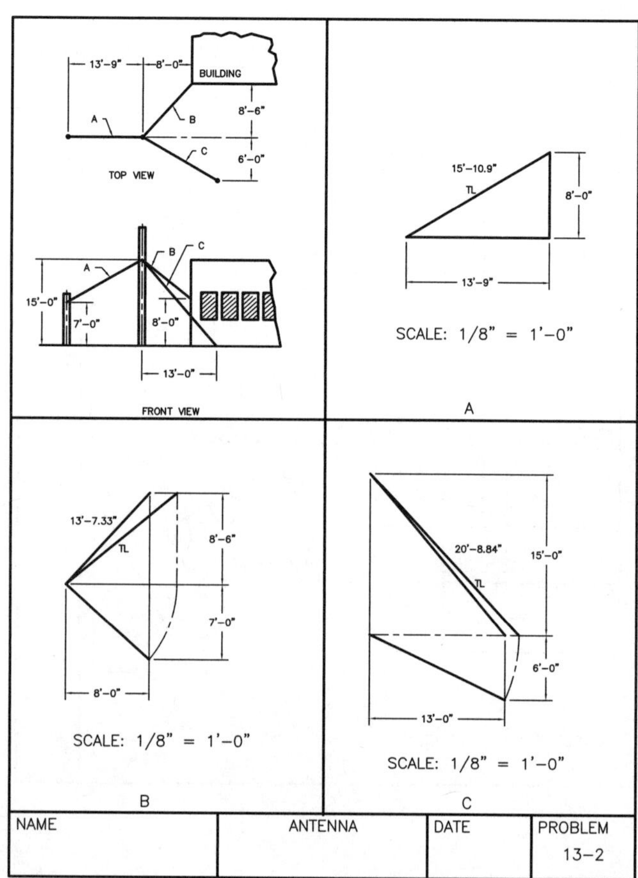

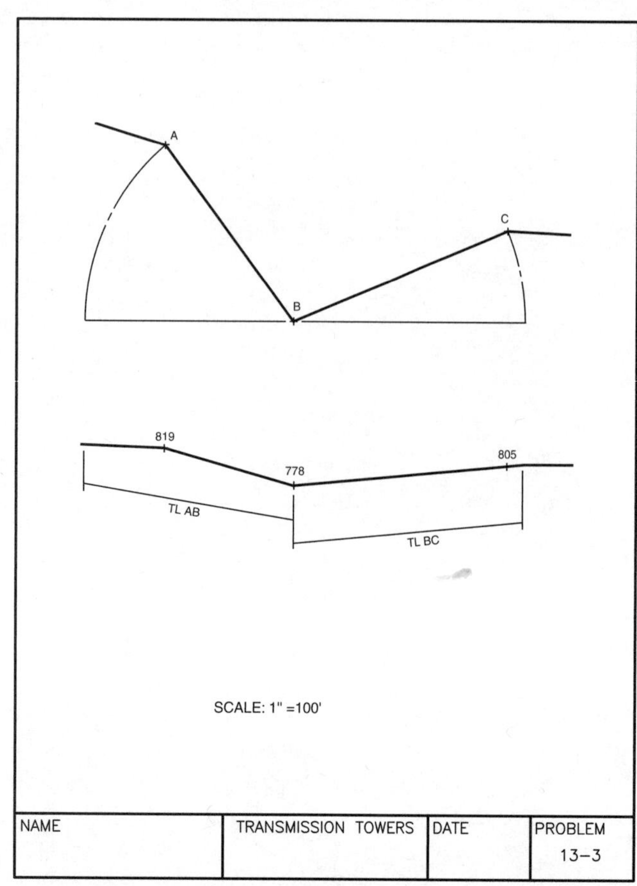

Solutions to Worksheets

Pages 107–113

Student work should look like the following drawings. The problem number and title are indicated on each problem sheet.

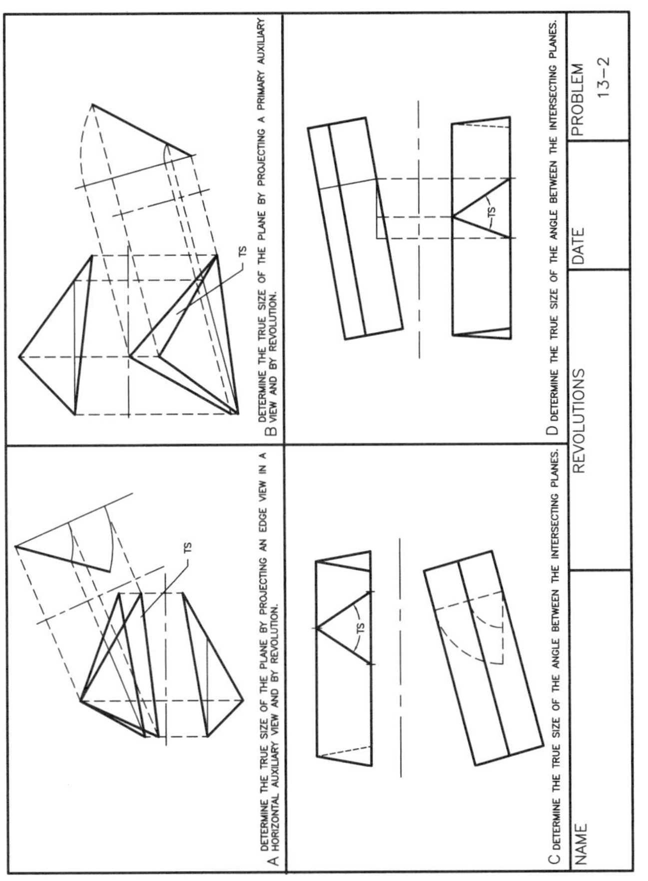

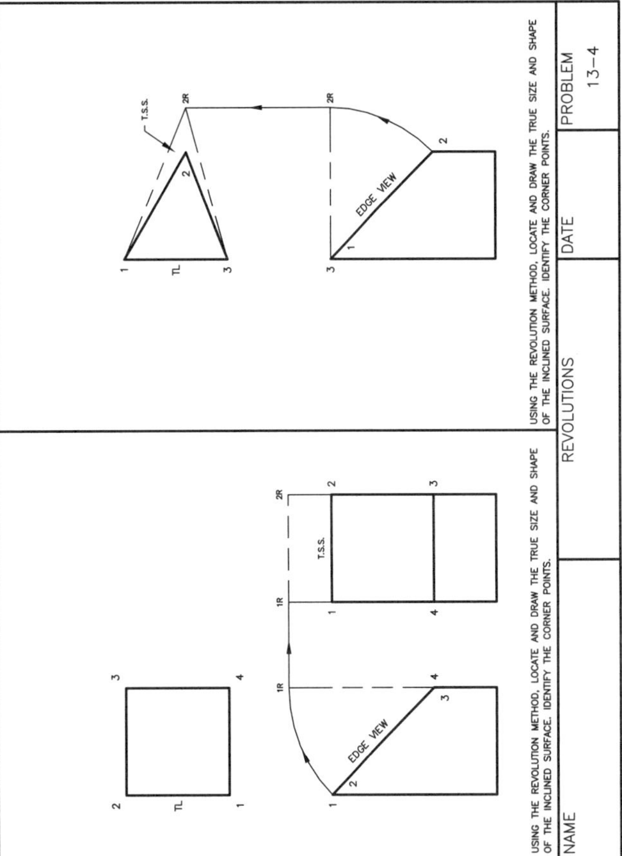

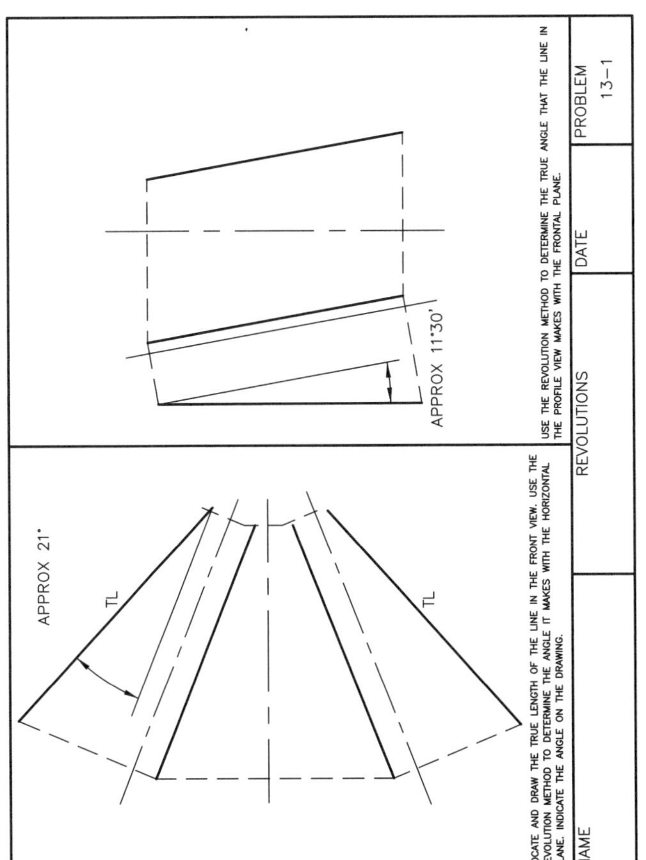

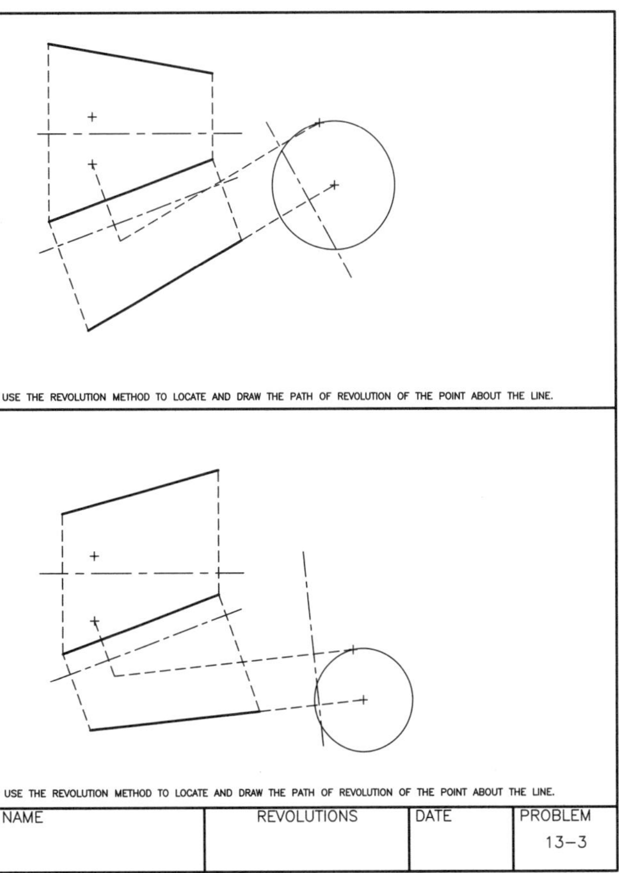

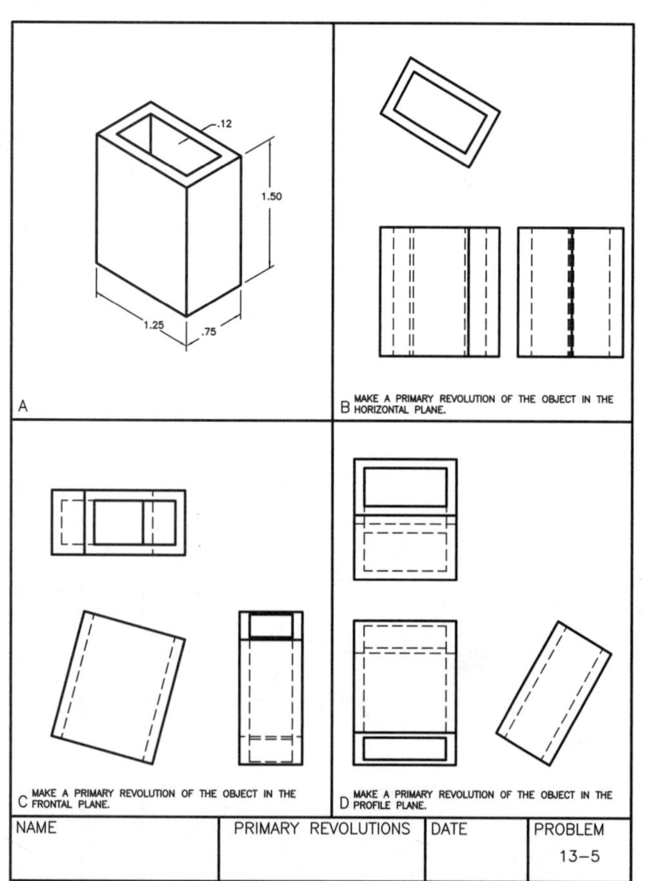

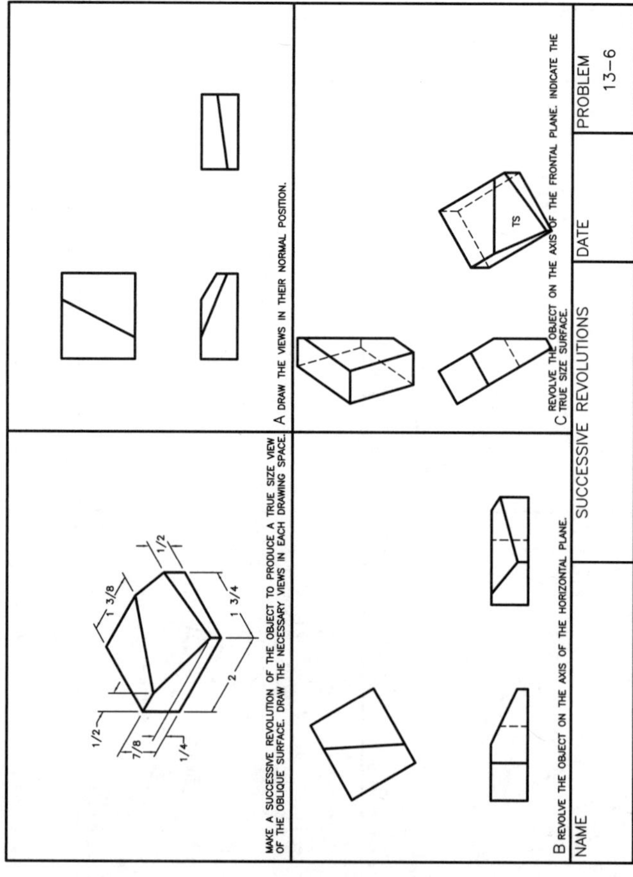

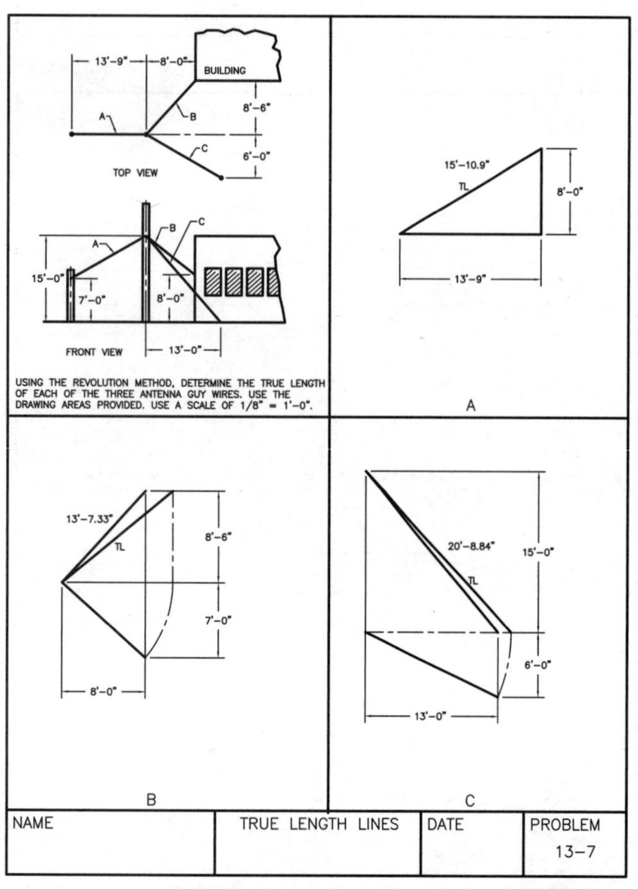

Answers to Chapter 13 Quiz

1. C. perpendicular to the line of sight in a normal view
2. B. successive revolutions
3. C. a right section through the two planes, revolving the section to the principal plane, and projecting it to the adjacent view
4. A. orthographic
5. Refer to the drawings given in the *Solutions to Problems and Activities, Text* section or the *Solutions to Drawing Problems, Text* section for the problem selected from the textbook.

Chapter Quiz 13

Revolutions

Name ______________________________

Period__________ Date__________ Score __________

Multiple Choice

Choose the answer that correctly completes the statement. Write the corresponding letter in the space provided.

_______ 1. The revolution method of determining the true length or size of a feature is simply a matter of viewing the feature _____.
  A. parallel to the line of sight
  B. in an adjacent view
  C. perpendicular to the line of sight in a normal view
  D. in a normal view

_______ 2. Determining the true size of an oblique surface by the revolution method requires the use of _____.
  A. a revolved section view
  B. successive revolutions
  C. a single primary revolution
  D. one primary revolution and one secondary revolution

_______ 3. The true angle between two planes whose line of intersection appears as its true length in a principal view can be found by drawing _____.
  A. successive revolutions
  B. an edge view in a primary revolution
  C. a right section through the two planes, revolving the section to the principal plane, and projecting it to the adjacent view
  D. an auxiliary view

_______ 4. Regular _____ drawing principles are used in projecting revolved views.
  A. orthographic
  B. isometric
  C. oblique
  D. perspective

Drafting Performance

5. Draw a solution of a problem selected by your instructor from Chapter 13 in your textbook. Leave construction lines on the drawing.

Revolution Method

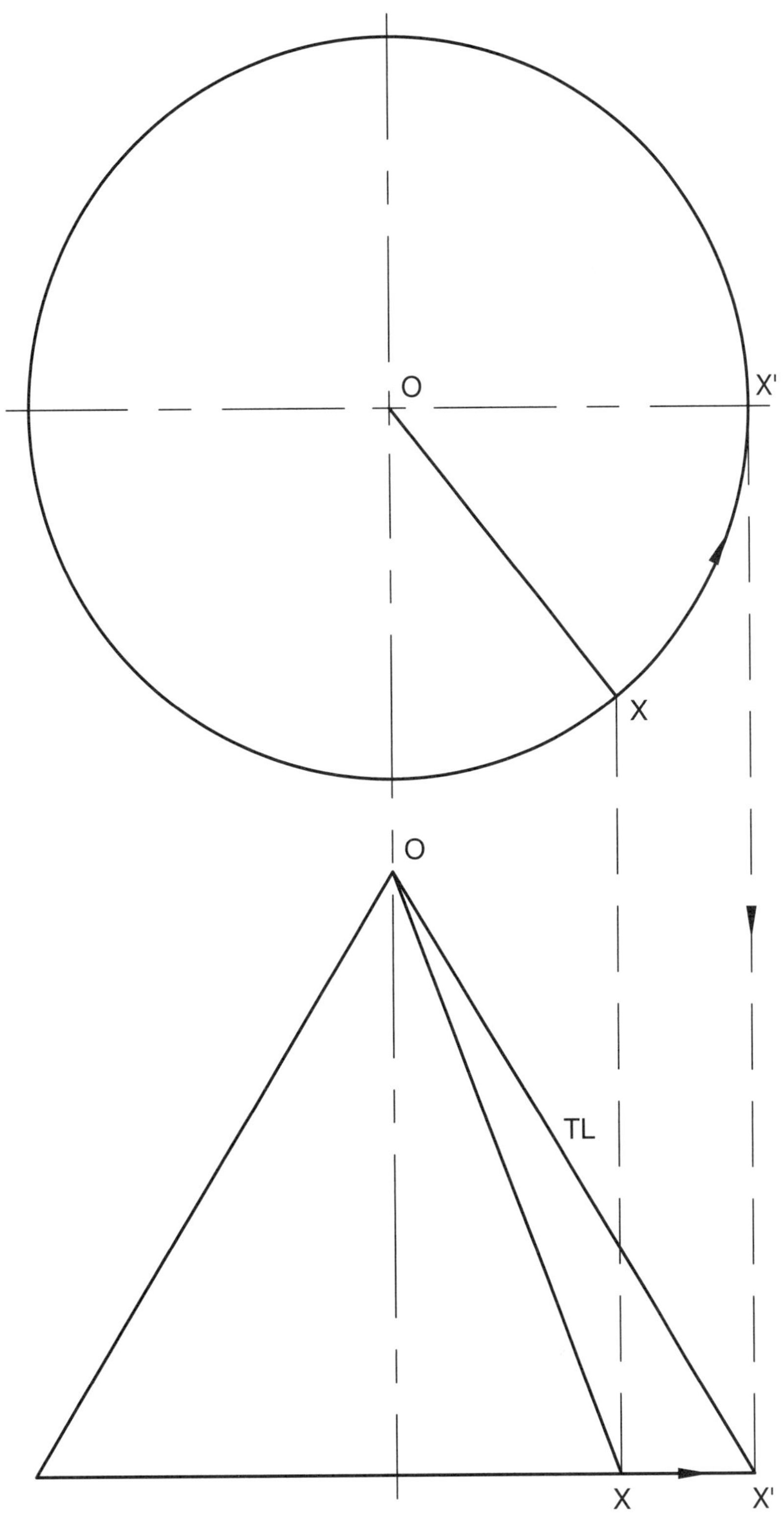

True Length of a Line

RM 13-1

Procedure Checklist

Revolutions

Name ____________________

Observable Items	Completed		Comments	Instructor Initials
	Yes	No		
1. Uses the revolution method to determine the true size of an angle between a line and a principal plane.				
2. Uses the revolution method to determine the true size of a plane.				
3. Uses the revolution method to determine the true angle between two intersecting planes.				
4. Constructs a true angle between two intersecting oblique planes.				
5. Revolves a point about an oblique axis to determine its path.				
6. Constructs primary revolutions.				
7. Constructs successive revolutions.				

Instructor Signature ____________________

Intersections

Learning Objectives

After studying this chapter, the student will be able to:

- List the basic types of geometric surfaces and intersections.
- Describe how intersections are formed and identify the common methods used in their construction.
- Construct intersections using manual and CAD procedures.
- List the applications of intersections in construction and manufacturing.

Instructional Resources

Text: pages 463–507

Review Questions, page 498

Problems and Activities, pages 498–507

Worksheets: pages 114–122

- Worksheet 14-1: *Intersections of Lines*
- Worksheet 14-2: *Intersections of Lines*
- Worksheet 14-3: *Line Visibility*
- Worksheet 14-4: *Piercing Points*
- Worksheet 14-5: *Piercing Points*
- Worksheet 14-6: *Perpendicular Lines*
- Worksheet 14-7: *Intersection of Planes*
- Worksheet 14-8: *Intersection of a Plane and Prism*
- Worksheet 14-9: *Intersection of Prisms*

Instructor's Resource

Instructional Tasks

Instructional Aids and Assignments

Chapter 14 Quiz

Reproducible Masters

- Reproducible Master 14-1: *Visibility of a Line and a Plane in Space.* The step-by-step procedure for determining the visibility of a line and a plane in space is shown.
- Reproducible Master 14-2: *Piercing Point of a Line and a Plane.* The step-by-step procedure for determining the piercing point of a line and a plane is shown.

Procedure Checklist

Color Transparencies (Binder/IRCD only)

- Transparency 14-1: *Types of Surfaces.* Intersections and their solutions are classified on the basis of the types of geometric surfaces involved. The broad classifications are shown in this transparency.
- Transparency 14-2: *Visibility of Crossing Lines in Space.* The step-by-step procedure for determining the visibility of crossing lines in space is shown.
- Transparency 14-3: *Intersection of Planes.* The procedure for determining the intersection of two planes is shown.

Instructional Tasks

1. Define the term *intersection.*
   - Discuss the applications of intersections in industry.
2. Discuss the two types of intersections: ruled geometrical surfaces and double-curve geometrical surfaces.
   - Use a transparency to illustrate ruled surfaces and double-curve surfaces.
3. Explain how to locate a point on a line.
   - Show students the procedure for locating a point on a line.
4. Explain how to identify intersecting and nonintersecting lines.
   - Demonstrate the procedure for distinguishing between intersecting and nonintersecting lines.
5. Determine the visibility of crossing lines in space.

- Demonstrate the procedure for determining the visibility of crossing lines.

6. Explain how to use orthographic projection to determine the visibility of a line and plane in space.
   - Use step-by-step instruction, and related transparencies, to aid students in determining the visibility of a line and a plane in space.
7. Explain how to use orthographic projection to locate the piercing point of a line and a plane.
   - Explain the meaning and importance of the term *piercing point*.
8. Explain how to use auxiliary views to locate the piercing point of a line and a plane.
   - Discuss and demonstrate how to locate the piercing point of a line and a plane using auxiliary views as opposed to orthographic projection.
9. Explain how to locate a line through a point and perpendicular to an oblique plane.
   - Discuss situations where locating a line through a point and perpendicular to an oblique plane might be useful.
10. Explain how to determine the intersection of two planes using orthographic projection.
    - Discuss the steps for locating the intersection of two planes using orthographic projection.
11. Explain how to determine the intersection of two planes using auxiliary views.
    - Discuss and demonstrate how to locate the intersection of two planes using auxiliary views.
12. Explain how to locate the intersection of an inclined plane and a prism by orthographic projection.
    - Use step-by-step instruction, with related transparencies, to demonstrate how to locate the intersection of an inclined plane and a prism by orthographic projection.
13. Explain how to locate the intersection of an oblique plane and a prism using the cutting-plane method.
    - Discuss the usefulness of the cutting-plane method.
    - Demonstrate the procedure of locating the intersection of an oblique plane and prism.
14. Explain how to determine the intersection of an oblique plane and an oblique prism using an auxiliary view.
    - Discuss and demonstrate how to determine the intersection of an oblique plane and an oblique prism.
15. Explain how to locate the intersection of two prisms using the cutting-plane method.
    - Discuss the steps for using the cutting-plane method to locate the intersection of two prisms.
16. Explain how to locate the intersection of two prisms using an auxiliary view.
    - Use geometric models to demonstrate the method of locating the intersection of two prisms using an auxiliary view.
17. Explain how to locate the intersection of a plane and a cylinder using orthographic projection.
    - Demonstrate the procedure for determining the intersection of a plane and a cylinder using orthographic projection.
18. Explain how to use the cutting-plane method to determine the intersection of an oblique plane and a cylinder.
    - Use models to demonstrate how to use the cutting-plane method to determine the intersection of an oblique plane and a cylinder.
19. Explain how to determine the intersection of an oblique plane and an oblique cylinder using auxiliary views.
    - Cite industrial applications where locating the intersection of an oblique plane and an oblique cylinder is required.
20. Explain how to locate the intersection of a cylinder and a prism.
    - Use transparencies with overlays to demonstrate how to locate the intersection of a cylinder and a prism.
21. Explain how to locate the intersection of two cylinders.
    - Discuss applications for determining the intersection of two cylinders.
22. Explain how to locate the intersection of an inclined plane and a cone.
    - Use step-by-step instruction, and related transparencies, to demonstrate how to locate the intersection of an inclined plane and a cone.
23. Explain how to locate the intersection of a cylinder and a cone.
    - Use geometric models to demonstrate how to locate the intersection of a cylinder and a cone.
24. Discuss the importance and purposes for the various methods of locating intersections.

- Review the three methods of locating intersections. Clarify the considerations made when choosing a method.

Instructional Aids and Assignments

1. Display models of geometric forms involving intersections. Paint the models a light color and identify the intersections with a dark color for contrast.
2. Display samples or photos of industrial parts involving intersections such as heating and air conditioning ducts or pipes.
3. Assign the drawing problems in the textbook. The number of problems is sufficient to assign a minimum number to all students and to identify problems that may be done for extra credit. Some problems may be used for the performance section of the chapter quiz.

Answers to Review Questions, Text

Page 498

1. The line formed at the junction of surfaces when two objects join or pass through each other.
2. Surfaces generated by moving a straight line.
3. Plane surfaces, single-curve surfaces, and warped surfaces.
4. developed
5. A warped surface.
6. A surface generated by a curved line revolving around a straight line in the plane of the curve.
7. single-plane
8. points
9. intersecting
10. visibility
11. The point of intersection between a plane and a line inclined to that plane.
12. piercing points
13. It is used to create section views of 3D models.
14. planes
15. The **Intersect** command.
16. The orthographic projection method, the cutting plane method, and the auxiliary view method.

Solutions to Problems and Activities, Text

Pages 498–507

Student work for Problems 1–11 should look like the following drawings. The problem number and title are indicated on each problem sheet. For Problem 2, check student work for accuracy and proper projection technique.

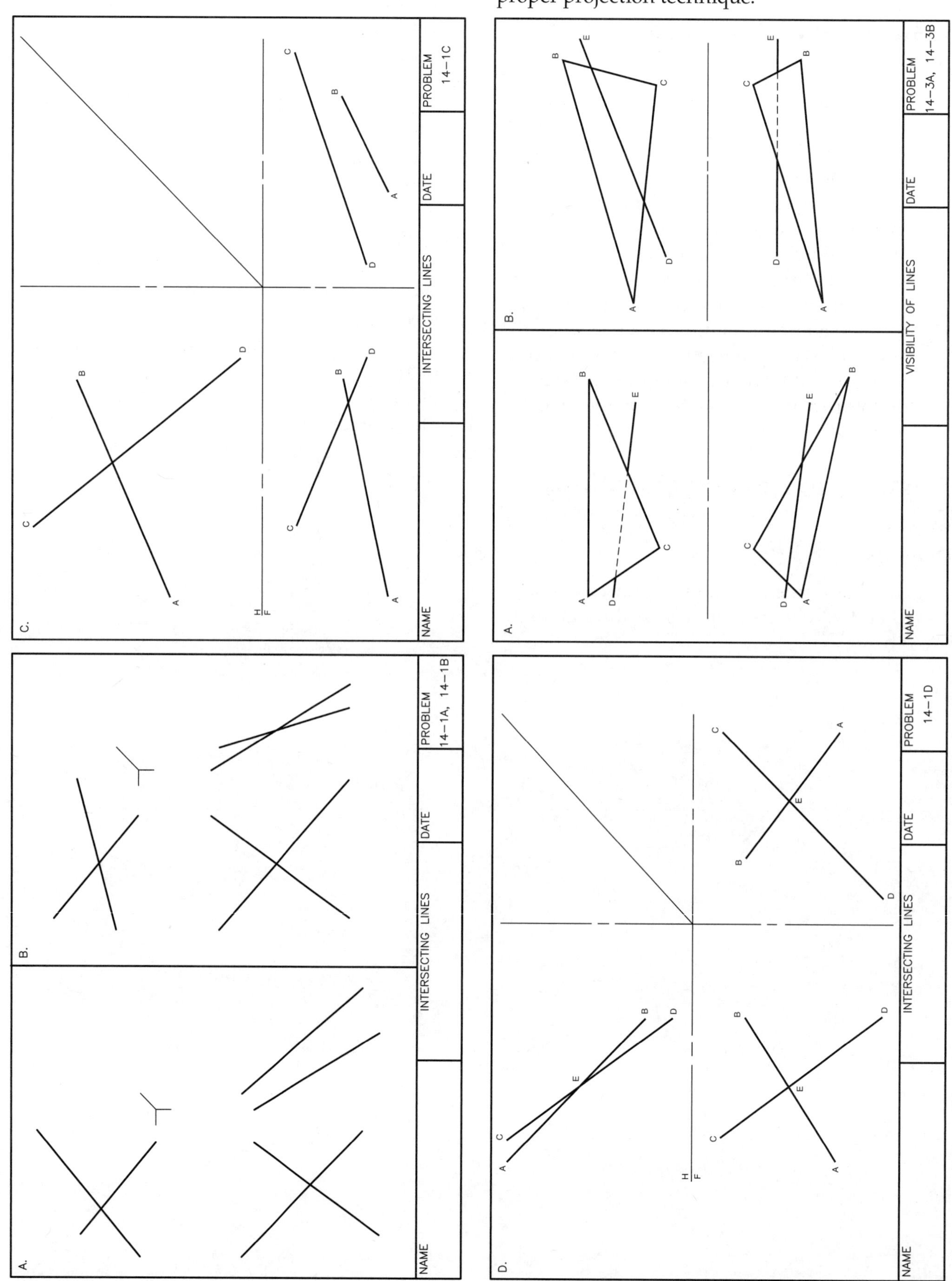

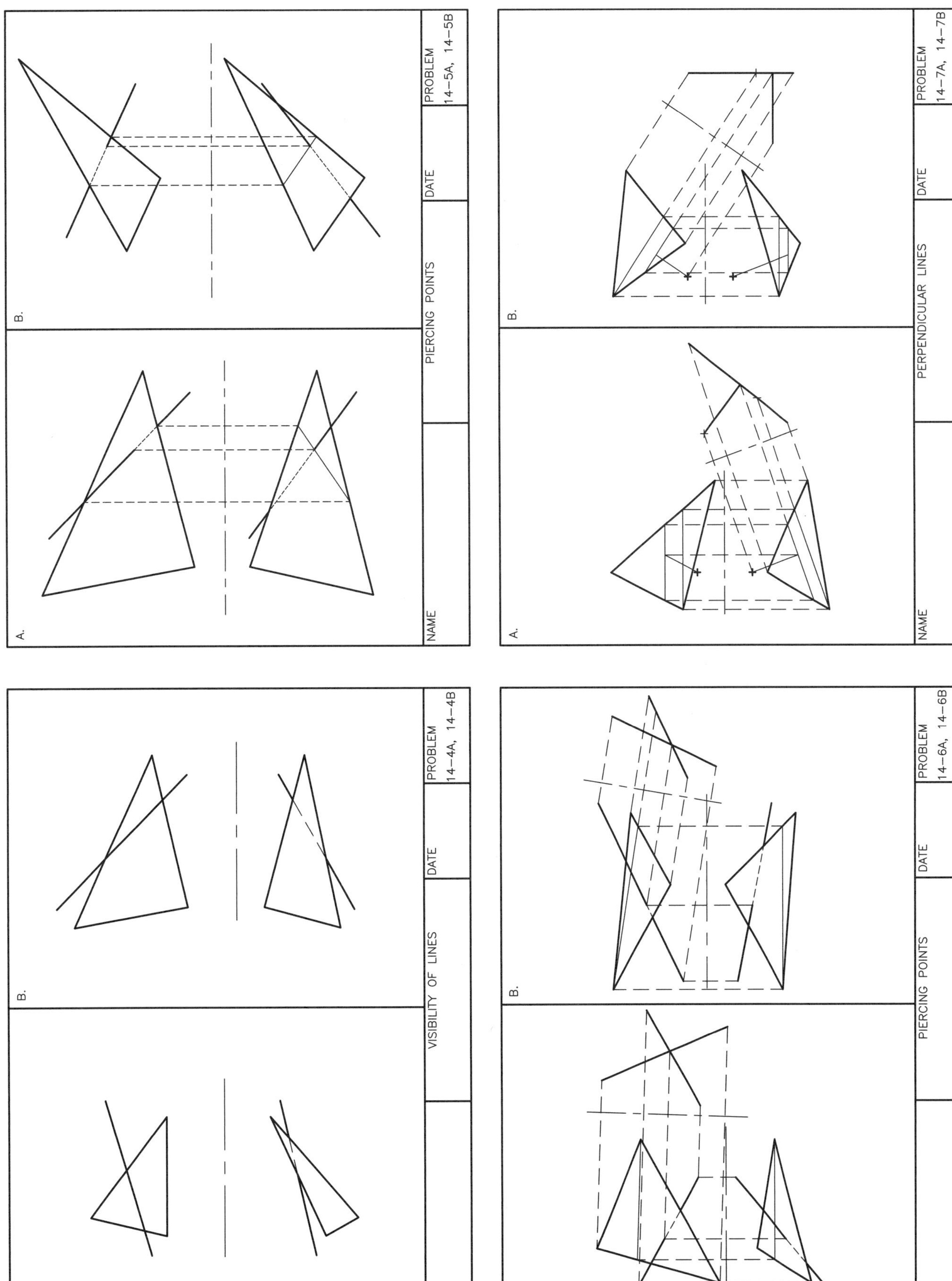
A.
B.
PROBLEM
14–5A, 14–5B
DATE
PIERCING POINTS
NAME
A.
B.
PROBLEM
14–7A, 14–7B
DATE
PERPENDICULAR LINES
NAME
A.
B.
PROBLEM
14–4A, 14–4B
DATE
VISIBILITY OF LINES
NAME
A.
B.
PROBLEM
14–6A, 14–6B
DATE
PIERCING POINTS
NAME

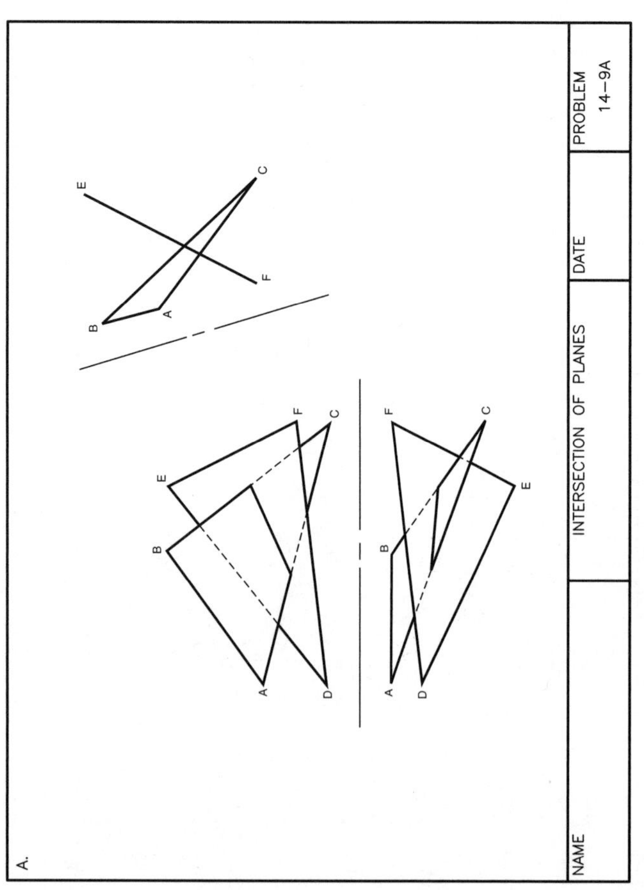
PROBLEM 14–9A
DATE
INTERSECTION OF PLANES
NAME
A.
E
C
F
B
A
D

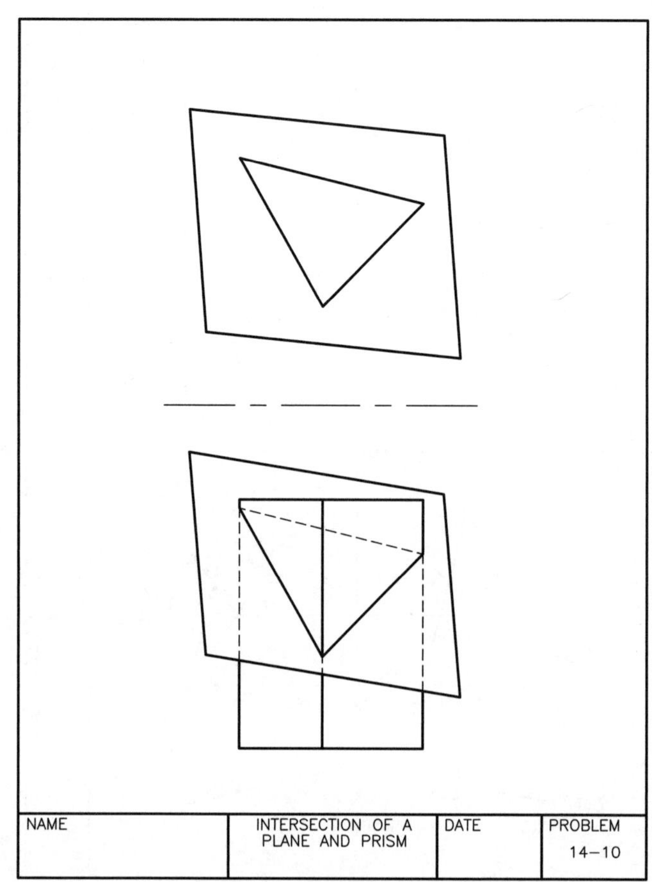
NAME
INTERSECTION OF A PLANE AND PRISM
DATE
PROBLEM 14–10

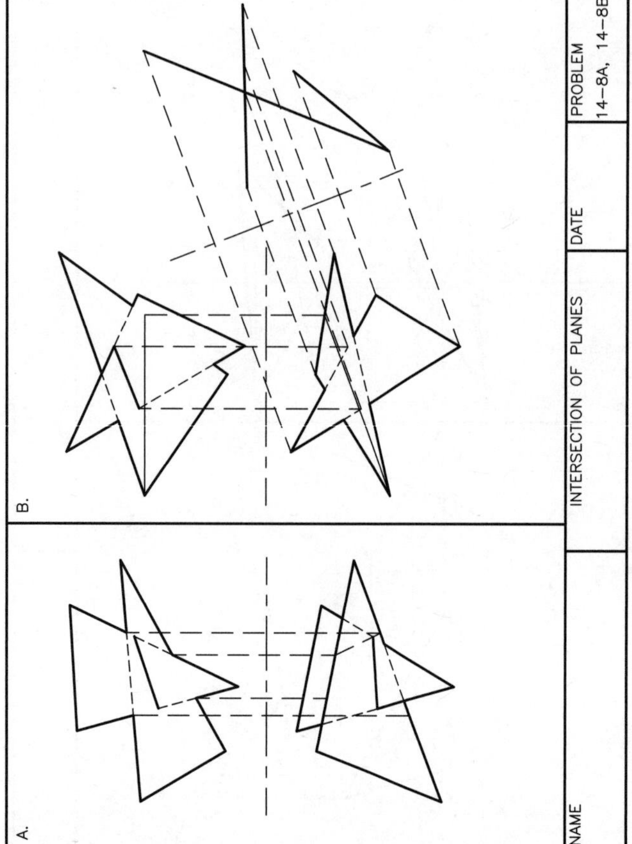
PROBLEM 14–8A, 14–8B
DATE
INTERSECTION OF PLANES
NAME
B.
A.

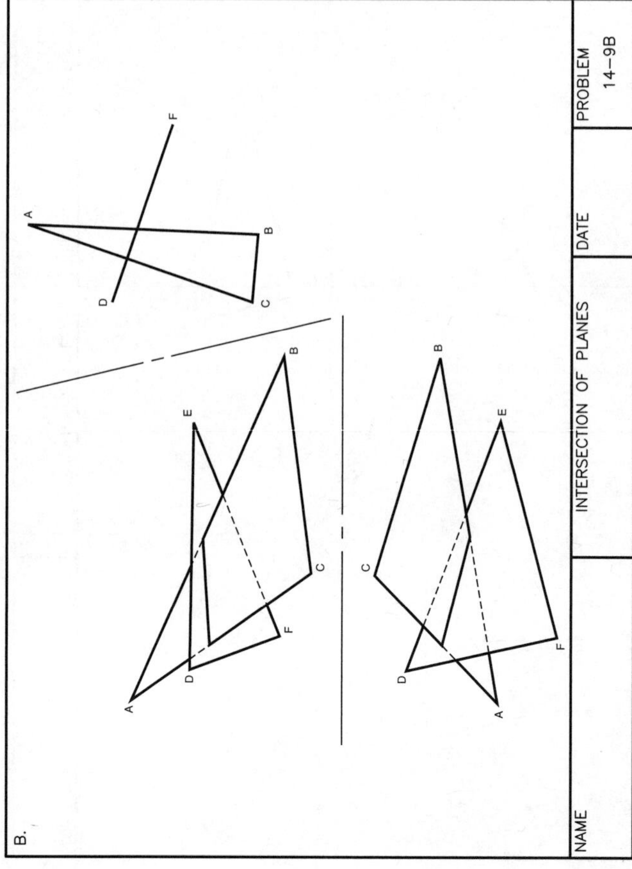
PROBLEM 14–9B
DATE
INTERSECTION OF PLANES
NAME
B.
A
B
C
D
E
F

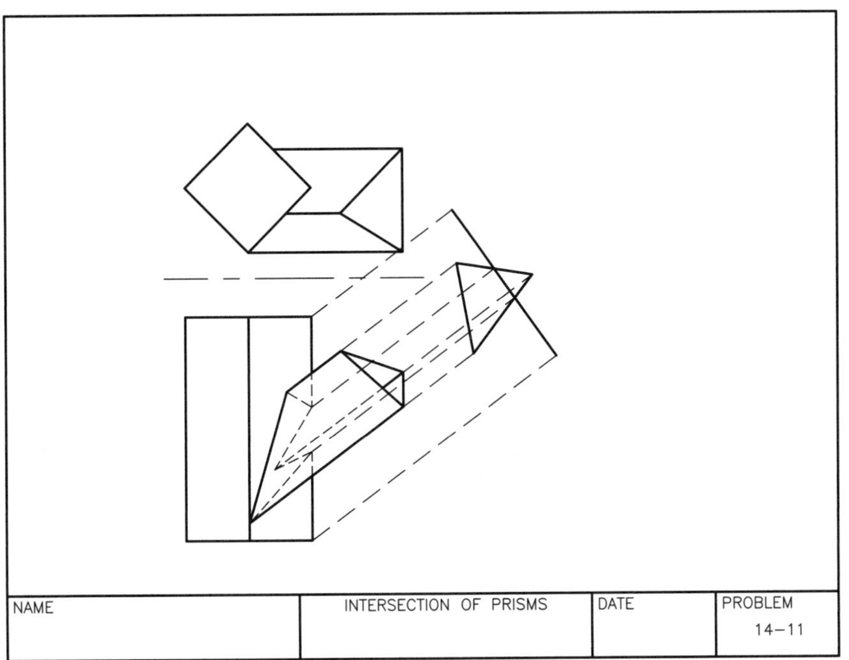
NAME
INTERSECTION OF PRISMS
DATE
PROBLEM
14–11

Solutions to Worksheets
Pages 114–122

Student work should look like the following drawings. The problem number and title are indicated on each problem sheet.

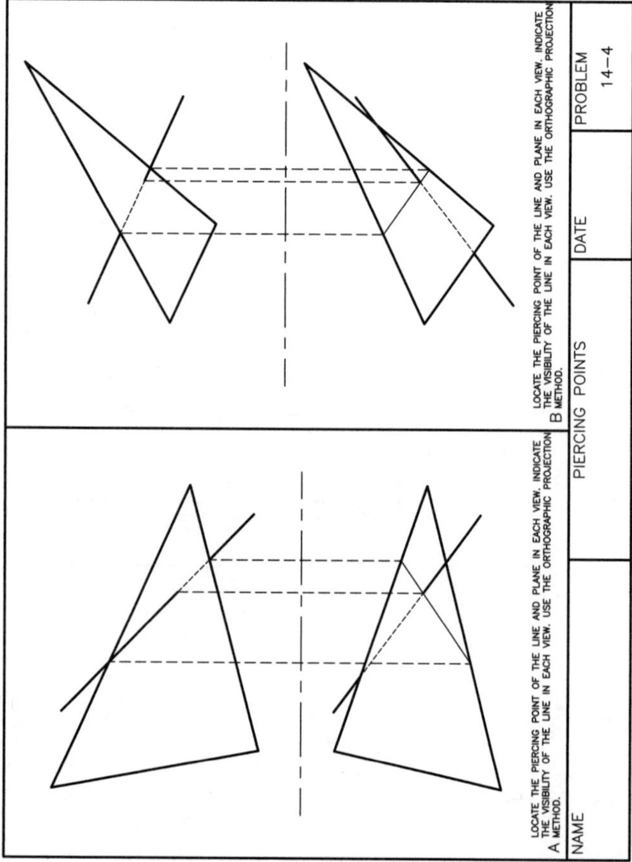

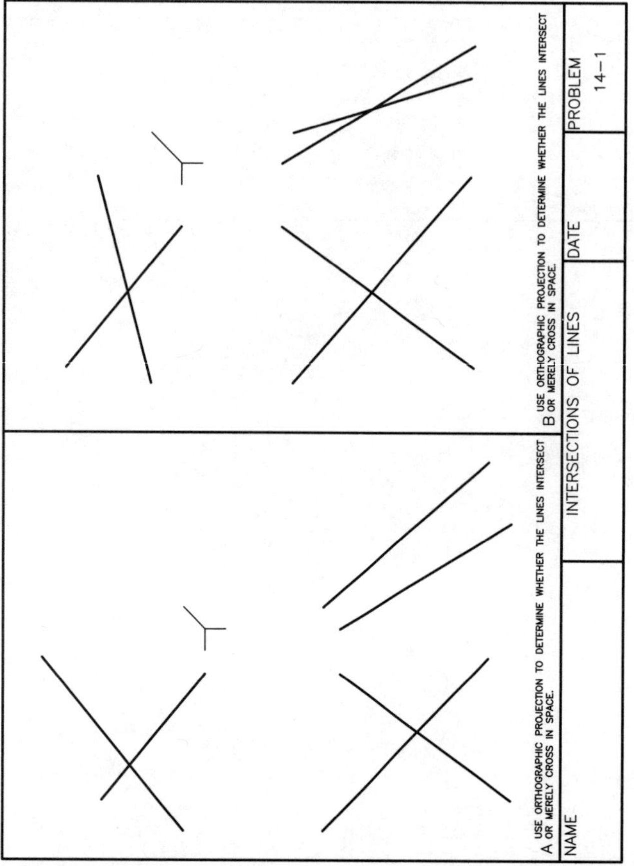

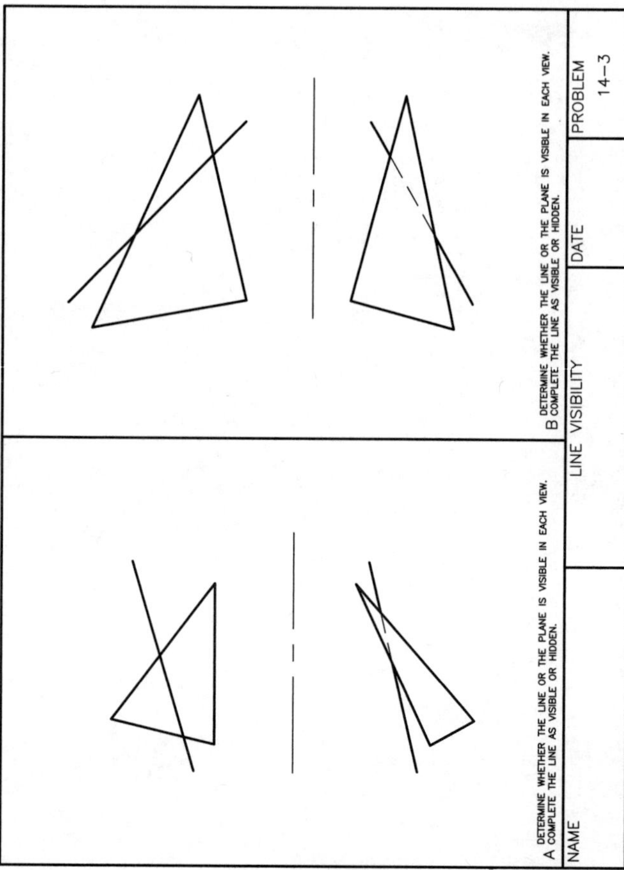

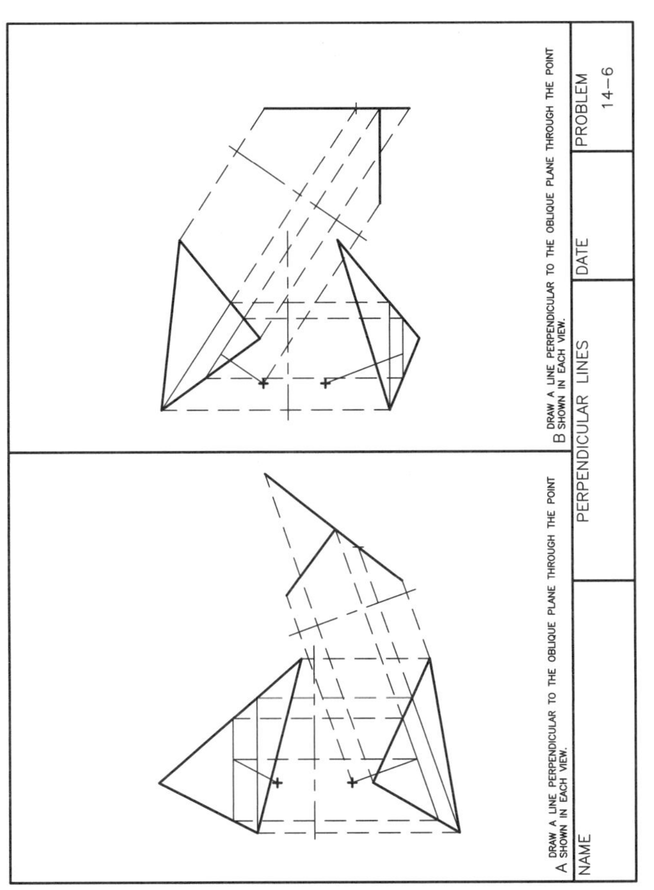
A DRAW A LINE PERPENDICULAR TO THE OBLIQUE PLANE THROUGH THE POINT SHOWN IN EACH VIEW.
B DRAW A LINE PERPENDICULAR TO THE OBLIQUE PLANE THROUGH THE POINT SHOWN IN EACH VIEW.
NAME
PERPENDICULAR LINES
DATE
PROBLEM
14–6

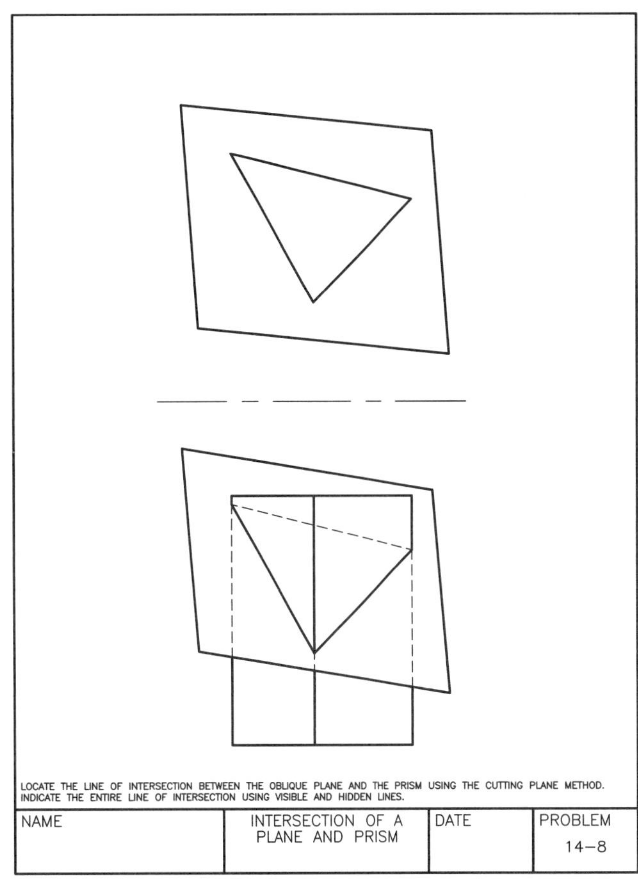
LOCATE THE LINE OF INTERSECTION BETWEEN THE OBLIQUE PLANE AND THE PRISM USING THE CUTTING PLANE METHOD.
INDICATE THE ENTIRE LINE OF INTERSECTION USING VISIBLE AND HIDDEN LINES.
NAME
INTERSECTION OF A PLANE AND PRISM
DATE
PROBLEM
14–8

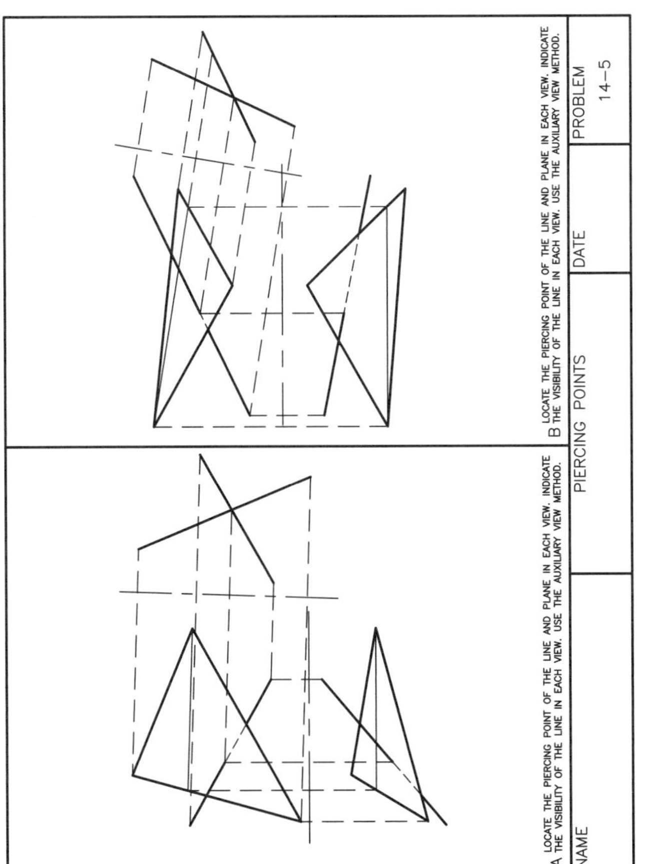
A LOCATE THE PIERCING POINT OF THE LINE AND PLANE IN EACH VIEW. INDICATE THE VISIBILITY OF THE LINE IN EACH VIEW. USE THE AUXILIARY VIEW METHOD.
B LOCATE THE PIERCING POINT OF THE LINE AND PLANE IN EACH VIEW. INDICATE THE VISIBILITY OF THE LINE IN EACH VIEW. USE THE AUXILIARY VIEW METHOD.
NAME
PIERCING POINTS
DATE
PROBLEM
14–5

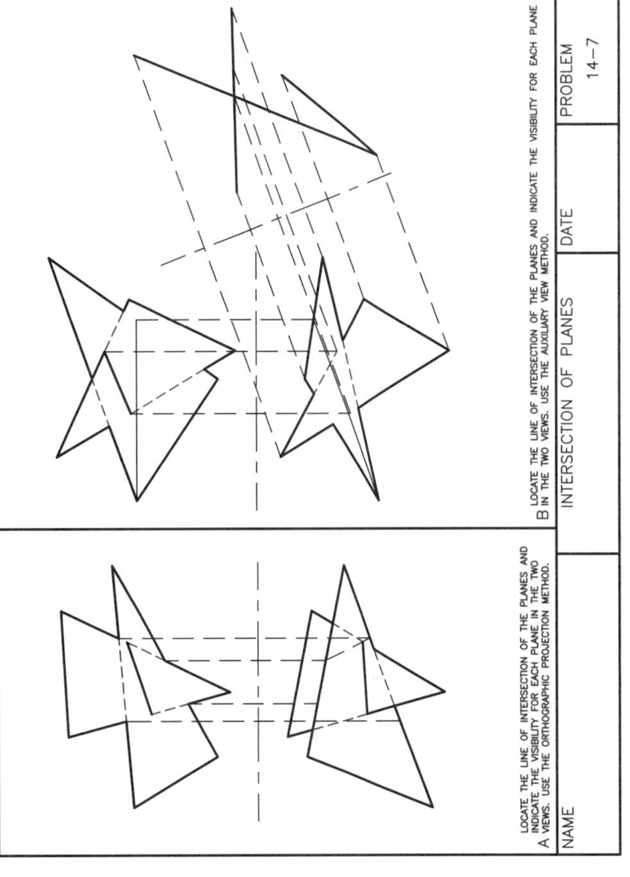
A LOCATE THE LINE OF INTERSECTION OF THE PLANES AND INDICATE THE VISIBILITY FOR EACH PLANE IN THE TWO VIEWS. USE THE ORTHOGRAPHIC PROJECTION METHOD.
B LOCATE THE LINE OF INTERSECTION OF THE PLANES AND INDICATE THE VISIBILITY FOR EACH PLANE IN THE TWO VIEWS. USE THE AUXILIARY VIEW METHOD.
NAME
INTERSECTION OF PLANES
DATE
PROBLEM
14–7

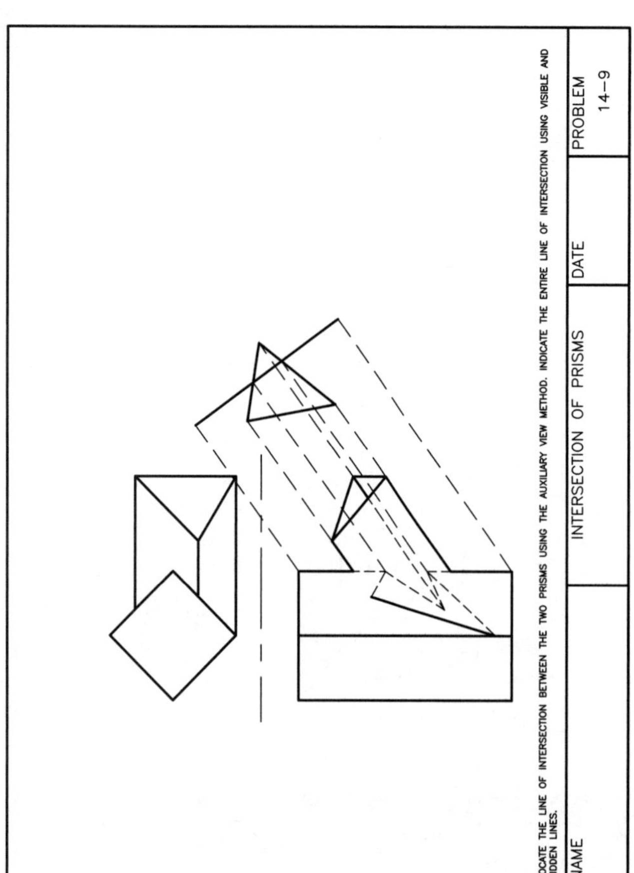

Answers to Chapter 14 Quiz

1. D. Ruled surfaces and double-curve surfaces.
2. C. Sphere
3. B. Lines that intersect in space will have a common point to both lines in any of the principal orthographic views.
4. A. By projecting the crossing point of the lines from an adjacent view.
5. B. Project an edge view of the plane.
6. A. Rectangular prism
7. C. auxiliary view
8. Refer to the drawings given in the *Solutions to Problems and Activities, Text* section for the problem selected from the textbook.

Chapter Quiz 14

Intersections

Name ______________________________

Period __________ Date __________ Score __________

Multiple Choice

Choose the answer that correctly completes the statement. Write the corresponding letter in the space provided.

_____ 1. What are the two broad classifications of geometrical surfaces?
A. Ruled surfaces and conoid surfaces.
B. Convoluted surfaces and ruled surfaces.
C. Double-curve surfaces and convoluted surfaces.
D. Ruled surfaces and double-curve surfaces.

_____ 2. What type of surface is *not* capable of being developed into a single plane surface?
A. Tetrahedron
B. Right circular cylinder
C. Sphere
D. Helical convolute

_____ 3. Lines that appear to cross in space do not necessarily intersect. What condition is necessary to prove that they do intersect?
A. If two lines appear to cross in the profile view, then they do intersect.
B. Lines that intersect in space will have a common point to both lines in any of the principal orthographic views.
C. Lines appearing to cross in space in two principal views do intersect in space.
D. Lines appearing to cross in space in three principal views must intersect.

_____ 4. How is the visibility of crossing lines established?
A. By projecting the crossing point of the lines from an adjacent view.
B. By drawing an auxiliary view.
C. By drawing a section view.
D. There is no way to establish the visibility of crossing lines without first finding the point view of one line.

_____ 5. What is the basic procedure for finding the piercing point of a line and a plane by the auxiliary view method?
A. Determine the true length of the line.
B. Project an edge view of the plane.
C. Determine the true size and shape of the plane and the true length of the line.
D. Draw a cutting plane through one view and project points to the adjacent view.

Name ____

________ 6. Which of the following can be developed into a single-plane surface?
A. Rectangular prism
B. Conoid
C. Torus
D. Right helicoid

________ 7. To find the intersection of an oblique triangular prism with a cylinder, the _____ method is used.
A. orthographic projection
B. cutting plane
C. auxiliary view
D. Either B or C.

Drafting Performance

8. Draw a solution of a problem selected by your instructor from Chapter 14 in your textbook. Leave construction lines on the drawing.

Visibility of a Line and a Plane in Space

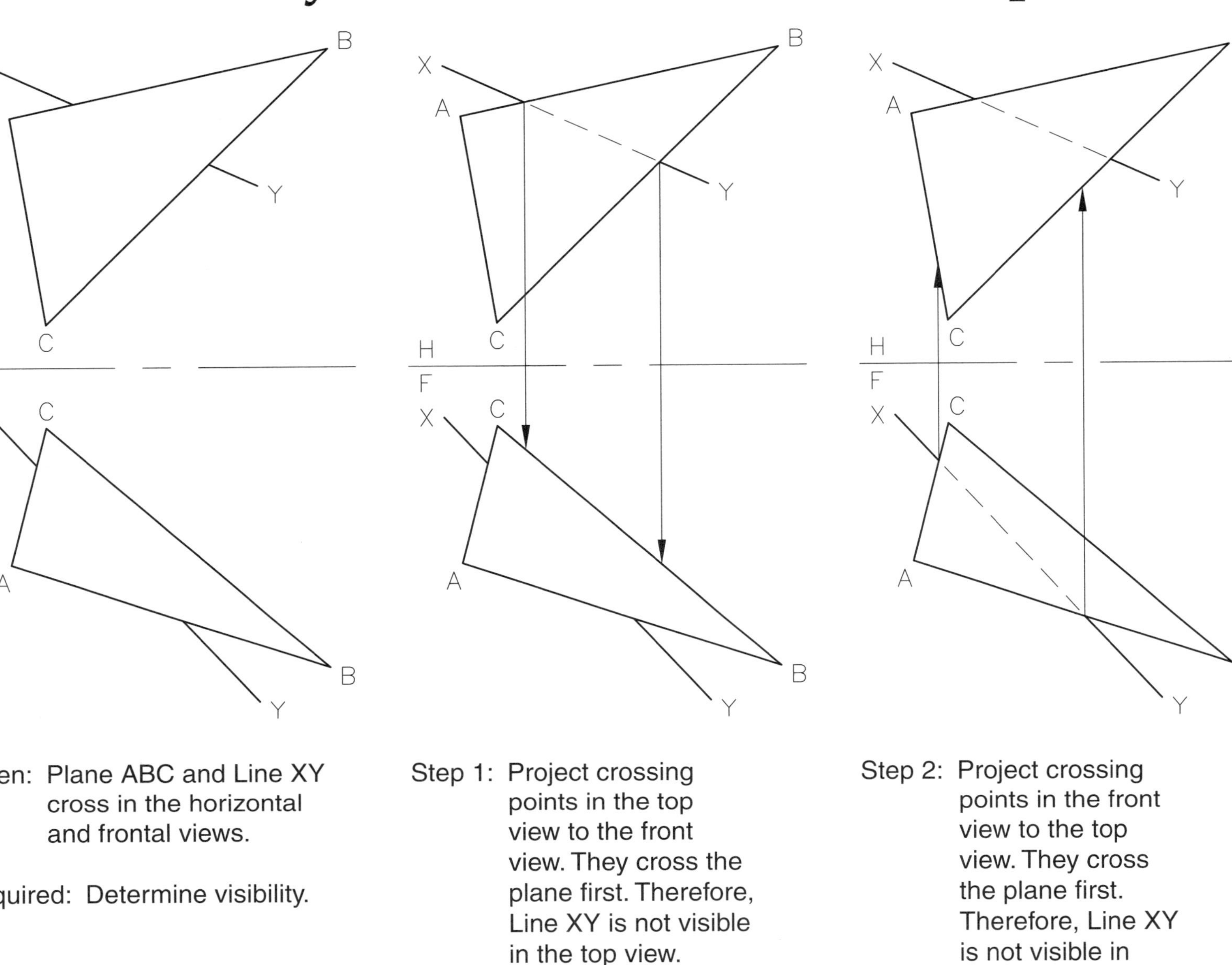

Given: Plane ABC and Line XY cross in the horizontal and frontal views.

Required: Determine visibility.

Step 1: Project crossing points in the top view to the front view. They cross the plane first. Therefore, Line XY is not visible in the top view.

Step 2: Project crossing points in the front view to the top view. They cross the plane first. Therefore, Line XY is not visible in the front view.

RM 14-1

Piercing Point of a Line and a Plane

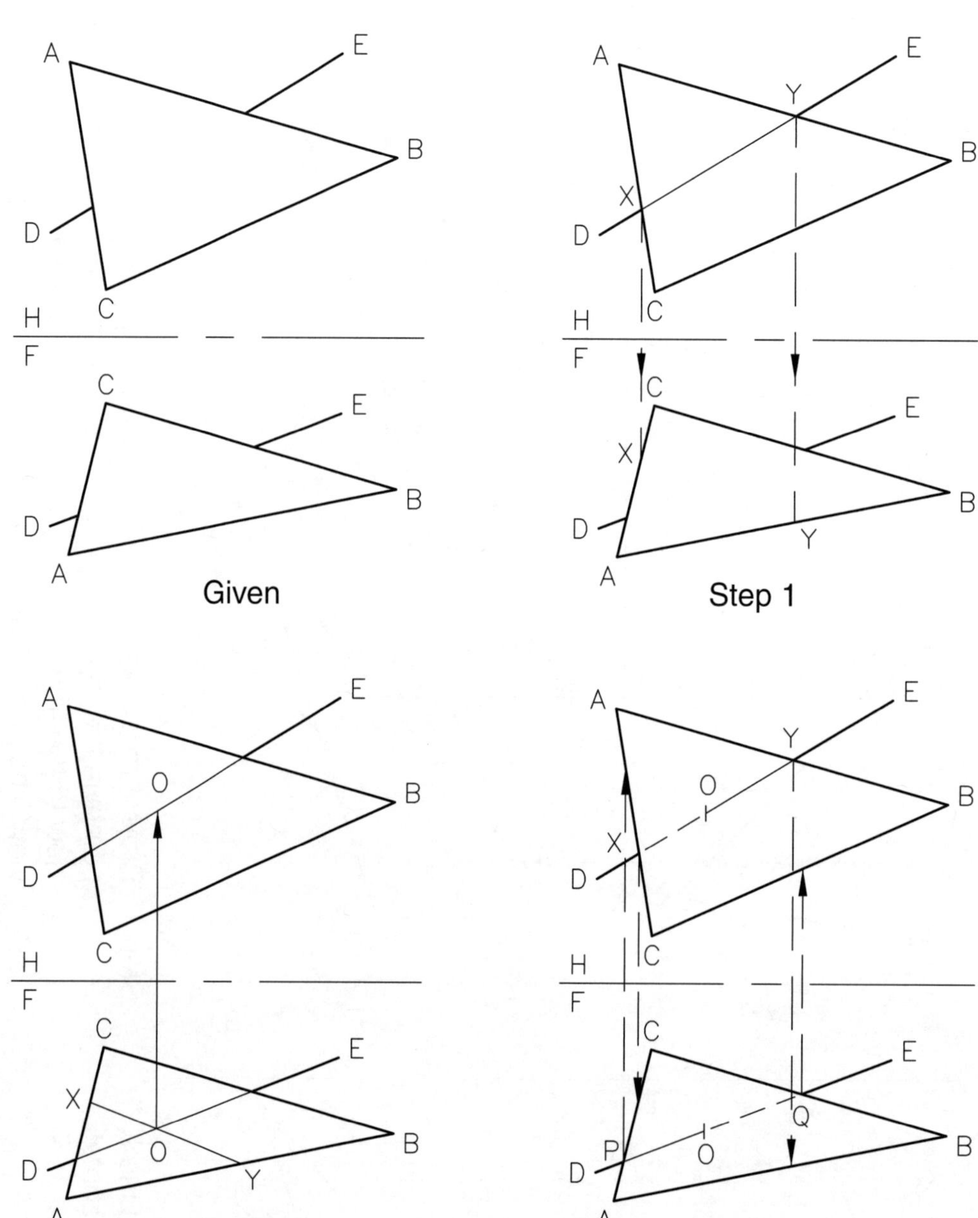

RM 14-2

Procedure Checklist

Intersections

Name ____

Observable Items	Completed		Comments	Instructor Initials
	Yes	No		
1. Determines the visibility of crossing lines in space.				
2. Determines the visibility of a line and plane in space.				
3. Locates the piercing point of a line and a plane in space using: A. The orthographic projection method.				
B. The auxiliary view method.				
4. Constructs a line through a point and perpendicular to an oblique plane.				
5. Locates the intersection of two planes using: A. The orthographic projection method.				
B. The auxiliary view method.				
6. Locates the intersection of an inclined plane and a prism using the orthographic projection method.				
7. Locates the intersection of an oblique plane and a prism using the cutting plane method.				
8. Locates the intersection of an oblique plane and an oblique prism using the auxiliary view method.				
9. Locates the intersection of two prisms using: A. The cutting plane method.				
B. The auxiliary view method.				
10. Locates the intersection of an oblique plane and a cylinder.				
11. Locates the intersection of an oblique plane and an oblique cylinder.				
12. Locates the intersection of two cylinders.				
13. Locates the intersection of a cylinder and a cone.				

Instructor Signature ____

Developments

Learning Objectives

After studying this chapter, the student will be able to:

- Explain the purpose of a development.
- List common applications for developed surfaces.
- Describe the principles of parallel line development, radial line development, and triangulation.
- Develop rectangular, oblique, and truncated objects.
- Create an approximate development of a warped surface.

Instructional Resources

Text: pages 509–547
  Review Questions, page 536
  Problems and Activities, pages 536–545
  Drawing Problems, pages 545–547

Worksheets: pages 123–134

- Worksheet 15-1: *Rectangular Prism Development*
- Worksheet 15-2: *Rectangular Prism Development*
- Worksheet 15-3: *Oblique Prism Development*
- Worksheet 15-4: *Truncated Cylinder Development*
- Worksheet 15-5: *Two-Piece Pipe Elbow Development*
- Worksheet 15-6: *Three-Piece Pipe Elbow Development*
- Worksheet 15-7: *Oblique Cylinder Development*
- Worksheet 15-8: *Truncated Pyramid Development*
- Worksheet 15-9: *Truncated Oblique Pyramid Development*
- Worksheet 15-10: *Cone Development*
- Worksheet 15-11: *Truncated Cone Development*
- Worksheet 15-12: *Transition Piece Development*

Instructor's Resource
  Instructional Tasks
  Instructional Aids and Assignments
  Chapter 15 Quiz

Reproducible Masters

- Reproducible Master 15-1: *Development of a Rectangular Prism.* The top view, front view, and development of a rectangular prism is shown.
- Reproducible Master 15-2: *Development of a Cylinder with an Inclined Bevel.* The stretchout of a cylinder with an inclined bevel is shown.

Procedure Checklist

Color Transparencies (Binder/IRCD only)

- Transparency 15-1: *Development of a Truncated Pyramid.* The development of a truncated pyramid is shown.
- Transparency 15-2: *Development of a Truncated Right Cone.* The development of a truncated right cone is shown. Several points are identified for reference.

Instructional Tasks

1. Define the term *development.*
   - Discuss the industrial applications of developments.
2. Explain the development of a rectangular prism with an inclined bevel.
   - Use a paper or plastic model to demonstrate the development of a rectangular prism with an inclined bevel.
3. Explain the development of an oblique prism.
   - Demonstrate the development of an oblique prism. Emphasize the steps that differ from the procedure for prisms that are not oblique.
4. Explain the development of a cylinder with an inclined bevel.
   - Display samples of industrial parts that utilize the development of a cylinder with an inclined bevel in their manufacture.
   - Demonstrate the development of a cylinder with an inclined bevel. Refer to the displayed samples for each step.

5. Explain the development of a two-piece and a four-piece elbow pipe.
   - Discuss and demonstrate the development of two-piece and four-piece elbow pipes.
6. Explain the development of an oblique cylinder.
   - Demonstrate the development of an oblique cylinder.
7. Explain the development of a pyramid.
   - Use step-by-step instruction, with related transparencies, to demonstrate the development of a pyramid.
8. Explain the development of a truncated pyramid.
   - Demonstrate the development of a truncated pyramid. Clarify the additional steps involved as compared to the development of a regular pyramid.
9. Explain the development of a pyramid inclined to its base.
   - Discuss how the development of a pyramid inclined to its base differs from the development of a right pyramid.
10. Explain the development of a cone.
    - Demonstrate the development of a cone.
11. Explain the development of a truncated right cone.
    - Demonstrate the additional layout steps required for the development of a truncated right cone as compared to the development of a regular cone.
12. Explain the development of a cone inclined to its base.
    - Using step-by-step instruction, demonstrate the development of a cone inclined to its base.
13. Explain the development of transition pieces.
    - Clarify and give examples of transition pieces used in industry.
    - Use transparencies with overlays to demonstrate the development of transition pieces.
14. Explain the construction of an approximate development of a warped surface.
    - Define and give examples of warped surfaces.
    - Demonstrate the construction of an approximate development of a warped surface.

Instructional Aids and Assignments

1. Display transparencies with overlays showing various development techniques.
2. Display paper, plastic, or sheet metal models of developments.
3. Display samples of industrial parts that have utilized "patterns" or "developments" in their manufacture. Examples of items you might use include heating and air conditioning ducts, pipe, ornamental sheet metal parts, or consumer products packages.
4. Assign the drawing problems in the textbook. The number of problems is sufficient to assign a minimum number to all students and to identify problems that may be done for extra credit. Some problems may be used for the performance section of the chapter quiz.

Answers to Review Questions, Text

Page 536

1. The layout of a pattern on flat sheet stock.
2. pattern, stretchout
3. Ruled surfaces and double-curved surfaces.
4. Parallel line development and radial line development.
5. Parallel
6. Radial
7. stretchout
8. auxiliary
9. Parallel line development.
10. Radial line development.
11. truncated
12. Radial line development.
13. The **Divide** command.
14. triangulation
15. transition
16. triangulation

Solutions to Problems and Activities, Text

Pages 536–545

Student work should look like the following drawings. The problem number and title are indicated on each problem sheet.

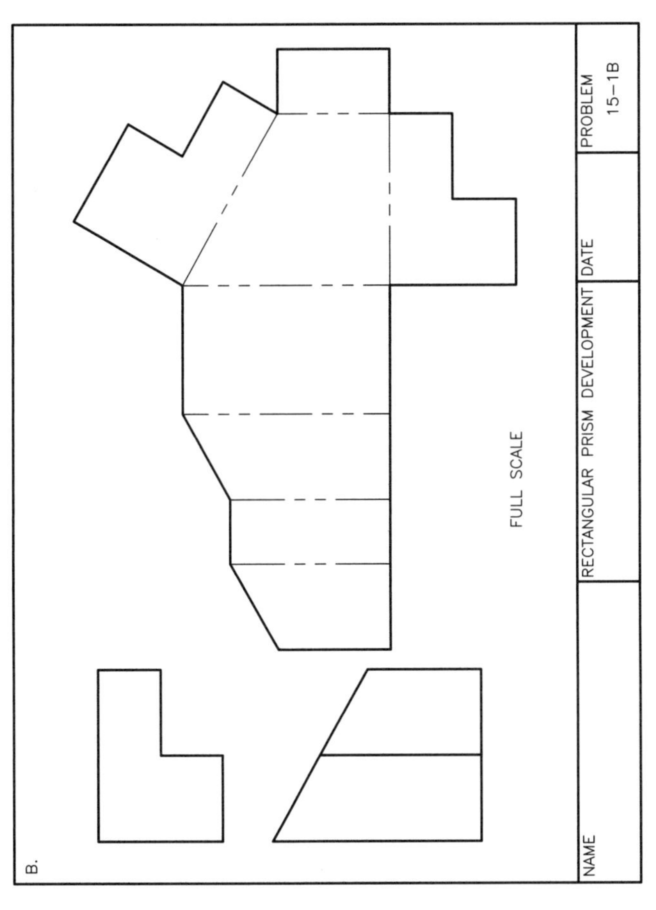
B.
FULL SCALE
NAME
RECTANGULAR PRISM DEVELOPMENT
DATE
PROBLEM
15–1B

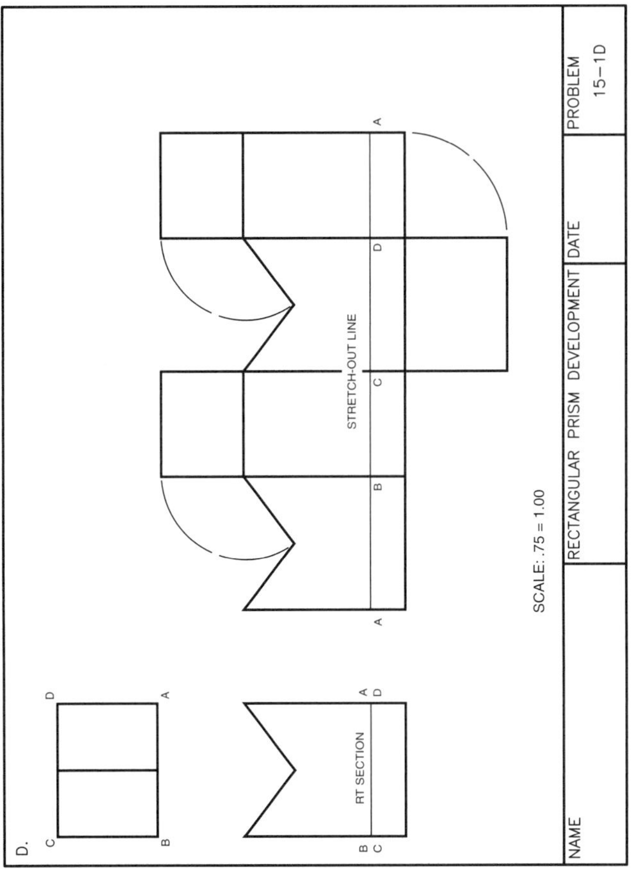
D.
RT SECTION
STRETCH-OUT LINE
SCALE: .75 = 1.00
NAME
RECTANGULAR PRISM DEVELOPMENT
DATE
PROBLEM
15–1D

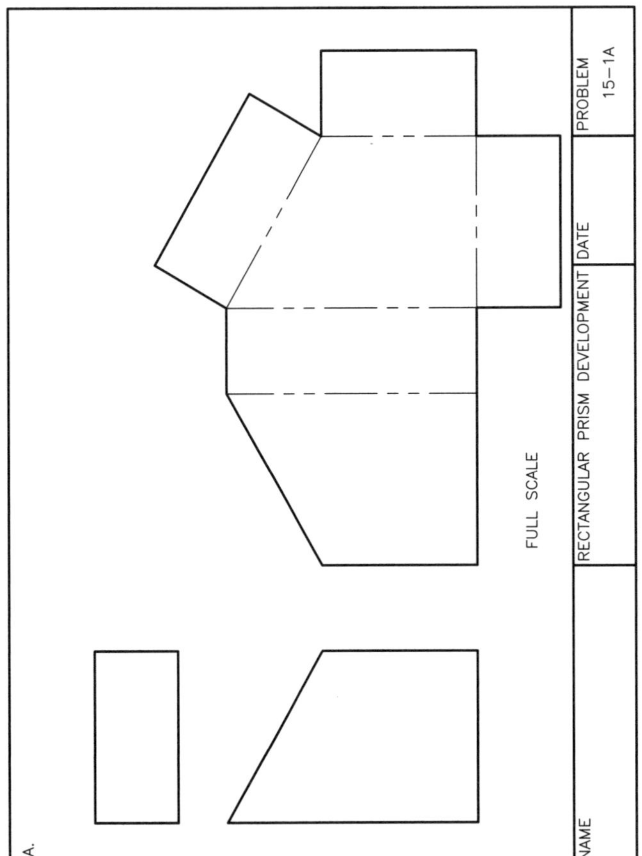
A.
FULL SCALE
NAME
RECTANGULAR PRISM DEVELOPMENT
DATE
PROBLEM
15–1A

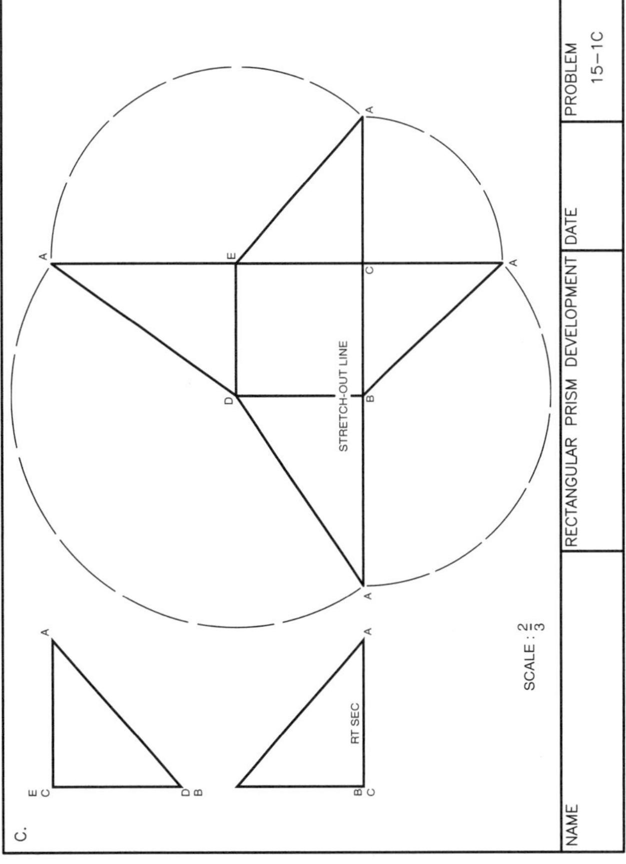
C.
RT SEC
STRETCH-OUT LINE
SCALE: 2/3
NAME
RECTANGULAR PRISM DEVELOPMENT
DATE
PROBLEM
15–1C

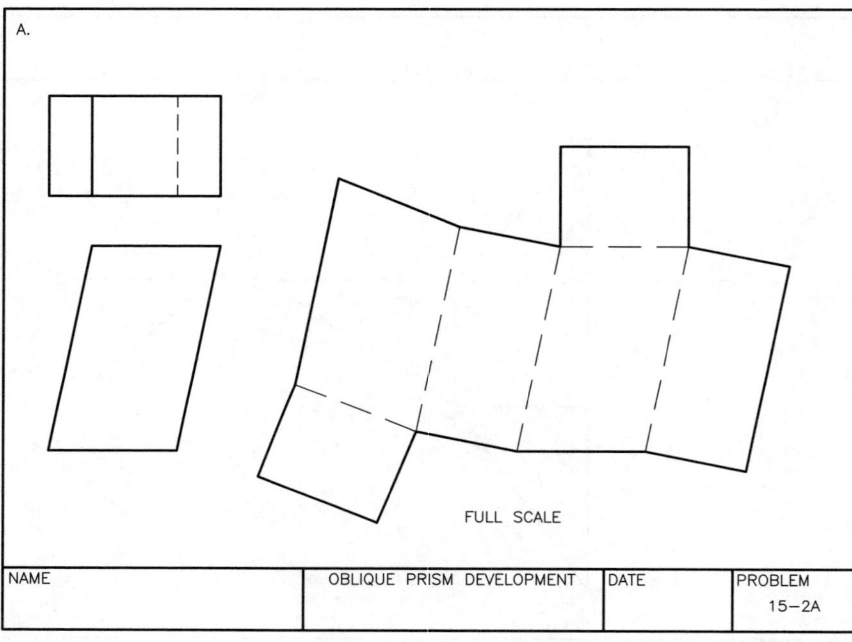
A.
FULL SCALE
NAME
OBLIQUE PRISM DEVELOPMENT
DATE
PROBLEM
15–2A

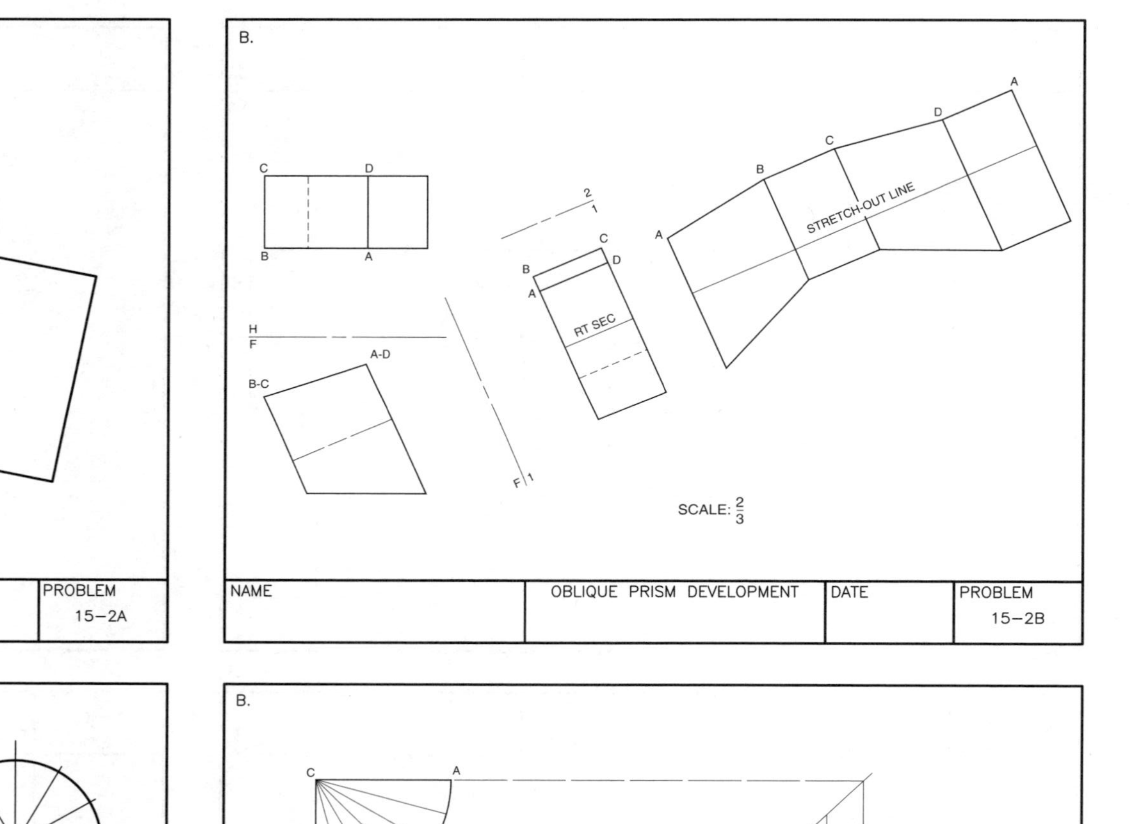
B.
STRETCH-OUT LINE
RT SEC
SCALE: 2/3
NAME
OBLIQUE PRISM DEVELOPMENT
DATE
PROBLEM
15–2B

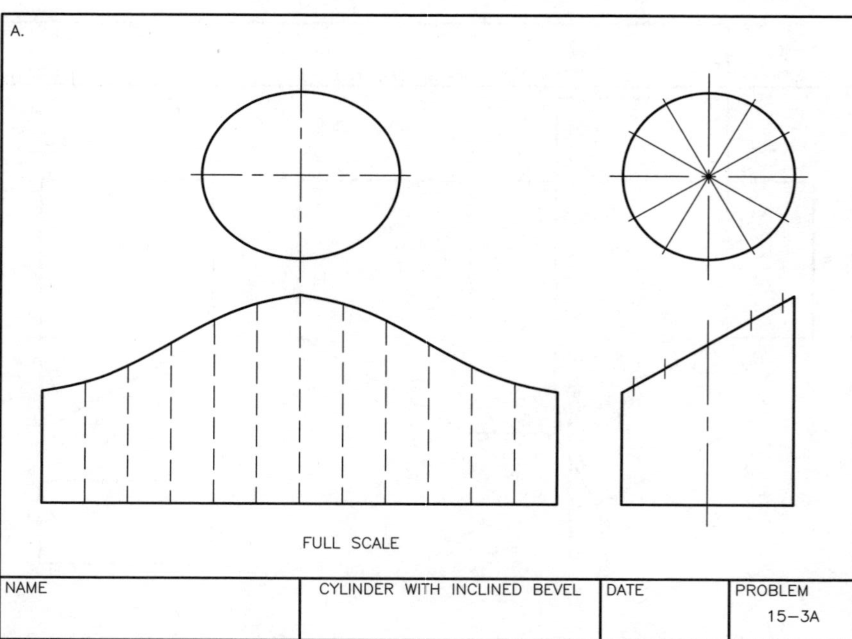
A.
FULL SCALE
NAME
CYLINDER WITH INCLINED BEVEL
DATE
PROBLEM
15–3A

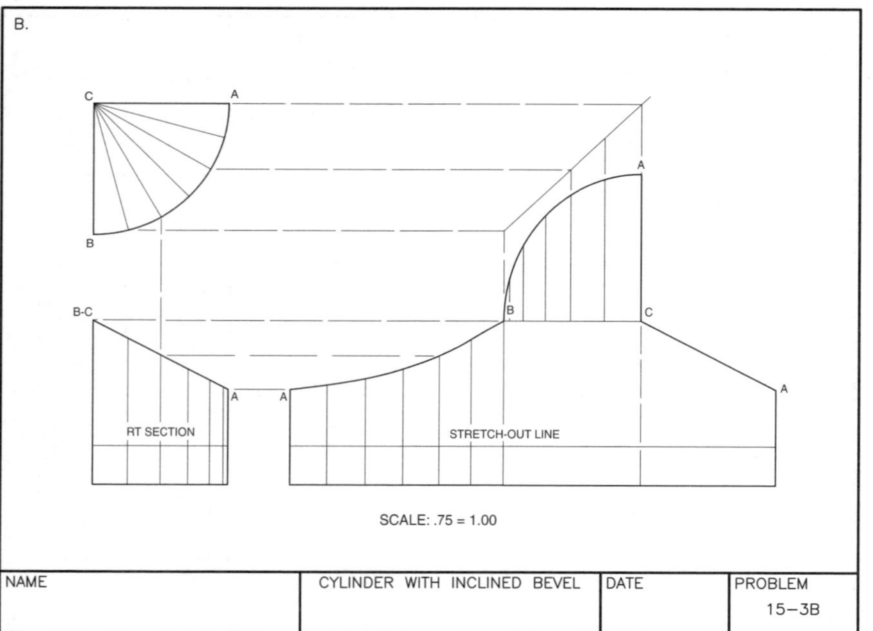
B.
RT SECTION
STRETCH-OUT LINE
SCALE: .75 = 1.00
NAME
CYLINDER WITH INCLINED BEVEL
DATE
PROBLEM
15–3B

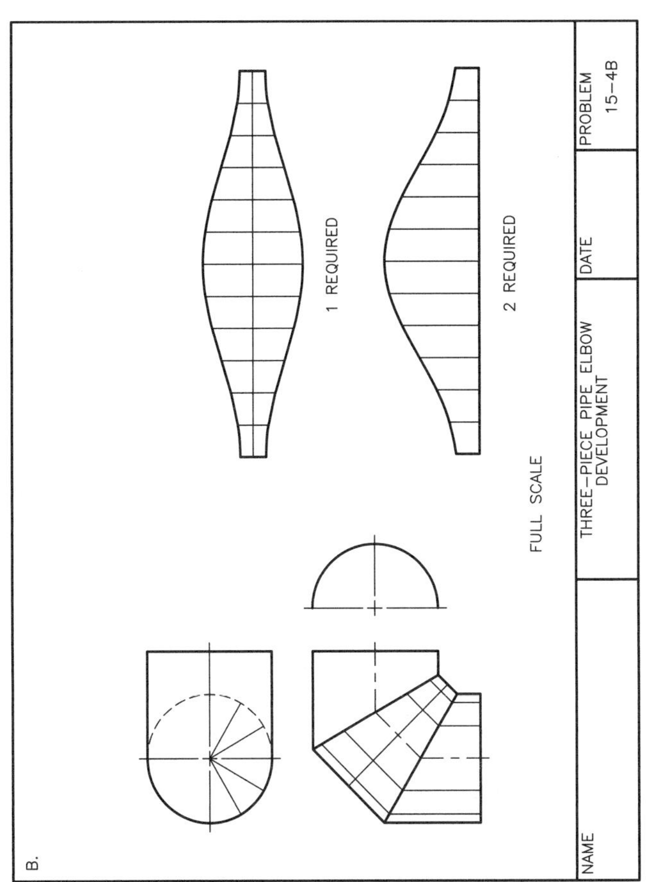
B.
1 REQUIRED
2 REQUIRED
FULL SCALE
NAME
THREE-PIECE PIPE ELBOW DEVELOPMENT
DATE
PROBLEM 15-4B

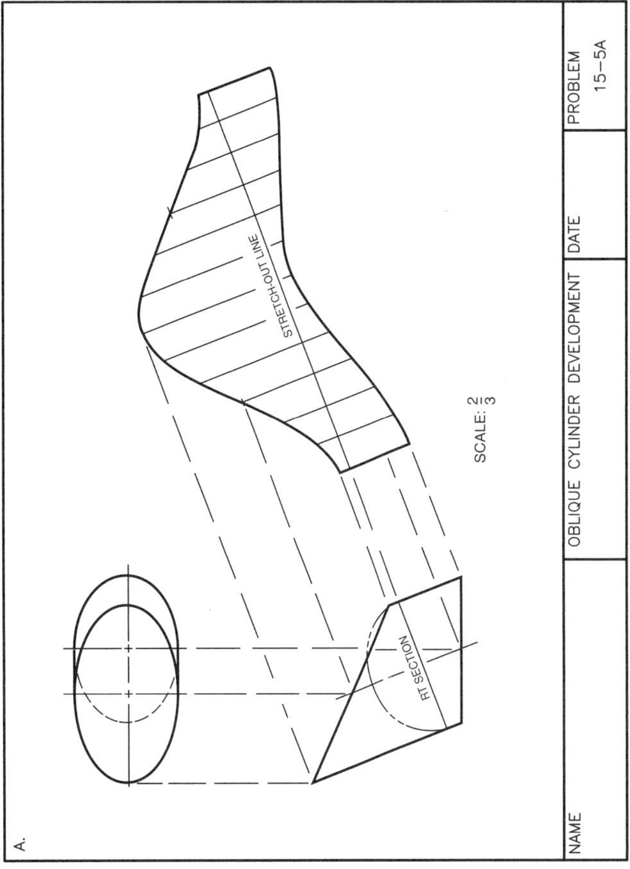
A.
STRETCH-OUT LINE
SCALE: 2/3
RT SECTION
NAME
OBLIQUE CYLINDER DEVELOPMENT
DATE
PROBLEM 15-5A

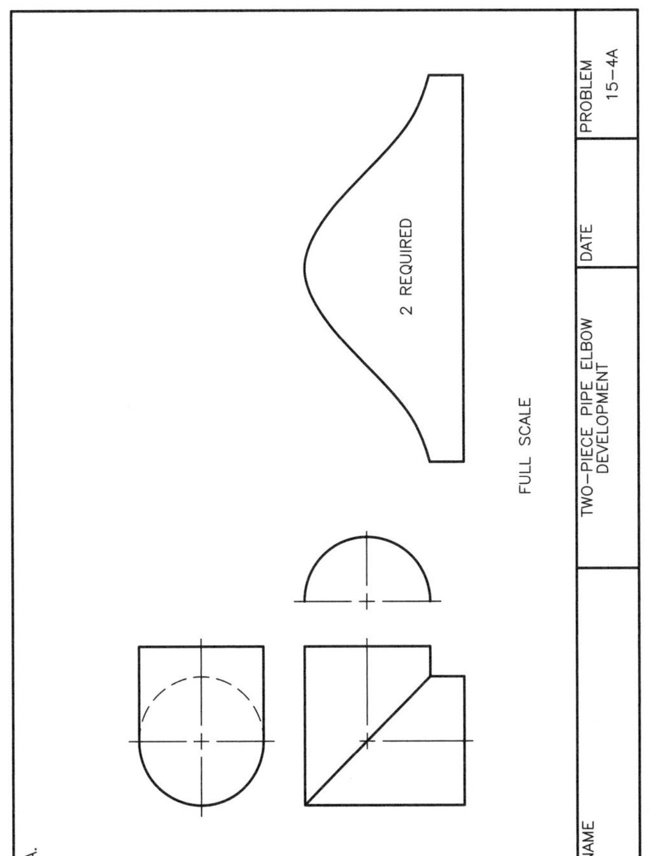
A.
2 REQUIRED
FULL SCALE
NAME
TWO-PIECE PIPE ELBOW DEVELOPMENT
DATE
PROBLEM 15-4A

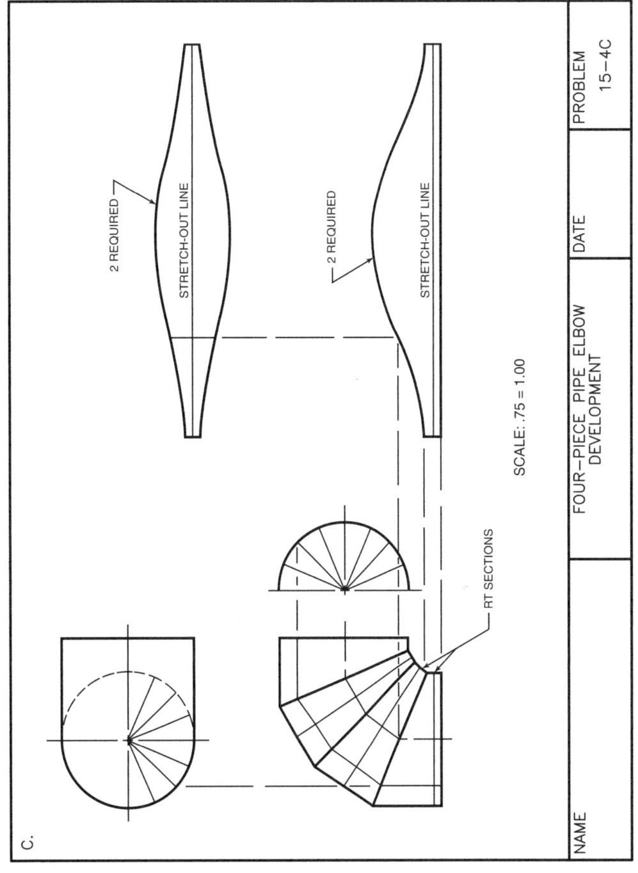
C.
2 REQUIRED
STRETCH-OUT LINE
2 REQUIRED
STRETCH-OUT LINE
SCALE: .75 = 1.00
RT SECTIONS
NAME
FOUR-PIECE PIPE ELBOW DEVELOPMENT
DATE
PROBLEM 15-4C

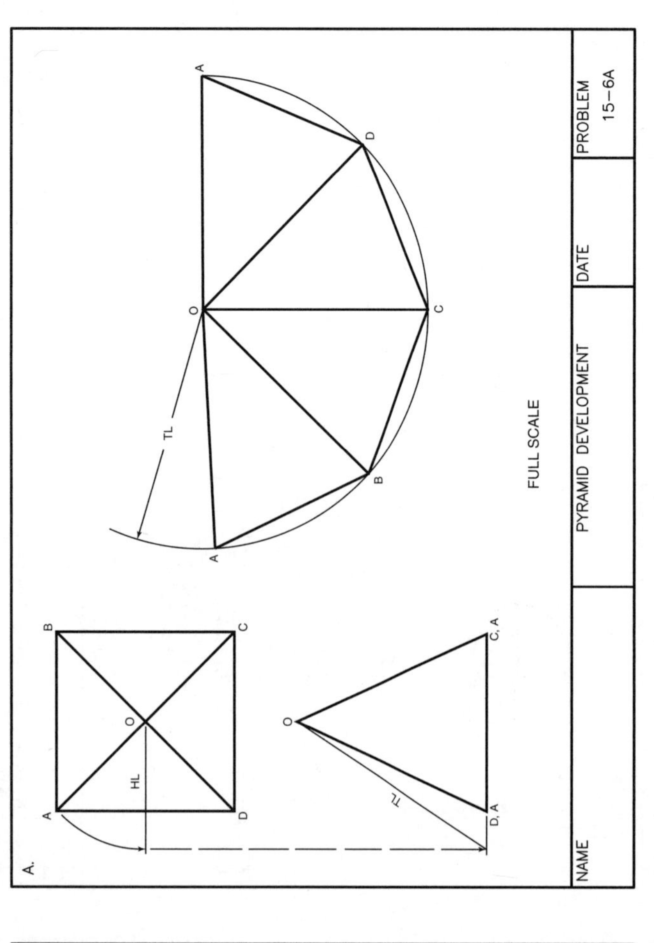
A.
B
C
O
HL
A
D
O
TL
C, A
D, A
A
D
O
C
B
A
TL
FULL SCALE
NAME
PYRAMID DEVELOPMENT
DATE
PROBLEM
15-6A

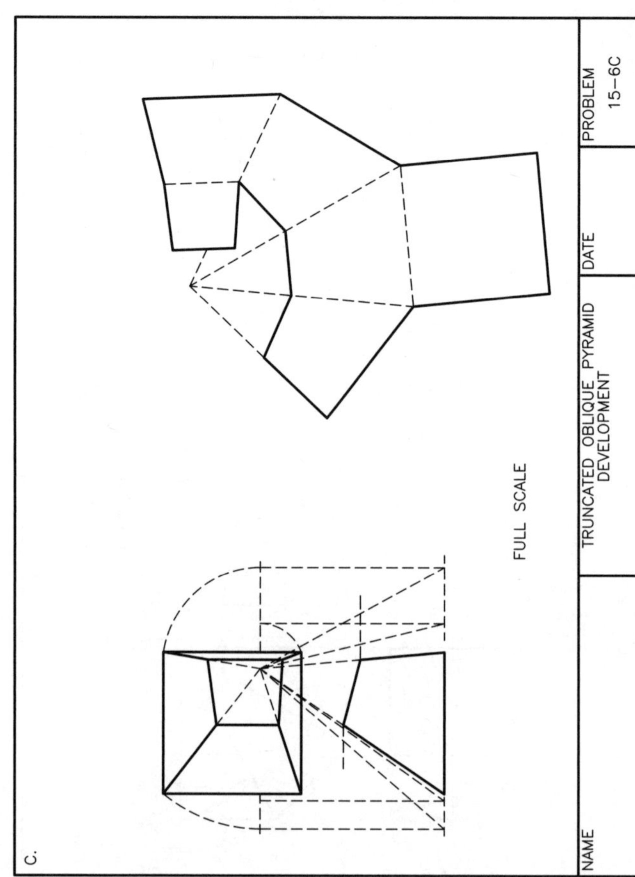
C.
FULL SCALE
NAME
TRUNCATED OBLIQUE PYRAMID DEVELOPMENT
DATE
PROBLEM
15-6C

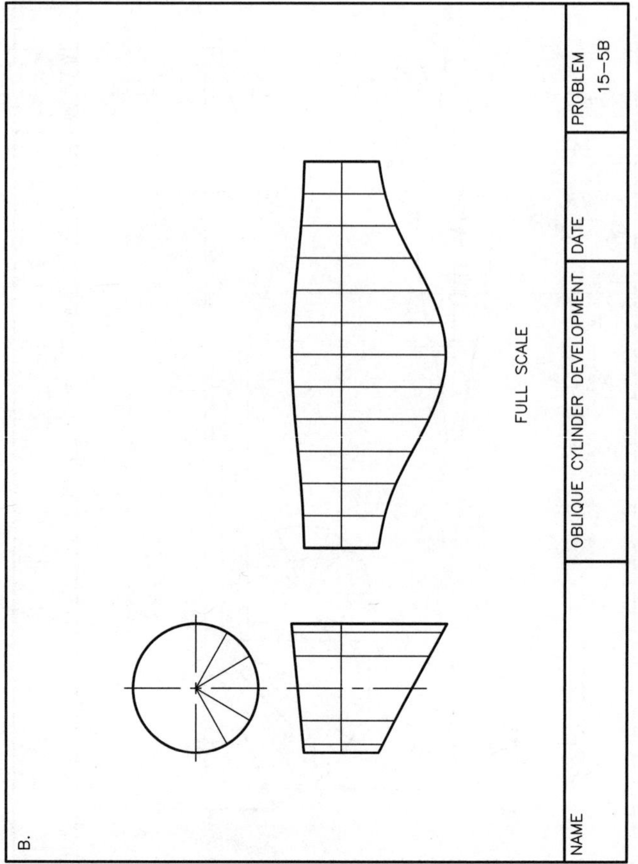
B.
FULL SCALE
NAME
OBLIQUE CYLINDER DEVELOPMENT
DATE
PROBLEM
15-5B

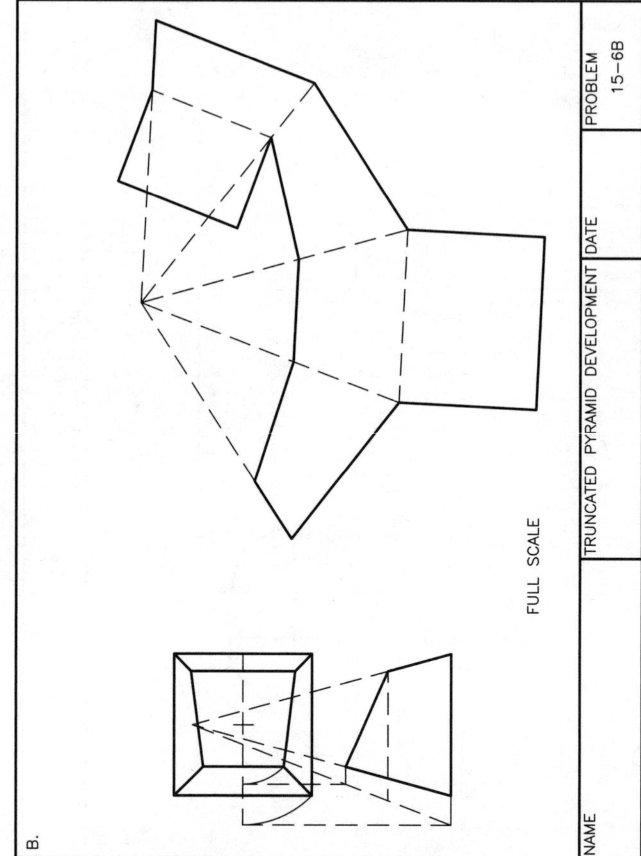
B.
FULL SCALE
NAME
TRUNCATED PYRAMID DEVELOPMENT
DATE
PROBLEM
15-6B

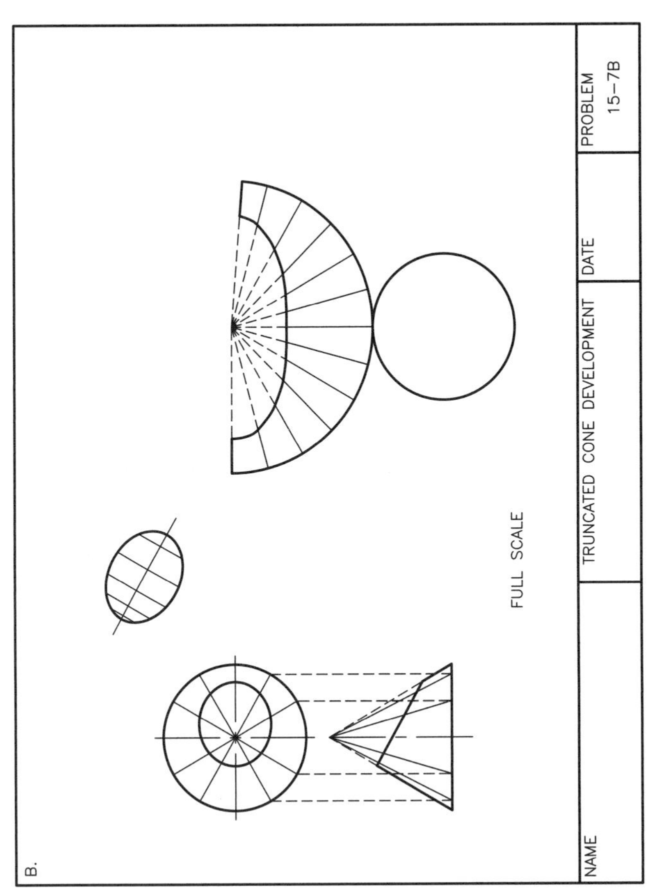
B.
FULL SCALE
NAME
TRUNCATED CONE DEVELOPMENT
DATE
PROBLEM
15–7B

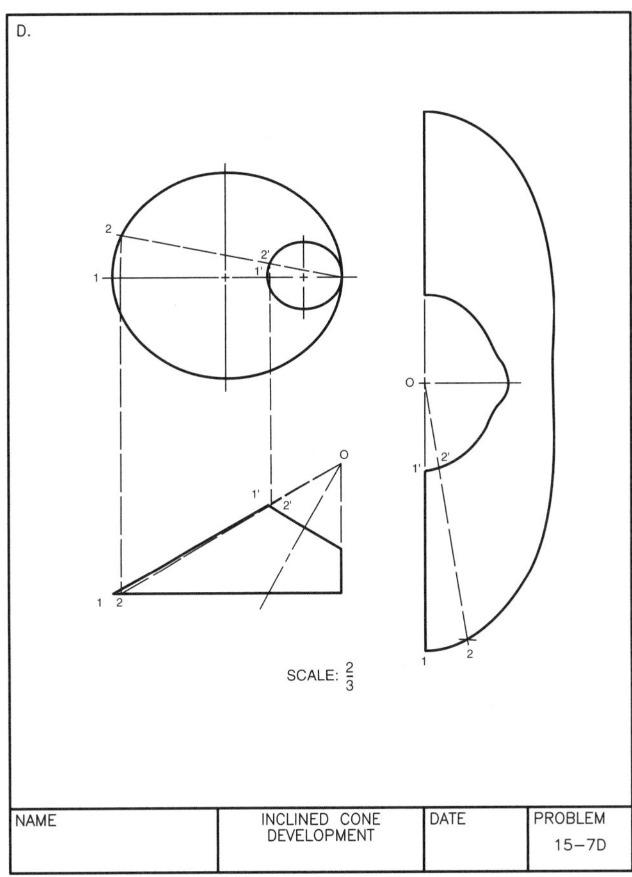
D.
2
1
2'
1'
O
1'
2'
1 2
O
1'
2'
1
2
SCALE: $\frac{2}{3}$
NAME
INCLINED CONE
DEVELOPMENT
DATE
PROBLEM
15–7D

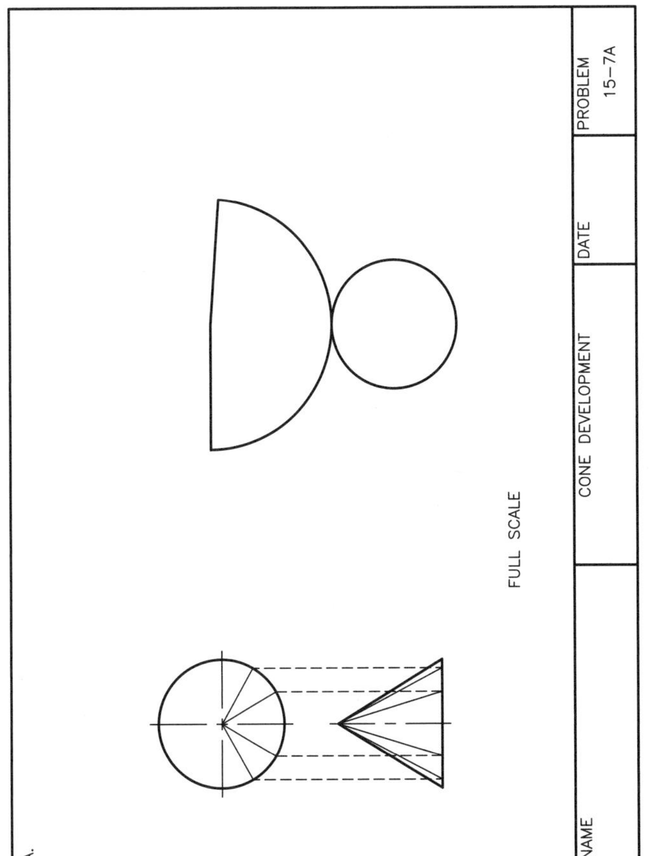
A.
FULL SCALE
NAME
CONE DEVELOPMENT
DATE
PROBLEM
15–7A

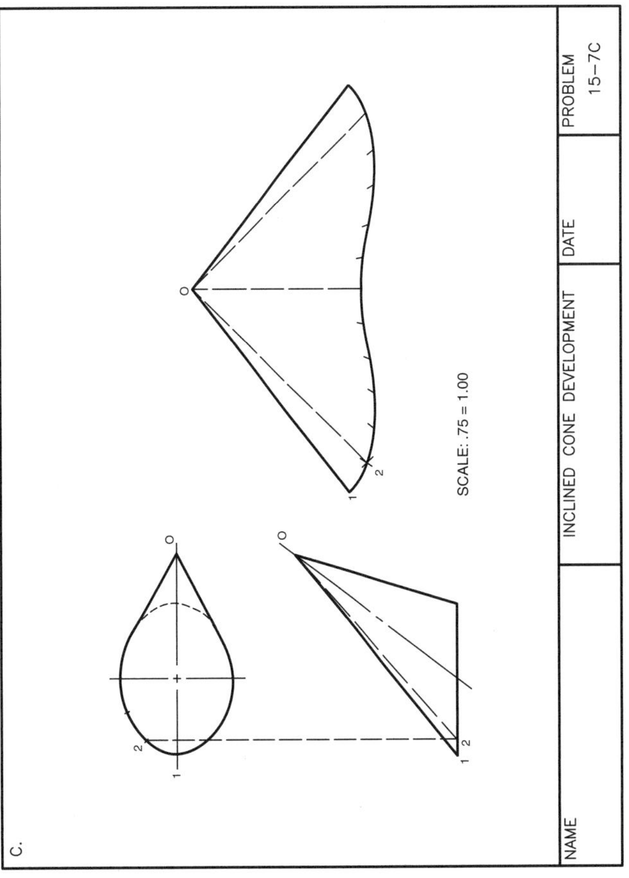
C.
O
1
2
SCALE: .75 = 1.00
O
2
1
O
1 2
NAME
INCLINED CONE DEVELOPMENT
DATE
PROBLEM
15–7C

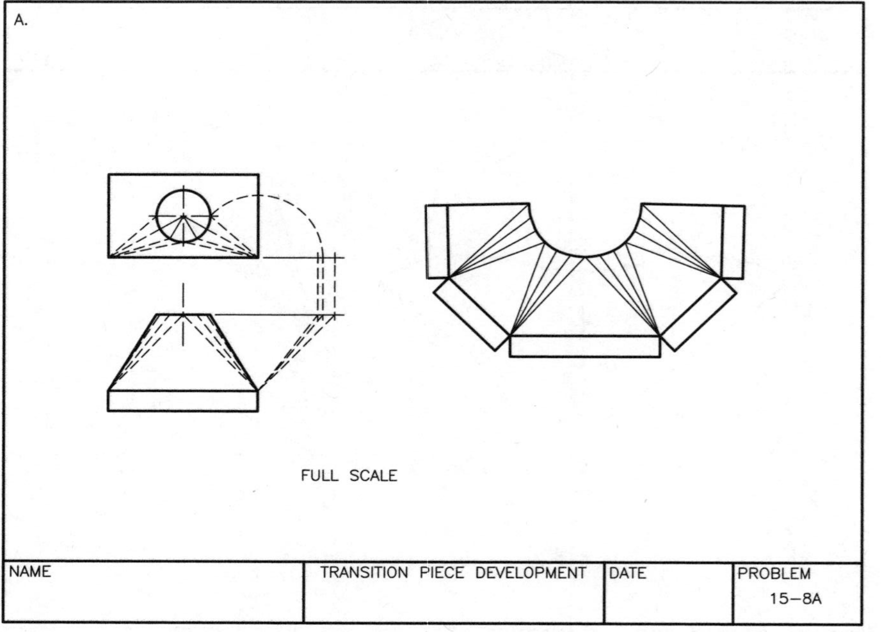
A.
FULL SCALE
NAME
TRANSITION PIECE DEVELOPMENT
DATE
PROBLEM
15–8A

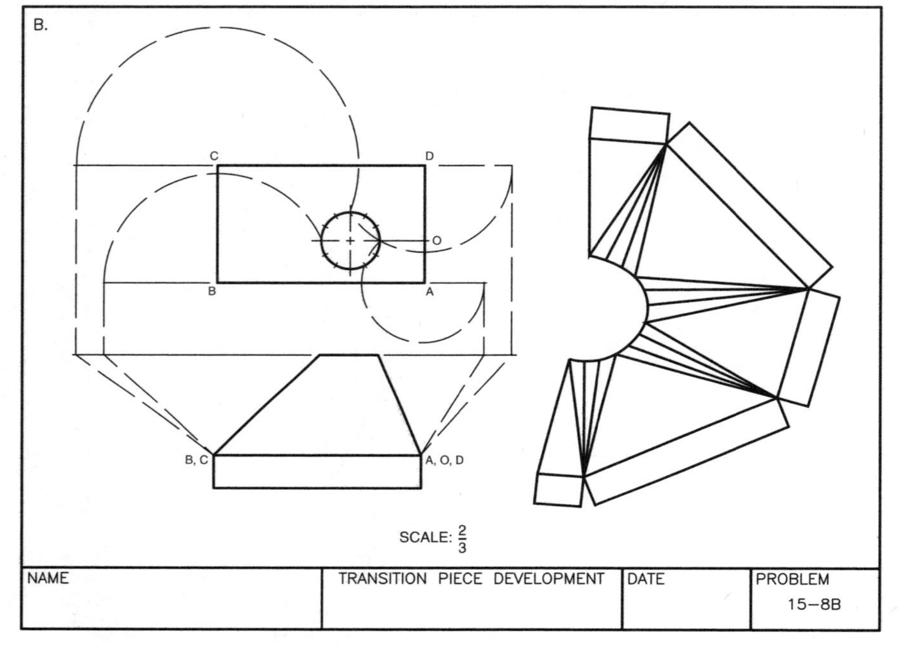
B.
C
D
O
B
A
B, C
A, O, D
SCALE: 2/3
NAME
TRANSITION PIECE DEVELOPMENT
DATE
PROBLEM
15–8B

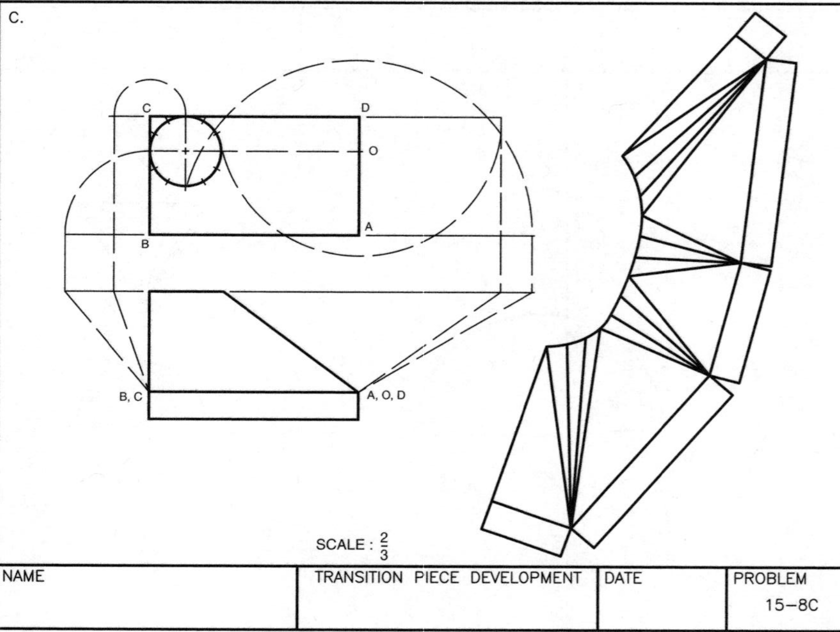
C.
C
D
O
B
A
B, C
A, O, D
SCALE: 2/3
NAME
TRANSITION PIECE DEVELOPMENT
DATE
PROBLEM
15–8C

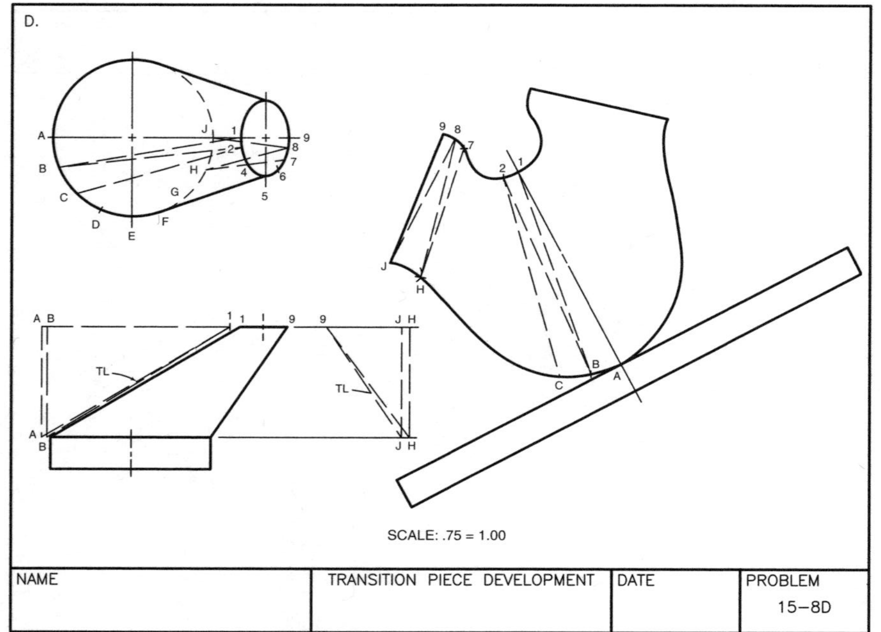
D.
A
B
C
D
E
F
G
H
J
1
2
4
5
6
7
8
9
A B
J H
TL
TL
SCALE: .75 = 1.00
NAME
TRANSITION PIECE DEVELOPMENT
DATE
PROBLEM
15–8D

Solutions to Design Problems, Text

Page 545

1. The solution may vary based upon the diameter and length of the tank designed. The following basic data apply:

    1 cubic foot = 7.4805 gallons (approx.)

    1000 gallons = 133.6809 cubic feet (approx.)

    Therefore:

    A. The student must first decide on the tank's design size by selecting a diameter in feet.

    B. The student must then calculate the area of the tank base in square feet (area of a circle = πr^2).

    C. The student needs to then divide the number of square feet in the base area into 133.6809 to determine the length of the tank to hold 1000 gallons.

    The following are two examples:

    Example A. The design size diameter of the tank is 4′.

    A. Area of base = $\pi r^2 = 3.1416 \times 2 \times 2 = 12.5664$ square feet

    B. Length of tank = $133.6809 \div 12.5564 =$ 10.637963′

    Example B. The design size diameter of the tank is 5′.

    A. Area of base = $\pi r^2 = 3.1416 \times 2.5 \times 2.5 =$ 19.635 square feet

    B. Length of tank = $133.6809 \div 19.635 =$ 6.8082964′

    The dimensions in the above examples are inside dimensions. The storage tank cylinder and 4″ pipe would be laid out using radial line development as discussed in the text. The drawing shown below is a solution for Example A.

2. Review proposed problems from students before they start. Students should prepare working drawings of the best solutions.
3. Review proposed problems from students before they start. Students should prepare working drawings of the best solutions.
4. Review proposed problems from students before they start. Students should prepare working drawings of the best solutions.
5. Review proposed problems from students before they start. Students should prepare working drawings of the best solutions.

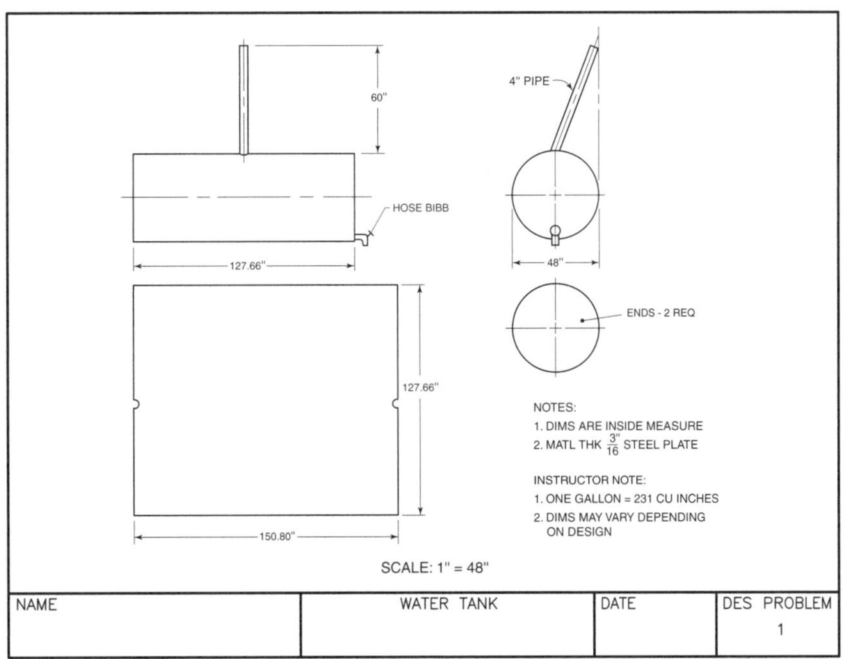

Example A

Solutions to Drawing Problems, Text

Pages 545–547

Student work should look like the following drawings. The problem number and title are indicated on each problem sheet.

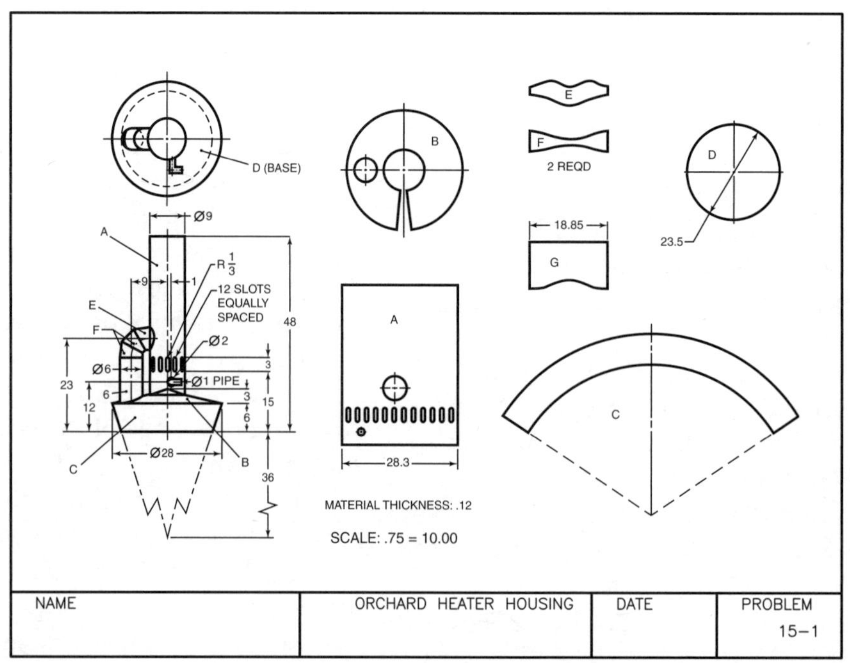

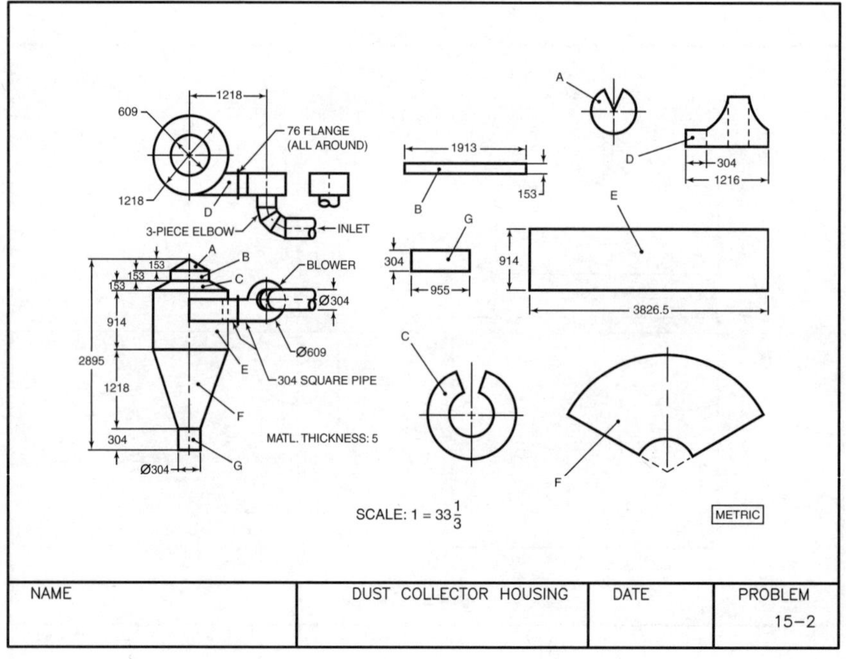

Solutions to Worksheets

Pages 123–134

Student work should look like the following drawings. The problem number and title are indicated on each problem sheet.

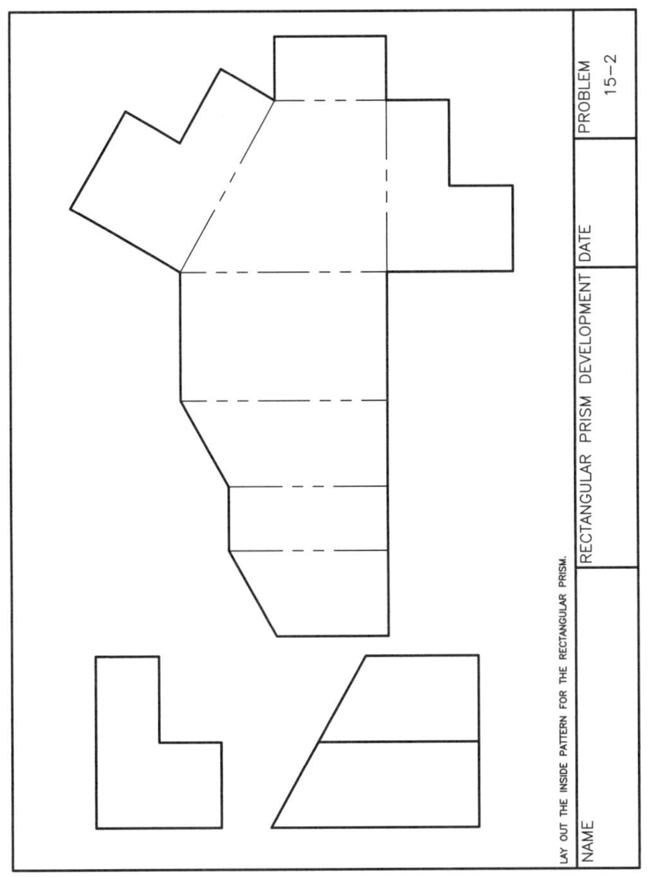

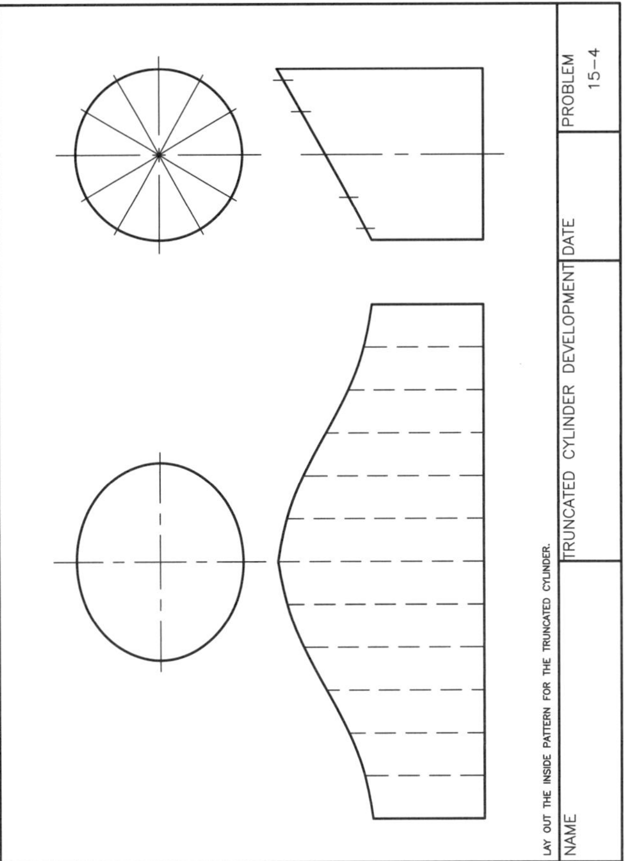

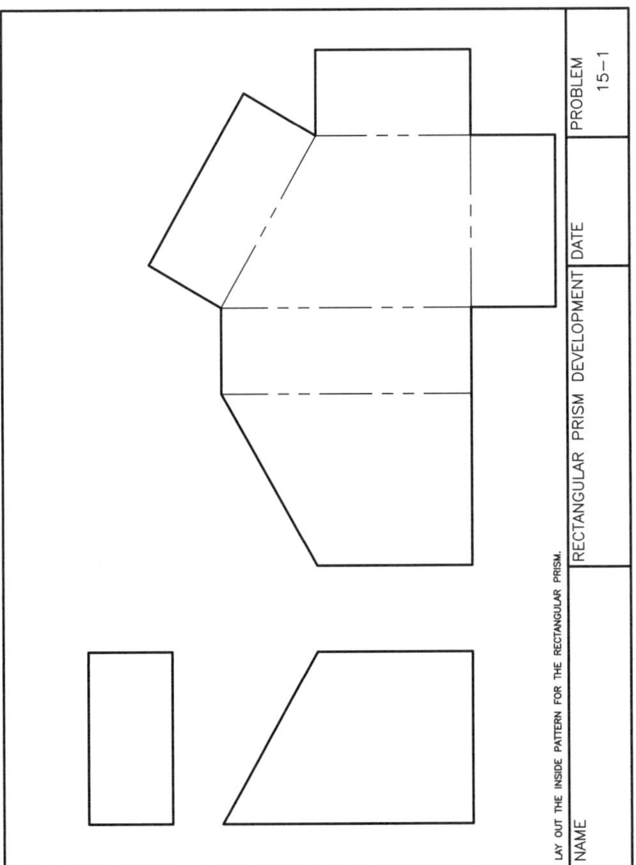

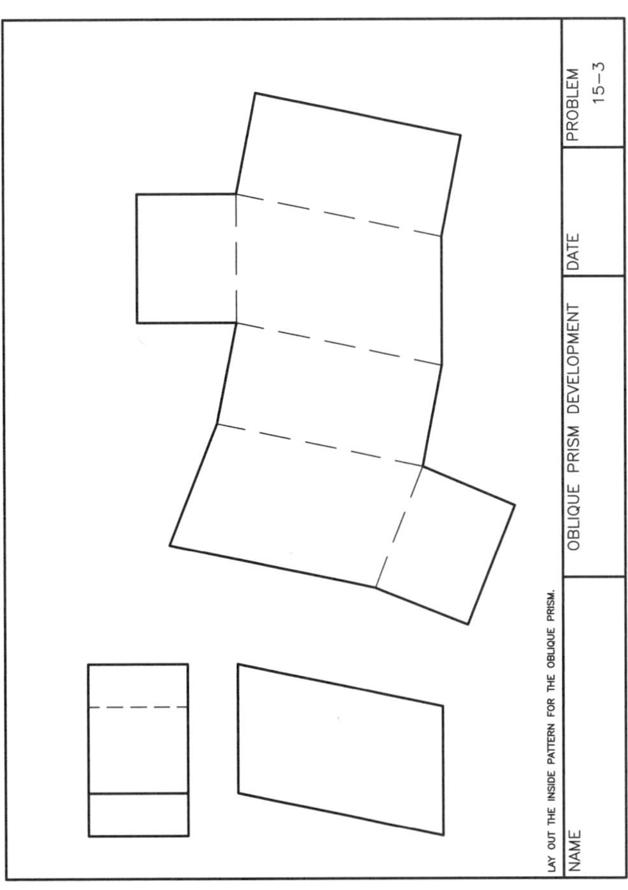

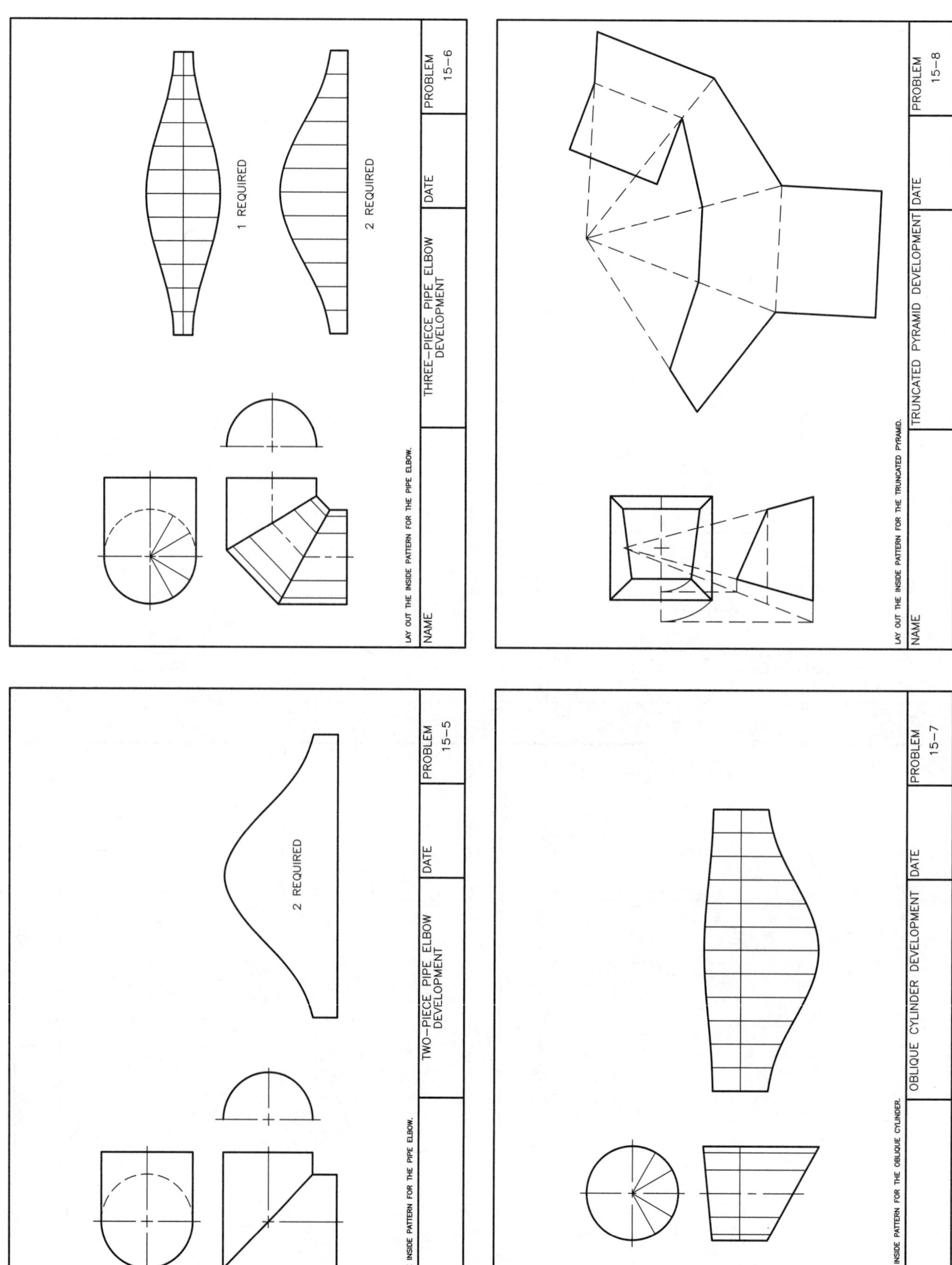

1 REQUIRED
2 REQUIRED
LAY OUT THE INSIDE PATTERN FOR THE PIPE ELBOW.
NAME
THREE-PIECE PIPE ELBOW DEVELOPMENT
DATE
PROBLEM 15-6
LAY OUT THE INSIDE PATTERN FOR THE TRUNCATED PYRAMID.
NAME
TRUNCATED PYRAMID DEVELOPMENT
DATE
PROBLEM 15-8
2 REQUIRED
LAY OUT THE INSIDE PATTERN FOR THE PIPE ELBOW.
NAME
TWO-PIECE PIPE ELBOW DEVELOPMENT
DATE
PROBLEM 15-5
LAY OUT THE INSIDE PATTERN FOR THE OBLIQUE CYLINDER.
NAME
OBLIQUE CYLINDER DEVELOPMENT
DATE
PROBLEM 15-7

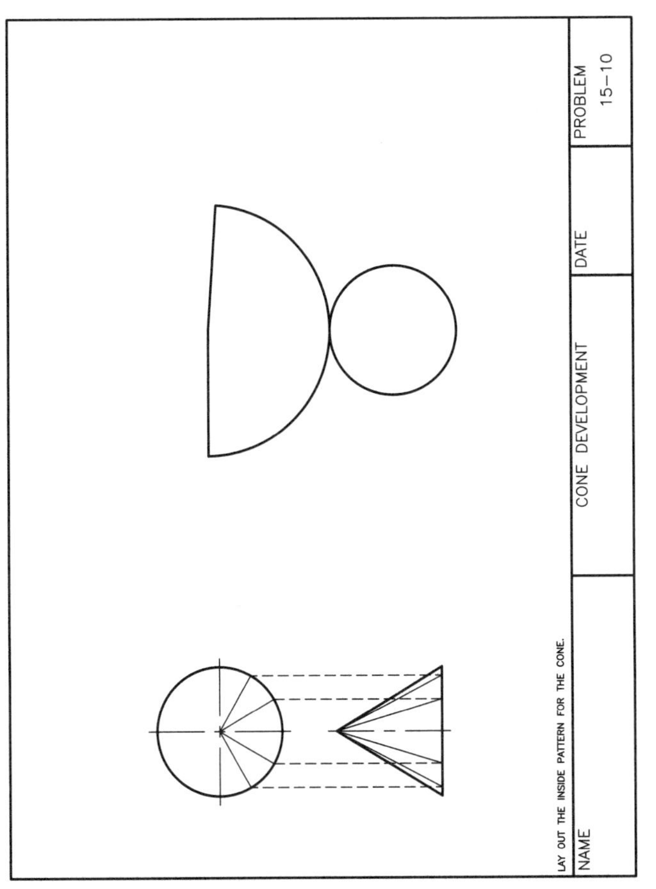
LAY OUT THE INSIDE PATTERN FOR THE CONE.
NAME
CONE DEVELOPMENT
DATE
PROBLEM
15–10

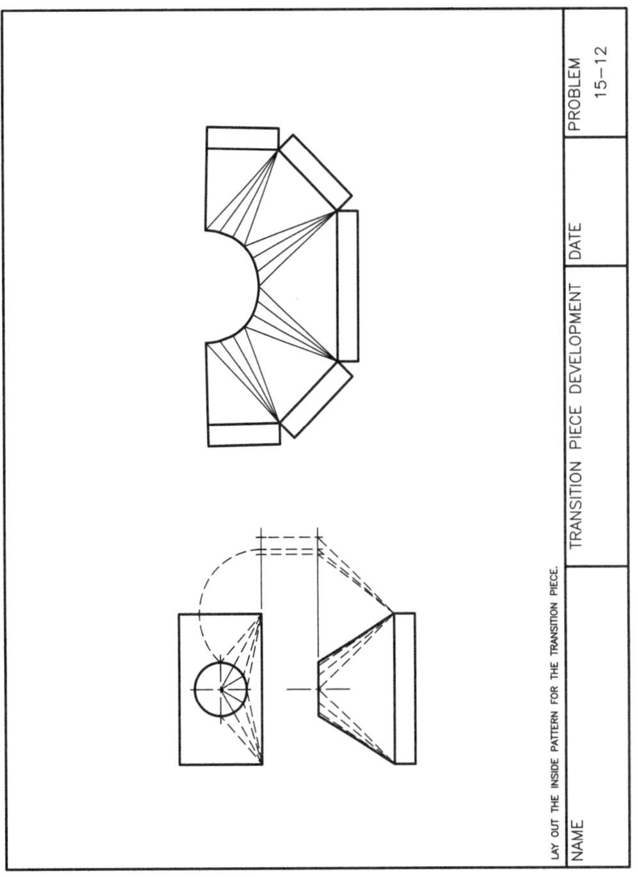
LAY OUT THE INSIDE PATTERN FOR THE TRANSITION PIECE.
NAME
TRANSITION PIECE DEVELOPMENT
DATE
PROBLEM
15–12

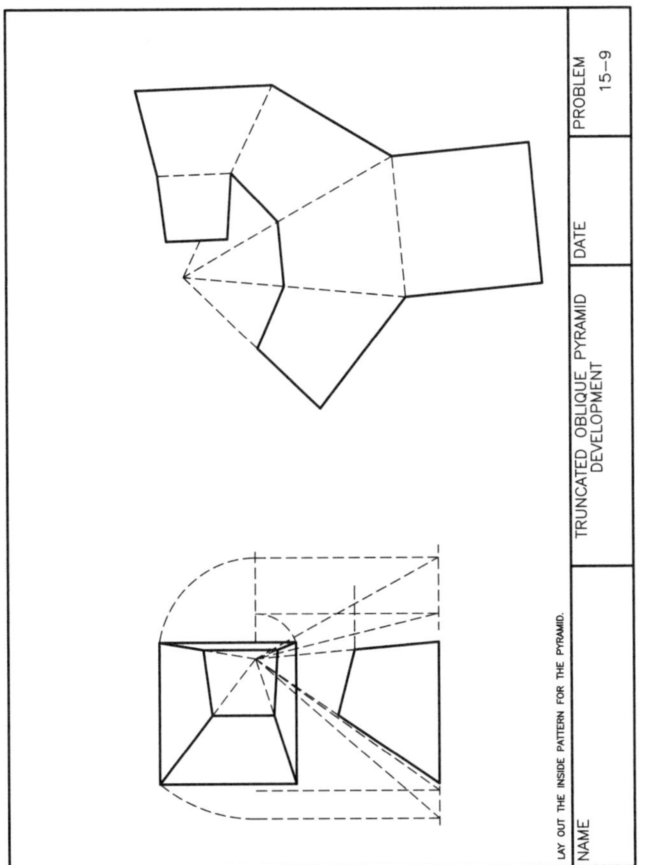
LAY OUT THE INSIDE PATTERN FOR THE PYRAMID.
NAME
TRUNCATED OBLIQUE PYRAMID DEVELOPMENT
DATE
PROBLEM
15–9

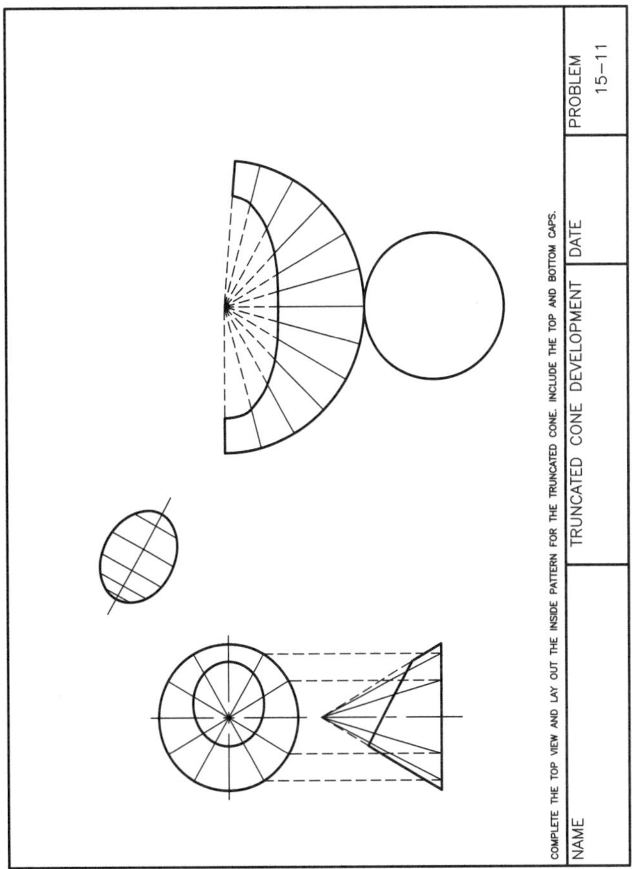
COMPLETE THE TOP VIEW AND LAY OUT THE INSIDE PATTERN FOR THE TRUNCATED CONE. INCLUDE THE TOP AND BOTTOM CAPS.
NAME
TRUNCATED CONE DEVELOPMENT
DATE
PROBLEM
15–11

Answers to Chapter 15 Quiz

1. B. Single-curve surfaces
2. C. Rectangular prism
3. C. parallel line development
4. B. auxiliary view
5. D. cone
6. A. triangulation
7. B. triangulation
8. Refer to the drawings given in the *Solutions to Problems and Activities, Text* section for the problem selected from the textbook.

Chapter Quiz 15

Developments

Name ____________________

Period____________ Date____________ Score ____________

Multiple Choice

Choose the answer that correctly completes the statement. Write the corresponding letter in the space provided.

_____ 1. What kinds of surfaces can be developed accurately into flat patterns?
A. Spherical surfaces
B. Single-curve surfaces
C. Double-curve surfaces
D. All of the above.

_____ 2. Which of the following objects can be developed using simple orthographic projection?
A. Oblique prism
B. Warped cone
C. Rectangular prism
D. All of the above.

_____ 3. The development of a cylinder with an inclined bevel involves _____.
A. orthographic projection
B. triangulation
C. parallel line development
D. successive auxiliary views

_____ 4. The development of an oblique cylinder is best done using the _____ method.
A. orthographic projection
B. auxiliary view
C. revolution
D. perspective projection

_____ 5. Development of a _____ involves radial line development.
A. rectangular prism
B. oblique prism
C. cylinder
D. cone

_____ 6. The development of approximate warped surfaces can be accomplished through the use of _____.
A. triangulation
B. parallel line development
C. successive auxiliary views
D. Approximate warped surfaces cannot be developed.

Name ____

________ 7. The development of a transition piece involves _____.
A. orthographic projection
B. triangulation
C. successive auxiliary views
D. parallel line development

Drafting Performance

8. Draw a solution of a problem selected by your instructor from Chapter 15 in your textbook. Draw the required views and develop an inside pattern.

Development of a Rectangular Prism

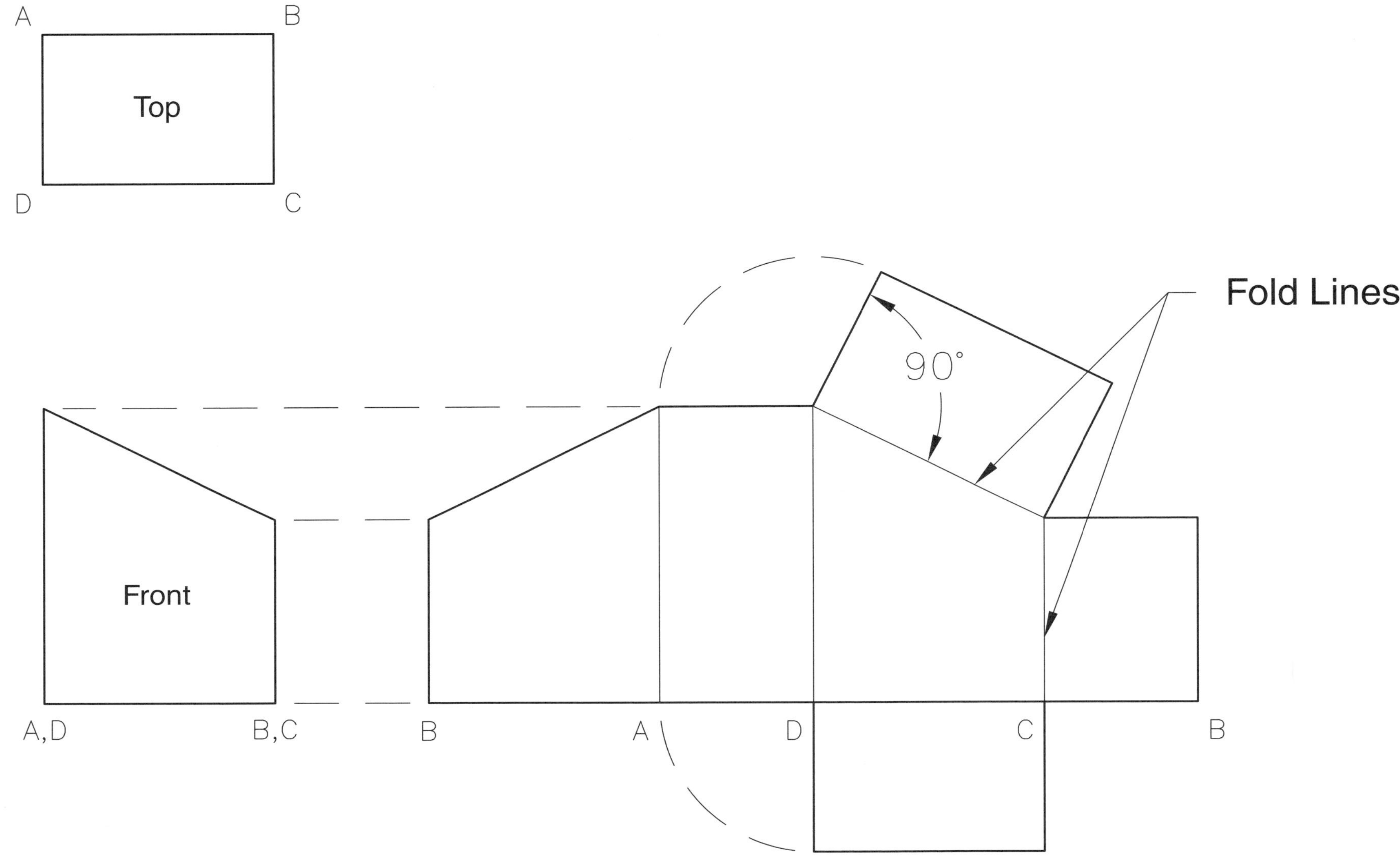

RM 15-1

Development of a Cylinder with an Inclined Bevel

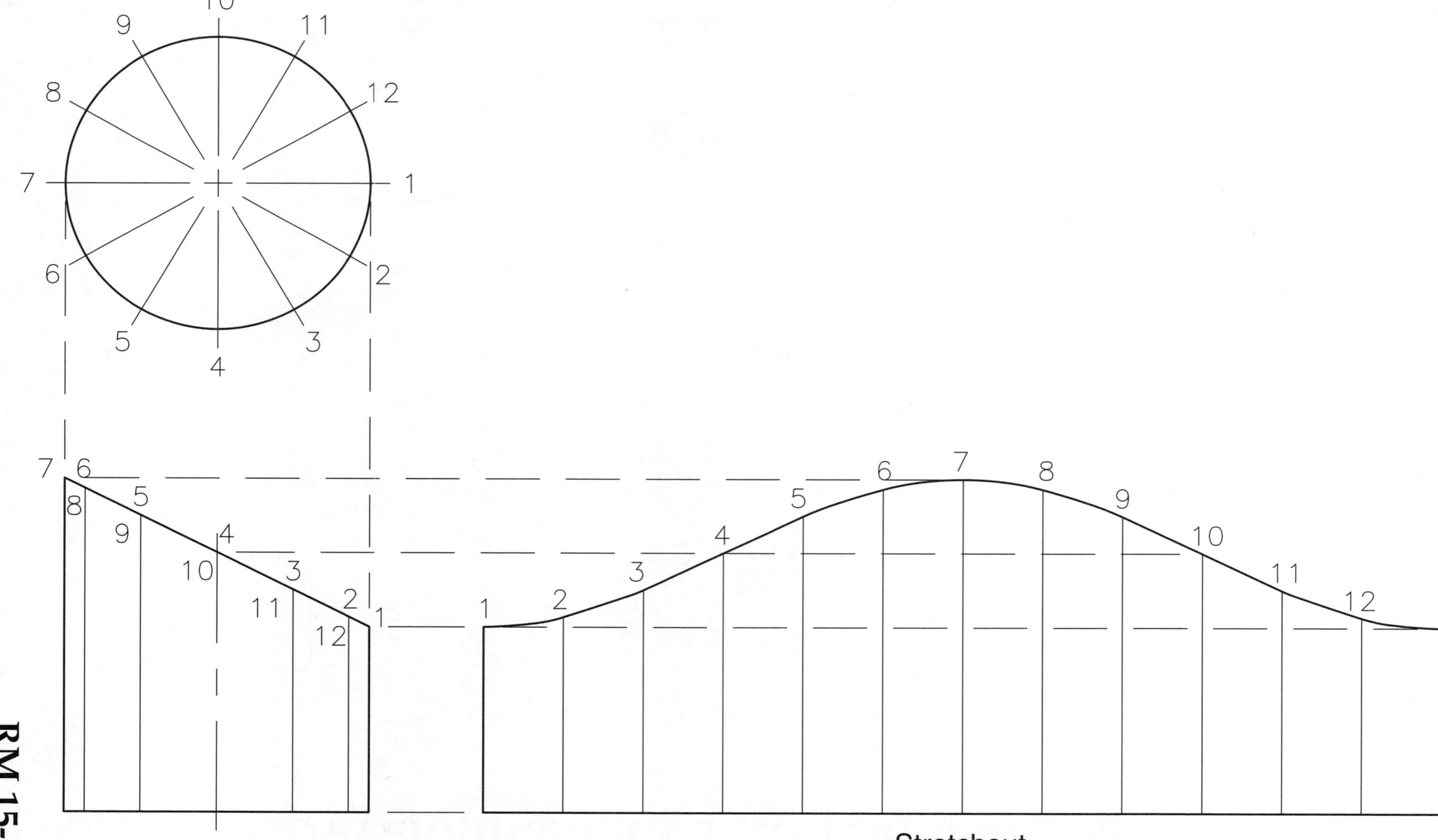

RM 15-2

Procedure Checklist

Developments

Name ____

Observable Items	Completed		Comments	Instructor Initials
	Yes	No		
1. Constructs the development of a rectangular prism.				
2. Constructs the development of a cylinder with an inclined bevel.				
3. Constructs the development of a two-piece elbow.				
4. Constructs the development of an oblique cylinder.				
5. Constructs the development of a pyramid.				
6. Constructs the development of a truncated pyramid.				
7. Constructs the development of a cone.				
8. Constructs the development of a cone inclined to the base.				
9. Constructs the development of a transition piece.				
10. Constructs an approximate development of a warped surface.				

Instructor Signature ____

Section 4 Advanced Applications

Geometric Dimensioning and Tolerancing 16

Learning Objectives

After studying this chapter, the student will be able to:

- Define the common terms used in geometric dimensioning and tolerancing applications.
- List and describe the different types of tolerances used to control fits for machine parts.
- Identify specific symbols used in geometric dimensioning and tolerancing applications.
- Explain the standard practices for applying tolerance dimensions to drawings.
- Describe how tolerance dimensions are created on CAD drawings.

Instructional Resources

Text: pages 549–586

Review Questions, pages 576–577

Drawing Problems, pages 578–586

Worksheets: pages 135–140

- Worksheet 16-1: *Differential Spider*
- Worksheet 16-2: *Slide Nut*
- Worksheet 16-3: *Alignment Block*
- Worksheet 16-4: *Ring Plate*
- Worksheet 16-5: *Left Z-Axis Support*
- Worksheet 16-6: *Y-Axis Drive Cover Bracket*

Instructor's Resource

Instructional Tasks

Instructional Aids and Assignments

Chapter 16 Quiz

Reproducible Masters

- Reproducible Master 16-1: *Geometric Characteristic Symbols and Modifying Symbols*. This handout shows the standard symbols used for geometric characteristics of part features. Also shown are modifying symbols and other dimensioning symbols used in the geometric dimensioning and tolerancing system.
- Reproducible Master 16-2: *Positional Tolerancing for Feature Pattern Location*. This handout shows the relationships of the Feature-Relating Tolerance Zone Framework (FRTZF) to the Pattern-Locating Tolerance Zone Framework (PLTZF) established by single-segment feature control frames.
- Reproducible Master 16-3: *Dimensioning Symbols*. Proper sizes and proportions of common dimensioning symbols are shown.
- Reproducible Master 16-4: *Geometric Dimensioning and Tolerancing Symbols*. Proper sizes and proportions of common geometric dimensioning and tolerancing symbols are shown.
- Reproducible Master 16-5: *Positional Tolerancing*. Standard practices for representing positional tolerances are shown.

Procedure Checklist

Color Transparencies (Binder/IRCD only)

- Transparency 16-1: *Applications of Tolerances*. Common systems for representing toleranced dimensions are shown.
- Transparency 16-2: *Feature Control Frame*. Shown is a feature control frame with each part identified.
- Transparency 16-3: *Surface Texture Symbol*. Shown is the standard surface texture symbol with the various parts identified.

Instructional Tasks

1. Identify and define common dimensioning and tolerancing terms.
   - Show a multimedia presentation or film on geometric dimensioning and tolerancing.
   - Invite an engineer or industrial designer to speak to the class on precision dimensioning requirements.
2. Explain how to apply toleranced dimensions to drawings.
   - Review industrial drawings for use of toleranced dimensions.

3. Describe the types of tolerances used to control fits for machine parts.
   - Discuss types of fits.
4. Identify common geometric dimensioning and tolerancing symbols and explain their use.
   - Discuss the meaning of common geometric dimensioning and tolerancing symbols.
5. Explain how to dimension drawings using geometric dimensioning and tolerancing symbols and explain their use.
   - Discuss the meaning of common geometric dimensioning and tolerancing symbols.
6. Discuss the importance of precision dimensioning to interchangeability of parts.
   - Show a multimedia presentation or film on modern manufacturing methods involving interchangeability of parts.

Instructional Aids and Assignments

1. Display transparencies with overlays showing applications of geometric dimensioning and tolerancing.
2. Display industrial drawings showing the proper application of geometric dimensioning and tolerancing.
3. Assign the drawing problems in the textbook. The number of problems is sufficient to assign a minimum number to all students and to identify problems that may be done for extra credit. Some problems may be used for the performance section of the chapter quiz.

Answers to Review Questions, Text

Pages 576–577

1. B. tolerancing
2. Positional
3. Form
4. An exact, untoleranced value used to describe the shape, size, or location of a feature.
5. By enclosing the dimension figure in a rectangular frame.
6. An exact plane, line, or point from which other features are located.
7. datum feature
8. D. nominal
9. B. basic
10. A. actual
11. allowance
12. The extreme dimensions allowed by the tolerance range.
13. Tolerance
14. unilateral
15. bilateral
16. Clearance, interference, and transition.
17. basic size
18. hole
19. shaft
20. Maximum material condition (MMC)
21. Least material condition (LMC)
22. limit
23. A process of selecting mating parts by inspection, and classification into groups according to actual sizes.
24. datum
25. RC
26. press
27. feature control
28. True position, concentricity, and symmetry.
29. A. Concentricity
30. B. Flatness
31. Surface texture
32. The **Tolerance** command.

Solutions to Drawing Problems, Text

Pages 578–586

Student work should look like the following drawings. The problem number and title are indicated on each problem sheet.

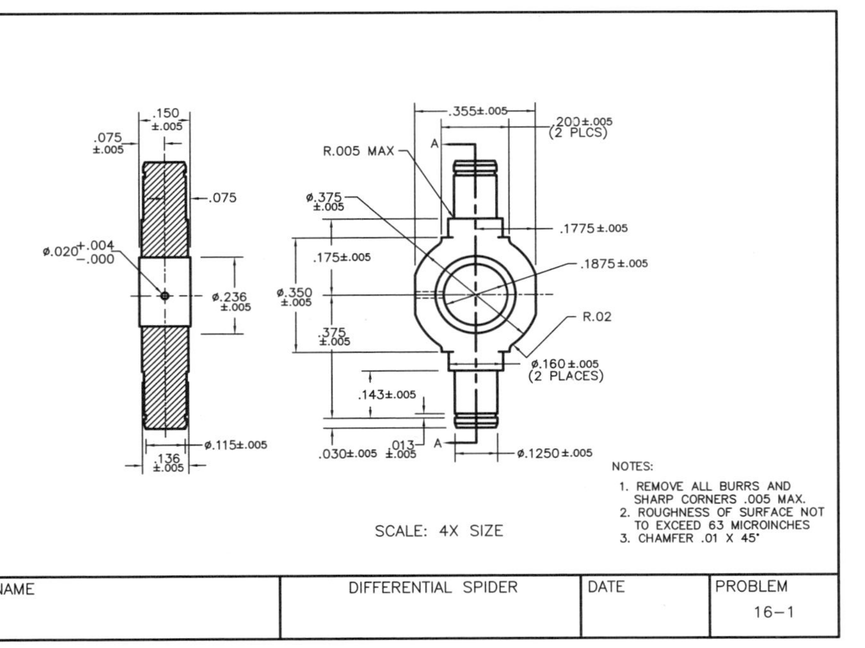
NOTES:
1. REMOVE ALL BURRS AND SHARP CORNERS .005 MAX.
2. ROUGHNESS OF SURFACE NOT TO EXCEED 63 MICROINCHES
3. CHAMFER .01 X 45°
SCALE: 4X SIZE
NAME
DIFFERENTIAL SPIDER
DATE
PROBLEM
16–1

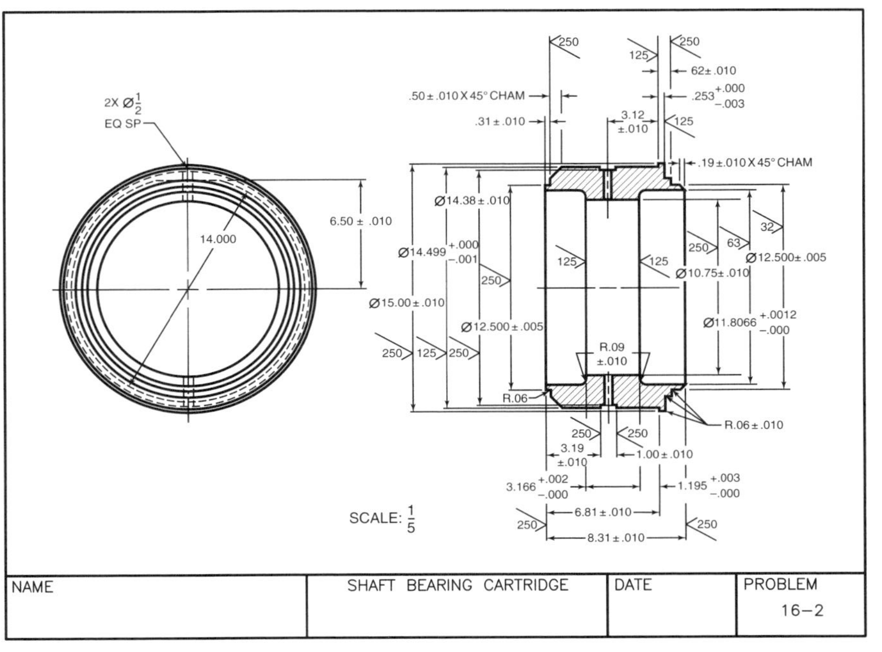
2X Ø1/2 EQ SP
SCALE: 1/5
NAME
SHAFT BEARING CARTRIDGE
DATE
PROBLEM
16–2

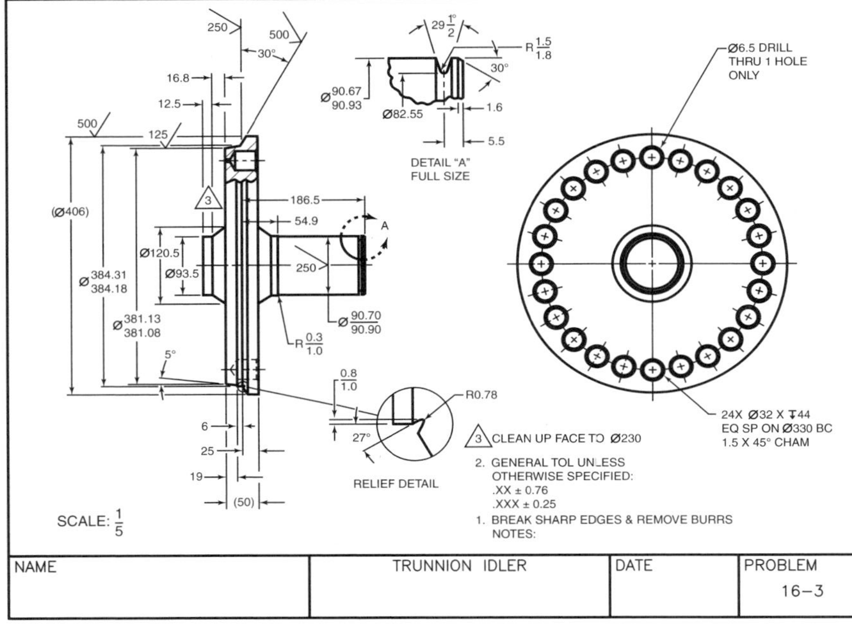
Ø6.5 DRILL THRU 1 HOLE ONLY
DETAIL "A" FULL SIZE
24X Ø32 X ⌴44 EQ SP ON Ø330 BC 1.5 X 45° CHAM
RELIEF DETAIL
3 CLEAN UP FACE TO Ø230
2. GENERAL TOL UNLESS OTHERWISE SPECIFIED: .XX ± 0.76 .XXX ± 0.25
1. BREAK SHARP EDGES & REMOVE BURRS
NOTES:
SCALE: 1/5
NAME
TRUNNION IDLER
DATE
PROBLEM
16–3

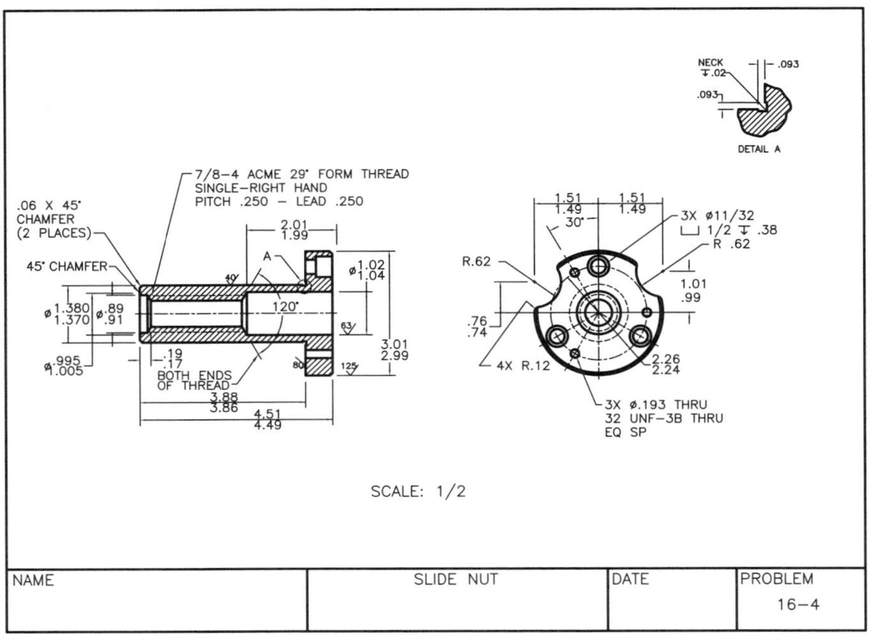
DETAIL A
7/8–4 ACME 29° FORM THREAD SINGLE–RIGHT HAND PITCH .250 – LEAD .250
.06 X 45° CHAMFER (2 PLACES)
45° CHAMFER
BOTH ENDS OF THREAD
3X ø11/32 ⌴ 1/2 ↧ .38 R .62
4X R.12
3X ø.193 THRU 32 UNF–3B THRU EQ SP
SCALE: 1/2
NAME
SLIDE NUT
DATE
PROBLEM
16–4

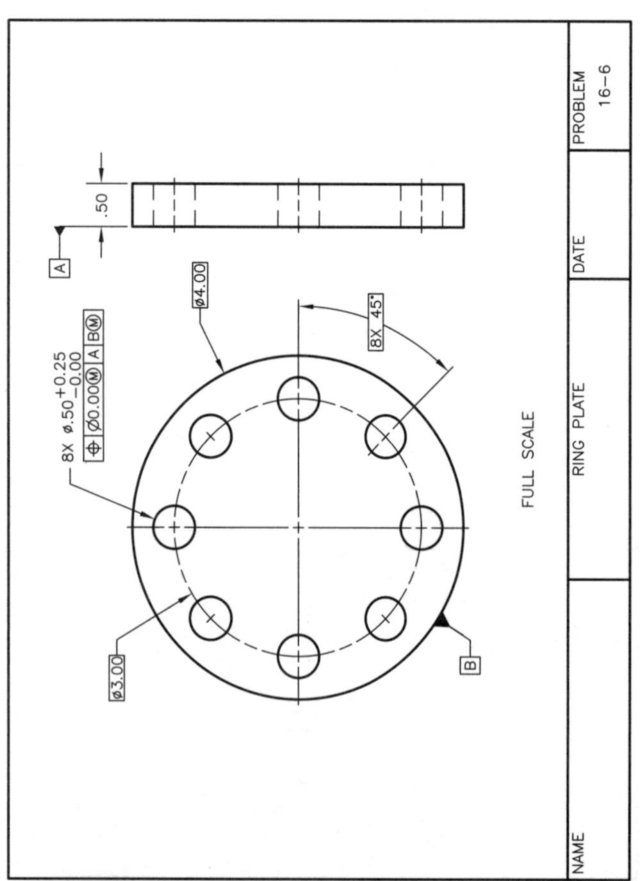
FULL SCALE
NAME
RING PLATE
DATE
PROBLEM
16–6

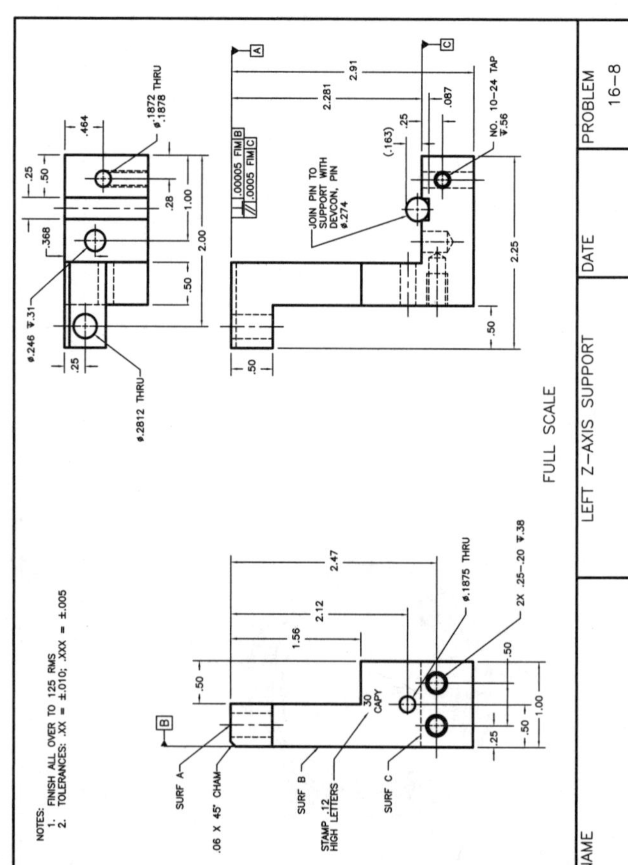
NOTES:
1. FINISH ALL OVER TO 125 RMS
2. TOLERANCES: .XX = ±.010; .XXX = ±.005
FULL SCALE
NAME
LEFT Z–AXIS SUPPORT
DATE
PROBLEM
16–8

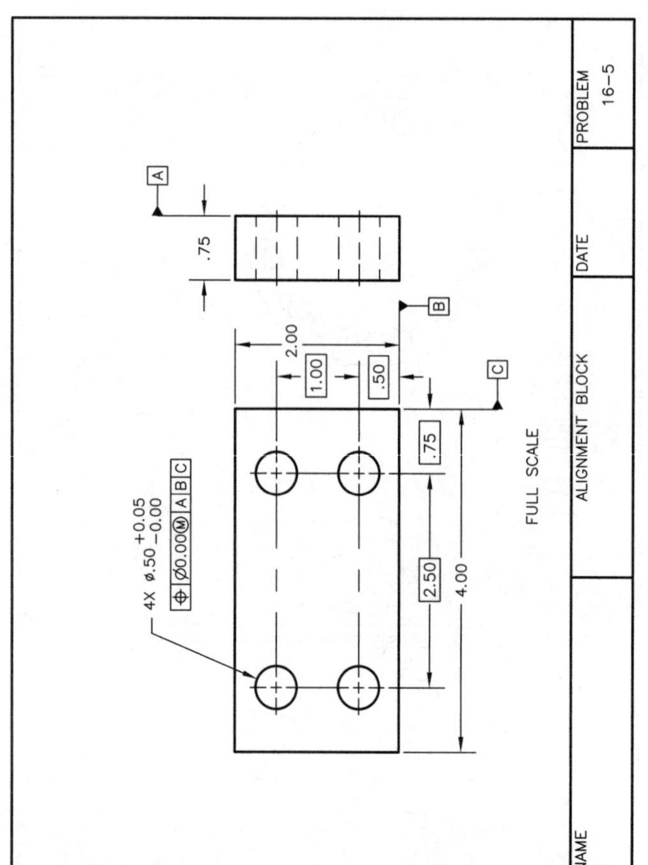
FULL SCALE
NAME
ALIGNMENT BLOCK
DATE
PROBLEM
16–5

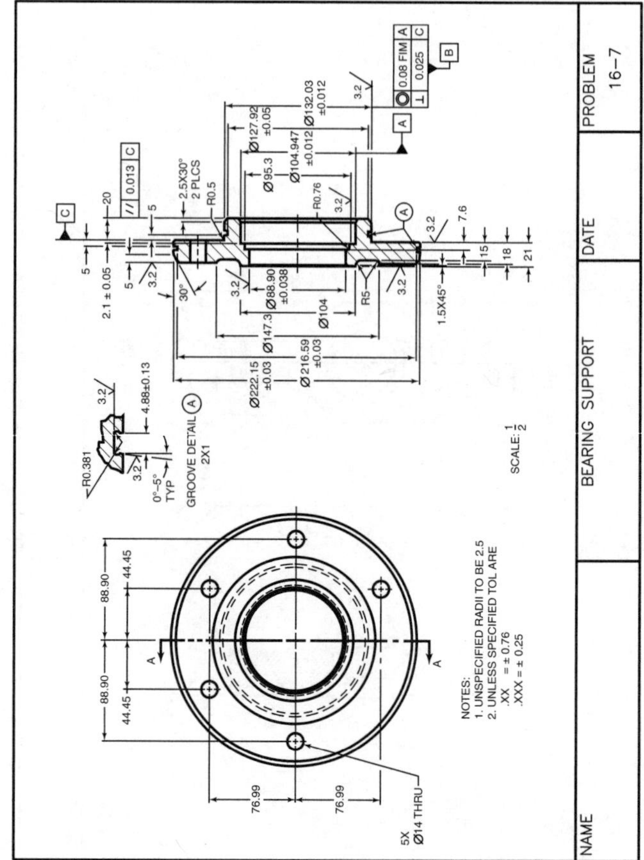
NOTES:
1. UNSPECIFIED RADII TO BE 2.5
2. UNLESS SPECIFIED TOL ARE
.XX = ± 0.76
.XXX = ± 0.25
NAME
BEARING SUPPORT
DATE
PROBLEM
16–7

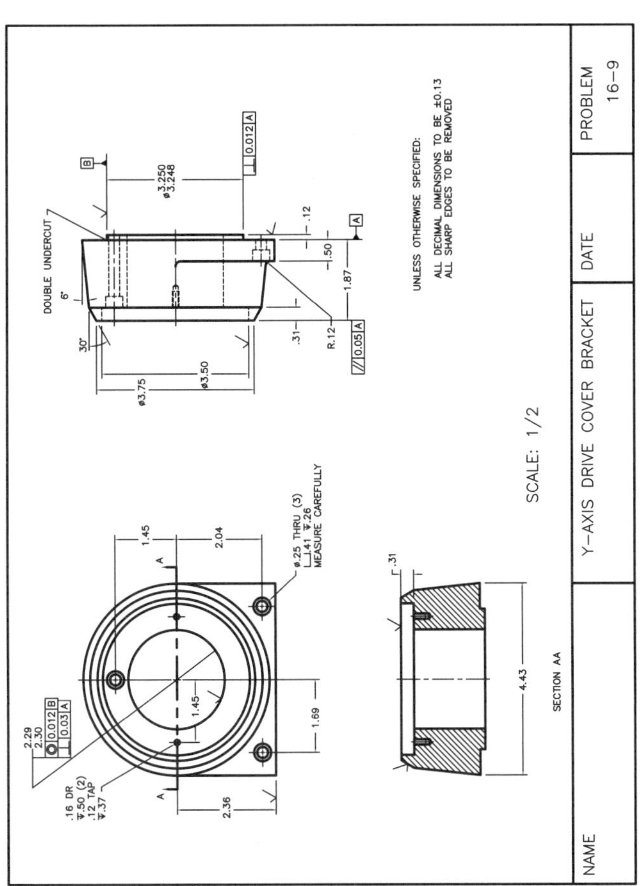

DOUBLE UNDERCUT
6°
30°
ø3.75
ø3.50
ø3.250
ø3.248
0.012 A
.12
.50
1.87
.31
R.12
0.05 A
B
A
UNLESS OTHERWISE SPECIFIED:
ALL DECIMAL DIMENSIONS TO BE ±0.13
ALL SHARP EDGES TO BE REMOVED
2.29
2.30
0.012 B
0.03 A
.16 DR
↧.50 (2)
.12 TAP
↧.37
1.45
2.04
1.45
1.69
2.36
ø.25 THRU (3)
⌴1.41 ↧.26
MEASURE CAREFULLY
.31
4.43
SECTION AA
SCALE: 1/2
NAME
Y–AXIS DRIVE COVER BRACKET
DATE
PROBLEM
16–9

Solutions to Worksheets

Pages 135–140

Student work should look like the following drawings. The problem number and title are indicated on each problem sheet.

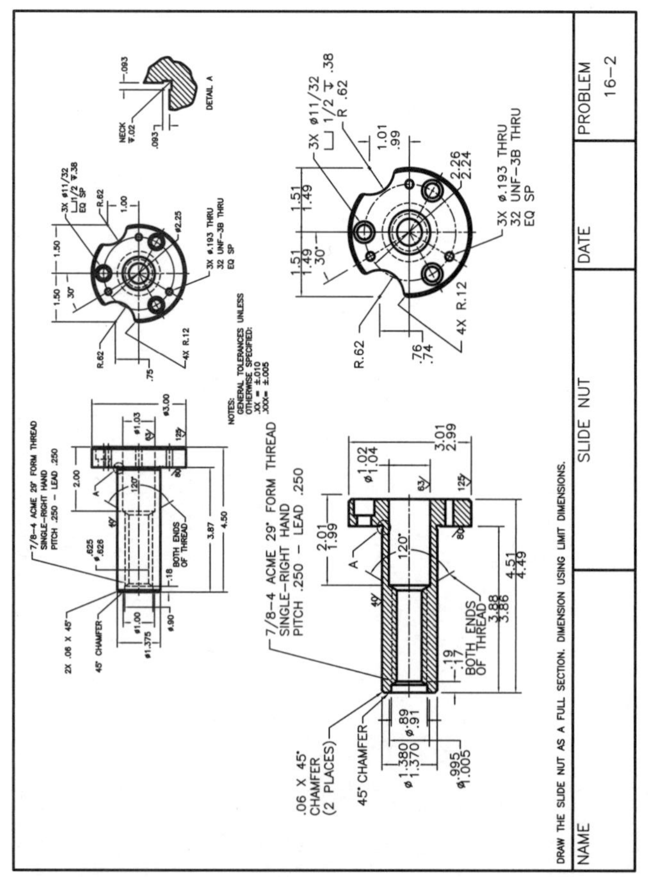

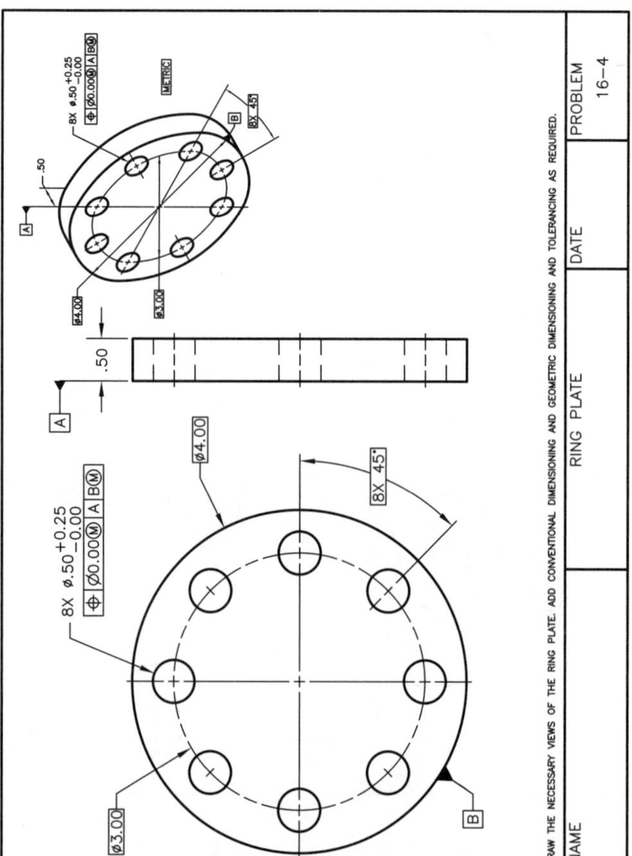

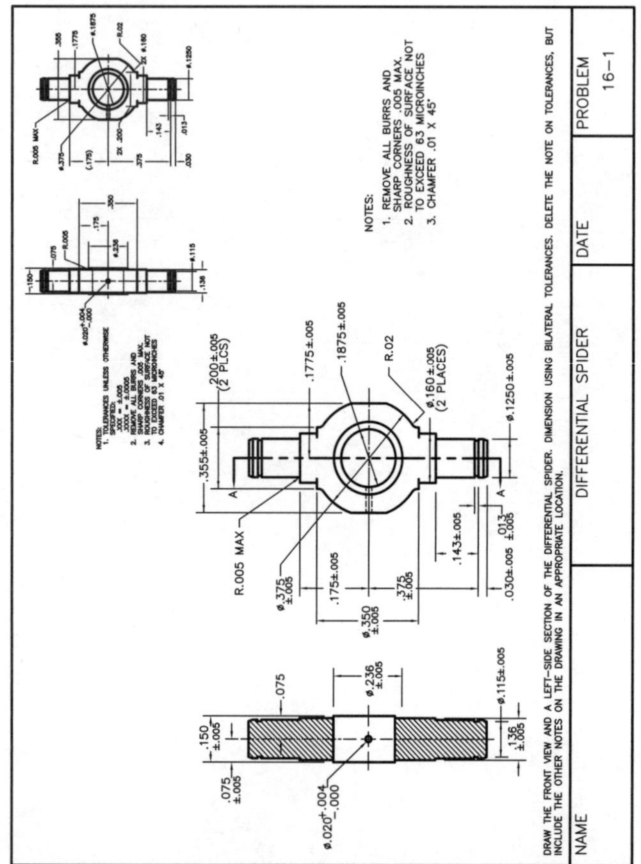

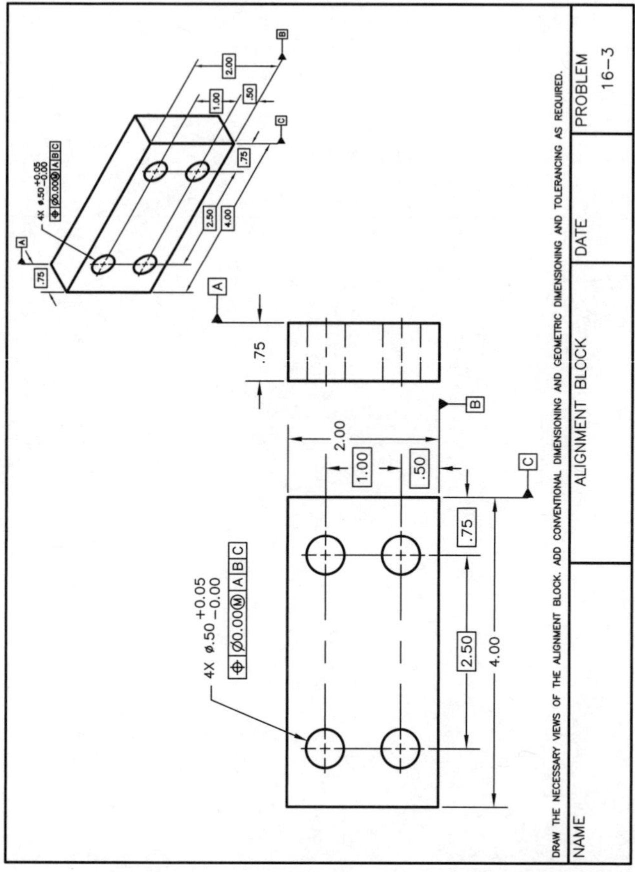

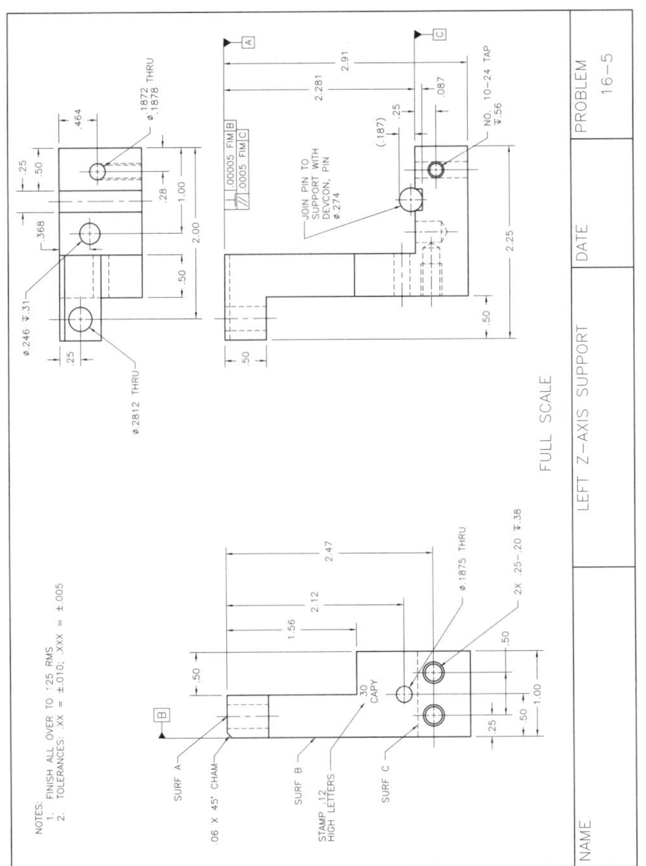

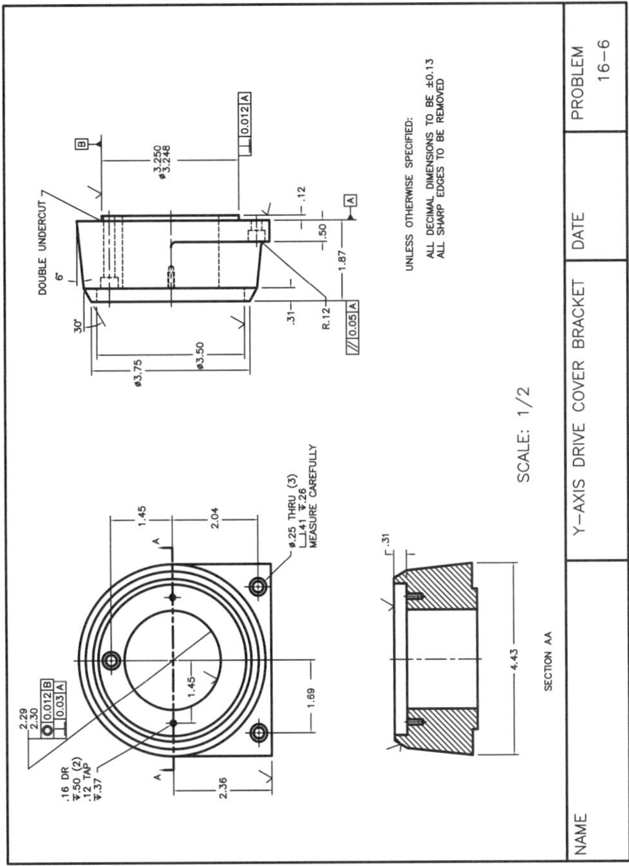

Answers to Chapter 16 Quiz

1. C. They are given for the convenience of engineering and manufacturing personnel.
2. A. clearance
3. B. allowance
4. C. datum
5. D. design
6. A. True position, concentricity, and symmetry.
7. B. a theoretically exact, untoleranced dimension
8. D. ⊥
9. The feature must lie in true position with Datum A within .0005″ diameter at maximum material condition.
10. The feature must be parallel to Datum B within .002″.
11. Refer to the drawings given in the *Solutions to Drawing Problems, Text* section for the problem selected from the textbook.

Chapter Quiz 16

Geometric Dimensioning and Tolerancing

Name ____

Period__________________ Date__________________ Score ______________

Multiple Choice

Choose the answer that correctly completes the statement. Write the corresponding letter in the space provided.

_______ 1. What is the purpose of reference dimensions?
   A. They are required for the manufacture of the part.
   B. They are used to track a part during production.
   C. They are given for the convenience of engineering and manufacturing personnel.
   D. They represent the exact dimensions.

_______ 2. When the limits of size are so prescribed that a clearance always results when mating parts are assembled, this is an example of a(n) _____ fit.
   A. clearance
   B. interference
   C. transition
   D. allowance

_______ 3. The intentional difference in the dimensions of mating parts to provide for different classes of fits is called _____.
   A. design size
   B. allowance
   C. actual size
   D. tolerance

_______ 4. When the distance between two features must be closely controlled without the use of an extremely small tolerance, _____ dimensioning should be used.
   A. aligned
   B. chain
   C. datum
   D. limit

_______ 5. The size of a part after an allowance for clearance has been applied and tolerances assigned is called the _____ size.
   A. actual
   B. nominal
   C. allowable
   D. design

Name ____

________ 6. What are the three basic types of positional tolerances?
A. True position, concentricity, and symmetry.
B. True position, symmetry, and form.
C. Concentricity, symmetry, and flatness.
D. Form, flatness, and true position.

________ 7. A *basic dimension* is _____.
A. a precision toleranced dimension
B. a theoretically exact, untoleranced dimension
C. another way of expressing a reference dimension
D. another way of expressing a limit dimension

________ 8. To indicate the squareness of one feature to another in a machine part, which of the following is the appropriate geometric tolerancing symbol?

A. ▱

B. ⌭

C. //

D. ⊥

Completion

In the space provided, explain the information provided by the geometric feature control.

9. | ⌖ | A | Ø.0005Ⓜ |

____

____

10. | // | B | .002 |

____

____

Drafting Performance

11. Draw a solution of a problem selected by your instructor from Chapter 16 in your textbook. Dimension the drawing using geometric dimensioning and tolerancing symbols to replace notes where applicable.

Geometric Characteristic Symbols and Modifying Symbols

Geometric Characteristic Symbols		
TYPE OF TOLERANCE	**CHARACTERISTIC**	**SYMBOL**
FORM	Straightness	—
	Flatness	⏥
	Circularity (roundness)	○
	Cylindricity	⌭
PROFILE	Profile of a line	⌒
	Profile of a surface	⌓
ORIENTATION	Angularity	∠
	Perpendicularity	⊥
	Parallelism	//
LOCATION	Position	⌖
	Concentricity	◎
	Symmetry	⌯
RUNOUT	Circular runout	↗*
	Total runout	⌰*

* Arrowheads may be filled or not filled.

Modifying Symbols	
TERM	**SYMBOL**
At maximum material condition	Ⓜ
At least material condition	Ⓛ
Regardless of feature size	NONE
Projected tolerance zone	Ⓟ
Diameter	∅
Spherical diameter	S∅
Radius	R
Spherical radius	SR
Arc length	⌒105
Between	↔
Datum target	06/A1 (in circle)
Target point	×
Dimension origin	⌖→
All-around	↙○—
Conical taper	⌲
Slope	⌳
Counterbore/spotface	⌴
Countersink	⌵
Depth/deep	↧
Square (shape)	□

RM 16-1

Positional Tolerancing for Feature Pattern Location

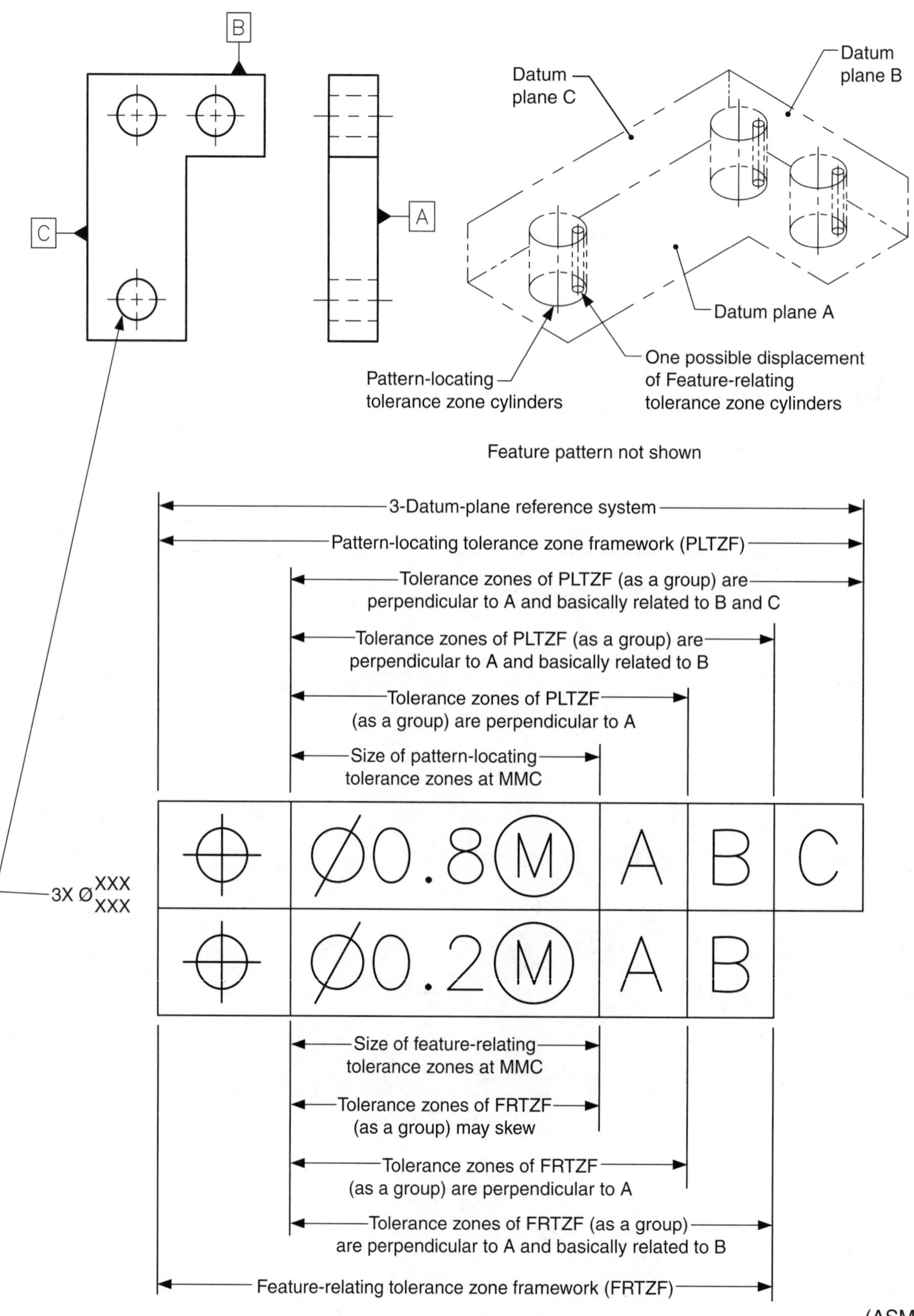

(ASME)

RM 16-2

Dimensioning Symbols

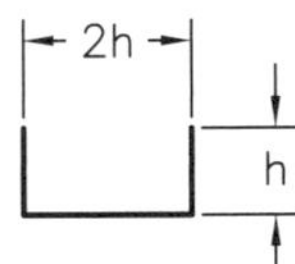

Counterbore
or Spotface

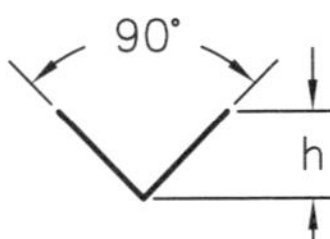

Countersink

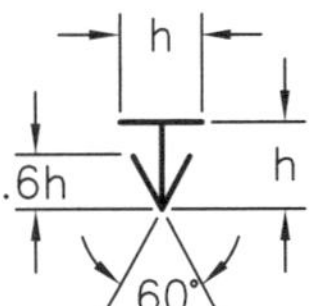

Depth
(or Deep)

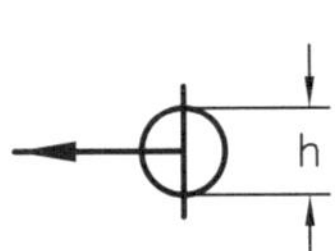

Dimension
Origin

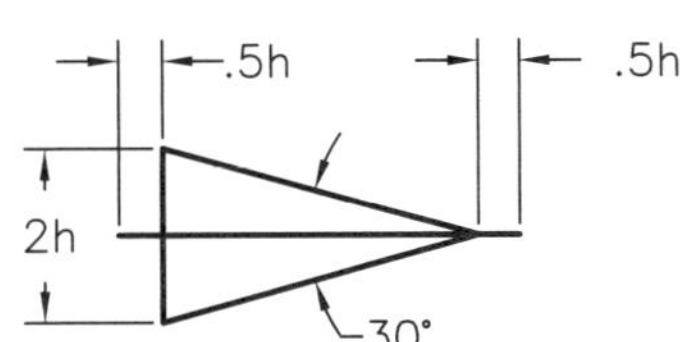

Conical Taper

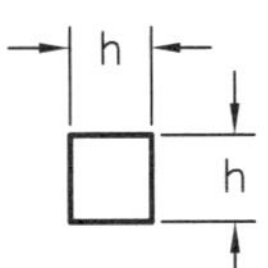

Square
(Shape)

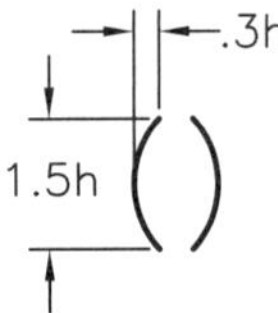

Reference

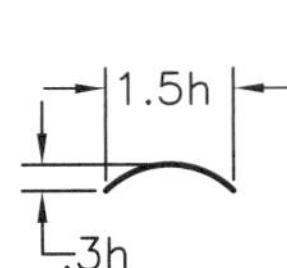

Arc Length

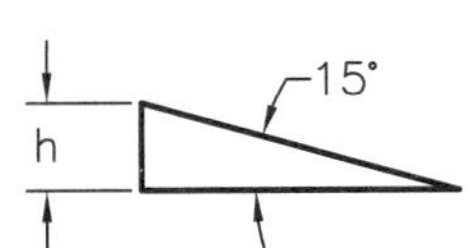

Slope

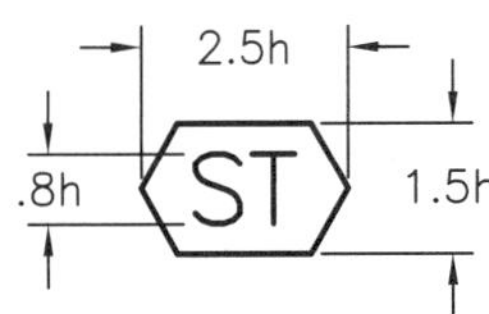

Statistical
Tolerance

h = Letter height

R	SR	SØ	CR	X
Radius	Spherical Radius	Spherical Diameter	Controlled Radius	Places or By

RM 16-3

Geometric Dimensioning and Tolerancing Symbols

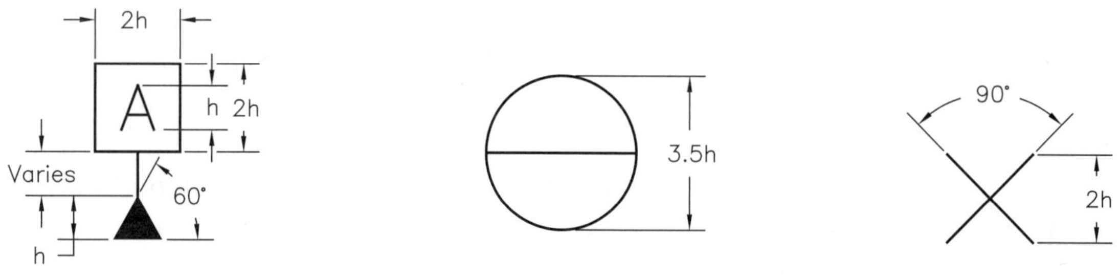

Datum Feature   Datum Target   Target Point

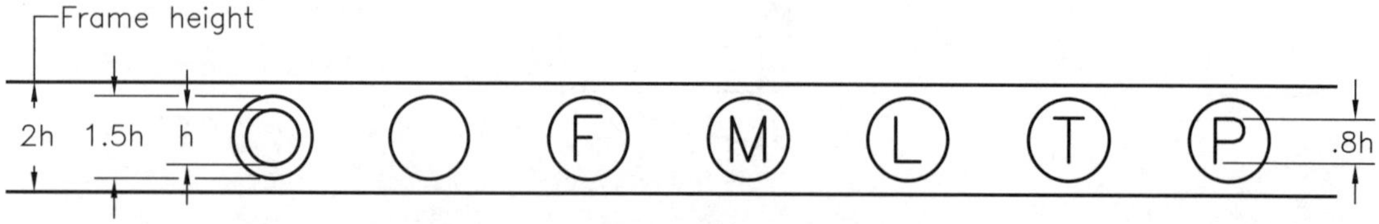

Frame height

Concentricity   Circularity   Free State   MMC   LMC   Tangent Plane   Projected Tolerance

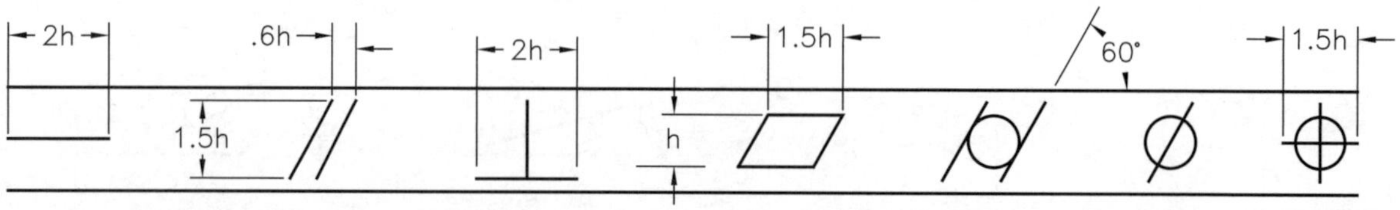

Straightness   Parallelism   Perpendicularity   Flatness   Cylindricity   Diameter   Position

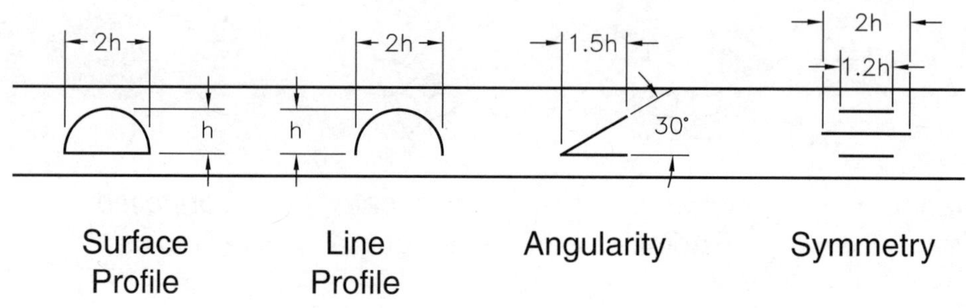

Surface Profile   Line Profile   Angularity   Symmetry

RM 16-4

Positional Tolerancing

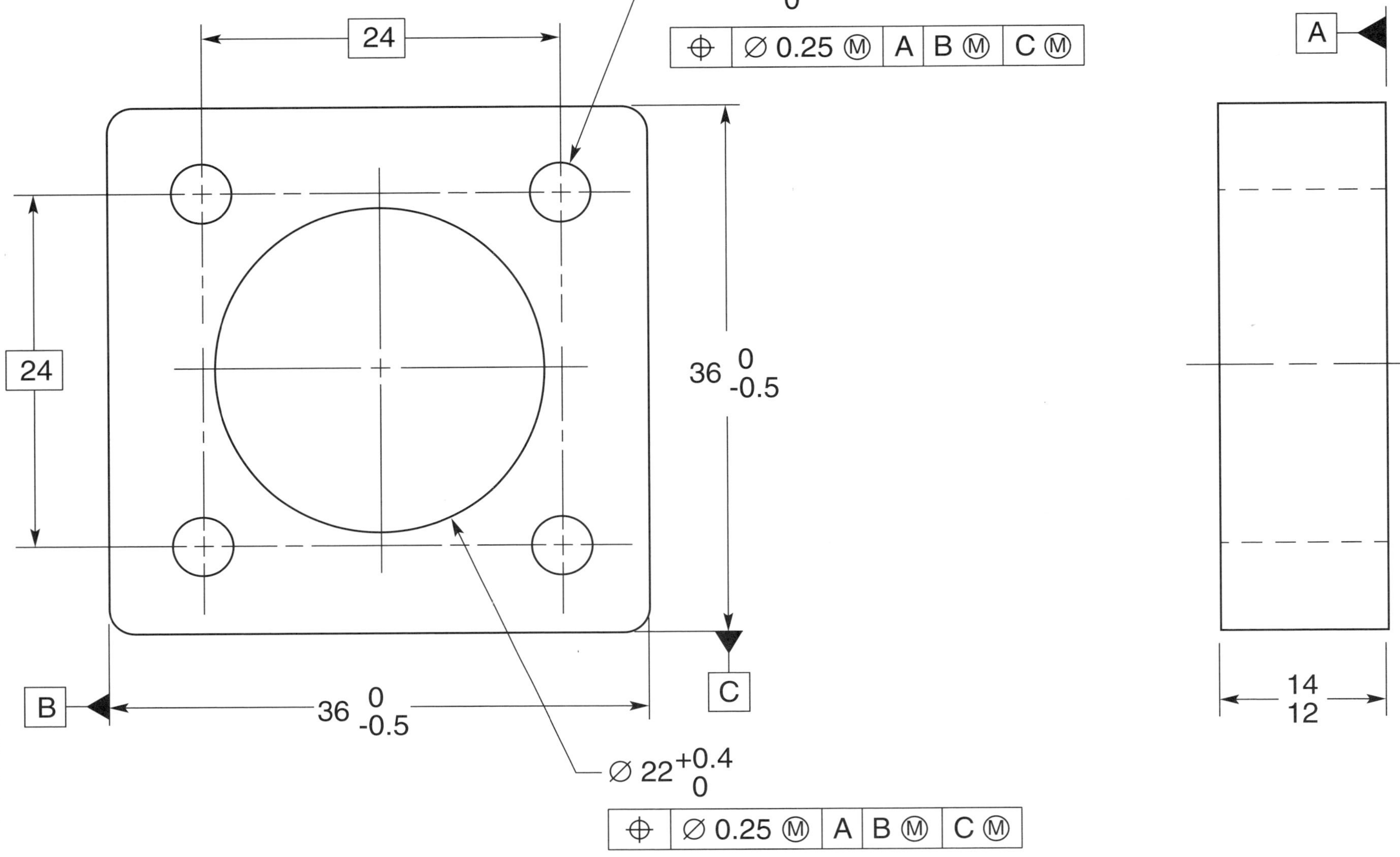

RM 16-5

Procedure Checklist

Geometric Dimensioning and Tolerancing

Name ______________________________

Observable Items	Completed		Comments	Instructor Initials
	Yes	No		
1. Applies limit dimensioning to a drawing.				
2. Draws basic dimensions.				
3. Applies chain dimensioning to a drawing.				
4. Applies datum dimensioning to a drawing.				
5. Draws reference dimensions.				
6. Draws geometric characteristic symbols.				
7. Applies tolerance dimensions to drawings.				

Instructor Signature ______________________________

Working Drawings

Learning Objectives

After studying this chapter, the student will be able to:

- Explain the purpose of working drawings.
- List the different types of working drawings and describe the information communicated by each type.
- Identify and explain the common elements used to convey information on working drawings.
- Explain how company and industry standards are incorporated on drawings.
- List the common applications for working drawings in major industries.
- Define functional drafting.

Instructional Resources

Text: pages 587–614
  Review Questions, page 603
  Drawing Problems, pages 603–613
  Design Problems, page 614

Worksheets: pages 141–157

- Worksheet 17-1: *Components Bracket*
- Worksheet 17-2: *Mating Components Bracket*
- Worksheet 17-3: *Cover Bracket*
- Worksheet 17-4: *Hanger Bolt*
- Worksheet 17-5: *Battery Bracket*
- Worksheet 17-6: *Valve*
- Worksheet 17-7: *Bracket*
- Worksheet 17-8: *Center Base Frame*
- Worksheet 17-9: *PC Card Bracket*
- Worksheet 17-10: *Gear Cover Plate*
- Worksheet 17-11: *Hydraulic Dechuck Piston*
- Worksheet 17-12: *Roller for Brick Elevator*
- Worksheet 17-13: *Metering Sleeve*
- Worksheet 17-14: *Tube Transfer*
- Worksheet 17-15: *Idler Gear Shaft*
- Worksheet 17-16: *Duct Casting*
- Worksheet 17-17: *Focusing Base*

Instructor's Resource
  Instructional Tasks
  Instructional Aids and Assignments
  Chapter 17 Quiz
  Reproducible Masters

- Reproducible Master 17-1: *Types of Working Drawings*. Common types of working drawings are identified and described in this handout.
- Reproducible Master 17-2: *Detail Drawing*. A detail drawing of a simple part is shown in proper orientation and format.
- Reproducible Master 17-3: *Assembly Drawing*. A manufacturer's assembly drawing for the front section of a bicycle is shown.
- Reproducible Master 17-4: *Exploded Assembly Drawing*. A typical exploded assembly drawing used in equipment literature is shown.
- Reproducible Master 17-5: *Freehand Sketch*. A freehand sketch of a custom muffler housing is shown.

  Procedure Checklist

Instructional Tasks

1. Define the term *working drawing*.
   - Obtain samples of working drawings from companies in the manufacturing and construction industries. Discuss the features of these drawings with the class.
2. Describe the common types of working drawings and their applications.
   - Display specific types of working drawings, such as freehand sketches, tabulated drawings, process drawings, or operation drawings.
3. Identify the types of information contained in the various block areas on a working drawing.
   - Discuss the purpose and format of the title block, materials block, and revision block.

4. Explain how working drawings are prepared.
   - Discuss the use of drafting standards.
   - Discuss the design and drafting process.
   - Discuss functional drafting techniques.
5. Discuss the applications of working drawings in various industries.
   - Display working drawings from various industries.

Instructional Aids and Assignments

1. Display copies of working drawings from various types of industries, such as the manufacturing, construction, and electronics industries.
2. Display copies of ASME drafting standards.
3. Display copies of drafting room manuals from local industries.
4. Assign the drawing problems in the textbook. The number of problems is sufficient to assign a minimum number to all students and to identify problems that may be done for extra credit. Some problems may be used for the performance section of the chapter quiz.

Answers to Review Questions, Text

Page 603

1. A working drawing provides all the necessary information to manufacture, construct, assemble, or install a machine or structure.
2. detail
3. tabulated
4. An assembly drawing.
5. Layout
6. In the lower right-hand corner.
7. In the revision block.
8. Casting
9. welding
10. patent
11. The process of making a drawing that conveys the necessary information with minimum time and effort without sacrificing quality and accuracy.

Solutions to Drawing Problems, Text

Pages 603–613

Student work should look like the following drawings. The problem number and title are indicated on each problem sheet.

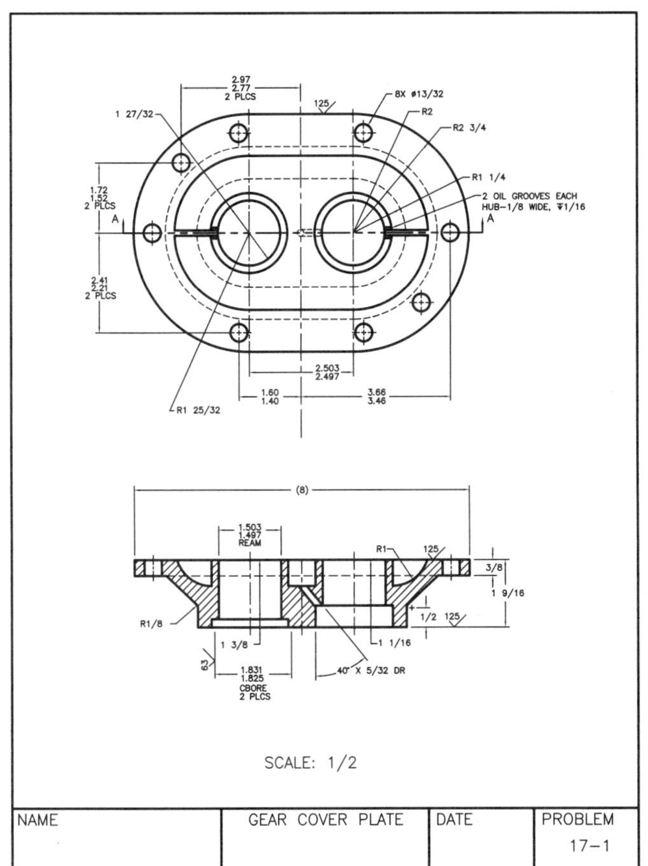
2.97
2.77
2 PLCS
125
8X ⌀13/32
R2
R2 3/4
1 27/32
1.72
1.52
2 PLCS
R1 1/4
2 OIL GROOVES EACH HUB–1/8 WIDE, ↧1/16
A
A
2.41
2.21
2 PLCS
2.503
2.497
1.60
1.40
3.66
3.46
R1 25/32
(8)
1.503
1.497
REAM
R1
125
3/8
1 9/16
1/2
125
R1/8
1 3/8
1 1/16
63
1.831
1.825
CBORE
2 PLCS
40° X 5/32 DR
SCALE: 1/2
NAME
GEAR COVER PLATE
DATE
PROBLEM
17–1

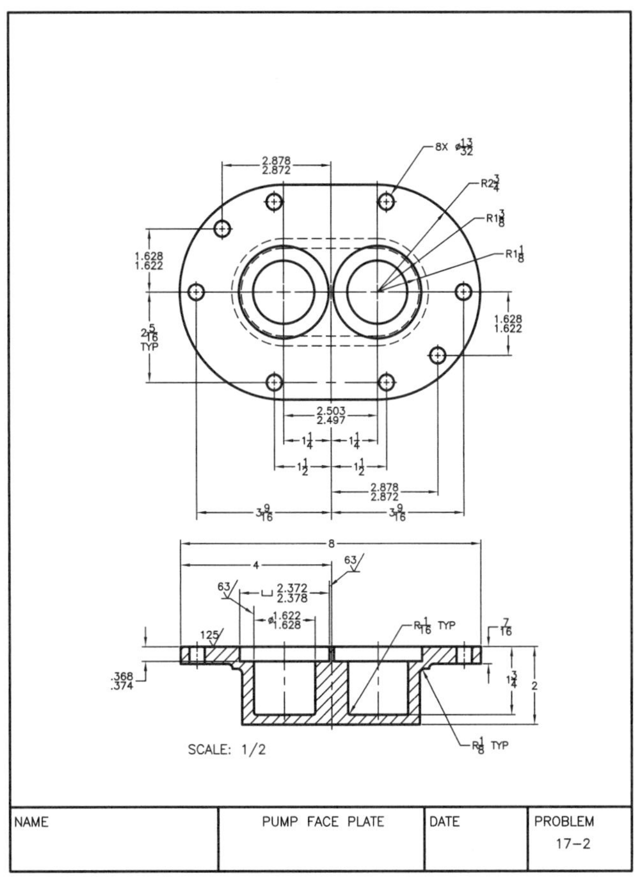
2.878
2.872
8X ⌀13/32
R2 3/4
R1 3/8
R1 1/8
1.628
1.622
2 5/16
TYP
1.628
1.622
2.503
2.497
1 1/4
1 1/4
1 1/2
1 1/2
2.878
2.872
3 9/16
3 9/16
8
4
63
63
2.372
2.378
⌀1.622
1.628
125
R 1/16 TYP
7/16
.368
.374
1 3/4
2
R 1/8 TYP
SCALE: 1/2
NAME
PUMP FACE PLATE
DATE
PROBLEM
17–2

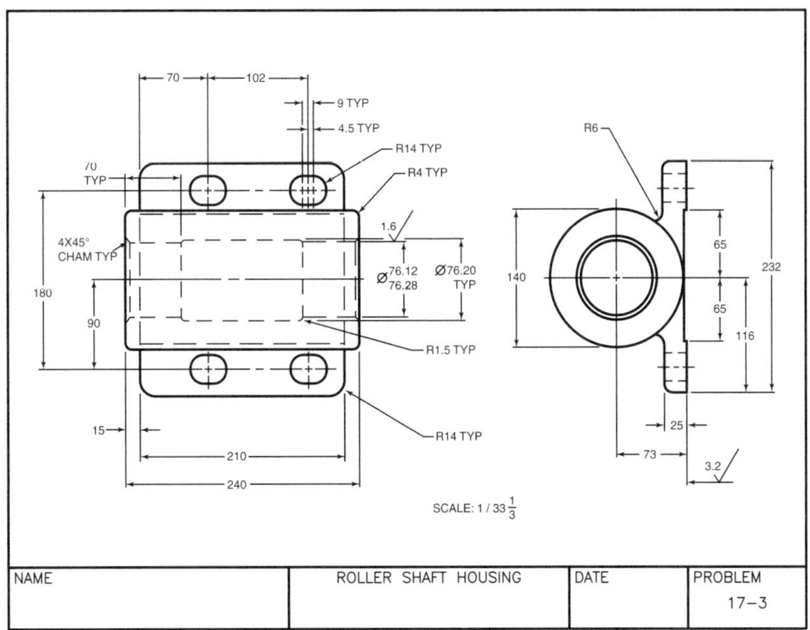
70
102
9 TYP
4.5 TYP
R14 TYP
R4 TYP
70
TYP
R6
4X45°
CHAM TYP
1.6
180
Ø76.12
76.28
Ø76.20
TYP
140
65
232
90
65
116
R1.5 TYP
15
R14 TYP
25
210
73
240
3.2
SCALE: 1 / 33 1/3
NAME
ROLLER SHAFT HOUSING
DATE
PROBLEM
17–3

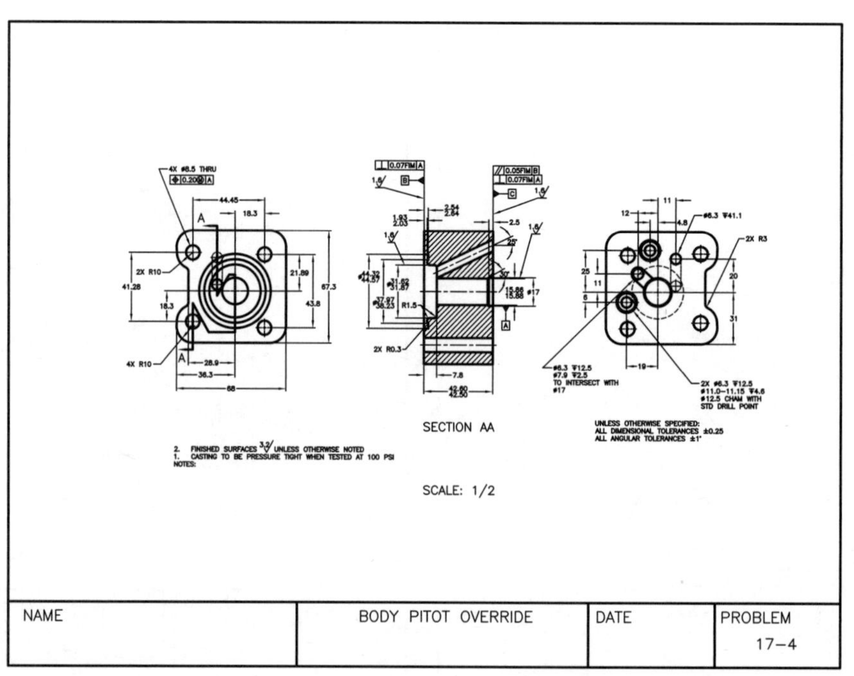

SECTION AA
UNLESS OTHERWISE SPECIFIED:
ALL DIMENSIONAL TOLERANCES ±0.25
ALL ANGULAR TOLERANCES ±1°
2. FINISHED SURFACES 3.2 UNLESS OTHERWISE NOTED
1. CASTING TO BE PRESSURE TIGHT WHEN TESTED AT 100 PSI
NOTES:
SCALE: 1/2
NAME
BODY PITOT OVERRIDE
DATE
PROBLEM
17–4

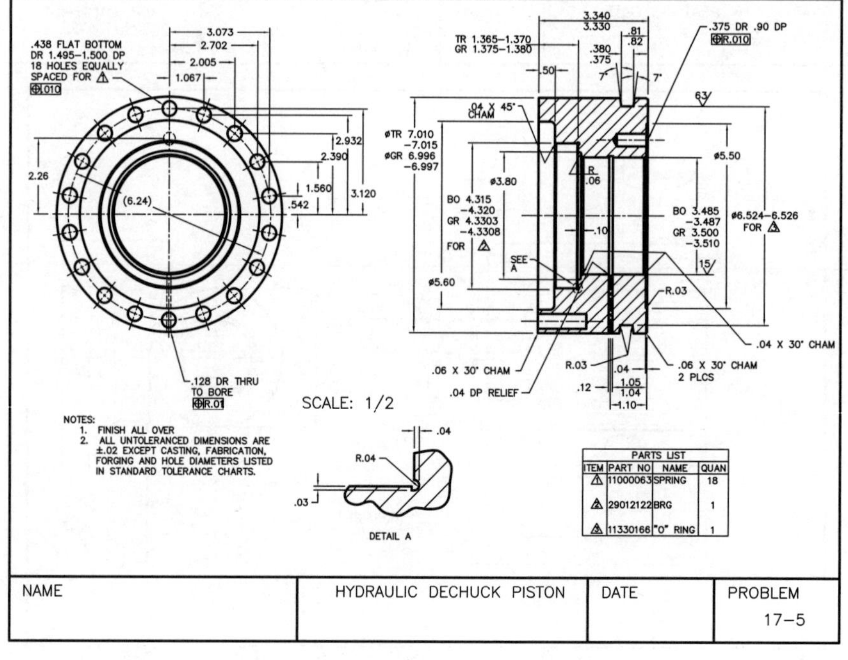

.438 FLAT BOTTOM
DR 1.495–1.500 DP
18 HOLES EQUALLY
SPACED FOR
.128 DR THRU
TO BORE
SCALE: 1/2
NOTES:
1. FINISH ALL OVER
2. ALL UNTOLERANCED DIMENSIONS ARE ±.02 EXCEPT CASTING, FABRICATION, FORGING AND HOLE DIAMETERS LISTED IN STANDARD TOLERANCE CHARTS.
DETAIL A
.06 X 30° CHAM
.04 DP RELIEF
.04 X 30° CHAM
.06 X 30° CHAM
2 PLCS
.375 DR .90 DP
PARTS LIST
ITEM | PART NO | NAME | QUAN
1 | 11000063 | SPRING | 18
2 | 29012122 | BRG | 1
3 | 11330166 | "O" RING | 1
NAME
HYDRAULIC DECHUCK PISTON
DATE
PROBLEM
17–5

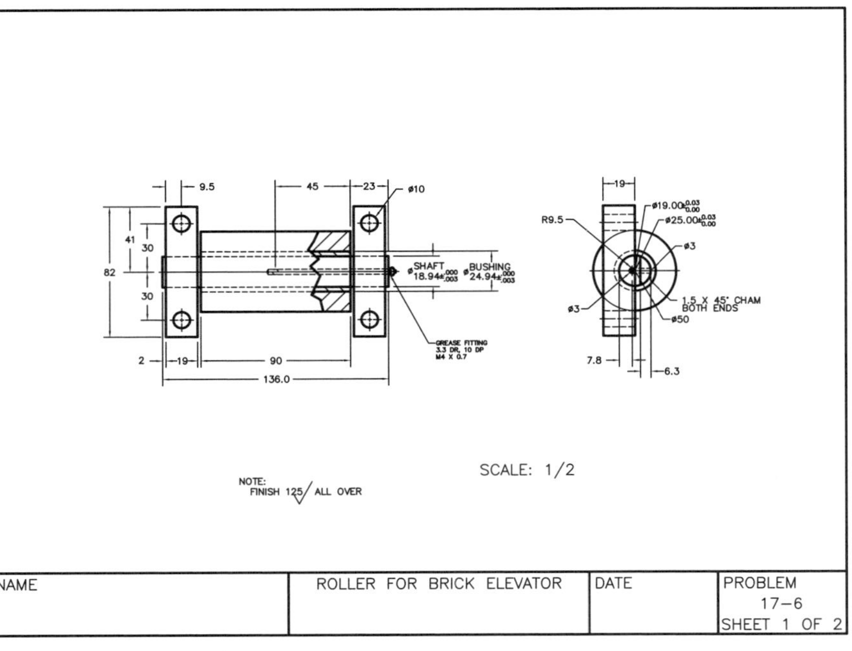

SCALE: 1/2
NOTE: FINISH 125 ALL OVER
NAME
ROLLER FOR BRICK ELEVATOR
DATE
PROBLEM 17–6 SHEET 1 OF 2

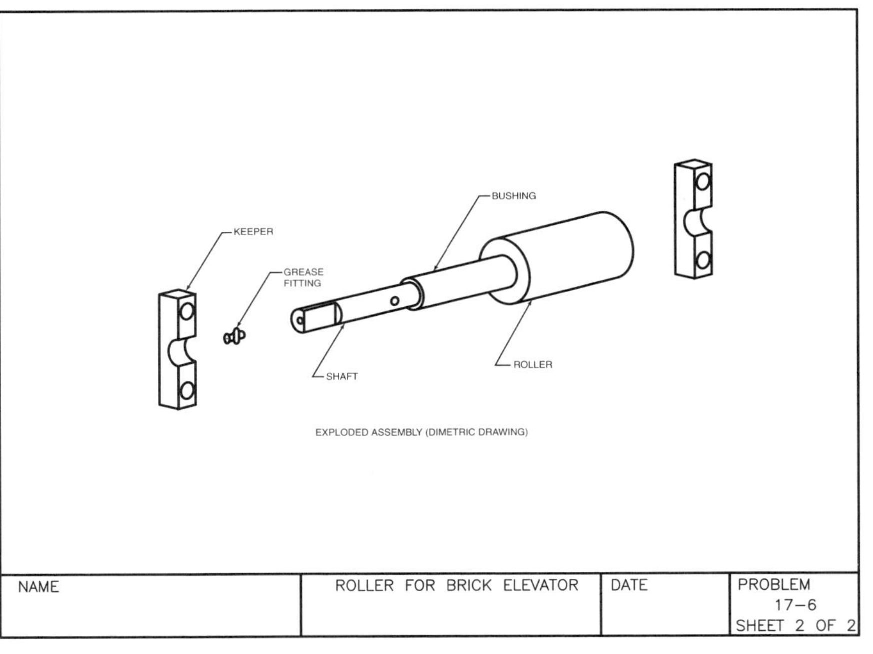

KEEPER
GREASE FITTING
SHAFT
BUSHING
ROLLER
EXPLODED ASSEMBLY (DIMETRIC DRAWING)
NAME
ROLLER FOR BRICK ELEVATOR
DATE
PROBLEM 17–6 SHEET 2 OF 2

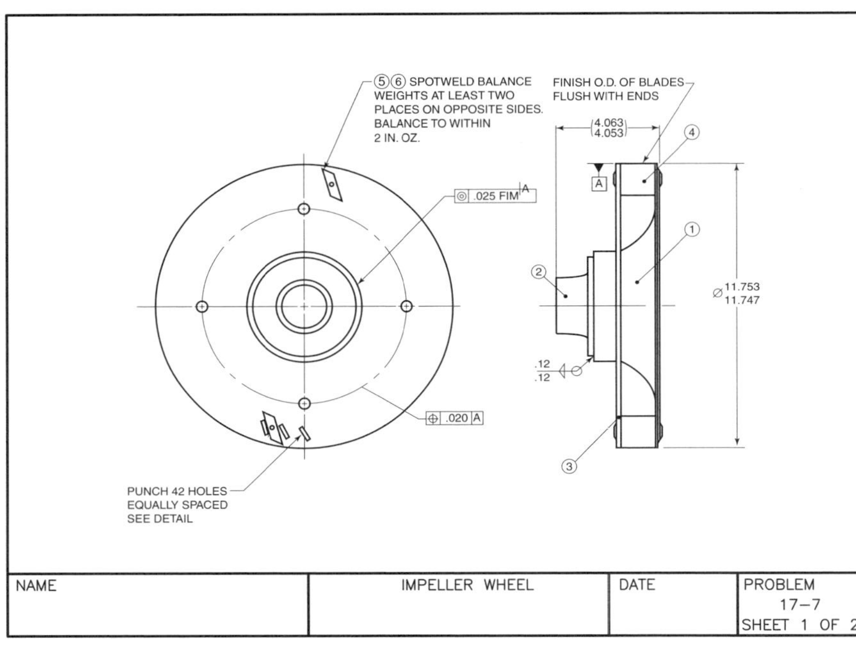

SPOTWELD BALANCE WEIGHTS AT LEAST TWO PLACES ON OPPOSITE SIDES. BALANCE TO WITHIN 2 IN. OZ.
FINISH O.D. OF BLADES FLUSH WITH ENDS
PUNCH 42 HOLES EQUALLY SPACED SEE DETAIL
NAME
IMPELLER WHEEL
DATE
PROBLEM 17–7 SHEET 1 OF 2

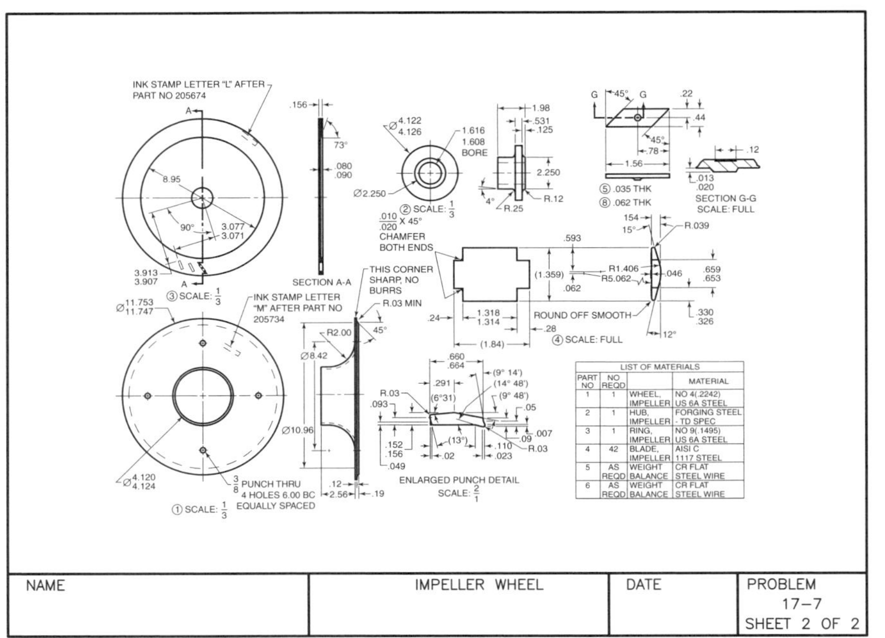

INK STAMP LETTER "L" AFTER PART NO 205674
SECTION A-A
INK STAMP LETTER "M" AFTER PART NO 205734
THIS CORNER SHARP, NO BURRS
CHAMFER BOTH ENDS
ROUND OFF SMOOTH
SECTION G-G SCALE: FULL
ENLARGED PUNCH DETAIL
LIST OF MATERIALS
NAME
IMPELLER WHEEL
DATE
PROBLEM 17–7 SHEET 2 OF 2

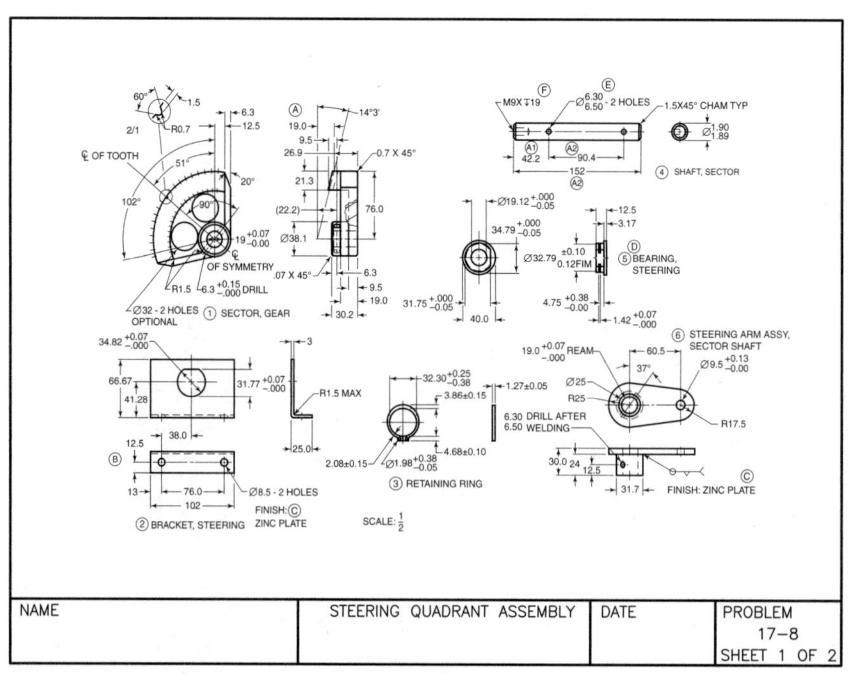

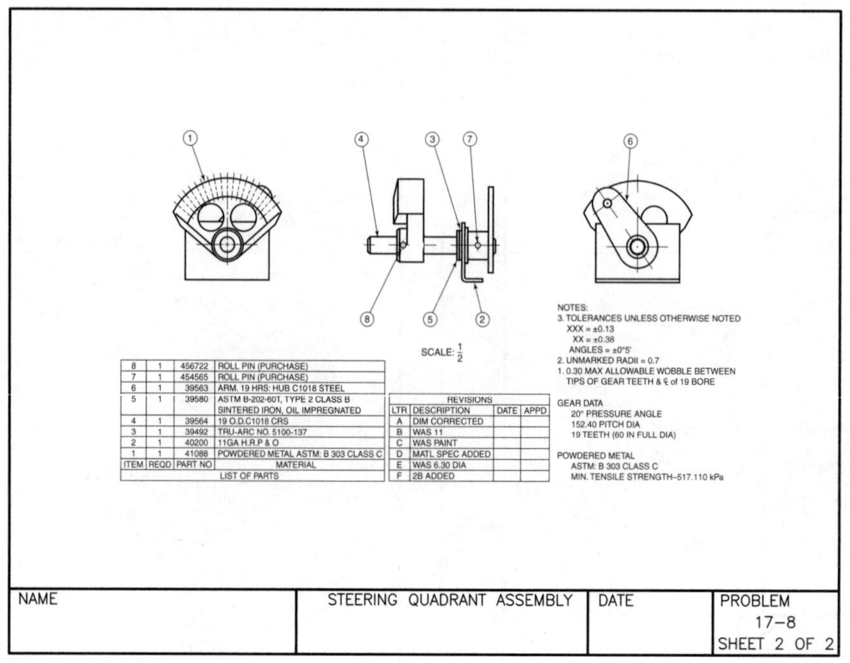

ITEM	REQD	PART NO	MATERIAL
8	1	456722	ROLL PIN (PURCHASE)
7	1	454565	ROLL PIN (PURCHASE)
6	1	39563	ARM. 19 HRS: HUB C1018 STEEL
5	1	39580	ASTM B-202-60T, TYPE 2 CLASS B SINTERED IRON, OIL IMPREGNATED
4	1	39564	19 O.D.C1018 CRS
3	1	39492	TRU-ARC NO. 5100-137
2	1	40200	11GA H.R.P & O
1	1	41088	POWDERED METAL ASTM: B 303 CLASS C

LIST OF PARTS

REVISIONS

LTR	DESCRIPTION	DATE	APPD
A	DIM CORRECTED		
B	WAS 11		
C	WAS PAINT		
D	MATL SPEC ADDED		
E	WAS 6.30 DIA		
F	2B ADDED		

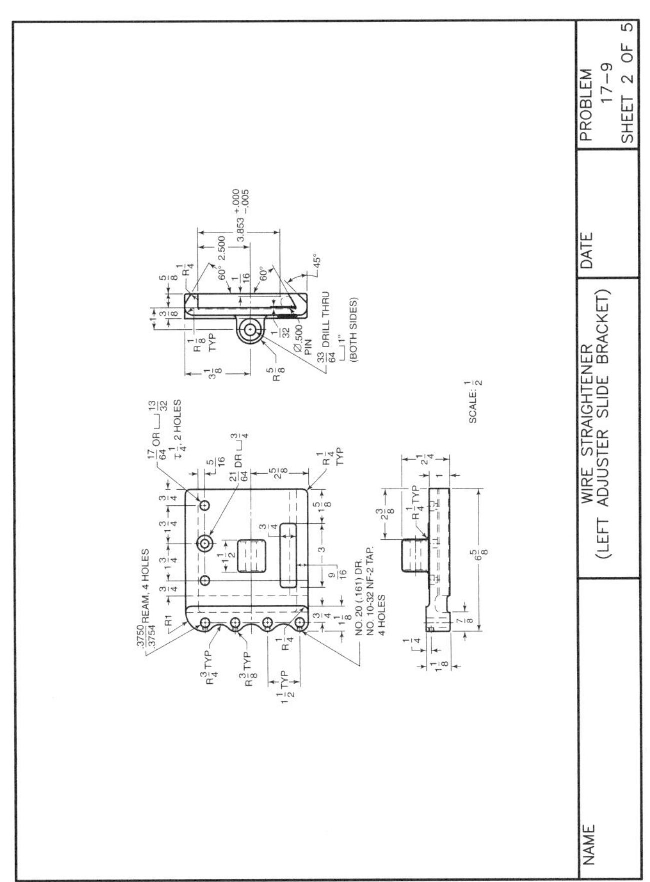
NAME
DATE
WIRE STRAIGHTENER
(LEFT ADJUSTER SLIDE BRACKET)
PROBLEM
17–9
SHEET 2 OF 5
SCALE: 1/2

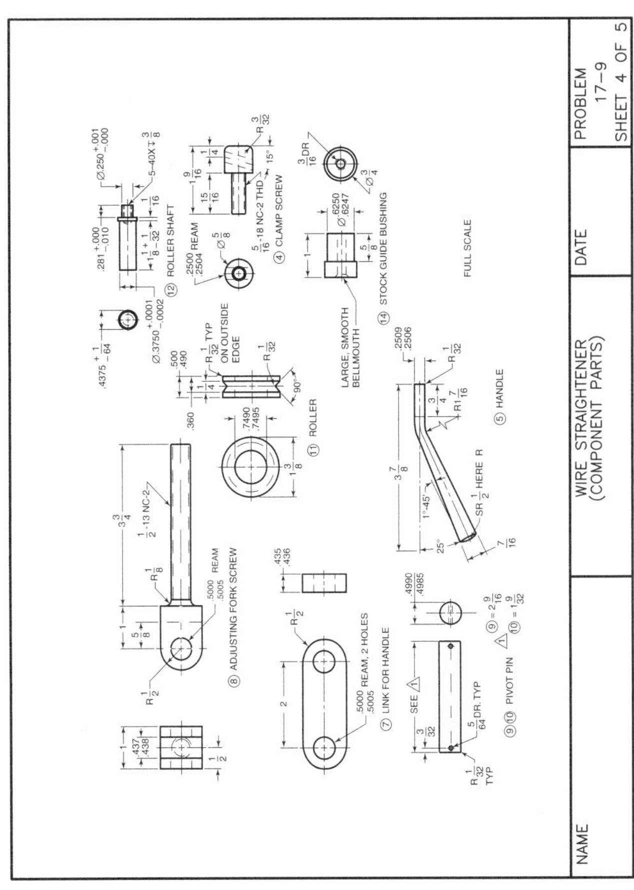
NAME
DATE
WIRE STRAIGHTENER
(COMPONENT PARTS)
PROBLEM
17–9
SHEET 4 OF 5
FULL SCALE

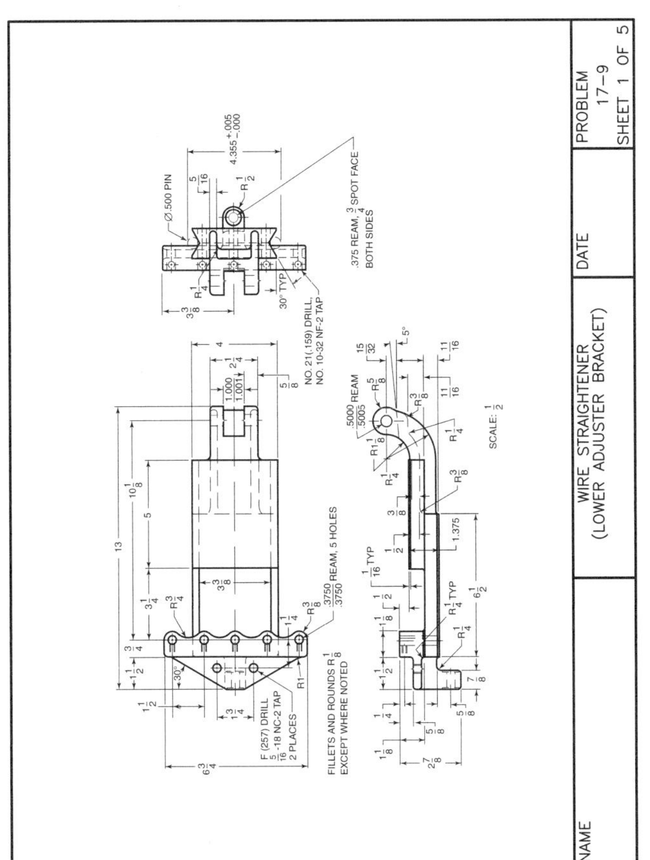
NAME
DATE
WIRE STRAIGHTENER
(LOWER ADJUSTER BRACKET)
PROBLEM
17–9
SHEET 1 OF 5
SCALE: 1/2

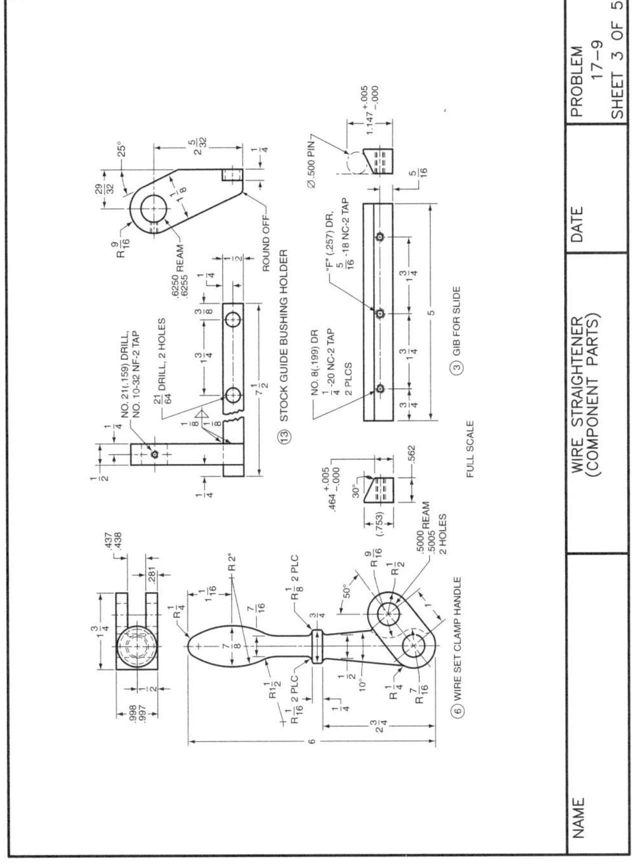
NAME
DATE
WIRE STRAIGHTENER
(COMPONENT PARTS)
PROBLEM
17–9
SHEET 3 OF 5
FULL SCALE

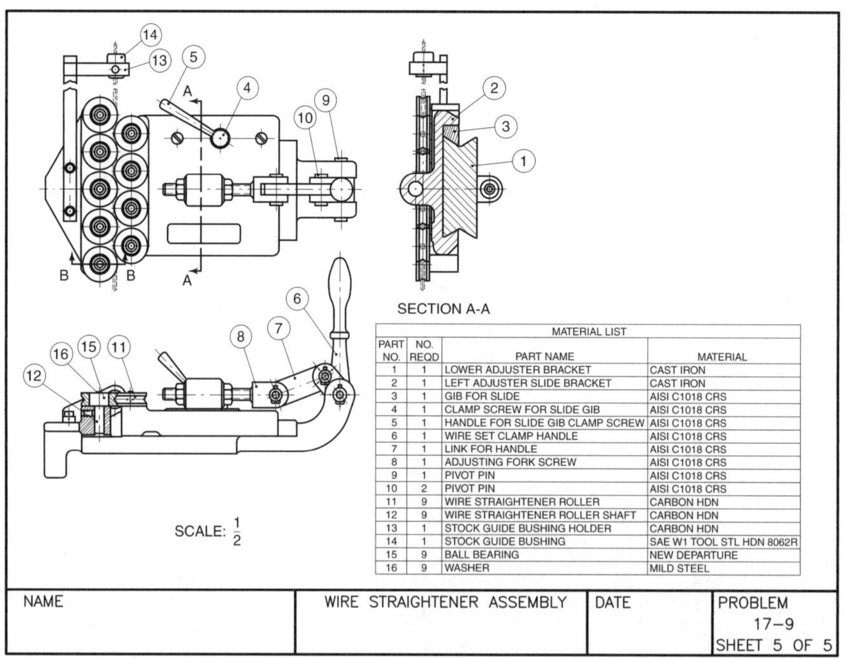

MATERIAL LIST			
PART NO.	NO. REQD	PART NAME	MATERIAL
1	1	LOWER ADJUSTER BRACKET	CAST IRON
2	1	LEFT ADJUSTER SLIDE BRACKET	CAST IRON
3	1	GIB FOR SLIDE	AISI C1018 CRS
4	1	CLAMP SCREW FOR SLIDE GIB	AISI C1018 CRS
5	1	HANDLE FOR SLIDE GIB CLAMP SCREW	AISI C1018 CRS
6	1	WIRE SET CLAMP HANDLE	AISI C1018 CRS
7	1	LINK FOR HANDLE	AISI C1018 CRS
8	1	ADJUSTING FORK SCREW	AISI C1018 CRS
9	1	PIVOT PIN	AISI C1018 CRS
10	2	PIVOT PIN	AISI C1018 CRS
11	9	WIRE STRAIGHTENER ROLLER	CARBON HDN
12	9	WIRE STRAIGHTENER ROLLER SHAFT	CARBON HDN
13	1	STOCK GUIDE BUSHING HOLDER	CARBON HDN
14	1	STOCK GUIDE BUSHING	SAE W1 TOOL STL HDN 8062R
15	9	BALL BEARING	NEW DEPARTURE
16	9	WASHER	MILD STEEL

Solutions to Design Problems, Text

Page 614

Students should present the problems they select to you before they begin work. Evaluate each proposal to make certain it is appropriate. When completing problems, students should follow the design method discussed in Chapter 1. Students should prepare working drawings for the solution.

Solutions to Worksheets

Pages 141–157

Student work should look like the following drawings. The problem number and title are indicated on each problem sheet.

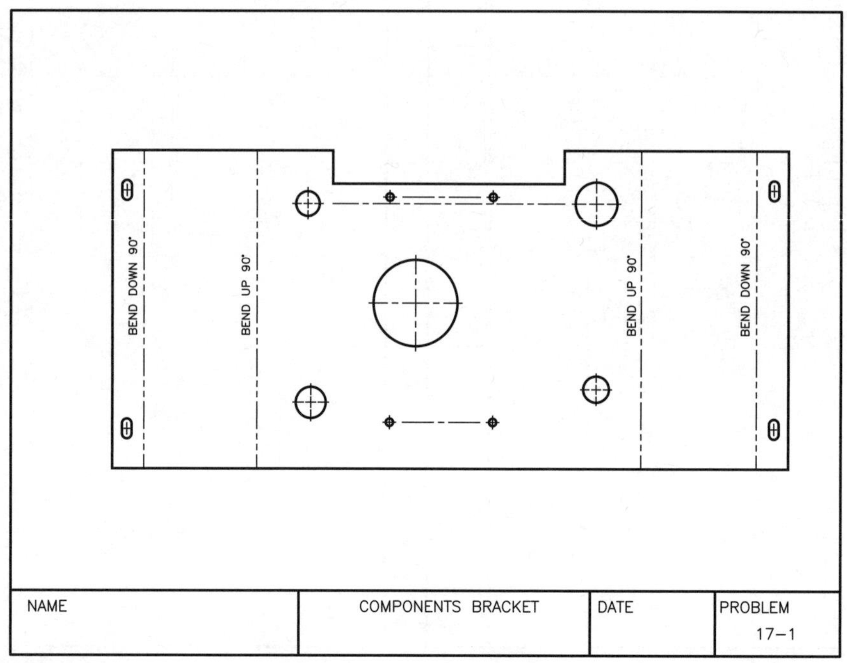

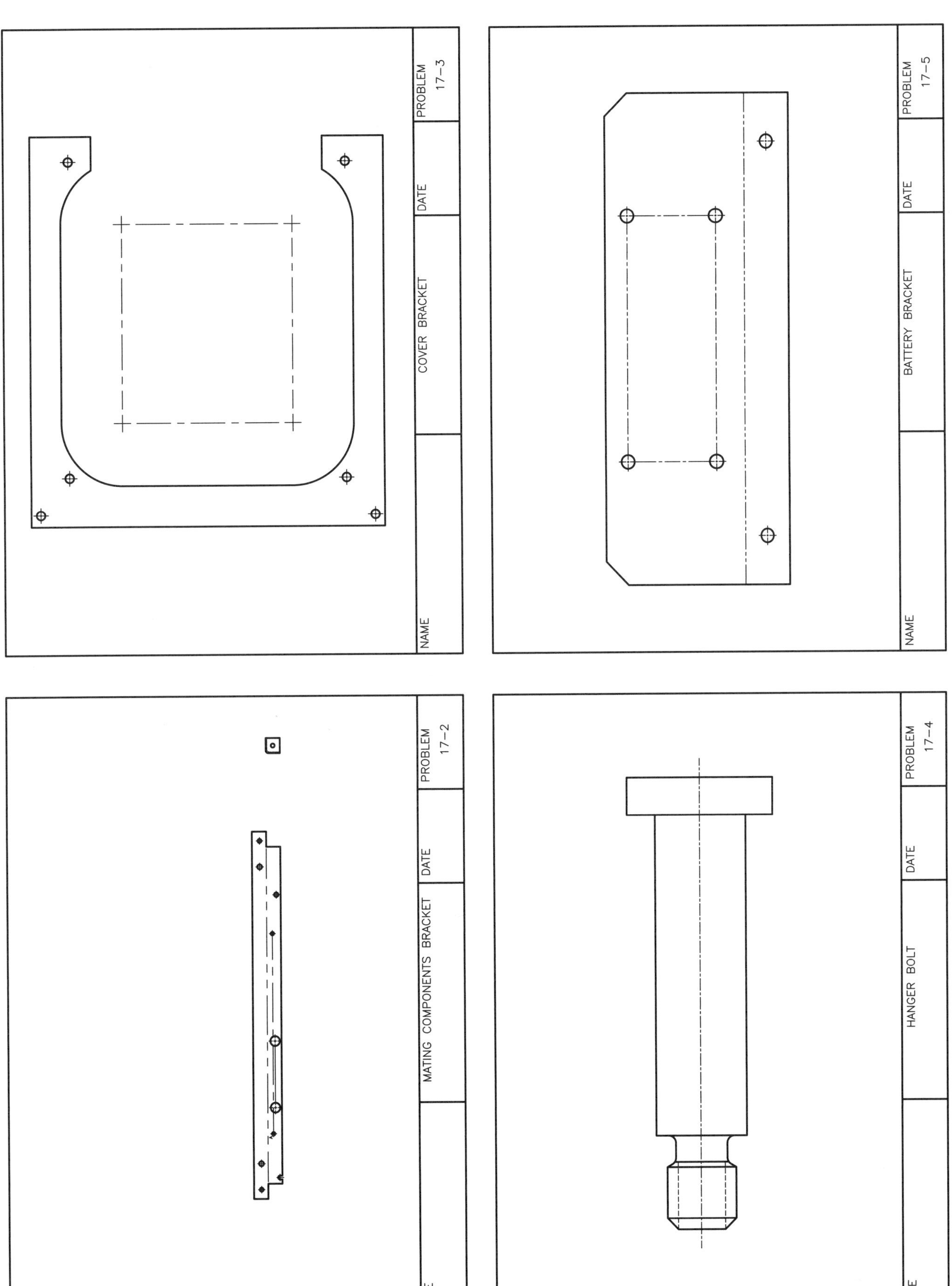
PROBLEM 17–3
DATE
COVER BRACKET
NAME
PROBLEM 17–5
DATE
BATTERY BRACKET
NAME
PROBLEM 17–2
DATE
MATING COMPONENTS BRACKET
NAME
PROBLEM 17–4
DATE
HANGER BOLT
NAME

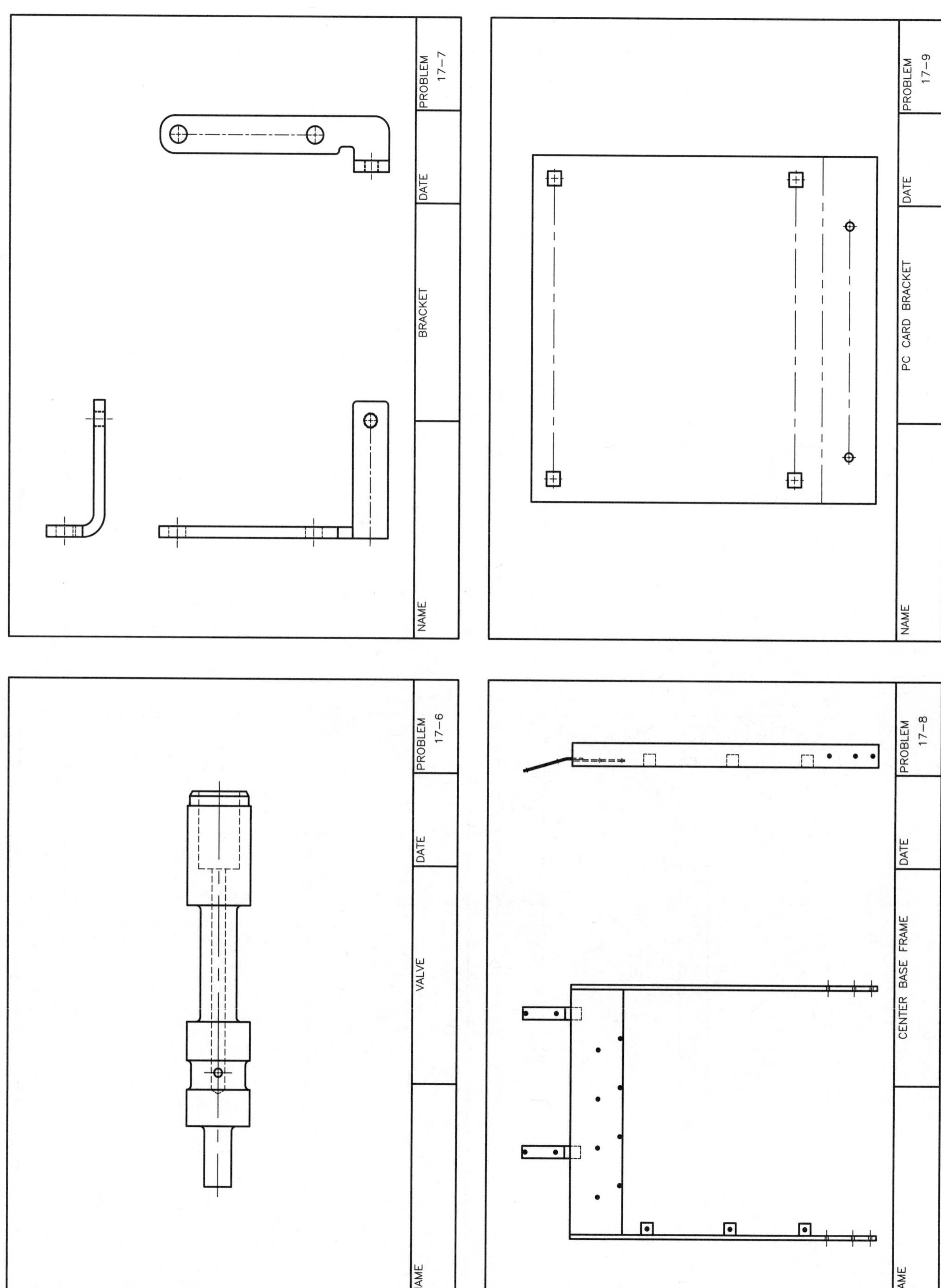
PROBLEM
17–7
DATE
BRACKET
NAME
PROBLEM
17–9
DATE
PC CARD BRACKET
NAME
PROBLEM
17–6
DATE
VALVE
NAME
PROBLEM
17–8
DATE
CENTER BASE FRAME
NAME

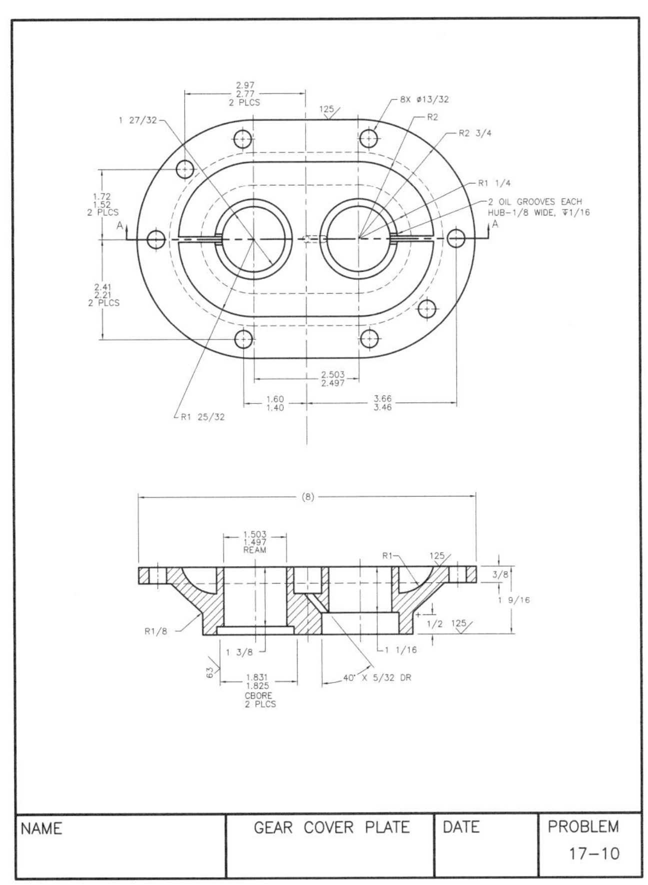
2.97
2.77
2 PLCS
1 27/32
125
8X ⌀13/32
R2
R2 3/4
R1 1/4
2 OIL GROOVES EACH
HUB–1/8 WIDE, ↧1/16
1.72
1.52
2 PLCS
A
A
2.41
2.21
2 PLCS
2.503
2.497
1.60
1.40
3.66
3.46
R1 25/32
(8)
1.503
1.497
REAM
R1
125
3/8
1 9/16
1/2
125
R1/8
1 3/8
1 1/16
63
1.831
1.825
CBORE
2 PLCS
40° X 5/32 DR
NAME
GEAR COVER PLATE
DATE
PROBLEM
17–10

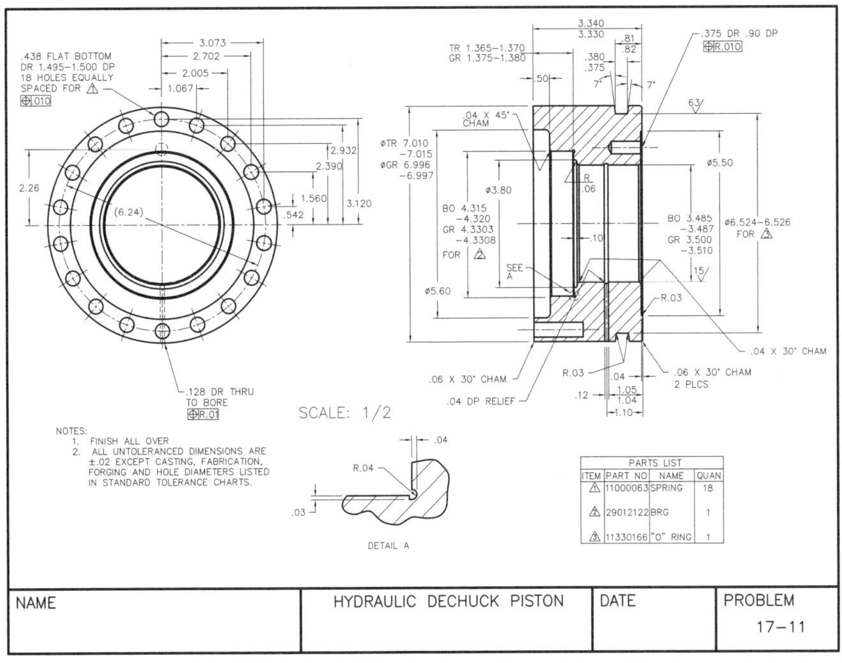
.438 FLAT BOTTOM
DR 1.495–1.500 DP
18 HOLES EQUALLY
SPACED FOR ⚠1
⌖.010
3.073
2.702
2.005
1.067
2.932
2.390
1.560
.542
3.120
2.26
(6.24)
.128 DR THRU
TO BORE
⌖R.01
SCALE: 1/2
NOTES:
1. FINISH ALL OVER
2. ALL UNTOLERANCED DIMENSIONS ARE ±.02 EXCEPT CASTING, FABRICATION, FORGING AND HOLE DIAMETERS LISTED IN STANDARD TOLERANCE CHARTS.
3.340
3.330
TR 1.365–1.370
GR 1.375–1.380
.81
.82
.380
.375
.50
7°
7°
.375 DR .90 DP
⌖R.010
63
.04 X 45° CHAM
⌀TR 7.010
–7.015
⌀GR 6.996
–6.997
⌀3.80
R
.06
⌀5.50
BO 4.315
–4.320
GR 4.3303
–4.3308
FOR ⚠2
.10
BO 3.485
–3.487
GR 3.500
–3.510
⌀6.524–6.526
FOR ⚠3
15
SEE A
⌀5.60
R.03
.04 X 30° CHAM
.06 X 30° CHAM
R.03
.04
.06 X 30° CHAM
2 PLCS
.12
1.05
1.04
1.10
.04 DP RELIEF
.04
R.04
.03
DETAIL A
PARTS LIST
ITEM | PART NO | NAME | QUAN
1 | 11000063 | SPRING | 18
2 | 29012122 | BRG | 1
3 | 11330166 | "O" RING | 1
NAME
HYDRAULIC DECHUCK PISTON
DATE
PROBLEM
17–11

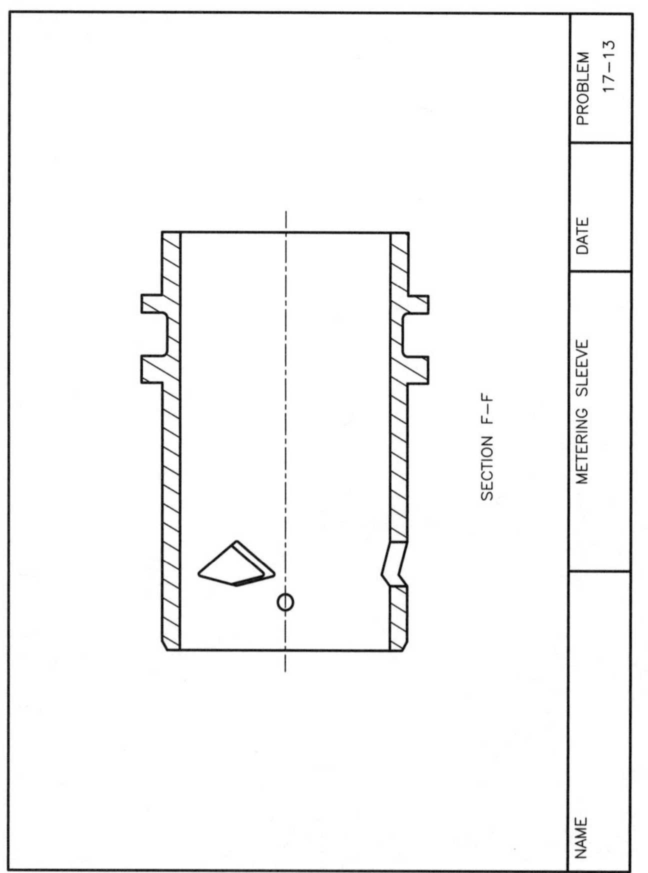
PROBLEM 17–13
DATE
METERING SLEEVE
NAME
SECTION F–F

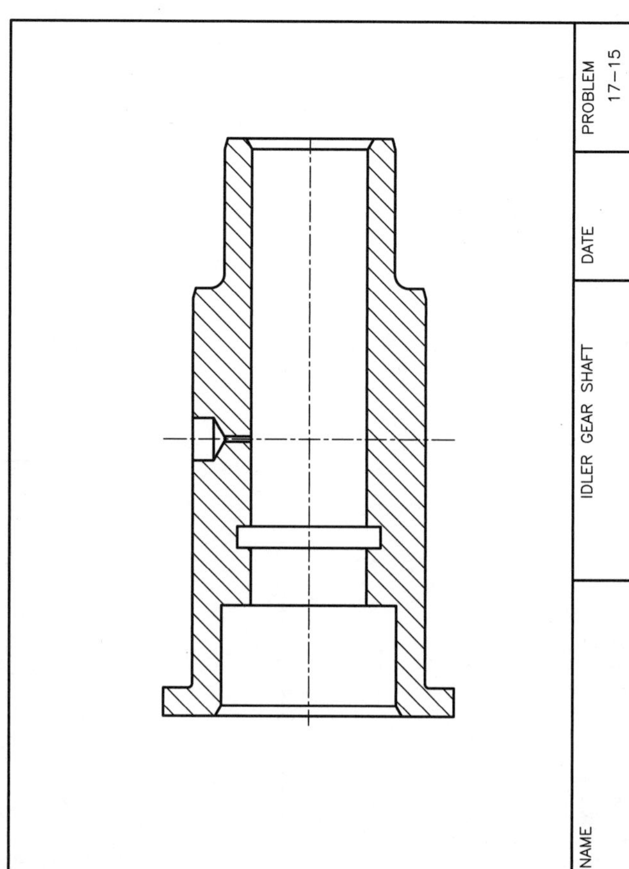
PROBLEM 17–15
DATE
IDLER GEAR SHAFT
NAME

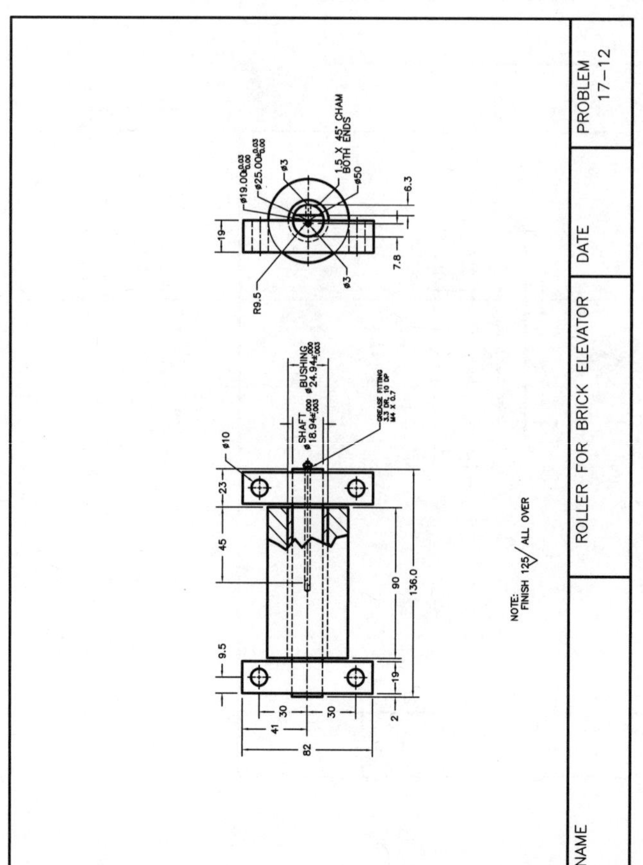
PROBLEM 17–12
DATE
ROLLER FOR BRICK ELEVATOR
NAME
NOTE: FINISH 125 ALL OVER
SHAFT
BUSHING
1.5 X 45° CHAM BOTH ENDS
ø50
ø3
ø10
R9.5
45
23
9.5
19
90
136.0
82
41
30
30
2
7.8
6.3

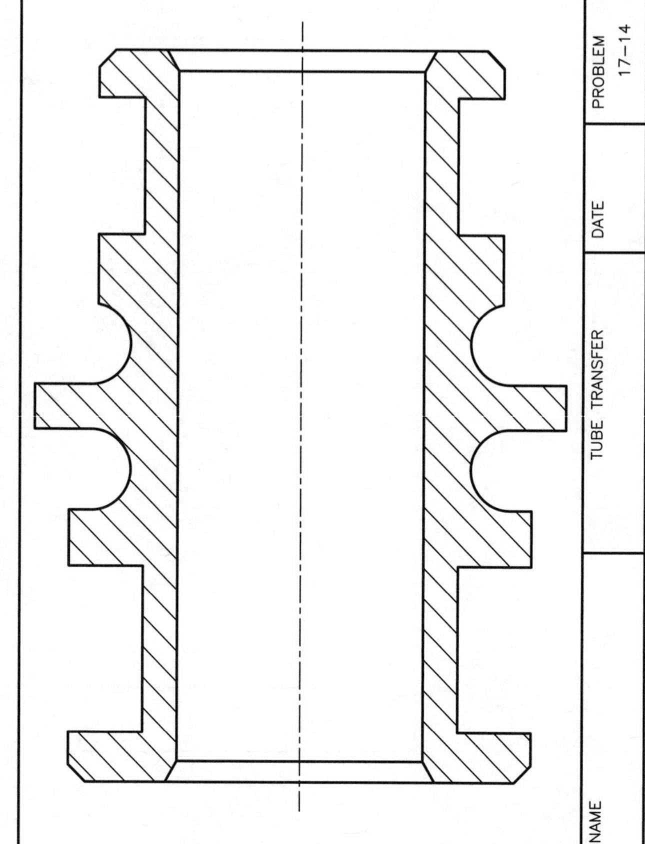
PROBLEM 17–14
DATE
TUBE TRANSFER
NAME

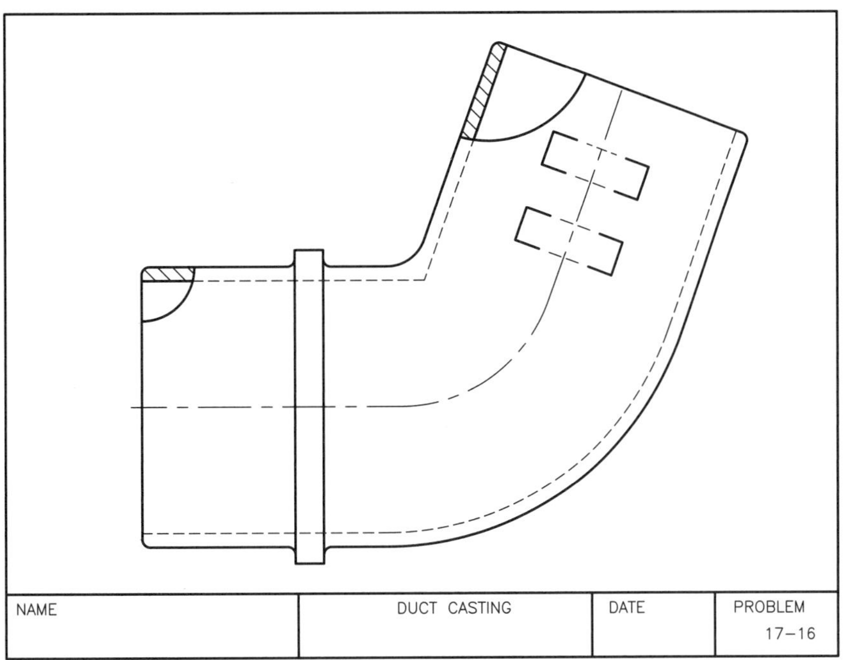

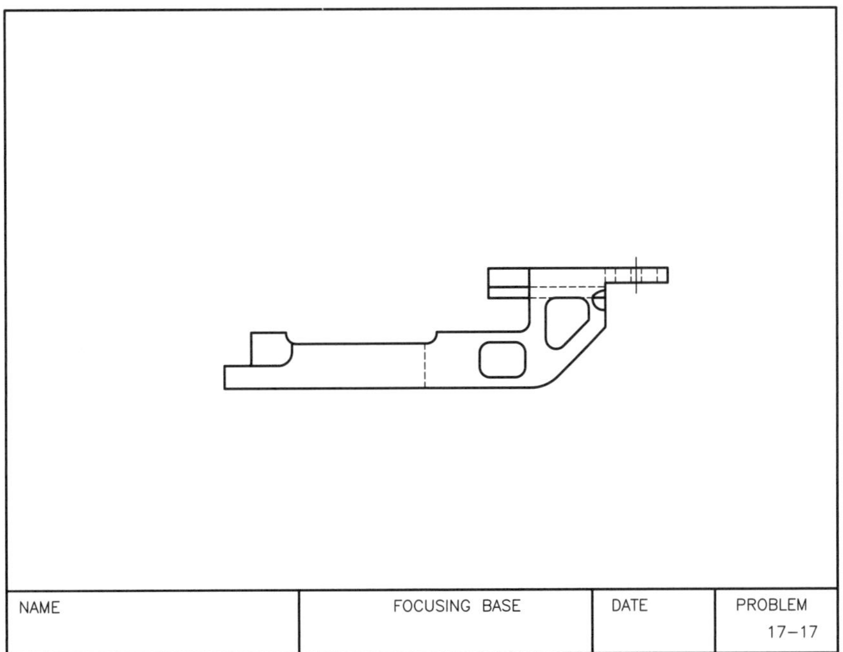

Answers to Chapter 17 Quiz

1. D. All of the above.
2. B. Assembly drawing
3. C. Layout drawing
4. A. operation
5. A. Use the maximum number of views possible.
6. D. tabulated
7. A. title
8. Refer to the drawings given in the *Solutions to Drawing Problems, Text* section for the problem selected from the textbook.

Chapter Quiz

Working Drawings

Name ____

Period ____________ Date ____________ Score ____________

Multiple Choice

Choose the answer that correctly completes the statement. Write the corresponding letter in the space provided.

_______ 1. Which of the following is a type of working drawing?
- A. Freehand sketch
- B. Detail drawing
- C. Assembly drawing
- D. All of the above.

_______ 2. What type of drawing shows the relationship or position of two or more detail parts that comprise a unit?
- A. Tabulated drawing
- B. Assembly drawing
- C. Detail drawing
- D. Operation drawing

_______ 3. What type of drawing may be used in the construction of a model or prototype but not as a production drawing?
- A. Detail drawing
- B. Assembly drawing
- C. Layout drawing
- D. Operation drawing

_______ 4. A(n) _____ drawing usually provides information for only one step in the making of a part.
- A. operation
- B. detail
- C. tabulated
- D. layout

_______ 5. Which of the following is *not* a standard practice used in functional drafting?
- A. Use the maximum number of views possible.
- B. Use a partial view, where adequate.
- C. Use symmetry to reduce drawing time.
- D. Avoid unnecessary repetition of detail.

Name ____

________ 6. A drawing that provides the necessary information to manufacture two or more parts that are basically identical but vary in a few characteristics is the ______ drawing.
A. assembly
B. operation
C. process
D. tabulated

________ 7. General tolerances when given on a drawing are usually included in the ______ block.
A. title
B. materials
C. revision
D. change

Drafting Performance

8. Draw a solution of a problem selected by your instructor from Chapter 17 in your textbook.

Types of Working Drawings

Working drawings may be divided into several subtypes, depending on their use. The following are common types of working drawings.

Freehand Sketches

A ***freehand sketch*** provides basic graphic information about a design idea or part. Freehand sketches are sometimes used for tooling, for jigs and fixtures, for test equipment setups, for prototypes, for research, for experimental parts, or for experimental assembly.

Detail Drawings

A ***detail drawing*** describes a single part that is to be made from a single piece of material. The drawing is complete with appropriate views, notes, dimensions, tolerances, and material and finish specifications.

Tabulated Drawings

A ***tabulated drawing*** provides information that is needed to fabricate two or more items that are basically identical but vary in a few characteristics. These variable characteristics typically involve dimensions, material, or finish.

Assembly Drawings

An ***assembly drawing*** shows the assembled relationship or positions of two or more detail parts, or of the parts and assemblies that make up a unit. An exploded assembly is one type of assembly drawing.

Operation Drawing

An ***operation drawing,*** also known as a ***process drawing,*** provides information for only one step or operation in making a part. This type of drawing is used by a machine operator when making a machine setup and performing single operations.

Layout Drawing

A ***layout drawing*** is often the original concept for a machine design or for placement of units. It is not a production drawing, but rather serves to record developing design concepts.

RM 17-1

Detail Drawing

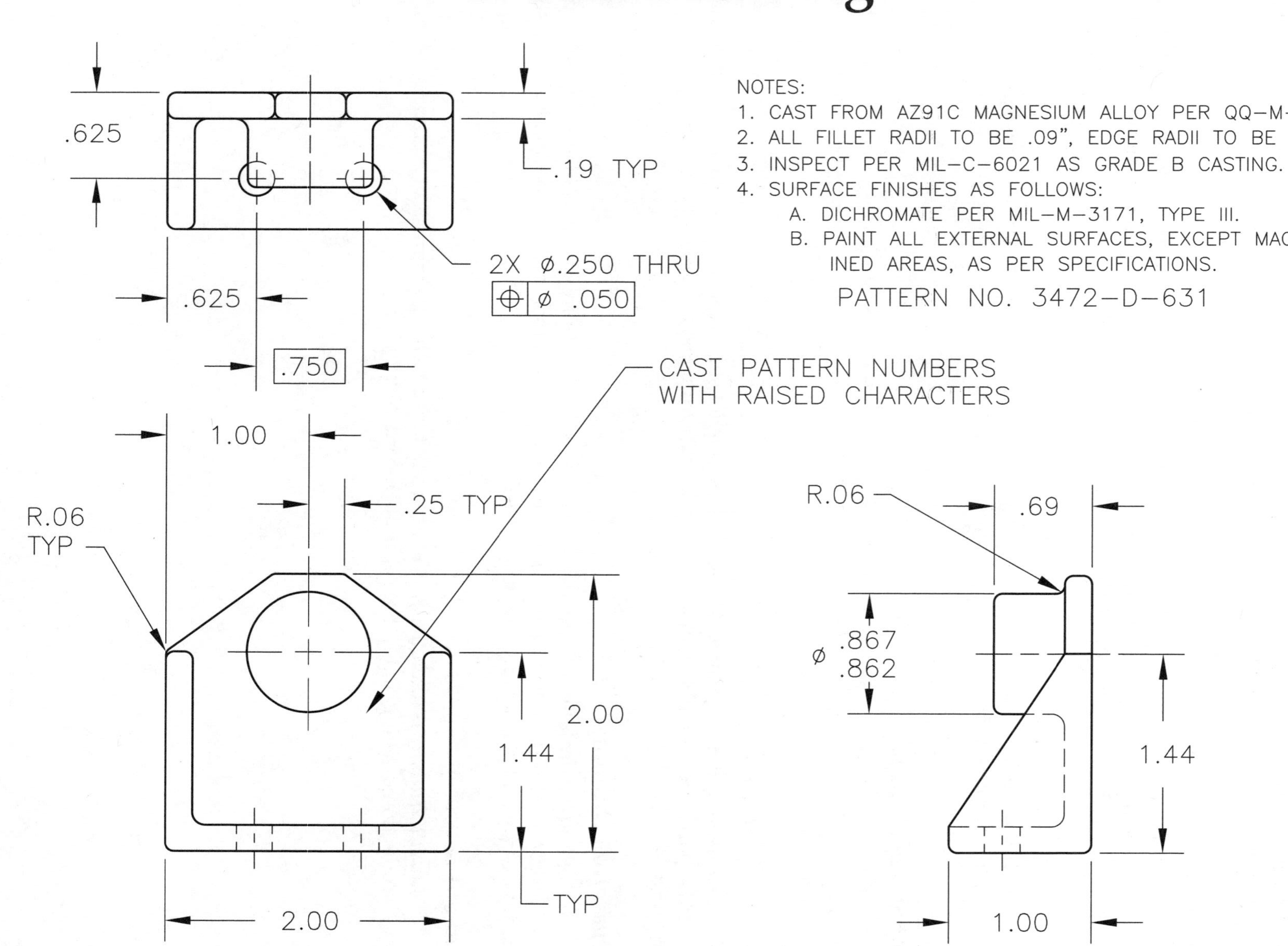

Assembly Drawing

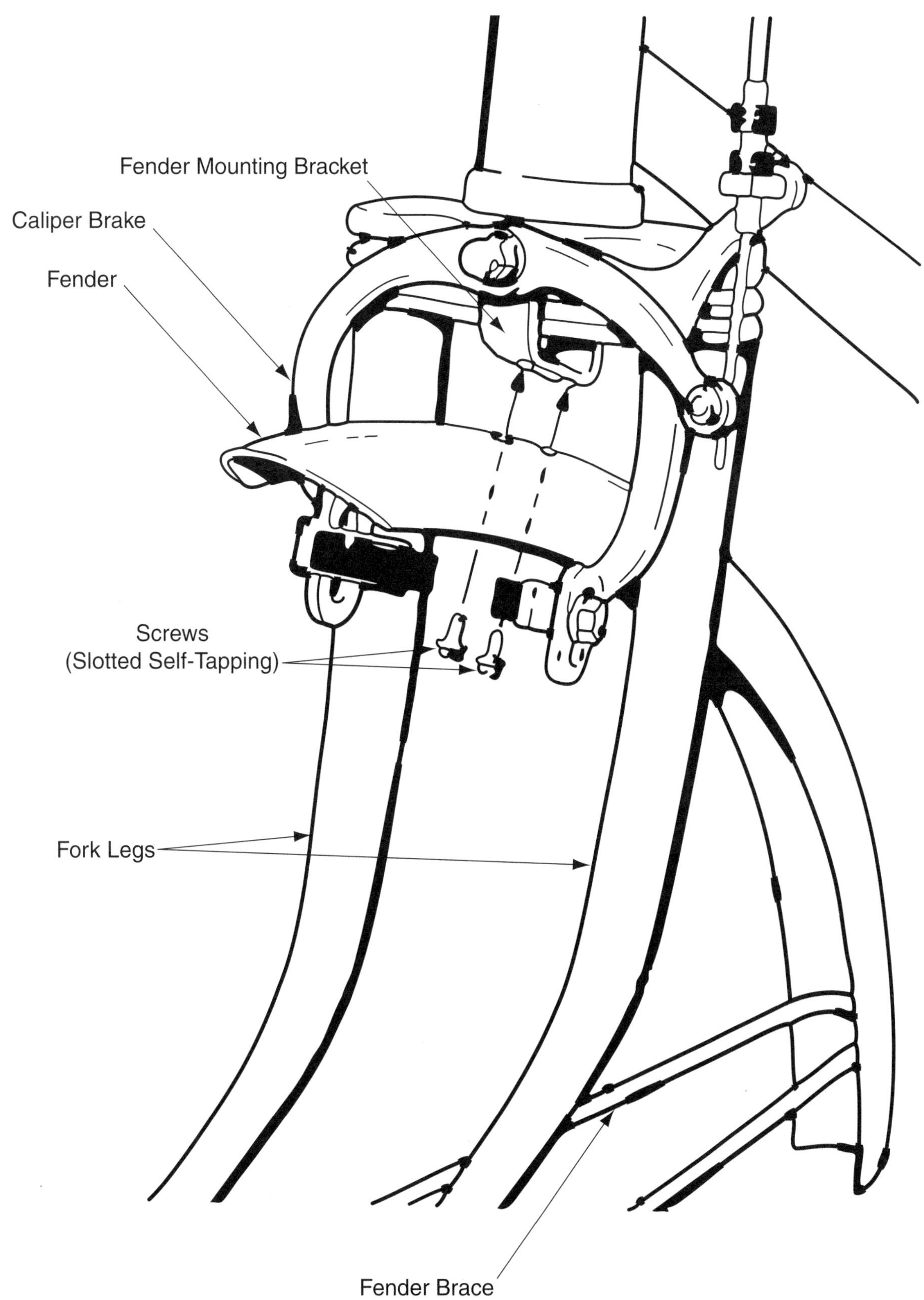

RM 17-3

Exploded Assembly Drawing

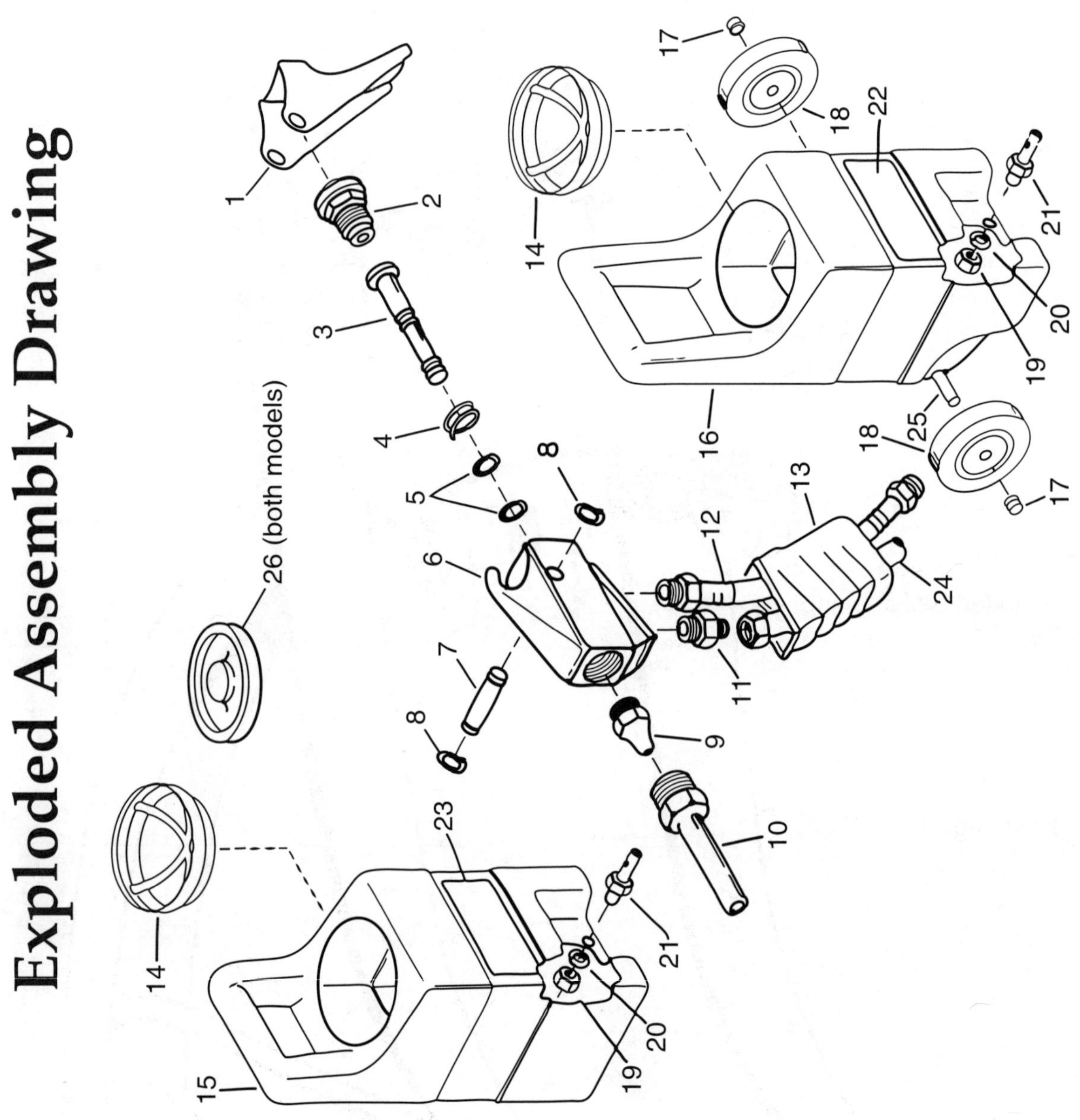

RM 17-4

Freehand Sketch

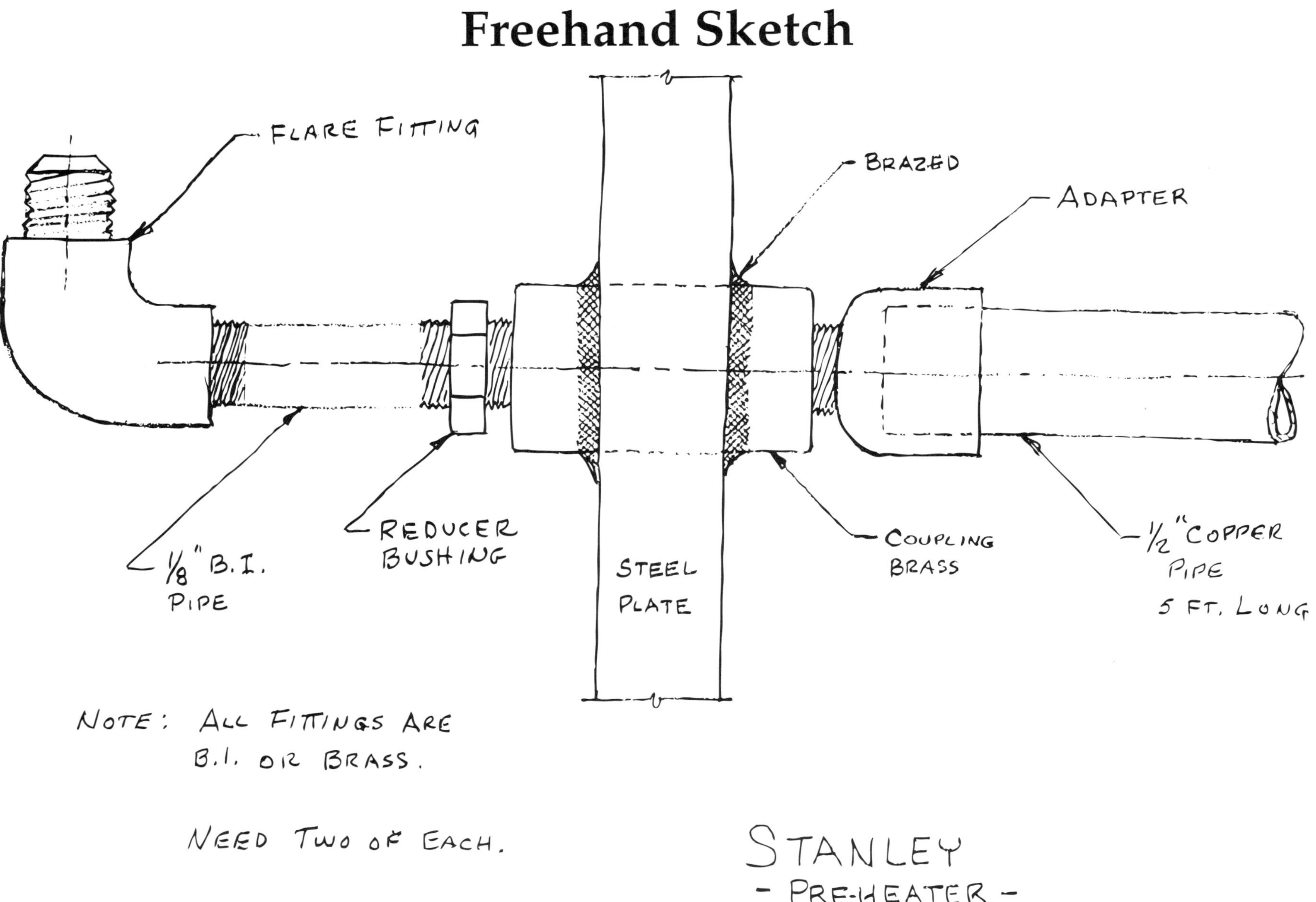

RM 17-5

Procedure Checklist

Working Drawings

Name ____

Observable Items	Completed		Comments	Instructor Initials
	Yes	No		
1. Draws freehand sketches.				
2. Prepares a detail drawing.				
3. Prepares a tabulated drawing.				
4. Prepares an assembly drawing.				
5. Prepares an operation or process drawing.				
6. Prepares a layout drawing.				

Instructor Signature ____

Threads and Fastening Devices 18

Learning Objectives

After studying this chapter, the student will be able to:

- Identify and explain common terms used to describe screw threads.
- Describe the standard methods used to represent threads on drawings.
- Identify different types of bolts, screws, and nuts and explain how they are drawn.
- Explain the purpose of washers and retaining rings.
- List applications for rivets, pin fasteners, and keys.

Instructional Resources

Text: pages 615–650

Review Questions, pages 642–643

Problems and Activities, page 644

Drawing Problems, pages 645–650

Worksheets: pages 158–162

- Worksheet 18-1: *Bolts and Nuts*
- Worksheet 18-2: *Threaded Block*
- Worksheet 18-3: *Special Adjusting Screw*
- Worksheet 18-4: *Spindle Ram Screw*
- Worksheet 18-5: *Shank*

Instructor's Resource

Instructional Tasks

Instructional Aids and Assignments

Chapter 18 Quiz

Reproducible Masters

- Reproducible Master 18-1: *Thread Terminology*. A drawing of external and internal threads is shown with thread terminology identified.
- Reproducible Master 18-2: *Thread Forms*. Eight standard thread forms are shown. The angle of thread is identified for each form.
- Reproducible Master 18-3: *Thread Note*. A thread specification note is shown. Each part of the note is identified.

Procedure Checklist

Color Transparencies (Binder/IRCD only)

- Transparency 18-1: *Thread Representations*. The different conventions used for representing external threads are shown.

Instructional Tasks

1. Identify common thread terms.
   - Discuss the importance of threads and fasteners.
   - Discuss thread terminology.
   - Discuss the different thread forms and their uses.
2. Explain how to interpret thread notes.
   - Discuss metric thread specifications.
3. Explain how to draw detailed representations of thread forms.
   - Use transparencies with overlays to demonstrate the procedure for drawing detailed thread representations.
4. Explain how to draw schematic thread representations.
   - Discuss uses for schematic thread representations.
5. Explain how to draw simplified thread representations.
   - Demonstrate the procedure for drawing simplified thread representations.
   - Discuss uses for simplified thread representations.
   - Demonstrate the procedure for drawing simplified thread representations. Use models as examples.
6. Explain how to draw pipe threads.
   - Discuss the types and uses of pipe threads.
   - Demonstrate the procedure for drawing pipe threads.
7. Explain how to draw bolt heads and screws.
   - Discuss the different types of bolts and screws. Also discuss their applications in industry.

- Demonstrate the procedures for drawing various bolts and screws. Label the drawings in the appropriate manner.

8. Explain how to draw washers, rings, and nuts.
    - Have students bring in washers, rings, or nuts and make drawings of them.
9. Explain how to draw rivets, pins, springs, and keys.
    - Using a supply catalog, demonstrate the various procedures for drawing rivets, pins, springs, and keys.

Instructional Aids and Assignments

1. Show a multimedia presentation or film on threads and fasteners.
2. Display charts showing various types of fasteners.
3. Show students catalogs from manufacturers of threaded fasteners or other types of fasteners.
4. Invite a speaker from industry or a manufacturer representative to talk about fastener requirements.
5. Assign the drawing problems in the textbook. The number of problems is sufficient to assign a minimum number to all students and to identify problems that may be done for extra credit. Some problems may be used for the performance section of the chapter quiz.

Answers to Review Questions, Text

Pages 642–643

1. A fastener is any mechanical device used to attach two or more pieces or parts together in a fixed position.
2. The Unified Screw Thread Series.
3. major diameter
4. pitch
5. D. root
6. profile
7. The American National and British Whitworth forms.
8. motion, power
9. friction
10. Coarse, fine, extra fine, and constant pitch.
11. Unified Coarse (UNC)
12. Unified Fine (UNF)
13. Unified Extra Fine (UNEF)
14. UN
15. B. lead
16. The nominal size, the number of threads per inch, the thread form and series, and the class of fit.
17. DOUBLE, TRIPLE
18. M
19. Detailed, schematic, and simplified representations.
20. blocks
21. clockwise
22. simplified
23. American Standard Regular, Dryseal, and Aeronautical.
24. 1, 16
25. A. bolt
26. D. stud
27. machine screw
28. D. Thread-forming screws
29. Flat, oval, and round.
30. Lock
31. Finishing
32. common
33. C. Locknuts
34. By the shank diameter and the shank length.
35. blind
36. B. Keys
37. Springs

Solutions to Problems and Activities, Text

Page 644

Student work should look like the following drawings. The problem number and title are indicated on each problem sheet.

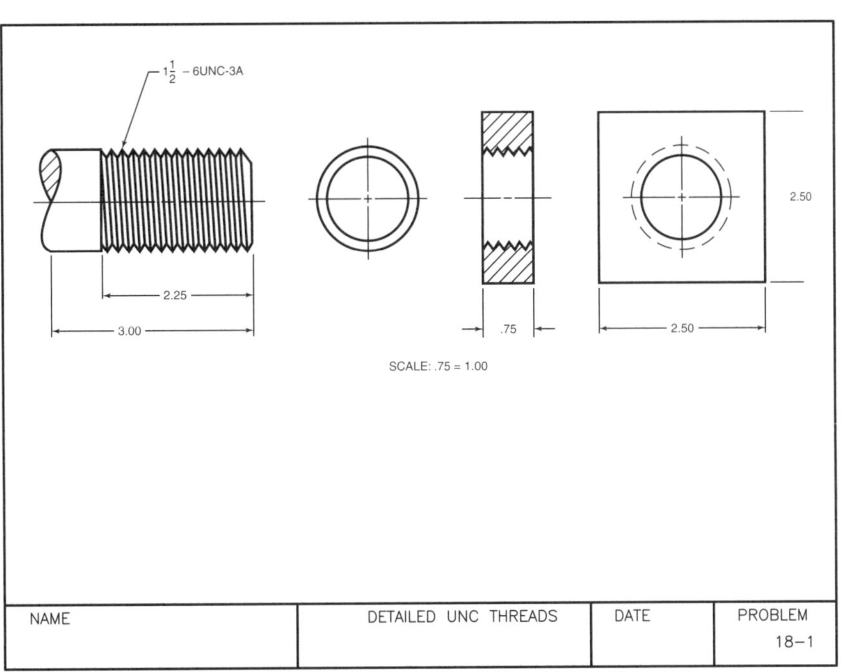
1½ – 6UNC-3A
2.25
3.00
.75
2.50
2.50
SCALE: .75 = 1.00
NAME
DETAILED UNC THREADS
DATE
PROBLEM
18–1

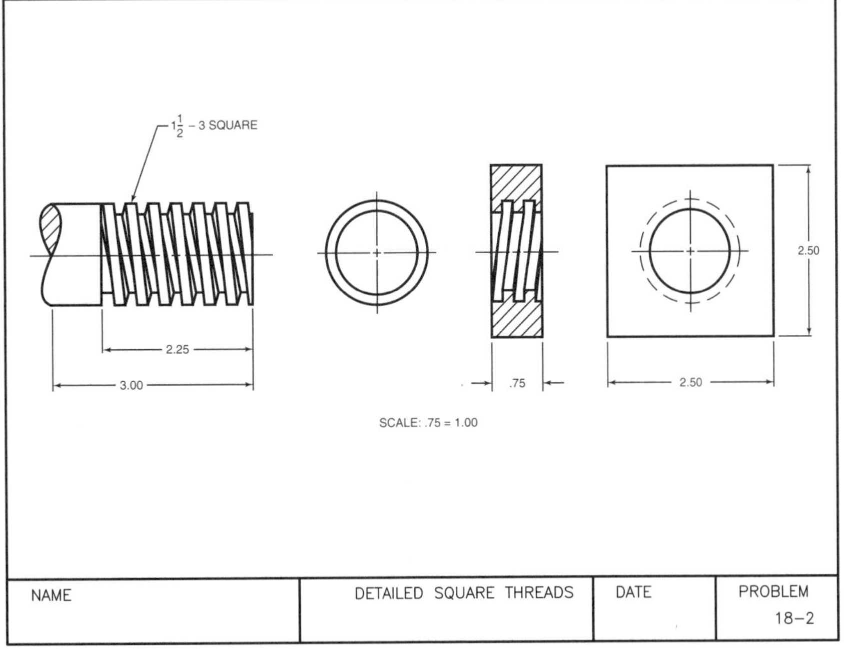
1½ – 3 SQUARE
2.25
3.00
.75
2.50
2.50
SCALE: .75 = 1.00
NAME
DETAILED SQUARE THREADS
DATE
PROBLEM
18–2

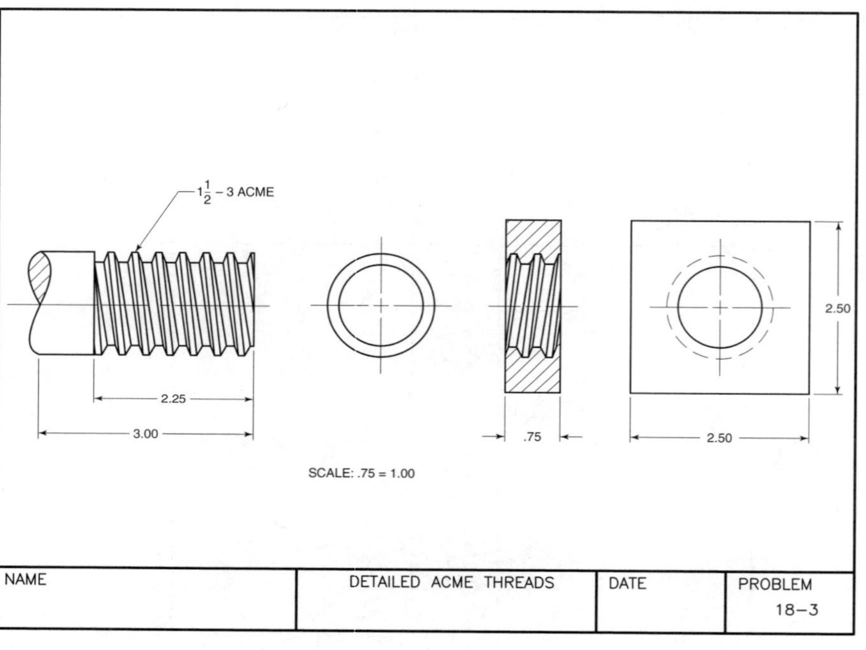
1 1/2 – 3 ACME
2.25
3.00
.75
2.50
2.50
SCALE: .75 = 1.00
NAME
DETAILED ACME THREADS
DATE
PROBLEM 18–3

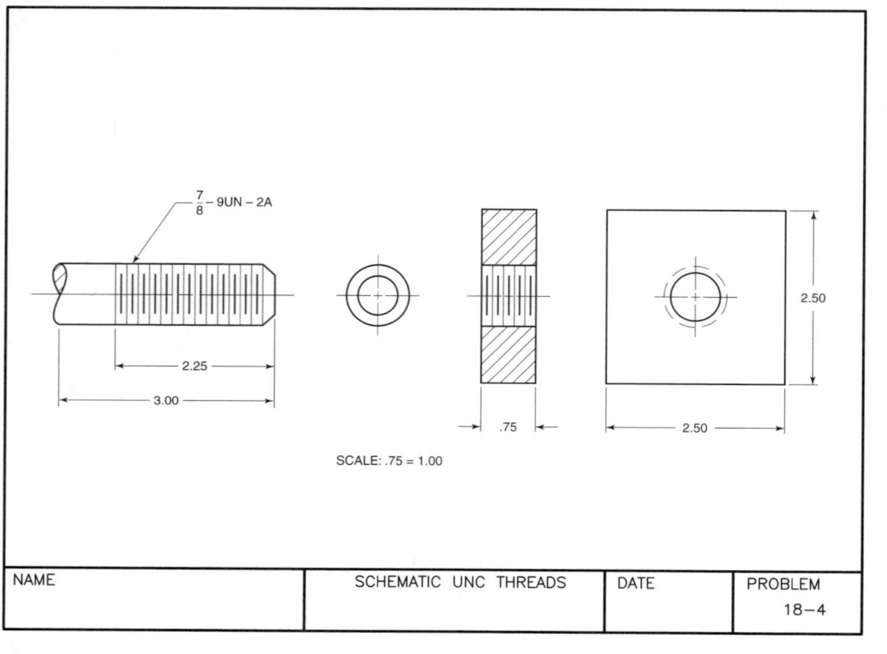
7/8 – 9UN – 2A
2.25
3.00
.75
2.50
2.50
SCALE: .75 = 1.00
NAME
SCHEMATIC UNC THREADS
DATE
PROBLEM 18–4

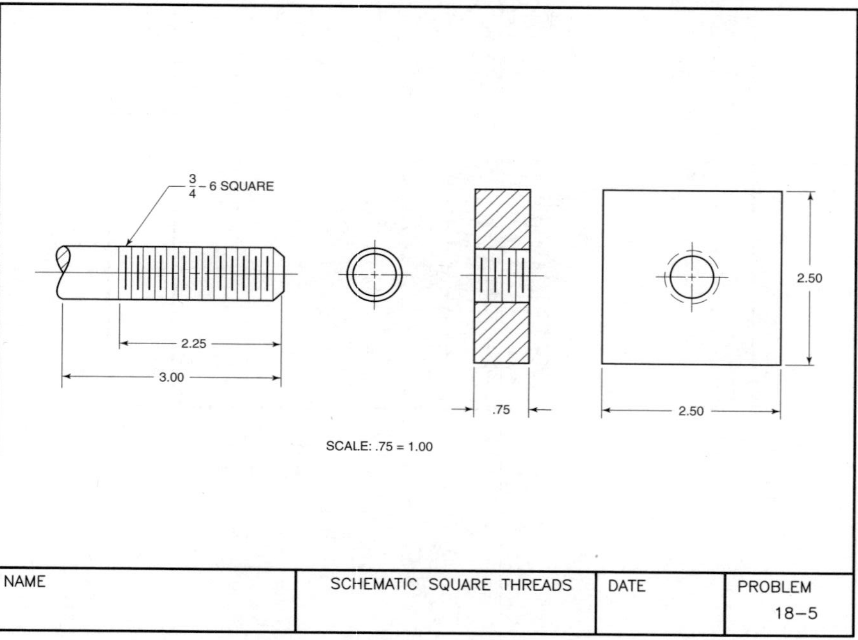
3/4 – 6 SQUARE
2.25
3.00
.75
2.50
2.50
SCALE: .75 = 1.00
NAME
SCHEMATIC SQUARE THREADS
DATE
PROBLEM 18–5

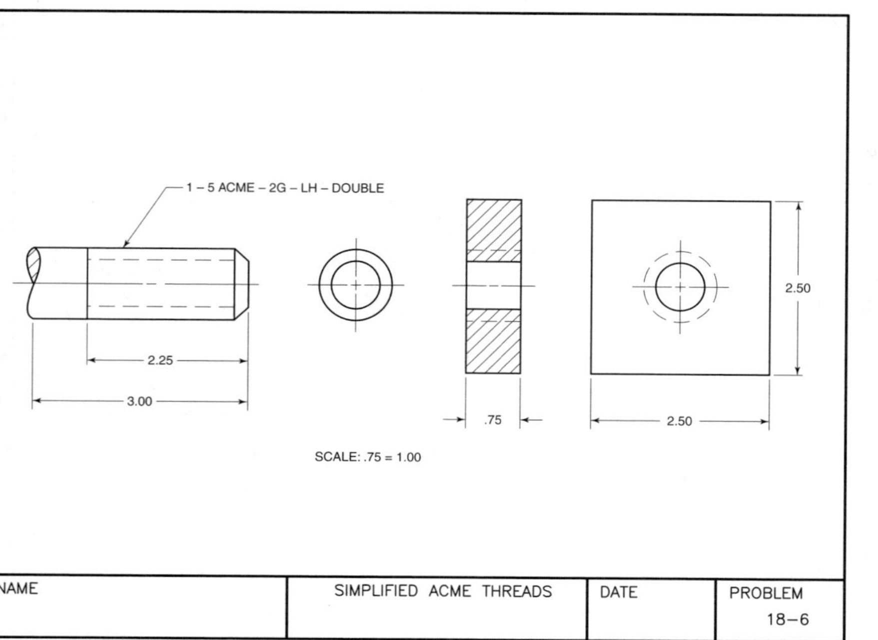
1 – 5 ACME – 2G – LH – DOUBLE
2.25
3.00
.75
2.50
2.50
SCALE: .75 = 1.00
NAME
SIMPLIFIED ACME THREADS
DATE
PROBLEM 18–6

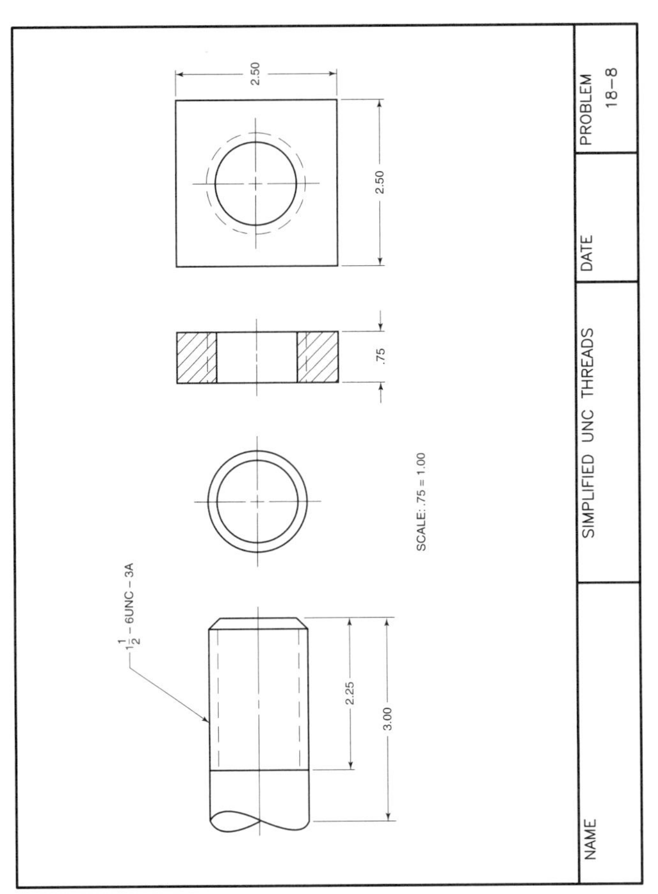
PROBLEM 18–8
DATE
SIMPLIFIED UNC THREADS
NAME
SCALE: .75 = 1.00
$1\frac{1}{2}$ – 6UNC – 3A
2.50
2.50
.75
2.25
3.00

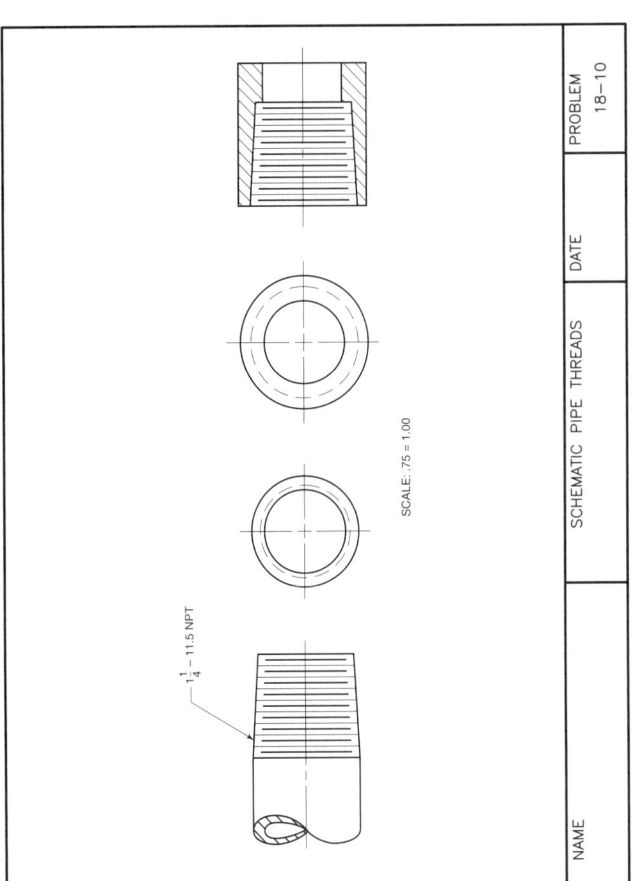
PROBLEM 18–10
DATE
SCHEMATIC PIPE THREADS
NAME
SCALE: .75 = 1.00
$1\frac{1}{4}$ – 11.5 NPT

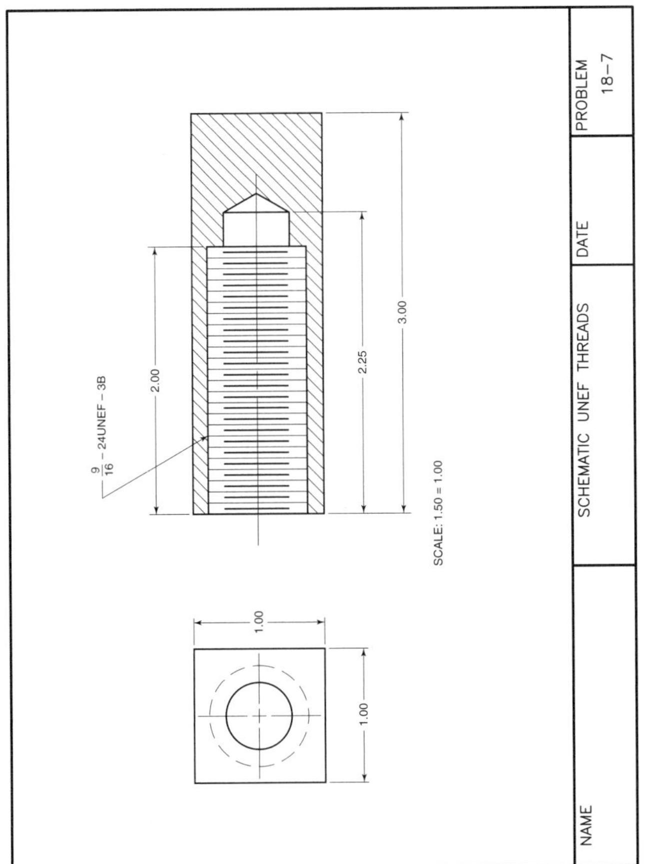
PROBLEM 18–7
DATE
SCHEMATIC UNEF THREADS
NAME
SCALE: 1.50 = 1.00
$\frac{9}{16}$ – 24UNEF – 3B
2.00
2.25
3.00
1.00
1.00

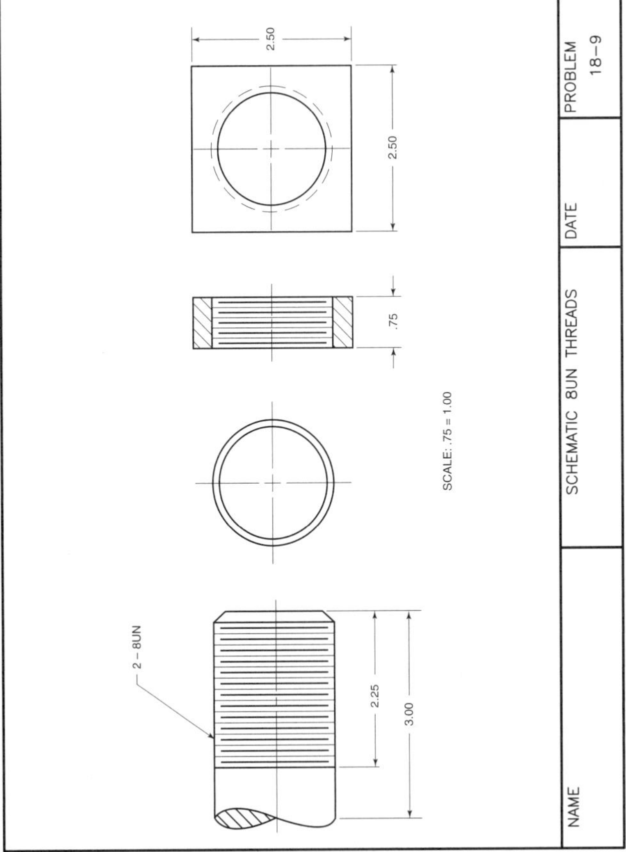
PROBLEM 18–9
DATE
SCHEMATIC 8UN THREADS
NAME
SCALE: .75 = 1.00
2 – 8UN
2.50
2.50
.75
2.25
3.00

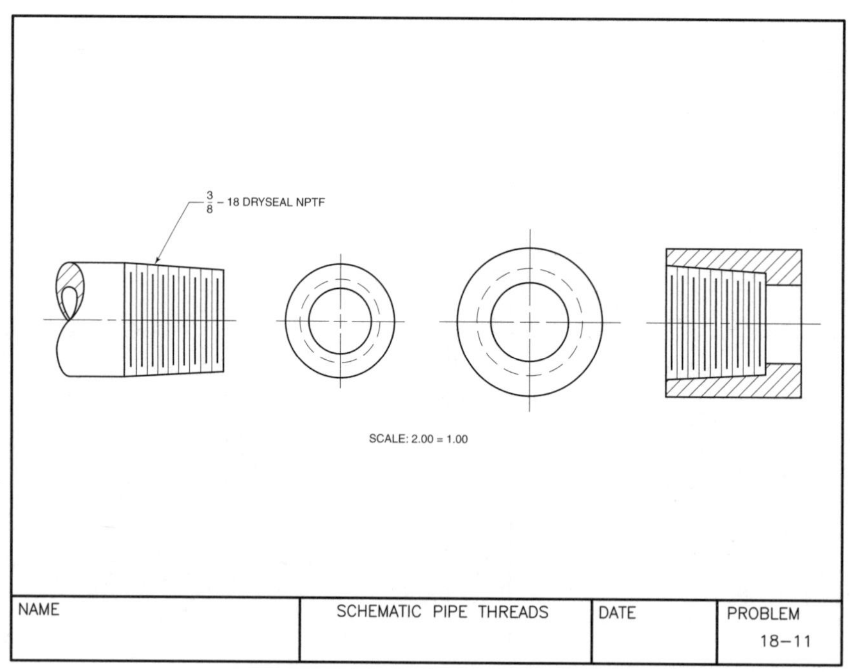

3/8 – 18 DRYSEAL NPTF
SCALE: 2.00 = 1.00
NAME
SCHEMATIC PIPE THREADS
DATE
PROBLEM
18–11

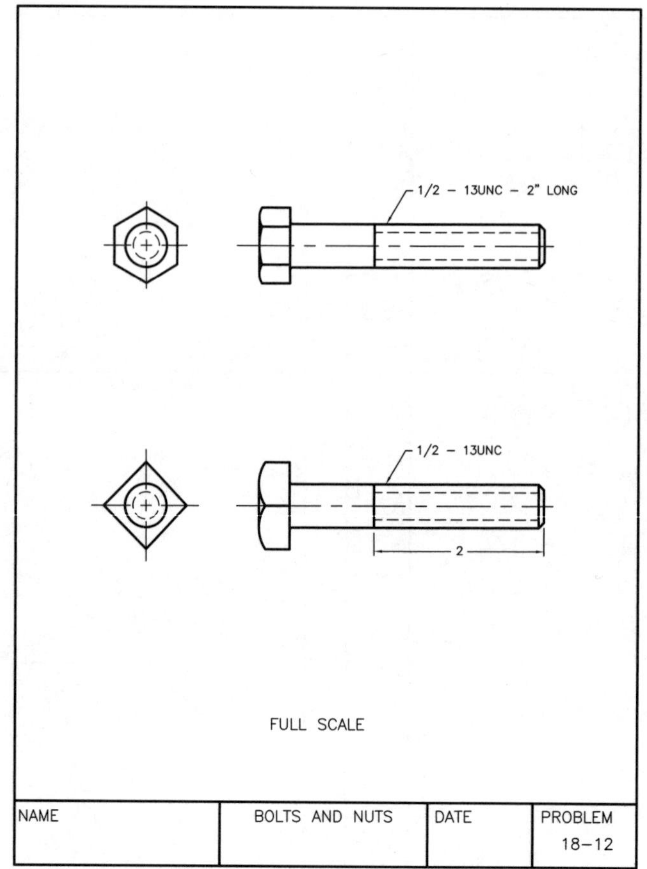

1/2 – 13UNC – 2" LONG
1/2 – 13UNC
2
FULL SCALE
NAME
BOLTS AND NUTS
DATE
PROBLEM
18–12

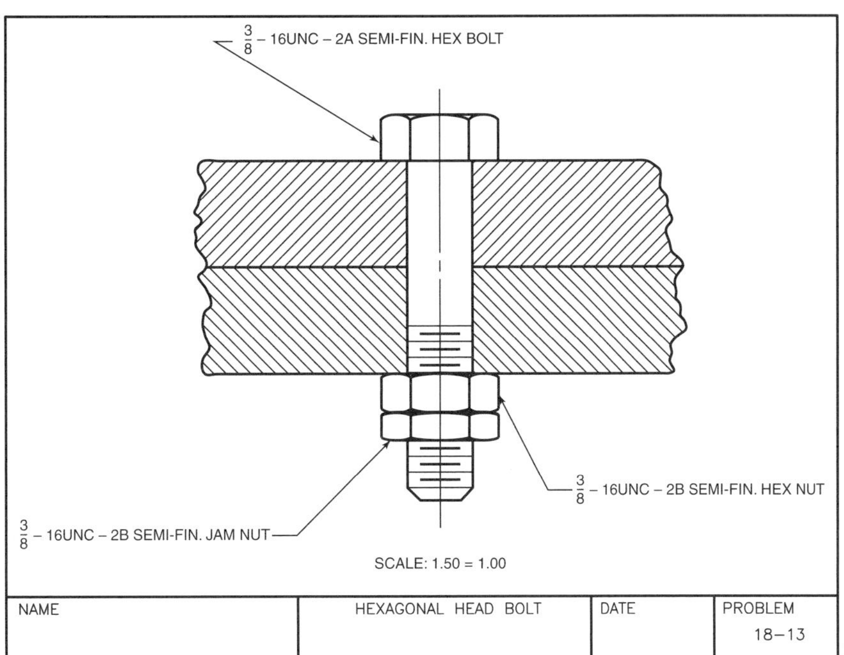

Solutions to Drawing Problems, Text

Pages 645–650

Student work should look like the following drawings. The problem number and title are indicated on each problem sheet.

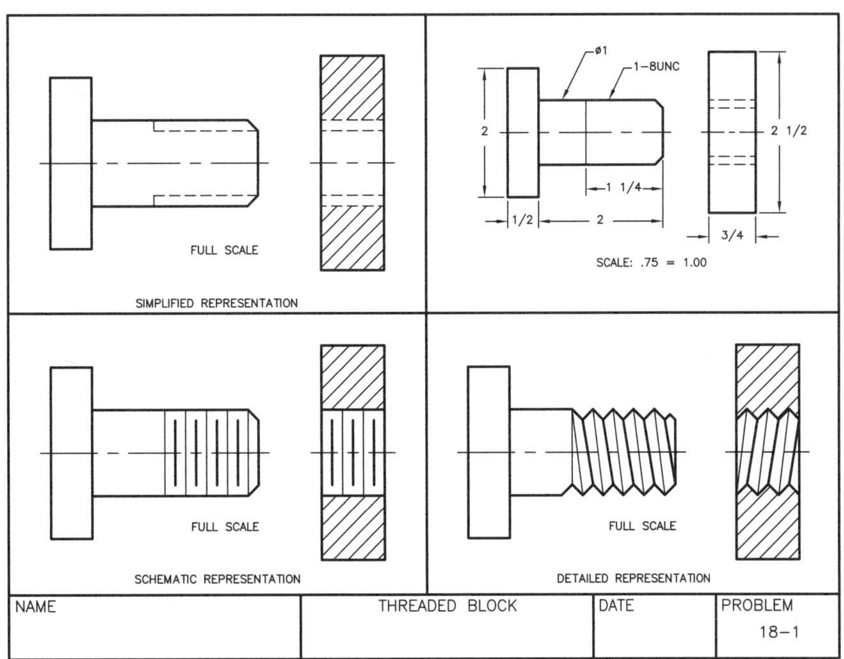

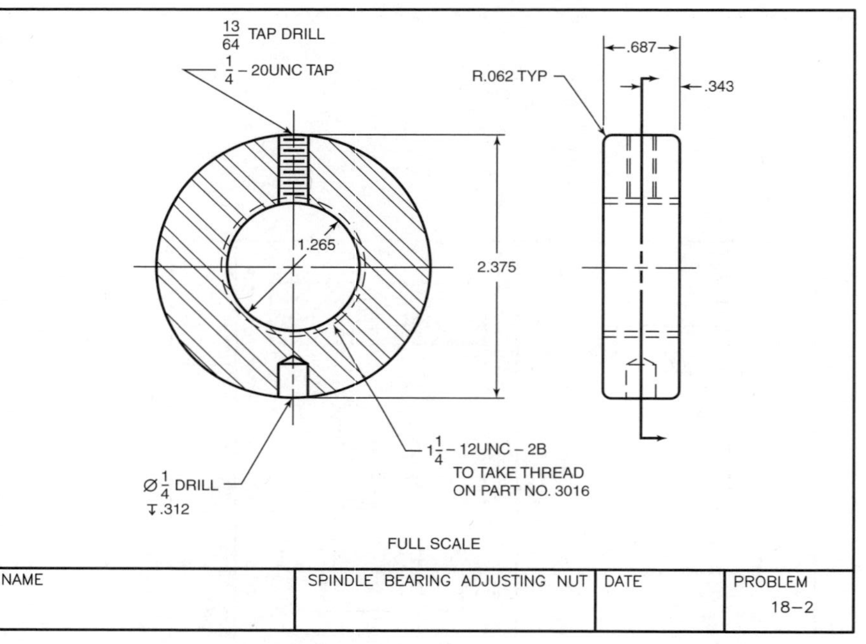
13/64 TAP DRILL
1/4 – 20UNC TAP
R.062 TYP
.687
.343
1.265
2.375
Ø 1/4 DRILL
↧.312
1 1/4 – 12UNC – 2B
TO TAKE THREAD
ON PART NO. 3016
FULL SCALE
NAME
SPINDLE BEARING ADJUSTING NUT
DATE
PROBLEM
18–2

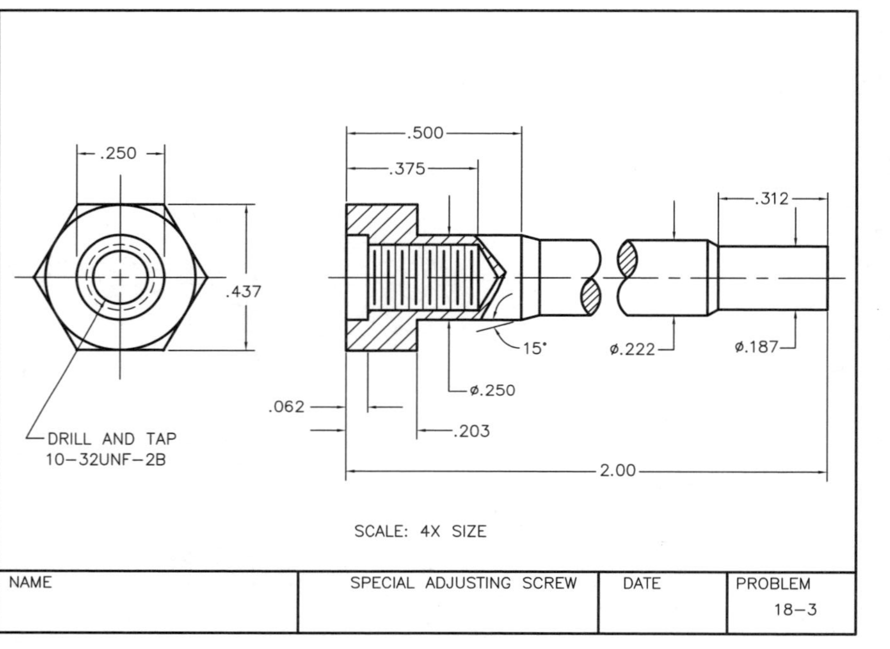
.250
.500
.375
.312
.437
15°
ø.222
ø.187
ø.250
.062
.203
DRILL AND TAP
10–32UNF–2B
2.00
SCALE: 4X SIZE
NAME
SPECIAL ADJUSTING SCREW
DATE
PROBLEM
18–3

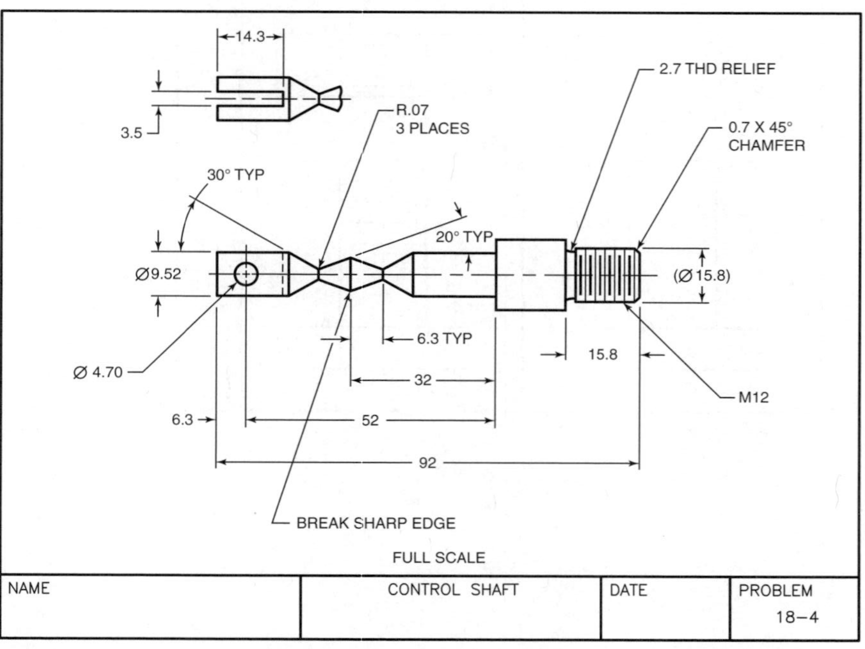
14.3
3.5
R.07
3 PLACES
2.7 THD RELIEF
0.7 X 45°
CHAMFER
30° TYP
20° TYP
Ø9.52
(Ø15.8)
6.3 TYP
15.8
Ø 4.70
32
M12
6.3
52
92
BREAK SHARP EDGE
FULL SCALE
NAME
CONTROL SHAFT
DATE
PROBLEM
18–4

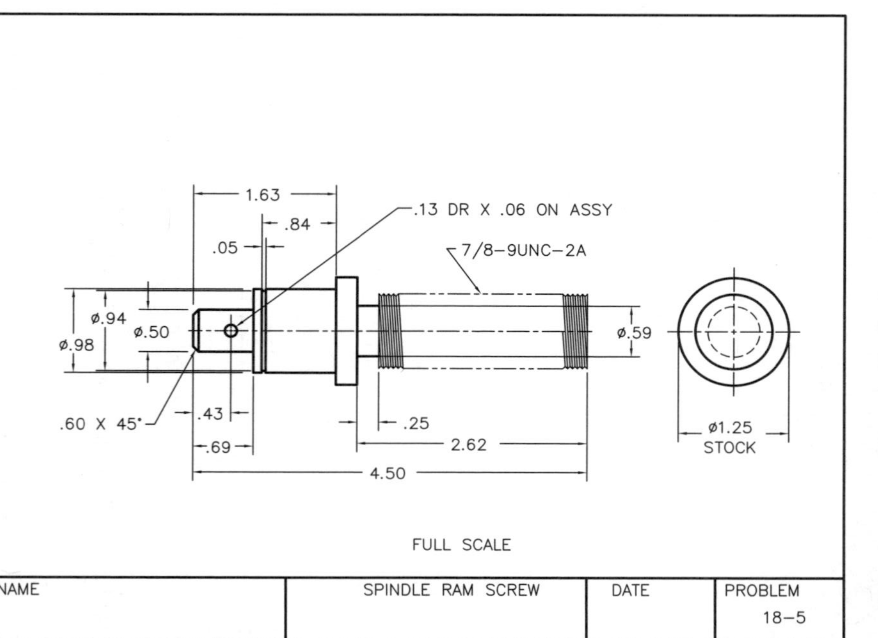
1.63
.84
.13 DR X .06 ON ASSY
.05
7/8–9UNC–2A
ø.94
ø.50
ø.98
ø.59
.60 X 45°
.43
.25
ø1.25
STOCK
.69
2.62
4.50
FULL SCALE
NAME
SPINDLE RAM SCREW
DATE
PROBLEM
18–5

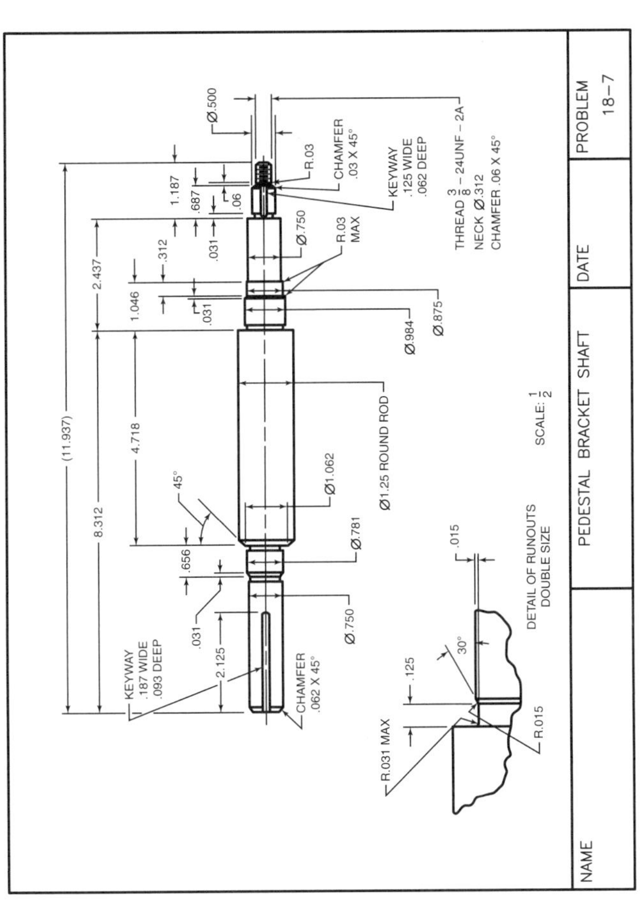
PROBLEM 18-7
DATE
PEDESTAL BRACKET SHAFT
NAME
SCALE: 1/2
DETAIL OF RUNOUTS DOUBLE SIZE
Ø1.25 ROUND ROD

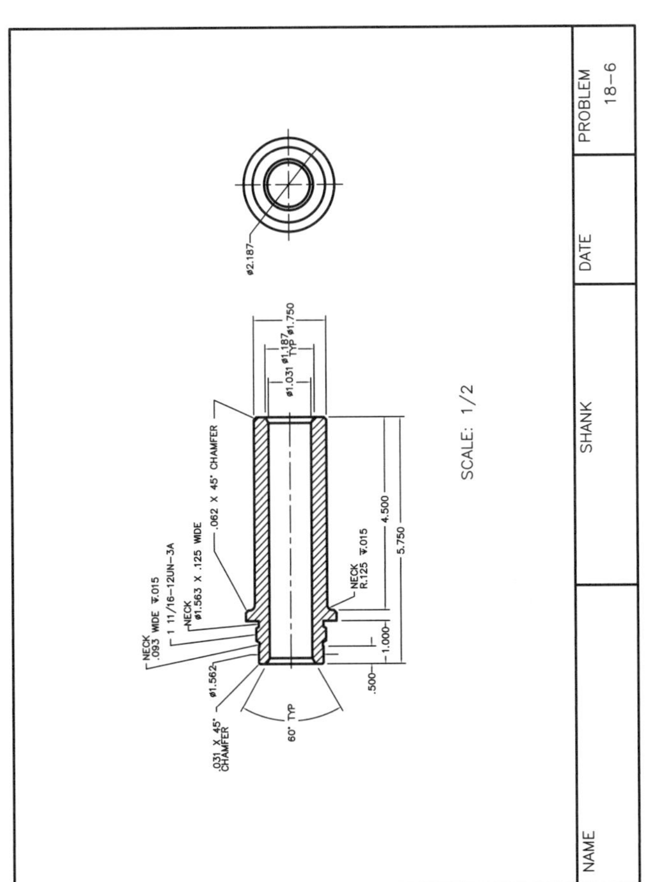
PROBLEM 18-6
DATE
SHANK
NAME
SCALE: 1/2

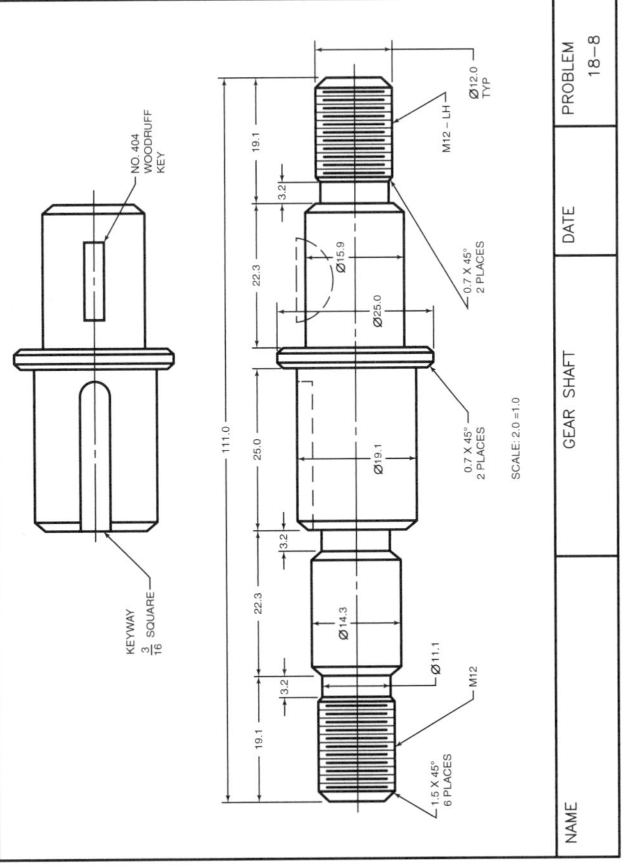
PROBLEM 18-8
DATE
GEAR SHAFT
NAME
SCALE: 2.0 = 1.0
NO. 404 WOODRUFF KEY

Solutions to Worksheets

Pages 158–162

Student work should look like the following drawings. The problem number and title are indicated on each problem sheet.

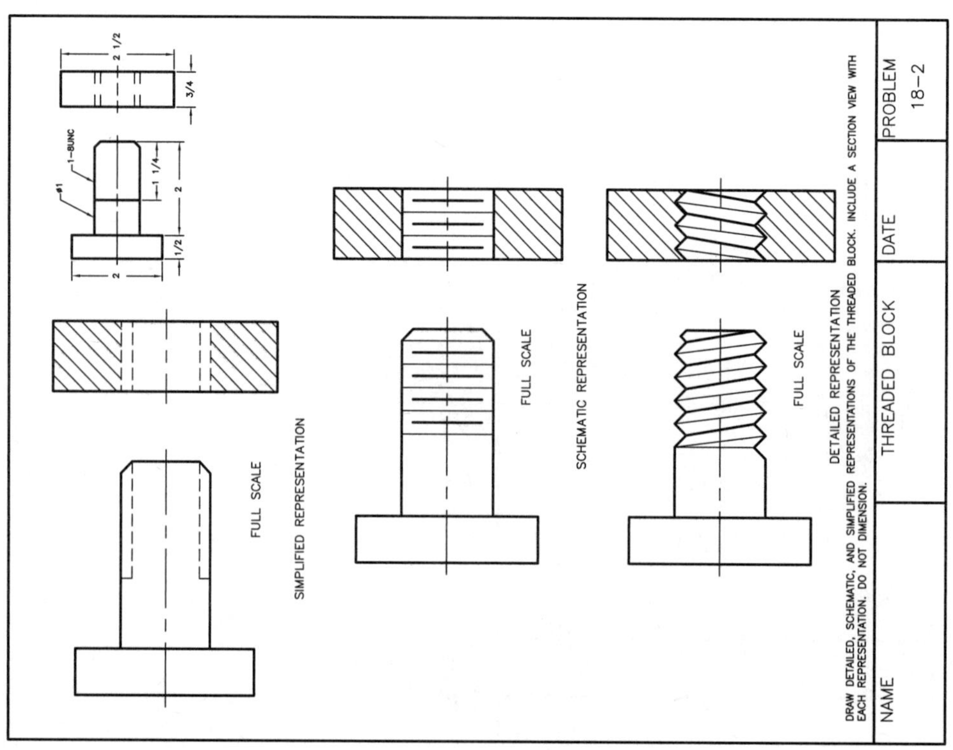

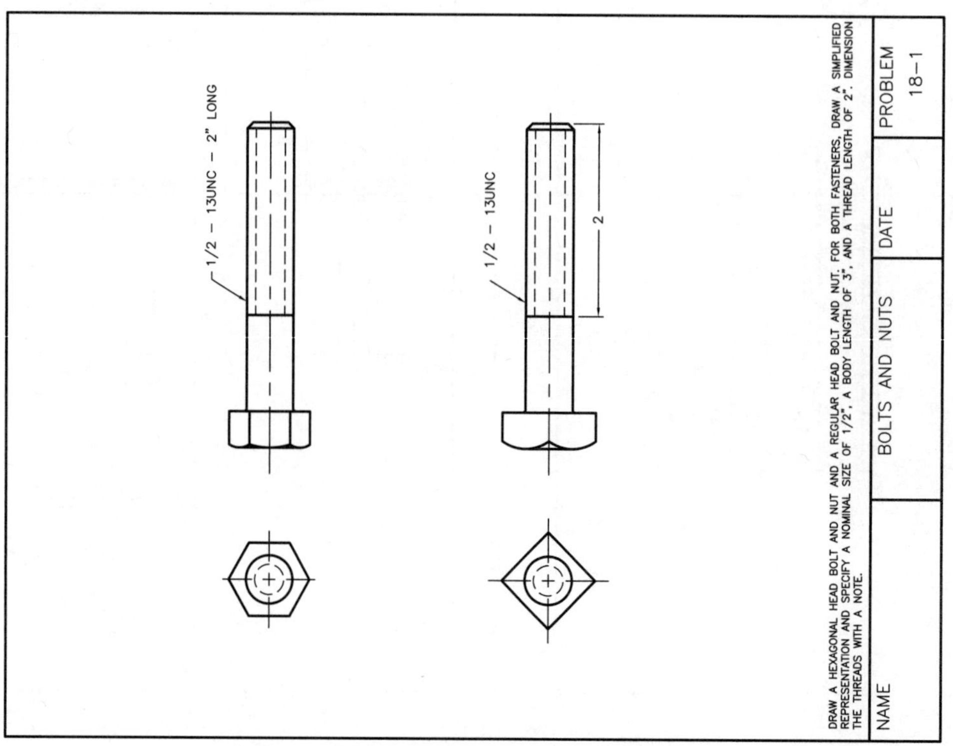

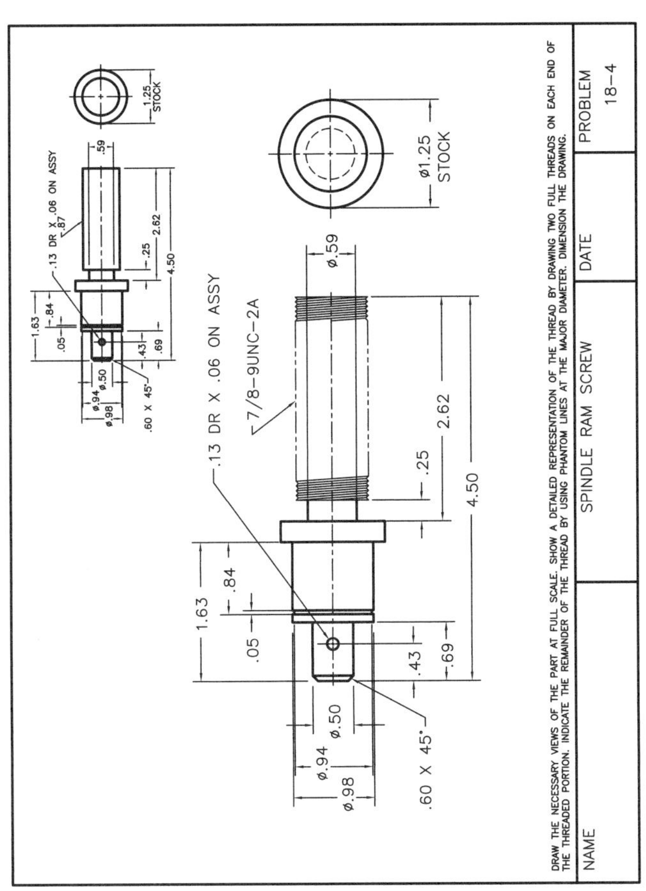

DRAW THE NECESSARY VIEWS OF THE PART AT FULL SCALE. SHOW A DETAILED REPRESENTATION OF THE THREAD BY DRAWING TWO FULL THREADS ON EACH END OF THE THREADED PORTION. INDICATE THE REMAINDER OF THE THREAD BY USING PHANTOM LINES AT THE MAJOR DIAMETER. DIMENSION THE DRAWING.
NAME
SPINDLE RAM SCREW
DATE
PROBLEM
18-4
.13 DR X .06 ON ASSY
7/8-9UNC-2A
1.63
.84
.05
.25
2.62
4.50
.43
.69
.60 X 45°
Ø.94
Ø.98
Ø.50
Ø.59
Ø1.25
STOCK

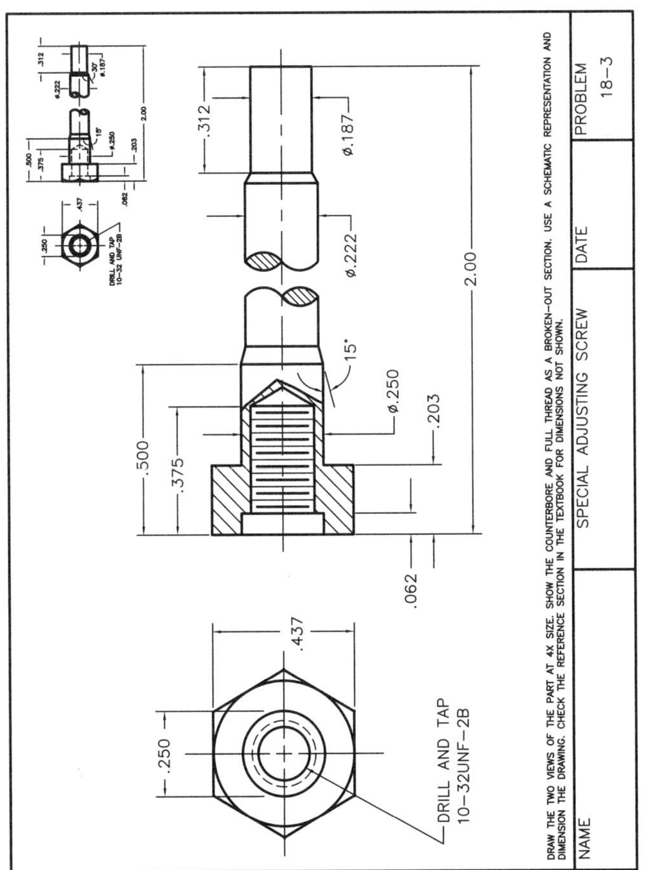

DRAW THE TWO VIEWS OF THE PART AT 4X SIZE. SHOW THE COUNTERBORE AND FULL THREAD AS A BROKEN-OUT SECTION. USE A SCHEMATIC REPRESENTATION AND DIMENSION THE DRAWING. CHECK THE REFERENCE SECTION IN THE TEXTBOOK FOR DIMENSIONS NOT SHOWN.
NAME
SPECIAL ADJUSTING SCREW
DATE
PROBLEM
18-3
.250
DRILL AND TAP
10-32UNF-2B
.437
.500
.375
.062
15°
Ø.250
.203
2.00
Ø.222
.312
Ø.187

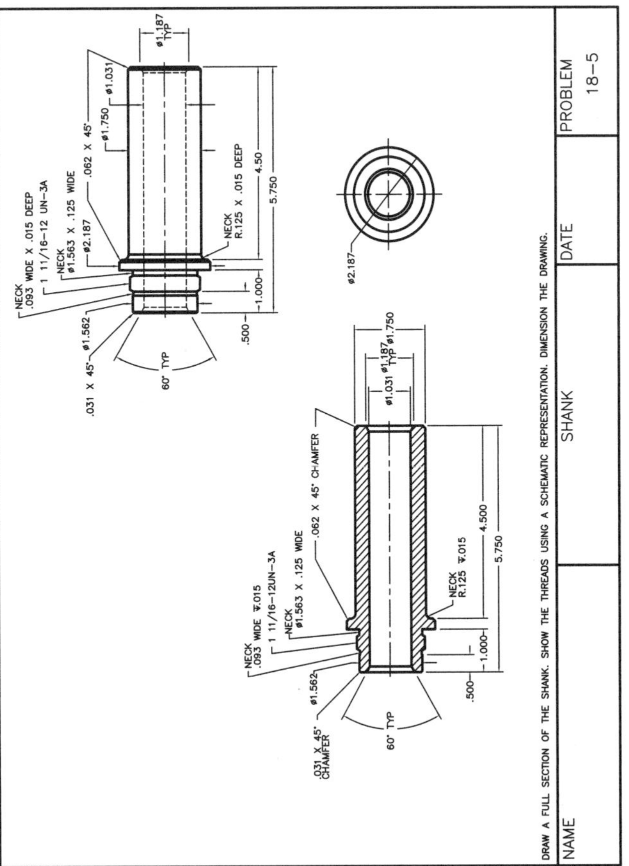

DRAW A FULL SECTION OF THE SHANK. SHOW THE THREADS USING A SCHEMATIC REPRESENTATION. DIMENSION THE DRAWING.
NAME
SHANK
DATE
PROBLEM
18-5

Answers to Chapter 18 Quiz

1. C. pitch
2. D. All of the above.
3. A. Unified
4. C. simplified
5. A. Regular
6. B. key
7. B. form
8. A. Nominal size (or major diameter)
   B. Threads per inch
   C. Form and series
   D. Class of fit
9. A. Metric thread designation
   B. Nominal size
   C. Pitch (fine thread only)
   D. Tolerance designation
10. Refer to the drawings given in the *Solutions to Problems and Activities, Text* section or the *Solutions to Drawing Problems, Text* section for the problem selected from the textbook.

Chapter Quiz

Threads and Fastening Devices

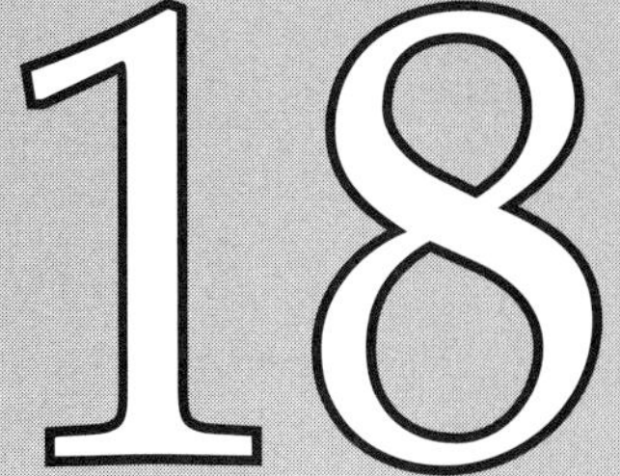

Name ____

Period____________________ Date____________________ Score ____________________

Multiple Choice

Choose the answer that correctly completes the statement. Write the corresponding letter in the space provided.

_______ 1. The diameter of an imaginary cylinder passing through the thread profiles at the point where the widths of the thread and groove are equal is the ______ diameter.
A. major
B. minor
C. pitch
D. root

_______ 2. What thread form is used to transmit motion and power?
A. Square
B. Acme
C. Worm
D. All of the above.

_______ 3. What thread form is used by the United States, Canada, and Great Britain as the standard for fasteners such as bolts, machine screws, and nuts?
A. Unified
B. American National
C. British Whitworth
D. Canadian National

_______ 4. The use of _____ thread symbols is the quickest way to represent threads on a drawing.
A. detailed
B. schematic
C. simplified
D. pictorial

_______ 5. What is the standard pipe thread form used in the plumbing trade?
A. Regular
B. Dryseal
C. Aeronautical
D. Acme

_______ 6. What type of fastener is used to prevent rotation between a shaft and machine part?
A. flat head machine screw
B. key
C. stud
D. bolt

Name ____

________ 7. Thread terms such as Unified, square, and Acme refer to thread ______.
A. class
B. form
C. series
D. pitch

Identification

8. Identify each designation item in the following American Standard thread specification.

________ A.

________ B.

________ C.

________ D.

.3125–24UNF–3A ↧1.00

A B C D

9. Identify each designation item in the following metric thread specification.

________ A.

________ B.

________ C.

________ D.

M8 X 1.0–6h6g

A B C D

Drafting Performance

10. Draw a solution of a problem selected by your instructor from Chapter 18 in your textbook.

Thread Terminology

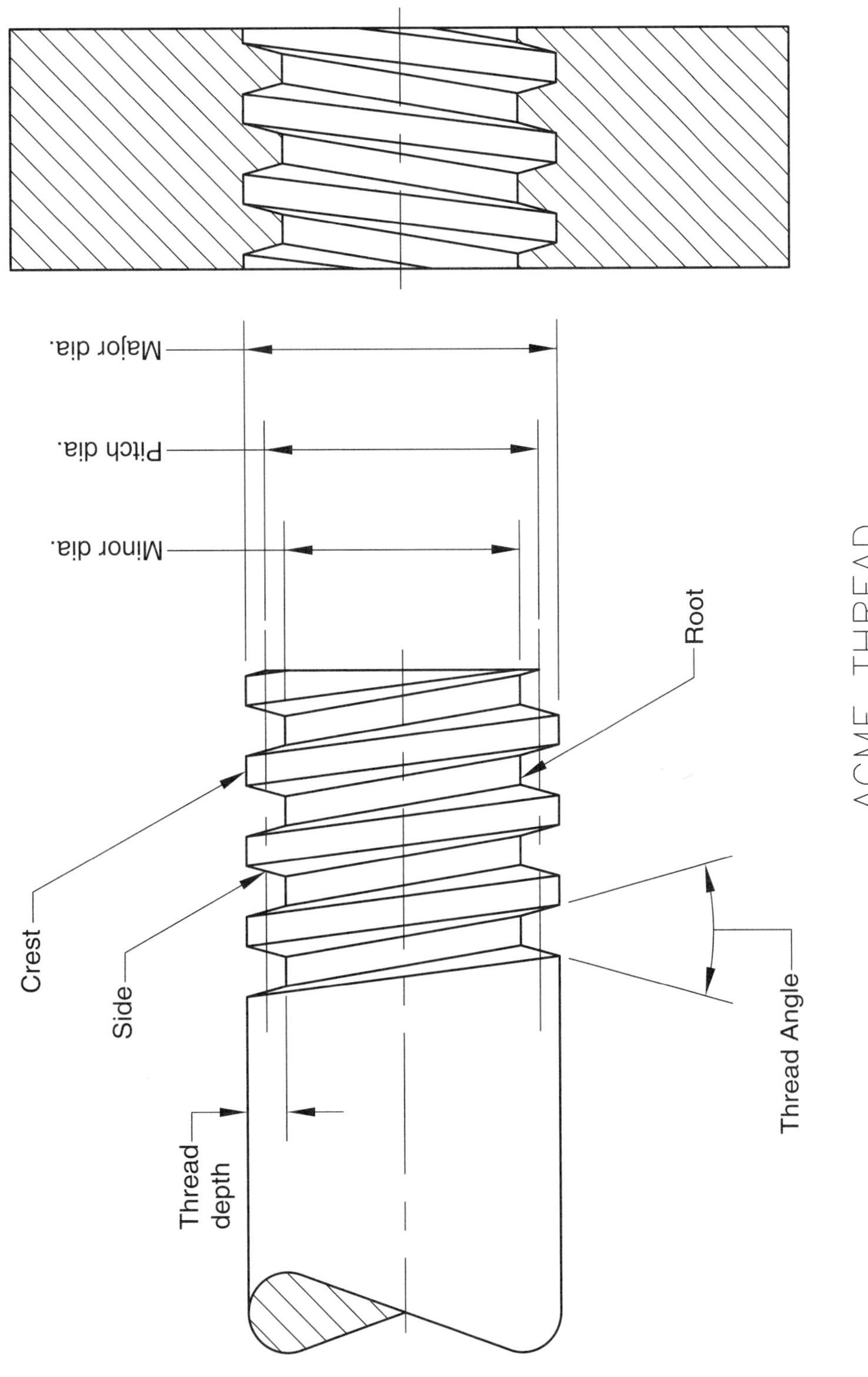

RM 18-1

Thread Forms

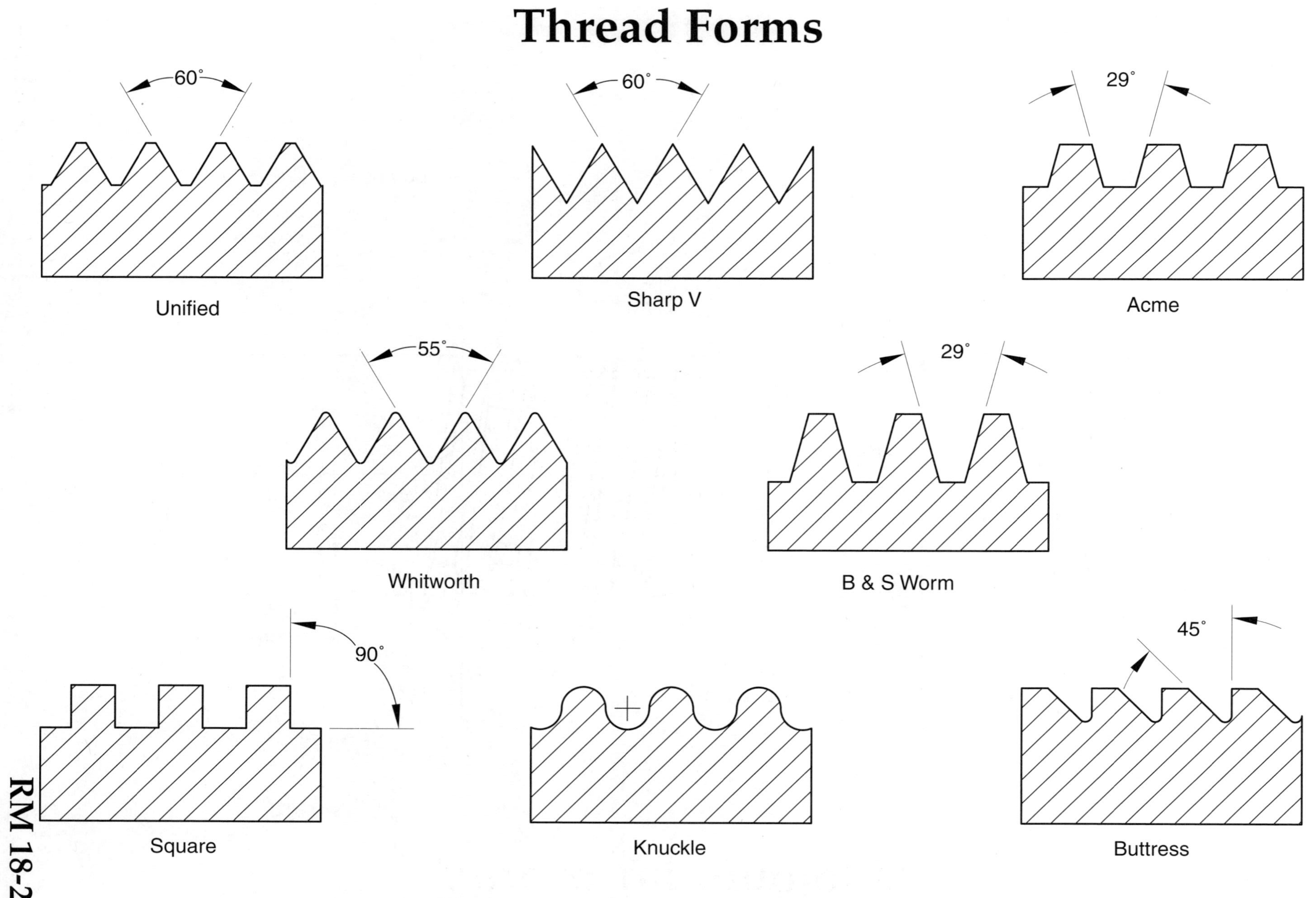

RM 18-2

Thread Note

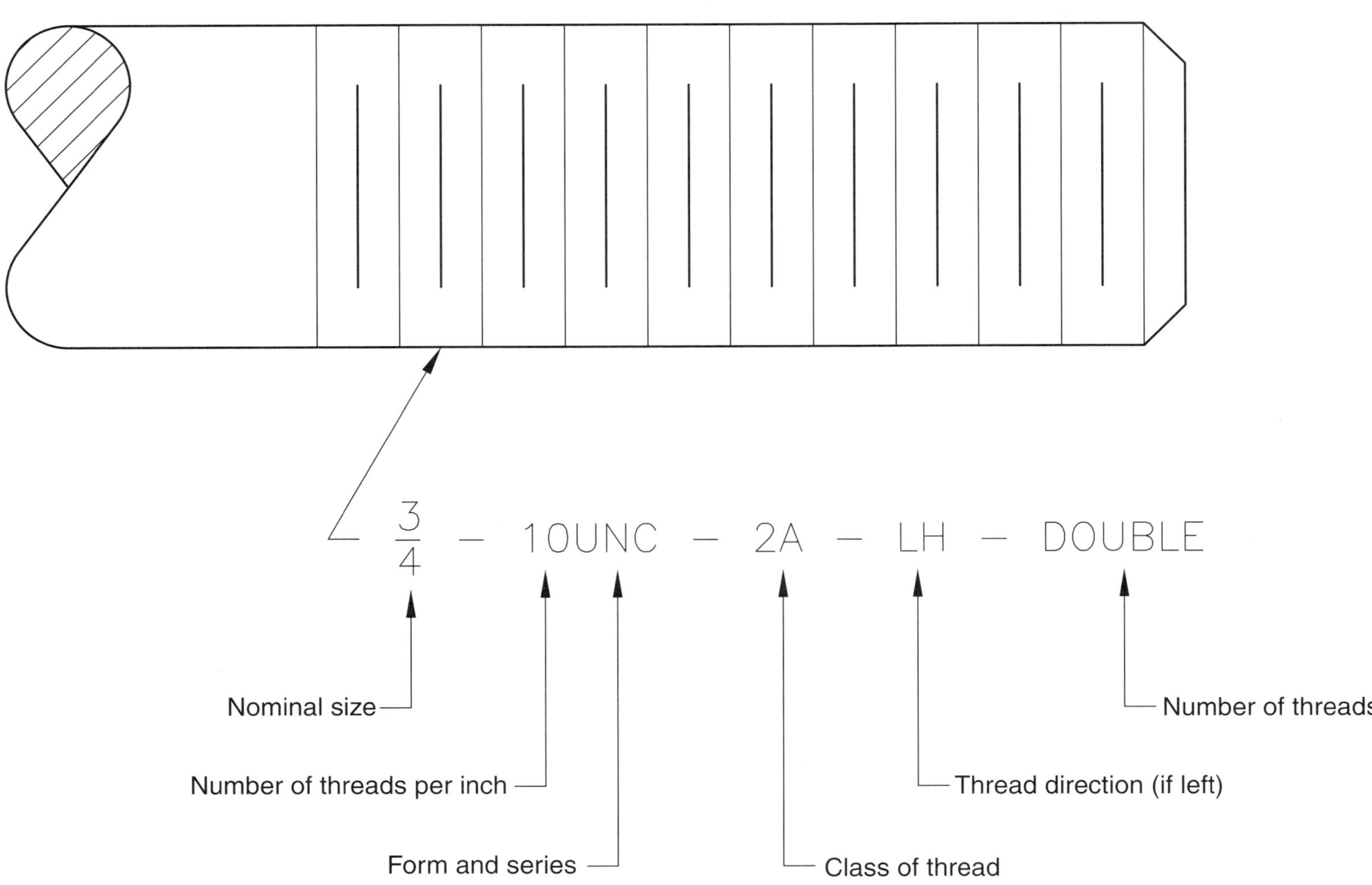

RM 18-3

Procedure Checklist 18

Threads and Fastening Devices

Name ____

Observable Items	Completed		Comments	Instructor Initials
	Yes	No		
1. Draws a detailed thread representation.				
2. Draws a schematic thread representation.				
3. Draws a simplified thread representation.				
4. Draws a pipe thread representation.				
5. Specifies thread notes on drawings.				
6. Draws hexagonal bolt heads and nuts.				
7. Draws cap screws.				
8. Draws machine screws.				
9. Draws setscrews.				
10. Draws rivets.				
11. Draws springs.				
12. Draws keys.				

Instructor Signature ____

Cams, Gears, and Splines

Learning Objectives

After studying this chapter, the student will be able to:

- Explain the purpose of cams.
- Identify and describe the basic types of cams.
- Describe the different types of cam motion.
- Explain how spur gears, bevel gears, and worm gears function.
- List and describe common terms related to gears, bevel gears, and worm gears.
- Explain the purpose of splines.
- Make working drawings of cams and gears.

Instructional Resources

Text: pages 651–680

Review Questions, page 678

Problems and Activities, pages 679–680

Worksheets: pages 163–167

- Worksheet 19-1: *Cam Layout*
- Worksheet 19-2: *Cam Design Problem*
- Worksheet 19-3: *Spur Gear*
- Worksheet 19-4: *Bevel Gear*
- Worksheet 19-5: *Gear Assembly*

Instructor's Resource

Instructional Tasks

Instructional Aids and Assignments

Chapter 19 Quiz

Reproducible Masters

- Reproducible Master 19-1: *Spur Gear Terminology*. A spur gear, pinion, and partial pictorial of each gear are shown with all parts identified.
- Reproducible Master 19-2: *Bevel Gear Terminology*. Two bevel gears in mesh are shown with all parts identified.
- Reproducible Master 19-3: *Worm Gear Terminology*. A worm and worm gear in mesh are shown with all parts identified.

Procedure Checklist

Color Transparencies (Binder/IRCD only)

- Transparency 19-1: *Cam Displacement Diagram and Cam Layout*. The constructions of a cam displacement diagram and cam layout are shown.

Instructional Tasks

1. Identify and define common cam terms.
   - Show a multimedia presentation or film on uses and applications of cams.
2. Explain how to construct cam layouts and displacement diagrams.
   - Use a transparency with a series of overlays to show cam layout and displacement.
3. Define common terms associated with spur gears.
   - Use a model to show the operation of gears.
   - Discuss the function of gears.
4. Calculate gear data using formulas.
   - Discuss gear measurement calculations.
5. Explain how to construct spur gear drawings.
   - Demonstrate the procedure for constructing spur gears. Use an industry example as a visual aid.
6. Define common terms associated with bevel gears.
   - Use a transparency that illustrates the proper use of bevel gear terminology.
7. Explain how to construct bevel gear drawings.
   - Use step-by-step instruction, with related transparencies, to demonstrate the procedure for constructing bevel gears.
8. Define common terms associated with worm gears.
   - Using a handout illustrating a worm gear mesh, instruct students to label the drawing using proper terminology.

9. Explain how to construct worm gear drawings.
   - Show the steps for proper construction of a worm and worm gear assembly.
10. Define common terms associated with splines.
   - Have students compile a list of industry applications for splines.

Instructional Aids and Assignments

1. Show multimedia presentations or films on cams, gears, and splines.
2. Display models and mockups that portray cam and gear motion.
3. Display sequential transparencies that depict cam and gear motion.
4. Display samples of various types of cams, gears, and splines.
5. Assign the drawing problems in the textbook. The number of problems is sufficient to assign a minimum number to all students and to identify problems that may be done for extra credit. Some problems may be used for the performance section of the chapter quiz.

Answers to Review Questions, Text

Page 678

1. A mechanical device that changes uniform rotating motion into reciprocating motion of varying speed.
2. Plate cams, groove cams, and cylindrical cams.
3. displacement
4. Uniform, harmonic, and uniformly accelerated motion.
5. uniform
6. one
7. Dwell represents a period of time when the cam follower displacement remains unchanged.
8. Gears are machine parts used to transmit motion and power by means of successively engaging teeth.
9. involute
10. shafts
11. pinion
12. A. diametral pitch
13. C. 16
14. C. dedendum
15. B. outside
16. D. root
17. C. whole depth
18. B. base
19. simplified conventional
20. A spur gear with its teeth spaced along a straight pitch line.
21. Bevel
22. Worm
23. Splines

Solutions to Problems and Activities, Text

Pages 679–680

Student work should look like the following drawings. The problem number and title are indicated on each problem sheet.

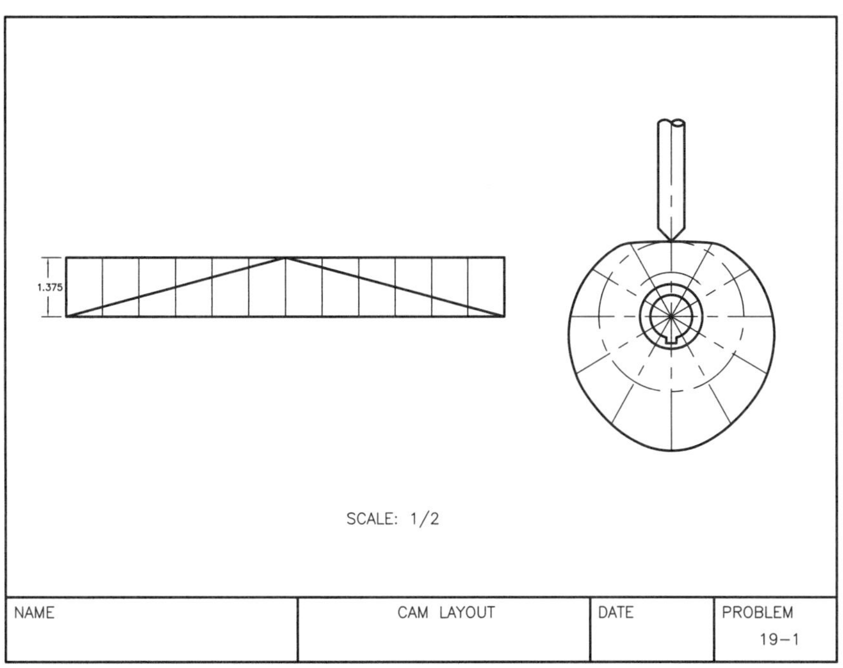

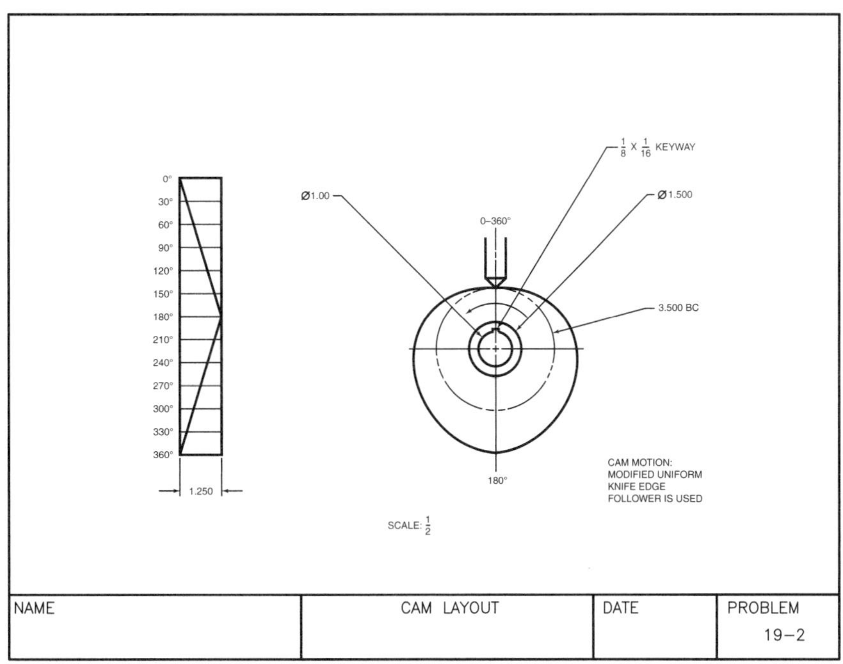

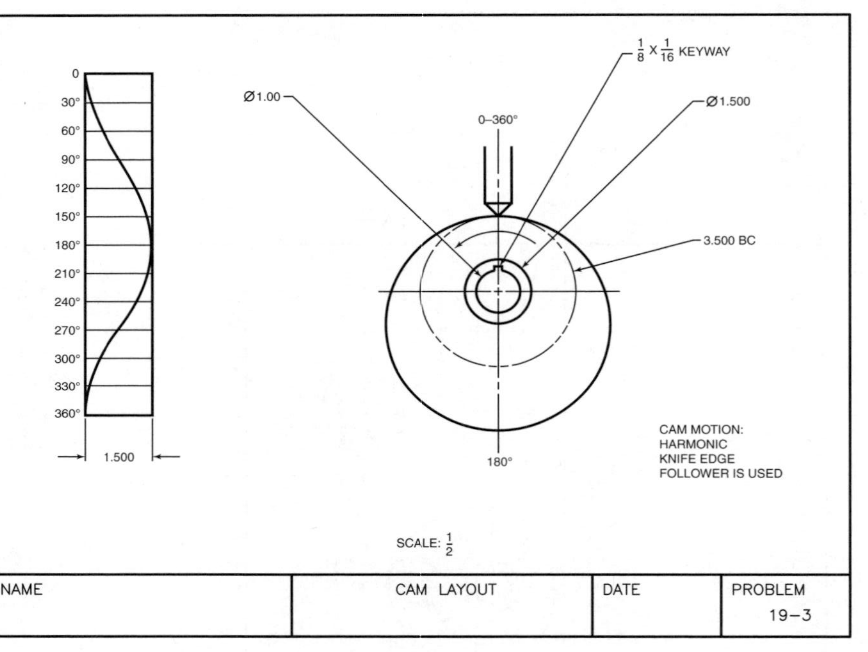

$\frac{1}{8} \times \frac{1}{16}$ KEYWAY
Ø1.00
Ø1.500
0–360°
3.500 BC
180°
CAM MOTION:
HARMONIC
KNIFE EDGE
FOLLOWER IS USED
SCALE: $\frac{1}{2}$
0
30°
60°
90°
120°
150°
180°
210°
240°
270°
300°
330°
360°
1.500
NAME
CAM LAYOUT
DATE
PROBLEM
19–3

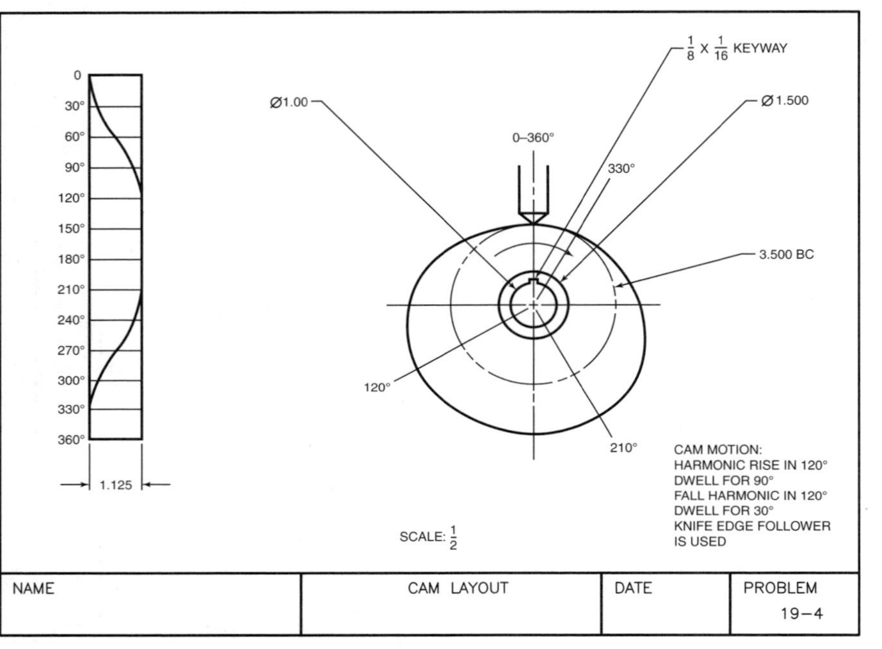

$\frac{1}{8} \times \frac{1}{16}$ KEYWAY
Ø1.00
Ø1.500
0–360°
330°
3.500 BC
120°
210°
CAM MOTION:
HARMONIC RISE IN 120°
DWELL FOR 90°
FALL HARMONIC IN 120°
DWELL FOR 30°
KNIFE EDGE FOLLOWER
IS USED
SCALE: $\frac{1}{2}$
0
30°
60°
90°
120°
150°
180°
210°
240°
270°
300°
330°
360°
1.125
NAME
CAM LAYOUT
DATE
PROBLEM
19–4

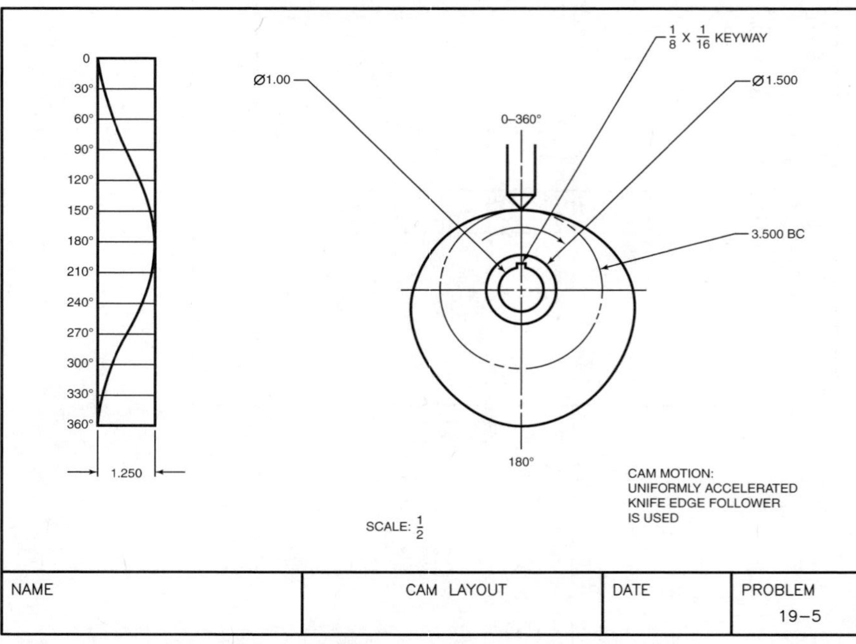

$\frac{1}{8} \times \frac{1}{16}$ KEYWAY
Ø1.00
Ø1.500
0–360°
3.500 BC
180°
CAM MOTION:
UNIFORMLY ACCELERATED
KNIFE EDGE FOLLOWER
IS USED
SCALE: $\frac{1}{2}$
0
30°
60°
90°
120°
150°
180°
210°
240°
270°
300°
330°
360°
1.250
NAME
CAM LAYOUT
DATE
PROBLEM
19–5

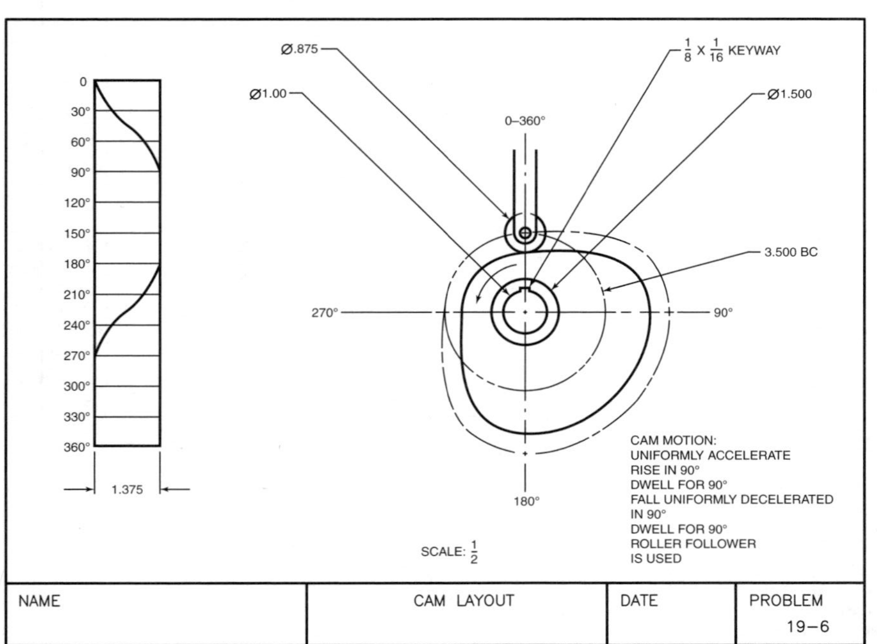

Ø.875
$\frac{1}{8} \times \frac{1}{16}$ KEYWAY
Ø1.00
Ø1.500
0–360°
3.500 BC
270°
90°
180°
CAM MOTION:
UNIFORMLY ACCELERATE
RISE IN 90°
DWELL FOR 90°
FALL UNIFORMLY DECELERATED
IN 90°
DWELL FOR 90°
ROLLER FOLLOWER
IS USED
SCALE: $\frac{1}{2}$
0
30°
60°
90°
120°
150°
180°
210°
240°
270°
300°
330°
360°
1.375
NAME
CAM LAYOUT
DATE
PROBLEM
19–6

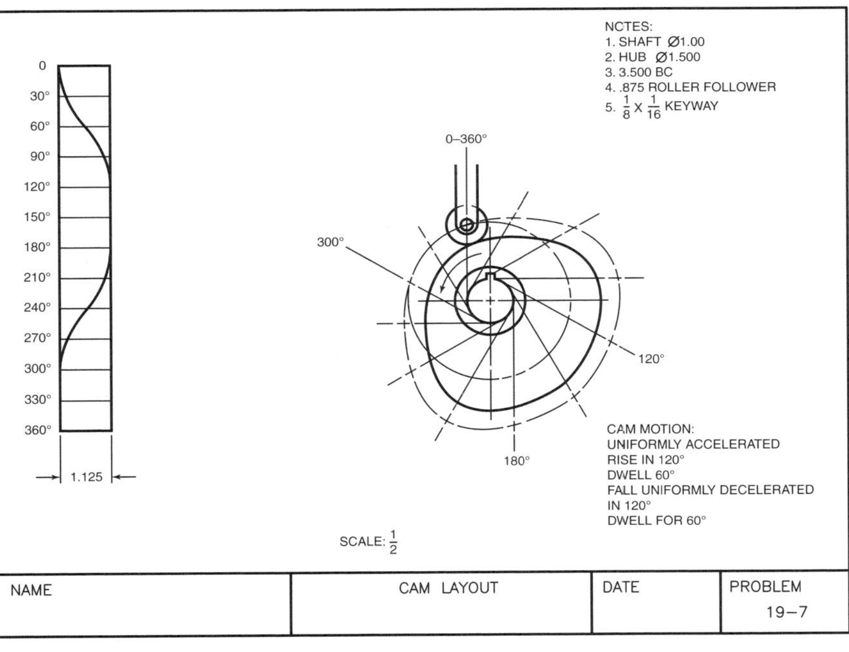

NCTES:
1. SHAFT Ø1.00
2. HUB Ø1.500
3. 3.500 BC
4. .875 ROLLER FOLLOWER
5. 1/8 X 1/16 KEYWAY
0
30°
60°
90°
120°
150°
180°
210°
240°
270°
300°
330°
360°
1.125
0–360°
300°
120°
180°
CAM MOTION:
UNIFORMLY ACCELERATED
RISE IN 120°
DWELL 60°
FALL UNIFORMLY DECELERATED
IN 120°
DWELL FOR 60°
SCALE: 1/2
NAME
CAM LAYOUT
DATE
PROBLEM
19–7

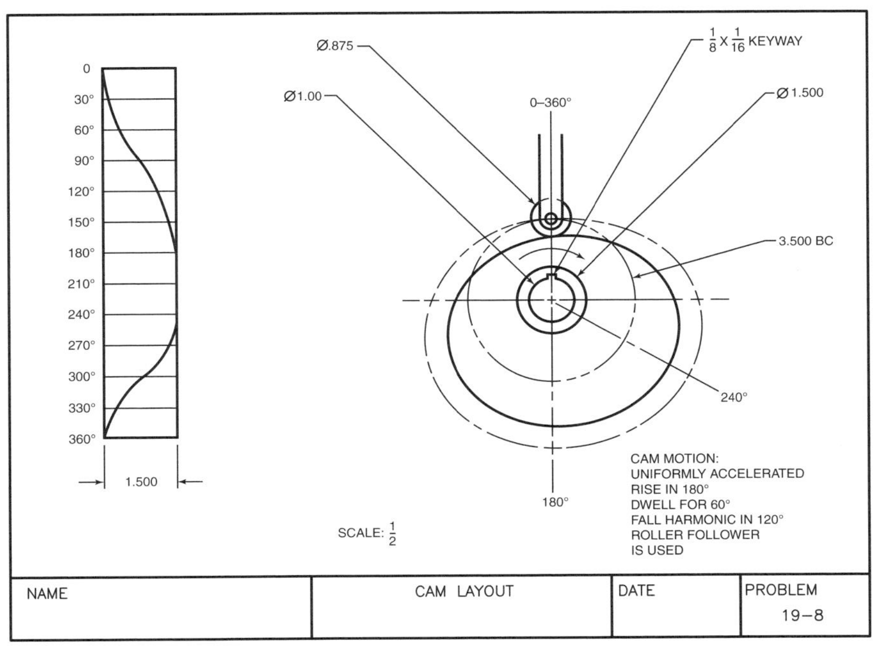

Ø.875
1/8 X 1/16 KEYWAY
Ø1.00
0–360°
Ø1.500
0
30°
60°
90°
120°
150°
180°
210°
240°
270°
300°
330°
360°
3.500 BC
240°
1.500
180°
CAM MOTION:
UNIFORMLY ACCELERATED
RISE IN 180°
DWELL FOR 60°
FALL HARMONIC IN 120°
ROLLER FOLLOWER
IS USED
SCALE: 1/2
NAME
CAM LAYOUT
DATE
PROBLEM
19–8

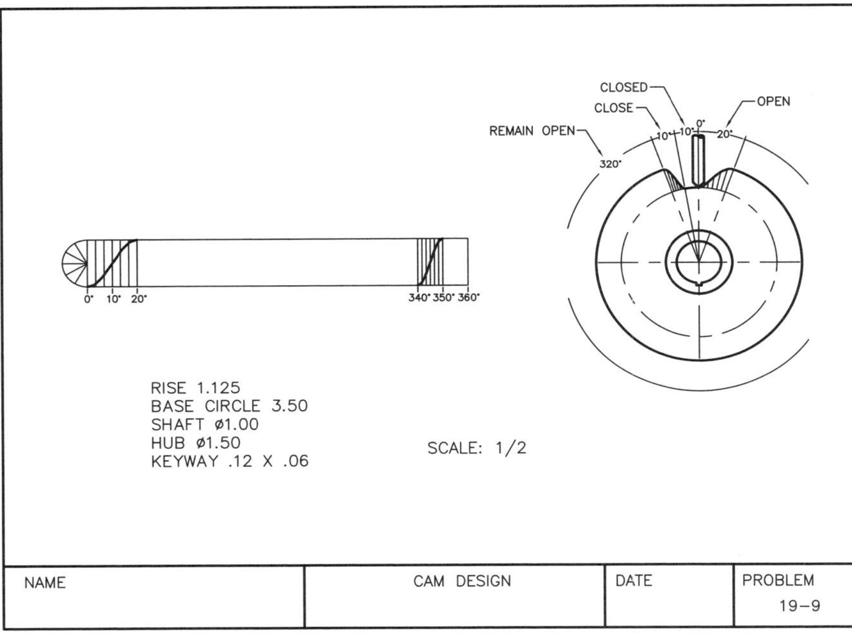

CLOSED
CLOSE
OPEN
REMAIN OPEN
320°
10°
10°
0°
20°
0° 10° 20°
340° 350° 360°
RISE 1.125
BASE CIRCLE 3.50
SHAFT Ø1.00
HUB Ø1.50
KEYWAY .12 X .06
SCALE: 1/2
NAME
CAM DESIGN
DATE
PROBLEM
19–9

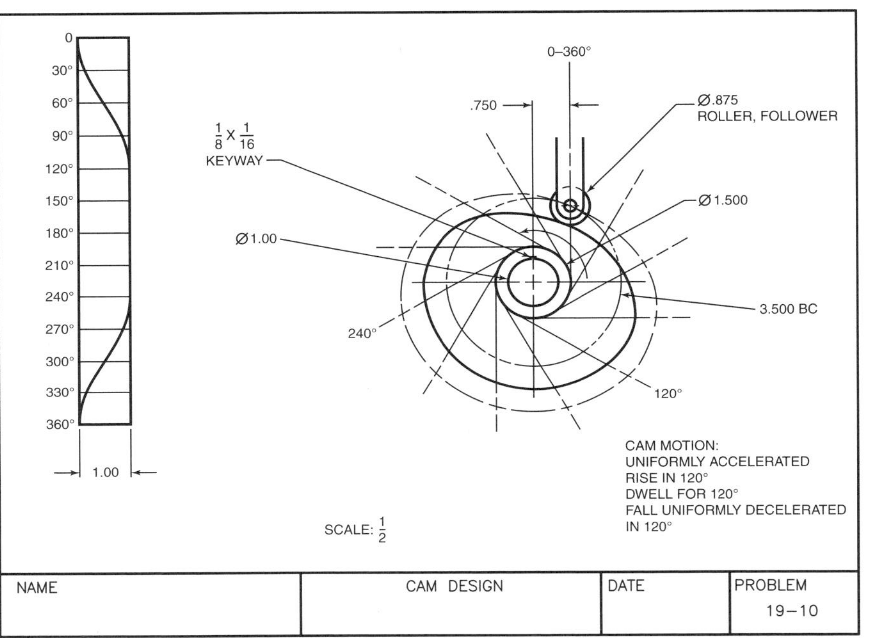

0
30°
60°
90°
120°
150°
180°
210°
240°
270°
300°
330°
360°
0–360°
.750
Ø.875
ROLLER, FOLLOWER
1/8 X 1/16
KEYWAY
Ø1.500
Ø1.00
3.500 BC
240°
120°
1.00
CAM MOTION:
UNIFORMLY ACCELERATED
RISE IN 120°
DWELL FOR 120°
FALL UNIFORMLY DECELERATED
IN 120°
SCALE: 1/2
NAME
CAM DESIGN
DATE
PROBLEM
19–10

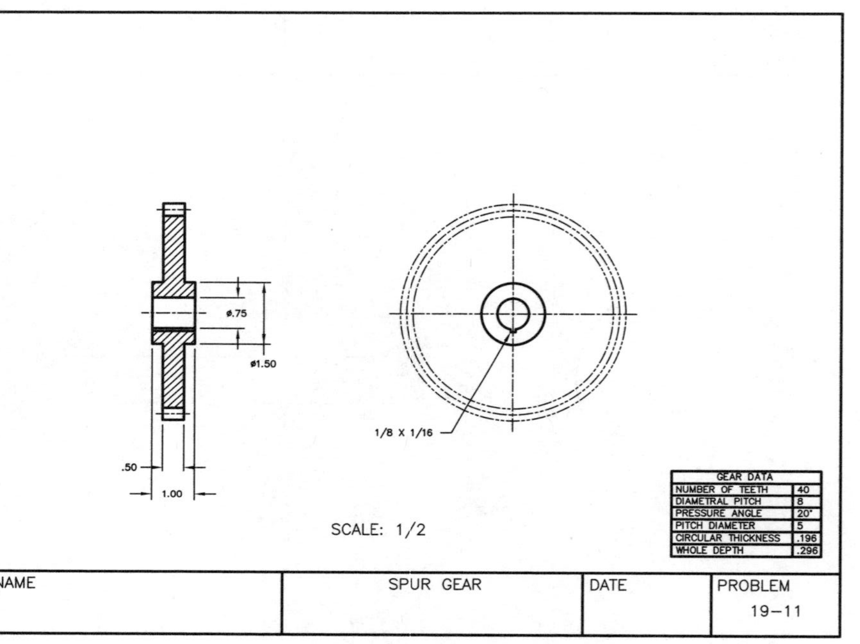

GEAR DATA	
NUMBER OF TEETH	40
DIAMETRAL PITCH	8
PRESSURE ANGLE	20°
PITCH DIAMETER	5
CIRCULAR THICKNESS	.196
WHOLE DEPTH	.296

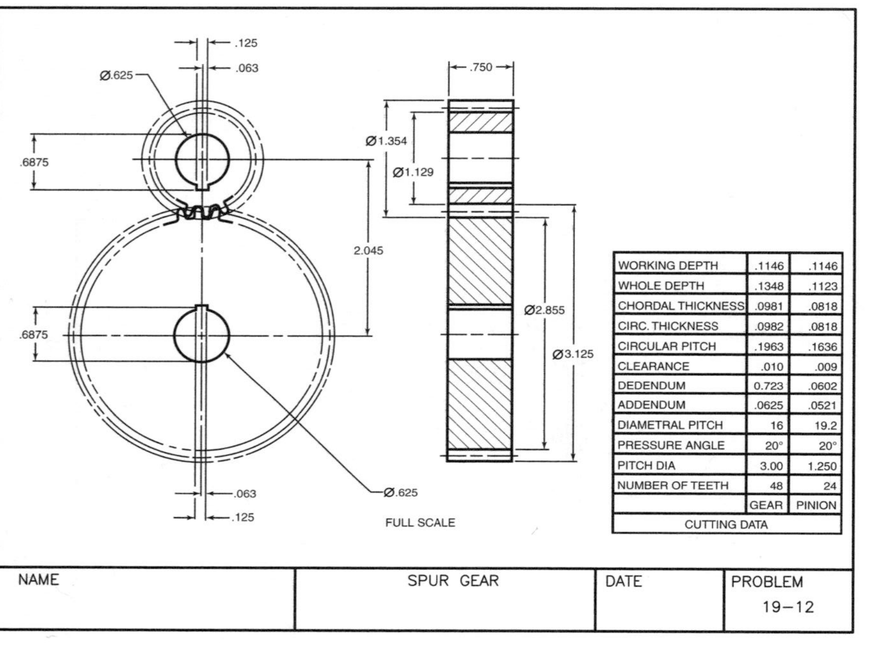

	GEAR	PINION
WORKING DEPTH	.1146	.1146
WHOLE DEPTH	.1348	.1123
CHORDAL THICKNESS	.0981	.0818
CIRC. THICKNESS	.0982	.0818
CIRCULAR PITCH	.1963	.1636
CLEARANCE	.010	.009
DEDENDUM	0.723	.0602
ADDENDUM	.0625	.0521
DIAMETRAL PITCH	16	19.2
PRESSURE ANGLE	20°	20°
PITCH DIA	3.00	1.250
NUMBER OF TEETH	48	24

CUTTING DATA

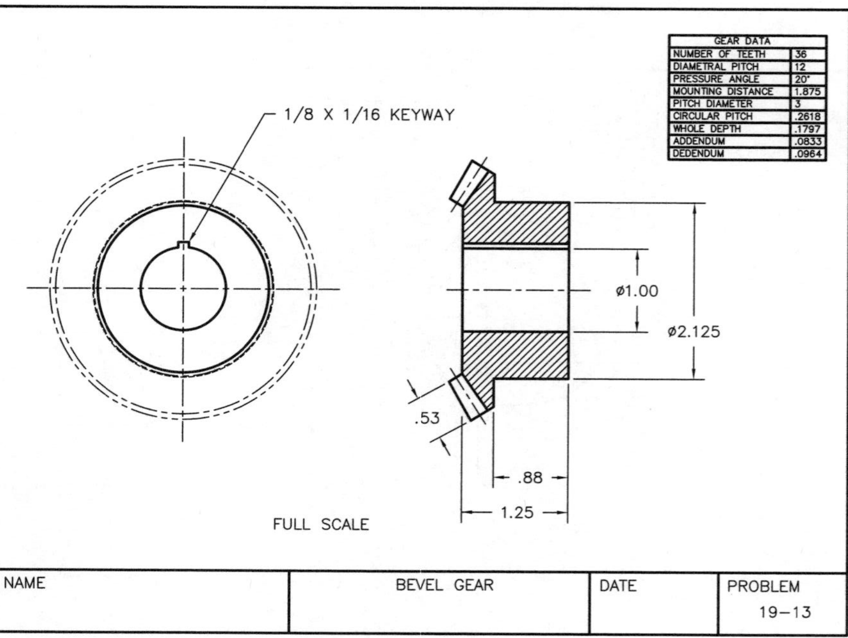

GEAR DATA	
NUMBER OF TEETH	36
DIAMETRAL PITCH	12
PRESSURE ANGLE	20°
MOUNTING DISTANCE	1.875
PITCH DIAMETER	3
CIRCULAR PITCH	.2618
WHOLE DEPTH	.1797
ADDENDUM	.0833
DEDENDUM	.0964

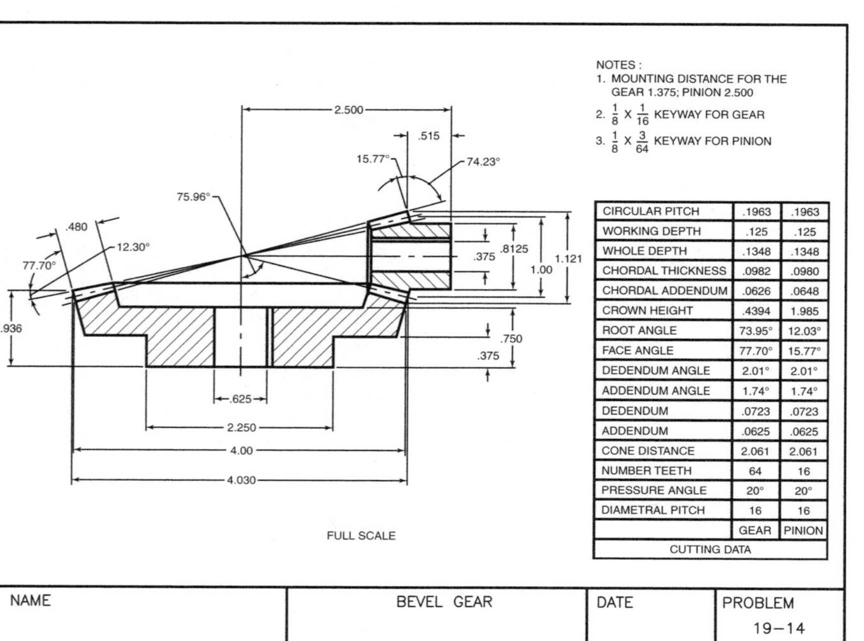

	GEAR	PINION
CIRCULAR PITCH	.1963	.1963
WORKING DEPTH	.125	.125
WHOLE DEPTH	.1348	.1348
CHORDAL THICKNESS	.0982	.0980
CHORDAL ADDENDUM	.0626	.0648
CROWN HEIGHT	.4394	1.985
ROOT ANGLE	73.95°	12.03°
FACE ANGLE	77.70°	15.77°
DEDENDUM ANGLE	2.01°	2.01°
ADDENDUM ANGLE	1.74°	1.74°
DEDENDUM	.0723	.0723
ADDENDUM	.0625	.0625
CONE DISTANCE	2.061	2.061
NUMBER TEETH	64	16
PRESSURE ANGLE	20°	20°
DIAMETRAL PITCH	16	16

CUTTING DATA

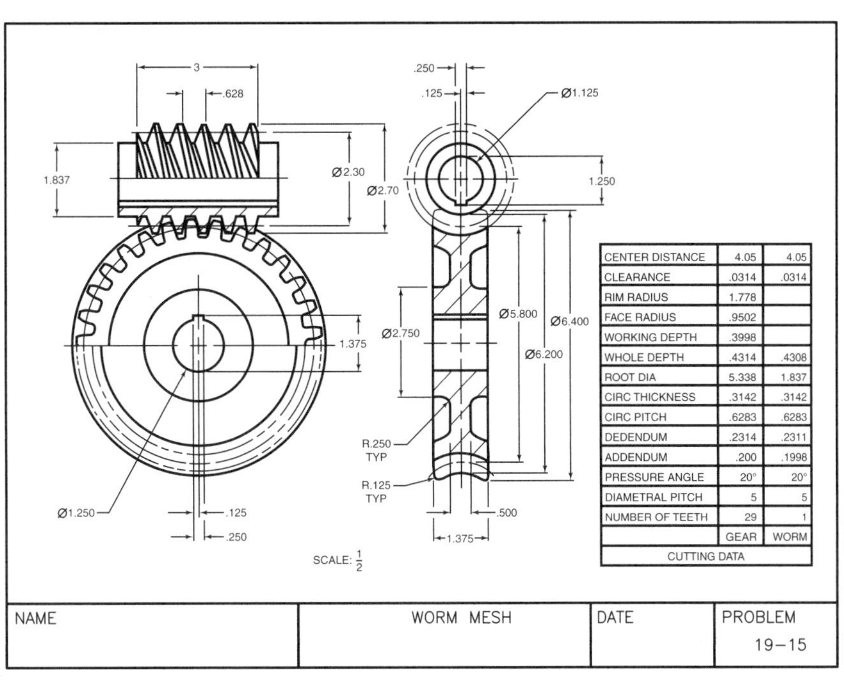

CENTER DISTANCE	4.05	4.05
CLEARANCE	.0314	.0314
RIM RADIUS	1.778	
FACE RADIUS	.9502	
WORKING DEPTH	.3998	
WHOLE DEPTH	.4314	.4308
ROOT DIA	5.338	1.837
CIRC THICKNESS	.3142	.3142
CIRC PITCH	.6283	.6283
DEDENDUM	.2314	.2311
ADDENDUM	.200	.1998
PRESSURE ANGLE	20°	20°
DIAMETRAL PITCH	5	5
NUMBER OF TEETH	29	1
	GEAR	WORM
CUTTING DATA		

ANSWER TO BE PROVIDED BY INSTRUCTOR.

NAME	GEAR ASSEMBLY DESIGN	DATE	PROBLEM 19–16

Solutions to Worksheets

Pages 163–167

Student work should look like the following drawings. The problem number and title are indicated on each problem sheet.

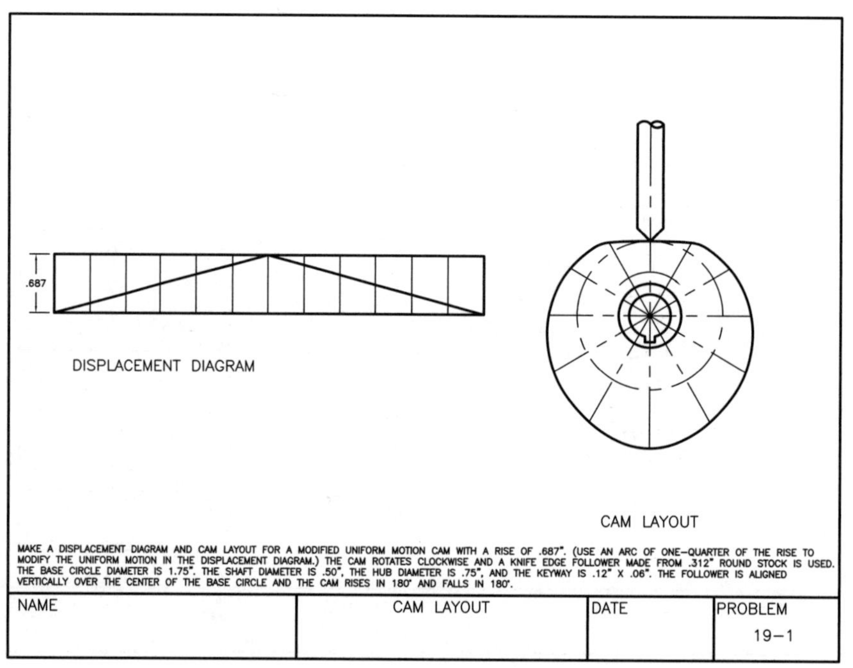

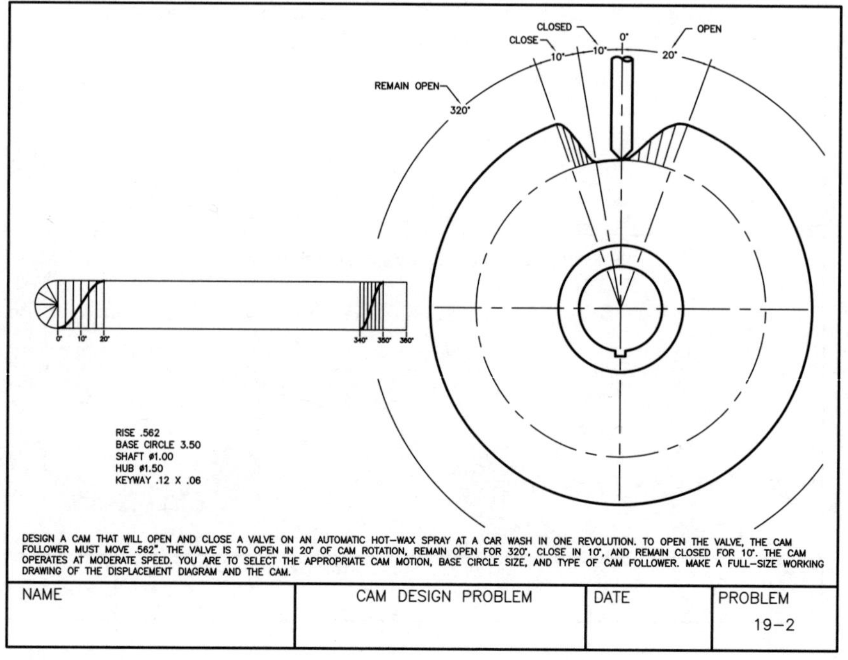

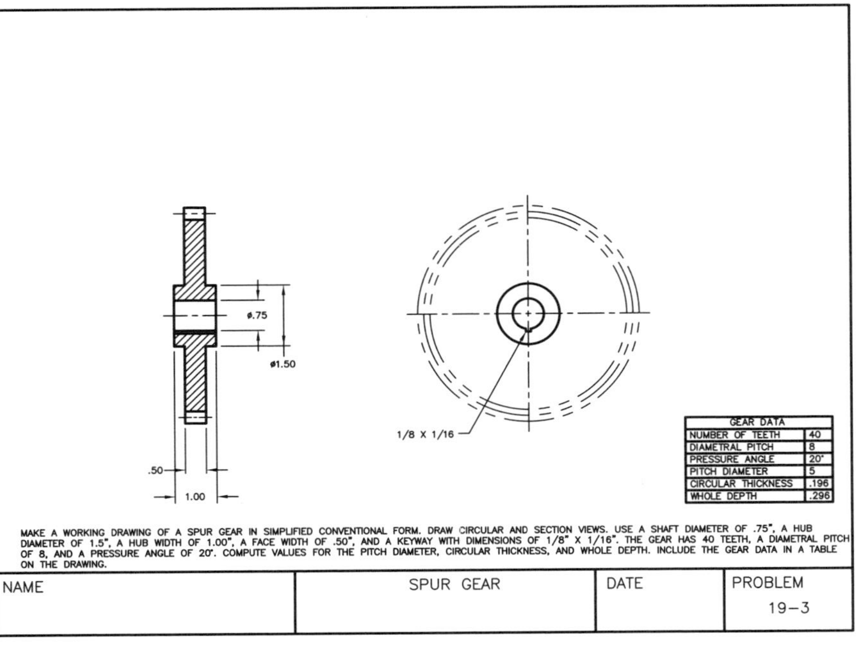
.50
1.00
ø.75
ø1.50
1/8 X 1/16
GEAR DATA
NUMBER OF TEETH 40
DIAMETRAL PITCH 8
PRESSURE ANGLE 20°
PITCH DIAMETER 5
CIRCULAR THICKNESS .196
WHOLE DEPTH .296
MAKE A WORKING DRAWING OF A SPUR GEAR IN SIMPLIFIED CONVENTIONAL FORM. DRAW CIRCULAR AND SECTION VIEWS. USE A SHAFT DIAMETER OF .75", A HUB DIAMETER OF 1.5", A HUB WIDTH OF 1.00", A FACE WIDTH OF .50", AND A KEYWAY WITH DIMENSIONS OF 1/8" X 1/16". THE GEAR HAS 40 TEETH, A DIAMETRAL PITCH OF 8, AND A PRESSURE ANGLE OF 20°. COMPUTE VALUES FOR THE PITCH DIAMETER, CIRCULAR THICKNESS, AND WHOLE DEPTH. INCLUDE THE GEAR DATA IN A TABLE ON THE DRAWING.
NAME
SPUR GEAR
DATE
PROBLEM
19–3

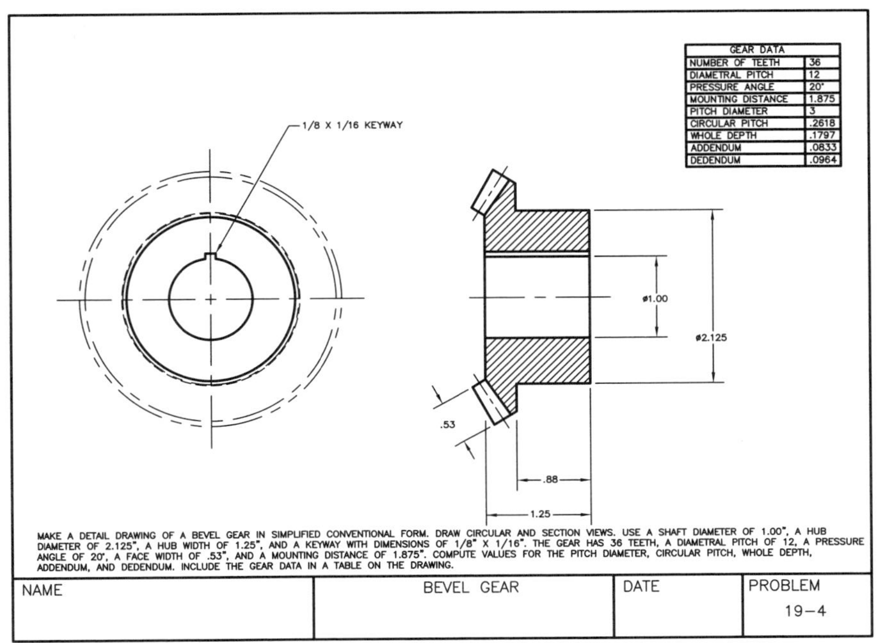
1/8 X 1/16 KEYWAY
GEAR DATA
NUMBER OF TEETH 36
DIAMETRAL PITCH 12
PRESSURE ANGLE 20°
MOUNTING DISTANCE 1.875
PITCH DIAMETER 3
CIRCULAR PITCH .2618
WHOLE DEPTH .1797
ADDENDUM .0833
DEDENDUM .0964
ø1.00
ø2.125
.53
.88
1.25
MAKE A DETAIL DRAWING OF A BEVEL GEAR IN SIMPLIFIED CONVENTIONAL FORM. DRAW CIRCULAR AND SECTION VIEWS. USE A SHAFT DIAMETER OF 1.00", A HUB DIAMETER OF 2.125", A HUB WIDTH OF 1.25", AND A KEYWAY WITH DIMENSIONS OF 1/8" X 1/16". THE GEAR HAS 36 TEETH, A DIAMETRAL PITCH OF 12, A PRESSURE ANGLE OF 20°, A FACE WIDTH OF .53", AND A MOUNTING DISTANCE OF 1.875". COMPUTE VALUES FOR THE PITCH DIAMETER, CIRCULAR PITCH, WHOLE DEPTH, ADDENDUM, AND DEDENDUM. INCLUDE THE GEAR DATA IN A TABLE ON THE DRAWING.
NAME
BEVEL GEAR
DATE
PROBLEM
19–4

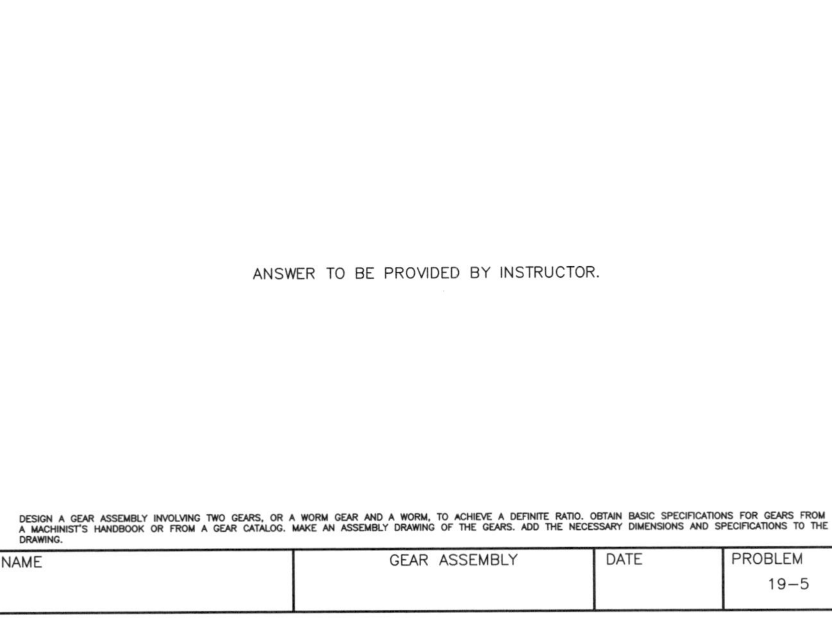
ANSWER TO BE PROVIDED BY INSTRUCTOR.
DESIGN A GEAR ASSEMBLY INVOLVING TWO GEARS, OR A WORM GEAR AND A WORM, TO ACHIEVE A DEFINITE RATIO. OBTAIN BASIC SPECIFICATIONS FOR GEARS FROM A MACHINIST'S HANDBOOK OR FROM A GEAR CATALOG. MAKE AN ASSEMBLY DRAWING OF THE GEARS. ADD THE NECESSARY DIMENSIONS AND SPECIFICATIONS TO THE DRAWING.
NAME
GEAR ASSEMBLY
DATE
PROBLEM
19–5

Answers to Chapter 19 Quiz

1. C. Cam
2. B. Displacement
3. D. Construct a displacement diagram.
4. A. Spur
5. B. pinion
6. C. spline
7. D. Uniformly accelerated motion.
8. A. diametral pitch
9. Refer to the drawings given in the *Solutions to Problems and Activities, Text* section for the problem selected from the textbook.

Chapter Quiz 19

Cams, Gears, and Splines

Name ____________________

Period ____________ Date ____________ Score ____________

Multiple Choice

Choose the answer that correctly completes the statement. Write the corresponding letter in the space provided.

_____ 1. What is the device that can be used to change the motion of a uniformly rotating shaft into a reciprocating motion of varying speed?
A. Gear
B. Spline
C. Cam
D. Key

_____ 2. _____ refers to the distance a cam follower moves in relation to the rotation of the cam.
A. Clearance
B. Displacement
C. Velocity
D. Dwell

_____ 3. What is generally the first step in designing a cam?
A. Draw a profile of the cam.
B. Draw a profile of the cam follower.
C. Determine the size of the cam.
D. Construct a displacement diagram.

_____ 4. _____ gears are used to transmit rotary motion between two or more parallel shafts.
A. Spur
B. Bevel
C. Miter
D. Worm

_____ 5. In mating gears, the smaller gear is referred to as the _____.
A. worm
B. pinion
C. rack
D. follower

_____ 6. The purpose of a _____ is to prevent rotation between a shaft and its related member.
A. cam
B. gear
C. spline
D. All of the above.

_______ 7. If you were to design a cam to operate at high speed, which of the following motions would you select?
A. Uniform motion.
B. Modified uniform motion.
C. Harmonic motion.
D. Uniformly accelerated motion.

_______ 8. The number of teeth in a spur or bevel gear per inch of pitch diameter is referred to as the _____.
A. diametral pitch
B. clearance
C. circular pitch
D. circular thickness

Drafting Performance

9. Draw a solution of a problem selected by your instructor from Chapter 19 in your textbook.

Spur Gear Terminology

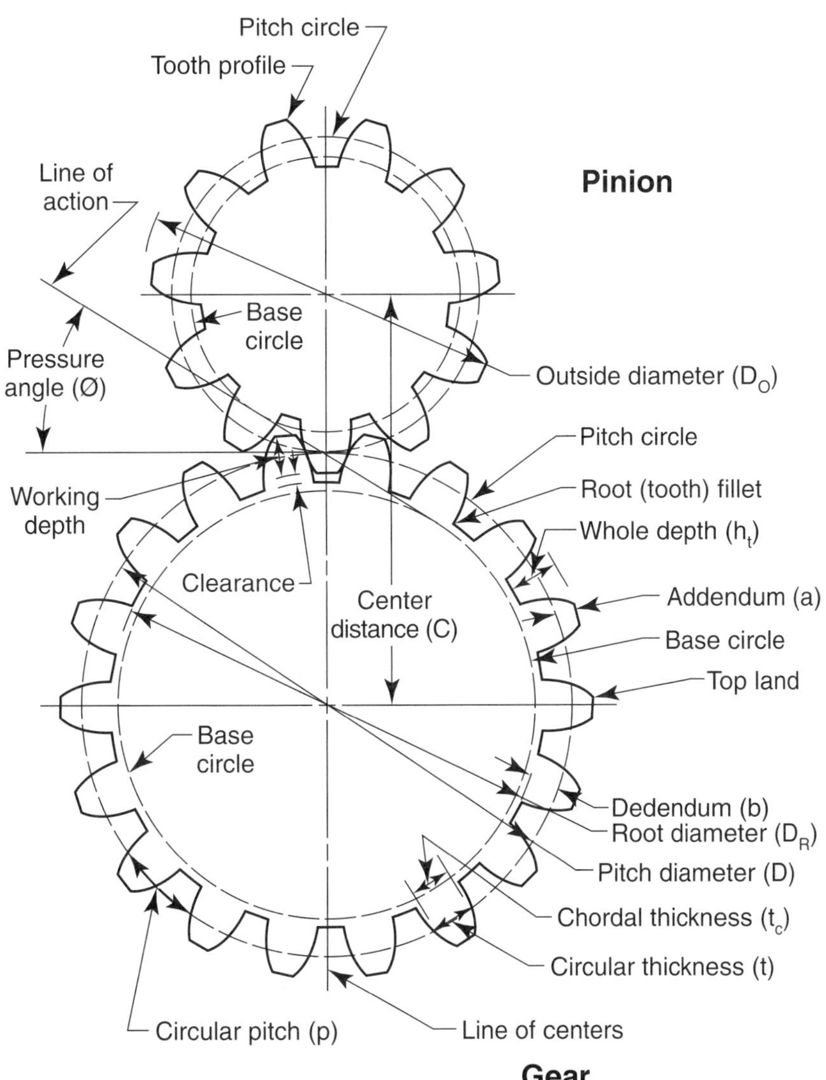

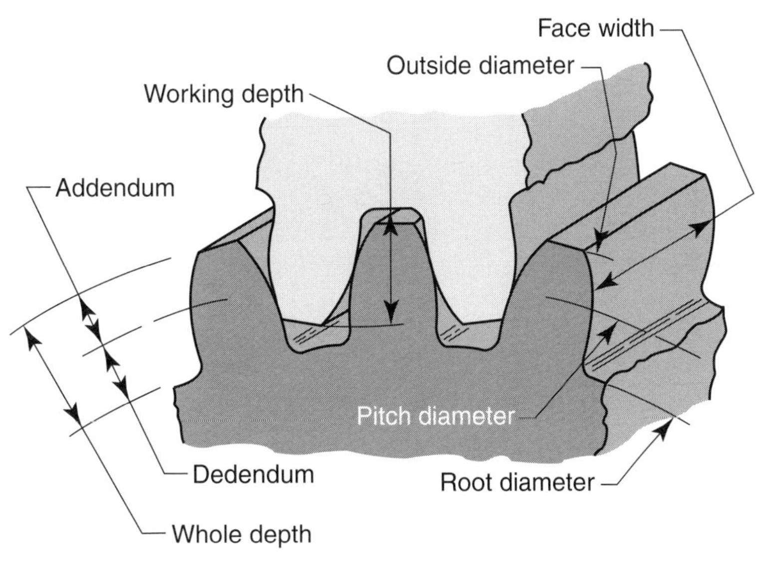

RM 19-1

Bevel Gear Terminology

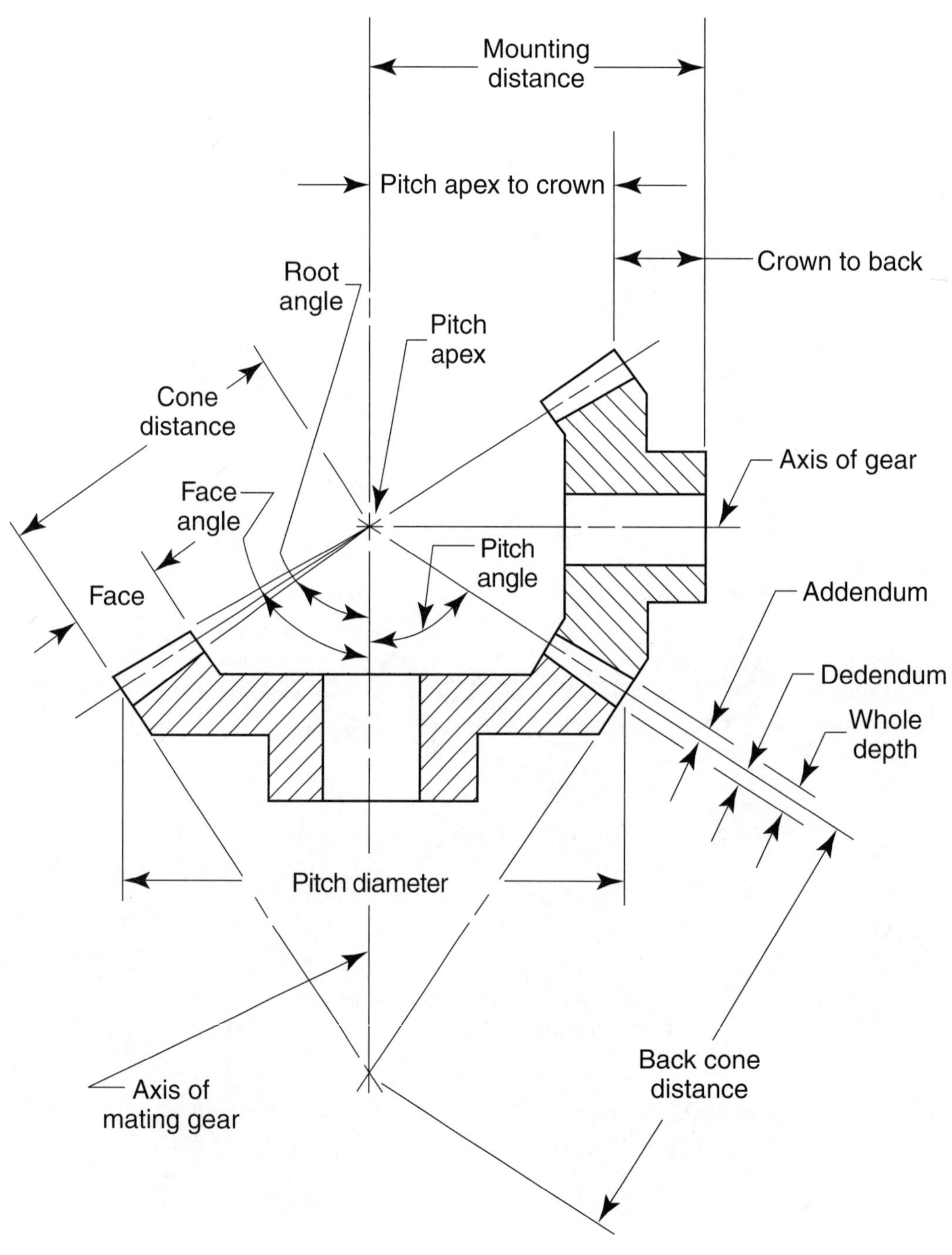

RM 19-2

Worm Gear Terminology

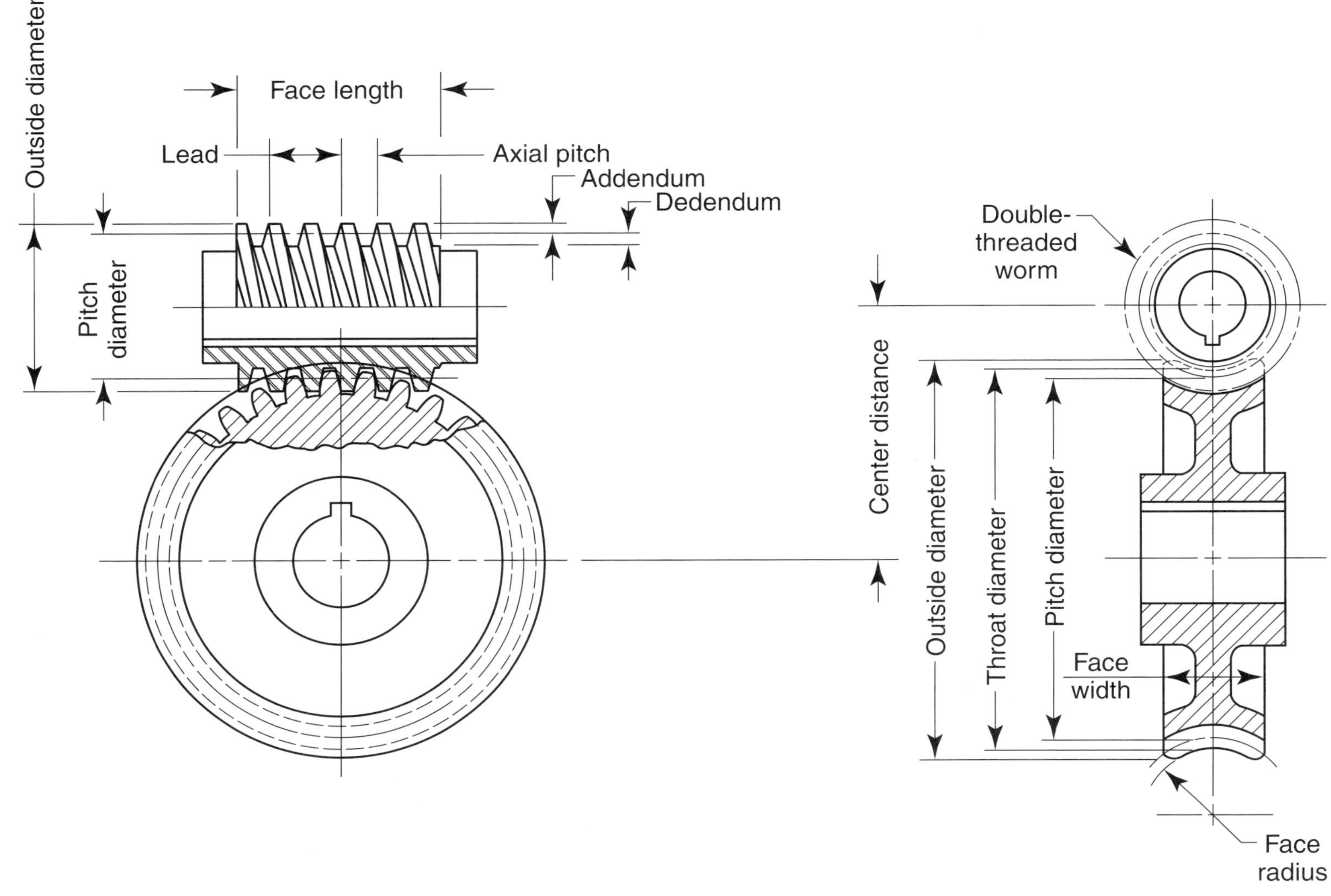

RM 19-3

Procedure Checklist

Cams, Gears, and Splines

Name ____________________

Observable Items	Completed		Comments	Instructor Initials
	Yes	No		
1. Draws a cam displacement diagram.				
2. Draws a cam layout.				
3. Draws a spur gear.				
4. Draws a bevel gear.				
5. Draws a worm gear.				
6. Draws a spline.				

Instructor Signature ____________________

Drawing Management

Learning Objectives

After studying this chapter, the student will be able to:

- List and describe the traditional ways used to reproduce drawings.
- Explain how drawings are prepared for microfilm storage.
- Describe the tools used in the reproduction and storage of CAD drawings.
- Explain the common distribution methods used for transferring CAD drawing files.

Instructional Resources

Text: pages 681–690

Review Questions, page 690

Problems and Activities, page 690

Instructor's Resource

Instructional Tasks

Instructional Aids and Assignments

Chapter 20 Quiz

Procedure Checklist

Color Transparencies (Binder/IRCD only)

- Transparency 20-1: *Reproduction Prints.* The common types of prints made from original drawings are listed and described.

Instructional Tasks

1. Identify and define terms associated with the reproduction of drawings.
   - Make one reproduction of a quality original drawing and another reproduction where the line work and lettering are inadequate. Discuss with the class the essentials of a quality original drawing.
2. Explain the microfilm process and its advantages.
   - Discuss the techniques required for quality microfilming.
3. Explain the photodrawing process.
   - Display examples of photodrawings.
4. Discuss the advantages of scissors drafting and its uses.
   - Have students prepare a "second original" drawing.
5. Describe the various processes of producing prints from drawings.
   - Obtain copies of various types of reproductions from industry. Lead the class in a discussion of the advantages and limitations of each type of reproduction.
   - Have students make a print reproduction of a drawing.
   - Arrange a class visit to a local printer or reproduction business and have the class observe the various processes used in the reproduction of drawings.

Instructional Aids and Assignments

1. Display samples of various types of industrial prints showing desirable print quality.
2. Display equipment supplier catalogs and instruction manuals.
3. Assign the problems in the textbook. You may want to identify problems that may be done for extra credit.

Answers to Review Questions, Text

Page 690

1. Microfilming, photodrafting, and scissors drafting.
2. A fine-grain, high-resolution film containing an image greatly reduced in size from the original.

3. Answer may include any three of the following: Less storage space is required; the retrieval time is nearly instantaneous; the data in drawings is used more because of the ready availability; and there is reduced handling.
4. 30
5. microfilm, aperture cards
6. photodrawing
7. A method in which part (or all) of one drawing is used to create part (or all) of a "second original" drawing.
8. print
9. blueprint
10. The diazo process.
11. electronic
12. Plotters and printers.
13. A package of files prepared from CAD drawings for distribution purposes.
14. discs, tapes
15. A master file or folder containing all of the files belonging to a project.
16. efficiency

Solutions to Problems and Activities, Text

Page 690

1. Check student work for line delineation and density. Minimum line width should be .01″. Open space between adjacent lines should be at least .06″. Features can be drawn slightly out of scale if needed. Removed views can be drawn at a larger scale to show details. Hidden lines should be shown only when necessary for clarity.

   Lettering (or text) should be clear, legible, and well formed. The minimum lettering height for drawing part numbers is .40″ on all drawings. Titles on A-size, B-size, and C-size drawings should be a minimum of .10″ in height. For D-size drawings, titles should be a minimum of .12″ in height. For E-size drawings, titles should be a minimum of .20″ in height. Spacing between parallel lines of lettering is a minimum of .06″. Each element of a fraction must have the same height as a whole number.
2. Students may use an industry photograph, or their own photograph of the part or assembly to be dimensioned. Check student dimensioning against good dimensioning practices for clarity.
3. Students should select a previously prepared drawing and modify it for a second original drawing. Check finished student reproductions for clarity and appearance.
4. Check student prints for clarity of line definition and lettering, and absence of "ghosting."
5. Check student prints for clarity of line definition and lettering, and absence of "smudges."
6. Have students report their findings to the class. Check to see how the student findings compare with accepted practices.
7. Have students report their findings to the class. Students should describe any new processes or materials found, and their significance to drafting and the reproduction industry.

Answers to Chapter 20 Quiz

1. C. .06″
2. B. intermediate
3. B. A photo of an actual object that has callouts and notes added.
4. D. All of the above.
5. B. diazo
6. B. scissors drafting

Chapter Quiz 20

Drawing Management

Name ____

Period ____________________ Date ____________________ Score ____________________

Multiple Choice

Choose the answer that correctly completes the statement. Write the corresponding letter in the space provided.

_______ 1. What is the standard minimum spacing between parallel lines when making drawings suitable for microfilming?
A. .02″
B. .04″
C. .06″
D. .08″

_______ 2. Which term refers to a suitable medium, such as vellum or photographic paper, that serves as a drawing medium when preparing a second original drawing?
A. archive
B. intermediate
C. negative
D. positive

_______ 3. What is a *photodrawing*?
A. A drawing of photo quality.
B. A photo of an actual object that has callouts and notes added.
C. A photograph of a drawing.
D. A drawing traced from a photo.

_______ 4. The term "print" is used loosely to refer to _____.
A. blueprints
B. direct line prints
C. all types of hard copy prints
D. All of the above.

_______ 5. The _____ process produces positive prints with dark lines sometimes referred to as whiteprints.
A. electrostatic
B. diazo
C. inkjet
D. blueprint

_______ 6. The process used to revise a reproduction of an original drawing by "cutting and pasting" it into a revised drawing is known as _____.
A. microfilming
B. scissors drafting
C. photodrawing
D. diazo printing

Procedure Checklist

Drawing Management

Name ____

Observable Items	Completed		Comments	Instructor Initials
	Yes	No		
1. Prepares a drawing for microfilming.				
2. Prepares a photodrawing.				
3. Prepares a second original drawing.				
4. Makes prints using different reproduction methods.				

Instructor Signature ____

Manufacturing Processes

Learning Objectives

After studying this chapter, the student will be able to:

- List and describe common machining operations.
- Specify dimensions for features to be machined using proper drafting conventions.
- Explain how computer numerical control machines carry out tool operations.
- Identify common positioning systems used for specifying distances and directions in CNC machining.
- Describe the principles of computer-aided manufacturing (CAM) and computer-integrated manufacturing (CIM).
- Explain the principles of just-in-time (JIT) manufacturing.

Instructional Resources

Text: pages 691–713

Review Questions, page 713

Instructor's Resource

Instructional Tasks

Instructional Aids and Assignments

Chapter 21 Quiz

Reproducible Masters

- Reproducible Master 21-1: *Machine Processes.* Drawings illustrating common machining processes are shown.
- Reproducible Master 21-2: *Automated Manufacturing System.* This handout shows a chart that illustrates the relationship between the various aspects of an automated manufacturing system.

Color Transparencies (Binder/IRCD only)

- Transparency 21-1: *Computer-Integrated Manufacturing.* The basic components of computer-integrated manufacturing are identified in this chart.

Instructional Tasks

1. Explain drafting conventions used for specifying machining processes.
   - Show a multimedia presentation or film on manufacturing processes and discuss the processes as they relate to drafting.
   - Review machine specifications on industrial drawings.
2. Explain the principles of computer numerical control (CNC) machining.
   - Take the class on a tour of a business that utilizes computer numerical control in the manufacturing process.
   - Invite an industry representative to speak about CNC manufacturing and drafting requirements.
3. Explain how drawings are dimensioned for CNC machining.
   - Review industrial drawings designed for CNC machining.
4. Explain how to specify surface texture.
   - Review industrial drawings including specifications for surface texture.
5. Discuss the importance of developments that have linked design and manufacturing.
   - Show a multimedia presentation or film on a computer-integrated manufacturing (CIM) plant.
   - Discuss the interaction of CIM components.
   - Compare the manufacture of parts prior to CIM and after CIM.
6. Discuss computer terms related to design and manufacturing and their meanings.
   - Prepare a chart of computer terms associated with design and manufacturing.
7. Discuss the advantages of CAD in the design process.
   - Show a multimedia presentation or film on CAD.

8. Describe the characteristics and development of CNC machines.
    - Show a multimedia presentation or film on automated manufacturing.
9. Discuss machining centers and flexible manufacturing systems.
    - Provide examples of typical products capable of being manufactured using CNC.
10. Define the terms *group technology* and *artificial intelligence.* Discuss the current state of these two technologies and their future development.
    - Have a group of students prepare a report on group technology and artificial intelligence. Have the students lead a class discussion on the current state of group technology and artificial intelligence and possible future development.
11. Describe a CIM facility and its component parts.
    - Invite an industry representative from a CIM facility (or partial CIM facility) to speak to the class on the status of CIM and future developments.

Instructional Aids and Assignments

1. Display samples of industrial machine parts that illustrate a manufacturing process. For example, show a machine part that has been milled and has ground surfaces. Other examples might be extruded metal parts and manufactured plastic parts.
2. Display trade journals in the field of manufacturing.
3. Show multimedia presentations or films on CAD, CAM, FMS, or CIM.
4. Display brochures from CAD or CIM suppliers.
5. Invite industry representatives and supplier representatives to speak to the class.

Answers to Review Questions, Text

Page 713

1. callout
2. Spotfacing is a cutting process used to clean up or level the surface around a hole to provide a bearing for a bolt head or nut.
3. Counterboring involves cutting deeper than spotfacing to allow fillister or socket head screws to be seated below the surface. A larger amount of metal is removed.
4. beveled
5. Broaching is the process of pulling or pushing a tool over or through the workpiece to form irregular or unusual shapes.
6. knurling
7. chamfer
8. A taper is a section of a part that increases or decreases in size at a uniform rate.
9. Computer numerical control machining is a computer-operated means of controlling the movement of machine tools.
10. Drawings for CNC machining do not differ significantly from other drawings, but the dimensioning system should be compatible with the reference point system of the CNC machine. Drawings for CNC machines using the absolute positioning system use datum dimensioning. Drawings for CNC machines using the incremental positioning system use chain dimensioning.
11. Surface texture is the smoothness or finish of a surface. It is measured using a profilometer or a similar device.
12. A network is a group of computers connected together to permit shared access to electronic data and resources. Networks used in large industrial operations make it possible for a number of sources to retrieve information from a database.
13. Evaluate responses individually.

14. CAD/CAM
15. A machining center is a CNC machine that is capable of performing a variety of material removal operations and is usually equipped with tool changing, storage, and part delivery functions. Machining centers are usually installed as integral parts of flexible manufacturing systems. The machining center is considered the smallest building block of a flexible manufacturing system.
16. ladder logic
17. Group technology is a manufacturing philosophy that consists of organizing components into families of parts for production.
18. To reduce work-in-progress to an absolute minimum.
19. artificial intelligence
20. Computer-integrated manufacturing (CIM) is the full automation and joining of all facets of an industrial enterprise.

Answers to Chapter 21 Quiz

1. B. spotfacing
2. C. honing or lapping
3. D. Profilometer
4. C. callout
5. D. counterboring
6. C. .06 × 45°
7. B. CAD and CAM
8. D. robot
9. A. machining center
10. B. Group technology
11. D. All of the above.

Chapter Quiz 21

Manufacturing Processes

Name ____

Period ________________ Date ________________ Score ________________

Multiple Choice

Choose the answer that correctly completes the statement. Write the corresponding letter in the space provided.

_____ 1. When a surface is to be cleaned up or leveled to provide a bearing for a bolt head or nut, the process is called _____.
A. broaching
B. spotfacing
C. boring
D. knurling

_____ 2. An extremely smooth machine finish as fine as 2 μin is usually accomplished with a _____ operation.
A. milling
B. surface grinding
C. honing or lapping
D. turning

_____ 3. What device is used to measure the smoothness of a surface texture or finish?
A. Rockwell hardness tester
B. Electrical discharge machine
C. Broach
D. Profilometer

_____ 4. The dimensional note on a drawing specifying a machine process is referred to as a _____.
A. general note
B. feature specification
C. callout
D. machine symbol

_____ 5. The machining process illustrated here is known as _____.
A. reaming
B. counterdrilling
C. countersinking
D. counterboring

.37

_____ 6. Which of the following is a correct chamfer specification?
A. CHAMFER .06
B. .06 CHAMFER
C. $.06 \times 45°$
D. $0.6 \times 45° \times .06$

_____ 7. What are the two subsystems of computer-integrated manufacturing (CIM)?
A. AI and FMC
B. CAD and CAM
C. FMS and FMC
D. CAM and FMC

_____ 8. A(n) _____ is a programmable multifunctional manipulator designed to move material, parts, tools, or specific devices through variable motions for the performance of a variety of tasks.
A. automatic guided vehicle
B. CNC machine
C. flexible manufacturing system
D. robot

_____ 9. A _____ is a machine tool that is capable of performing a variety of metal removal operations on a part.
A. machining center
B. robot
C. flexible arm
D. automated guided vehicle

_____ 10. _____ refers to a grouping of parts that have similar design characteristics into families of parts for production.
A. Just-in-time manufacturing
B. Group technology
C. Artificial intelligence
D. Expert systems

_____ 11. Which of the following characteristics is associated with artificial intelligence (AI)?
A. Speech recognition
B. Language interpretation
C. Visual interpretation
D. All of the above.

Machine Processes

For certain features, machine processes are specified on the drawing. The following machine processes are most common.

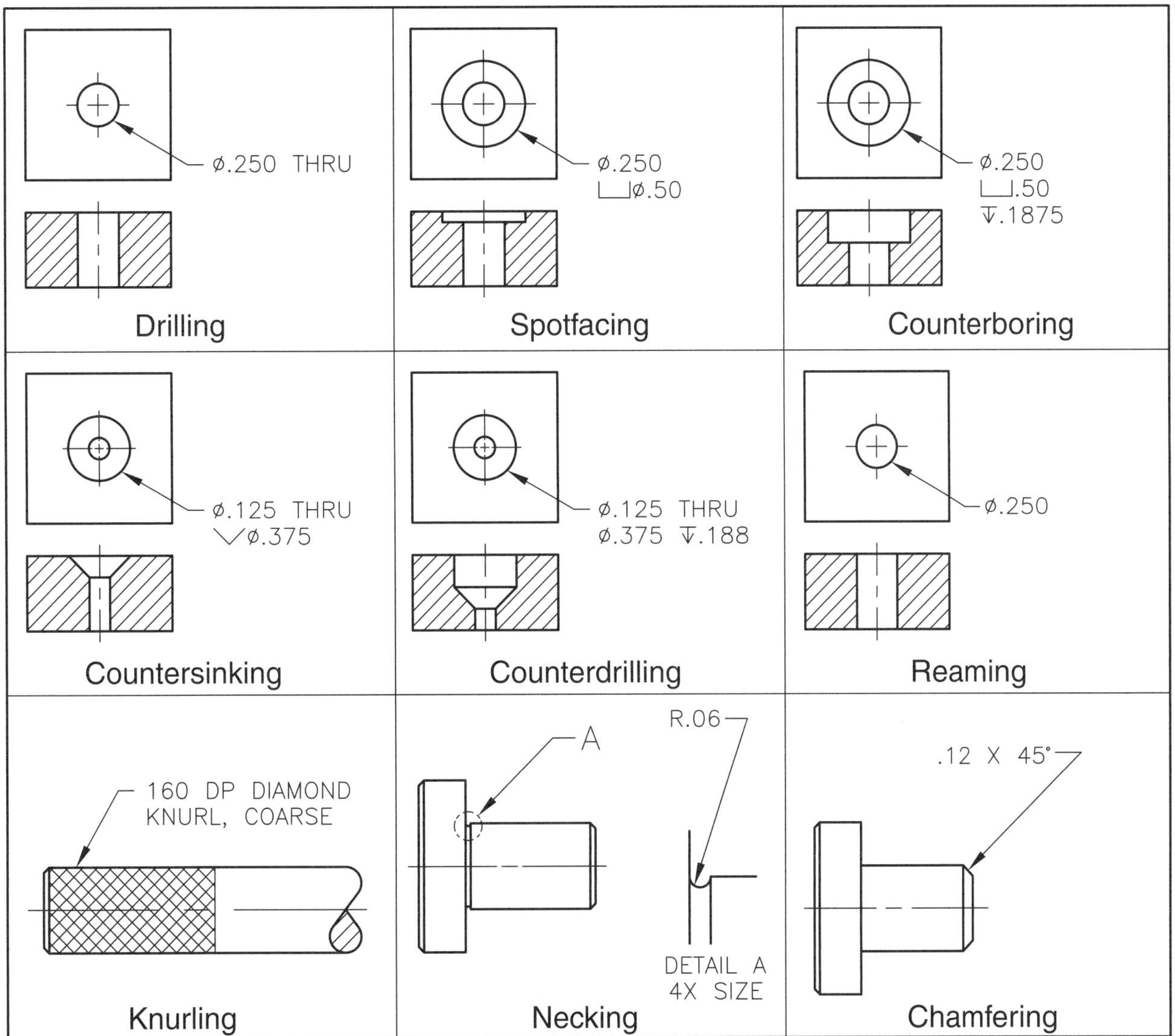

RM 21-1

Automated Manufacturing System

In an automated manufacturing system, the central computer database links design and manufacturing.

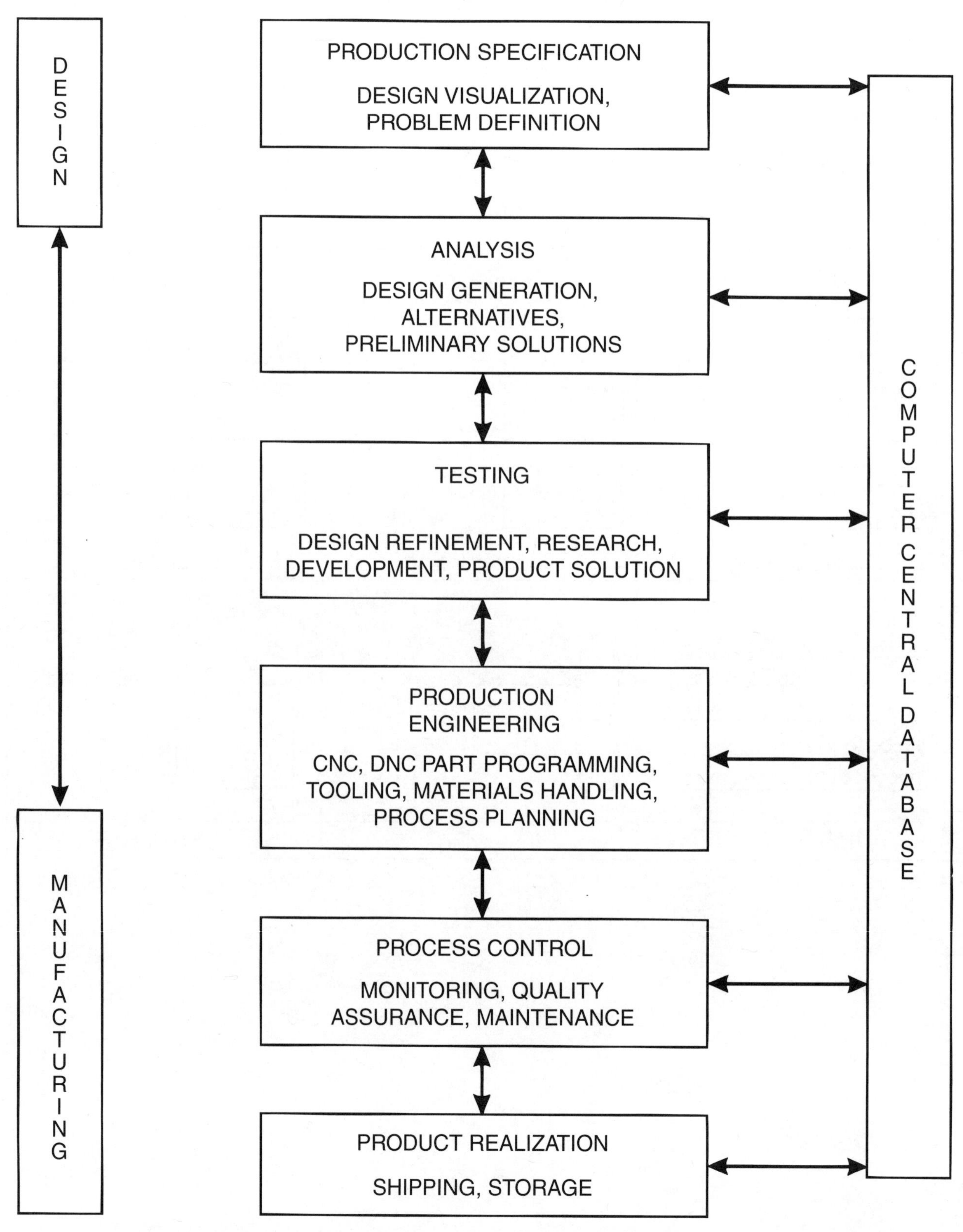

RM 21-2

Section 5 Drafting and Design Specializations

Architectural Drafting

Learning Objectives

After studying this chapter, the student will be able to:

- Explain the types of drawing skills and knowledge necessary to produce acceptable drawings used in the architectural drafting field.
- List the different types of drawings in a set of architectural plans and explain the purpose of each type.
- Describe the purpose of presentation drawings.
- List the common types of architectural models and explain the applications for each type.

Instructional Resources

Text: pages 715–734

Review Questions, page 732

Problems and Activities, pages 733–734

Worksheets: page 168

- Worksheet 22-1: *Architectural Drawings*

Instructor's Resource

Instructional Tasks

Instructional Aids and Assignments

Chapter 22 Quiz

Reproducible Masters

- Reproducible Master 22-1: *Architectural Material Symbols.* Shown are common material symbols used on plan, elevation, and section drawings.
- Reproducible Master 22-2: *Floor Plan.* Shown is a typical residential floor plan.

  Procedure Checklist

Color Transparencies (Binder/IRCD only)

- Transparency 22-1: *Plot Plan.* A typical plot plan is shown.
- Transparency 22-2: *Floor Plan.* A residential floor plan is shown.
- Transparency 22-3: *Presentation Model.* Shown is a computer-generated rendering of a proposed building design.

Instructional Tasks

1. Discuss lettering styles used on architectural drawings.
   - Have students practice architectural lettering and dimensioning.
2. Explain how to prepare a floor plan.
   - Have students study the common features of floor plans and common floor plan symbols.
   - Demonstrate the procedure for preparing a floor plan.
3. Explain how to prepare foundation plans and basement plans.
   - Demonstrate the various procedures for drawing foundation plans and basement plans. Use transparencies with overlays to assist in the demonstration.
4. Explain how to prepare an electrical plan.
   - Have students study the common symbols used on electrical plans.
5. Explain how to draw an exterior elevation.
   - Demonstrate the procedure for drawing an exterior elevation. Use a sample photograph of a house as an example.
6. Explain how to prepare door and window schedules.
   - Have students study the schedules from a set of plans.
7. Explain how to prepare cabinet elevations.
   - Show the steps for the proper completion of cabinet elevations.
8. Explain how to prepare architectural models.
   - Arrange for a display of various models.

Instructional Aids and Assignments

1. Show multimedia presentations or films on architecture and construction.
2. Display catalogs from architectural and building suppliers.

3. Display models and cutaway sections of architectural and building components.
4. Collect and display architectural and construction journals.
5. Assign the drawing problems in the textbook. The number of problems is sufficient to assign a minimum number to all students and to identify problems that may be done for extra credit. Some problems may be used for the performance section of the chapter quiz.

Answers to Review Questions, Text

Page 732

1. The area of design and drafting that specializes in the preparation of drawings for the building of structures.
2. Architectural drawings have a more "artistic" style of lettering, make greater use of presentation drawings, and use drawing symbols not found on technical drawings.
3. D. site
4. C. plot
5. B. foundation
6. A. floor
7. elevation
8. plumbing
9. B. 1/4″ = 1′-0″
10. Answer may include any three of the following: The electrical meter, the distribution panel box, electrical outlets, switches, and special electrical features.
11. climate control
12. construction detail
13. presentation
14. renderings
15. Small-scale solid models, structural models, and presentation models.
16. Exterior and interior views developed as perspectives, rendered elevation drawings, and presentation floor plan drawings.

Solutions to Problems and Activities, Text

Pages 733–734

For Problems 1–5, evaluate student work for accuracy and appearance. Each drawing should be made to an appropriate scale. Check that symbols are properly drawn and that each drawing is dimensioned properly.

Solutions to Worksheets

Page 168

For Problem 22-1, evaluate student work for accuracy and appearance. Each drawing should be made to an appropriate scale. A separate drawing sheet should be used for each drawing. Check that each drawing is dimensioned properly.

Answers to Chapter 22 Quiz

1. D. The type of structure.
2. B. Plot plan
3. A. elevation
4. A. floor
5. A. 1/8″ = 1′-0″
6. C. HVAC
7. D. All of the above.
8. Evaluate student work for accuracy and appearance. The drawing should be made to an appropriate scale and dimensioned properly.

Chapter Quiz

Architectural Drafting

Name ____________________

Period ____________ Date ____________ Score ____________

Multiple Choice

Choose the answer that correctly completes the statement. Write the corresponding letter in the space provided.

_______ 1. In a set of construction drawings, what has the most influence on the type and number of drawings required for a structure?
A. The cost of the project.
B. The preference of the designer.
C. Building code requirements.
D. The type of structure.

_______ 2. Which drawing in a set of construction drawings shows the location of the structure on the site?
A. Foundation plan
B. Plot plan
C. Floor plan
D. Basement plan

_______ 3. A(n) _____ shows a view of the side of a structure.
A. elevation
B. foundation plan
C. plot plan
D. site plan

_______ 4. Drawings showing the systems of a structure, such as plumbing plans and electrical plans, are typically traced from the _____ plan.
A. floor
B. foundation
C. plot
D. site

_______ 5. Drawing scales for floor plans are usually 1/4″ = 1′-0″ for residential buildings and _____ for commercial buildings.
A. 1/8″ = 1′-0″
B. 1/4″ = 1′-0″
C. 1/2″ = 1′-0″
D. 1″ = 1′-0″

_______ 6. A(n) _____ plan shows the location of heating and cooling ducts and registers in a structure.
A. plot
B. foundation
C. HVAC
D. site

_______ 7. Construction detail drawings are typically made to show information about _____.
A. kitchens
B. fireplaces
C. stairs
D. All of the above.

Drafting Performance

8. Draw a solution of a problem selected by your instructor from Chapter 22 in your textbook.

Architectural Material Symbols

MATERIAL	PLAN	ELEVATION	SECTION
EARTH	NONE	NONE	
CONCRETE			SAME AS PLAN VIEW
CONCRETE BLOCK	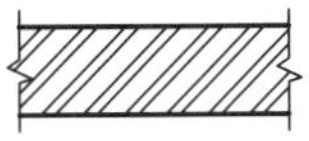	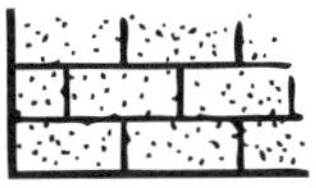	
GRAVEL FILL	SAME AS SECTION	NONE	
WOOD	FLOOR AREAS LEFT BANK	 SIDING PANEL	FINISH  FRAMING
BRICK	 FACE  COMMON	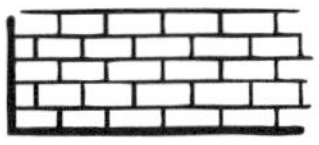 FACE OR COMMON	SAME AS PLAN VIEW
STONE	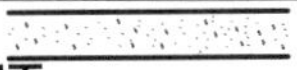 CUT  RUBBLE	 CUT RUBBLE	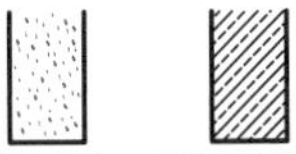 CUT RUBBLE
STRUCTURAL STEEL		INDICATED BY NOTE	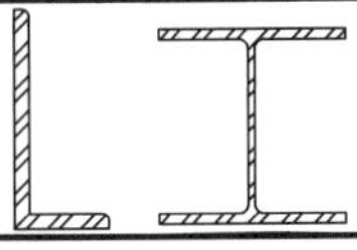
SHEET METAL FLASHING	INDICATED BY NOTE		 SHOW CONTOUR
INSULATION	SAME AS SECTION	 INSULATION	 LOOSE FILL OR BATT  BOARD
PLASTER	SAME AS SECTION	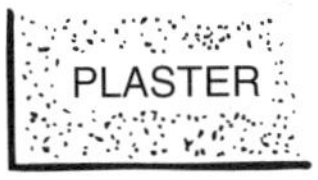 PLASTER	 STUD LATH AND PLASTER
GLASS			 LARGE SCALE SMALL SCALE
TILE	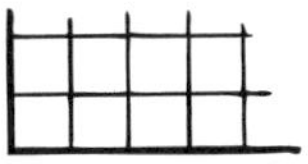	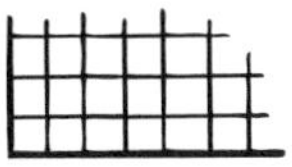	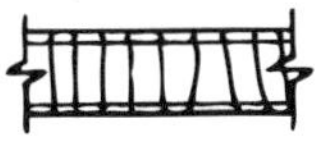

RM 22-1

Floor Plan

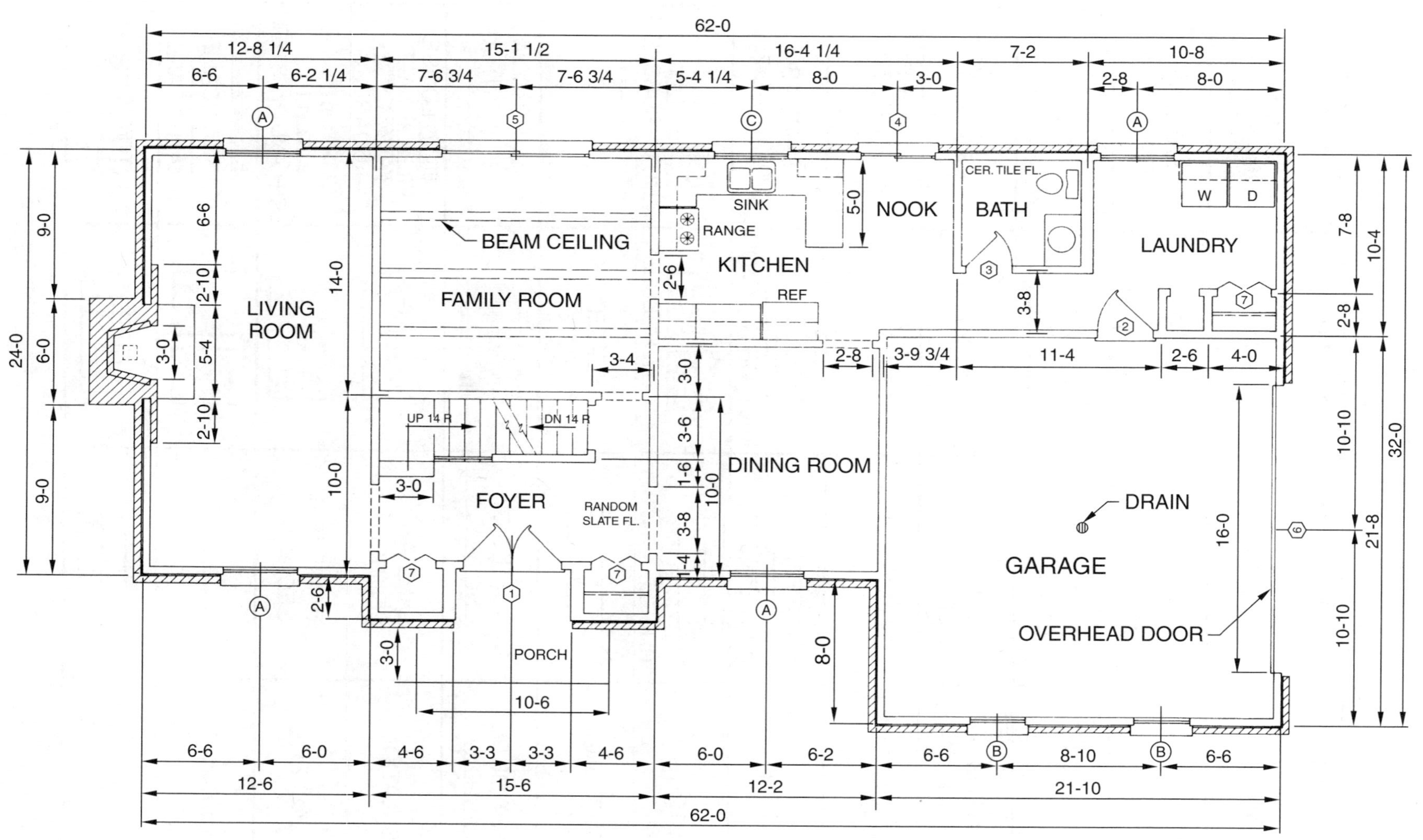

FIRST FLOOR PLAN
SCALE—1/4" = 1'-0"

RM 22-2

Procedure Checklist

Architectural Drafting

Name ______________________________

Observable Items	Completed		Comments	Instructor Initials
	Yes	No		
1. Draws a site plan.				
2. Draws a plot plan.				
3. Draws a foundation plan.				
4. Draws a floor plan.				
5. Draws an exterior elevation.				
6. Draws a plumbing plan.				
7. Draws an electrical plan.				
8. Draws an HVAC plan.				
9. Makes detail drawings.				

Instructor Signature ______________________________

Structural Drafting

Learning Objectives

After studying this chapter, the student will be able to:

- List the types of structures for which drawings are prepared.
- List and describe the common types of drawings made by structural drafters.
- Identify and explain the types of components used in structural wood construction.
- Describe the common structural shapes used in steel construction.
- List and describe the common types of concrete construction.

Instructional Resources

Text: pages 735–747

Review Questions, pages 746–747

Problems and Activities, page 747

Instructor's Resource

Instructional Tasks

Instructional Aids and Assignments

Chapter 23 Quiz

Reproducible Masters

- Reproducible Master 23-1: *Welded Wire Reinforcement Sizes*. Shown are US Customary sizes and styles of welded wire reinforcement.
- Reproducible Master 23-2: *Beam Data*. Sizes and load data for S-beams and W-beams used in structural steel construction are shown.

Procedure Checklist

Color Transparencies (Binder/IRCD only)

- Transparency 23-1: *Post and Beam Construction*. Shown is a roof truss and the use of steel plates and bolts for beam and framing connections.
- Transparency 23-2: *Steel Construction*. Shown is a steel bridge designed for motorist, train, and pedestrian traffic.

Instructional Tasks

1. Discuss the types of drawings used in structural drafting.
   - Display typical structural drawings for the class to examine.
   - Show typical connectors and other structural elements.
2. Show photos of each of the primary types of structural materials.
   - Discuss wood frame structures.
   - Discuss structural steel structures.
   - Discuss reinforced concrete structures.
3. Discuss structural wood construction.
   - Identify the principal types of structural timber.
   - Compare the strengths of various wood materials.
   - Show various types of timber fasteners.
   - Define wood post and beam construction.
   - Define curtain walls.
4. Discuss structural steel construction.
   - Identify the basic structural steel shapes.
   - Describe the methods of fastening structural steel shapes.
   - Show engineering design and shop drawings.
   - Make available industry resources such as *Architectural Graphic Standards*.
5. Discuss the types of concrete construction.
   - Show drawings or photos of cast-in-place concrete roof and floor systems.
   - Show illustrations of structures using precast concrete construction.
   - Describe standard-shaped prestressed concrete panels.
   - Share concrete construction drawings with the class.

Instructional Aids and Assignments

1. Show a film of the construction of a famous structure (a building, bridge, or dam).
2. Collect and display typical structural materials used in construction.
3. Assign the drawing problems in the textbook. The number of problems is sufficient to assign a minimum number to all students and to identify problems that may be done for extra credit.

Answers to Review Questions, Text

Pages 746–747

1. Wood, structural steel, and reinforced concrete.
2. Answer may include any four of the following: Douglas fir, spruce, redwood, southern yellow pine, oak, and poplar.
3. strength, weight
4. Joists, trusses, beams, columns, and braces.
5. strength
6. 3 1/2″ × 5 1/2″
7. 19
8. posts, beams, planks
9. posts
10. The weight to be supported, the soil bearing capacity, and local building codes.
11. Answer may include any five of the following: Common bars, plates, angles, channels, beams, tees, pipe, and tubing.
12. Structural steel shapes may be fastened together by welds, bolts, or rivets.
13. The American Society for Testing and Materials (ASTM)
14. Shop
15. engineering
16. Concrete that has steel bars, rods, or wire mesh embedded in it to increase its tensile strength.
17. Prestressed
18. construction
19. The pan joist, waffle, flat plate, and flat slab systems.
20. Tilt-up construction is reasonable in cost, requires low maintenance, provides durability, and allows for suitable speed in construction.
21. Double-tee units, single-tee units, and hollow-core panels.
22. Engineering and placing drawings.

Solutions to Problems and Activities, Text

Page 747

For Problems 1–3, evaluate student work for accuracy and appearance. Each drawing should be made to an appropriate scale. Check that structural components are properly drawn and that each drawing is dimensioned properly.

Answers to Chapter 23 Quiz

1. B. bolts and lag screws
2. C. 1/2″
3. A. posts
4. D. Lag screws
5. C. pan joist construction
6. Evaluate student work for accuracy and appearance. The drawing should be made to an appropriate scale and dimensioned properly.

Chapter Quiz 23

Structural Drafting

Name ________________________________

Period ______________ Date ______________ Score ______________

Multiple Choice

Choose the answer that correctly completes the statement. Write the corresponding letter in the space provided.

_______ 1. For better holding power, _____ are commonly used to fasten structural members in timber construction.
- A. nails
- B. bolts and lag screws
- C. rivets
- D. steel bars

_______ 2. Wood framing members that are 5″ and thicker and 5″ and wider (measured by nominal size) have an actual dimension that is _____ less than the nominal size.
- A. 1/8″
- B. 1/4″
- C. 1/2″
- D. 1″

_______ 3. In a post and beam structure, most of the weight is supported by _____.
- A. posts
- B. walls
- C. headers
- D. tilt-up panels

_______ 4. Which of the following connection methods is *not* used to fasten together structural steel shapes?
- A. Bolts
- B. Welds
- C. Rivets
- D. Lag screws

________ 5. The method of cast-in-place concrete construction shown here is known as _____.

A. flat plate construction
B. flat slab construction
C. pan joist construction
D. waffle construction

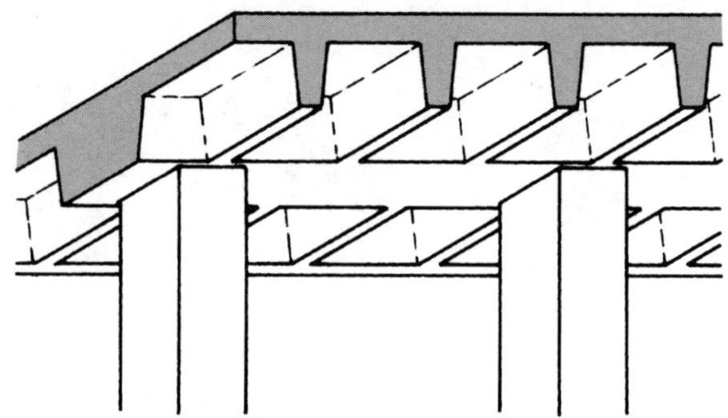

Drafting Performance

6. Draw a solution of a problem selected by your instructor from Chapter 23 in your textbook.

Welded Wire Reinforcement

Stock Sizes

Type of Construction	Recommended Style	Remarks
Basement Floors	6 × 6 – W1.4 × W1.4 6 × 6 – W2.1 × W2.1 6 × 6 – W2.9 × W2.9	For small areas (15' maximum side dimension) use 6 × 6 – W1.4 × W1.4. As a rule of thumb, the larger the area or the poorer the subsoil, the heavier the gauge.
Driveways	6 × 6 – W2.9	Continuous reinforcement between 25' to 30' contraction joints
Foundation Slabs (Residential Only)	6 × 6 – W1.4 × W1.4	Use heavier gauge over poorly drained subsoil, or when maximum dimension is greater than 15'.
Garage Floors	6 × 6 – W2.9 × W2.9	Position at midpoint of 5" or 6" thick slab.
Patios and Terraces	6 × 6 – W1.4 × W1.4	Use 6 × 6 – W2.1 × W2.1 if subsoil is poorly drained.
Porch Floor A. 6" thick slab up to 6' span B. 6" thick slab up to 8' span	 6 × 6 – W2.9 × W2.9 4 × 4 – W4 × W4	Position 1" from bottom form to resist tensile stresses.
Sidewalks	6 × 6 – W1.4 × W1.4 6 × 6 – W2.1 × W2.1	Use heavier gauge over poorly drained subsoil. Construct 25' to 30' slabs as for driveways.
Steps (Free Span)	6 × 6 – W2.9 × W2.9	Use heavier style if more than five risers. Position reinforcement 1" from bottom of form.
Steps (On Ground)	6 × 6 – W2.1 × W2.1	Use 6 × 6 – W2.9 × W2.9 for unstable subsoil.

RM 23-1

Beam Data

Size of beam	Weight of beam per foot	Maximum allowable uniform loads for American standard S-beams with lateral support Span in feet																		
		4	6	8	10	12	14	16	18	20	22	24	26	28	30	32	34	36	38	40
4″ x 2-3/4″	7.7	10	7	5																
	9.5	11	7	6																
5″ x 3″	10.0	16	11	8	6															
	11.3	20	13	10	8															
6″ x 3-1/8″	12.5	24	16	12	10	8														
	17.3	29	19	15	12	10														
7″ x 3-3/4″	15.3	35	23	17	14	12	10													
	20.0	40	27	20	16	15	13													
8″ x 4″	18.4	47	32	24	19	16	14	12												
	23.0	53	36	27	21	18	15	13												
10″ x 4-3/4″	25.4	80	54	41	33	27	23	20	18	16										
	35.0	97	65	49	39	32	28	24	22	20										
12″ x 5″	31.8	110	80	60	48	40	34	30	27	24	22	20								
	35.0	126	84	63	50	42	36	32	28	25	23	21								
12″ x 5-1/4″	40.8	144	100	75	60	50	43	37	33	30	27	25								
	50.0	168	112	84	67	56	48	42	37	34	31	28								
15″ x 5-1/2″	42.9	160	131	98	79	65	56	49	44	39	36	33	30	28	26	25				
	50.0	214	143	107	86	71	61	54	48	43	39	36	33	31	29	27				
18″ x 6″	54.7		196	147	118	98	84	74	66	59	54	49	45	42	39	37	35	33	31	
	70.0		226	170	136	113	97	85	76	68	62	57	52	49	45	43	40	38	36	
20″ x 6-1/4″	65.4		260	195	156	130	111	97	87	78	71	65	60	56	52	49	46	43	41	39
	75.0		281	211	169	140	120	105	94	84	77	70	65	60	56	53	50	47	44	42

Loads are in kips. 1 kip = 1,000 pounds

Size of beam	Weight of beam per foot	Maximum allowable uniform loads for wide flange W-beams with lateral support Span in feet																		
		4	6	8	9	10	12	14	18	20	22	24	26	28	30	32	34	36	38	40
8″ x 5-1/4″	17	47	31	24	19	16	13	12												
8″ x 6-1/2″	24		46	35	28	23	20	17												
8″ x 8″	31		60	46	37	30	26	23	20	18	16									
10″ x 5-1/4″	21	62	48	36	29	24	21	18	16	14										
10″ x 8″	33		74	58	47	39	33	29	26	23										
10″ x 10″	49			88	73	61	52	46	40	36	33	30	28	26						
12″ x 6-1/2″	27		74	57	45	38	32	28	25	23	21	19								
12″ x 8″	40		87	69	58	49	43	38	35	32	29									
12″ x 10″	53			108	94	79	67	59	52	47	43	39								
12″ x 12″	65				117	98	84	73	65	59	53	49	45	42	39					
14″ x 6-3/4″	30		93	70	56	46	40	35	31	28	25	23	21	20	19					
14″ x 8″	43			105	84	70	60	52	46	42	38	35	32	30	28					
14″ x 10″	61				123	102	88	77	68	62	56	51	47	44	41					
14″ x 12″	78				156	135	115	101	90	81	73	67	62	58	54					
14″ x 14-1/2″	87					152	132	115	102	92	84	77	71	66	61	57	54	51		
16″ x 7″	36		124	94	75	63	54	47	42	38	34	31	29	27	25	24	22			
16″ x 8-1/2″	58			157	126	105	90	78	70	63	57	52	48	45	42	39	37			
16″ x 11-1/2″	88				202	168	144	126	112	101	92	84	78	72	67	63	59			
18″ x 7-1/2″	50			148	119	99	85	74	66	59	54	49	46	42	40	37	35	33	31	
18″ x 8-3/4″	64			188	156	130	111	98	87	78	71	65	60	56	52	49	46	43	41	
18″ x 11-3/4″	96				224	189	176	154	137	123	112	103	95	88	82	77	72	68	65	
21″ x 8-1/4″	62			211	169	141	120	105	94	84	77	70	65	60	56	53	50	47	44	42

Loads are in kips. 1 kip = 1,000 pounds

(American Institute of Steel Construction)

RM 23-2

Procedure Checklist

Structural Drafting

Name ______________________________

Observable Items	Completed		Comments	Instructor Initials
	Yes	No		
1. Develops a plan view drawing showing structural members for a building.				
2. Draws construction details.				
3. Develops an engineering design drawing.				
4. Develops a shop drawing.				
5. Develops an engineering drawing.				
6. Develops a placing drawing.				

Instructor Signature ______________________________

Electrical and Electronics Drafting

Learning Objectives

After studying this chapter, the student will be able to:

- List and describe the types of devices for which electrical and electronics drawings are prepared.
- Identify special graphic symbols used on electrical and electronics drawings.
- List and explain the different types of drawings and diagrams used in electrical and electronics drafting.
- Explain the methods used in making drawings for integrated circuits and printed circuit boards.

Instructional Resources

Text: pages 749–760

Review Questions, page 757

Problems and Activities, pages 757–760

Worksheets: pages 169–171

- Worksheet 24-1: *Electrical Symbols*
- Worksheet 24-2: *Electrical Power System*
- Worksheet 24-3: *Schematic Diagram*

Instructor's Resource

Instructional Tasks

Instructional Aids and Assignments

Chapter 24 Quiz

Reproducible Masters

- Reproducible Master 24-1: *Industrial Control Schematic Diagram*. A typical schematic diagram is shown.

Procedure Checklist

Instructional Tasks

1. Identify and discuss electrical and electronics component symbols.
   - Show a multimedia presentation or film on graphic symbols used in electrical and electronics drawings.
2. Explain how to draw block diagrams.
   - Obtain a block diagram to show to the class. Explain the meaning of the diagram.
3. Explain how to draw schematic diagrams.
   - Demonstrate the procedure for drawing schematic diagrams.
   - Tour a drafting firm that prepares electrical and electronics drawings. Observe the drafting processes of the various drawings discussed in the chapter.
4. Explain how to draw connection and interconnection wiring diagrams.
   - Discuss and demonstrate the procedures for drawing connection and interconnection wiring diagrams.

Instructional Aids and Assignments

1. Show a multimedia presentation or film on electrical and electronics drafting.
2. Display copies of electrical and electronics drawings from industry.
3. Display electrical and electronic components identified with their graphic symbols.
4. Display copies of instruction manuals for electrical and electronics equipment.
5. Display copies of standards published by the American National Standards Institute (ANSI) and the Institute of Electrical and Electronics Engineers (IEEE).
6. Assign the drawing problems in the textbook. The number of problems is sufficient to assign a minimum number to all students and to identify problems that may be done for extra credit.

Answers to Review Questions, Text

1. The use of special symbols to represent electrical circuits and wiring devices.

2. A simplified representation of a complex circuit or an entire system.
3. primary
4. horizontal, vertical
5. A diagram that uses block shapes to present an overview of a system in its simplest form.
6. input, output
7. signal path
8. Schematic
9. wiring
10. connections
11. Continuous line, interrupted line, and tabular.
12. A complete electronic circuit, usually very small in size, composed of various electronic devices such as transistors, resistors, capacitors, and diodes.
13. chips
14. printed circuit board

Solutions to Problems and Activities, Text

Pages 757–760

For Problem 1, review and approve the object before the student makes the pictorial drawing. Evaluate student work for accuracy and appearance. The drawing should have components identified and should be in proportion.

For Problems 2–6, student work should look like the following drawings. The problem number and title are indicated on each problem sheet.

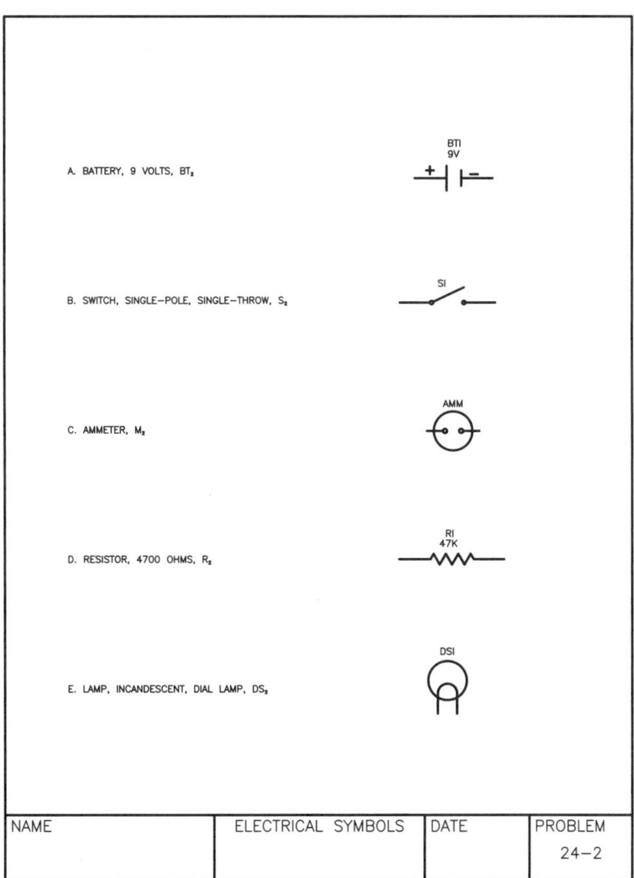

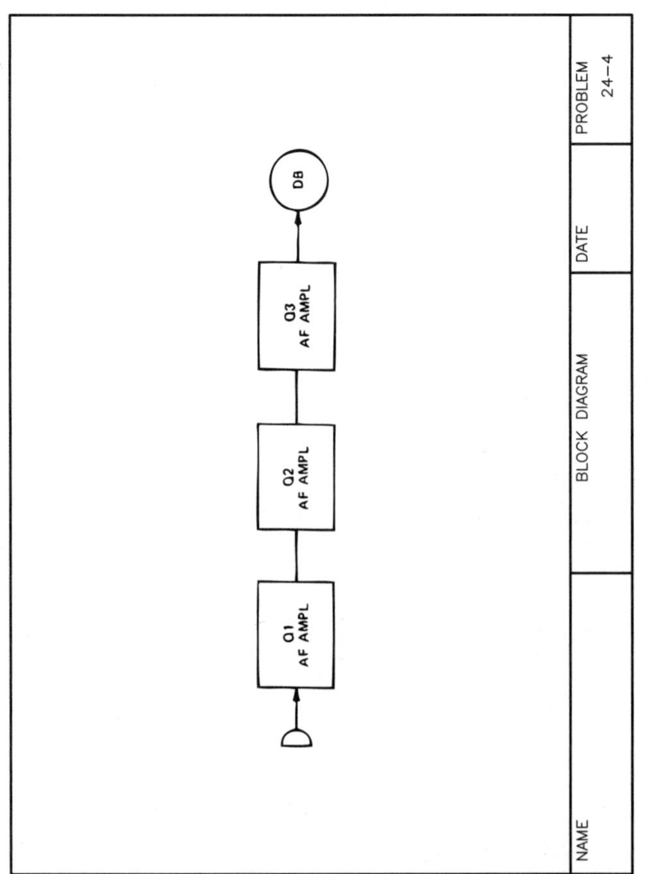

Q1
AF AMPL
Q2
AF AMPL
Q3
AF AMPL
DB
NAME
BLOCK DIAGRAM
DATE
PROBLEM
24–4

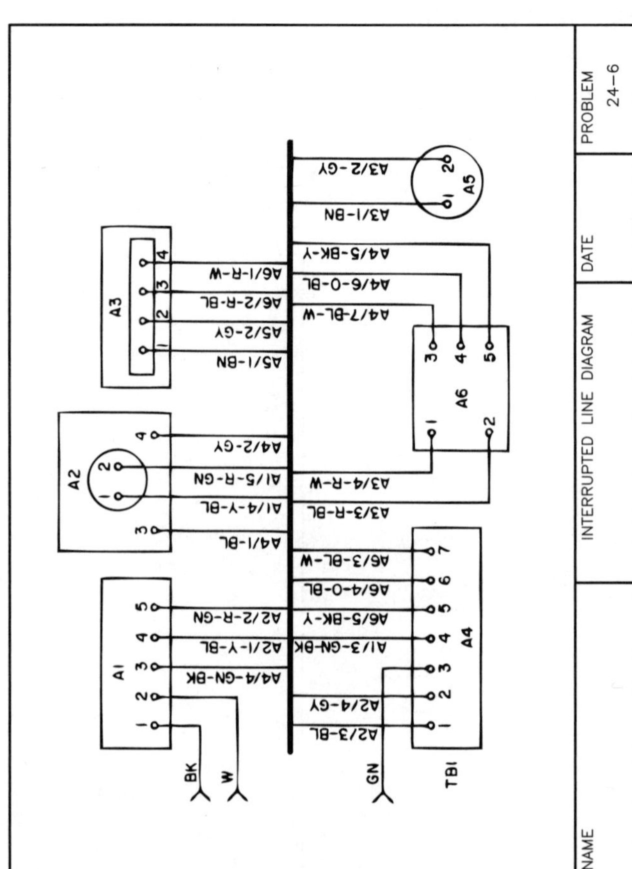

A1
A2
A3
A4
A5
A6
TB1
BK
W
GN
A4/4-GN-BK
A2/1-Y-BL
A2/2-R-GN
A4/1-BL
A1/4-Y-BL
A1/5-R-GN
A4/2-GY
A5/1-BN
A5/2-GY
A6/2-R-BL
A6/1-R-W
A2/3-BL
A2/4-GY
A1/3-GN-BK
A6/5-BK-Y
A6/4-O-BL
A6/3-BL-W
A3/3-R-BL
A3/4-R-W
A4/7-BL-W
A4/6-O-BL
A4/5-BK-Y
A3/1-BN
A3/2-GY
NAME
INTERRUPTED LINE DIAGRAM
DATE
PROBLEM
24–6

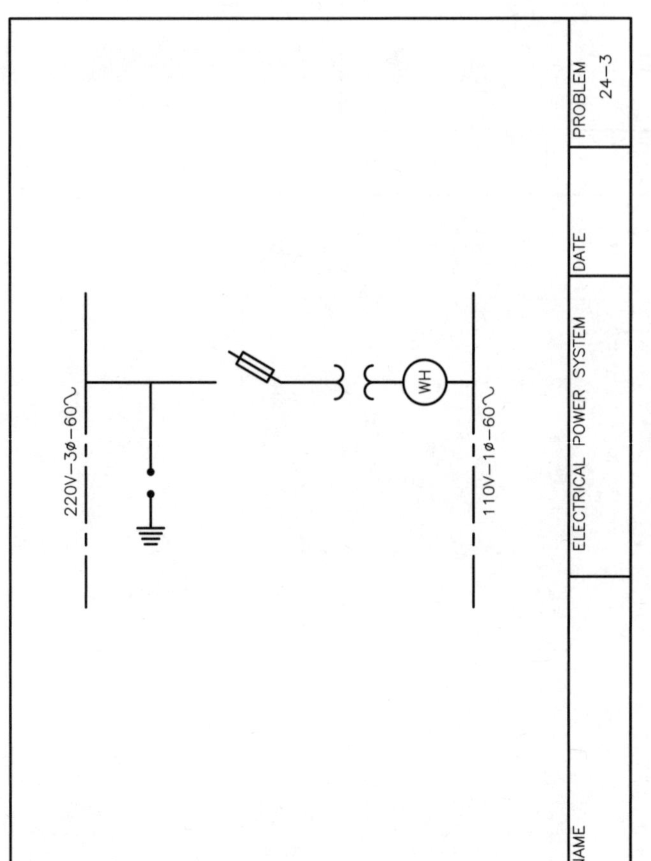

220V–3ø–60∿
WH
110V–1ø–60∿
NAME
ELECTRICAL POWER SYSTEM
DATE
PROBLEM
24–3

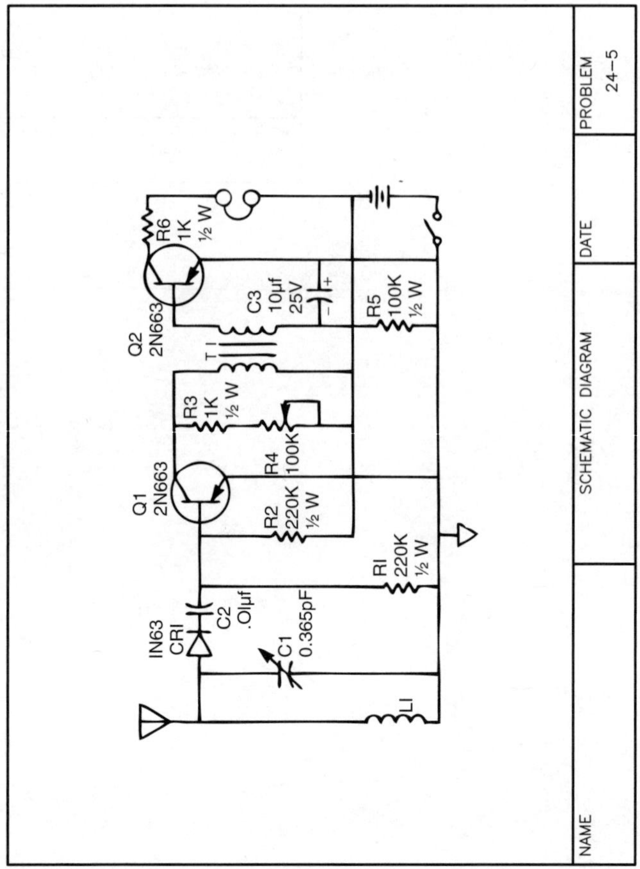

IN63
CRI
C2
.01μf
C1
0.365pF
LI
Q1
2N663
R2
220K
½ W
RI
220K
½ W
R3
1K
½ W
R4
100K
T1
Q2
2N663
C3
10μf
25V
R5
100K
½ W
R6
1K
½ W
NAME
SCHEMATIC DIAGRAM
DATE
PROBLEM
24–5

Solutions to Worksheets

Pages 169–171

Evaluate student work for accuracy and appearance. Student work should look like the corresponding problems from the textbook given in the *Solutions to Problems and Activities, Text* section.

Answers to Chapter 24 Quiz

1. C. They can be read by personnel not familiar with graphic symbols.
2. A. left to right
3. C. schematic diagram
4. B. interrupted line
5. C. interconnection
6. Refer to the drawings given in the *Solutions to Problems and Activities, Text* section for the problem selected from the textbook.

Chapter Quiz 24

Electrical and Electronics Drafting

Name ______________________________

Period ______________ Date ______________ Score ______________

Multiple Choice

Choose the answer that correctly completes the statement. Write the corresponding letter in the space provided.

_______ 1. Why are pictorial drawings of electrical components used?
- A. They are faster to draw.
- B. There are not enough electrical symbols for all the different parts.
- C. They can be read by personnel not familiar with graphic symbols.
- D. All of the above.

_______ 2. Block diagrams should be arranged in rows and columns, with the main signal path progressing from _____.
- A. left to right
- B. right to left
- C. top to bottom
- D. bottom to top

_______ 3. The most frequently used drawing in the electronics field is the _____.
- A. block diagram
- B. pictorial drawing
- C. schematic diagram
- D. wiring schedule

_______ 4. A(n) _____ diagram is arranged so that all connecting paths are routed to a common baseline.
- A. block
- B. interrupted line
- C. continuous line
- D. tabular

_______ 5. A(n) _____ diagram shows only external connections between unit assemblies or equipment.
- A. block
- B. elementary
- C. interconnection
- D. single-line

Drafting Performance

6. Draw a solution of a problem selected by your instructor from Chapter 24 in your textbook.

Industrial Control Schematic Diagram

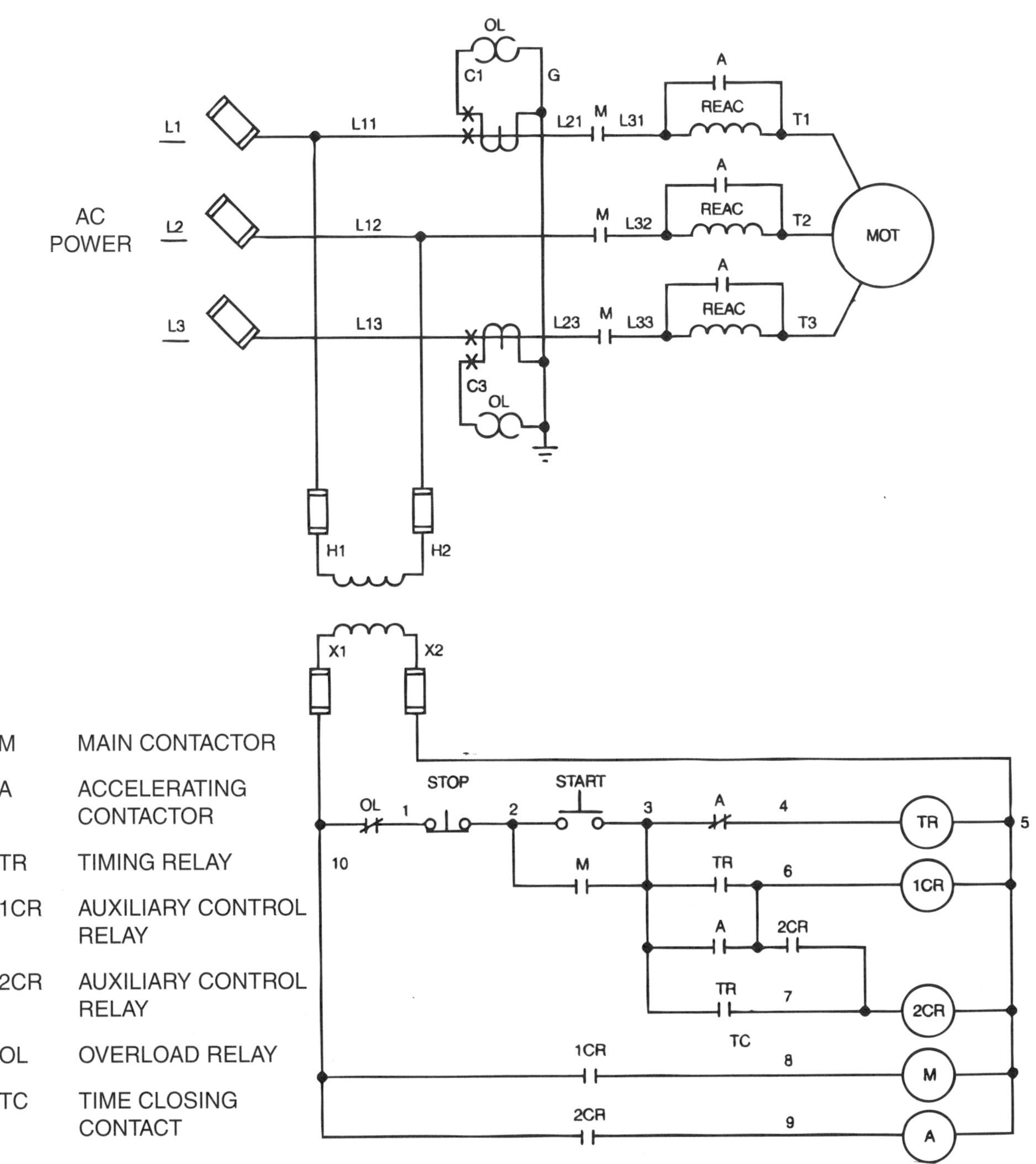

M MAIN CONTACTOR
A ACCELERATING CONTACTOR
TR TIMING RELAY
1CR AUXILIARY CONTROL RELAY
2CR AUXILIARY CONTROL RELAY
OL OVERLOAD RELAY
TC TIME CLOSING CONTACT

RM 24-1

Procedure Checklist

Electrical and Electronics Drafting

Name ______________________________

Observable Items	Completed		Comments	Instructor Initials
	Yes	No		
1. Draws a block diagram.				
2. Draws a schematic diagram.				
3. Draws connection diagrams.				

Instructor Signature ______________________________

Map and Survey Drafting

Learning Objectives

After studying this chapter, the student will be able to:

- List and explain common terms associated with map drafting.
- Identify and describe the common types of drawings used in map drafting.
- Explain common methods used for data collection in mapmaking.
- Describe the special kinds of drafting required in the preparation of map drawings.

Instructional Resources

Text: pages 761–778

Review Questions, pages 775–776

Problems and Activities, pages 777–778

Worksheets: pages 172–173

- Worksheet 25-1: *Topographic Map*
- Worksheet 25-2: *Map Traverse*

Instructor's Resource

Instructional Tasks

Instructional Aids and Assignments

Chapter 25 Quiz

Procedure Checklist

Color Transparencies (Binder/IRCD only)

- Transparency 25-1: *Contour Map*. Shown is a contour map of a mountain with a profile view drawn from elevation data.

Instructional Tasks

1. Define and discuss map and surveying terms.
    - Show a multimedia presentation or film on methods of gathering map data, such as surveying, photogrammetry, and geographic information system (GIS) technology.
2. Identify common types of maps and their uses.
    - Visit a map drafting department and have students observe the types of maps being prepared.
3. Identify and explain common format elements found on maps.
    - Demonstrate how to lay out the map title and scale.
    - Demonstrate how to draw notes and map symbols.
4. Identify and describe methods of gathering map data.
    - Invite a cartographer or surveyor to speak to the class.

Instructional Aids and Assignments

1. Show a multimedia presentation or film on map and survey drafting.
2. Arrange a visit to the state, county, parish, or city map drafting department to observe the type of drawings being made.
3. Display sample survey data and map drawings from industry or government.
4. Display a model of a plot of land with a cross section cut in order to show contour lines.
5. Assign the drawing problems in the textbook. The number of problems is sufficient to assign a minimum number to all students and to identify problems that may be done for extra credit.

Answers to Review Questions, Text

Pages 775–776

1. cartography
2. The angle of a line measured from either north or south.
3. contour
4. A technique used to locate, by proportion, intermediate points between given data in contour plotting problems.
5. plat

6. C. geographic
7. Geology
8. topographic
9. cadastral
10. An engineering map.
11. 10
12. bottom, right-hand
13. true
14. The means of collecting data for use in making maps.
15. Photogrammetry
16. A software-based program used to gather and manage spatial data for analysis and design purposes.
17. point
18. profile
19. A rectangular grid with identified elevation points at the grid intersections used to plot contour lines.

Solutions to Problems and Activities, Text

Pages 777–778

Student work should look like the following drawings. The problem number and title are indicated on each problem sheet.

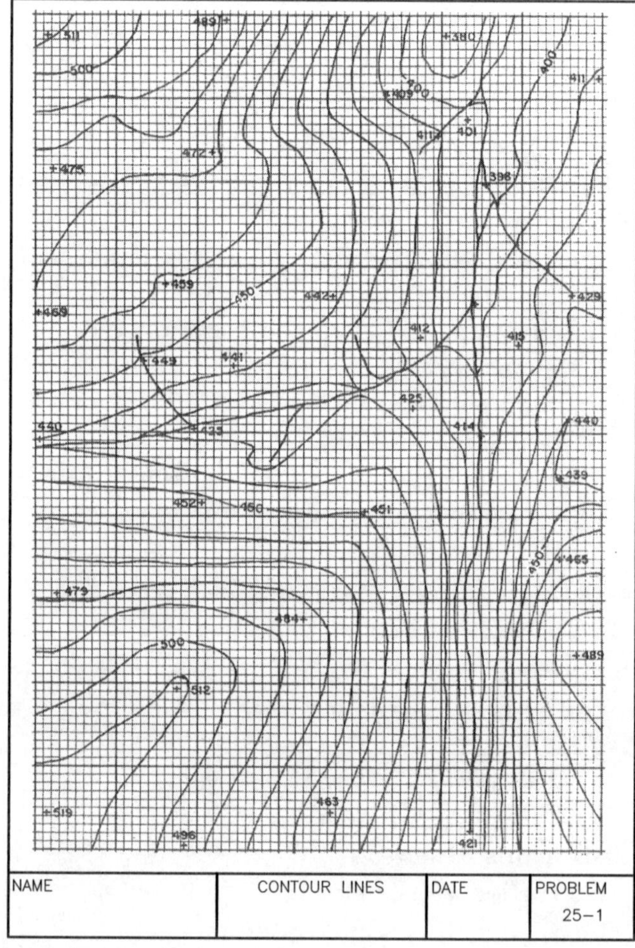

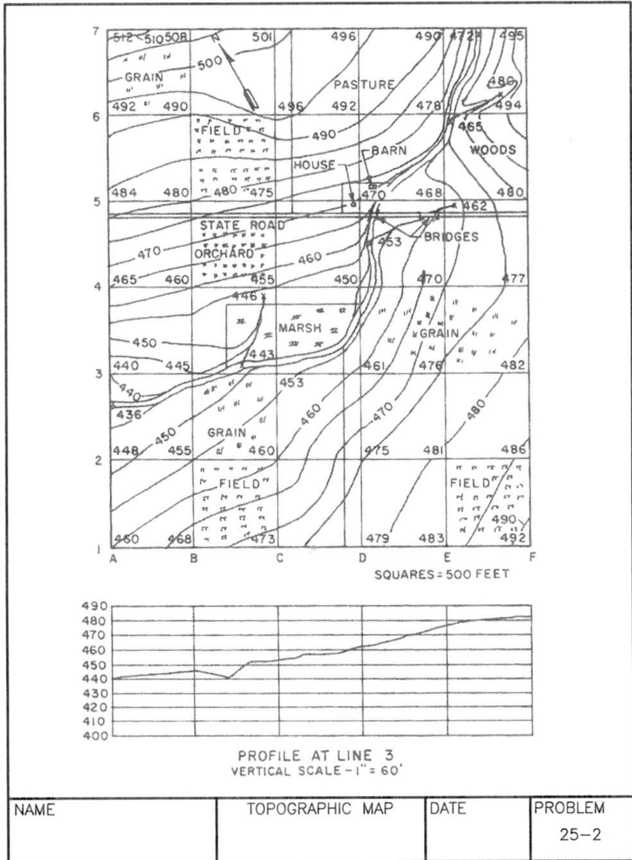
GRAIN
PASTURE
FIELD
HOUSE
BARN
WOODS
STATE ROAD
ORCHARD
BRIDGES
MARSH
GRAIN
GRAIN
FIELD
FIELD
SQUARES = 500 FEET
PROFILE AT LINE 3
VERTICAL SCALE - 1" = 60'
NAME
TOPOGRAPHIC MAP
DATE
PROBLEM
25–2

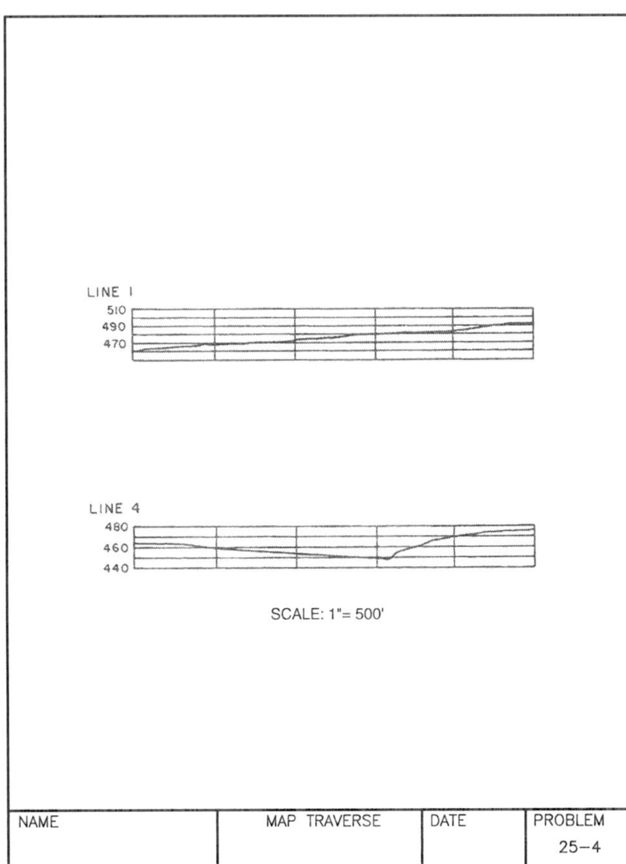
LINE 1
LINE 4
SCALE: 1"= 500'
NAME
MAP TRAVERSE
DATE
PROBLEM
25–4

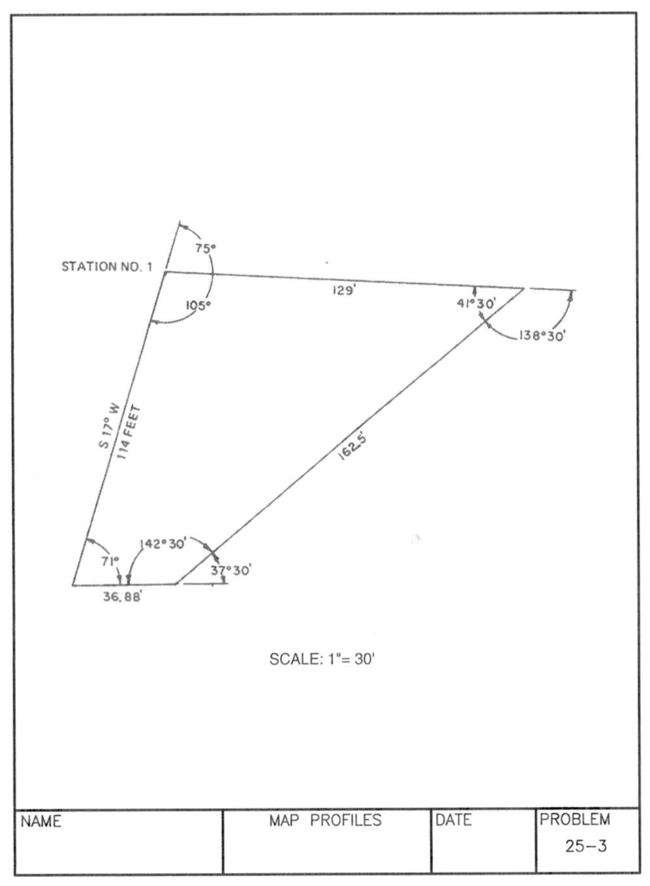
STATION NO. 1
75°
105°
129'
41°30'
138°30'
S 17° W
114 FEET
162.5'
71°
142°30'
37°30'
36.88'
SCALE: 1"= 30'
NAME
MAP PROFILES
DATE
PROBLEM
25–3

Solutions to Worksheets

Pages 172–173

Evaluate student work for accuracy and appearance. Student work should look like the corresponding problems from the textbook given in the *Solutions to Problems and Activities, Text* section.

Answers to Chapter 25 Quiz

1. A. traverse
2. C. station
3. D. parabolic
4. A. engineering
5. D. Photogrammetry
6. Refer to the drawings given in the *Solutions to Problems and Activities, Text* section for the problem selected from the textbook.

Chapter Quiz 25

Map and Survey Drafting

Name ______________________________

Period ______________ Date ______________ Score ______________

Multiple Choice

Choose the answer that correctly completes the statement. Write the corresponding letter in the space provided.

______ 1. A map _____ refers to a series of lines laid out by means of angular and linear measurements.
- A. traverse
- B. curve
- C. range
- D. contour

______ 2. An established point on a map traverse or drawing is known as a(n) _____.
- A. azimuth
- B. bearing
- C. station
- D. mosaic

______ 3. A vertical curve in the grade of a roadway (shown in a profile view) is usually achieved by means of a _____ curve.
- A. hyperbolic
- B. helical
- C. harmonic
- D. parabolic

______ 4. A(n) _____ map shows construction details for a given building project.
- A. engineering
- B. cadastral
- C. geographic
- D. geological

______ 5. _____ is the use of photography, either aerial or land-based, to produce useful data for the preparation of contour and profile maps.
- A. Interpolation
- B. Rendering
- C. Photodrafting
- D. Photogrammetry

Drafting Performance

6. Draw a solution of a problem selected by your instructor from Chapter 25 in your textbook.

Procedure Checklist

Map and Survey Drafting

Name ______________________________

Observable Items	Completed		Comments	Instructor Initials
	Yes	No		
1. Draws a contour map.				
2. Draws a profile view from a contour map.				
3. Lays out a grid survey.				
4. Lays out a map traverse.				

Instructor Signature ______________________________

Welding Drafting 26

Learning Objectives

After studying this chapter, the student will be able to:

- List and describe some of the most common welding processes.
- Identify the basic types of welded joints.
- Describe the purpose of weld symbols and identify the different types used on drawings.
- Explain the elements making up a welding symbol and interpret the information provided.

Instructional Resources

Text: pages 779–794

Review Questions, pages 788–789

Problems and Activities, page 789

Drawing Problems, pages 789–794

Worksheets: pages 174–175

- Worksheet 26-1: *Joint Designs*
- Worksheet 26-2: *Lubricator Tank Base*

Instructor's Resource

Instructional Tasks

Instructional Aids and Assignments

Chapter 26 Quiz

Reproducible Masters

- Reproducible Master 26-1: *Welding Processes.* Common types of welding processes are listed and explained.
- Reproducible Master 26-2: *Types of Welds.* Common types of welds are shown. Each type is illustrated with the appropriate drawing representation.
- Reproducible Master 26-3: *Weld Symbols.* Standard weld symbols developed by the American Welding Society (AWS) are shown.
- Reproducible Master 26-4: *Elements in a Welding Symbol.* The proper locations of elements in a welding symbol are shown.

Procedure Checklist

Instructional Tasks

1. Identify and describe the various welding processes.
   - Show a multimedia presentation or film on welding processes.
2. Identify and discuss different types of welded joints.
   - Display samples of welded joints.
3. Explain how to detail types of welds on drawings.
   - Discuss the elements of a welding symbol.
   - Discuss basic weld symbols.

Instructional Aids and Assignments

1. Show a multimedia presentation or film on welding processes.
2. Display samples of welded joints and types of welds.
3. Display copies of industrial drawings specifying welds.
4. Display transparencies showing welds and welding symbols.
5. Assign the drawing problems in the textbook. The number of problems is sufficient to assign a minimum number to all students and to identify problems that may be done for extra credit. Some problems may be used for the performance section of the chapter quiz.

Answers to Review Questions, Text

Pages 788–789

1. assembly
2. The process of joining metals by adhesion with a low melting point filler metal.

3. In brazing, the metals are joined by the adhesion of a low melting point metal that does not melt the parent metal. Oxyfuel gas welding causes the parent metal to melt and "fuse" into one piece, joining metals by cohesion.
4. oxyacetylene welding
5. electrode
6. tungsten inert gas (TIG)
7. argon, helium
8. D. All of the above.
9. Welding metals 1/4" thick or thicker.
10. Gas tungsten arc welding is used for lightweight nonferrous metal. A tungsten electrode is used, and a metal filler rod may or may not be added. Gas metal arc welding is used with heavier metals 1/4" thick or thicker. A filler wire serves as the electrode and is fed into the weld automatically.
11. current flow
12. Spot welding, seam welding, and flash welding.
13. The heat generated for the weld is produced by the resistance of the metal to the flow of an induced electric current. The welding action may occur with or without pressure.
14. A high-intensity beam of electrons focused in a small area at the surface to be welded.
15. Butt joints, corner joints, T-joints, lap joints, and edge joints.
16. A weld symbol designates the specific type of weld to be performed. A welding symbol designates all pertinent information required for welding.
17. The location of welds with respect to a joint is controlled by the placement of the weld symbol on the reference line of the welding symbol. Welds that are to be made on the arrow side of the joint are shown by placing the weld symbol on the side of the reference line toward the reader. Welds that are to be made on the side opposite the arrow are considered to be on the other side of the joint, so the weld symbol is shown on the side of the reference line away from the reader. When the joint is to be welded on both sides, the weld symbol is shown on both sides of the reference line.
18. libraries

Solutions to Problems and Activities, Text

Welding Symbols, Page 789

Student work should look like the following drawings. The problem number and title are indicated on each area of the sheet.

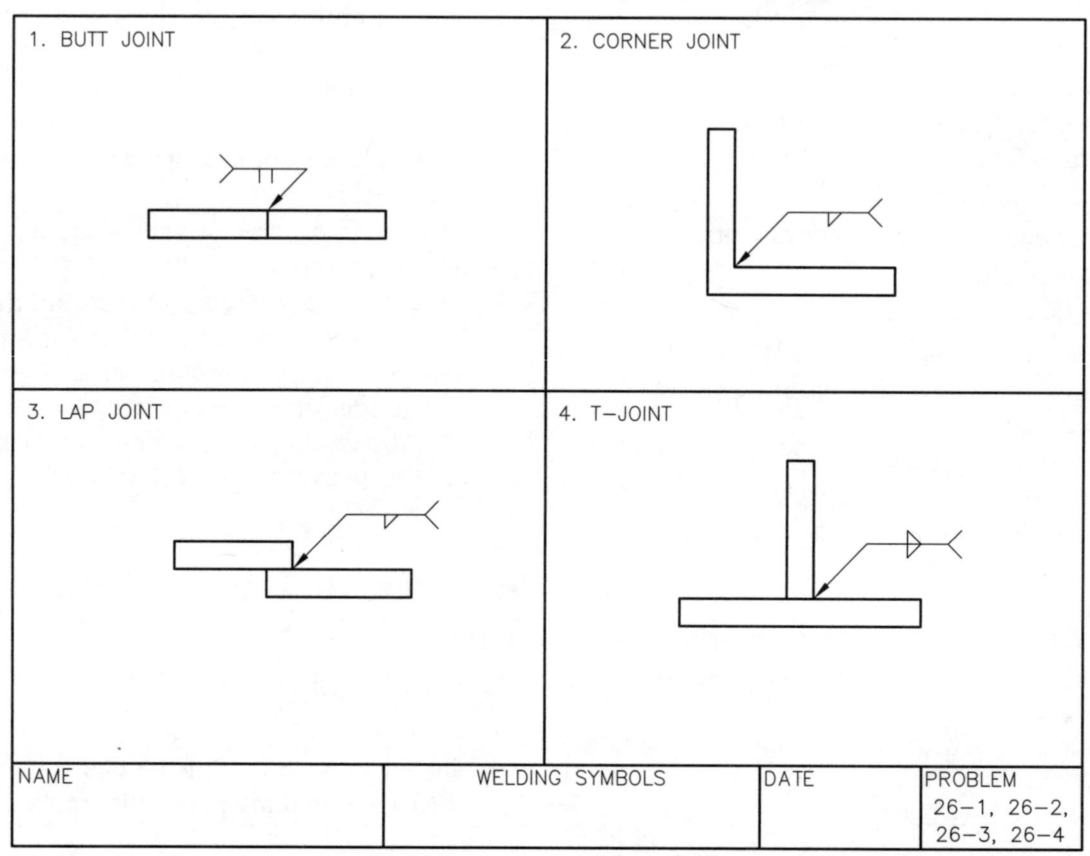

Outside Activities, Page 789

1. Individual student design project. Verify welds specified with an experienced welder.
2. Individual student design project. Verify welds specified with an experienced welder.

Solutions to Drawing Problems, Text

Pages 789–794

Student work should look like the following drawings. The problem number and title are indicated on each problem sheet.

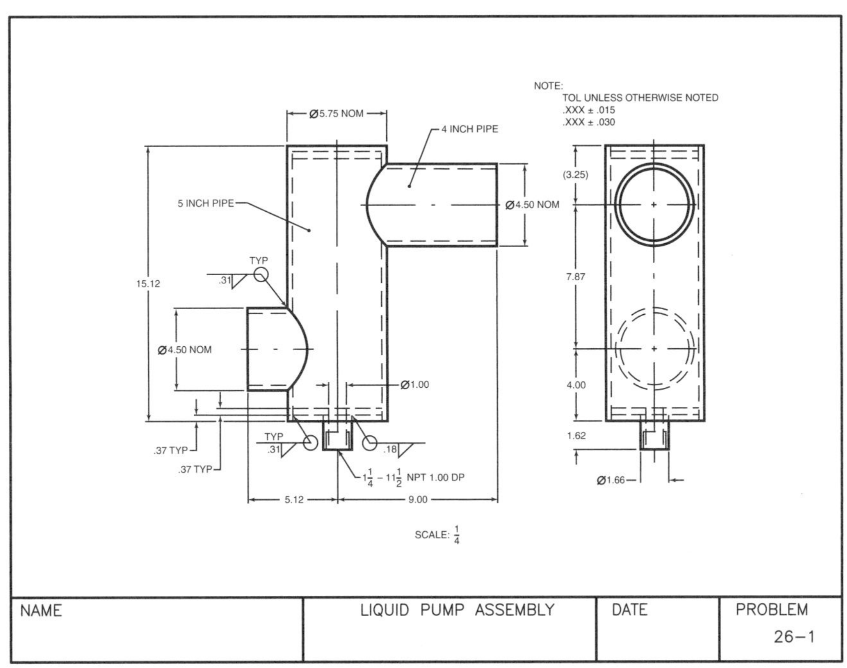

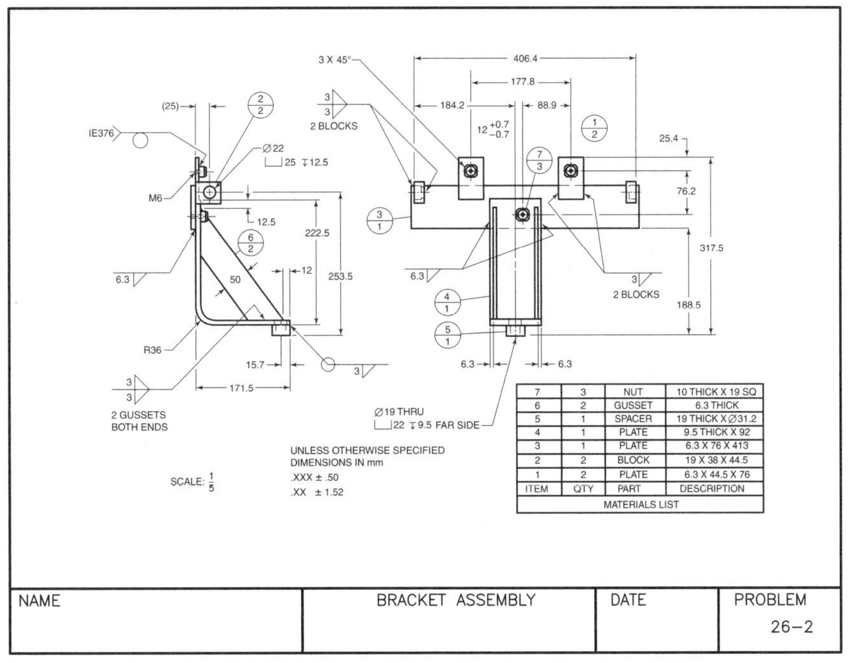

7	3	NUT	10 THICK X 19 SQ
6	2	GUSSET	6.3 THICK
5	1	SPACER	19 THICK X Ø31.2
4	1	PLATE	9.5 THICK X 92
3	1	PLATE	6.3 X 76 X 413
2	2	BLOCK	19 X 38 X 44.5
1	2	PLATE	6.3 X 44.5 X 76
ITEM	QTY	PART	DESCRIPTION
MATERIALS LIST			

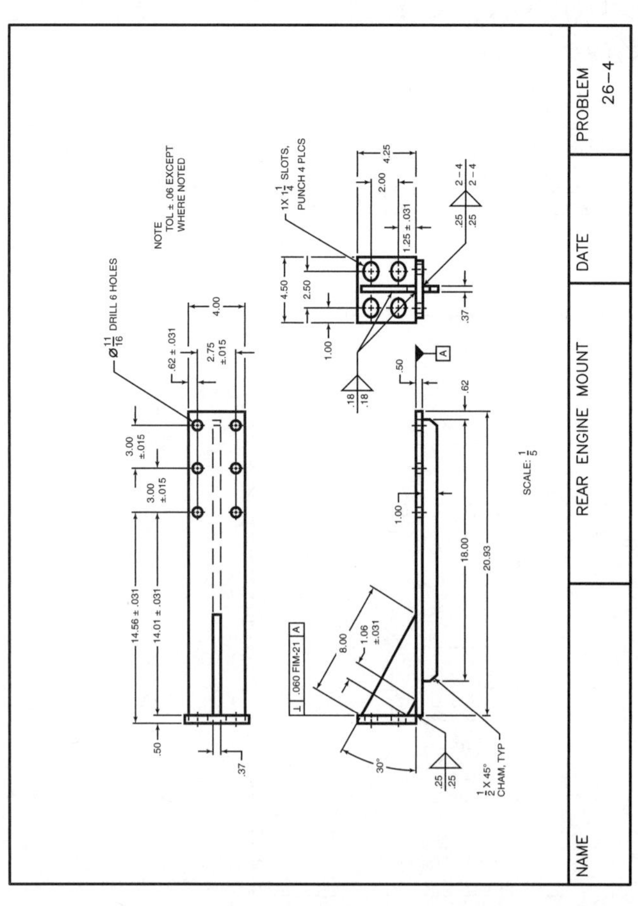

NAME
REAR ENGINE MOUNT
DATE
PROBLEM 26–4
SCALE: 1/5
NOTE TOL ± .06 EXCEPT WHERE NOTED

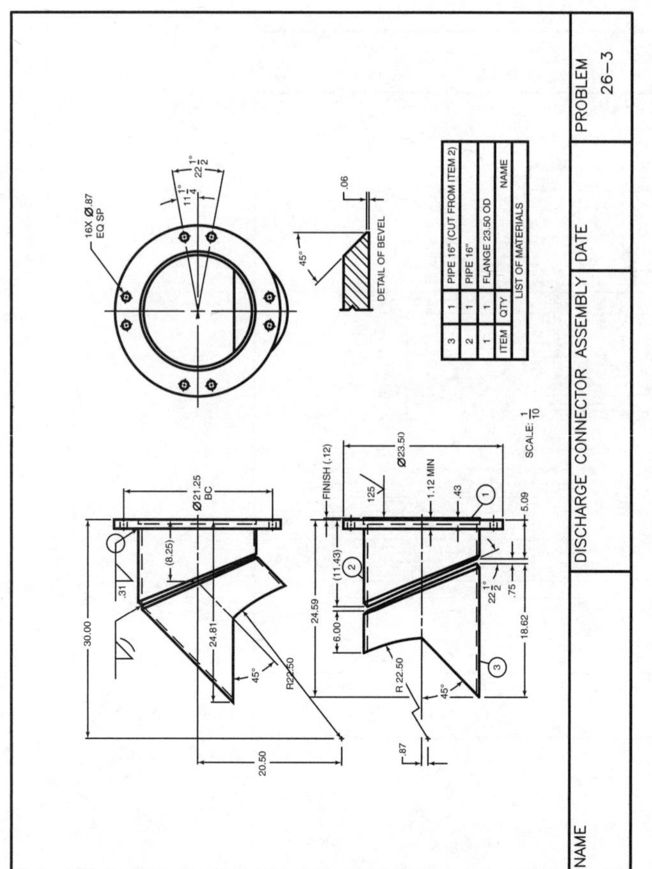

NAME
DISCHARGE CONNECTOR ASSEMBLY
DATE
PROBLEM 26–3
SCALE: 1/10
DETAIL OF BEVEL
LIST OF MATERIALS

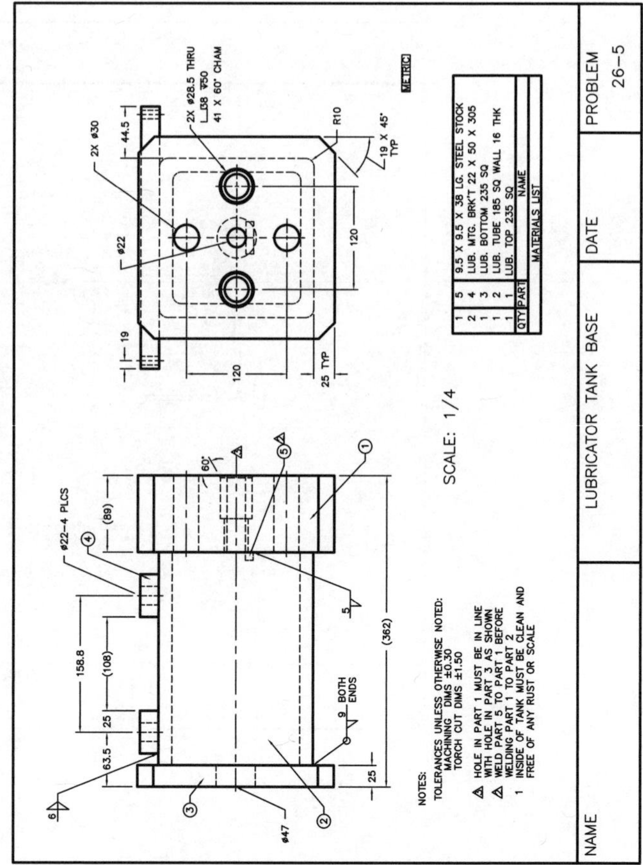

NAME
LUBRICATOR TANK BASE
DATE
PROBLEM 26–5
SCALE: 1/4
METRIC
MATERIALS LIST

Solutions to Worksheets

Pages 174–175

Student work should look like the following drawings. The problem number and title are indicated on each problem sheet.

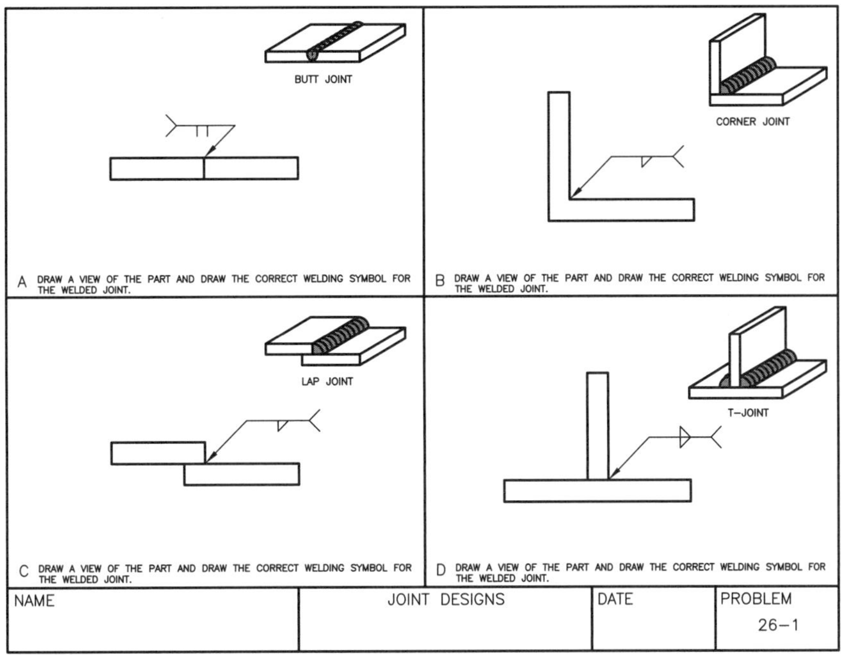

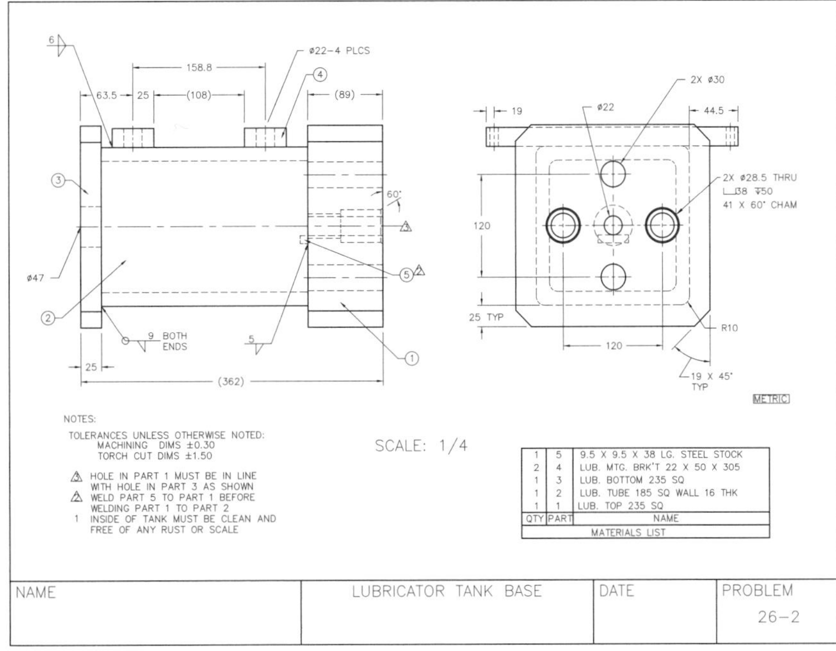

Answers to Chapter 26 Quiz

1. B. Brazing
2. C. Welding lightweight nonferrous metals.
3. A. The type of weld, size, location, and welding process.
4. C. Electron beam
5. D. resistance
6. Refer to the drawings given in the *Solutions to Problems and Activities, Text* section or the *Solutions to Drawing Problems, Text* section for the problem selected from the textbook.

Chapter Quiz 26

Welding Drafting

Name ____

Period ____________________ Date ____________________ Score ____________________

Multiple Choice

Choose the answer that correctly completes the statement. Write the corresponding letter in the space provided.

_______ 1. What welding process does *not* melt the parent metal?
- A. Oxyacetylene welding
- B. Brazing
- C. Arc welding
- D. Gas tungsten arc welding (GTAW)

_______ 2. What is gas tungsten arc welding (GTAW) best suited for?
- A. Welding heavy ferrous metals.
- B. Welding thin steel.
- C. Welding lightweight nonferrous metals.
- D. Welding underwater.

_______ 3. What information is included in the standard welding symbol?
- A. The type of weld, size, location, and welding process.
- B. The type of weld, location, welding process, and equipment to be used.
- C. The type of weld, size, welding process, and strength.
- D. All of the above.

_______ 4. _____ welding is performed in a vacuum.
- A. Induction
- B. Resistance
- C. Electron beam
- D. Oxyfuel gas

_______ 5. Spot welding is a type of _____ welding.
- A. induction
- B. electron beam
- C. oxyfuel gas
- D. resistance

Drafting Performance

6. Draw a solution of a problem selected by your instructor from Chapter 26 in your textbook. Use appropriate symbols to specify welds.

Welding Processes

Numerous welding processes have been developed to meet the needs for joining both like and unlike metals. The following are some of the processes commonly used in industry.

Brazing

Brazing is the joining of metals by adhesion with a low melting point filler metal. Brazing does not melt the parent metal.

Oxyfuel Gas Welding

Oxyfuel gas welding is a process in which the heat generated by burning gases causes the parent metal to melt and "fuse" into one piece. A filler metal is used in some cases.

Arc Welding

In *arc welding*, heat is produced by an electric arc between a welding electrode and the parent metal, causing the metal to melt and fuse. Two common arc welding processes are gas tungsten arc welding (GTAW) and gas metal arc welding (GMAW).

Resistance Welding

In *resistance welding*, an electric current is the source of heat and the parts fuse together at the point of contact.

Induction Welding

Induction welding is similar to resistance welding. However, the heat generated in induction welding is produced by the resistance of the metal parts to the flow of an induced electric current. The welding action may occur with or without pressure.

Electron Beam Welding

Electron beam welding is performed in a vacuum. The source of heat is a high-intensity beam of electrons focused in a small area at the surface to be welded.

RM 26-1

Types of Welds

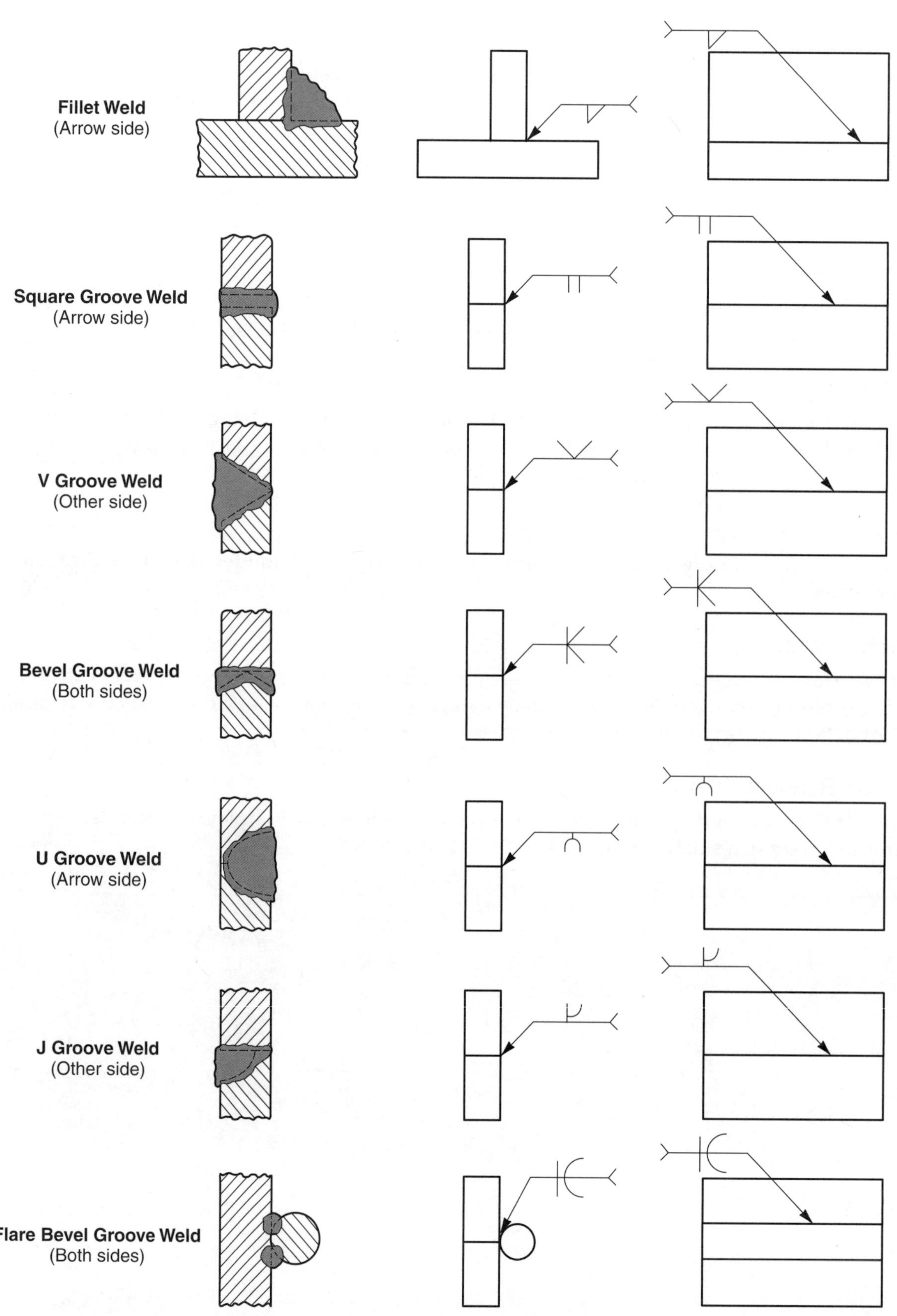

RM 26-2

Weld Symbols

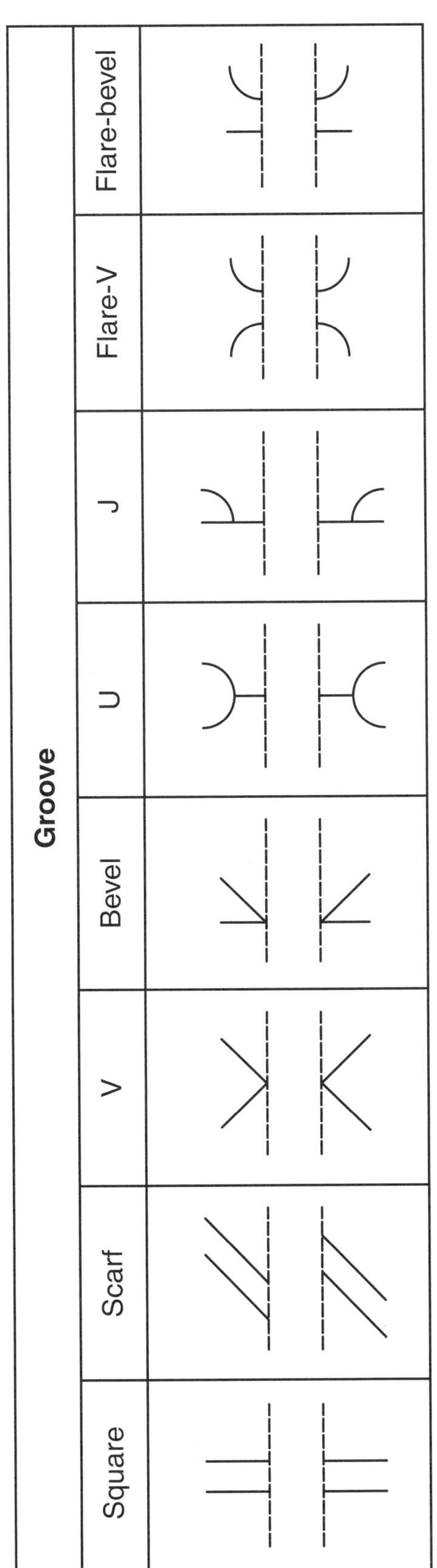

Edge

Surfacing

Back or Backing

Seam

Spot or Projection

Stud

Plug or Slot

Fillet

RM 26-3

Elements in a Welding Symbol

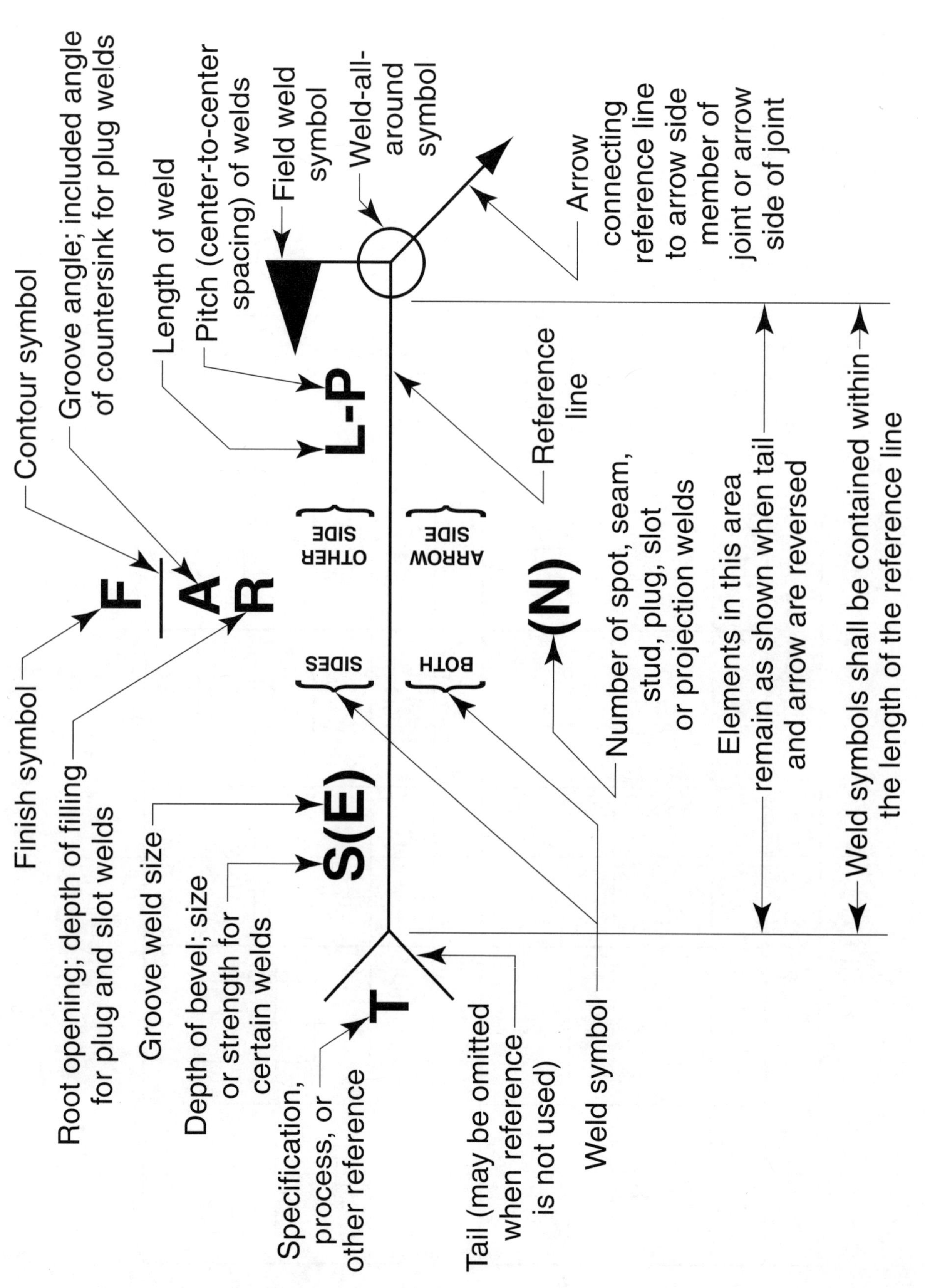

RM 26-4

Procedure Checklist

Welding Drafting

Name ______________________________

Observable Items	Completed		Comments	Instructor Initials
	Yes	No		
1. Makes a detail drawing for a welded part.				
2. Specifies a weld type on a drawing.				
3. Specifies weld size on a drawing.				
4. Indicates a field weld on a drawing.				
5. Indicates a welding process on a drawing.				

Instructor Signature ______________________________

Technical Illustration

Learning Objectives

After studying this chapter, the student will be able to:

- Describe the purpose of technical illustration.
- Identify the types of drawings made by technical illustrators.
- Explain the common techniques used to produce technical illustrations.

Instructional Resources

Text: pages 795–804

Review Questions, page 803

Problems and Activities, page 804

Worksheets: pages 176–177

- Worksheet 27-1: *Bearing Mount*
- Worksheet 27-2: *Slotted Angle Plate*

Instructor's Resource

Instructional Tasks

Instructional Aids and Assignments

Chapter 27 Quiz

Reproducible Masters

- Reproducible Master 27-1: *Technical Illustrations.* Common types of technical illustrations are shown.

Procedure Checklist

Color Transparencies (Binder/IRCD only)

- Transparency 27-1: *CAD-Generated Technical Illustration.* Shown is a photorealistic computer-generated rendering of an instrument panel.

Instructional Tasks

1. Identify and describe the various types of drawings used in technical illustration.
   - Invite an experienced technical illustrator to present a lecture on illustration techniques used in industry.
   - Ask members of the class to gather examples of technical illustrations from professional journals, technical journals, and equipment operation manuals. Have the class identify the techniques used in the preparation of each illustration.
2. Explain how to prepare an illustration using the outline shading method.
   - Demonstrate the outline shading technique.
3. Explain how to prepare an illustration using line shading.
   - Demonstrate line shading of flat and curved surfaces. Also demonstrate the line shading technique on threads.
4. Explain how to prepare an illustration using smudge shading.
   - Demonstrate smudge shading techniques.
5. Explain how to prepare an illustration using the pencil shading method.
   - Use an unshaded illustration to demonstrate pencil shading techniques.

Instructional Aids and Assignments

1. Display samples of professionally drawn technical illustration work.
2. Display samples of technical illustration work from former class members.
3. Display instructional pamphlets and catalogs from suppliers of such equipment and materials as airbrushes, shading films, transfer type, and art supplies.
4. Assign the drawing problems in the textbook. The number of problems is sufficient to assign a minimum number to all students and to identify problems that may be done for extra credit.

Answers to Review Questions, Text

Page 803

1. pictorial
2. Engineering and production illustrations and publication illustrations.
3. assembly
4. light
5. model
6. line
7. foreground
8. light
9. smudge
10. architectural
11. stipple
12. airbrush
13. retouching

Solutions to Problems and Activities, Text

Page 804

For Problems 1–4, approve selected problems before the students begin work. Evaluate student work for accuracy and appearance.

Solutions to Worksheets

Pages 176–177

Evaluate student work for accuracy and appearance. For Problems 27-1 and 27-2, student work should look like the following drawings. The problem number and title are indicated on each problem sheet.

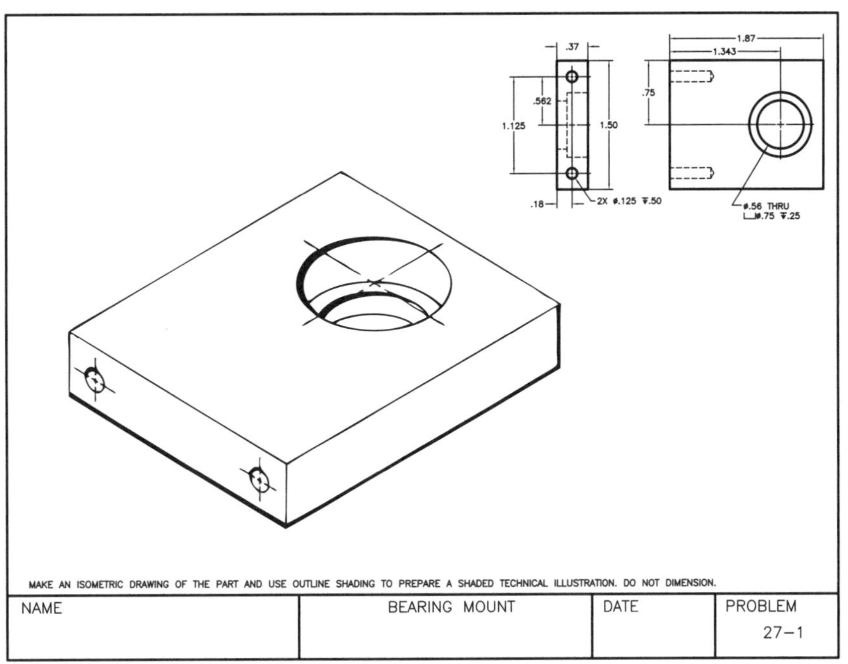

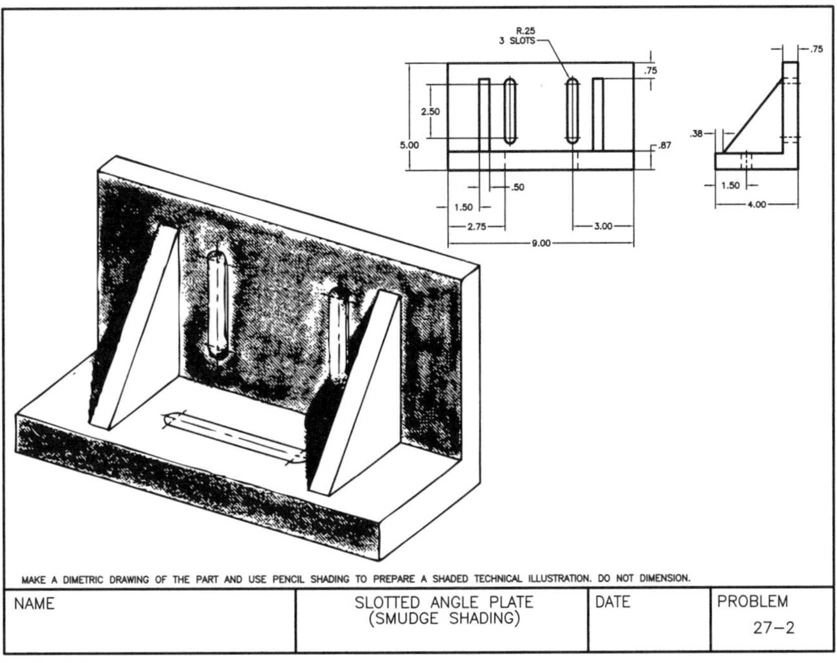

Answers to Chapter 27 Quiz

1. B. outline
2. A. line
3. C. Stipple
4. C. Smudge shading
5. B. frisket
6. Evaluate student work for accuracy and appearance.

Chapter Quiz 27

Technical Illustration

Name ____

Period ____________ Date ____________ Score ____________

Multiple Choice

Choose the answer that correctly completes the statement. Write the corresponding letter in the space provided.

_____ 1. Drawing lines at different line weights to establish light and dark areas on a drawing is known as _____ shading.
A. line
B. outline
C. smudge
D. airbrush

_____ 2. Drawing lines of varying spacing and length to establish light and dark areas on a drawing is known as _____ shading.
A. line
B. outline
C. smudge
D. airbrush

_____ 3. _____ shading is the application of patterns of dots to different object surfaces to simulate shadows.
A. Outline
B. Line
C. Stipple
D. Sponge

_____ 4. _____ is accomplished by going over the area to be shaded with a soft lead pencil and rubbing the graphite into the paper with a stub of paper or cloth.
A. Line shading
B. Airbrush shading
C. Smudge shading
D. Photo retouching

_____ 5. In airbrushing, parts of the drawing that are not to be sprayed should be protected by a paper template or _____.
A. sponge
B. frisket
C. transfer sheet
D. trammel

Drafting Performance

6. Draw a solution of a problem selected by your instructor from Chapter 27 in your textbook.

Technical Illustrations

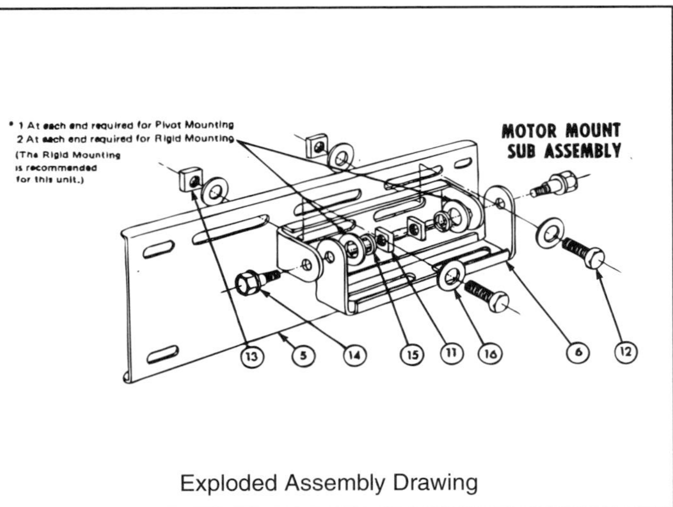

Exploded Assembly Drawing

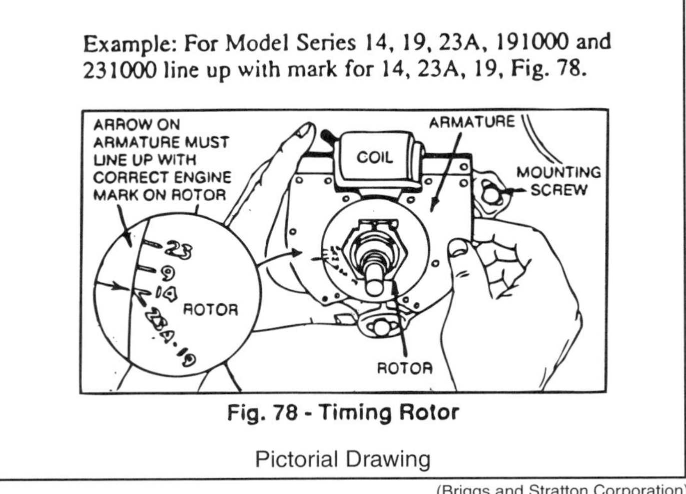

Fig. 78 - Timing Rotor

Pictorial Drawing

(Briggs and Stratton Corporation)

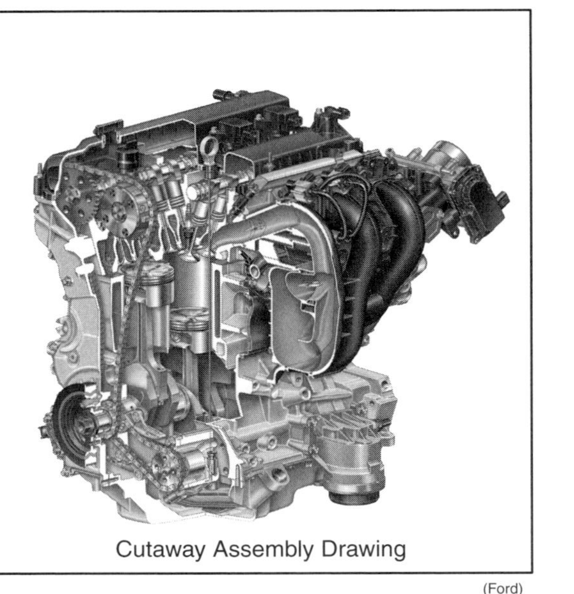

Cutaway Assembly Drawing

(Ford)

RM 27-1

Procedure Checklist

Technical Illustration

Name ______________________________

Observable Items	Completed		Comments	Instructor Initials
	Yes	No		
1. Illustrates an object using outline shading.				
2. Illustrates an object using line shading.				
3. Illustrates an object using smudge shading.				
4. Makes a pencil rendering.				
5. Makes an ink rendering.				

Instructor Signature ______________________________

Graphs and Charts

Learning Objectives

After studying this chapter, the student will be able to:

- List and describe the types of graphs and charts prepared by drafters.
- Explain how graphs and charts are developed.
- Identify common applications for constructing graphs and charts.

Instructional Resources

Text: pages 805–813

Review Questions, page 812

Problems and Activities, page 813

Worksheets: page 178

- Worksheet 28-1: *Line Graph*

Instructor's Resource

Instructional Tasks

Instructional Aids and Assignments

Chapter 28 Quiz

Procedure Checklist

Color Transparencies (Binder/IRCD only)

- Transparency 28-1: *Index Bar Graph*. A typical index bar graph is shown.

Instructional Tasks

1. Identify and describe the various types of graphs used to analyze and clarify data.
    - Collect a number of graphs and charts. Arrange them in an interesting display on a wall, or make reproductions suitable for an overhead projector and present them to the class for discussion.
2. Explain how to construct line graphs.
    - Discuss the characteristics and principal uses of line graphs.
    - Demonstrate line graph construction techniques.
3. Explain the different types of bar graphs.
    - Clarify how bar graphs are constructed.
    - Use bar graphs from newspapers or magazines to explain the type of data that can be presented.
    - Present a hypothetical situation that requires the construction of a bar graph. Use this example to demonstrate bar graph construction techniques.
4. Explain how to construct area graphs.
    - Demonstrate area graph construction techniques.
5. Explain how to construct pie graphs.
    - Instruct students to bring examples of pie graphs to class. Discuss the strong and weak points of each graph.
    - Demonstrate pie graph construction techniques.
6. Identify and describe the various types of charts used to analyze and clarify data.
    - Discuss the characteristics and functions of charts.
7. Explain how to construct a nomograph.
    - Discuss the characteristics of a nomograph.
    - Demonstrate nomograph construction.
8. Explain how to construct flow charts.
    - Ask students to suggest data that would be presented best by being projected in chart form.
    - Demonstrate flow chart construction.
9. Explain how to construct organizational charts.
    - Ask students to suggest data that would be presented best by being projected in chart form.
    - Using a hypothetical corporation, demonstrate organizational chart construction.

Instructional Aids and Assignments

1. Display catalogs from suppliers of graph and chart materials.
2. Display annual reports of major companies that include several graphs and charts for illustration.
3. Display current news magazines with illustrations of graphs and charts.

Answers to Review Questions, Text

Page 812

1. Graphs and charts are used for contract proposals, analysis, and marketing.
2. graph
3. chart
4. A line graph is used to show relationships of quantities to a time span.
5. A bar graph is used to show relationships between two or more variables.
6. Index bar graphs and range bar graphs.
7. subdivided
8. paired
9. A pie graph.
10. A nomograph is a graph that usually contains three parallel scales graduated for different variables. When a straight line connects values of any two scales, the related value may be read directly from the third scale at the point intersected by the line.
11. flow
12. It shows relationships between individuals and departments within an organization and the operations or services each performs.

Solutions to Problems and Activities, Text

Page 813

For Problems 1–6, approve selected subjects before the students begin work. Evaluate student work for accuracy and appearance.

Solutions to Worksheets

Page 178

Student work should look like the following drawing.

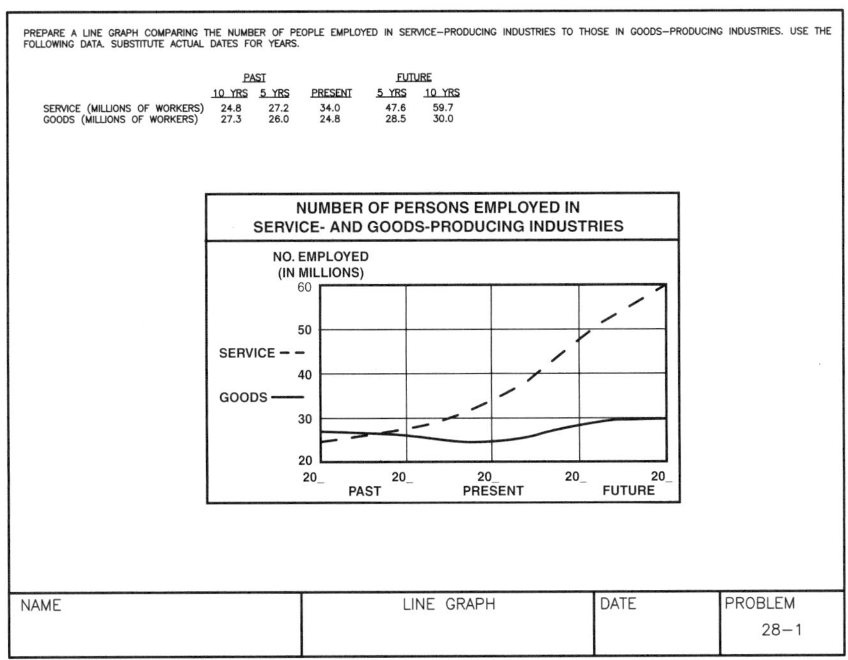

PREPARE A LINE GRAPH COMPARING THE NUMBER OF PEOPLE EMPLOYED IN SERVICE–PRODUCING INDUSTRIES TO THOSE IN GOODS–PRODUCING INDUSTRIES. USE THE FOLLOWING DATA. SUBSTITUTE ACTUAL DATES FOR YEARS.

	PAST			FUTURE	
	10 YRS	5 YRS	PRESENT	5 YRS	10 YRS
SERVICE (MILLIONS OF WORKERS)	24.8	27.2	34.0	47.6	59.7
GOODS (MILLIONS OF WORKERS)	27.3	26.0	24.8	28.5	30.0

NAME	LINE GRAPH	DATE	PROBLEM 28–1

Answers to Chapter 28 Quiz

1. A. graph
2. A. Index and range.
3. C. percentage
4. D. pie graph
5. C. organizational chart
6. Evaluate student work for accuracy and appearance.

Chapter Quiz 28

Graphs and Charts

Name ____

Period ________________ Date ________________ Score ________________

Multiple Choice

Choose the answer that correctly completes the statement. Write the corresponding letter in the space provided.

_______ 1. The purpose of a _____ is to show the relationship between two or more factors.
A. graph
B. organizational chart
C. flow chart
D. personnel chart

_______ 2. What are the two types of bar graphs?
A. Index and range.
B. Index and pie.
C. Range and line.
D. Surface and area.

_______ 3. A _____ bar graph uses subdivided bars to compare data.
A. deviation
B. paired
C. percentage
D. grouped

_______ 4. A _____ is commonly used to contrast individual parts with the whole.
A. nomograph
B. flow chart
C. line graph
D. pie graph

_______ 5. Authority for certain functions within a company can best be illustrated with a(n) _____.
A. nomograph
B. flow chart
C. organizational chart
D. line chart

Drafting Performance

6. Draw a solution of a problem selected by your instructor from Chapter 28 in your textbook.

Procedure Checklist

Graphs and Charts

Name ____

Observable Items	Completed		Comments	Instructor Initials
	Yes	No		
1. Constructs a line graph.				
2. Constructs a bar graph.				
3. Constructs a surface graph.				
4. Constructs a pie graph.				
5. Constructs a flow chart.				
6. Constructs an organizational chart.				

Instructor Signature ____